HUMAN COGNITIVE NEUROPSYCHOLOGY

Human Cognitive Neuropsychology

A Textbook with Readings

Andrew W. Ellis

University of York, UK

Andrew W. Young

MRC Applied Psychology Unit, Cambridge, UK

Psychology Press
Taylor & Francis Group

LONDON AND NEW YORK

First published 1988 by
Psychology Press Ltd, Publishers
27 Church Road,
Hove, East Sussex BN3 2FA, UK

711 Third Avenue,
New York, NY 10017

Psychology Press is an imprint of the Taylor and Francis Group, an informa business

First issued in hardback 2015

British Library Cataloguing in Publication Data

A catalogue record for this book is available from the British Library

    ISBN 978-0-86377-715-8 (pbk)
    ISBN 978-1-138-13101-9 (hbk)

Contents

This augmented edition of *Human Cognitive Neuropsychology* contains selected readings
from books and journals, which are gathered together at the end of the book, starting on
page 345. The readings are listed here below the chapter to which they relate.

Preface to the Augmented Edition

This book first appeared in 1988 and we are pleased that it has generally been well received and widely used. If there had been no other demands on our time, we would like to think that we would now be announcing a rewritten second edition. But there have been other demands. Both of us have endured spells as head of department since 1988. Then there are the pressures that dominate academic life in Britain in the 1990s: to win grants, maintain research teams, and publish journal articles. Writing textbooks is currently regarded as a somewhat self-indulgent pastime that distracts the individual from more the important business of writing the next grant application or submitting the next paper.

That is, we believe, an unfortunate and short-sighted attitude. Good textbooks summarise and organise material that is otherwise dispersed among countless individual articles, hence they can be of value even to researchers active in the field. Textbooks also serve as the introduction to an area for beginners, hopefully instilling in them an interest and enthusiasm for the topic. Without good textbooks, there is a serious danger that the stream of young talent that is vital to maintaining the vigour of an area will dry up. And successful textbooks help to pay for their authors' family holidays.

This is not the second edition we would like to be announcing. It is—and there is no point avoiding this fact—a stopgap, even if the gap it stops may prove to be a rather long one. We are indebted to Michael Forster of

Psychology Press (formerly Erlbaum, UK) for suggesting to us the idea of producing an augmented version of the first edition in which selected articles are used to introduce the reader to developments since 1988. The more we thought about this, the more positive we became. The addition of readings allows us to bring in material written by leading authorities in each field, and the inclusion of some primary-source case reports gives a much clearer idea of the work that goes into a really first-rate case study, bringing the topic literally and metaphorically to life. We may even continue the concept if and when we manage to write a true second edition.

The first part of this expanded edition of *Human Cognitive Neuropsychology* is, then, just the old first edition with the Further Readings at the end of each chapter revised, and a few minor errors corrected. The second part is a series of papers that expand upon, or bring up to date, the contents of each chapter. We have written a short Introduction to the one or two papers selected to complement each chapter, indicating how they relate to the material in the chapter. One of the reasons we warmed to this device is that we can imagine these additional papers being used as readings for seminars and tutorials in courses on neuropsychology and cognitive psychology. We have therefore deliberately stopped short of summarising the contents of each paper in a way that would eliminate the necessity for the student actually to read them.

We thank the authors and publishers of the reprinted papers for permission to use their work in this way. We are acutely aware that this is not the second edition that many people would have liked to see, but we hope they will find that it has genuine value.

Andy Ellis
York

Andy Young
Cambridge

June 1996

1 | What is Cognitive Neuropsychology?

In any well-made machine one is ignorant of the working of most of the parts—the better they work the less we are conscious of them . . . it is only a fault which draws our attention to the existence of a mechanism at all.

Kenneth Craik, *The Nature of Explanation* (1943)

INTRODUCTION

On 5th August, 1982 a 19-year-old man who we shall refer to by his initials as PH was involved in an accident in which he was knocked off his motorcycle. He lost his right arm, and suffered a severe closed head injury. He was in a coma for over 12 days.

Like many head-injury patients PH has, with the help of rehabilitation services, made quite a good recovery. Some four years after his accident his language abilities seemed normal in conversation, and he could read without difficulty. His I.Q. on verbal tests (91) was probably close to what it was before the accident. His short-term memory abilities were normal and, although he scored poorly on formal tests involving long-term retention, he was able to remember the things that were important to his daily life without apparent difficulty.

However, one of PH's problems was most resistant to rehabilitation; he could not recognise people's faces. As soon as a familiar person spoke he would know who it was but, to PH, all faces seemed unfamiliar. He could tell if a face belonged to a man or a woman, an old or a young person, and he could describe the general appearance and facial features

1

reasonably accurately. But PH had no sense of recognising people who had previously been very familiar to him. In neuropsychological terms, his accident had left PH *prosopagnosic*—able to see, but unable to recognise many once-familiar faces (De Haan, Young, & Newcombe, 1987a).

EST was a well-educated, 65-year old man whose difficulties lay not in perception or recognition, but in speaking. His attempts to converse were hampered by the fact that he could no longer call to mind many words that had once been part of his ordinary, everyday vocabulary. The cause of EST's *anomia* (as his condition is known) was not a head injury, but a large slow-growing tumour in the left hemisphere of his brain which was successfully removed when he was 53 years old. Whereas normal people just occasionally find themselves caught in a "tip of the tongue" state, temporarily unable to remember a word, EST seemed to be trapped in such a state almost every minute because EST's word-finding problems extended to commonplace words like "piano", "spider", and "lamp". He knew perfectly well what such objects were, and what one could do with them, but was often unable to remember what they were called. His understanding of speech was good, and he could comprehend written words, though his attempts to read aloud were hindered by the same word-finding problems as affected his speaking (Kay & Ellis, 1987; Kay & Patterson, 1985).

The difficulties experienced by PH and EST are just two of the vast range of different problems that can be caused by brain injury. In this book we shall encounter many of them, though there are many more that we have not had space to include. Chapter 4, for example, reviews different forms of face recognition disorder, including the sort of prosopagnosia suffered by PH, whereas Chapters 5 and 9 examine disorders of speech production, including EST's type of anomia. Other conditions we shall look at include disorders affecting object recognition, spatial knowledge and orientation, speech comprehension, reading, writing, and memory.

Human cognitive neuropsychology is, however, much more than just a catalogue of the different problems that brain injury can give rise to. Cognitive neuropsychologists believe that by studying patients like PH and EST (with their co-operation and consent), fundamental insights can be gained into the way the human mind works. These insights should then feed back to provide a better understanding of the problems of brain-injured patients, and should lead in turn to the development of better therapies (e.g. Howard & Hatfield, 1987).

As an approach to understanding the mind and the brain, cognitive neuropsychology is both old and new—old to the extent that the issues it addresses are ones which have exercised the minds of philosophers, psychologists, neurologists and others for hundreds, even thousands, of years; and new because it is only within the last 15 years or so that cognitive neuropsychology has become established and has articulated its distinctive approach. This chapter is intended to acquaint the reader with what cognitive neuropsychologists are trying to do. We shall discuss the sort of questions they ask, the methods they adopt in trying to answer them, the assumptions they make, and some of the potential pitfalls that await them along the way. In doing so we shall try to be brief for two reasons. First, we believe that the vigour and usefulness of cognitive neuropsychology is best established through illustrating its practical application in different areas: If any converts are to be made, they will be won over by the demonstrations in later chapters of how cognitive neuropsychology can illuminate the processes involved in human perception, language, and memory. Secondly, cognitive neuropsychology is an approach in evolution. Matters to be reviewed in this chapter, such as the appropriate methodology and the underlying assumptions, are matters of lively current debate, and we are only too well aware that opinion on these topics is likely to continue to evolve in the years to come. But the fact that we can make extensive use in the chapters to come of observations and conclusions made by earlier researchers whose theoretical viewpoints were different from our own shows that the main substance of the book has a fair chance of surviving a wide range of changes in theoretical fashion.

QUESTIONS AND POSSIBLE ANSWERS

Assuming we have spent some time investigating a case like the anomic patient EST mentioned earlier, two questions arise naturally:

1. What has happened to this patient to cause him to show the particular symptoms he does?
2. Can his pattern of impaired and intact capabilities teach us anything about the way the normal mind and brain are organised?

If we consider first the question of what has happened to EST to cause his anomia, then it soon becomes clear that the question can be answered in at least two very different ways. Brain scans have shown that the tumour which caused EST's anomia occupied a large area in his left cerebral hemisphere, affecting in particular the temporal and temporo-parietal areas (Kay & Patterson, 1985). As we have seen, the consequence of the resulting brain injury was that EST could no longer remember, or "find", many words which had once been well-established parts of his vocabulary. Is it better to say of EST, "He is anomic because of damage to his left cerebral hemisphere" or "He is anomic because of damage to the psychological processes which mediate spoken word finding?" Although there are those who believe that one of these two modes of explanation is intrinsically superior to the other, we would suggest that they are both valid in their own way. Only the second explanation is a cognitive neuropsychological explanation, however. Accordingly, the emphasis in this book will be on *explaining the symptoms of brain-injured patients in terms of impairment to psychological operations which are necessary for normal, efficient perception, language and memory*, though we shall see that there are times when a knowledge of the relevant anatomy and physiology is of positive benefit when it would be churlish to ignore biological evidence.

Our main subject matter, however, is *cognitive* neuropsychology. Cognitive psychology (without the neuro- prefix) is the study of those mental processes which underlie and make possible our everyday ability to recognise familiar objects and familiar people, to find our way around in the world, to speak, read and write, to plan and execute actions, to think, make decisions and remember (Eysenck, 1984; Smyth, Morris, Levy, & Ellis, 1987). Neuropsychology is the study of how particular brain structures and processes mediate behaviour, and encompasses such things as appetites and emotions as well as cognitive aspects of mental life. As its name suggests, cognitive neuropsychology represents a convergence of cognitive psychology and neuropsychology. In Campbell's (1987a) words: "Neuropsychology is *cognitive* to the extent that it purports to clarify the mechanisms of cognitive functions such as thinking, reading, writing, speaking, recognising, or remembering, using evidence from neuropathology."

Cognitive neuropsychology has, then, two basic aims (Coltheart, 1986; Ellis, 1983). The first is *to explain the patterns of impaired and intact cognitive performance seen in brain-injured patients in terms of damage to one or more of the components of a theory or model of normal cognitive functioning*. Thus PH's prosopagnosia and EST's anomia might be explained in terms of damage to one or more of the processes required to effect normal face recognition and speech production, respectively.

The second aim of cognitive neuropsychology is largely responsible for the recent upsurge of interest in the approach. It is *to draw conclusions about normal, intact cognitive processes from the patterns of impaired and intact capabilities seen in brain-injured patients*. In pursuing this second aim, the cognitive neuropsychologist wishes to be in a position to assert that observed patterns of symptoms could not occur if the normal, intact cognitive system were not organised in a certain way. We shall make claims of this sort with respect to patients PH and EST in Chapters 4 and 5.

Dissociations and Associations

Assertions about the way the intact mind must be organised are often based on what are termed *dissociations*. If patient X is impaired on task 1 but performs normally on task 2, then we may claim to have a dissociation between the two tasks. For instance, if task 1 is reading words and task 2 is recognising famous faces, then we would state that patient X shows a dissociation between reading, which is impaired, and face recognition, which is intact. On such evidence alone, many cognitive neuropsychologists would feel justified in saying that the normal cognitive system must be organised with face recognition and written word recognition handled by different sets of cognitive processes, thereby allowing one set to be impaired while the other continues to function normally.

Other cognitive neuropsychologists might be more circumspect, however. They would point out that logically possible alternative accounts of patient X can be put forward. It might be, for example, that written word recognition is in some way easier than face recognition and that X's brain injury has rendered him incapable of difficult recognition tasks, while leaving him still able to perform easy ones. This type of alternative account could be ruled out, however, if a second patient, Y, could be discovered in whom written word recognition was intact whereas face recognition was impaired. That patient when contrasted with patient X would provide us with a *double dissociation* between face recognition and written word recognition. There is no doubt that double dissociations are more reliable indicators that there are cognitive processes involved in the performance of task 1 that are not involved in the performance of task 2, and vice versa (Shallice, 1979a; Teuber, 1955; Weiskrantz, 1968). Double dissociations can also be established without requiring that either patient should perform normally on either task: It would often be sufficient to show that patient Y performed reliably and significantly better on task 1 than on task 2 whereas patient X performed reliably and significantly better on task 2 than on task 1 [for the technically-minded, Jones (1983) discusses cases in which this would *not* be sufficient evidence].

There are times, however, when arguments based on such things as the relative simplicity of two tasks seem so implausible that cognitive neuropsychologists are willing to venture claims about normal cognitive organisation on the basis of single dissociations (where a patient performs well on one set of tasks but badly on another), and we shall encounter several examples of such reasoning later in the book. Also, it would be unwise to regard the search for double dissociations as some sort of royal road to understanding the structure of the mind. Having unearthed a double dissociation, there is a lot of work to be done in determining just what cognitive processes mediate aspects of tasks 1 and 2 independently, and what processes, if any, the two tasks share in common. This requires intensive investigation of the patients in order to discover just why they perform badly when they do, and just where in the total cognitive system their breakdowns have occurred.

Much more problematical than arguments based on either double or single dissociations are arguments based on *associations* between symptoms. It is common in neuropsychology to discover that patients who are impaired on task 1 are also typically impaired on tasks 3, 4 and 5. Now, it might be that this association of deficits occurs because a cognitive process required for the successful execution of task 1 is also required for the successful execution of tasks 3, 4 and 5, so that a patient in whom that process is damaged will experience problems with all these tasks. Unfortunately, deficits can also tend to co-occur for reasons that are of neurological importance, but of less interest specifically to the cognitive neuropsychologist.

It could be, for example, that tasks 1, 3, 4, and 5 have no overlap in terms of the cognitive processes required for their execution, but that four discrete sets of cognitive processes are mediated by four adjacent areas of the brain. If this is so, then a brain injury which damages one of those areas will tend also to damage the others, so that deficits on the four tasks which depend on those four regions will tend to be associated. This point as applied to language disorders was well expressed by Lord Brain (1964, p.7) in the following passage:

> ...let us consider two aspects of language which we will merely call *a* and *b* to indicate that we habitually distinguish them in our own minds and give them different labels. Let us further suppose that they are both depressed [*i.e., impaired*] in a particular aphasic patient. There are several possible explanations of this. The primary disturbance may involve *a*, and the disturbance of *b* may be secondary to this, or conversely, we may implicate some general function *c* and say that both *a* and *b* are particular examples of disorder *c*. These are all functional or dynamic [*cognitive*] interpretations. But there is also the possibility that there is no functional relationship between *a* and *b*. They are involved together merely because their pathways, though separate in terms of neurones, run close enough together to be damaged by the same lesion.

Associations which occur for anatomical reasons rather than cognitive-psychological reasons will be encountered on several occasions in this book. They are revealed in their true colours when the exceptional patient is discovered whose lesion affects some but not all of the anatomically adjacent regions and which, therefore, affects some but not all of the cognitive tasks mediated by those regions. In sum, theoretical arguments based on observed associations between symptoms can be very appealing because there are often good psychological reasons for expecting two or more deficits to co-occur as a result of damage to a single cognitive process, but such arguments should always be advanced with caution and are never as secure as arguments based on dissociations.

COGNITIVE NEUROPSYCHOLOGICAL METHODS

We have just seen that *differences* between patients play a very important role in the development of theories in cognitive neuropsychology. In contrast, similarities between patients, in the form of shared sets of associated symptoms, are viewed with caution if not suspicion. Several important dissociations between symptoms have been discovered in patients whom traditional neuropsychology would have grouped together as members of the same syndrome category.

This difference in emphasis is perhaps what most distinguishes modern cognitive neuropsychology from traditional neuropsychology. The latter approach used common co-occurrences of symptoms to group patients together into syndromes. Thus patients with language disorders following brain injury (aphasias) were grouped into categories labelled Broca's aphasia, Wernicke's aphasia, conduction aphasia, etc. on the basis of shared symptoms. The assumption made would be that patients with Broca's aphasia are effectively interchangeable, and quite strong claims would sometimes be made concerning symptom complexes that *had* to co-occur (if patient Z shows symptom q, she will also show symptoms r, s, and t, etc.).

It is now generally acknowledged in cognitive neuropsychology that traditional syndrome categories are too coarse-grained and often form groupings on the basis of symptoms that co-occur for anatomical rather than functional reasons (Poeck, 1983). This is understandable, because one of the original purposes of such syndromes was to assist in the determination of probable lesion sites in the days before more direct brain scanning techniques became available, but most cognitive neuropsychologists would now accept Caramazza's (1984) advice that "research based on classical syndrome types should not be carried out if the goal of the research is to address issues concerning the structure of cognitive processes".

The problem lies in deciding how best to proceed once one has acknowledged that classical syndromes are unsuitable for cognitive neuropsychological analysis. On this issue cognitive neuropsychologists fall into two broad camps. The first wishes to replace the old, broad groupings with newer, finer, more theoretically motivated categories. These could be developed by subdividing the old syndrome categories to take account of dissociations as they arise, or they could be developed *de novo* (as with the classification of acquired reading disorders into "deep dyslexia", "surface dyslexia", "phonological dyslexia" etc.—see Chapter 8). Shallice (1979a) strongly advocates this approach, though acknowledging that it will inevitably lead to the postulation of ever more syndromes of increasing complexity and specificity.

Other cognitive neuropsychologists react to the manifest inadequacies of the classical syndromes by suggesting that there may simply be no need to group patients into categories in order to practise effective cognitive neuropsychology (e.g. Caramazza, 1984; 1986; Ellis, 1987). If it were possible to group patients into homogeneous categories, then that would represent a valuable saving because cognitive neuropsychologists would only need to produce an explanation for each syndrome, not each individual patient. Unfortunately, advocates of the revised syndrome viewpoint have not yet managed to come up with a single, lasting homogeneous category. Thus, the categories of acquired reading disorder mentioned earlier, which are only 10 or 15 years old at the time of writing, are already fractionating as theoretically important individual differences are found among patients in the same categories. As the rest of this book shows, similar fates are befalling all other attempts to delineate new syndrome categories.

One possible response to this situation is to argue that cognitive neuropsychologists should treat each patient as a unique case requiring separate explanation. Single patients could serve the same role in cognitive neuropsychology as single experiments do in experimental cognitive psychology—each is a separate test of cognitive theory (Ellis, 1987). This does not mean that all comparisons between patients are excluded: There are times in the book, for example, when we wish to highlight similarities between two or more patients. Typically, however, this happens because they share a single particular *symptom* which may be given the same explanation in each case. The point is that the other symptoms these patients show may be very different: The patients are alike in one respect but are different in several others and could not plausibly be combined into a syndrome category. In the remaining chapters of this book, we tend to retain traditional neurological terms (aphasia, dyslexia, agnosia, etc.) simply as a shorthand convenience for referring to particular broad classes of symptoms: We do *not* wish to imply that patients with a common symptom will necessarily show that symptom for the same reason.

We do not wish to labour this point about the usefulness or otherwise of syndrome groupings (which we see as just one of the teething troubles of a new scientific approach trying to establish how best to proceed). Advocates of new syndromes still talk to advocates of the single-patient approach. The two groups share the same theoretical models of reading, object recognition, memory or whatever, and each uses the others' case studies to develop those theories. Although we have our own views on this issue, we have tried not to let them dominate this book, which we hope will find acceptance among cognitive neuropsychologists of all denominations.

Case Studies

What an increasing number of cognitive neuropsychologists now agree upon is that the approach is best served by intensive single-case studies of patients with deficits in different areas of cognitive processing. This stands in contrast to traditional neuropsychology where the dominant approach has often been one in which the performance on one or more tasks of a group of patients of a given type is contrasted either with the performance of another group of patients of a different type or with a group of normal "control" subjects. Such studies commonly report only the average score on each task for each group. Unfortunately, much potentially valuable information can be lost in such an averaging procedure, notably information about individual differences between patients assigned to the same groups (Shallice, 1979a).

Accordingly, even cognitive neuropsychologists who believe in the usefulness of syndrome groupings now tend to present data on each individual patient separately. Many publications in cognitive neuropsychology are devoted to presenting and interpreting data from just one patient with a disorder of particular theoretical interest. Generalisability of theories comes in two ways: First, a theory or model of a particular cognitive function is meant to account for *all* reported cases of disorder of that function, so that the theory is *not* a theory of a single patient; and secondly, these are theories of normal, intact cognitive functioning which are used to explain disorders. As such they must explain all the available data from experimental cognitive psychology as well as all the available neuropsychological data. Few areas of psychology place such exacting demands on their theories.

Shallice (1979a) made several recommendations about how single-case studies should proceed. He suggested, for example, that when comparisons between patients are appropriate they would be facilitated if "baseline" data from a range of standard neuropsychological tests were supplied. Beyond that point the particular tasks given to the patient are likely to be tailor-made and designed to evaluate a particular hypothesis as to the nature of the patient's disorder. Such tests should be given under conditions that are as controlled as possible, and their results should be analysed statistically using tests applied as standard in experimental cognitive psychology. Tasks which are of particular theoretical importance should be given on more than one occasion to establish the replicability of their results, and theoretical conclusions should be supported wherever possible by data from more than one task.

In fact, although we have described traditional neuropsychology as being devoted to group studies, that is an over-simplification. Rare or exceptional disorders have always been reported as single-case studies, and in the decades between about 1870 and 1910 a succession of important case studies were published. As we shall see shortly, there are several respects in which modern cognitive neuropsychology can justly be regarded as a return to this turn-of-the-century approach, though the theories and methods employed have become more sophisticated.

MODULARITY

It has already been argued that if one patient shows an impairment of reading but not face recognition, whereas another shows an impairment of face recognition but not reading, then that double dissociation indicates that there are cognitive processes involved in recognising faces that are not involved in reading words, and vice versa. As the remainder of this book will reveal, such dissociations abound in cognitive neuropsychology. If we follow through the logic of our argument, that means that the cognitive skills of the sort we shall be discussing are mediated by large numbers of semi-independent cognitive processes or systems, each capable of separate impairment.

This view of how the mind and brain are organised has come to be known as the *modularity hypothesis*. According to the modularity hypothesis, our mental life is made possible by the orchestrated activity of multiple cognitive processors or *modules*. There may, for example, be one set of modules responsible for various aspects of face recognition, another set for recognising written words, a third set for maintaining our orientation in the geographical environment, and so on. Every module engages in its own form of processing independently of the activity in modules other than those it is in direct communication with. Modules are also distinct within the brain, so that brain injury can affect the operation of some modules while, at the same time, leaving the operation of other modules intact (hence a patient can, for example, experience difficulties in face recognition following brain injury without necessarily experiencing difficulties with reading).

Current interest in the modularity hypothesis stems in large part from the work of Marr (1976; 1982) and Fodor (1983). Building on his experience in both vision research and the simulation of complex human abilities in computers, Marr suggested that complex systems, like minds and brains, are very likely to evolve towards a modular organisation in the course of their development. This is because it is easier, according to Marr, both to detect and correct errors and to improve complex systems whose organisation is modular. Thus, Marr (1976) writes:

> Any large computation should be split up and implemented as a collection of small subparts that are as nearly independent of one another as the overall task allows. If a process is not designed in this way a small change in one place will have consequences in many other places. This means that the process as a whole becomes extremely difficult to debug or to improve, whether by a human designer or in the course of natural evolution, because a small change to improve one part has to be accompanied by many simultaneous compensatory changes elsewhere.

An Analogy

An analogy may help at this point. Modern hi-fi systems are often highly modular, consisting of separate and separable record decks, cassette decks, radio tuners, amplifiers, speakers, headphones, and so on. In contrast, all-in-one "radiograms" of the sort seen in the 1950s were much less modular. One advantage of the modularity of a modern hi-fi is that it assists in tracing the source of a malfunction because disorders can be confined to particular modules leaving the operation of the others intact. Thus, if the record you are playing sounds dreadful, you can decide whether the fault lies in the deck, amplifier or speakers by trying a cassette, listening through headphones instead of through the speakers, and so on.

Many amplifiers have spare slots which allow you to add on new components as they come on the market (adding a compact disc player to an existing hi-fi for example). All that is required is that the new component should provide an output which is compatible with the requirements of the existing components. Similarly, the modular organisa- tion of our minds and brains may allow us to develop new cognitive components and interface them with old ones to create new skills and capabilities. The development in childhood of modules for reading and writing would be an example; reading and writing have only become widespread in very recent history, yet we will see that they appear to be modularised within the brain. Finally, a new, improved type of record deck may come onto the market. If your system is modular you can simply replace your old deck with one of the new type without needing to touch any of your other components, thereby illustrating Marr's point about modular systems being easier to improve.

Diagrams and Diagram Makers

If you were in the position of wanting to assemble a hi-fi system from scratch then you might find it useful to sketch a simple diagram showing the components you need and how they will interconnect. Diagrams are very useful expository devices wherever modular systems are under consideration (Ellis, 1987; Morton, 1981). They were used extensively by the school of neuropsychologists which flourished between 1870 and 1910 (Morton, 1984).

Figure. 1.1 shows the diagram put forward by Lichtheim (1885) as a model of the recognition and production of spoken and written words. It comprises five different "centres" or modules interlinked in certain ways. Centre A is a module whose function is to recognise the spoken forms of words when listening to a speaker and also to provide spoken word-forms when you are speaking yourself. Centre B houses word concepts or meanings, and is similarly employed in both the production and comprehension of language. Centre O, the centre for visual word images, recognises written words and also makes their spellings available in the act of writing. Finally, Centre M holds "motor images" ready to guide the groups of muscles which will articulate the words.

Diagrams like this were used to explain different forms of language disorder in terms of damage either to the centres themselves or to the pathways connecting them. A patient who had problems understanding or producing both spoken and written words might, for example, be

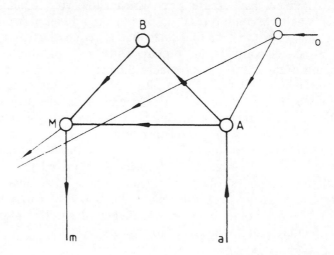

FIG. 1.1 Lichtheim's (1885) model of word recognition and production (reproduced with permission from Howard and Hatfield, 1987).

assumed to have suffered damage to centre B, whereas a patient whose problems lay in articulating words in speech would be said to have an impairment affecting centre M. A patient who could both understand and produce spoken words, but had difficulties in repeating heard words, might be interpreted as having suffered damage to the connection between A and M, and so on.

The popularity of diagrams like Lichtheim's must tell us something about their usefulness for neuropsychologists in practice. They did, however, have their problems (Marshall, 1982; Morton, 1984). First, the diagrams were only of real use in interpreting disorders that affected the comprehension, production or repetition of single words: They had little to say about disorders affecting, for example, grammatical processes involved in sentence construction. Secondly, the theorists had very little idea as to how their centres might actually work. They lacked the vocabulary of computational, information-processing concepts that now enables us to talk about the possible internal operations of the modules we postulate. Thirdly, whereas a modern cognitive theory has to account for data from experimental cognitive psychology as well as data from neuropsychology, the diagrams of the late nineteenth century were only constrained by neuropsychological evidence. The danger was that a diagram could be modified in a fairly *ad hoc* manner in order to fit the particular pattern of impairment seen in any particular patient. Some of these modifications were arbitrary and manifestly unsatisfactory. A theory that can "explain" any patient who comes along simply by redrawing the diagram is unfalsifiable. Unfalsifiable theories may seem attractive to the novice, but because they set no constraints on the claims or predictions that can be made, they are of little real use.

Finally, the majority of the turn-of-the-century diagrams were superimposed upon an outline of the left cerebral hemisphere of the brain. The diagrams therefore incorporated both a cognitive theory as to what the appropriate centres and their interconnections were, and a neuropsychological theory as to where the centres were located in the brain and where the tracts ran between them. If a patient was discovered whose symptoms were not those one would predict, given the site of the patient's brain injury, there was no way of knowing whether the cognitive component of the diagram—the proposed set of centres and connections—was at fault, or whether it was the proposed localisation of the centres and connections that was in error.

Today's cognitive neuropsychologists are much more careful to distinguish between theories as cognitive models and questions as to where a proposed set of modules may be localised within the brain. Some cognitive neuropsychologists refuse almost as a matter of principle to discuss issues of possible localisation; others consider such issues to be of interest but acknowledge that they are separate from the evaluation of the model as a cognitive theory. Our own view is that many of the deficits we will discuss are related to damage to particular areas of the brain. Thus we will mention lesion sites from time to time, but we do *not* give them *explanatory* status.

In his influential book, *The Modularity of Mind*, Fodor (1983) acknowledged several antecedents of the notion of modularity, but curiously failed to mention the nineteenth-century diagram makers. Yet these theorists are arguably closer than anyone to current thinking, as Morton (1984) demonstrates in his point-by-point comparison of nineteenth-century diagrams with information-processing diagrams proposed by cognitive psychologists in recent times. We shall make quite extensive use of modular diagrams in this book to help us understand disorders shown by patients, though some of the weaknesses of nineteenth-century diagrams, such as their problems in giving an account of grammatical and other high-level disorders, remain.

Fodor's Proposed Attributes of Cognitive Modules

In *The Modularity of Mind* Fodor listed what he thought to be the properties of cognitive modules. Important among these was the property of *informational encapsulation*, meaning that a module must carry out its own form of processing in complete ignorance of, and isolation from, the processes going on elsewhere in the total cognitive system. If, for example, there is a module or set of modules which process the emotional expression on a face, and a separate module or set of modules which recognise the face and determine who the person is, then informational encapsulation demands that the modules processing the emotion on the face must operate independently of any activity within those modules processing the identity of the face.

According to Fodor, modules must also be *domain-specific*, meaning that each module can only accept one particular sort of input. For example, the module processing the emotional expression of faces would not also be able to process the emotional tone of voices; such processing would require a separate domain-specific module. As Shallice (1984) pointed out, if the assumptions of informational encapsulation and domain specificity are combined with an assumption of *neurological specificity*, whereby modules are distinctly represented within the brain itself, then cognitive neuropsychology becomes a viable enterprise, because the possibility arises that brain lesions will selectively impair certain modules while leaving the others intact and operating at normal, pre-injury levels of efficiency.

The notions of informational encapsulation and domain specificity are ones which commentators upon Fodor's thesis have found easiest to accept (see, for example, the commentaries which accompany Fodor, 1985). Other properties of modules that Fodor proposed have received less unanimous acclaim. For example, Fodor argued that the operation of modules is *mandatory*. This means that modules are unstoppable— they are beyond voluntary control, and if the appropriate input is present a module will carry out its particular source of processing whether the owner of that module wishes it or not. We shall discover that many modules do indeed show the property of mandatory operation, particularly the modules involved in various aspects of recognition and processing of sensory information, but there may be modules whose operation is not mandatory. For example, the system from which the names of people and things are retrieved appears to have many of the required properties of modules, yet the retrieval of the name of a person or object seems to be more voluntary than mandatory. We cannot stop ourselves recognising a familiar person we see, but we do seem to have some voluntary control over whether or not we activate the module from which the person's name is retrieved. Conceivably, mandatoriness is more a property of input modules than of output modules.

Another property of modules which Fodor suggested but which has come in for some criticism is the notion that cognitive modules are of necessity *innate*, i.e. they are part of our genetic endowment. As Schwartz and Schwartz (1984) among others noted, some of the best cognitive neuropsychological evidence for the existence of modular systems comes from studies of acquired reading and writing disorders (dyslexias and dysgraphias). The skills of reading and writing appear to be made possible by the concerted and orchestrated activity of several cognitive modules each of which is capable of separate impairment, and those modules in the skilled reader and writer apparently behave just like any other cognitive modules. Yet reading and writing are artificial, culturally trans- mitted skills which until recently have only ever been acquired by a very small minority of people, and few psychologists are willing to entertain the notion that the modules required to read and write are part of our biological heritage (though see Marshall, 1987). It in no way threatens Fodor's general thesis to argue that modules can be established through a process of learning as well as being inherited genetically.

One of Fodor's most controversial suggestions was that whereas input processes to do with the perception of the external world (and possibly output processes to do with the control of action upon the world) are modular, there may also be central parts of the mind which are not modular in their organisation. Fodor suggests that higher-level thinking processes such as are involved in reasoning, decision making, the forma- tion of beliefs, etc., are the product of operations which are not informationally encapsulated, not mandatory, not domain-specific, and so on. He even went so far as to suggest that because these central processes are not modular they are not amenable to scientific investigation. Readers interested in pursuing this aspect of Fodor's line of thought are directed to the commentaries in Fodor (1985).

From a cognitive neuropsychological perspective it is true that the dissociation methodology has largely been applied to input and output processes, and dissociations have not been sought among higher-level mental operations. If Fodor is right, then the quest for dissociations among input and output modules will be a quest directed at carving Nature at her joints, but trying to find dissociations among higher mental processes would be like trying to carve a meat loaf at its joints. That said, even if Fodor is right, there is still room for a cognitive neuropsychology of higher mental processes, because dissociations are not the only weapon in the armoury of the cognitive neuropsychologist. One of the techniques that cognitive neuropsychologists use in order to formulate hypotheses about the possible internal workings of cognitive systems is to look at the sorts of errors those systems make when they are partially but not completely disrupted. We shall look, for example, at the sorts of errors made by patients with speech production deficits or spelling impairments in order to try to understand something about the internal workings of modules which mediate the production of spoken and written words. One can equally look at the sorts of errors made by patients with disorders of higher mental functions and the sorts of difficulties they experience on different tasks in order to learn something about how those higher mental functions can be disrupted and impaired. One would hope in the process to learn something about how higher mental processes actually operate. The work of Shallice (1982) and Duncan (1986) represent steps in this direction.

SOME FURTHER ASSUMPTIONS OF COGNITIVE NEUROPSYCHOLOGY

The philosopher of science, Imre Lakatos, has argued that every science has at its core a set of assumptions which are not directly testable (Lakatos, 1974). These assumptions may be right or they may be wrong—the only way that the scientist working in a particular area will know whether its assumptions are right or wrong is by seeing whether the whole approach advances or flounders. As cognitive neuropsychology has become established in recent times, so its practitioners have sought to identify some of the core assumptions upon which it rests. The work of Shallice (1979a; 1981a), Saffran (1982) and Caramazza (1984; 1986) is of particular importance here.

Modularity is arguably one of the core assumptions of cognitive neuropsychology—something which can never be ultimately proved or disproved, but upon whose validity the enterprise as currently articulated rests. Another key assumption, following Shallice (1981a), is what we have already called *neurological specificity*, and what others have called *isomorphism*. This is the assumption that there is some correspondence between the organisation of the mind and the organisation of the brain. In the words of Lashley (1941): "The discovery that the various capacities which independently contribute to intellectual performance do correspond to the spatial distribution of cerebral mechanisms represents a step towards the recognition of similar organisation in neurological and mental events."

This assumption is not one that neuropsychologists in all periods have been willing to make. Brain (1964, p. 6) wrote that:

> The older neurologists, and even some today, thought that the different varieties of aphasia produced by lesions in different situations could be classified in psychological terms... but this presupposes first that in the nervous system speech is organised in such a way that anatomical centres correspond to psychological functions, and then that destruction of such a centre merely impairs a particular psychological element in speech. This view has largely been abandoned.

The view which Brain thought abandoned is one which has been revived by cognitive neuropsychologists and one which underpins much of the cognitive neuropsychological enterprise. This does not mean that it is right, and if it is wrong (as Brain thought) then the early promise of cognitive neuropsychology will not be borne out in its further development. We should note, however, that at minimum all that cognitive neuropsychology needs to claim is that impairments of cognitive processes can be selective. It may well be possible to see selective deficits following injury to systems in which the storage of information is "distributed" rather than being organised into physically discrete centres (modules) corresponding to psychological functions. If so, then cognitive neuropsychology can proceed with its research programme.

Another assumption of cognitive neuropsychology is the assumption of *transparency*, which requires that "The pathological performance observed will provide a basis for discerning which component or module of the system is disrupted" (Caramazza, 1984). That is, careful analysis of the pattern of intact and impaired performance and the pattern of errors shown by a patient after brain injury must be capable of leading us to valid conclusions about the nature and functions of the impaired processing components. To this end, Caramazza (1984) suggests that the performance of a given patient will reflect four factors. These are:

1. The contribution attributable to the "true" effect of the hypothesised disruption of one or more processing components (modules).
2. Normal individual variation in performance.
3. The effects of compensatory operations.
4. Effects that result from disruptions to processing mechanisms other
than the hypothesised component.

Clearly some of these factors present obstacles to the interpretation
of the pattern of symptoms shown by a particular patient. Caramazza's
mention of normal individual variation in performance highlights the fact
that we are not all alike in so-called normality. Even within the normal
population of individuals without brain injuries some people's modules
work better for some things than do other people's, so that some people
are naturally better than others at, say, verbal skills or spatial skills.
Before one attributes a patient's poor performance on certain tasks to
brain injury, it is necessary to satisfy oneself that the patient was not
constitutionally poor on those tasks even before his or her brain injury.
There is a real danger of diagnosing an impairment of geographical
orientation in a patient who always used to get lost when he turned round
twice, or an impairment of spelling in a patient who has never been able
to spell at all well. The usual (but not infallible) way of preventing such
possibilities is to show that the patient's performance is seriously impaired
in comparison to appropriately chosen control subjects.

Caramazza's third factor, that of "compensatory operations", refers
to the widely acknowledged fact that aspects of a brain-injured patient's
performance may reflect cognitive systems working in ways rather different
from those in which they worked before the brain was damaged. For
example, some patients read words in a letter-by-letter manner, naming
each letter before saying what the word is and often before understanding
it (see Chapter 8). Letter-by-letter reading is not something that normal
readers ever do, nor something that these patients would ever have done
before their brain injury; rather it seems to be a way that non-damaged
cognitive systems can operate so as to effect a form of reading in a new
and unusual way when other parts of the system have been damaged.
What matters for cognitive neuropsychology is not that old modules can
be put to new uses, but that new modules should not be coming into
existence following brain injury.

The important assumption that the performance of a brain-injured
patient reflects the total cognitive apparatus minus those systems which
have been impaired, is what Saffran (1982) termed the assumption of
subtractivity. It is assumed—and there is as yet no good evidence to

cast doubt on this assumption—that the mature brain is not capable of sprouting new modules after brain injury. Only if we make this assumption can we use our models and other theoretical accounts of intact cognitive operations to interpret a patient's behaviour in terms of damage to the formerly intact cognitive system. As Caplan (1981) observes: "If the lesioned brain develops systems that are radically different than normal, that is an interesting and medically important fact, but not one relevant to normal functions." The injured brain may develop new *strategies* for coping in a particular task or situation, but it must do so using pre-existing *structures*. We shall encounter several examples of such strategies in the course of the book (e.g. patients who identify people using single salient visual features, or patients who read words by first naming all their letters). Such bizarre strategies need to be explained in terms of old modules and connections being put to new uses, though it is probably fair to say that such abnormal strategies are less helpful than other disorders when it comes to helping us understand the organisation of normal cognitive processes.

Caramazza's (1984) fourth requirement—that effects seen in brain-injured patients should not result from disruptions to processing mechanisms other than those hypothesised to be impaired—alludes to the fact that most brain injuries are substantial and cause damage to multiple processing components. There is a danger of ascribing to one component effects which are in fact due to a second, separate component which also happens to be damaged in that patient. In essence, this is the point made earlier in the chapter that co-occurrences of symptoms are much more hazardous things to base theoretical conclusions upon than are dissociations between symptoms. We will encounter several instances in this book where two or more symptoms, which at one time have plausibly been attributed to the impairment of one cognitive component, have later proved to be dissociable and must now be attributed to impairments to two separate cognitive components.

We should note that the assumption of transparency, whereby a patient's pattern of performance will provide a guide—albeit a complex one—to the nature of the underlying disruption, is one on which opinions have varied quite widely. Heeschen (1985, p. 209) quotes the neuropsychologist Kurt Goldstein as "emphatically pointing out over and over again that the brain-damaged patients' spontaneous behaviour never reflects the deficit itself, but rather the patients' reactions to the deficit". This does not undermine cognitive neuropsychology because "the true behavioural deficit shows up... under more carefully controlled and restricted formal testing conditions", but it suggests that we should be thinking in terms of an assumption of potential if sometimes clouded visibility rather than crystal transparency.

CONVERGING OPERATIONS

We have mentioned a number of similarities between today's cognitive neuropsychology and that practised by the "diagram makers" of the late nineteenth century. There are also, however, some important differences. One of these is that the diagram makers came to a cognitive neuropsychology from a background in medicine and neurology. In contrast, most of today's cognitive neuropsychologists either come from a background in experimental cognitive psychology or work in collaboration with mainstream cognitive psychologists. This means that cognitive neuropsychology is much closer in aims and in theories to experimental cognitive psychology than has ever been the case in the past. This is in part responsible for cognitive neuropsychology's current vigour.

It is noticeable that the subjects on which cognitive neuropsychology cut its teeth in the late 1960s and early 1970s were subjects for which there was a strong tradition in experimental cognitive psychology and for which there were viable theories of normal functioning. For example, Shallice and Warrington (1970) used existing theories of the organisation of short-term memory and long-term memory as a framework within which to interpret the performance of their patient KF in whom short-term verbal recall was impaired although long-term recall was preserved. Shallice and Warrington argued that such a pattern of performance was, in fact, incompatible with prevailing theories of memory structure, such as that put forward by Atkinson and Shiffrin (1968), but was interpretable in terms of a somewhat modified memory model.

Although Shallice and Warrington eventually disagreed with and sought to modify pre-existing memory models, nevertheless those models and techniques which derived from experimental cognitive psychology shaped and guided their investigation of patient KF. Similarly, Marshall and Newcombe (1973) were able to make use of models of normal reading performance which existed at the time in their analysis of different forms of reading disorder (acquired dyslexia). Once again their cognitive neuro-psychological work led them to propose modifications to certain existing models, but their work was nevertheless closely guided and shaped by the theories and methods of cognitive psychology. Unlike the diagram makers, who had to devise their own theories of normal performance while simultaneously using those theories to explain different patterns of disorder, the more recent generation of cognitive neuropsychologists have often been able to begin their investigations of disorders in particular areas with reference to theories of normal performance put forward by mainstream experimental cognitive psychologists.

Modern-day cognitive neuropsychologists also bring to the study of patients the techniques of analysis developed in experimental psychology, including techniques for the statistical interpretation of results. Indeed, many cognitive neuropsychologists retain a foot in the experimental camp, because it is not uncommon for work with a patient to generate predictions about how normal subjects will behave in particular tasks or under particular conditions. Cognitive neuropsychologists can find themselves alternating between the hospital ward or patient's home and the cognitive laboratory in their pursuit of the understanding of how a particular area of cognition works.

We noted above that cognitive neuropsychology rests on a number of fundamental assumptions. So, equally, does experimental cognitive psychology. But the assumptions of the two approaches are to some extent different. This means that a conclusion about the nature of cognition which is supported by evidence from both experimental and neuropsychological studies is more reliable than a conclusion which is supported by evidence from only one source, because the conclusion supported by two lines is that much less likely to be artifactual or to rest on a faulty assumption. Seeking support for a theoretical conclusion from two or more different sources is what Garner, Hake, and Eriksen (1956) termed *converging operations*, and the quest for converging operations has provided much of the vigour of cognitive neuropsychology in recent decades.

The quest for converging evidence is seen very clearly in the work of Shallice, McLeod, and Lewis (1985). They sought evidence for the independence of cognitive modules from experiments with normal subjects involving "dual-task" performance. They reasoned that if neuropsychological data suggests that two tasks are dissociable and therefore mediated by separate sets of cognitive modules, then in the normal subject it should be possible for those two sets of modules to sustain their separate tasks independently without detriment to either. Therefore, two tasks which each depend for their execution on different sets of modules should be capable of being executed together simultaneously almost as efficiently as either can be executed on its own. Shallice et al. (1985) tested this prediction in a dual-task experiment where normal subjects were required simultaneously to read aloud written words and to monitor a list of heard names for particular target names. They found that their subjects were capable of reading aloud while monitoring heard names almost as well as they could either read aloud alone or monitor heard names alone. This matches similar work, such as that of Allport, Antonis, and Reynolds (1972) who found that skilled pianists with a little practice could simultaneously repeat passages of prose they were hearing over headphones and sight-read music they had seen beforehand for only 10 seconds with little detriment to either task. This line of convergence promises to provide a good way of assessing whether modules which neuropsychological evidence suggests are capable of functioning independently of one another can in fact do so in the normal, intact person.

A rather different form of convergence between data from patients and data from normal subjects comes when normal subjects display "symptoms" similar to those shown by brain-injured patients. We shall see in Chapter 5 how the word-finding difficulties of some "aphasic" patients closely resemble the occasional difficulties which normal people can experience when caught in a tip-of-the-tongue state. Similarly, in Chapter 7 we shall show how patients with certain forms of writing disorder can make habitual spelling errors which resemble the occasional spelling difficulties of normal subjects. Chapter 8 discusses a form of acquired reading disorder known as "attentional dyslexia" in which patients often report having seen words which are made up of letters taken from words actually present on the written page but rearranged to form a new word (for example, seeing the word *peg* when the words in front of them are *pad* and *leg*). Normal subjects will occasionally make this sort of error when reading (Cowie, 1985) but will make these same errors much more frequently if shown groups of words for very short intervals. That simple experimental manipulation greatly increases the number of errors to a level which can come close to that of "attentional dyslexics" (Allport, 1977). The crucial difference, of course, is that the "attentional dyslexics" make these errors when they have unlimited time to inspect words.

The importance of this sort of converging evidence lies in the support it provides for the subtractivity assumption—the assumption that what we see in a brain-injured patient is just the previous, intact cognitive system minus those components which have been lost or impaired through brain injury. Where the errors made by neurological patients resemble errors made by normal people then we feel confident in saying that the cognitive systems which are impaired in the patient, and give rise to the habitual errors of those patients, are the same systems which very occasionally malfunction in normals, or which can be made to malfunction more often when stressed by various experimental manipulations. We do not need to postulate the growth of new cognitive processes or even of new strategies in the patient in order to explain the occurrence of symptoms which have counterparts in normal behaviour and normal errors.

Converging operations are extremely important in present-day cognitive neuropsychology. The aim is to develop theories of normal, intact cognitive functioning which are also capable of accounting for the different patterns of disorder that can be seen in neurological patients. Sometimes the development of those theories will be better served by laboratory experiments with normal subjects; sometimes by careful study of brain-injured patients. We should be willing to turn to either source of evidence as necessary. The continuing vigour of cognitive neuropsychology will depend to a large extent on whether or not it is able to keep abreast of developments in cognitive psychology. If cognitive neuropsychology were to lose touch with mainstream cognitive science, then it would be in real danger of losing much of its momentum.

We said at the outset of this chapter that we think the strength of cognitive neuropsychology is best appreciated through experience of its achievements in helping to unravel cognitive processes. Accordingly, we shall wind up our introduction at this point in order to turn to a consideration of specific applications of the cognitive neuropsychological approach. Each of the following chapters will end with an Overview, a Summary, and a list of Further Reading. The Overview will make some general theoretical points about the cognitive function under consideration, while the Summary will provide a précis of the main points. Because this entire chapter is, in a sense, an Overview, we shall forego such a section here.

SUMMARY

Cognitive neuropsychology has undergone a revival since around 1970. It is an approach which attempts to understand cognitive functions such as recognising, speaking or remembering through an analysis of the different ways those functions can be impaired following brain injury. More specifically, cognitive neuropsychology seeks to explain the patterns of impaired and intact cognitive performance seen in brain-injured patients in terms of damage to one or more of the components of a theory or model of normal cognitive functioning and, conversely, to draw conclusions about normal, intact cognitive processes from the observed disorders.

Dissociations, in which one aspect of performance is impaired whereas others are preserved, are taken to imply the existence of separate cognitive subsystems or *modules* responsible for different cognitive operations. The hypothesised organisation of these modules may (according to taste) be expressed in terms of an "information processing" diagram. Frequently, observed *associations* between deficits are harder to interpret because of the danger that they may arise for anatomical rather than functional reasons (e.g. cognitively distinct modules depend on adjacent regions of cerebral cortex and thus tend to be impaired together).

In contrast to traditional neuropsychology which tended to study groups of patients, cognitive neuropsychologists typically investigate single cases of theoretical importance. The results of these investigations are interpreted in terms of a set of assumptions which are still being articulated and changed as the approach evolves. The assumption of *isomorphism* states that the cognitive structure of the mind is reflected in, and arises out of, the physiological organisation of the brain. The assumption of *transparency* holds that, given the wit and the time, it will be possible to deduce the nature of the underlying cognitive disorder in a patient from the pattern of preserved and impaired capabilities (including the pattern of errors). This process will be aided by the assumption of *subtractivity* according to which the performance of a brain-injured patient is explained in terms of the capabilities of the normal, intact cognitive system minus those components which have been lost as a result of the injury. In other words, the mature brain is assumed to be incapable of developing new cognitive structures following injury.

Cognitive neuropsychologists believe that we can draw general conclusions about the way the intact mind and brain work from studying neurological patients, but such conclusions can obviously also be drawn from observational and experimental studies of normal subjects. Some theoretical questions may be more easily resolved by the study of patients, others by the study of normals. The most reliable conclusions, however, will be those supported by independent evidence from the two separate lines of enquiry.

FURTHER READING

We can begin with the two papers that initially excited many people and awakened them to the possibilities of cognitive neuropsychology:

Shallice, T. & Warrington, E.K. (1970). Independent functioning of verbal memory stores: a neuropsychological study. *Quarterly Journal of Experimental Psychology, 22,* 261–273. Used data from patient KF to argue against the prevailing view of the organisation of short-term and long-term memory as sequential memory stores in favour of a parallel entry model (see Chapter 10).

Marshall, J.C. & Newcombe, F. (1973). Patterns of paralexia: a psycholinguistic approach. *Journal of Psycholinguistic Research, 2,* 175–199. A review of classical research on reading disorders plus new data supporting a "dual route" model of normal reading processes (see Chapter 8). Introduced, for better or for worse, the terms "visual dyslexia", "surface dyslexia", and "deep dyslexia". Still a joy to read.

Then we recommend three readings that examine the reasons why detailed investigations of individual patients are particularly important in cognitive neuropsychology:

Shallice, T. (1988). *From neuropsychology to mental structure* (Section I, pp. 1–37) Cambridge: Cambridge University Press. Introducing cognitive neuropsychology. More detailed introduction to topics discussed here.

Caramazza, A. & McCloskey, M. (1988). The case for single–patient studies. *Cognitive Neuropsychology, 5,* 517–528. Part of a special issue of the journal *Cognitive Neuropsychology,* which was devoted to methodology. The paper argues that only single-case studies allow valid inferences about normal cognitive processes from acquired disorders and rejects clinical syndrome classifications.

Ellis, A.W. (1987). Intimations of modularity, or the modularity of mind: doing cognitive neuropsychology without syndromes. In M. Coltheart, G. Sartori, & R. Job (Eds), *The cognitive neuropsychology of language*. Hove, UK: Lawrence Erlbaum Associates Ltd. Queries the wisdom of replacing old neuropsychological taxonomies of patients with new cognitive neuropsychological ones. Argues that the results of case studies should be related directly to theoretical models without the intervention of syndrome categories

Finally, here are two readings that look carefully at recent theoretical developments:

Shallice, T. (1988). *From neuropsychology to mental structure*. Cambridge: Cambridge University Press. Section III (pp. 203–266): Inferences from neuropsychological findings. Critique of ultra-cognitive neuropsychology and detailed discussion of inferences that can be made from neuropsychological dissociations.

Quinlan, P. (1991). *Connectionism and psychology: a psychological perspective on new connectionist research*. New York: Harvester Wheatsheaf. Chapter 5 (pp. 195–237): Higher-order aspects of cognition. Intelligent discussion of some connectionist accounts of neuropsychological phenomena.

2 Object Recognition

INTRODUCTION

The area of neuropsychology that has received the most attention, both from the traditional localisationalist approach and in the more recent studies in which the disorders are considered from a psychological perspective, is language use. There are several reasons for this, including the marked cerebral asymmetries in the control of language which seem well suited to investigation in terms of the localisation of functions in particular areas of the brain. The structural properties of language itself also offer a ready choice of factors to manipulate and investigate in more psychologically oriented studies. In addition, disorders of language are commonly encountered in stroke patients and in other patients with cerebral injuries, and can take remarkably specific forms.

The use of language, however, presupposes something to talk about. So let us begin by considering impairments in an individual's ability to understand the world around her or him; a world of objects and people. In doing this we will first consider the ability to recognise objects (this chapter), then broaden our discussion to examine a wider range of visual and spatial abilities (Chapter 3), and then consider the ability to recognise other people and to interpret their feelings and expressions (Chapter 4). These are vast topics, and in order to keep the range and quantity of material to a manageable level we will concentrate on the understanding of the visually perceived world, and on the face as a source of information used to identify people and interpret their feelings. Although the cognitive analysis of such impairments has not been nearly as widely pursued as has the cognitive analysis of disorders of language, we think that it holds great promise and that there are exciting discoveries to be made. This is not, however, to underestimate the size of the obstacles that will be encountered along the way.

Before considering neuropsychological studies of object recognition, we examine briefly some of the factors involved in recognising objects, and develop a simple theoretical framework to describe the functional components (modules) involved.

UNDERSTANDING OBJECT RECOGNITION

Most people are able to recognise everyday objects with ease across quite wide ranges of distances, orientations and lighting conditions. This is necessary for normal life, because we encounter the objects concerned under many different circumstances. In pointing out that an object can usually be recognised despite such transformations we do not wish to imply that the transformations have no effect. Gross or unusual transformations of distance, lighting or orientation can, for instance, be used to make puzzles in which everyday objects become hard to recognise. Our point is only that the brain's object recognition system has the potential to cope with such transformations and that under everyday conditions their effects are not usually noticed.

We can also readily recognise depictions of objects on a two-dimensional surface in the form of photographs, coloured pictures, or line drawings that may or may not include implied pictorial depth. Realistic depictions of these types make use of some but not all of the cues that can be used to recognise real objects.

Two important points can be deduced from this preliminary consideration of object recognition. The first is that descriptions of the structures of all of the objects we know must in some sense be stored in the brain, so that we are able to recognise one we have met before even if it is seen from a new angle. Object recognition can thus be considered to involve a comparison of the structure of a seen object with the structures of objects that are already known. The second point is that although this comparison will often demand knowledge of the three-dimensional structure of the objects concerned, there are certain cases in which outline shape can be sufficient to effect recognition. Recognition from outline shape probably requires that the object concerned is both well known and has a particularly characteristic shape, and will often also require that it is seen (or depicted) from one of a limited range of viewing positions.

The most powerful theoretical analysis of object recognition to date was presented by Marr (1980, 1982). Marr took as his starting point the assumption that vision involves the computation of efficient symbolic descriptions or representations from images cast by the world upon the retina. The basic questions he addressed were thus those of what types of representations are necessary for vision and what computational problems their construction poses. He suggested an analysis that proceeds through a sequence of three types of representation:

1. An initial representation, which Marr called the primal sketch. He thought that this would represent intensity (brightness) changes across the field of vision, and the two-dimensional geometry of the image. Such features as edges will usually produce abrupt intensity changes.

2. A viewer-centred representation, which Marr called the $2^1/_2$-D sketch. This would represent the spatial locations of visible surfaces from the viewer's position. Marr's idea was that conventional sources of information concerning depth and location (stereopsis, texture gradients, shading, and so on) are computed as part of the primal sketch and then assembled in the the $2^1/_2$-D sketch. The disadvantage of the $2^1/_2$-D sketch is that it lacks generality since it describes the object only from the observer's viewpoint.

3. An object-centred representation, which Marr called the 3-D model representation. This is a representation of the seen objects and surfaces which is independent of the viewer's position, and specifies the real shape of these objects and surfaces and how they are positioned with respect to each other.

Because the object-centred (3-D model) representation specifies the three-dimensional structure of the object in a relatively standard form, recognition by means of looking up this structure in some kind of store of all known object structures would then be possible.

A problem in understanding how objects are recognised that has often received comment concerns the fact that the level in the hierarchy of things in the world at which recognition is required can vary. A motor car might, for instance, be identified under different circumstances as a vehicle, a car, a Ford car, a Ford Escort, or as your friend's car. This point is important because it emphasises the flexibility of the human cognitive system.

We think, however, that the significance of our potential for flexibility of approach in object recognition can be overemphasised. Although it is certainly true that the car can be identified at any of the levels described by someone with the requisite knowledge, it does not follow either that all levels of recognition can be achieved with the same ease or that one level is not typical of everyday use. A particularly convincing case has been made by Rosch and her colleagues that categorisations of concrete objects are not arbitrary, but determined by their natural properties into certain basic categories (Rosch, Mervis, Gray, Johnson, & Boyes-Braem, 1976; Rosch, 1978). The basic category for our example would be "car". These basic categories were found to exist at a level at which objects in different categories could be most readily differentiated from each other in terms of attributes and shapes; they were also the earliest categories to be sorted and named by children. Of particular importance to the present discussion is Rosch et al.'s (1976) finding that objects could be classified as members (or not members) of the basic category more quickly than they could be classified as members (or not members) of superordinate or subordinate categories. Thus you would be quicker to identify your friend's car as a car than as a vehicle (superordinate category) or as a Ford car (subordinate category). This suggests that identification as a member of superordinate or subordinate categories may often be achieved via an initial identification at the basic level.

A MODEL OF OBJECT RECOGNITION AND NAMING

A model of the functional components involved in object recognition and naming consistent with the points we have discussed is presented in Fig. 2.1. This is by no means the only possible theoretical model, but we believe that it is adequate for present purposes. The model makes use of Marr's idea that three levels of representation of the visual input can be distinguished; we have called these initial, viewer-centred and object-centred. It also makes use of the idea that recognition is effected by comparing viewer-centred and object-centred representations to stored structural descriptions of known objects. We have called these stored descriptions object recognition units, and they act as an interface between visual and semantic representations (see Humphreys & Riddoch, 1987b; Seymour, 1979; Warren & Morton, 1982, for related conceptions of object recognition). A visual representation (separated here into initial, viewer-centred and object-centred) describes what the object looks like, whereas a semantic representation specifies its properties and attributes. One recognition unit is held to exist for each known object. This recognition unit can access the object's semantic representation when the visual representation of a seen object corresponds to the description of the object stored in the recognition unit. The object recognition units can be "primed" by recent experience or by context to be more easily activated (i.e. to "expect" certain objects to occur). Like most contemporary theories of object and word recognition (see Seymour, 1979) we tend to think that any particular stimulus has a semantic representation that can be accessed by different types of input (object, picture, written

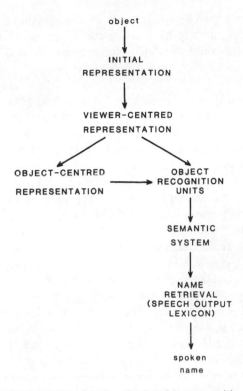

FIG. 2.1.   Functional model for object recognition.

name, spoken name, etc.) rather than a different semantic representation for every type of input.

Object naming, which is a task commonly given to neuropsychological patients, is dealt with in our model by assuming that the semantic system does not contain the object's name, but can retrieve the name from a separate store or "lexicon", which we shall discuss in Chapter 5 under the heading of the "speech output lexicon". There is no direct link between the object recognition units and this name store; all retrieval of object names occurs via a semantic representation.

THE CONCEPT OF AGNOSIA

GL, an 80-year-old salesman, returned exhausted from one of his business trips after a severe storm had blown him against a wooden fence, knocking his head. He retired to bed for a few days, complaining that he was no longer able to see as well as before.

GL's problems were obvious when he got up. Although he could still see, he no longer recognised the things about him. Instead, he looked around in a perplexed manner, as if everything was unfamiliar. He thought that pictures in his room were boxes, and tried to search in them for things he could not find. He mistook his jacket for a pair of trousers, and at mealtimes he could not recognise the pieces of cutlery on the table.

Detailed investigations showed that GL still had almost normal visual acuity for his age, and that he could draw quite accurate copies of seen objects that he could not recognise; thus his vision was in at least some respects intact. Neither had he lost his knowledge of objects; he referred to them appropriately in conversation, and he could recognise them immediately if he handled them, or from characteristic sounds. When shown a whistle, for example, he had no idea what it was, yet he recognised it straight away when it was blown.

GL's problems form a good example of *visual agnosia*. The term agnosia is derived from the Ancient Greek language, and roughly translates as "not-knowing". Use of the term agnosia is usually taken to imply that the recognition disorder is not a consequence of general intellectual deterioration, language impairment, or basic sensory dysfunction at the level we have described as the initial representation. The patient can still see things, but fails to recognise what they are. GL's case is, in fact, of particular interest because it was one of the first to be reported. His accident occurred in 1887, and his case was described in a classic paper by Lissauer (1890; see Shallice & Jackson, 1988).

Agnosias may be in visual (inability to recognise seen objects), tactile (inability to recognise felt objects) or auditory (inability to recognise heard objects) modalities (see Oppenheimer & Newcombe, 1978; Rubens, 1979; Vignolo, 1982). Within a particular modality they can occur for different classes of stimuli such as colours, objects or faces. Often, however, the same patient will be agnosic for more than one modality or for more than one class of stimuli within a particular modality. An excellent review of the clinical features of agnosic disorders is given by Rubens (1979). We will give most attention here to the nature of the underlying cognitive impairments found in cases of agnosia for visually presented objects. These are very disabling, and Humphreys and Riddoch (1987a) provide a sympathetic account of the impact of the condition on everyday life.

There seem to be several different causes of visual object agnosia. Lissauer (1890) himself realised this, and distinguished between what he termed "apperceptive" and "associative" agnosias. He proposed that visual recognition can be separated into apperceptive and associative stages, and that each when impaired has its own characteristic agnosia. The apperceptive stage would correspond to the final stage of purely "perceptual" processing; it was considered to be intact if the patient could accurately copy items s/he could not recognise. The associative stage would give the percept meaning by linking it to previous experience.

Lissauer's apperceptive or associative distinction is still often used as a starting point in identifying the various types of agnosia, but we will not make much use of it here because, as we will see, the issues raised by modern studies of agnosia demand a richer type of theory.

Disconnection Hypotheses

Lissauer's explanation of apperceptive agnosia was in terms of *damage* to the perceptual mechanisms themselves, whereas his explanation of associative agnosia was closer to that of a *disconnection* between intact perception and stored associations. Damage and disconnection continue to be used as explanatory concepts in modern studies of agnosia, and disconnection explanations were given a particular boost by the work of Geschwind (1965a; 1965b), who demonstrated that certain neurological syndromes fit disconnection explanations very neatly.

Although it was not central to his argument, Geschwind (1965b) proposed that visual object agnosia can result from disconnection of areas of the brain responsible for vision and for speech. Such a disconnection could, for instance, happen when serious injury of the posterior part of the left cerebral hemisphere deprived the left hemisphere's speech areas of visual input by destroying simultaneously both the left hemisphere's own visual areas and the connections (via the corpus callosum) to the left hemisphere's speech area from the remaining visual areas of the right cerebral hemisphere. The patient would still have an intact (right hemisphere) visual area and an intact (left hemisphere) speech area, but these intact areas would be disconnected from each other (for most patients there is no right hemisphere speech area). This is actually an over-simplification of Geschwind's suggestion, but it is sufficient to establish the basic point that such disconnections are anatomically possible. Moreover, cases of difficulties in object recognition for which disconnection provides a plausible and appealing explanation have certainly been described (e.g. Mack & Boller, 1977; Newcombe & Ratcliff, 1974, case 3; Rubens & Benson, 1971). As we will see, however, disconnection cannot account for the problems of all agnosic patients, and the basic distinction of vision and speech is in any case too simple to cope with the complexity of the issues that emerge. The first cases we will discuss involve shape processing impairments. They are what Lissauer (1890) would have considered to be apperceptive agnosias (but see Warrington, 1987, for a different view), and are not susceptible to disconnection explanations.

HCP—B*

SHAPE-PROCESSING IMPAIRMENTS

Benson and Greenberg (1969) reported their observations of a young soldier, Mr S, who had suffered accidental carbon monoxide poisoning. Mr S seems to have possessed an initial representation of visual stimuli that was at least to some extent intact. His visual fields were normal to 10 mm and 3 mm white objects, and he was able to maintain fixation. He could name colours and describe at least some other perceptual qualities; for instance he described a safety pin as being "silver and shiny like a watch or nail clipper". He was said to appear attentive to his surroundings, and he could navigate the hospital corridors successfully in his wheelchair. He was also able to distinguish small differences in stimulus brightness and wavelength on psychophysical testing, and could detect movements of small objects.

On any task requiring shape or form perception, however, Mr S was very severely impaired. His eye movements seemed random when he scanned pictures, and he was virtually unable to recognise objects, pictures of objects, body parts, letters, numbers, faces or geometrical figures from vision alone. He was unable to copy letters or simple figures and could not match a sample figure to an identical figure in a set of four. In marked contrast, he was able to identify and name objects from tactile, olfactory and auditory cues. No defects were noticed in his memory, spontaneous speech, or comprehension.

Mr S showed impaired ability to analyse visual form. We could interpret the case as being one of severe impairment in constructing the viewer-centred representation, because there is some evidence of sparing of the simple perceptual properties given by the initial representation despite almost total deterioration on tasks requiring shape information including copying, matching and identification. Efron (1968) provides further information on Mr S's shape-processing impairment.

A more recent case described by Abadi, Kulikowski, and Meudell (1981), and investigated subsequently by Campion and Latto (1985), however, suggests that impairment of the initial representation might contribute to this type of problem. Like Mr S, Campion and Latto's patient, RC, had suffered accidental carbon monoxide poisoning. He also showed an impairment of object recognition, being able to identify only 17 out of 27 objects with considerable difficulty. He could not copy line drawings, or even trace them with his finger. In contrast, he could negotiate obstacles, reach out for seen objects, name objects from touch or sound, and comment on the colour and texture of seen objects. His visual acuity was normal, yet he maintained that his vision was "not clear".

Initial investigation of RC's visual fields showed only that there was an area of blindness in the lower right-hand portion. Such visual field defects are often found after neurological injury, but this alone could not account for RC's object recognition impairment, because many patients with worse visual field defects do not have the same problem. More careful testing revealed, however, that small areas of blindness were scattered across the whole of RC's field of vision. Campion and Latto (1985) suggest that this "peppering" of the visual field resulted from diffuse damage to the visual cortex of the brain: Because of their cortical origin, RC would not be aware of these numerous small areas of blindness when he looked at things (in the same way as we are not normally aware of the blind spot in our own field of vision where the optic nerve leaves the retina). Figure 2.2 gives an idea of how difficult this hypothesised scattering of blind areas throughout the visual field might make object recognition.

We are touching here on the much debated issue of the contribution of impairments of basic perceptual abilities to agnosias. RC's case makes clear that such impairments may contribute to at least some cases of disordered object recognition ability. The suspicion that all visual object agnosias may be a consequence of subtle (and, by implication, probably overlooked) alterations in perceptual function has been particularly difficult to shake off, but it is now widely accepted that sensory impairments show no necessary relation to object identification difficulties, and that many patients who are in no sense agnosic show greater sensory defects than those who are (Ettlinger, 1956; Young & Ellis, 1988). Moreover, as we will see, even the most careful testing has failed to reveal sensory defects in a few of the agnosic patients who have been described.

RECOGNITION OF DEGRADED STIMULI, AND IMPAIRMENTS OF OBJECT CONSTANCY

Degraded Stimuli

We have already commented on the facility with which normal people can recognise objects across a relatively wide range of perceptual transformations. Several studies of groups of patients with posterior lesions of the left or right cerebral hemispheres have, however, shown that patients with right hemisphere injuries do not show this facility to the same degree as normal people. These patients are not agnosic, in the sense that their everyday recognition abilities are not dramatically affected by the disorder, but they show clear impairments on certain types of task. They experience, for instance, disproportionate difficulty in identifying objects which are drawn overlapping each other (De Renzi & Spinnler, 1966), or in identifying objects from pictures degraded by the removal of some

FIG. 2.2. A: Photograph of a scene, and B: the same photograph covered with a random dot mask to simulate what the world might look like to R.C. It is assumed that the patient would not actually be aware of the dots but would be left with the consequent disruption of contour necessity for form perception. Note the differential masking effect of the same mask on different objects. Thus, the child's face completely disappears, whereas the wheelbarrow remains visible. The bucket contour is disrupted to an intermediate extent. (Reproduced with permission from Campion, 1987.)

36

edge information (De Renzi & Spinnler, 1966; Warrington & James, 1967a).

A number of other examples of this type could be given. What they all share is the finding that in difficult object recognition tasks the performance of patients with right hemisphere injuries is more affected than the performance of normal control subjects or patients with left hemisphere injuries. Warrington (1982, p. 18) remarks that "the hallmark of this syndrome appears to be a difficulty in perceiving meaningful visual stimuli when the redundancy normally present within the figure is reduced or degraded".

This impairment in difficult recognition tasks does not seem to be a direct consequence of impairment at the level of what we have called the initial representation. Several examples of this point are given by Warrington (1982), who shows that despite their impairment on object identification tasks, patients with right posterior injuries can achieve what she calls an "adequately structured percept". Their impairments in visual sensory efficiency, figure-ground discrimination and contour discrimination are no greater than those of other patients (usually patients with left hemisphere injuries) who do not experience difficulty in object identification tasks.

The difficulties in identification tasks are thus thought to reflect impairments at a post-sensory level of visual information processing, such as the viewer-centred and object-centred representations. The deficits are seen as sufficient to interfere with difficult identification tasks while leaving performance on relatively simple identification tasks within normal limits. Comparable impairments in right hemisphere patients have also been shown for the recognition of degraded letters (Warrington & James, 1967a) and for deciding whether pictures of faces distorted by the exaggeration of lighting effects were those of a man, woman, old man, old woman, boy or girl (Newcombe, 1969; 1974). The parallel between these tasks and those causing impairment of object identification in right hemisphere patients is easy to see, though it should not be too quickly assumed that they all measure the same deficit, because Warrington (1982) has presented evidence for dissociations between comparable impairments with different types of visual stimulus material.

Unusual Views

In a series of papers Warrington (1982; Warrington & Taylor, 1973; 1978) has argued that object recognition requires some means of assigning equivalent stimuli to the same perceptual category, in order to cope with transformations of orientation, lighting, distance, and so on. It is this perceptual categorisation that she thinks defective in patients with posterior injuries of the right cerebral hemisphere. In terms of our own model Warrington's idea of perceptual categorisation involves the combined action of the functional components described as viewer-centred representation, object-centred representation, and object recognition units (i.e. stored descriptions of the structures of familiar objects).

The evidence presented by Warrington and Taylor (1973; 1978) is intriguing. They showed patients photographs of objects taken from conventional and unusual views. Although Warrington and Taylor do not attempt to define what constitutes a conventional or an unusual view, the idea is not difficult to pick up, and an example of what is meant is given in Fig. 2.3. Warrington and Taylor (1973) point out that they chose the unusual views so that they were not necessarily unfamiliar views. Their unusual view of a bucket, for instance, involves looking almost directly into it; yet buckets are not uncommonly seen from this angle.

Two different versions of tests using conventional and unusual views have been devised by Warrington and Taylor. The first version (Warrington & Taylor, 1973) involved photographs of the same 20 common objects taken from both conventional and unusual views. Subjects were first required to identify the object shown in each of the unusual views, and then to identify the same objects from each of the conventional views. Their findings were that few errors were made from the conventional view, but a group of patients with posterior injuries of the right hemisphere were poor at identifying objects from an unconventional view.

We would suggest that at least part of this deficit in identifying objects from unconventional views may be explainable in terms of an impairment in constructing object-centred representations. As already stated, Warrington's idea of perceptual categorisation seems to encompass what we have described as the viewer-centred representation, object-centred representation and object recognition units. However, the unimpaired performance of the patients with right posterior injuries on conventional views suggests that the viewer-centred representation and object recognition units are relatively intact. The key feature of many (though by no means

UNUSUAL VIEW   USUAL VIEW

FIG. 2.3. Examples of usual and unusual views of an object. (Figure kindly supplied by Professor E. K. Warrington.)

all) of the unusual views used by Warrington and Taylor (1973) is most likely to be the foreshortening of the object's principal axis of elongation. This foreshortening would make it particularly difficult to derive an object-centred representation (Marr & Nishihara, 1978) and would thus highlight any impairment at this level.

In the second version of their conventional and unusual views test Warrington and Taylor (1978) presented pairs of photographs of objects, with one conventional view and one unusual view in each pair. The task was to decide whether the photographs in each pair were pictures of the same object; Warrington and Taylor (1978) describe this task as involving matching by physical identity. An impairment in a group of patients with posterior injuries of the right cerebral hemisphere was again found. This result is particularly striking because it implies that these patients cannot form an adequate representation of the object in the unusual view *despite* being able to derive an explicit hypothesis as to what it might be from their unimpaired performance with the conventional view photographs. When the same patients were later asked to identify the objects from photographs of conventional and unusual views presented one at a time, an impairment was again found for the unusual views.

It is clear, then, that patients with posterior (usually parietal lobe) lesions of the right cerebral hemisphere show impairments on some object recognition tasks which do not seem to be a direct consequence of an impairment in the initial representation of visual stimuli. Warrington has interpreted these difficulties as reflecting impaired perceptual categorisation, whereas we have preferred to emphasise the importance of object-centred representations. We see this as a variant of Warrington's explanation rather than a challenge to it. Both accounts locate the impairment at a level of visual information processing that can be described as post-sensory but pre-semantic.

Object Constancy

Humphreys and Riddoch (1984; 1985) have extended Warrington's work by carrying out investigations of individual patients with impairments of object constancy. By object constancy, Humphreys and Riddoch mean the ability to recognise that an object has the same structure across changes in view. They propose that we have two independent means of achieving object constancy; one by making use of an object's distinctive features, and the other by describing its structure relative to its principal axis of elongation. "Unusual" views might then impair object constancy either because they obscure a distinctive feature or because they foreshorten the object, making its principal axis of elongation more difficult to determine.

To disentangle these possibilities Humphreys and Riddoch used a matching task in which two photographs of the same object were presented together with a third photograph showing a visually similar distractor.

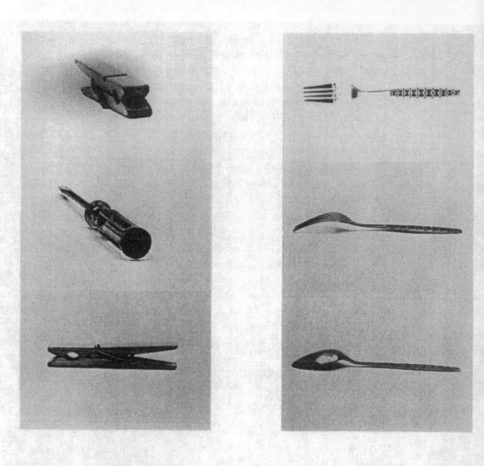

FORESHORTENED MATCH   MINIMAL FEATURE MATCH

FIG. 2.4. Examples of the foreshortened and minimal-feature conditions of Humphreys and Riddoch's (1984) matching task. (Stimuli kindly supplied by Dr. G. Humphreys & Dr. J. Riddoch.)

Patients and control subjects were asked to pick the two photographs which showed the same object. The target objects were carefully chosen to have a primary distinctive feature and a principal axis of elongation. One member of the correct pair of photographs always showed the target object in a "prototypical" view, in which its distinctive feature and axis of elongation were clearly visible. The other member of the correct pair of photographs showed the same object with its axis of elongation foreshortened or with the saliency of its primary distinctive feature reduced; these are called the foreshortened and minimal-feature conditions, respectively. It is easy to get the idea by examining the examples shown in Fig. 2.4.

Humphreys and Riddoch (1984; 1985) present data for five patients— four of these had right posterior cerebral lesions and the fifth, HJA, had a severe visual object agnosia caused by bilateral occipital lobe lesions. Because the performances of the four patients with right hemisphere lesions were so similar we have selected one representative, JL. On tests of basic form perception involving length, orientation and position discrimination with two-dimensional shapes, both JL and HJA were within the normal range of performance.

Data from the matching task for JL, HJA and control subjects are shown in Fig. 2.5, together with data indicating how often JL and HJA could name successfully the objects used from the different views. It was only the foreshortened pictures that created serious problems for JL, and these problems were equally severe whether the task was one of matching or naming. Thus, as we suggested for Warrington's patients with right posterior lesions, JL seems to have difficulty deriving the object-centred representation that would be needed to make a successful match or a successful identification in the foreshortened conditions. Humphreys and Riddoch (1984) in fact note that JL tended to fail to utilise available depth cues with the foreshortened objects, treating them instead as if they were almost two-dimensional, and that JL's performance was improved if extrinsic depth cues (in the form of a textured background) were provided.

HJA's problems are clearly quite different. The most notable feature is that he was much better at matching the objects than at identifying them by name. His performance at matching the foreshortened views was much better than JL's, yet he was as poor as JL at naming them. Thus HJA seems to have access to some form of object-centred representation (because he can match foreshortened views quite well) yet he did not seem to be able to use this very successfully to identify the objects concerned. HJA's case is one of the most fascinating (and thoroughly documented) in the literature of visual agnosia, and we will return to consider the case in detail later in this chapter.

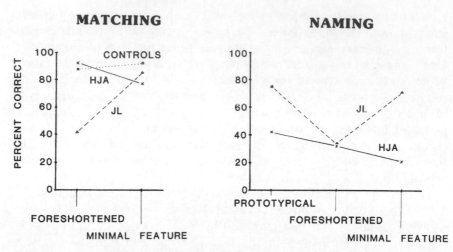

FIG. 2.5.   Performance of JL, HJA and control subjects on object matching and naming tasks. Data from Humphreys & Riddoch (1984; 1985); the naming data consider omissions as errors.

SEMANTIC IMPAIRMENTS

Sometimes inability to recognise objects after brain injury can be caused by impairment to the semantic system itself. That is, knowledge of the object's category membership, functions, and so on, is degraded or inaccessible. This can be seen both in the findings of group studies and single-case studies.

Group Studies

Although patients with right hemisphere injuries can show impairments of object recognition to degraded or unusual views, De Renzi, Scotti, and Spinnler (1969) found that it was patients with left (rather than right) hemisphere injuries who were the most impaired when asked to match real objects to pictures of objects with very different appearances but the same names. This task, however, allows the match to be made at the level of object recognition units, semantic representations, or names. This problem of interpretation was eliminated by Warrington and Taylor (1978) who grouped stimuli, so that a photograph of an object was presented together with a photograph of a different object of a somewhat similar appearance and a photograph of another object with a similar function. When they were asked to pick the photograph of the object that matched the original object in function, patients with left and patients with right posterior injuries both showed significant impairments. For the patients with right posterior injuries, however, the impairments were found to be linked to misidentifications of the photographed objects, whereas the patients with the left posterior injuries made few mis-identifications but were still impaired on this matching by function task. Thus there is evidence of dissociable deficits of recognition and classification by function, or in Warrington's (1982) terms, of perceptual and semantic categorisation.

Single-case Studies

Single-case studies of recognition impairments due to damage to the semantic system were initially reported by Taylor and Warrington (1971) and Warrington (1975). The four cases described in these reports all involved progressive cerebral atrophy, and thus present particular problems of description and interpretation because of the changes in the patients' condition. Warrington (1975), however, points out that for these patients at least the pattern of abilities and disabilities remained constant as their condition deteriorated. In effect, what can be done with each patient is to present a "snapshot" of his or her abilities at a certain stage in the disease's progression. From these four cases we have selected that of a former civil servant, AB (Warrington, 1975), for discussion here because of the combination of relatively severe object recognition difficulties and at least some preserved intellectual abilities.

Initially, AB was referred to the National Hospital in London for investigation of his deteriorating memory. He did indeed show impairments on conventional memory tests, yet he obtained a verbal I.Q. of 122 (well above average). His understanding of verbal instructions was good and he was able to converse fluently using a somewhat impoverished vocabulary.

Performance on a variety of perceptual tests was within normal limits. AB's visual fields, visual acuity and hearing were normal. He was able to distinguish shapes, and to make figure-ground discriminations at various levels of background noise. He could also match pictures of different views of faces satisfactorily (25/28 correct), and on Warrington and Taylor's (1978) task of matching conventional and unusual views of objects his performance (17/20 correct) was also within normal limits. In our terms this would indicate a preserved ability to derive an adequate object-centred representation.

In contrast to this pattern of remarkably intact perceptual abilities, AB was severely impaired in recognition tasks. Although he could identify colours, numbers, and letters, he was unable to name successfully any of a series of 12 common objects, and could name only 2 of a set of 15 photographs of the faces of contemporary personalities. In addition to these visual object and face recognition problems he was also unable to identify meaningful sounds such as a telephone ringing or a dog barking (2/12 correct). His comprehension of spoken words presented individually (i.e. without any supporting context to aid interpretation) was also impaired. Similarly, although he could read words he often did not understand what he had read, and he was also found to be poor at reading irregular words. He could, for instance, read "classification" but not "nephew". This combination of poor comprehension and difficulty with irregular words suggests that he relied a lot on spelling to sound correspondences in reading single words (see Chapter 8).

As well as being poor at object naming, AB was poor at naming pictures, and this deficit extended to both conventional (11/20 correct) and unusual (12/20 correct) views. When he could not identify an item he would usually state that it was "familiar" or that he had "forgotten" it. The other types of error mentioned by Warrington included being able to identify an object but not name it, being only able to place the item in a superordinate category (identifying a daffodil as "some kind of flower"; a hammer as "some kind of tool"), and substitutions of an incorrect item from the same category (identifying a donkey as a "horse"; a dog as a "cat").

When asked to identify the same items from pictures and spoken words (by naming the objects shown in the pictures or by describing the function of the same objects presented as spoken words) AB was impaired on both tasks, but was a little more successful with spoken words (27/40 correct) than with pictures (19/40 correct). The presence of an impairment on both tasks introduces the possibility favoured by Warrington (1975) that he is suffering from an impairment of semantic memory. This would correspond to an impairment of what we have called the semantic system and would imply some loss of knowledge of the "meanings" of objects (what they do, what they are made of, what category they belong to, where they are found, etc.).

In order to investigate this idea Warrington showed AB 40 photographs of animals and objects. These were given one at a time in random order, and he was asked to decide whether or not each was a photograph of an animal. The animal photographs were then presented one at a time and he was asked whether each one was a bird, whether each one was foreign, and whether each one was bigger than a cat. Similarly, with the object photographs he was asked whether each one was made of metal, used indoors, and heavier than a telephone directory.

The results of these tests are summarised in Table 2.1, together with the performance of five control subjects. AB is clearly impaired on most of the tests, but he is able to judge quite well whether or not photographs are of animals (37/40 correct). This confirms the observation that he could sometimes identify objects only to the level of a superordinate category

TABLE 2.1
Performance of Warrington's (1975) Patient AB on Semantic Judgement Tasks
(Number of Items Correct)

Stimulus Items	Task	Items Presented as Photographs		Items Presented as Spoken Words	
		AB's Performance	Mean Performance of Control Subjects[a]	AB's Performance	Mean Performance of Control Subjects[a]
Animals and objects	Animal?	37/40	39.6	29/40	39.8
Animals	Birds?	13/20	19.6	15/20	19.4
	Foreign?	9/20	18.4	14/20	18.8
	Size?	11/20	16.0	13/20	15.2
Objects	Metal?	16/20	19.8	11/20	19.6
	Indoors?	18/20	19.4	15/20	19.2
	Weight?	8/20	14.8	12/20	15.8

[a]($n=5$)

(e.g. identifying a daffodil as "some kind of flower"). Further evidence of a selective semantic impairment comes from the finding from another task that AB was poor at defining low-frequency concrete words yet able to define low-frequency abstract words. He was, for instance, able to define abstract words like supplication ("making a serious request for help") and pact ("friendly agreement"), while being unable to define needle ("forgotten") or geese ("an animal but I've forgotten precisely").

AB thus presents a pattern of intact initial, viewer-centred and object-centred representations, together with impairments on semantic tasks, suggesting the possibility of a selective impairment of some aspects of semantic memory. Although his memory was also impaired in other ways these additional memory impairments are not in themselves a satisfactory explanation of his recognition difficulties, because even globally amnesic patients are not usually agnosic, as Warrington (1975) and Ratcliff and Newcombe (1982) point out.

Category-specific Semantic Impairments

A remarkable feature of semantic memory impairments is that, for some patients, they can be category-specific. The patient JBR from the series of four patients described by Warrington and Shallice (1984) forms a good example. Like Warrington and Shallice's (1984) other patients, JBR was recovering from herpes simplex encephalitis, which causes extensive damage to the temporal lobes. His scores on intelligence tests were average (Verbal I.Q. 101, Performance I.Q. 103), though probably lower than his premorbid level (he had been an electronics undergraduate). He was amnesic, and disoriented in time and place. Like AB he could match conventional and unusual views well (20/20 correct), but performed poorly on tests of object recognition.

JBR's impairment was, however, particularly noticeable to living things. Table 2.2 shows data obtained when he was asked to identify 48 coloured pictures of animals and plants (living things), and 48 pictures of inanimate objects matched to the animals and plants for frequency of use as a word. He was then asked to define the same items when they

TABLE 2.2
Performance of Warrington and Shallice's (1984) Patient JBR
at Identifying Objects from Coloured Pictures and Defining
Them to Their Spoken Names (Percent Correct)

	Living Things	Inanimate Objects
Recognition from picture	6	90
Successful definition of spoken name	8	79

were presented to him as spoken words instead of pictures, and the data are again shown in Table 2.2. The superiority of inanimate objects over living things is most striking. JBR could define an item such as a compass ("tools for telling direction you are going"), yet produced the response "don't know" when asked what a parrot is. The category-specific impairment was found irrespective of whether JBR was tested on verbal description, naming, mimed responses, or picture–word matching. Often he could get superordinate information to living things (e.g. that a daffodil is a "plant"; a snail is "an insect animal"), but even in terms of access to the superordinate category he was still impaired in comparison with inanimate objects.

Warrington and Shallice (1984) are careful to make clear that the living/non-living distinction may not be the one that captures *every* aspect of these category-specific semantic impairments. JBR, for instance, was poor at identifying (inanimate) musical instruments yet good at (living) body parts. They suggest that semantic systems may be organised differently (and hence vulnerable to selective impairment) for things that have significance in terms of the way we use them (household objects, tools, etc.) and things that we know primarily in terms of their visual form (animals, plants, etc.). For those of us who are not musicians, musical instruments, the inanimate category JBR was poor at identifying, are known primarily from their appearance whereas our own bodies, i.e. the parts of living things JBR could identify well, are used all the time.

PAUSE FOR CONTEMPLATION

So far, we have developed a model (Fig. 2.1) in which an initial representation of a seen object is used to construct viewer-centred and object-centred representations which have parallel access to stored descriptions of the structures of known objects (object recognition units), allowing access to semantic representations. We were then able to use this model to account for cases involving shape-processing impairments (which would traditionally be classified as involving apperceptive agnosia) in terms of impairment to the viewer-centred (and perhaps initial) representations, and to account for other object recognition impairments in terms of impairment to the semantic system itself. We were also able to account for some of the problems experienced by patients with right posterior cerebral lesions by proposing that they experience difficulties in constructing object-centred representations, and were able to explain why these patients are not agnosic (because access to object recognition units from viewer-centred representations remains unimpaired).

If we stopped discussing object recognition impairments now, everything would seem neat. But there are other cases in the literature that do not fit this tidy story so well. Because they force us to reconsider, and perhaps revise, our notions these cases are of exceptional theoretical interest. We will now discuss four such patients, two (MS and HJA) involving "higher-order" perceptual impairment, and two (JF and JB) involving a condition known as optic aphasia.

HIGHER-ORDER PERCEPTUAL IMPAIRMENT

MS had been a police cadet until he suffered a febrile illness. This left him blind in part of his former field of vision and with disturbed colour vision. He also had serious memory difficulties, but he was still able to achieve a verbal I.Q. of 101 (normal level). Object and face recognition were very poor. His case has been described by Newcombe and Ratcliff (1974, case 2) and Ratcliff and Newcombe (1982).

When shown a series of 36 line drawings of objects, MS was only able to name 8 of them correctly. This poor performance cannot be attributed solely to the area of blindness in his left visual field, because most other patients with comparable or even more severe visual field defects would experience little difficulty with a task of this type. For most (20) of these drawings he did not give any suggestions as to what the object might be, but when he did make an error of identification it tended to resemble the stimulus. He thought, for example, that a drawing of an anchor showed an umbrella. The same types of error were evident to photographs and to real objects, though there were signs of improved performance for real objects (in a 10-item test he recognised 4 real objects, 1 photograph and 1 drawing). He was poor at describing the appearance of objects from memory. When asked to recognise objects presented in sense modalities other than vision, MS also showed an impairment in tactual recognition by both left and right hands, but his ability to recognise environmental sounds was within normal limits.

When Newcombe and Ratcliff (1974) asked MS to name each of the 36 objects used in their drawing naming task from a verbal description of its function or use he was able to name 20 correctly. This is certainly an improvement on the eight he could name from drawings, so that it does seem that any semantic or name retrieval problems are not sufficient to account for his agnosia. Further evidence for this conclusion comes from the finding (Ratcliff & Newcombe, 1982) that MS was much better able to make semantic judgements about printed words than pictures, which again suggests an impairment of object recognition over and above any semantic disturbance. However, MS did show uneven performance when asked to define objects himself. He could, for instance, explain successfully what an anchor is ("a brake for ships") but not what a nightingale is (Ratcliff & Newcombe, 1982); the possible parallel with Warrington and Shallice's (1984) patient JBR is obvious. These observations suggest that MS may also be experiencing some disturbance of the semantic system, but that (unlike JBR) it is not in itself sufficient to account for his agnosia.

The impairment of visual object recognition stands in marked contrast to some of MS' other abilities. In particular, we will draw attention to his preserved ability to read, and to his ability to copy drawings and to match identical stimuli. In each of these respects MS was quite unlike patients such as those described by Benson and Greenberg (1969) and Campion and Latto (1985).

On tasks involving naming printed words, MS was very accurate. This preserved ability to read is important because it suggests that the visual analysis needed to recognise words may be different to that required for object recognition, though Humphreys and Riddoch (1987a) have noted that reading *accuracy* is not a particularly sensitive measure, and that at least some agnosic patients may read accurately but letter-by-letter. The question as to the relation between reading impairments and the different types of visual agnosia may thus merit more systematic investigation.

MS also showed good ability to copy drawings and to match identical stimuli. His copy of a picture of an anchor is shown in Fig. 2.6. This was an object he had identified as an umbrella, yet the copy is remarkably accurate. It was achieved, however, only by the use of considerable care and a line-by-line copying strategy; when drawing objects without a model to copy from, his attempts were poor (but not always unrecognisable). When asked to match objects as being the same or different to each other MS performed almost perfectly on visual, tactual and cross-modal (one object presented to vision and one by touch) matches.

His ability to copy and match stimuli successfully suggests that, in contrast to Benson and Greenberg's (1969) patient, MS was able to construct adequate viewer-centred representations of the objects he viewed. Despite the evidence of intact viewer-centred representations, however, MS failed to identify many objects and pictures (such as the anchor) for which shape alone would seem to provide a powerful cue. Thus MS would seem to have an impairment to the stored descriptions of the structures of known objects (object recognition units). This is also suggested by the fact that MS was poor at describing the appearance of objects from memory. In addition, however, object-centred representations seemed to be impaired for MS. This can be seen in his performance on Warrington and Taylor's (1978) task involving the matching of objects photographed from conventional and unusual views. On this task, MS's performance was close to chance level despite his good performance on simpler matching tasks, for which viewer-centred representations would be adequate.

MS's problems in object recognition seem to derive primarily from impairment of "higher" visual functions. We have argued that the principal causes of his visual agnosia might be a combination of impairments of object-centred representations and object recognition units. This view is consistent with those of Newcombe and Ratcliff (1974) and Ratcliff and Newcombe (1982), though our theoretical model differs from theirs in some respects. However, the second case of "higher-order" perceptual impairment we will consider, HJA, cannot be reconciled with our model so easily.

ORIGINAL   COPY

FIG. 2.6.   Copy of a picture of an anchor by MS. He had misidentified the original as an umbrella. (Figure kindly supplied by Dr. F. Newcombe.)

Integrative Agnosia

HJA suffered a stroke when he had an appendicitis operation at the age of 61. Following this stroke he complained of loss of colour vision, impaired reading (initially, he could only read slowly and letter-by-letter), and severe problems in recognising objects and faces. Investigation of his visual fields revealed blindness in the upper-left and -right quadrants (i.e. he had lost the top half of the normal field of vision), but for the lower quadrants acuity was normal. Again, we must note that this visual field defect is not in itself a sufficient explanation of HJA's agnosia; there are other patients with the same visual field loss who can recognise objects without difficulty.

As well as having normal visual acuity, HJA showed normal discrimination of length, orientation and position. He was susceptible to visual illusions such as the Muller-Lyer and Ponzo illusions (which are often thought to depend on implied depth), and he could still see depth from disparity between images presented to each eye (stereopsis). Initial representation of perceptual qualities would thus seem intact.

HJA's object recognition impairments have been carefully investigated by Riddoch and Humphreys (1987a). He was better able to identify real objects (21/32) than photographs of the same objects from a prototypical view (12/32), and worst of all at recognising line drawings. When he could identify a stimulus it was usually only after careful, feature-by-feature examination, leading to response latencies of around 25 seconds for correct responses. All of his errors involved either misidentification as a visually similar item or omission (i.e. failure to come up with an answer). He could not mime the use of objects he could not identify.

Like MS, HJA could copy drawings of objects that he could not recognise. His copy of a drawing of an eagle, which he identified as "a cat sitting up", is shown in Fig. 2.7. To the extent that copying demands use of a viewer-centred representation, HJA's viewer-centred representations seem intact. Moreover, as Fig. 2.5 showed (using data from Humphreys & Riddoch, 1984), HJA's ability to match foreshortened to prototypical views of objects was also unimpaired; thus he seems able to construct some form of object-centred representation.

There was no evidence of any impairment to HJA's semantic system; he was easily able to define objects that he could not recognise. When asked what a duck is, for instance, he said that it:

> is a water bird with the ability to swim, fly and walk. It can be wild or kept domestically for eggs; when wild it can be the target of shooting. In the wild it has a wingspan between 15 and 18 inches and weighs about 2 or 3

HJA

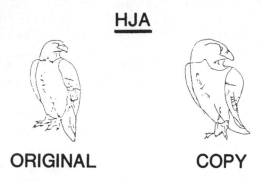

ORIGINAL   COPY

DRAWING FROM MEMORY

FIG. 2.7.   HJA's copy of a picture of an eagle, and his drawing of an eagle from memory. (Reproduced with permission of Oxford University Press from Riddoch and Humphreys, 1987a.)

pounds. Domestic ducks are heavier, up to about 6 pounds perhaps. Wild ducks are multicoloured, mainly brown but with green and yellow breasts. Domestic ducks are white or khaki.

An interesting feature of HJA's object definitions was that, as above, they often included information about the *appearance* of the objects concerned. It seemed as if his stored knowledge of objects (i.e. object recognition units) was intact and accessible from the semantic system, and this was demonstrated convincingly by his ability to draw from memory. Figure 2.7 shows HJA's drawing of an eagle; clearly he remembers what eagles look like. Figure 2.7 is thus very informative about HJA's problems. He can see a drawing of an eagle well enough to copy it accurately, and he can remember what the bird looks like sufficiently well to draw it from memory, yet he cannot recognise an eagle when shown a picture of one. It is as if he can no longer achieve an accurate mapping between his intact perception and his intact stored knowledge of the appearance of objects. We might argue, then, that object recognition units can no longer be accessed properly from viewer-centred or object-centred representations.

This does seem at least in part correct. HJA's ability to decide whether line drawings represented real objects or meaningless objects made by combining different real objects was at chance level (69/120; mean for control subjects 115.7/120). This finding conforms exactly to the view that he is no longer properly able to relate what he sees to his stored knowledge of visual forms.

We could fit HJA to our model by suggesting that intact object recognition units can no longer be accessed effectively from viewer-centred and object-centred representations which are themselves largely intact. To maintain that viewer-centred and object-centred representations are *intact* we would, however, have to overlook an aspect of his attempts at recognition which Riddoch and Humphreys (1987a) see as crucial—the laboured, feature-by-feature descriptions. These were sometimes accompanied by incorrect grouping of the local parts of objects. HJA thought, for instance, that a photograph of a paint-brush with a wooden handle might show "two things close together; a longish wooden stick and a darker, shorter object".

Riddoch and Humphreys (1987a) suggest that HJA finds it difficult to integrate local form information into a coherent overall visual description of the seen object. He picks up the details, but cannot "see" the whole properly. This idea is reminiscent of anecdotes in the literature in which agnosic patients complain that things they look at seem fragmented.

To support this "integration deficit" theory of HJA's difficulties, Riddoch and Humphreys (1987a) point out that his ability to recognise line drawings was reduced both by decreasing exposure duration and by overlapping one drawing on top of another. Moreover, he was better able to decide whether or not a silhouette (i.e. outline shape) represented a real or meaningless object than he was able to make the same decision about line drawings (63/88 silhouettes correct, whereas for line drawings he had been at chance level; mean for controls 77.73/88 silhouettes correct). It is as if the internal detail present in line drawings hindered HJA's performance instead of facilitating it; thus people with normal vision find line drawings easier than silhouettes in this task, but HJA found silhouettes easier than line drawings.

For Riddoch and Humphreys (1987a), then, HJA's perception is impaired, but it is impaired at the highest level of visual analysis. His is an integrative agnosia. He can pick up local features, shape cues, depth cues, and so on, but Riddoch and Humphreys think that he does not readily integrate these into a coherent representation of what he is looking at.

This is an intriguing idea, and we note Young and Deregowski's (1981) suggestion that a similar process is quite generally implicated in picture perception, because under certain conditions children will pick up local depth and feature cues correctly but fail to integrate these into a coherent representation of the depicted object, leading to problems strikingly similar to those experienced permanently by HJA.

One possible way of accommodating the idea of an agnosic integration deficit to our model would be to propose that construction of an adequate object-centred representation involves at least two steps: (1) finding the object's axis of elongation; and (2) integrating local details correctly with respect to this. Patients with posterior lesions of the right hemisphere would then be impaired for the first step, but HJA only for the second step. We would still, though, have to propose that HJA has an additional impairment in accessing object recognition units from viewer-centred representations; perhaps integration is as important to the construction of effective viewer-centred representations as it is to object-centred representations.

More work will be needed before we can know how fruitful such speculations will be (see Humphreys & Riddoch, 1987b, for related suggestions). In the meantime, HJA illustrates well the challenges and insights that a well-documented case study can provide.

OPTIC APHASIA

Optic aphasia was first described by Freund in 1889. The key features of optic aphasia are problems in naming or verbally identifying visually presented objects, which are accompanied by the ability to demonstrate by miming their use that the objects have been recognised, and by unimpaired tactual naming. Thus we are faced in optic aphasia with a naming defect that is specific to the visual modality.

In January, 1970 JF, a retired French electrician, experienced visual disturbances and pins and needles on the right side of his body while driving his car. He had suffered a stroke involving the left posterior cerebral artery. At first he did not seek medical advice and resumed his normal life, though he had become blind in the right side of his former field of vision and unable to read. Some months later, however, he became suspicious and aggressive; he thought that his wife intended to poison him.

In the period following June, 1970 JF was examined at the Salpêtrière Hospital in Paris. He was found to have a complete loss of vision in his right visual field. No disturbances were evident in his spoken language or comprehension, and he obtained a verbal I.Q. of 93 on the Wechsler

Bellevue Test. He was also able to write adequately, both spontaneously and to dictation, and was able to draw well. He was, however, somewhat amnesic and showed a variety of memory difficulties on formal testing, with a Memory Quotient (M.Q.) of 77 on the Wechsler Memory Scale.

JF was found to have problems in naming visually presented stimuli which were carefully investigated by Lhermitte and Beauvois (1973). He was able to name objects presented tactually to his left or right hand (109/120 correct) and he could also name environmental sounds (24/25 correct). He was, however, impaired at naming colours, seen objects (23/30 corrrect), pictures (72/100 correct), and photographs of famous people's faces. He was also severely alexic, being able to name only a few letters and no words at all. When asked to define the spoken name of objects he had misnamed, however, he succeeded on 96 of 100 trials, thus clearly indicating that his object naming difficulty was not due to his impaired memory.

JF's poor performance on visual object naming tasks did not usually derive from failures to produce a name, but from the production of incorrect names. Various types of error were observed by Lhermitte and Beauvois. A number of these were perseverations, in which the name of a previously identified object was repeated; thus he called a fork a comb when it followed a comb in a series of objects, and he called a tomato a strawberry when it occurred a few trials after a strawberry in a series of fruits. He also made a lot of errors in which he produced the name of a semantically related object, including "shoes" for trousers and "grass-hopper" for a slug. Some of his errors were visual in nature, such as "hazel nuts" for coffee beans, and there were others in which it was not entirely clear whether the production of the incorrect names was linked to visual or to semantic factors, or some combination of the two ("glass" for a bottle, "toothbrush" for a comb).

The most notable feature of the case, however, was that JF could indicate that he had understood what a visually presented object was, despite his inability to name it. He did this by miming its use. Thus, for instance, when shown a comb he correctly pretended to use it even though he called it a toothbrush. None of his mimes were found to be incorrect. When asked to draw an object he had just misnamed, he usually drew what he had seen rather than what he had called it. Although he seems to have been aware of his visual field defect and alexia, Lhermitte and Beauvois (1973) state that JF was apparently unaware of his problems in naming visually presented objects.

Optic aphasia poses a challenge to theories that postulate a common set of semantic representations for known objects that can be accessed from any sensory modality. The patient "knows" what seen objects are (in the sense of being able to gesture their use), and knows what felt objects are, but can only name the ones that have been handled.

One way of resolving this paradox is to maintain that different parts of the semantic system can become disconnected from each other. Beauvois (1982) adopts this position. Her claim is that JF has more or less normal vision in the intact part of his visual field, and that visual semantic processes are normal. He also has normal speech and verbal semantic processes, but the visual semantic processes and the verbal semantic processes have become disconnected from each other, whereas tactile input still has access to verbal semantics.

The possibility of separation of visual and verbal semantic processes is supported by Schwartz, Marin, and Saffran's (1979) finding that a patient with a progressive dementing disease, WLP, could mime the use of objects despite a severe impairment of semantic memory. Her mimes were so precise that observers could distinguish easily her "use" of a depicted spoon or fork, pipe or cigarette, and so on. Yet WLP could not identify these objects verbally, or even show understanding of their names in a classification task.

Optic Aphasia as a Semantic Access Impairment

One problem with Beauvois' (1982) account of optic aphasia is how to make more clear the distinction between visual and verbal semantic processes. Work by Riddoch and Humphreys (1987b) has helped by suggesting a somewhat different basis for the distinction and a more precise hypothesis concerning a potential cause of optic aphasia.

Riddoch and Humphreys studied JB, who had sustained a left hemisphere injury in a road traffic accident. This left him unable to read or write, but with intact oral spelling. His speech was not affected, but he was initially amnesic. Although he had a right hemianopia, JB's vision did not seem to be otherwise much affected. He could copy simple drawings, and his ability to match prototypical to minimal-feature or foreshortened views of objects was within the range of control subjects (minimal-feature 26/26; foreshortened 20/26).

JB's ability to name seen objects was poor, and was unaffected by view (42% prototypical view; 40% foreshortened view; 43% minimal-feature view). Like JF, he made several semantic errors. He could, however, provide specific gestures indicating the uses of seen objects that he could not otherwise identify. Object naming from tactile presentation was better than naming from vision.

Thus far, the main difference between JB and the agnosic patient HJA is that whereas JB could mime the functions of the objects he saw, HJA could not. When JB was asked to decide whether line drawings represented real objects or meaningless objects made by combining different real objects, however, he was much better than HJA (HJA 69/120; JB 110/116—JB performed within the range of control subjects). Thus JB was able to access stored knowledge of object structures (object recognition units) from vision, whereas HJA could not do this. JB's performance on this object decision task remained in the normal range even when the task was made very difficult by deriving the meaningless objects from items in the same semantic category (for example, combining features of two different types of animal).

Riddoch and Humphreys (1987b) thus describe JB's impairment as involving semantic access from vision; although he can recognise objects as familiar, he is poorer at accessing semantic knowledge from pictures than from touch or from spoken names. This problem proved to be bidirectional: JB was equally poor at accessing knowledge of an object's appearance from semantics. His ability to draw objects from memory was poor, and he commented that "I know what it (the object he was asked to draw) is, but I just can't picture it."

For JB, then, the ability to mime the use of seen objects occurs in the context of intact access to object recognition units. It would seem that knowledge of how to use objects is linked to their structural rather than their semantic properties. Whether this would also have been true for Lhermitte and Beauvois' (1973) patient JF we do not, of course, know. It may be the case (as we are inclined to think) that intact access to object recognition units is *necessary* for correct gestures to be made, or it may be that there are different forms of optic aphasia. Only further detailed investigations of individual cases can reveal the answer.

Optic aphasia forces us to think more carefully about the different types of information we can access from seen objects. An outline of a possible account of optic aphasia is given in Fig. 2.8. Here we propose that intact miming reflects preserved access to a system of stored motor programs for object use, whereas the naming impairment reflects a disconnection between object recognition units and the (verbal) semantic system.

OVERVIEW

The basic lessons of cognitive neuropsychology, which will be encountered throughout this book, can be learnt from studies of disorders of object recognition.

The first lesson is that quite specific impairments can occur. There are patients who do not recognise the objects they see, yet have well-preserved language, memory, and other intellectual functions. These people are not blind and they can still use their vision effectively for many purposes,

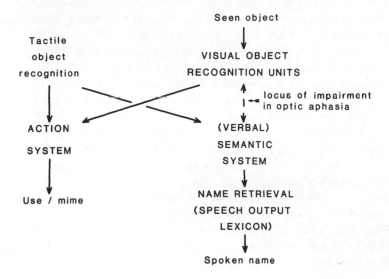

FIG. 2.8. A possible account of optic aphasia as a disconnection between visual object recognition and the verbal semantic system.

but the things they see have little meaning for them, or meanings that are only attained with difficulty. Such cases are rare, but this rarity is probably due to anatomical reasons (see Chapter 1). The key point is that they can exist at all.

Neuropsychological impairments do not, however, affect object recognition as if it were a single, homogeneous faculty. Instead, what we encounter are different *types* of recognition impairment. One person may be unable to perceive the shapes of seen objects properly, another can perceive shape but fails to form an effective integrated representation that combines local and global features, and another can recognise object forms as familiar and even mime their use, while remaining unable to give any verbal identification. The organisation of complex abilities such as object recognition seems to be into a number of separable functional components or modules, any one of which may be impaired selectively.

Of course, every neuropsychological patient is unique; exactly the same injury is no more likely to recur than people are likely to have the same fingerprints. But the patterns of impairment that are found do not turn out to be unlimited. There are, for instance, no accounts of patients who show impaired processing of shape information and yet recognise seen objects without difficulty. Thus, among the myriad of observed patterns, it is possible to discern a sense of order.

The easiest way to comprehend this orderliness of neuropsychological breakdown is in terms of an explicit theoretical model. A satisfactory model needs to explain what functional components are involved in the ability of interest, and how these are organised with respect to each other. It should be able not only to account for the patterns of impairment observed, but also for those that are *not* found. In our model (Fig. 2.1), for instance, it is clear that anyone who shows impaired shape processing *must* have impaired object recognition ability, because the viewer-centred representations which would include shape information have to be constructed before recognition can take place. The demonstration of one case in which this was not so would be sufficient to force revision (or abandonment) of a model of this type.

With a reasonably adequate theoretical model, then, it is possible to account for existing patterns of impairment, to predict new types of pattern that might be found, and to use newly discovered patterns that do not conform to revise our understanding. That is why cognitive neuropsychology can be so exciting.

SUMMARY

We can think of object recognition as requiring that viewer-centred and object-centred representations of seen objects are matched to stored descriptions of the structures of known objects (object recognition units) which then allow access to semantic representations (see Fig. 2.1). Cases in which there is a severe impairment of form perception and inability to copy seen objects may then be considered to involve impairment of the ability to construct viewer-centred representations. Problems with matching unusual or foreshortened views derive from impaired object-

FURTHER READING

Bruce, V. & Humphreys, G.W. (1994). Recognizing objects and faces. *Visual Cognition, 1,* 141–180. Introduction to a special issue on object and face recognition of the journal *Visual Cognition,* which discusses the visual processing of objects (and faces).

Farah, M.J. & McClelland, J.L. (1991). A computational model of semantic memory impairment: modality specificity and emergent category specificity. *Journal of Experimental Psychology: General, 120,* 339–357. Shows how category-specific impairments can be simulated in a computer model in which semantic knowledge is subdivided into partially separable visual and functional components.

Hodges, J.R., Patterson, K.E. & Tyler, L.K. (1994). Loss of semantic memory: implications for the modularity of mind. *Cognitive Neuropsychology, 11,* 505–542. Describes a detailed investigation of a person with a neurodegenerative disease, demonstrating how semantic memory is and is not modular.

Humphreys, G.W. & Riddoch, M.J. (1987). *To see but not to see: a case study of visual agnosia.* Hove, UK: Lawrence Erlbaum Associates Ltd. Readable introduction to HJA's case, with interesting sections explaining the impact of the disorder on his life.

Humphreys, G.W., Riddoch, M.J., Quinlan, P.T., Price, C.J., & Donnelly, N. (1992). Parallel pattern processing and visual agnosia. *Canadian Journal of Psychology, 46,* 377–416. Uses visual search paradigms to show that HJA has a particular type of perceptual grouping problem.

Humphreys, G.W. & Riddoch, M.J. (1993). Object agnosias. In C. Kennard (Ed.), *Baillière's clinical neurology: international practice and research. Vol. 2, No. 2: Visual perceptual defects* (pp. 339–359). London: Baillière Tindall. Useful discussion of forms of visual object agnosia, which explores different classification systems.

Newcombe, F., Mehta, Z., & de Haan, E.H.F. (1994). Category specificity in visual recognition. In M.J. Farah & G. Ratcliff (Eds), *The neuropsychology of high-level vision: collected tutorial essays* (pp. 103–132). Hillsdale, N.J.: Lawrence Erlbaum Associates Inc. Update on category-specific deficits.

Rubens, A.B. (1979). Agnosia. In K.M. Heilman & E. Valenstein (Eds), *Clinical neuropsychology.* Oxford: Oxford University Press. Still an excellent introduction from the clinical perspective.

Warrington, E.K. (1982). Neuropsychological studies of object recognition. In D.E. Broadbent & L. Weiskrantz (Eds), *The neuropsychology of cognitive function.* London: The Royal Society. Also available in *Philosophical Transactions of the Royal Society, London, B298,* 15–33. Explains Warrington's influential ideas of perceptual and semantic categorisation and her model of object recognition.

Warrington, E.K. & Shallice, T. (1984). Category-specific semantic impairments. *Brain, 107,* 829–854. Includes detailed investigation of JBR and other patients with semantic impairment.

VIDEOS

Two videos in the series edited by E. Funnell & G.W. Humphreys: *Teaching programmes in cognitive neuropsychology* (Hove, UK: Lawrence Erlbaum Associates Ltd.) illustrate topics discussed in this chapter. They are *Peripheral agnosia: disorders of object recognition* and *Central agnosia: loss of knowledge about objects.*

3 Visual and Spatial Abilities

INTRODUCTION

In Chapter 2 we looked at what cognitive neuropsychological studies have revealed about how we recognise objects. However, for normal life we use vision for a much wider range of purposes. We can recognise other types of stimuli than everyday objects, such as printed words or people's faces, we can see colour and movement, and we can assess accurately the locations of seen objects both with respect to ourselves and in relation to each other.

Our visual experience has such a unified quality that it is initially surprising to discover that, as for object recognition, a range of quite specific impairments of visual information processing can be found after brain injury. The processes responsible for vision are organised into a number of functionally separable modules. This modular organisation makes good sense in terms of keeping the nerve connections involved as tidy as possible and in terms of allowing one process to be modified without affecting others that are unrelated to it (Cowey, 1985; Marr, 1982), and there is good agreement between studies of humans and studies of other species concerning the types of functional module that exist (Cowey, 1982; 1985; Ratcliff & Cowey, 1979; Zeki, 1978). None the less, one cannot help being puzzled as to how our visual experience can have its unified quality when it is produced by a number of separate processing modules. We will not attempt to answer this question here, but will concentrate instead on introducing some of the dissociable disorders that can be observed. Impairments of word and face processing are dealt with elsewhere (Chapters 4, 5, 6, and 7), and in this chapter we examine some of the other deficits that are found. We will not discuss every possible disorder; for those seeking it, a more detailed listing can be found in Benton (1979). Instead, we will illustrate the range of problems that can arise. We begin with colour processing and movement perception, which may be considered to be fairly "basic" visual abilities. These are followed by a discussion of the phenomena associated with "blindsight", which have important implications for our conception of the relation between visual experience and perceptual mechanisms. We then turn to look at impairments affecting abilities that are best considered to be more "spatial" in nature—visual location, spatial attention, and spatial knowledge and thought.

Although modular organisation is a widely agreed feature of visual and spatial abilities, there is as yet no generally accepted theoretical framework that can specify the complete underlying pattern (see Young & Ratcliff, 1983). Obviously, the various processing modules must be interconnected into some kind of coherent system, but we do not yet know how. An important clue, however, is that mechanisms responsible for the recognition of different types of visual pattern seem to be organised into separate systems to those involved in space perception. Thus patients experiencing object recognition difficulties may be relatively unimpaired on spatial tasks, and patients who are spatially disorientated may yet remain able to identify objects without difficulty.

Such observations are borne out by more formal studies. Newcombe and Russell (1969), for instance, studied a group of men with brain lesions due to shrapnel and gunshot wound injuries sustained some 20 years previously. They found that men with right hemisphere injuries could show severe problems in spatial tasks (such as maze learning) or in more directly "visual" tasks likely to relate to pattern recognition, but that these deficits did not relate to each other. Newcombe, Ratcliff, and Damasio (1987) present detailed information on two cases from this series, one with each type of impairment. Such findings, and related studies of the monkey's brain, have been developed by Ungerleider and Mishkin (1982) into the view that there are effectively parallel visual systems in the cerebral cortex responsible for appreciation of an object's identity and its spatial location. Interestingly, Levine, Warach, and Farah (1985) have pointed out that the same dissociation occurs for impairments affecting mental imagery.

COLOUR PROCESSING

Impairments of colour processing due to brain injury can be grouped into three main types affecting what we might roughly describe as colour perception, colour knowledge and colour naming. Of course, many patients experience what would have to be regarded as hybrid impairments under this classification scheme, but this seems justifiable as some relatively pure cases have been described.

Impairments of colour *perception* are called achromatopsias. Patients with cerebral achromatopsia complain that they cannot see colours, and that everything is like a black and white picture, or that colours have lost their brightness (Meadows, 1974b). In some cases the loss of colour perception relates only to part of the field of vision (Damasio, 1985). Even when the whole of the visual field is involved, however, everyday objects can still be recognised provided that colour is not a critical cue; there need not be any impairment of form perception itself. Pallis's (1955) patient, for instance, stated that he could usually identify everyday objects, but gave as examples where his loss of colour perception caused him problems the fact that his shirts all looked dirty and he could not tell them apart, and that he could not tell until he had opened a jar (and smelt or tasted the contents) whether it would contain jam or pickles. Warrington (1987) provides documented cases of dissociations between impairments affecting the processing of colours, locations and shapes.

The cerebral achromatopsias are quite different to the types of colour blindness found in the absence of brain damage, which are due to deficiencies in the retina of the eye (Mollon, 1982). Mollon, Newcombe, Polden, and Ratcliff (1980) showed, for instance, that the patient MS, who experienced achromatopsia as well as his object agnosia (see Chapter 2), none the less retained the usual three functional cone mechanisms with normal spectral sensitivities (cones are the retina's colour-sensitive cells). In threshold tasks MS was found to be able to respond to signals from any of the three classes of cone normally associated with colour blindness; his complete achromatopsia was thus due to a deficit affecting his ability to make proper *use* of the signals that the different types of cone continued to send. He could respond to wavelength without being able to match, sort, or name different hues.

Clinically, achromatopsias are often found in conjunction with problems in recognising familiar faces (prosopagnosia) and familiar places. In some cases, however, colour perception may be impaired without loss of ability to recognise faces or places and, conversely, it remains intact in some reported cases of prosopagnosia (Heywood, Wilson, & Cowey, 1987; Meadows, 1974a; 1974b; see Chapter 4 for further discussion of this point). Thus it seems that these functions are carried out by separate information processing modules, but that these lie in adjacent or even partially overlapping cortical areas that are often damaged simultaneously.

A quite different type of deficit seems to involve impairment of colour *knowledge*. For these patients colour perception is intact, but errors are made in tasks that demand use of stored information about colour.

Patients may be unable to answer from memory questions such as "What colour is a strawberry?", and may choose the wrong coloured crayons if asked to colour in line drawings of the objects concerned (Kinsbourne & Warrington, 1964; Oxbury & Humphrey, 1969, case 2). This deficit often occurs in the context of more general language difficulties (De Renzi, Faglioni, Scotti, & Spinnler, 1972), but, apparently, it can also occur in an isolated form (see Meadows, 1974b). Unlike achromatopsia, the impairment is not found only in "perceptual" tasks, because it is as great in what is apparently a purely verbal task such as stating the colour of a specified object—a task which would not cause an achromatopsic patient particular difficulty.

Impairments of colour knowledge need to be distinguished from problems affecting colour *naming*. Geschwind and Fusillo (1966) described a 58-year-old man who, following a stroke, became unable to name seen colours. This patient could state the usual colours of familiar objects like bananas, or the sky, but he could not put a name to the colour of objects (such as items of clothing) for which there was no learnt association to rely on. Similarly, he could not point to the correct colour when a particular colour name was specified.

These colour naming problems are often found in combination with forms of reading impairment involving letter-by-letter reading, or the complete inability to read. Geschwind and Fusillo's (1966) patient was also unable to read (alexic), and they interpreted his colour naming defects as demanding a similar explanation to his reading problems; in essence, their argument is that there is a disconnection between the brain's visual and language areas. Colour naming problems and alexia do, however, dissociate in rare cases which weaken Geschwind and Fusillo's (1966) argument. For example, Greenblatt (1973) described an alexic patient who could name colours, whereas Mohr, Leicester, Stoddard, and Sidman's (1971) patient could read but was impaired at colour naming. Davidoff and Ostergaard (1984) describe a patient with a colour naming impairment who was none the less able to point to named colours, which again suggests that the explanation of colour anomia is not as simple as disconnection theories often assume. It may prove more enlightening to link impairments of colour naming to other reports of naming disorders specific to certain semantic categories (see Chapter 5).

Colour processing impairments, then, both demonstrate the separability of colour processing from other aspects of vision, and form an interesting and reasonably coherent pattern. Much more work needs to be done, however, before an adequate model of the deficits can be proposed, because there are already signs that the simple classification scheme we have adopted need not always apply (see, especially, Beauvois & Saillant, 1985).

MOVEMENT PERCEPTION

Riddoch (1917) was one of the first people to take a serious interest in disorders of movement perception. He showed that for soldiers with brain injuries due to gunshot and shrapnel wounds there were dissociations between movement perception and form perception abilities in impaired parts of the visual field. In addition, movement perception and form perception could show different courses of recovery. Riddoch (1917) used these findings to argue that movement involves a special type of visual perception.

Isolated disturbances of movement perception are a most uncommon sequel of brain injury, but a very convincing case has been investigated in detail and reported by Zihl, Von Cramon, and Mai (1983). Their patient, LM, complained of a loss of movement perception following a venous thrombosis that produced bilateral lesions of temporo-occipital cortex. She saw the world almost entirely in terms of a series of "snapshots", especially if the movements involved were quite fast. Her perception was affected for movements in all spatial dimensions (horizontal movements, vertical movements, and movements toward or away from her), and the condition was very disabling. Thus LM experienced difficulty in crossing the road because she could no longer judge the movements of cars, yet she could identify the cars themselves without difficulty. She had problems in pouring tea or coffee into a cup because the liquid seemed to be frozen, like a glacier, and she did not know when to stop pouring because she could not see the level in the cup rising. In a room where people were moving about they would seem to LM to be first in one place and then suddenly in another place, and she complained of problems in following conversations because she could not see facial, and especially mouth, movements (people rely on these to a surprising extent, as we will explain in Chapter 4).

On formal tests LM proved to be perfectly able to locate stationary objects by sight; her saccadic eye movements to target lights presented up to 40° from fixation were very accurate. Thus she was able to control her eye movements. Yet her pursuit eye movements to moving targets were markedly abnormal for target velocities greater than 8° per second, with her eyes jumping from one point to another instead of tracking the moving target smoothly. At target velocities below 8° per second LM often did track the target light successfully with her eyes, and when she was successful she always reported seeing movement.

LM also had trouble moving parts of her body under visual control. She could easily trace the path of a raised wire with her finger when she was blindfolded and had to rely on tactile information. But when a sheet of glass was placed over the wire (to eliminate the tactile information) and the blindfold was removed she could only follow the path if she moved her finger slowly.

Other tests carried out by Zihl et al. (1983) confirmed that LM's disorder of movement perception was confined to the visual modality; her perception of movements specified via hearing or touch was unimpaired. Her visual perception of movements in depth was completely abolished but, as we have seen, there was some preservation of movement perception to targets moving slowly along horizontal or vertical axes up to around 15° from fixation. LM did not show visual motion after effects, and she no longer experienced the phi phenomenon, in which *apparent* visual movement is generated between sequentially presented lights.

Despite her impaired ability to see movement, LM remained able to discriminate colours adequately on the Farnsworth-Munsell 100 hue test, and her tachistoscopic recognition thresholds for visually presented objects and words were quite normal. Binocular visual functions, including stereoscopic depth perception were also normal.

BLINDSIGHT

We have described cases in which brain injury can lead to specific impairments of aspects of visual experience, such as colour or movement perception. Now we will consider a quite different type of impairment, in which conscious visual experience is entirely lost for at least part of the field of vision, yet the ability to respond to visual stimuli under certain testing conditions remains. The patient has no sense of seeing these stimuli, yet can make accurate responses if encouraged to guess or given a forced choice. Weiskrantz's term "blindsight" neatly encompasses the paradoxical nature of the condition. Part of the visual field is blind in terms of both standard clinical tests and subjective report, yet behavioural evidence indicates that accurate responses can be made to visual stimuli presented in this blind area. These accurate responses are made without awareness of visual experience on the patient's part.

At this point it is necessary to understand the causes of visual field defects in a little more detail. Loss of vision in part of the normal visual field is a common consequence of injury to posterior regions of the cerebral cortex. Nerve fibres from the retina of each eye project, via the lateral geniculate bodies, to the striate cortex in the occipital lobe of each cerebral hemisphere. The striate cortex is itself organised in a manner described as "retinotopic", meaning that different areas of the visual field are projected onto it in a quite systematic way. Damage to different parts of the geniculo-striate pathway can thus produce loss of sensation in corresponding parts of the visual field. These visual field defects often take the form of hemianopias (loss of vision for stimuli falling to the left or to the right side of fixation), or of impairments to one or more quadrants of the field of vision. Sometimes the central part of the visual field, or macula, is differentially spared or affected (for more details on the causes of visual field defects see Kolb and Whishaw, 1985).

Visual field defects have been investigated carefully for many years, because of their clinical importance. Before the introduction of modern brain imaging techniques, they formed one of the few available methods for determining the loci of cerebral lesions. Many of the neurological conditions described in this book are typically accompanied by characteristic visual field defects. These field defects are, however, coincidental with problems such as achromatopsia and prosopagnosia, and do not themselves directly cause the conditions. The association of particular conditions with particular field defects is often due to the close contiguity of cerebral areas, and in such cases it has no functional significance. Thus, for instance, other patients with the same or with more severe field defects than prosopagnosic patients may remain able to recognise faces without difficulty. For this reason we have not discussed visual field defects in this book except in cases where they have been thought to be, or might reasonably be thought to be, of functional importance in creating the impairment observed.

It has been known for some time that visual field defects can be associated with reduced visual sensitivity rather than an absolute loss. Weiskrantz (1986) reviews many such findings, and we have already noted Riddoch's (1917) observations on movement perception and form perception. One of the most important reports is that by Pöppel, Held, and Frost (1973), who presented a briefly flashed light at different locations in visual field defects caused by gunshot wounds, and asked their ex-servicemen to look toward the flash. Although Pöppel et al.'s (1973) patients thought this an odd request, because they could not consciously "see" anything, their eye movements did in fact approximate to the correct positions.

The key feature of Pöppel et al.'s (1973) technique is that they did not rely on their subjects' reports of what they could see, but instead encouraged them to guess and measured their behaviour to the visual stimulus. This has been the hallmark of the investigations of the patient DB carried out by Weiskrantz and his colleagues (Weiskrantz, Warrington, Sanders, & Marshall, 1974; Weiskrantz, 1980; 1986). DB underwent an operation in 1973 to remove an arteriovenous malformation at the pole of the right occipital lobe that was causing severe and recurrent migraine attacks. This operation involved removal of the striate cortex of the right hemisphere and some of the adjacent calcarine cortex, but left intact other areas of cerebral cortex that would typically be affected in cases of cerebral injury due to stroke, tumour or gunshot wound.

After the operation DB experienced, as would be expected, hemianopia affecting almost the whole of his left field of vision, without sparing of the central macular area. This field defect contracted during the next few years until it occupied the lower left quadrant, but it is the visual information processing abilities found within DB's area of subjective blindness that are of most interest here, rather than its extent or the course of any recovery. Weiskrantz et al. (1974) showed that, like Pöppel et al.'s (1973) patients, DB was able to make eye movements toward a light flashed in his visual field defect that he claimed to be unable to see. These movements were clearly related to the position of the target, though they were not particularly accurate. DB's ability to reach out or point toward the stimulus was, however, much more accurate despite the fact that he was given no feedback as to the correctness or incorrectness of his performance until the entire test was complete. When shown the accuracy of his results at the end of the session, DB was astonished; he thought that he had been guessing. DB was also found to be able to discriminate line orientations, and to make simple form discriminations, such as distinguishing X from O, provided that the stimuli were of sufficient size.

Following the initial report by Weiskrantz et al. (1974), DB has been investigated intensively, and Weiskrantz (1986) reports several further studies which have both confirmed and refined the original findings. As well as being able to locate stimuli presented within the "blind" part of his visual field, DB could detect accurately their presence or absence even when the light stimulus was introduced or extinguished quite slowly. He could also distinguish moving from stationary stimuli. His visual acuity for static stimuli falling within the field defect was found to be poorer than that of his intact field and, unlike normal vision, acuity in the field defect increased as the stimuli were moved to positions further away from fixation. Only limited shape discrimination abilities were found within the visual field defect, and Weiskrantz (1986) suggests that the ability to discriminate simple shapes, such as X or O, found by Weiskrantz et al. (1974) may have been based on DB's ability to discriminate orientation of lines.

Investigations of blindsight pose a number of exacting technical demands, which have been highlighted by Campion, Latto, and Smith (1983). Weiskrantz (1986), however, demonstrates that he has solved these problems satisfactorily, and it should also be noted that studies of blindsight in other patients than DB have revealed broadly comparable patterns of abilities (e.g. Barbur, Ruddock, & Waterfield, 1980; Perenin, 1978; Perenin & Jeannerod, 1978). This comparability of findings from different patients should not, however, be taken to imply that blindsight will be found within *any* visual field defect. The phenomena are only to be expected in field defects caused by lesions of certain types, and it will require extensive work to specify precisely what the necessary and sufficient conditions are.

A key issue concerns whether or not the visual abilities found in blindsight are produced in the geniculo-striate visual system itself, or by alternative visual pathways that may have different functions. Weiskrantz (1986) points out that whereas the geniculo-striate pathway involves about 90% of optic nerve fibres, there are nevertheless at least six other branches of the optic nerve projecting to midbrain and subcortical areas, one of which contains some 100,000 nerve fibres. It is thus possible that the visual abilities found in field defects are supported by one or more of these alternative pathways, and the fact that blindsight seems in some respects to involve a qualitatively different pattern of visual abilities rather than a degradation of those measured in the intact field would support this possibility. Weiskrantz (1986) discusses parallels with studies of other animal species that point in the same direction.

Of particular interest to the cognitive neuropsychologist is the fact that studies of blindsight promise to provide insights into the intriguing question of the relationship between the analysis of visual stimuli and conscious awareness. Several people have used cases of blindsight as a demonstration that awareness is *not* integral to the operation of visual information-processing mechanisms in the way that we commonly suppose (e.g. Marcel, 1983). There are, however, complex issues involved here. Often some degree of practice or "shaping" of responses can be needed before blindsight phenomena can be demonstrated (Weiskrantz, 1980). It is as if patients are able to learn to attend to something, yet that something is seldom described as being like a visual experience. DB, for instance, gradually came to say that he had a sense that "something was there", and roughly where it was, but that he did not in any sense "see" it (Weiskrantz, 1980, p. 374). Another patient, EY, sensed "a definite pinpoint of light" but then claimed that "it does not actually look like a light. It looks like nothing at all" (Weiskrantz, 1980, p. 378).

It is, of course, possible to insist that DB and other patients must in some sense be aware of the visual stimuli to which they respond, and that their descriptions of their experiences are of no scientific value, but this seems to us to take the whole issue into an intractable argument about when we can trust someone else's statement that she or he is—or is not—aware of something. Weiskrantz (1986) himself sidesteps this obstacle by defining blindsight as involving "visual capacity in a field defect in the absence of acknowledged awareness".

Cases of preserved ability to locate stimuli that have not been consciously "perceived" are not confined to the visual modality. Paillard, Michel, and Stelmach (1983) studied a patient with a severe impairment of touch perception for the right side of her body. This impairment was so severe that she would sometimes cut or burn herself without noticing, yet she could point to the position where her right arm had been touched even though she was not aware of its having been touched. She commented: "But I don't understand that! You put something here. I don't feel anything and yet I go there with my finger. How does that happen?" (Paillard et al., 1983, p. 550).

Although Paillard et al.'s (1983) patient was considerably better than chance in her ability to locate stimuli she could not feel, her performance was well below that of a control subject. She was also able to make gross discriminations between the sizes of objects palpated (but not subjectively "felt") by her right hand. As Paillard et al. (1983) observe, their case seems to form an interesting analogue of blindsight in the tactile modality.

VISUAL LOCATION

Although disorders affecting visual location had been described previously (e.g. Bálint, 1909), the most detailed of the early reports relate to soldiers who had sustained bullet or shrapnel wounds during the First World War (Holmes, 1918; 1919; Holmes & Horrax, 1919; Riddoch, 1917, case 3; Smith & Holmes, 1916; Yealland, 1916). Even though they did not have the benefit of modern experimental techniques, the descriptions given by Holmes and his colleagues have yet to be bettered.

In the papers he published around this time, Holmes presented his observations of eight people who had disturbances of spatial orientation. Their most obvious problems were in determining the location of seen objects. Holmes (1919, p. 231) described one of them trying to eat a meal:

> When he tried to take a piece of bread he brought his hand under the table rather than above it, and on attempting to seize the cup he found his fingers first in the tea, and, in his second attempt on a plate to one side of it.

The disorder was limited to the visual modality, with the patients being able to localise sounds accurately. When blindfolded they were easily able to point in the direction of a noise, or walk toward someone who called them. Similarly, the ability to locate touched objects remained intact. Thus Holmes described one of his patients eating soup, who succeeded in placing the spoon in the bowl only after repeated attempts. Once he had located the bowl, however, he could aways bring the spoon accurately to his mouth. This preserved ability to put a spoon in his mouth shows that the patient remained able to make accurate use of his own bodily sensations for locating things, and it also shows that he had not simply lost proper control over the movements of his muscles. Holmes confirmed these observations by allowing him to touch the soup bowl with his left hand; he then fed himself without difficulty.

Although Holmes's patients had lost the ability to locate seen objects they remained able to identify them:

> When I held up a pocket-knife in front of one man he said at once "that's a pocket-knife"; but though his eyes were directed on it he stretched out his arm in a totally wrong direction when he was told to take hold of it (Holmes, 1919, p. 231).

This provides a striking example of the point that deficits affecting object identification can dissociate from those of a more "spatial" nature.

The picture that we have built up so far is one in which the patients are able to specify object locations from touch or hearing, but not from vision. Despite the inability to derive information about the location of seen objects, they can be identified with ease. This was expressed succinctly by Private M (Holmes, 1918), who explained that though he could see an object he was not sure where it was. Such problems stand in marked contrast to those found in visual object agnosia (see Chapter 2), where patients who are unable to identify objects can usually locate them without difficulty.

We will look more closely at Private M's case, the first to be reported by Holmes (Holmes, 1918, case 1; Smith & Holmes, 1916), and one which is fairly typical. Private M was wounded by a shrapnel bullet. In some respects he recovered rapidly, and did not develop weakness or paralysis of his limbs, or any loss of hearing. His speech was at first a little disturbed, but quickly returned to normal. His intellectual abilities did not seem diminished, but he was unable to remember events that occurred during a period preceding his injury. His emotional reactions, however, were not considered normal as he was inclined to laugh at inappropriate things.

Private M's visual acuity was normal for central vision, and he could detect the presence of a static object to normal limits in his peripheral vision. He could also detect movement in all parts of his visual fields, though he could only do so with difficulty in the lower right quadrant. He could recognise seen objects, and he could also recognise letters and read words and short sentences.

Although Private M's vision would not seem too seriously impaired on the basis of these tests, they were very difficult to carry out because he experienced great problems in controlling the movements of his eyes. He found it difficult to move his eyes in a specified direction; he tended to make incorrect movements or to succeed only after a number of attempts. The inability to control his eye movements properly meant that he had difficulty reading anything other than short sentences. He could not follow a moving object with his eyes, he did not react to objects that were rapidly approaching him, and his eyes did not converge on slowly approaching objects. He had difficulty bringing objects he noticed into the centre of his field of vision, and when they were in central vision he was unable to maintain fixation. He did, however, make accurate eye movements in the direction of unexpected noises.

In addition to these problems of eye movements, Private M was unable to determine the locations of the objects he saw. Although he could detect the presence of moving stimuli he had no sense of their location, and was only aware of "something moving somewhere". There is an interesting contrast here between Private M, who was aware of movement but could not determine its location, and Zihl et al.'s (1983) patient LM, who could determine location but had lost the ability to see many types of movement.

Private M could not reach out accurately to grasp a seen object; sometimes he would project his arm in a totally wrong direction, or he would bring his hand to the appropriate position and then grope about until he came into contact with it. His errors not only took the form of reaching to the left or right of the object, but of stopping short of it or past it. This problem of visual location was worse for objects seen in peripheral than in central vision. For peripheral vision his errors were often gross, but in central vision he could use the groping strategy. Holmes (1918, p. 453) described him getting a box of matches from his locker:

> He sat up in bed, turned his head and eyes towards the locker, stared vacantly at one spot for a moment, then slowly and deliberately moved his eyes into other directions, until, after several seconds, the matchbox, as if by chance, came into his central vision; then he put his hand out to take hold of it, but succeeded in reaching it only after repeated gropings.

What we have described is a problem involving the absolute location of seen objects. However, Private M's problems were just as severe for relative location. He was shown two similar objects (silver and copper coins, or pieces of white and green paper), and then asked if another two objects were in the same relative positions. Whether the objects were positioned to one side of each other, with one above the other, or with one in front of the other, he made many errors. When he was asked to explain why he could not say which of the two objects was the nearer to him he replied: "When I look at one it seems to go further away, when I try to see which is the nearer they seem to change in position every now and then; that one at which I look directly seems to move away" (Holmes, 1918, p. 453).

In contrast to this problem in seeing relative locations, Private M could determine them without difficulty by touch. Thus when his finger was moved between two objects that he could not locate by vision, he could give accurate information immediately about their relative positions.

We are so used to locating objects by vision that it takes an effort to realise how disabled we would be without this ability. Its absence affected Private M across a wide range of activities. He could not count seen objects accurately, because he was unable to keep track of which ones he had already counted. He could only move about slowly and cautiously, and kept bumping into objects, and even walking into walls. When he found an object such as a chair in his way he had great problems in finding his way round it.

As we have already commented, Private M's case is typical of those described by Holmes. In most of these cases the visual location of objects was grossly deficient, yet the patient's experience was not that the world appeared "flat". Individual items were experienced as "normal" solid objects by all except one of the patients Holmes described (Holmes & Horrax, 1919).

Despite their being relatively pure cases, Holmes's patients also often had additional problems. In particular, some had general visual memory difficulties, and all had some degree of loss of topographical memory (for further information on this problem, see the last section of this chapter). We have not discussed these additional problems in detail here because they are all problems that can occur in people who do not experience any difficulty in visual location. Thus we do not think that they contribute to the problems in visual location.

Cases of specific loss of ability to locate seen objects are rare. All of Holmes's patients had bilateral lesions of the parietal lobes, and he commented that he had not seen similar symptoms produced by unilateral lesions. Subsequent studies have, however, shown that disorders of visual location can exist in the visual half field contralateral (i.e. opposite) to a unilateral cerebral lesion (Brain, 1941; Cole, Schutta, & Warrington, 1962; Ratcliff & Davies-Jones, 1972; Riddoch, 1935). Thus patients with left parietal lesions may have a specific difficulty locating objects seen in the right visual field, and patients with right parietal lesions may have a specific difficulty locating objects seen in the left visual field. These location problems can occur in the absence of any other visual defect.

A curious aspect of visual location difficulties is the contrast with blindsight, in which location is performed accurately. In blindsight, however, patients are not aware of seeing anything despite the intact visual location ability, whereas in impairments of visual location the patient cannot locate things accurately that she or he can otherwise see clearly.

It may be the case that it is the same visual location ability which remains intact in blindsight and is impaired in disorders of visual location (see Ratcliff, 1982), but a more intriguing possibility is that there is more than one type of visual location ability and that patients with visual location impairments cannot make use of location abilities equivalent to those available in blindsight. Impairments of visual location are closely related to impairments affecting movement under visual guidance (Damasio & Benton, 1979). Thus, the continued ability of patients with visual location impairments to consciously "see" may interfere with the expression of any residual location abilities.

SPATIAL ATTENTION

Overt and Covert Shifts of Attention

The world about us is extremely complex, and it may at times be useful to use attentional mechanisms to cut down the amount of information we have to deal with. For vision, shifts in attention are often accompanied by eye movements intended to bring the stimulus of interest onto the most sensitive central area of the retina, but shifts of attention to one part of space or another can also be made without eye movements. You can continue to look at a fixed point while directing your attention elsewhere; Posner (1980) calls these shifts in *covert* attention, to distinguish them from shifts involving an *overt* eye movement.

Posner and his colleagues have carried out several investigations of the ability to shift attention in both normal subjects and patients with different types of cerebral injury (e.g. Posner, 1980; Posner, Cohen, & Rafal, 1982; Posner, Walker, Friedrich, & Rafal, 1984; Posner, Rafal, Choate, & Vaughan, 1985). A noteworthy feature of their studies is that they have developed what amounts to a common set of experimental tasks that are given to all groups of subjects.

One of Posner's techniques involves asking people to fixate centrally and, while central fixation is maintained, to press a button as quickly as possible when they detect the presence of a specified stimulus. This stimulus may appear to the left or to the right of the fixated position, and is itself preceded by a cue indicating the left or right position. For normal subjects, detection of the target stimulus is faster if it appears on the cued side. Interestingly, this facilitation is found even when the cue is as likely to be invalid (the target then appears on the opposite side to the cue) as valid (the target then appears on the same side as the cue), so it seems to represent an involuntary attentional reaction outside of conscious strategic control.

Posner et al. (1982) used this general method with patients suffering from a condition known as progressive supranuclear palsy, which interferes with the ability to make voluntary eye movements. They showed that although their responses were rather slow these patients remained able to shift attention covertly, as measured by the facilitatory effect of cueing the target location. Thus the processes responsible for covert orienting of attention are not completely tied to those involved in overt shifts in the form of eye movements; these patients are able to make covert shifts in their visual attention in ways that they would find very difficult to accomplish by means of overt eye movements.

In contrast to the effects of progressive supranuclear palsy, which can leave at least some aspects of covert attentional mechanisms intact, parietal lobe injuries produce marked changes in such abilities. Posner et al. (1984) distinguished three aspects of covert shifts of attention: disengagement of attention from its current focus, moving attention to the target, and engagement of the target. They showed that patients with unilateral parietal lobe injuries find it difficult to disengage their attention from stimuli in the ipsilateral visual field (i.e. in the visual field corresponding to the side of the parietal lesion). Thus patients with right parietal lesions find it difficult to disengage their attention from a right visual field stimulus, but can readily disengage their attention from a left visual field stimulus. In terms of the experiment we described, their reaction times are very slow when the cue is presented to the right and the target appears to the left of fixation, but are unaffected when the cue is presented to the left and the target then appears on the right. Conversely, patients with left parietal lesions find it difficult to disengage their attention from a left but not from a right visual field stimulus.

Visual Extinction

Posner et al.'s (1984) findings form, as they note, an interesting parallel to the phenomenon of visual extinction found after parieto-occipital lesions. Patients with visual extinction can identify a single stimulus presented in any part of the visual field, but when stimuli are presented simultaneously in the left and right visual fields they do not seem to notice the stimulus falling in the visual field opposite (contralateral) to the site of the cerebral lesion. Thus a patient with visual extinction following a right parieto-occipital lesion would be able to identify a pair of scissors when they were presented individually in the left visual field or in the right visual field, but if the scissors fell in the left visual field and a pen was presented simultaneously in the right visual field, he or she would only report seeing the pen.

Visual extinction can happen even though the patient's visual fields may be intact on routine clinical examination (which typically involves testing for perception of a single stimulus). The problem is thus not due to a visual field defect as such, but to a higher-order attentional difficulty. In fact considerable analysis of the "extinguished" stimulus can take place. Volpe, LeDoux, and Gazzaniga (1979) have shown that accurate "same or different" comparisons between the extinguished and unextinguished stimuli are possible even when patients deny the presence of the extinguished stimulus. In our example, the patient would only report seeing a pen after simultaneous presentation of scissors in the left visual field and a pen in the right visual field, but would be able to say that the two stimuli were "different" from each other.

The parallel between visual extinction and Posner et al.'s (1984) demonstration of problems in disengaging attention from stimuli presented in the visual field ipsilateral to the lesion site is clear. Cases of clinically obvious visual extinction are, however, much more common following right rather than left cerebral injury. This observation is not inconsistent with Posner et al.'s (1984) findings, since they noted that although changes in covert orienting of attention were present after left or after right parietal injury, the effects were more marked in the case of right parietal injuries.

Unilateral Neglect and Denial

Visual extinction is closely related to one of the most intriguing of all spatial disorders—unilateral neglect. Like extinction, neglect is usually encountered in patients with right cerebral injuries, for whom it affects the left side of space. Patients with left-sided neglect following right

FIG 3.1.   Performance by a patient with visual neglect on a crossing-out task. She was asked to mark all the circles.

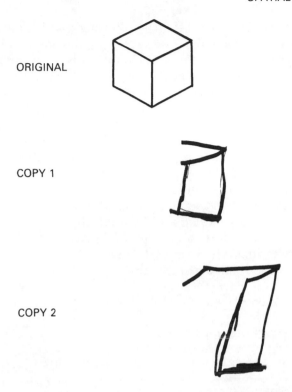

ORIGINAL

COPY 1

COPY 2

FIG. 3.2. Copies of a figure by a patient with visual neglect. Before copying it she had identified the figure as a cube.

hemisphere injury seem to ignore stimuli that fall to their left. A simple way of demonstrating this is by crossing-out tasks (Albert, 1973). Figure 3.1 shows a page of random circles and crosses: A neglect patient has been asked to put a mark through all the circles. There is a clear (and characteristic) boundary between the area on the right of the page for which the instruction has been followed and that on the left where it is effectively ignored. It is as if the patient has not noticed that the left side of the page is there; yet the right side has been searched diligently.

Neglect can also be detected in drawing and copying tasks. Figure 3.2 shows two attempts by a neglect patient to copy a line drawing of a cube. She easily identified the figure as a cube, yet only the right-hand side has been copied; she was apparently quite satisfied with her efforts, and did not try to change them when given verbal hints as to their inadequacies. Notice that the stimulus figure is symmetrical, so there is no intrinsic reason why the left side should be harder to copy.

Neglect often affects a wide range of everyday activities. Patients may show errors affecting the left side in reading (see Chapter 8), moving around (bumping into things on their left), dressing (putting on clothes only on the right side of the body), and eating (leaving food on the left side of a plate). These problems can exasperate relatives, because it can be curiously difficult to bring them to the patient's notice.

Patients with visual neglect often have a left hemianopia (blindness for stimuli presented in the left visual field). It is thus tempting to attribute their problems to the hemianopia, but this would be incorrect; the defect is found in tasks that allow free movement of the eyes. In addition, some patients show left neglect without any visual field defect and, conversely, there are many patients with left visual field defects without left neglect. Moreover, neglect need not be confined to the visual modality, and can affect the left side of tactile and auditory space as well.

In some cases neglect is associated with an inability to recognise that one is disabled, a denial or "anosognosia". Bisiach (1988) gives an example of a patient with a left visual field defect and left sided paralysis, who was anosognosic for both impairments:

Examiner: Do you know where you are?
Patient: In a hospital.
E: Why are you in a hospital?
P: Something went wrong.
E: What went wrong? [No reply.] Is your left arm alright?
P: Yes.
E: Give me your left hand.
P: Here you are [without performing any movement].
E: Where is it?
P: [Still motionless]...Here, in front of you.
E: [The examiner ostentatiously raises his forefinger in the patient's right visual field and asks]... Grasp my finger with your left hand... Well?... Can't you move your left hand at all?
P: [The patient hesitates]...Just give me time to proceed from thought to action.
E: Why don't you need any time to proceed from thought to action when you use your right hand? Maybe you *can't* move your left hand?
P: I can move it alright. Only,...sometimes there are illogical reactions in behaviour; some positive and some negative...
E: [The examiner places the patient's left hand in the patient's right visual field]...Whose hand is this?
P: Your hand.
E: [The examiner then places the patient's left hand between his own hands]...Whose hands are these?
P: Your hands.

E: How many of them?
P: Three.
E: Ever see a man with *three* hands?
P: A hand is the extremity of an arm. Since you have three arms
            it follows that you must have three hands.

In this example one has the impression of a type of neglect that leaves the patient unaware of the left side of his own body.

A number of different theories have been proposed to try to account for unilateral neglect, and Heilman (1979) provides a useful introduction to these. The term "neglect" implies that the disorder is attentional in nature, so we have chosen to consider it with other disorders of spatial attention. There is some evidence to support an attentional explanation. Riddoch and Humphreys (1983) investigated the effects of cueing in a line bisection task. When asked to bisect horizonal lines patients with unilateral neglect tend to choose a point that is to the right of the true midpoint. Riddoch and Humphreys (1983) showed that this tendency could be reduced if a cue, such as a digit, was presented at the left-hand end of the line, but that cueing was only effective if patients were made to report the cue; the mere presence of a cue did not reduce neglect. Riddoch and Humphreys distinguish between automatic aspects of attentional orienting, which should be elicited by the mere presence of a cue, and the more deliberate attentional demands involved when the cue must be reported. Because cues were only effective when they had to be reported, they suggest that neglect may involve a more serious impairment of automatic than deliberate aspects of attentional orienting.

Riddoch and Humphreys' (1983) work helps to form a link between investigations of neglect and the basic attentional mechanisms studied by Posner and his colleagues. In some symptoms of neglect, however, the disorder must involve very central mechanisms. The studies of Bisiach and Luzzatti (1978) and Bisiach, Capitani, Luzzatti, and Perani (1981) provide dramatic illustrations. Bisiach and his colleagues asked their (Italian) patients to *imagine* that they were in the central square (Piazza del Duomo) of Milan, facing the cathedral, and to describe what they would be able to see. The descriptions given by patients with left neglect were mostly found to involve the buildings on the right side of the square as seen from the patient's imagined viewpoint; buildings on the left of the square were not described. This neglect of the left side of a mental image is a remarkable phenomenon. The patients were then asked to describe the square from a different perspective; they were to imagine themselves standing on the steps of the cathedral, looking away from it. Immediately they described the buildings they had "neglected" to describe before, because these now fell to their right in the imagined view, and neglected to describe the buildings now to their left, which were of course those they had described in response to the initial request! This ingenious control condition neatly demonstrates that the patients' *memory* of the buildings is intact. Thus, they neglect to report buildings that they actually know are there.

Any explanation of Bisiach's findings in terms of an attentional hypothesis would, as we have said, have to involve central attentional mechanisms. Baddeley and Lieberman (1980), for instance, suggest that the process of internally scanning what they call the "visuo-spatial scratch pad" might be defective. Bisiach, however, dislikes the idea of making a distinction between the mental representation of an event and attentional processes that are supposed to "scan" this representation, and suggests instead that it is simpler to think of the deficit as one that involves the *construction of mental representations*. In Bisiach's view neglect is due to damage to an internal spatial framework that then interferes with the patient's ability to form a mental representation of the left side of real or imagined space.

To support this interpretation Bisiach, Luzzatti, and Perani (1979) studied the ability of patients with left neglect to detect differences between successively presented pairs of cloud-like patterns. In one condition of Bisiach et al.'s (1979) study the patterns were presented in their entirety, but in the other condition they were viewed as if passing from left to right or from right to left behind a stationary vertical slit, 1.5 × 12 cm, so that only a strip of one of the patterns was present at any given moment. Unlike control subjects, the neglect patients made more errors when the differences were on the left sides of the patterns, and this was true for both presentation conditions. Thus patients neglected the left side of a pattern even when it was only seen moving past a central area, and this held for both directions of movement, i.e. regardless of whether the left side was the first or the last part of the pattern to be shown. This finding again demonstrates that neglect can affect the left side of internal, mental representations.

The debate between proponents of attentional and representational theories of neglect looks set to continue for some years, and will no doubt reveal many other interesting findings. In our view, however, the central point is that neglect may not be a unitary condition, but a cluster of interrelated deficits that must be teased apart. Thus we doubt whether a unitary explanation of all aspects of neglect should be considered necessary. Not all neglect patients, for instance, neglect the left side of mental images, not all have dressing problems, and only some are anosognosic. It may be that these deficits are only found in the most severe cases, or it may be that they are caused by damage to functionally distinct mechanisms. In favour of this suggestion are the findings of Bisiach and his colleagues indicating dissociations between neglect of personal space (one's own body) and extrapersonal space, and between neglect and anosognosia (Bisiach, Perani, Vallar, & Berti, 1986a; Bisiach, Vallar, Perani, Papagno, & Berti, 1986b).

There are also hints in the literature of dissociations between symptoms of neglect found for the visual and auditory (Bisiach, Cornacchia, Sterzi, & Vallar, 1984) and visual and tactile modalities (Chedru, 1976), and between symptoms found for different materials within the visual modality (Heilman & Watson, 1978), though such dissociations do not, of course, apply to all patients (Caplan, 1985). One problem in investigating them is that neglect is not always a very stable condition. Often it clears up within a few months of the brain injury and, in addition, the performances of neglect patients can be quite variable from day to day, or even within a single testing session. There are some neglect patients with stable symptoms, however, and detailed comparisons between individual cases would seem desirable.

SPATIAL KNOWLEDGE AND SPATIAL THOUGHT

Bisiach and Luzzatti's (1978) study showed that their patients neglected to report buildings on the left of their mental image of Milan's Piazza del Duomo even though they "knew" the position of those buildings, as evidenced by their ability to report previously neglected buildings when they imagined that they were facing in the opposite direction. Thus their spatial knowledge concerning the arrangement of buildings around the square was intact, but their neglect interfered with their ability to express this knowledge in the chosen task.

Other patients, however, may show genuine impairments of spatial knowledge. A more detailed introduction to these impairments can be found in Ratcliff (1982), a comprehensive account is given by De Renzi (1982a), and Benton (1982) provides an interesting survey of the history of ideas about spatial disorders in neurological patients.

We will begin by considering problems in finding one's way about, which clinicians call loss of topographical memory. In fact, there are at least two distinct forms of topographical memory loss. In one form spatial knowledge is preserved, but the patient gets lost easily because he or she cannot recognise the familiar buildings that act as landmarks. Whiteley and Warrington (1977) report a patient, JC, who complained of difficulty in recognising familiar buildings and streets. JC could describe buildings he was looking at, and match simultaneously presented pictures of unfamiliar buildings without difficulty, yet he said that even the street in which he lived seemed unfamiliar, and each day he might be going along it as if for the first time. He had to recognise his own house by the number, or by his car parked outside it. In contrast, he could read maps easily and relied heavily on making maps and plans to get about in his unfamiliar world.

This problem seems like a form of visual recognition difficulty, and indeed it can be found together with problems in familiar face recognition (Landis, Cummings, Benson, & Palmer, 1986; Levine, Warach, & Farah, 1985; see also Chapter 4), so we mention it here only to contrast it with the forms of topographical memory impairment that do involve the loss of spatial knowledge. In these latter forms patients can recognise landmarks, but no longer know how to get from one landmark to another. One of De Renzi, Faglioni, and Villa's (1977b) patients, MA, could not find her way about the hospital ward, and kept stopping to look about her for some familiar landmark to tell her where she was. If she ventured onto a different floor of the hospital she had great trouble finding her way back, and she always got lost in the hospital gardens. Despite her problems remembering routes MA did not show a more general memory impairment, and De Renzi et al. (1977b) contrast her case with that of another patient, RA, who was severely amnesic but quite able to find his way about.

Interestingly, orientation in large-scale spaces may be independently impaired in comparison to other tasks that also seem to have a pronounced "spatial" component. This was demonstrated by Ratcliff and Newcombe (1973) using patients with shrapnel and gunshot wounds. They compared the performance of these patients on finding a path through a maze of 2×2 cm blocks (stylus maze) which had been learned by visual guidance, with their performance at following a path between nine points that were 150 cm apart by using a simple map (locomotor maze). Striking dissociations were found. One man with a right parietal lesion, for example, failed to learn the stylus maze task in 25 trials but made only one error on the locomotor maze whereas another man, with a bilateral posterior cerebral lesion, learnt the stylus maze in only 5 trials but made 40 errors (out of a possible 57) on the locomotor maze. Ratcliff and Newcombe (1973) point out that on the locomotor maze task the subject's orientation changes as he walks around, and attribute the poor performance of patients with bilateral posterior lesions to a failure to maintain orientation in a changing environment.

Impairments of spatial knowledge thus fall into different types. We can begin to make a distinction between loss of knowledge of the topography of familiar places, as shown by De Renzi et al.'s (1977b) patient MA, and loss of ability to maintain spatial orientation, as in Ratcliff and Newcombe's (1973) locomotor maze. A patient with impaired knowledge of familiar places might well remain spatially oriented (in the sense of being able to return to his or her starting point) in an unfamiliar place, whereas a patient with impaired spatial orientation would be lost whether the place was familiar or unfamiliar. A further distinction drawn by clinicians is that between personal space (one's own body) and extrapersonal space, where dissociable impairments of spatial knowledge again occur (Ogden, 1985; Semmes, Weinstein, Ghent, & Teuber, 1963).

Dissociations between impairments affecting short-term and long-term memory for spatial locations have also been found. De Renzi, Faglioni, and Previdi (1977a) used a task initially devised by Corsi. The equipment for this task consists of nine wooden cubes fixed at random locations on a small wooden board. The experimenter touches a number of these cubes in sequence, and the subject's task is to reproduce this sequence in the same order; the size of the sequence (in terms of the number of cubes) can be varied in order to determine the subject's immediate memory span. De Renzi et al. (1977a) found that patients with lesions of posterior areas of the left or right cerebral hemispheres could be impaired on this task, but that only patients with right posterior lesions were impaired on a comparable long-term memory task in which they were required to learn a sequence of block positions that was longer than their immediate memory span. Thus the patients with left posterior lesions have impaired short-term but intact long-term memory for spatial locations. Reports of two individual cases of impaired short-term and intact long-term spatial memory can be found in De Renzi and Nichelli (1975).

There are also impairments that affect spatial thought. Morrow, Ratcliff, and Johnston (1985) showed that patients with right cerebral hemisphere lesions who could estimate accurately the distances between arbitrary symbols marked on a piece of paper, and could locate cities correctly on an outline map of the U.S.A., were none the less impaired in comparison to control subjects at estimating the distances between major cities in the U.S.A. (where they lived). Because they could estimate the distances between symbols, and locate the cities involved on a map, their problems could not be due to ignorance of the city locations or inability to estimate distances. Before being asked to estimate the distances between cities, Morrow et al.'s (1985) subjects had been shown an outline map of the U.S.A. and told its overall dimensions in miles. In order to estimate the distances between cities they were asked to make use of a mental image. Morrow et al. emphasise, however, that defective estimation of distances was found for cities on the right (East) side of the U.S.A. as well as for those on the left (West) side; so the phenomenon would seem to be independent of the neglect-related imaging disorder studied by Bisiach and his colleagues.

A neat demonstration of impaired spatial thought was made by Ratcliff (1979), who showed patients with gunshot and shrapnel wounds a drawing of a man with one of the hands marked with a black disc (see Fig. 3.3).

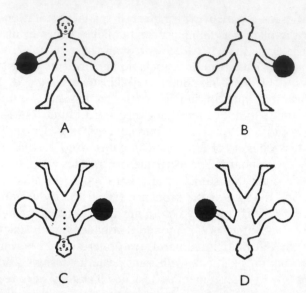

FIG. 3.3. Examples of stimuli used by Ratcliff (1979.) (Reproduced with permission of Pergamon Press from *Neuropsychologia*, 1979, *17*, 51.)

The figure was seen in upright or upside-down orientation, and in front or back view. The patients were asked to indicate whether the black disc marked the man's left or his right hand. Patients with posterior lesions of the right cerebral hemisphere showed a clear impairment on this task, but only when the stimuli were upside-down. Thus they could easily tell left from right when the stimulus was upright, but they seemed unable to "mentally rotate" the upside-down stimuli into their normal orientation.

It would be interesting to know more about the relation between impairments of spatial thought and impairments of spatial short-term memory. If Baddeley's (1983; 1986) conception that spatial short-term memory abilities form part of an organised "working memory" system is correct (see Chapter 10) these types of impairment may well prove to be closely related.

OVERVIEW

Neurophysiologists have been telling us for years that the human visual system has a precise and intricate organisation. Even so, the specificity of some of the disorders of visual and spatial abilities that are beginning to be revealed is very impressive. Highly selective impairments of different aspects of colour processing, movement perception, and visual location have been described. There is evidence, too, that different functional components of the visual system are organised into dissociable systems concerned primarily with the analysis of different types of visual pattern (objects, faces, words, etc.) or with space perception.

Abilities such as visual location might be considered to represent very basic aspects of our analysis of the spatial positioning of the objects around us. However, there is also evidence of modular organisation (as revealed by selective impairments) in the organisation of "higher" spatial abilities. We saw from the evidence reviewed in Chapter 2 that the processes involved in object recognition are highly organised; exactly the same conclusion would seem to be justified with regard to processes involved in space perception, though we have less idea as yet what the outlines of this organisation might be. Identifying the different dissociable impairments of visual and spatial abilities offers the possibility of helping to determine what modular functional components are involved.

Some disorders of visual and spatial abilities, however, turn out to involve different aspects of awareness. In blindsight, for instance, the patient is not aware of seeing anything, yet can make accurate responses based on some form of visual analysis. In visual extinction, patients may deny the presence of one of two simultaneously presented stimuli, yet be able to say whether or not it is the same as or different to one that is overtly reported as present. In visual neglect, awareness of part of external space seems to be compromised, and in anosognosia the patient seems to show an unawareness of one or more of his or her own disabilities. The investigation of such disorders holds great promise for helping us to understand questions about consciousness and awareness that have been puzzled over for centuries, and forms one of the most fascinating areas in contemporary cognitive neuropsychology.

SUMMARY

In this chapter we have examined a number of different types of impairment affecting visual and spatial abilities. Impairments of colour vision were divided into those involving inability to see colour (achromatopsias), impairment of colour knowledge (in which colour perception is intact, but errors occur in tasks that require use of stored information about colour), and difficulties involving colour naming. For movement perception we considered the remarkable case of LM, who had lost the ability to see movement under all except a rather limited range of conditions. To LM most moving things were like a series of arbitrary, static "snapshots". We then discussed contrasting impairments involving spatial location. Blindsight, in which a patient (DB) had no sense of seeing anything presented in the defective areas of his field of vision yet could make accurate judgements of location, was contrasted with a

disorder of visual location in which another patient (Private M) was well aware of seeing things and could even recognise them without difficulty, but did not know where they were positioned in external space. "Higher-order" spatial problems were then considered. Some of these involve impairments of spatial attention, and a dissociation between impairments affecting shifts of overt and shifts of covert attention can be observed. Certain aspects of unilateral neglect (such as the influence of cueing) are also consistent with an attentional explanation, but others (such as neglect of mental images) are perhaps more readily explained in terms of a "representational" theory. Neglect is probably a complex phenomenon involving a number of potentially dissociable aspects. For impairments of spatial knowledge a distinction can be drawn between impaired knowledge of the topography of familiar places and impaired ability to maintain spatial orientation. Other types of impairment can affect short-term memory for spatial locations, and spatial thought.

FURTHER READING

Bisiach, E. (1994). Perception and action in space representation: evidence from unilateral neglect. In G. d'Ydewalle, P. Eelen, & P. Bertelson (Eds), *International perspectives on psychological science, Vol. 2, The state of the art* (pp. 51–66). Hove, UK: Erlbaum. Reviews evidence pointing to a relative differentiation of perceptual from premotor forms of unilateral neglect.

Cowey, A. (1994). Cortical visual areas and the neurobiology of higher visual processes. In M.J. Farah & G. Ratcliff (Eds), *The neuropsychology of high-level vision: collected tutorial essays* (pp. 3–31). Hillsdale, N.J.: Lawrence Erlbaum Associates Inc. Useful update on the neurophysiology of the visual pathways and its implications.

Halligan, P.W. & Marshall, J.C. (1994). Toward a principled explanation of unilateral neglect. *Cognitive Neuropsychology, 11*, 167–206. Looks at different forms of neglect and tries to integrate these within an overall account.

Heywood, C.A., Cowey, A., & Newcombe, F. (1994). On the role of parvocellular (P) and magnocellular (M) pathways in cerebral achromatopsia. *Brain, 117*, 245–254. A good example of the rich interplay between neurobiological and psychological studies, with fascinating observations of responses to wavelength without any corresponding experience of seeing colour.

McLeod, P., Heywood, C., Driver, J., & Zihl, J. (1989). Selective deficit of visual search in moving displays after extrastriate damage. *Nature, 339*, 466–467. Further investigation of LM's perception of movement.

Meadows, J.C. (1974). Disturbed perception of colours associated with localized cerebral lesions. *Brain, 97*, 615–632. Still a good introduction to impairments of colour vision.

Milner, A.D. & Goodale, M.A. (1996). *The visual brain in action.* Oxford Psychology Series, 27. Oxford: Oxford University Press. Thought-provoking book that sets the study of visuo–spatial impairments firmly in the context of visual pathways specialised for the control of action.

Weiskrantz. L. (1986). *Blindsight: a case study and implications.* Oxford Psychology Series, 12. Oxford: Oxford University Press. Pathbreaking investigations of case DB.

VIDEOS

Videos: *Attentional dysfunctions: Problems in visual orienting* in the series *Teaching programmes in cognitive neuropsychology*, edited by E. Funnell & G.W. Humphreys, illustrates topics discussed in this chapter. Examples of visual neglect can be seen in a video by P. Halligan and J.C. Marshall: *The experience of visual neglect; Illustrations of visual neglect* and *Art and visuo-spatial perception*, all published by Erlbaum (UK) Taylor & Francis, Hove, UK.

4 Face Processing

INTRODUCTION

Other people's faces provide us with a wealth of social information. We are highly skilled at recognising the faces of people we know, and we can assess characteristics such as age or sex fairly accurately even when a face is unfamiliar. We are also adept at interpreting facial expressions, and make much use of these in regulating patterns of social interaction.

Given the range of different types of information we gain from faces, and the variety of uses to which these are put, it is perhaps not too surprising that different types of face processing disorder can be observed in people with cerebral injuries. Investigations of these disorders have been of central importance to the development of functional models of face processing.

A FUNCTIONAL MODEL OF FACE PROCESSING

We will use the functional model presented by Bruce and Young (1986) to organise our discussion of disorders of face processing. Detailed discussion of the studies of normal subjects that support a model of this type can be found in H. D. Ellis (1986a) and Bruce (1988). A slightly simplified version of the Bruce and Young model is shown in schematic form in Fig. 4.1. Bruce and Young (1986) propose that following structural encoding of the face's appearance (which we will equate loosely with formation of a facial percept), different types of information are extracted from the face in parallel. These include the analysis of facial expressions, analysis of the mouth and tongue movements involved in speaking (facial speech analysis), and the types of directed visual processing needed to manipulate facial representations intentionally so that we can, for example, see the similarities and differences between faces of unfamiliar people.

Recognition of familiar faces is also considered by Bruce and Young (1986) to occur in parallel with expression analysis, facial speech analysis, and directed visual processing. They postulate a set of "face recognition units" that form a link between structural encoding of the face's appearance and "person identity nodes" that provide access to stored information concerning known people (their occupations, personal characteristics, etc.). Each face recognition unit is held to contain the structural description of a known person's appearance. The recognition unit "fires" when a seen face resembles the description it holds. Recognition of familiar people from other cues, such as voices, would involve the use of separate access routes to the person identity nodes (not shown in Fig. 4.1). You should be familiar with this type of theoretical model from our discussion of object recognition in Chapter 2.

PROSOPAGNOSIA

The most striking type of face processing disorder is prosopagnosia, or inability to recognise familiar faces. Prosopagnosic patients are often

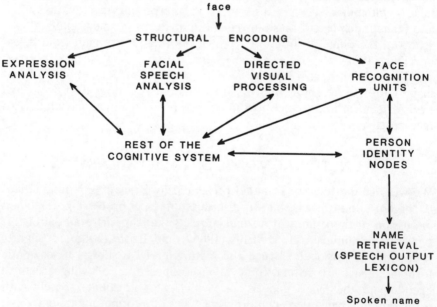

FIG. 4.1.   Functional model for face processing (based on Bruce & Young, 1986.)

unable to identify *any* familiar faces including famous faces, friends, family, and their own faces when seen in a mirror (Hécaen & Angelergues, 1962). Clinical features of this disorder have been summarised by Benton (1980) and Hécaen (1981), and neurological aspects are discussed by Meadows (1974a) and Damasio, Damasio, and Van Hoesen (1982).

Prosopagnosic patients know when they are looking at a face, but cannot say who the face belongs to. Instead they must rely on other cues such as voice, gait, clothing, or context in order to recognise people. Such methods are not very reliable, and it is possible that they are rendered even less effective than they might be by their inconsistency with the defective face recognition mechanisms. Tiberghien and Clerc (1986), for instance, mention that their patient, AH, could identify the voice of a politician on the television without seeing him, but that if AH saw and heard that person at the same time he could no longer recognise him.

Prosopagnosia is, of course, no more a unitary disorder than object agnosia, dyslexia or amnesia. We use the term "prosopagnosia" here simply as a convenient shorthand for "inability to recognise familiar faces" and, as we will show, this may have various causes. Thus, strictly, we should speak of "the prosopagnosias". Identification of the different types of prosopagnosia has, however, been made difficult by the fact that it is especially rare as an isolated deficit. In the historic cases described by Charcot (1883) and Wilbrand (1892), for instance, inability to recognise faces was found in the context of quite widespread perceptual and memory difficulties, and the distinct nature of impairments of familiar face recognition was not generally recognised until Bodamer (1947) published his own observations and coined the term "prosopagnosia". We will examine more closely the relation between impairments affecting the recognition of faces and other types of visual object later in this chapter (pp. 101–105).

Although the different types of prosopagnosic difficulty have yet to be delineated convincingly, it is widely believed that the cases reported to date fall into at least two distinct groups (Hécaen, 1981; De Renzi, 1986). For one group of patients the ability to *perceive* faces is manifestly impaired; in Bruce and Young's terms the defect affects structural encoding. The other group of patients seem to have relatively intact perceptual abilities, but cannot *recognise* or in some other way process the faces they seem to perceive satisfactorily.

DEFECTIVE PERCEPTION OF FACES

The first two patients described by Bodamer (1947) form good examples of prosopagnosia in the context of impaired perception of faces. We will consider his case 2, Unteroffizier (Uffz.) S. This 24-year-old noncommissioned officer was wounded in the head in March 1944. Following this injury he was unable to identify once-familiar faces. He maintained that he could still image the faces of people he knew before his injury, but that the faces of people he was actually looking at all looked the same. They were like strangely flat, white oval plates, with emphatically dark eyes.

Uffz. S could differentiate between faces and most other types of object, but made some errors with animal faces. He identified a rabbit's face from its ears correctly, but thought that a dog's face was that of an unusually hairy human. When looking at people's faces he could pick out individual features correctly, such as the nose, mouth or eyes, but had no sense of the face's individuality. Even very well known faces produced no feeling of familiarity, and he failed to recognise his own mother in a chance meeting.

As well as being unable to recognise individuals, Uffz. S also could not determine the age or sex of seen faces except by inferring these from the hairstyle. His ability to interpret facial expressions was also defective. He said that he could see the movements involved when people made angry or smiling facial expressions, but that these had no meaning for him. When looking in a mirror together with a number of other people Uffz. S could see the movements on his face when he spoke, without recognising the face as his own.

In interpreting the nature of the perceptual disorder involved, Bodamer (1947) placed emphasis on the fact that Uffz. S could distinguish the individual elements of a face but could not appreciate its unique character. Later observers also often return to this idea. As Pallis's (1955, p. 219) patient put it: "I can see the eyes, nose, and mouth quite clearly but they just don't add up. They all seem chalked in, like on a blackboard. I have to tell by the clothes or voice whether it is a man or a woman."

It is difficult to know what to make of such cases of impaired face perception beyond the fact that this can happen. Uffz. S seemed to experience impaired perception both of individual features *and* the facial configuration, whereas from Pallis's (1955) patient's description it would seem that the deficit in seeing the configuration formed by the individual features was perhaps more severe. Pallis's patient's description of his problems is in some ways reminiscent of Riddoch and Humphreys' (1987a) object agnosic patient, HJA (see Chapter 2), who was also prosopagnosic, but Pallis reports that his patient could identify everyday objects without difficulty provided that colour was not a necessary cue (his colour vision was severely impaired). The contrast between the problems of Uffz. S and patients such as Pallis's (1955) patient or HJA suggests that there are probably different types of perceptual deficit that can affect face recognition, and Hay and Young (1982) and H. D. Ellis (1986b) offer suggestions as to what these might be. But the patients are clearly trying to describe types of perceptual experience for which there is no normal shared vocabulary, and it may be unwise to rely too much on their subjective reports.

A further complication is that not all problems affecting face perception cause prosopagnosia. Bodamer (1947) contrasted a third case with his other two patients: This patient saw faces as distorted. He described a nurse's face as having its nose turned sideways by several degrees, one eyebrow higher than the other, the mouth askew, and hair shifted like an ill-fitting cap. This kind of perceptual distortion is often termed "metamorphopsia". According to Bodamer's (1947) third patient, only faces looked distorted in this way; but he remained able to recognise them.

Hécaen and Angelergues (1962) also point out that metamorphopsic patients often remain able to recognise familiar faces to some extent. Perhaps the distortions they experience are not sufficiently severe to prevent recognition (which we know from everyday experience can cope with a wide range of perceptual variations), or perhaps the perceptual impairments that can lead to prosopagnosia are not of the metamorphopsic type.

PROSOPAGNOSIA AS AN IMPAIRMENT OF FACE MEMORY

We have seen that prosopagnosia can arise in a context of impaired perception of faces. For some prosopagnosic patients, however, face perception is relatively intact, leading to the idea that it may be more useful to consider this type of disorder as if it were a material-specific memory impairment (De Renzi, 1982b; Tiberghien & Clerc, 1986; Warrington & James, 1967b; see also Chapter 10 for a discussion of other types of memory impairment). We will consider the patient Mr W, described by Bruyer, Laterre, Seron, Feyereisen, Strypstein, Pierrard, and Rectem (1983).

Mr W was a 54-year-old Belgian farmer who had been unable to identify familiar people for a year. His difficulties in recognising people had initially begun during a spell of hospital treatment for cardiac problems, and had now become stable. His scores on standard intelligence tests did not seem affected (Verbal I.Q. 90; Performance I.Q. 95), but neurological examination (CT scan) revealed bilateral occipital lobe lesions.

Subjectively, Mr W's complaint was that faces seemed "less beautiful" than before and that, although he could still see them and their constitutive parts well, he could not recognise them. Investigation of this complaint showed that he was able to pick out the human faces in an array of photographs of five human faces (photographed with a white hood covering the hairstyle), five dog faces, five car fronts, and five housefronts. He performed this task without error, and could also pick out the dogs, cars, and houses without difficulty. He was able to make accurate copies of line drawings of faces, and to identify correctly the sex of 16 faces (8 male, 8 female) photographed with a white hood covering the hairstyle.

Facial expressions were accurately perceived and interpreted. Mr W could match correctly photographs of faces as showing same or different expressions, could pick out faces having the same expression as a specified target picture, and could judge the appropriateness of facial expressions to pictures meant to elicit an emotional state (a clown, a funeral, etc.).

Mr W's ability to match unfamiliar faces was also good. He could discriminate between pairs of line drawings in which one or more features were altered (13/16 correct, mean score for normal subjects = 14.5). He achieved a normal level of performance when asked to pick out a photographed target face from an array of nine possible faces, and his performance on this task deteriorated in a "normal" manner if the stimuli were blurred. Had his ability to perceive faces already been impaired, blurring might not have produced any further effect. When shown two photographs of the same face in three-quarter and full-face views Mr W correctly stated that the photographs showed the same person on all six trials. He could also match the identities of unfamiliar faces (wearing white hoods so that hairstyle was not a cue) across different expressions. When shown a 4 × 4 matrix of photographs of four different people with each of four different expressions he made 14/16 correct choices of the photographs showing the same person as a target face with a neutral expression.

Given Mr W's ability to discriminate correctly between faces of different unfamiliar people, and to see that different views of the same unfamiliar face belonged to the same person, it is difficult to believe that his problems in recognising familiar people were due to an inability to construct an adequate facial "percept". Instead, it seems that he could no longer use differences that he could see between faces to effect recognition. We do not, however, mean to claim that his perceptual abilities were *entirely* intact. Bruyer et al. (1983) point out, for instance, that Mr W was unable to see bruises on potatoes, and he did sometimes show performances on their tests of face perception that were slightly below normal. These relatively subtle perceptual deficits may, however, have been coincidental; they do not seem sufficient to account for Mr W's recognition problems (patients can have far worse perceptual impairment without showing Mr W's prosopagnosic symptoms).

The face recognition impairment was severe in Mr W's case. When shown photographs of ten famous faces, five of which had been "cued" by being named in a previous discussion, he could only identify one (mean for normal subjects = 9.7). He was shown videotapes of the faces of himself, his doctor, his neuropsychologist, a patient he was friendly with, and two unfamiliar people, all wearing hoods to hide their hairstyles. Mr W could not recognise anyone, and thought that all of the faces were unfamiliar, though he was a little doubtful about his own face. When the hoods were removed he recognised himself after a long delay, thought that his friend's face seemed familiar, and that he might know the neuropsychologist. Even when asked only to decide whether or not faces were those of familiar people Mr W rejected 12 of 20 familiar faces shown to him. The eight faces he accepted as familiar in this task were all those of people he knew personally (and were thus probably of very high familiarity indeed); he invariably rejected celebrities' faces as unfamiliar.

We might summarise Mr W's face recognition problems by saying that in tasks demanding precise identification (e.g. by naming) he was very severely impaired, but that he did seem to retain some sense of the familiarity of faces that had previously been extremely well known to him. His difficulties seemed to lie in accessing previously stored memories concerning the people whose faces he saw—a problem that Damasio et al. (1982) have called "contextual evocation".

The attempts to explain prosopagnosia as a material-specific memory difficulty need to be approached carefully. The claim is *not* simply that prosopagnosics are amnesic. Mr W, for example, could remember perfectly well the people whose faces he could not recognise if he was presented with their names, voices, and so on. His problem was thus one of *access to* these memories from the face itself. In terms of Bruce and Young's (1986) approach Mr W's problem seems to lie in defective operation of face recognition units. His structural encoding processes were relatively intact, as indicated by his near normal performance on tests of face perception, and person identity nodes were also clearly intact because he could recognise people from names and voices, but the recognition units no longer formed an effective link. This conception is analogous to the idea of a material-specific memory difficulty, because face recognition units can be seen as equivalent to a memory store of the faces Mr W had encountered previously.

Mr W certainly did have problems with face memory. Bruyer et al. (1983) demonstrated this by showing him six faces and then asking him to find three that he had just seen in another array of six faces. Whether the faces used were those of familiar or unfamiliar people, Mr W only managed to get one correct. In contrast, when faces with emotional expressions were used in this type of task he did not make any errors because he could use a strategy of labelling the expressions. This shows neatly that it is Mr W's memory for faces, rather than his memory in any general sense, that was defective. The claim is supported by the finding that in paired associate learning tasks Mr W found it easier to associate people's names with meaningless drawings or even with pictures of car fronts than with faces.

SEMANTIC IMPAIRMENTS

In discussing the view that some cases of prosopagnosia might be considered to involve a material-specific memory problem, we drew attention to the point that prosopagnosia should none the less be distinguished from other forms of amnesia because prosopagnosic patients remain able to remember familiar people and to recognise them from their names or voices. Thus it is access to person identity nodes from faces that is impaired in prosopagnosia, and the memory representations of familiar people remain intact and readily accessible in other ways.

This is not the case for many amnesic patients. A number of studies have shown that amnesic memory deficits can affect memories of familiar people (Marslen-Wilson & Teuber, 1975; Sanders & Warrington, 1971). Such problems affect the recognition of people from their faces but, of course, they extend equally to recognition from names and voices, and problems are also shown in recall tasks involving famous people (Albert, Butters, & Levin, 1979; Hamsher & Roberts, 1985; Meudell, Northen, Snowden, & Neary, 1980b). In cases of semantic memory impairments, such as Warrington's patients AB and JBR (see Chapter 2), failure to recognise overtly familiar people may also occur.

A remarkable impairment affecting the semantic representations of familiar people is seen in the "Capgras syndrome". Capgras syndrome is one of a number of different types of misidentification syndromes (see Joseph, 1986), and was first described by the French psychiatrists Capgras and Reboul-Lachaux in 1923. The Capgras syndrome has been widely believed to be psychodynamic in origin, but recent reports have emphasised that it has a clear organic basis in several cases (e.g. Joseph, 1986; Lewis, 1987; MacCallum, 1973; Weston & Whitlock, 1971; Wilcox & Waziri, 1983).

The key feature of the Capgras syndrome is that the patient believes that one or more familiar people has been "replaced" by an impostor. Often, but not always, this impostor is thought to have harmful intentions. We will make use of the case described by Alexander, Stuss, and Benson (1979). This 44-year-old man suffered a severe brain injury in a road accident, leading to bilateral frontal and extensive right hemisphere damage. Prior to the accident he had been experiencing auditory hallucinations and delusions following a period of prolonged stress, but never acted on them.

When Alexander et al. (1979) met this patient, some two and a half years after his accident, he informed them that he had two families of identical composition. In each family his wife had the same name and very similar appearance and manner. There were five children in each family, with the same names and sexes, though he thought that the children in the original family were about one year younger than in his second family. The change had, he maintained, taken place in December, 1975 (about a month after the accident), when his "new" wife had turned up to take him home from hospital for the weekend. It is perhaps significant that he had not been informed that he was going home that weekend. He said he had not seen his original wife or family since, but he described positive feelings towards both wives and did not seem upset by his first wife's desertion.

Alexander et al. (1979) noted that their patient realised the implausibility of his story, but continued to assert it. He seemed unable to change his beliefs. They quote the following interview (p. 335):

E. Isn't that [two families] unusual?
S. It was unbelievable!
E. How do you account for it?
S. I don't know. I try to understand it myself, and it was virtually impossible.
E. What if I told you I don't believe it?
S. That's perfectly understandable. In fact, when I tell the story, I feel that I'm concocting a story.... It's not quite right. Something is wrong.

Despite being pressed in this way, and told that he was incorrect on several occasions, Alexander et al.'s patient continued to experience the delusion.

The Capgras syndrome may be seen as an example of a general class of "reduplicative paramnesias" (Alexander et al., 1979; Benson, Gardner, & Meadows, 1976; Patterson & Mack, 1985). The term paramnesia is used to refer to a distortion rather than a loss of memory. Capgras' patients reduplicate people, whereas for other reduplication patients it is often places that are affected, with the patient maintaining that their home or hospital is a duplicate of the one they actually live in. For example, Geschwind (1982) quoted the case of a patient in the Beth Israel Hospital in Boston, U.S.A., who said that he was in Concord, New Hampshire. This patient knew that he was in the Beth Israel Hospital, but maintained that he was in a (non-existent) branch of that hospital located in Concord. Sometimes the same patient will reduplicate both people and places (e.g. Patterson & Mack, 1985).

The fact that reduplication can occur to people or to places forms a curious parallel to the observation that defective recognition of places is often found in association with prosopagnosia (Landis et al., 1986). Perhaps this is no more than a coincidence, and it is really the emotional significance of people and of places that underlies the tendency to reduplicate them. Some reports, however, have demonstrated that Capgras' patients show deficits on tests of unfamiliar face matching (Shraberg & Weitzel, 1979; Tzavaras, Luaute, & Bidault, 1986). Although such face processing impairments cannot be sufficient to produce Capgras syndrome, because other patients with equally or more severe impairments do not reduplicate people, it is conceivable that they may play some contributory role.

NAME RETRIEVAL PROBLEMS

In Bruce and Young's (1986) model of face processing access to person identity nodes occurs before name retrieval. Problems involving name retrieval are common in everyday life (Reason & Lucas, 1984; Young, Hay, & Ellis, 1985a), and experiments with normal subjects have shown that people's names are harder to remember than various other kinds of semantic information (Cohen & Faulkner, 1986; McWeeny, Young, Hay, & Ellis, 1987).

Thus we would expect to find examples of patients who, following brain injury, remain able to access semantic information about people but cannot remember their names. This happens in a form of language disorder known as anomia (see Chapter 5), but anomias usually involve not only people's names but also names of objects, places and so on. McKenna and Warrington (1980), however, present a report of an anomia that affected people's names selectively. Their patient, GBL, could only name 3 of 20 photographs of famous people, yet was able to describe accurately who 18 of the 20 people were. In contrast, she correctly named 16 out of 20 European towns and 12 of 12 English towns from their locations on a map.

COVERT RECOGNITION IN PROSOPAGNOSIA

The impairments of familiar face recognition we have already discussed fit Bruce and Young's (1986) model quite well (see Fig. 4.1). Cases of defective face perception (such as Uffz. S) can be considered to involve impaired structural encoding, the material-specific memory deficit (Mr W) would involve face recognition units, semantic impairments would arise at the level of person identity nodes, and there are also distinct problems of name retrieval.

A remarkable feature of some recent studies of prosopagnosic patients, however, is that they can be shown to demonstrate a considerable degree of recognition of familiar faces if tested on tasks that do not demand explicit awareness that recognition has been achieved. The key feature of such tasks would seem to be that recognition is tested *implicitly* (Schacter, McAndrews, & Moscovitch, 1988). These phenomena are not in principle inconsistent with the type of model used here (Fig. 4.1), but they will need to be investigated carefully in order to see how they can be related to it.

Bruyer et al. (1983) tested Mr W's ability to associate names with several types of stimuli. Although Mr W could not identify the faces of celebrities, he found it much easier to learn correct than incorrect names to photographs of their faces. Thus it seems that some degree of recognition of the familiar faces must have taken place; otherwise correct or incorrect names would be equally easy to learn. Curiously, though, it would seem that Mr W was not aware of having recognised the faces.

This phenomenon of "recognition without awareness" in prosopagnosia has been more fully investigated by Bauer (1984), Tranel and Damasio (1985), De Haan, Young, and Newcombe (1987a; 1987b), and Young and De Haan (1988). Bauer (1984) and Tranel and Damasio (1985) used autonomic measures; they found that the skin conductance responses of their prosopagnosic patients showed discrimination between familiar and unfamiliar faces (Tranel & Damasio, 1985) and between correct and incorrect names when viewing a familiar face (Bauer, 1984) even though their patients had no sense of conscious, overt recognition. We will use De Haan et al.'s (1987a; 1987b) work to look more closely at this phenomenon of "covert" recognition in prosopagnosia.

De Haan et al. (1987a; 1987b) worked with PH, who had sustained a severe closed head injury in a motorcycle accident when he was aged 19. His language abilities were well preserved, and he had normal short-term memory, but he showed poor performance on long-term memory tasks and on some visuospatial tasks. He could read satisfactorily, and could recognise many (but not all) seen objects, but he was completely unable to recognise familiar faces. On formal tests he recognised none of 20 highly familiar faces and performed at chance level (18/36 correct) on a task requiring classification of faces as belonging to familiar or unfamiliar people. Even in a forced choice task in which he was only asked to pick which one of two simultaneously presented faces (one familiar, one unfamiliar) was the familiar person, PH still performed at chance level (65/128 correct), yet he was much more accurate (118/128) on a parallel task involving those people's names (Young & De Haan, 1988).

PH's visual acuity was normal for his right eye, but impaired for his left eye, probably because of a longstanding untreated squint. His field of vision for his right eye was somewhat constricted, and there was some loss of contrast sensitivity for all spatial frequencies greater than 1.5 cycles per degree. These visual impairments do not, however, seem sufficient to account for PH's prosopagnosia, because other patients with more severely impaired vision remain able to recognise people. Moreover, PH was able to match different views of unfamiliar faces as belonging to same or different people, and he could interpret facial expressions; his performances on such tasks tended to be impaired in comparison to those of normal people of his age, but well above chance level. His inability to recognise faces could also not be attributed to his other memory problems, because he *could* recognise people from their names. Thus he had not simply "forgotten" the people concerned; in Bruce and Young's (1986) terms, person identity nodes were relatively intact. The nature of his prosopagnosia would thus seem to bear some resemblance to that of Mr W, but for PH the face recognition deficit (on overt tasks) was more severe and occurred in the context of a wider range of other impairments.

Despite his very severe impairment on overt recognition tasks, De Haan et al. (1987a; 1987b) found that PH showed effects of face familiarity on his performance of various tasks that did not demand explicit recognition. Thus when required to judge as rapidly as possible whether two simultaneously presented photographs were of the same or different people he was faster for familiar than unfamiliar faces. As is found for normal subjects (Young, Hay, McWeeny, Flude, & Ellis, 1985b), PH was only faster at matching photographs of familiar faces when matches had to be based on the faces' internal (eyes, nose, mouth) rather than external (hair, chin) features. This normal pattern of responses to familiar and unfamiliar faces was found despite PH's inability to identify explicitly the people involved.

Because PH could recognise printed names without difficulty, De Haan et al. (1987a; 1987b) were able to investigate whether or not the presence of irrelevant "distractor" faces would interfere with name classification. When normal people classify names into semantic categories (for example, as names of politicians or of television personalities) their reaction times are increased by the presence of a distractor face drawn from a different category to the name being classified. PH was also found to show this interference effect in three separate experiments. Figure 4.2 shows examples of stimuli from De Haan et al.'s (1987b) task. Names and faces of four politicians and four television personalities were used as stimuli. These were combined with each other so that a name was presented with the same person's face (SAME PERSON condition), with the face of another person from the same category (RELATED condition; for example, a politician's name with another politician's face), or with the face of another person from the other category (UNRELATED condition; for example, a politician's name with a television personality's face). PH

FIG. 4.2.   Examples of stimuli from De Haan, Young, & Newcombe's (1987b) study. The name of the politician David Steel is combined with his own face (top; SAME PERSON), with the face of the politician Peter Walker (middle; RELATED), and with the face of the non-politician Michael Aspel (bottom; UNRELATED). (Reproduced with permission of The Press Association and Masson Italia Editori from *Cortex*, 1987, *23*, 312.)

was asked to decide as quickly as possible whether each *name* was that of a politician or a television personality. He was instructed to ignore the faces. His reaction times, measured from the onset of each stimulus by means of a manual response, are shown in Table 4.1.

TABLE 4.1

Mean Reaction Times (in Milliseconds) for PH's Classification of Names Accompanied by Different Types of Distractor Faces (Data From De Haan, Young, & Newcombe, 1987b)

Type of Face Distractor		
Same Person	Related	Unrelated
1059	1122	1234

Although the same names and faces were used in each condition, and the task only required him to assign the names to one of the sets of four politicians or four television personalities, PH shows a clear interference effect from the faces. His reaction times for classifying the names in the UNRELATED condition are significantly longer than those for classifying the same names in the RELATED condition; the reaction times for the RELATED and SAME PERSON conditions do not differ significantly. This is the same pattern of interference effects as is found in normal subjects for this type of task (Young, Ellis, Flude, McWeeny, & Hay, 1986). PH's reaction times are rather longer than would be usual for normal people, but a general slowing of reaction time is not uncommon after closed head injury (Van Zomeren & Deelman, 1978). The more important point is that the *patterning* of PH's reaction times across the different conditions looks normal.

The faces used by De Haan et al. (1987b) had been carefully matched so that cues such as age or hairstyle would not allow politicians and television personalities to be discriminated from each other. When PH was asked to classify explicitly these faces as those of politicians or television personalities he performed at chance level (30/48 correct). Thus the faces interfered with his ability to classify names despite the fact that accurate overt classification of these faces was not possible.

De Haan et al. (1987a) also showed that, like Mr W, PH learnt true face–name pairings (face + person's actual name) more easily than untrue (face + another person's name) pairings, and that the same finding held for face–occupation pairings. In addition, he learnt true pairings of faces and names more easily than untrue pairings even when tested with faces of people he had only met *since* his accident (and that he had, in consequence, *never* recognised overtly). Thus his face recognition system has continued to store representations of familiar faces seen since his accident, despite the fact that explicit recognition is no longer achieved.

Work on covert recognition in prosopagnosia is all quite recent, and it may be some time before its precise implications can be evaluated correctly. It seems unlikely, however, that such effects will be established for all prosopagnosic patients. It is difficult to believe, for instance, that someone with a structural encoding deficit as severe as that experienced by Uffz. S would show "recognition without awareness". A more likely possibility is that future studies will show the phenomenon to be confined to those patients with the "material-specific memory defect" form of the disorder, and possibly only to a subset of these. This would make sense, because there are some parallels to be drawn between covert recognition and the types of memory that truly amnesic patients can show if tested on "implicit" tasks (Schacter, 1987; Schacter et al. 1988; see also Chapter 10). One possibility is that covert recognition represents the performance of a recognition system that is itself relatively intact, but can no longer interact with the rest of the cognitive system in ways that would signal what has been recognised (see Young, 1988, and Young & De Haan, 1988, for further discussion of this idea).

SPECIFICITY OF FACE RECOGNITION IMPAIRMENTS

A question that is often discussed concerns the extent to which prosopagnosic disorders are *specific* to face recognition. The issue is not yet fully resolved, largely because the condition is seldom encountered in a "pure" form. A number of prosopagnosic patients can read, so they have not lost the ability to recognise *any* visual stimulus. But there are usually additional types of visual recognition difficulty present, particularly achromatopsia (loss of colour vision) and object agnosia. These disorders do not, however, inevitably occur together. Pallis's (1955) patient, for example, showed impairment of colour vision and prosopagnosia but not object agnosia, whereas a patient described by Levine (1978) had object agnosia and prosopagnosia but not loss of colour vision. Occasionally, too, a patient is reported for whom prosopagnosia is present without severe object agnosia *or* achromatopsia. Mr W would serve as an example of this. He could recognise objects without difficulty, and only showed errors of colour naming in relatively subtle tasks (saying, for instance, that brown was "dark red" and that grey was "pale blue").

Although a number of prosopagnosic patients do not show signs of object agnosia, many object agnosic patients are also unable to recognise familiar faces. Moreover, when prosopagnosia and visual object agnosia occur together, the prosopagnosia is usually the more severe deficit in the sense that the patient can identify a smaller proportion of faces (often none at all) than objects. Thus it might be thought that there is a kind of hierarchy in which increasingly fine discriminations lead to the identification first of different categories of object (faces, cars, houses, etc.) and then of individual objects *within* each category. Object agnosia would then be seen as a breakdown in the initial between-category recognition mechanism, and prosopagnosia would be considered to involve impairment of within-category recognition.

This hierarchical conception, in which between-category recognition is followed by within-category recognition, has a certain logical appeal, and it is consistent with the observation that prosopagnosia is often found together with a less severe object agnosia. The idea that prosopagnosia involves a general breakdown of within-category recognition is also bolstered by the fact that most prosopagnosic patients also experience difficulties in identifying individual objects in other visually homogeneous categories (Blanc-Garin, 1986). Bornstein (1963), for instance, described a prosopagnosic patient who had also lost the ability to identify species of birds which had formerly been well known to her. She commented that "All the birds look the same." Similarly, Bornstein, Sroka, and Munitz (1969) reported the case of a prosopagnosic farmer who could no longer identify his own livestock. Previously he had been able to recognise his cows as individuals, but he could no longer do this. He could identify his horse because he only kept one, but felt that had there been more horses he would not have been able to recognise those either. Of the prosopagnosic patients we have considered in detail here, Uffz. S could not discriminate between animals with similar outlines, and PH was severely impaired in his ability to identify different types of flowers or cars—we will say more about Mr W later.

Notice, however, that the arguments for a recognition hierarchy rest entirely on the *association* of different deficits. As we noted in Chapter 1, such arguments are weak because there are many possible reasons why deficits might be associated, not all of which have any functional significance. The existence of cases in which deficits that are thought to be causally linked are not found together is sufficient to falsify the argument.

Such cases do seem to exist. There have been reports of patients who show object agnosia without prosopagnosia, or for whom the object agnosia seems more severe than the prosopagnosia. If prosopagnosia was caused by a breakdown of the higher levels in a recognition hierarchy, this could not happen. The high-level recognition mechanisms could not remain intact while the ability to make the allegedly lower-level between-category discriminations involved in object recognition was lost. This is an important point, so it is disappointing that the known cases have not been more thoroughly investigated with respect to their face processing abilities. The observations of preserved face recognition have arisen incidentally in descriptions of patients with visual object agnosias.

The only cases of object agnosia in which face recognition seemed to be fully preserved are those of Hécaen, Goldblum, Masure, and Ramier (1974) and Ferro and Santos (1984). Hécaen et al.'s (1974) patient was able to recognise hospital staff and all photographs of celebrities presented to him, despite his object agnosia. Ferro and Santos's (1984) patient was also able to identify all of the faces shown to him, though he could not always name them. Thus he identified the face of a former Portuguese politician called Pintassilgo (goldfinch) by saying "I know her. This is the lady that was in power. She has the name of a bird" (Ferro & Santos, 1984, p. 124). On object-naming tasks Ferro and Santos's patient could only succeed on 7 out of 30 trials. However, when presented with an object he could not name he could almost always mime its use. Thus it is unclear to us whether this is not a case of optic aphasia (see Chapter 2) rather than visual agnosia *per se*, and the appropriateness of the comparison with face recognition is brought into question as his performance at *naming* faces was also defective.

In the only other relevant published cases known to us there was some impairment of face recognition, but the object recognition problems were more severe (Albert, Reches, & Silverberg, 1975; McCarthy & Warrington, 1986). Matters are further complicated, however, by the fact that the performance of Albert et al.'s (1975) patient on object recognition tasks improved rapidly during the period in which he was being tested. There is some evidence, then, that object agnosia can be dissociated from prosopagnosia, but more detailed investigations of convincing cases of object agnosia without prosopagnosia are needed.

A second type of dissociation that weakens the straightforward "recognition hierarchy" argument is that different types of within-category discrimination can dissociate from each other. Mr W, for instance, was not impaired at making *any* within-category discrimination. Like Bornstein et al.'s (1969) patient he was a farmer, yet Mr W *could* identify his cows and dogs. He could also identify particular houses and streets that were known to him. None the less, he did still have problems with coins, and with playing cards he found it difficult to distinguish suits of the same colour and jacks from kings.

The most "pure" case of prosopagnosia reported to date is that of patient 4 in the series described by De Renzi (1986). This former public notary showed well preserved verbal abilities and could identify objects (30/30), line drawings (30/30), and overlapping figures (36/36) without error. In contrast, he had to rely on voices to recognise relatives and close friends, and his secretaries had to assist him by identifying clients for him. His performance on unfamiliar face-matching tasks (Benton Test) was poor but, as De Renzi (1986) points out, no worse than that of many other patients who are not prosopagnosic. He also performed poorly on tests of face memory.

The specificity of the defect shown by De Renzi's (1986) patient was remarkable. He could pick out his own belongings when they were mixed in with several distractor objects chosen to resemble them. He could identify his own handwriting among nine samples of the same sentence written by other people. He could pick out a Siamese cat among photographs of other cats. He could recognise his own car in a car park. He could sort domestic (Italian) coins from foreign coins. Thus, on all the tests De Renzi used, this patient could make within-category discriminations with ease for all visual stimuli except faces.

The case for the existence of face-specific recognition deficits is thus becoming quite strong. There does seem to be a functionally distinct system for at least some aspects of face processing. A sceptic might, however, want to shift the grounds of the argument by maintaining that face-specific recognition problems can arise in occasional cases simply because face recognition demands the finest of all perceptual discriminations. On this view other within-category discriminations might be preserved because they are not as fine as those demanded by face recognition.

This argument now looks to be wrong. Assal, Favre, and Anderes (1984) described the case of the farmer MX. When seen by Assal et al. in January, 1983, MX complained of problems in recognising places (rooms in his flat, his farm buildings, etc.), his livestock (cows, calves, and heifers), and human faces (friends and family). When formally tested in June and July, 1983, however, his prosopagnosia had recovered. He recognised 18 of 20 faces of famous people, and he obtained normal scores on tests of unfamiliar face matching. He could also interpret facial expressions correctly. The only test involving faces on which he performed at all poorly involved face memory, where his performance was somewhat below that of normal control subjects (26/40 vs 34/40). Assal et al. (1984) point out, however, that his performance on this test was better than that of other patients with right hemisphere injuries (mean 16.5/40) and that when the test was given to a prosopagnosic patient a score of only 8 out of 40 was attained.

It seems, then, that by July, 1983, MX was no longer prosopagnosic; he had recovered his ability to recognise faces. He could also recognise without difficulty individual members of certain other categories of visual stimuli including fruits, flowers, vegetables, and trees. He remained, however, unable to recognise familiar places or to recognise his livestock. He said that places had lost their familiarity, and he made errors in recognising 6 of 10 photographs of local houses. He could not recognise his cows from their heads, coats, or silhouettes. He could remember all their names, but was unable to recognise them. When shown photographs of the "faces" of the cows he only recognised 2 out of 15 correctly, whereas his coworkers managed 10 out of 15 and 14 out of 15 respectively. For pictures of the whole cow he got 3 out of 10 whereas his coworkers each scored 8 out of 10. He could distinguish pictures of cows from other species of animals, but could not distinguish his own cows from other cows.

MX provides another example demonstrating that different types of within-category recognition impairment can dissociate from each other. The particularly interesting thing about MX, however, is that his pattern of ability to recognise human but not cow faces is *exactly the opposite* of that shown by Mr W, who could recognise his livestock but not people.

Evidence is thus beginning to favour the view that the inability to recognise familiar faces is not inevitably linked to other problems of visual recognition. It seems that recognition difficulties involving only faces can occur.

DIFFERENT TYPES OF FACE PROCESSING ABILITY

We have seen that some prosopagnosic patients do not complain of impaired face perception, and are able both to match views of unfamiliar faces and to interpret facial expressions correctly. It might thus be thought that the matching of unfamiliar faces and the analysis of facial expressions are carried out at a level of analysis preceding that at which recognition of familiar faces can be achieved. Bruce and Young (1986), however, prefer to think of familiar face recognition as proceeding *in parallel* with the analysis of facial expressions and with the "directed visual processing" needed to match unfamiliar faces. Evidence in favour of this suggestion can be found both in studies of normal subjects and in studies of the effects of cerebral injuries. For the neuropsychological literature the key point is that there are findings that imply double dissociations between impairments involving familiar face recognition and impairments involving expression analysis or unfamiliar face matching.

Unfamiliar Face Matching

We will begin by considering unfamiliar face matching. Warrington and James (1967b) noted that patients with right cerebral hemisphere lesions tended to show impairments of familiar face recognition and of recognition of unknown faces in an immediate memory task, but that there was no correlation between these two types of deficit. Their immediate memory task involved finding the face that had just been shown in a booklet of eight male and eight female faces; this is quite different to the relatively long-term tasks on which prosopagnosic patients often show defective memory for unfamiliar faces. The absence of a correlation in Warrington and James' (1967b) findings implies that one patient might be impaired at familiar face recognition but not at immediate memory for unfamiliar faces, whereas another patient might be impaired at immediate memory but not at recognition of familiar faces.

This point is clearly seen in the descriptions of two patients given by Malone, Morris, Kay, and Levin (1982). Initially, the first patient was unable to recognise familiar faces, but had regained this ability by the time that formal neuropsychological tests were given (10–22 weeks after the onset of his symptoms), when he was able to identify 14 out of 17 photographs of famous statesmen. On tests requiring the matching of views of unfamiliar faces, however, he was still impaired. The second patient showed the opposite pattern. Although, initially, he was also unable to recognise familiar faces or to match unfamiliar faces, the ability to match unfamiliar faces recovered to a normal level whereas the familiar face recognition impairment persisted (only 5/22 famous faces identified correctly).

Malone et al.'s (1982) second case is comparable to others in which prosopagnosic patients perform at normal levels on tests of unfamiliar face matching (e.g. Benton & Van Allen, 1972; Bruyer et al., 1983). Since Malone et al.'s first case showed exactly the opposite pattern, with impaired unfamiliar face matching being accompanied by intact recognition of familiar faces, the evidence that familiar face recognition is independent from the directed visual processing required for unfamiliar face matching tasks is strong. There is a double dissociation between impairments affecting the recognition of familiar faces and impairments affecting unfamiliar face matching. The only reservation that needs to be expressed is that it is probably advisable to provide more direct evidence of normal matching of unfamiliar faces in prosopagnosic patients. What has been shown to date is that some prosopagnosics can achieve an overall level of performance comparable to that of normal subjects on unfamiliar face matching tasks. It is possible, however, that this may reflect an effective use of unusual strategies.

Newcombe (1979), for instance, found that the prosopagnosic patient she studied seldom made errors in unfamiliar face matching tasks. However, he performed these tasks by a careful and very time-consuming strategy of searching for an informative individual feature such as the hairline. When faces were presented in an oval frame that masked the hairline, Newcombe's patient experienced great difficulty in performing matching tasks. It would thus be useful to know to what extent other prosopagnosic patients rely on such strategies when matching unfamiliar faces.

Expression Analysis

Impairments affecting the analysis of facial expression have also been shown to be dissociable from impairments of face recognition. Bornstein (1963) noted that some prosopagnosic patients show a degree of recovery of ability to identify familiar faces while remaining unable to interpret facial expressions. Similarly, Kurucz and Feldmar (1979) and Kurucz, Feldmar, and Werner (1979) found that certain patients with diffuse brain damage could not interpret facial expressions correctly yet were still able to identify photographs of American Presidents. For these patients there was no correlation between their performance on recognising expression and identity from faces.

These studies indicate that disorders affecting the analysis of facial expressions are dissociable from disorders affecting familiar face recognition. Studies of patients with right hemisphere injuries have also shown that disorders affecting the analysis of facial expressions can dissociate from disorders affecting unfamiliar face matching (see Etcoff, 1985, for a review). In addition, Bowers and Heilman (1984) described a patient who could match pairs of photographs of unfamiliar faces for identity (same or different person) or expression (same or different expressions; these were portrayed by the same actor in the test used), yet showed impaired ability to identify what the facial expressions were (i.e. which emotional state they corresponded to). Thus he could not interpret facial expressions even though he could match them on a purely "visual" basis.

Because of the evidence of dissociable deficits affecting familiar face recognition, unfamiliar face matching, and analysis of facial expressions, Bruce and Young (1986) suggested that following structural encoding of a seen face's appearance different types of information are accessed in parallel. In addition to the parallel operation of face recognition units, directed visual processing, and expression analysis, they also proposed that facial speech analysis is independently achieved.

Lipreading

The importance of seen movements of the lips and tongue to the perception of speech has only been properly appreciated in recent years. Obviously, we are able to hear what someone is saying even when we are not looking at her or his face. This fact may, however, have obscured the extent to which we all "lipread". This point was shown dramatically by McGurk and MacDonald (1976), who demonstrated an illusion in which a mismatch between heard and seen (mouthed) phonemes can result in the perceiver blending the two. If, for instance, the sound "*ba*" is superimposed on a film of the face of a person saying "*ga*", people watching the resulting film find that they *hear* the sound as "*da*". This surprising use of facial speech information is found even in infancy (Kuhl & Meltzoff, 1982; MacKain, Studdert-Kennedy, Spieker, & Stern, 1983), and may form an important part of the process of language acquisition (Studdert-Kennedy, 1983).

A neuropsychological dissociation between expression analysis and facial speech analysis is described by Campbell, Landis, and Regard (1986). The dissociation was observed in two female patients. One lady, D, was prosopagnosic. She could not recognise familiar faces, she was poor at judging what sex they were, and she could not categorise facial expressions correctly. She could, in contrast, achieve a normal level of performance on unfamiliar face matching tasks if given sufficient time. Her visual recognition problems included not only familiar faces but also familiar places, and she could not recognise her own handwriting. Her reading and speech comprehension abilities were, however, unimpaired.

Although D could not determine the meaning of facial expressions she could imitate both emotional and non-emotional expressions accurately, which suggests that the problem in analysing expressions did not have a perceptual basis. She could also judge correctly what phonemes were being mouthed in photographs of the faces of speaking people, and was susceptible to the McGurk and MacDonald (1976) illusion. Thus, despite her problems with expressions, facial speech analysis remained intact.

The second lady, T, had a severe reading impairment (she read letter-by-letter), but did not show impairments on most face processing tasks. She could both recognise familiar faces and interpret correctly their expressions without difficulty. Her analysis of facial speech was, however, defective. She was impaired at judging what phonemes were being mouthed in photographs of faces, and she was *not* susceptible to the McGurk and MacDonald (1976) illusion.

This double dissociation between impairments of facial speech analysis (lipreading) and expression analysis is particularly striking because the information required for lipreading and expression comprehension is, to a considerable extent, extracted from the same area of the face. This reinforces the idea that the reason for the dissociable deficits in face processing lies in the different types of cognitive operations involved, and cannot be entirely attributed to differences in the facial features that must be analysed.

OVERVIEW

The social and biological importance of faces is such that quite extensive areas of neural tissue must be involved in one way or another with face processing tasks. It does not, however, necessarily follow that these parts of the brain should deal with faces exclusively. We could imagine, for instance, that areas of the brain involved in recognising everyday objects might also be employed for the task of recognising the faces we encounter in our daily lives.

As we have seen, the available evidence suggests that this is *not* the case. To some extent, at least, different functional components seem to be involved in face and object recognition. This is probably in response to the different *demands* of face and object recognition. Often when we recognise everyday objects we need only assign them to a general category. We look for a pen, for a tin opener, for the scissors, and so on; it is only sometimes that we need to distinguish between the pen with the blue top that will not work and the one with the chewed end and the fine nib. In addition, we frequently encounter new exemplars of these categories—someone else's scissors, a shopful of pens, etc.—but can immediately classify them into the appropriate category.

The demands of face recognition are quite different. It is of little use to us to look at a photograph in the newspaper and only recognise that it shows a person's face. We want to know *whose* face it is, and we accept that differences between different people can sometimes be slight. For faces, then, we discriminate between the members of a class of rather homogeneous visual stimuli (all with eyes, nose, mouth, and more or less oval shape) and assign individual identities to those we know.

One reason why face recognition and object recognition can show dissociable impairments, then, is probably that different types of perceptual mechanism are needed to cope with recognition tasks that demand between-category or within-category discriminations. It is now becoming clear, however, that there are also dissociations between impairments of different within-category recognition mechanisms, such as those involved in recognising familiar faces and those used to recognise familiar places. The types of information needed to effect the discriminations involved would also seem to be an important factor.

We also need to be able to extract different kinds of information from faces. We can recognise the people we know, examine the appearance of unfamiliar faces, identify facial expressions, and read speech information from mouth and tongue movements. Impairments of these different aspects of face processing can dissociate from each other, suggesting that different functional components are involved; these seem to be arranged so that the different types of information are independently derived.

Disorders of face processing, then, offer a promising area for further investigation by cognitive neuropsychologists, and the findings of neuropsychological studies relate well to those obtained in studies of normal subjects (Bruce & Young, 1986; H. D. Ellis, 1986a; 1986b). A particularly interesting recent finding, however, has been that certain "automatic" aspects of recognition may be preserved in prosopagnosic patients. If tested on tasks that do not require explicit identification, patients such as PH seem to be able to recognise faces, yet they are not aware that any degree of recognition has taken place. Such cases form an intriguing parallel to some of the disorders discussed in Chapter 3, which we noted could also be seen as involving loss of different aspects of awareness. Explaining how this can happen offers an interesting challenge.

SUMMARY

A number of different causes of inability to recognise familiar faces (prosopagnosia) exist. For some patients (Uffz. S) face perception is clearly impaired, and there are probably several types of perceptual disorder. For other patients (Mr W), however, any perceptual impairment is minor, and cannot be seen to play a causative role. This has led to the suggestion that some cases of prosopagnosia should be considered to involve a material-specific memory impairment; this idea can be considered analogous to that of defective operation of face recognition units. Conversely, these are also cases in which inability to recognise faces arises in the context of a more general impairment of semantic memory, and these patients do not overtly recognise familiar people from their names or voices either.

For some prosopagnosic patients, however, a high degree of recognition of familiar faces can be shown to take place if it is measured on tasks that do not demand awareness of recognition. PH, for instance, showed covert recognition of familiar faces in matching, learning, and interference tasks. It would seem that certain automatic aspects of the operation of recognition mechanisms may be preserved without the patient being aware of this.

Face recognition impairments can dissociate from impairments affecting the recognition of other classes of visual stimuli and, in very rare cases, remarkably specific deficits have been found. Specific impairments of different aspects of face processing have also been revealed. Thus there are dissociations between problems affecting recognition of familiar faces, matching of unfamiliar faces, expression analysis, and lipreading. The existence of dissociable impairments suggests that these types of information are extracted from seen faces by functionally independent mechanisms.

FURTHER READING

Adolphs, R., Tranel, D., Damasio, H., & Damasio, A.R. (1995). Fear and the human amygdala. *Journal of Neuroscience, 15,* 5879–5891. Detailed study of a very specific deficit in the recognition of facial expressions.

Campbell, R., Heywood, C.A., Cowey, A., Regard, M., & Landis, T. (1990). Sensitivity to eye gaze in prosopagnosic patients and monkeys with superior temporal sulcus ablation. *Neuropsychologia, 28*, 1123–1142. Interesting work on sensitivity to gaze direction that integrates neuropsychological and neurophysiological studies.

De Renzi, E., Faglioni, P., Grossi, D., & Nichelli, P. (1991). Apperceptive and associative forms of prosopagnosia. *Cortex, 27*, 213–221. Investigates the idea of different types of prosopagnosia from the clinical viewpoint.

Ellis, H.D., & Young, A.W. (1990). Accounting for delusional misidentifications. *British Journal of Psychiatry, 157*, 239–248. Theoretical paper showing how the cognitive neuropsychological approach can be extended to delusional misidentification.

Evans, J.J., Heggs, A.J., Antoun, N., & Hodges, J.R. (1995). Progressive prosopagnosia associated with selective right temporal lobe atrophy: a new syndrome? *Brain, 118*, 1–13. Investigation of a person with a neurodegenerative disease, initially showing problems in recognising faces, then problems in recognition from face or name.

Milders, M.V. & Perrett, D.I. (1993). Recent developments in the neuropsychology and physiology of face processing. In C. Kennard (Ed.), *Baillière's clinical neurology: international practice and research. Vol. 2, No. 2: Visual perceptual defects* (pp. 361–388). London: Baillière Tindall. As the title says. A useful update.

Young, A.W. (1994). Face recognition. In G. d'Ydewalle, P. Eelen, & P. Bertelson (Eds), *International perspectives on psychological science. Vol. 2, The state of the art* (pp. 1–27). Hove, UK: Lawrence Erlbaum Associates Ltd. Gives more detail concerning the interplay of studies of neuropsychological impairments and studies of the unimpaired recognition system.

Young, A.W. (1994). Covert recognition. In M.J. Farah & G. Ratcliff (Eds.), *The neuropsychology of high-level vision: collected tutorial essays* (pp. 331–358). Hillsdale, N.J.: Lawrence Erlbaum Associates Inc. Review of studies of recognition without awareness in prosopagnosia.

5

Producing Spoken Words

INTRODUCTION

In the book so far we have focussed on processes of perception and their associated disorders. The human brain can, however, do more than just perceive the world; it can also talk about it, and understand others talking about it. Our capacities for speaking and understanding speech are the subject matter of this chapter, and also Chapters 6 and 9. Let us begin by sketching very briefly some of the cognitive processes we are likely to need in order to be able to talk sensibly about the world around us.

Imagine that the picture shown in Fig. 5.1 has been placed in front of you and that you have been asked to describe the goings on in it. There is a lot happening in the picture so you let your eyes roam over it to take it all in. "Taking it in" here includes doing precisely those operations we have discussed in Chapters 2 to 4—identifying the objects depicted, working out their spatial relationships one to another, and so on. You must also comprehend the actions being performed; the fact that the bull is *chasing* the boy scout, that another scout is *looking* through binoculars while another is *sitting* on the bank. As you inspect the picture you build up an understanding of it. That understanding is not initially couched in words, though it can be *translated* into words; instead you have some form of conceptual representation which is presumably similar to that built up by intelligent non-verbal animals like chimpanzees. What language allows us to do is to communicate the conceptual representation in our heads to others.

In attempting to describe the picture you may decide to start with the

FIG. 5.1.   A complex picture used to elicit speech from aphasic patients. (The attempt of patient RD to describe the picture is given on p.124.)

activity at the top centre. Here there is a scout and a bull, and one is chasing the other. Recognising a bull or a scout serves to activate within you all the stored knowledge you possess about those objects—their *meanings* in a sense. Linguists use the term *semantics* when discussing issues relating to the meanings of words, so we shall refer to the internal representations of the meanings (e.g. properties and uses) of words and things as their *semantic representations*. Semantic representations do not include the spoken names of concepts—those must be retrieved separately. For instance, you may readily recognise the three-legged object in the centre of the scout camp picture, and you may know that its function is to suspend cooking implements over a fire, but if more years have elapsed than you care to admit since you last went camping, then it may take you quite some considerable time to retrieve the name of the object in question (a "trivet"). When you eventually do manage to retrieve that name it is presumably from some form of memory store whose purpose and function is to make available to you the spoken forms of words appropriate to the meanings you wish to express. We shall call this memory store for the pronunciations of words the *speech output lexicon*. Other authors have referred to that store as the "speech output logogen system" (Morton, 1980a; Morton & Patterson, 1980), the "phonological lexicon" (Allport & Funnell, 1981), or the "phonemic word production system" (Ellis, 1984b). Whatever name we give it, the memory store in question normally works efficiently and yields up its contents with ease: Only when a word eludes you or becomes caught on the tip of your tongue do you become aware of the speech output lexicon's role in efficient speech production.

When the spoken forms of words are retrieved from the speech output lexicon it is presumably as strings of speech sounds which can then be articulated. The distinctive sounds that a language uses (English has 46 or so) are called its *phonemes*. Phonemes in English should not be confused with letters: Phonemes are units of the spoken language whereas letters are units of the written language, and there is not a one-to-one correspondence between them. Thus, whereas *lip* has three letters and three phonemes, *teeth* has five letters but still only three phonemes (*t, ee*, and *th*). *Bull* has four letters for three phonemes (*b, u*, and *ll*), whereas *scout* has five letters for four phonemes (*s, c, ou*, and *t*).

We can envisage the speech output lexicon as translating between conceptual, semantic representations of words and their phonemic labels or names. In some theories (e.g. Morton, 1980a), when the entry or "node" for a particular word in the lexicon is activated by its meaning, the lexicon releases a phonological (sound-based) "code" which is held in a short-term memory store before being articulated. In other theories (e.g. Stemberger, 1985), when a node in the lexicon is activated it does not release any form of code, but rather transmits *activation* down to nodes at a lower, phoneme level, activating the nodes for those phonemes which make up the word to be spoken. We shall indicate later why we prefer the latter account to the former, but for now we would emphasize their common features, in particular their assumption that the semantic system, the speech output lexicon, and the phoneme level constitute

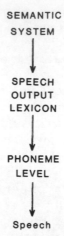

FIG. 5.2.   Simple functional model for word retrieval in speech production (naming).

distinct and separable cognitive components or "modules" which should, therefore, be subject to different types of impairment giving rise to different patterns of symptoms. This common assumption can be represented in simple diagrammatic form as in Fig. 5.2.

There is, of course, more to language than attaching names to concepts; words must be arranged properly into grammatical sentences or they remain just word lists. Some aphasic patients have particular difficulties with the structuring of spoken sentences, and we shall examine these difficulties in Chapter 9. The remainder of this chapter will be devoted to aphasic language disorders that afflict the translation between concepts and sounds (i.e. that afflict word meanings, word retrieval, and articulation). We shall begin by looking at some aphasic "word-finding" disorders which have been studied in some detail, namely the *anomias* and *neologistic jargonaphasia*. We shall then go on to examine how closely the problems and errors of these and other aphasics resemble the occasional word-finding problems experienced by normal people. In Chapter 6 we shall examine the perception and comprehension of spoken words, and will consider the extent to which the production and comprehension of spoken words are mediated by common or distinct cognitive processes.

ANOMIAS

The simple model in Fig. 5.2 assumes that the semantic system, the speech output lexicon, and the phoneme level are distinct cognitive components capable of separate, independent impairment. If this is so, then problems in retrieving and articulating words could arise at any of these three levels, though the precise nature of the patient's difficulties and the accompanying symptoms should help in identifying the locus of the impairment. Note, however, that it may be an unusual patient in whom one level is impaired, whereas the others continue to function completely normally. Brain injuries are often extensive and are no respectors of cognitive theories, so most patients with naming problems are likely to exhibit mixed symptoms arising from impairment to two or more components. That said, there are now sufficient detailed case reports in the literature that we can pick out the exceptional patients with fairly pure deficits. We shall begin with patients whose word-finding problems in speaking can plausibly be attributed to impairment in or around the semantic system.

Anomia Arising at the Semantic Level

The clearest evidence for semantic involvement in naming difficulties comes from reports of patients who can name objects in some semantic categories but not others. In fact we have already mentioned some of these cases in our discussion of object recognition (see pp. 42–47). Warrington and Shallice's (1984) patient, JBR, was considerably better at naming pictures of inanimate objects like a torch or a briefcase than pictures of living things like a parrot or a daffodil. This impairment was not, however, limited to naming because he had problems comprehending both pictures of the living things he could not name and comprehending their spoken names. Three other patients tested in less detail by Warrington and Shallice (1984) showed the same pattern. Warrington and Shallice suggest that JBR and the other patients suffered from a degradation of the semantic representations of certain categories of things (notably living objects), hence those representations were unavailable to sustain either full comprehension of those objects or the comprehension and production of their names.

The naming difficulties of patient MD (Hart, Berndt, & Caramazza, 1985) were focussed on the semantic categories of fruit and vegetables. Thus he could name an abacus and the Sphinx but not a peach or an orange. When asked to sort pictures into semantic categories he had no problems with animals or vehicles, made two errors to food products (classifying butter and cheese as vegetables), and made more errors to fruits and vegetables (classifying 3/24 fruits as vegetables and 6/23 vegetables as fruits). However, unlike Warrington and Shallice's (1984) patients, MD could comprehend the names he was not able to produce. When MD was required to point to one of two pictures drawn from the same semantic category in response to a heard word he made no mistakes on either fruit or vegetables. He could also categorise correctly the written names of fruits and vegetables whose pictures he had been unable to classify.

MD's good performance with heard and read words suggests that the actual semantic representations of fruit and vegetables are not themselves degraded; rather he has problems accessing those representations from objects or pictures and problems using them to initiate spoken naming (he was poor at generating exemplars of fruit and vegetables, so the deficit is not restricted to confrontation naming).

A Non-category-specific Semantic Anomia: Patient JCU

The patients just discussed had naming impairments of semantic origin that were more severe in some semantic domains than others. There are other patients, however, whose naming difficulties also appear to arise in or around the semantic representations, but in whom the deficit does not seem to be any more severe for one category than for another.

Howard and Orchard-Lisle's (1984) patient, JCU, could name very few object pictures unaided, but retrieved many more if given the initial phoneme of the word as a cue. She could also, however, be induced to make semantic naming errors if the initial phoneme of a close associate of the picture was supplied instead (e.g. shown a picture of a tiger and given the cue "l", JCU said "lion"). She rejected spontaneously only 24% of these semantic errors though she rejected 86% of unrelated responses (these were often perseverations of a name produced earlier). In addition, if an experimenter asked of a picture, "Is this an X?", she accepted 56% of close semantic associates but only 2% of unrelated names.

The results of two further tests led Howard and Orchard-Lisle to conclude that JCU's object recognition and comprehension were not defective. In the first test she was required to match one picture to a choice of two others on the basis of real-world associations (e.g. matching a picture of a pyramid to one of a palm tree rather than a deciduous tree). Here JCU scored 18 out of 20 correct. The second test required pictures to be matched on the basis of a shared semantic category (e.g. matching an onion to a pea—both vegetables—rather than to an apple), and JCU scored 16 out of 20 on this test. This was significantly worse than a normal control group, but sufficiently good when combined with her performance on the real-world associations task for Howard and Orchard-Lisle to reject impairment of processes of conceptual recognition as the source of JCU's naming deficit. They argued instead for a semantic impairment; more precisely, they proposed that semantic information available to the patient was insufficient to specify the exact target name, with the result that the phonological forms of close semantic associates were also being activated to the same level in a phonological lexicon. Thus, the semantic information that JCU can use is sufficient to enable her to reject entirely unrelated names profferred by the experimenter, but is often insufficient to allow her to distinguish a semantic associate from the correct name. Thus JCU might experience naming problems because of a general, non-specific impairment to the semantic representations.

Anomia without Semantic Impairment: Patient EST

Kay and Ellis (1987) report the case of a patient, EST, who experienced word-finding problems for words whose meanings were available to him in full detail. He knew precisely what he wanted to say but could not remember many of the words he needed in order to express his thoughts and intentions. His attempt to describe a kitchen scene from a test by Goodglass and Kaplan (1972) ran as follows:

> Er. . . two children, one girl one male . . . the . . . the girl, they're in a. . . and their, their mother was behind them in in, they're in the kitchen. . . the boy is trying to get. . . a. . . er, a part of a cooking. . . jar. . . He's standing on. . . the lad, the boy is standing on a. . . standing on a. . . standing on a. . . I'm calling it a seat, I can't. . . I forget what it's, what the name of it is. . . . It is cr a higher, it's a seat, standing on that, 'e's standing on that. . . this boy is standing on this, seat. . . getting some of this er stuff to. . . biscuit to eat. As he is doing that, the post, it's not a post, it's the, seat, is falling down, is falling over. . .

EST's speech output is fluent and reasonably grammatical but short on specific object (and action) names. Words he cannot access are usually replaced in spontaneous speech by other, more general words, or by circumlocutions which avoid the difficult word. He has considerable difficulty naming pictures of objects though both his understanding of the objects themselves and his understanding of their spoken names was very good. In picture-naming tasks he would often be at pains to show that he recognised pictures he could not name (e.g. of a snowman he said: "It's cold, it's a man. . . cold. . . frozen"). He was very good at sorting pictures into semantic categories, even when this could not be done on obvious visual cues (e.g. wild animals *vs.* domesticated animals). He also performed at normal levels on Howard and Orchard-Lisle's (1984) task which required pictures to be matched on the basis of real-world associations rather than category membership (e.g. matching a picture of a pyramid to a palm tree rather than to a deciduous tree, because pyramids and palm trees both belong in Egypt).

EST's auditory-vocal repetition of words he had previously been unable to access in a naming task was good, though not perfect (43/50), and better than his repetition of invented non-words (25/50). On a task requiring him to select the picture that matched a heard word from a set of four semantically related items he performed flawlessly (25/25) and he also performed at normal levels (50/52) on a version of the "palm trees and pyramids" task where he was required to choose which of two pictures had the closest real-world association to a heard word. Unlike patient JCU discussed earlier, EST would not accept close associates of an object name when profferred by an experimenter (e.g. he would not accept "lion" as the name to match a picture of a tiger).

EST's semantic representations of the object names he had difficulty accessing in spontaneous speech thus seem to have been intact and he was capable of sustaining good comprehension of spoken (and written) words. We cannot, therefore, locate the source of his anomia within the semantic system. A close analysis of his successes and failures in object naming provided clues as to where the impairment might lie.

In six 1-hour sessions spread over as many weeks EST was asked to name a set of 260 line drawings of objects taken from Snodgrass and Vanderwart (1980). He named 97 pictures correctly without hesitation and a further 27 after a delay or after "working up" to the word (e.g. "five in it, begins with a 't', table"). There were a further 22 pictures which EST could not name correctly but for which he produced without cueing what Kay and Ellis (1987) call a "phonological approximation" to the word. Examples of such approximations include "sumberry" for strawberry, "balla" and "ballow" for balloon, and "gritch" and "grief" for grapes.

If EST failed to provide either the correct name or an approximation to the name of a picture he was cued with the initial phoneme of the name. This allowed him to name a further 27 pictures correctly and produce phonological approximations to 37 more. The remaining 50 pictures he remained unable either to name or approximate, though his comments usually made it clear that he recognised the object for what it was.

Of course some words, including some object names, are used more frequently than others. Word-frequency counts (e.g. Francis & Kucera, 1982) provide a rough measure of the relative frequencies of usage of words in the language (rough because they are usually based on written rather than spoken English). A clear pattern emerged when the name frequencies were compared for the pictures eliciting different types of response from EST. Specifically, those pictures he could name immediately had the most frequently used names of all. Next most frequent were the names he produced after a delay, followed by the names for which he could generate, uncued, a phonological approximation. The names he needed to be cued on were least frequent of all. Thus, the probability that EST could name an object seems to be related to the number of times he is likely to have used that name in the course of his past life.

In fact, a glance at EST's spontaneous speech shows that virtually all the words he uses in normal conversation are of high frequency. This includes the nouns, verbs and adjectives he still has available and also the function words like "the", "on", "not", and "to" that he uses with ease. Marshall (1987) noted that one can create a fair replica of anomic speech using just the 100 most common words in the English language, thus:

> I have one or more of them. It's a... I like them. It must be over there in the... by the... but it's not. My... also made one for some... that he had been with in the... as a... it was before he had his... most of them are like that. They can also be had from the... a man has them, many of them, but a new one would be even more of a.... Did you have one when you were with them? You said that you had one from the time that you were at.... No, if that were so, you could not have made so much... at it all these years. Even then it's not the first new one that I must have been through.

It may be that for *some* anomic aphasics (like EST) what determines their success or failure in accessing a word is not its meaning, nor its grammatical class, but its sheer frequency of usage. EST's good comprehension of words he could not use in speech, the frequency effect he showed, and the presence of phonological approximations led Kay and Ellis (1987) to propose that the source of his anomia lay in a deficit in activating entries for words within the speech output lexicon.

More particularly, Kay and Ellis (1987) supported models like that of Stemberger (1985) in which the role of the speech output lexicon is to channel activation down from the semantic system to the phoneme level, permitting the set of phonemes that comprise a word's spoken form to be activated when that word's semantic representation is activated. It is a common assumption of such models that entries in the lexicon which are frequently activated develop higher *resting* levels of activation. This means that they achieve full activation more quickly and more easily from a given semantic input than do nodes which are less frequently activated. Such a proposal helps to explain why even normal subjects find high-frequency words easier to access than low-frequency words. Thus pictures with commonly used names are named more rapidly than pictures with infrequently used names (Oldfield & Wingfield, 1965) though the two types of picture differ little in terms of speed of recognising them for what they are (Wingfield, 1968). Similarly, slips of the tongue in which normal speakers inadvertently use a wrong word in place of the intended one usually involve the replacement of a less frequent word by a more frequent one (Beattie & Butterworth, 1979).

The frequency bias in EST's speech could be explained by some form of impairment to the lexicon itself, but Kay and Ellis (1987) argue against this on two grounds. First, EST sometimes retrieved a word after extensive effort, and, secondly, he sometimes retrieved a word on one occasion that he had been unable to find on another, earlier occasion. Neither of these observations is new (cf. the patient of Franz, 1930, who when shown a picture of a box of strawberries said: "I like them; I ought to be able to say it. My wife bought some boxes yesterday, and she was making them up into jam. I know, but it has just escaped me... [then after a long pause]... strawberries"), but both suggest that EST's problem is not that certain words have been lost from the speech output lexicon, but that they have become inaccessible. An explanation in terms of inaccessibility would also account for observations of patients who recover from anomia with a speed which suggests re-accessing rather than re-learning their vocabulary (e.g. case 4 of Benson, 1979).

One way to explain how the speech output lexicon might remain intact though many of its entries have become more or less inaccessible is to propose, as Kay and Ellis (1987) did, that following the brain injury, the *amount* of activation reaching the (intact) speech output lexicon from the (intact) semantic system is much reduced (cf. Rochford & Williams, 1965). This reduced activation is still enough to boost up to full activation entries whose resting levels are already high (i.e. entries for frequently-used words), but entries for infrequently-used words whose resting levels are low can no longer be boosted sufficiently to allow all their phonemes to be activated and articulated.

EST could name correctly most pictures with high-frequency names and could make no reasonable attempt at words with low-frequency names. There was a middle range of names, however, for which he could often generate a close approximation. These approximations were sometimes real words, sometimes not (it is not easy to determine whether some approximations like "sludge" for sledge merely happened by chance to be real words in English). In the case of these medium-frequency words, sufficient activation seems to be reaching the phoneme level to activate some, but not all, of the phonemes in the target word. The missing phonemes apparently have to be guessed when an attempt must be made at the word. (N.B. EST made few approximation errors in spontaneous speech: He seemed to know when a word was proving elusive and would typically opt for either an alternative of higher frequency or a circumlocution. Approximations were only common in confrontation naming tasks where the specific names of objects were demanded.)

The notion that EST's speech output lexicon is intact though much of its contents are inaccessible was supported by Kay and Ellis (1987). They showed that EST's auditory-vocal repetition is better for words he can no longer access in his spontaneous speech or naming than for invented non-words created by changing one or two of the consonants of the real words. Thus there was some form of support available from the lexicon to assist the repetition of normally inaccessible words and to boost their repetition accuracy above that of matched non-words. That support would not have been possible had the entries for inaccessible words in the lexicon actually been destroyed.

Semantic versus Output Lexicon Anomias

In sum, then, word-finding difficulties can apparently arise either at the semantic level or at the level of the speech output lexicon. The two forms of anomia seem, however, to have rather different patterns when observed in their pure forms (note that many patients are likely to display a combination of the two sets of symptoms because their brain injury affects both levels).

Patients with semantic level impairments may show a degree of category specificity, having greater naming problems in some semantic domains than others. They make semantic errors in naming and are subsequently poor at detecting those errors as incorrect in comprehension tasks. In general, they perform poorly on comprehension tasks which require precise semantic knowledge. A number of investigators have noted a correlation between the number of semantic errors a patient makes in production and the degree of impairment in comprehension (Butterworth, Howard, & McLoughlin, 1984; Gainotti, 1976; Gainotti, Miceli, Caltagirone, Silveri, & Masullo, 1981). This association has been interpreted as implying that there is just one semantic system employed in both comprehension and production, so that damage to it will be reflected in comparable degrees of impairment to input and output. Such a proposal would help to explain why patients who make semantic errors in speech also make semantic errors in other tasks which do not require spoken responses (Alajouanine, Lhermitte, Ledoux, Renaud, & Vignolo, 1964; Zurif, Caramazza, Myerson, & Galvin, 1974).

On our account, patients with impairment to the output lexicon itself will not show category specificity and will not make semantic naming errors. Their comprehension of the words they find hard to access for speech will be unimpaired. The probability of their being able to produce a word correctly will be strongly affected by its frequency of use, and they will make approximation errors (or "neologisms") to some words they cannot fully access.

NEOLOGISTIC JARGONAPHASIA

The spontaneous speech of anomic aphasics typically contains few phonological approximations, though they may appear in object-naming tasks. There are other aphasics whose spontaneous speech contains large numbers of these errors. They are sometimes regarded as a type of "Wernicke's aphasia", and sometimes treated as a separate group of aphasics termed "neologistic jargonaphasics" (Buckingham & Kertesz, 1976; Butterworth, 1979; 1985; Butterworth, Swallow, & Grimston, 1981; Caramazza, Berndt, & Basili, 1983; Ellis, Miller, & Sin, 1983; Miller & Ellis, 1987). As before, we shall not be concerned with issues of labelling so much as with explaining and interpreting the symptoms of these patients.

The following transcript is part of the attempt by RD, the patient reported by Ellis et al. (1983), to describe the goings on in the scout camp picture (Fig. 5.1). Neologisms are printed in italics, and the target words which RD is presumed to have been attempting are in capital letters within brackets. (A fuller version with the neologisms transcribed in phonemic notation can be found in Ellis et al., 1983):

> A *bun, bun* (BULL)... a *buk* (BULL) is *cherching* (CHASING) a boy or *skert* (SCOUT). A *sk*... boy *skut* (SCOUT) is by a *bone poe* (POST) of pine. A... post... *pone* (POST) with a, er, *tone toe* (LINE?) with *woshingt* (WASHING) hanging on including his socks *saiz* (?). A... a *nek* (TENT) is by the washing. A b-boy is *swi'ing* (SWINGING) on the bank with his hand (FEET) in the *stringt* (STREAM). A table with *orstrum* (SAUCEPAN?) and... I don't know... and a three-legged *stroe* (STOOL) and a *strane* (PAIL)— table, table... near the water. A er *trowlvot* (TRIVET), three-legged er er means for hanging a *tong, tong* (PAN?) on the *fiyest* (FIRE) which is blowed by a boy-boy. A boy *skrut* (SCOUT) is up a tree and looking at... through... *hone*(?) glasses. A man is knocking a paper... paper with a *notist* (NOTICE) by the er t-tent, tent er *tet* (TENT) er tent.

What impairment to the speech production processes could cause such neologisms to occur? We would appear to be able to rule out a conceptual or semantic disorder from the available evidence. RD, whose speech we have just seen an extract of, had very good understanding of written words and pictures. He could sort written words into categories despite being able to read very few of them aloud correctly, and could match pictures to written names. He could also sort pairs of written words into those having similar meanings (e.g. *corner–angle; exhaustion–fatigue*) or dissimilar meanings (e.g. *hurricane–troops; oven–ghost*), and could sort written sentences into those which made sense (e.g. *He sat reading a paper*) and those which, though grammatical, were nonsensical (e.g. *She played her favourite window*). Similarly, JS, the patient reported by Caramazza et al. (1983), could categorise written words and pictures, and could match pictures to words correctly.

We would also seem able to eliminate an articulatory deficit as a cause of JS's and RD's errors. It does not appear to be the case that these patients can retrieve the spoken forms of words correctly which then become distorted during articulation (Buckingham, 1977). Both RD and JS were less likely to produce a neologism as an attempt at a common word than as an attempt at a less common (but still familiar) word, even though the less common word may have been shorter and simpler to articulate than the more common one. Thus in a picture-naming task RD correctly named a "policeman" and a "cigarette" while making errors on the simpler but less common words "frog" and "swan". Word length had little or no effect on whether or not he could say a word correctly, and there was no detectable tendency for incorrect phonemes to resemble the phonemes they replaced (Miller & Ellis, 1987).

It is interesting to look at the grammatical class of the target words which RD mispronounced (which can usually be deduced from their verbal contexts). In the full description of the scout picture from which we have given an extract, Ellis et al. (1983) reckoned that RD made a total of 28 errors. Of these, 24 occupied positions where a noun appears to have been the target (e.g. *trowlvot* for TRIVET), whereas the remaining 4 occupied verb slots (e.g. *cherching* for CHASING). This pattern has been reported by several previous investigators including Green (1969), Buckingham and Kertesz (1976), and Butterworth (1979), and has led a number of theorists to suggest that in patients of this type we are looking at a deficit which has selectively impaired the use of information-transmitting "content words" (nouns, verbs, and adjectives) and spared the use of grammatical "function words" like *a, with, of, and, by*, and *is* (e.g. Garrett, 1982; 1984; Marin, Saffran, & Schwartz, 1976). However, we have already noted that RD and JS were both less prone to make errors on common compared to less common words, and it is a fact of language that function words occur, on average, far more frequently in speech than do content words. When Ellis et al. asked RD to read aloud written content and function words which were equated on frequency of occurrence he was no more successful on the function words (14/20 and 16/24 correct) than on the content words (16/20 and 17/24 correct), suggesting that the apparent preservation of function words in his speech is due to their higher average frequency of usage.

Buckingham and Kertesz (1976) proposed that a word-finding problem similar to that of anomics with output lexicon deficits lies at the heart of "neologistic jargonaphasia". Butterworth (1979) provided support for this proposal by showing that the errors made by his patient KC followed longer pauses than correctly spoken words. The long pauses were construed as indicating an unsuccessful search of the speech output lexicon. The deficit would seem, then, to be at the level of the speech output lexicon. Like the anomics with output lexicon impairments, patients like KC and RD are still able to retrieve the spoken phonological forms of words they have used many times in their lifetimes, including most of the function words. Sometimes only partial information can be retrieved, in which case a phonological approximation error—what Butterworth (1979) calls a "target-related neologism"—is made (such as "balons" for *balloon*, or "peharst" for *perhaps*). Sometimes little or nothing can be retrieved in which case the error may be wildly deviant (e.g. "senstenz" for *penguin*, or "orstrum" for *saucepan*). Individual patients appear to differ in the proportion of target-related neologisms they produce. Some jargonaphasics produce only masses of utterly unintelligible speech, like some foreign tongue: These may be patients who can retrieve no usable phonological information at all from their speech output lexicons (e.g. Perecman and Brown, 1981).

Anomia and Neologistic Jargonaphasia Compared

The account we have just given of RD and other similar patients is effectively the same as the account we gave in the previous section for EST and other anomics with speech output lexicon impairments. Both types of patient can show preserved semantic knowledge with a frequency-related word-finding problem in speech. The chief difference between the two is that the spontaneous speech of neologistic jargonaphasics like RD is littered with approximations to target words whereas anomics like EST only produce high levels of approximation errors in confrontation naming tasks. Part of the explanation of this difference may lie in the speech comprehension of the two types of patient. Understanding of spoken words was effectively nil in RD (a neologistic jargonaphasic), whose comprehension had to be assessed using written words. Caramazza, Berndt, and Basili (1983) analysed in detail the speech perception problems of their patient JS, who was very similar to RD, and attributed his loss of speech comprehension to an inability to make the fine discriminations between speech sounds that speech comprehension demands (see the section on "pure word deafness" in Chapter 6).

Anomics like EST, in contrast, show intact speech perception and comprehension. This may mean that they can monitor the accuracy of their attempts to say words in a way that neologistic jargonaphasics cannot. Thus, RD seemed not to know whether or not he had spoken a word correctly and would sometimes include the correct pronunciation of a word in the course of a sequence of attempts without appearing to know when he got the pronunciation right. Repeated attempts at words showed no tendency to be any better approximations to the target (Miller & Ellis, 1987; see also Joanette, Keller, & Lecours, 1980).

Impaired speech perception can occur in the context of intact speech production in patients with word deafness (e.g. Goldstein, 1974; Saffran, Marin, & Yeni-Komshian, 1976a), so that impairment in neologistic jargonaphasics cannot be held fully responsible for their speech production disorder. We are, however, willing to contemplate the possibility that neologistic jargonaphasia arises through anomia of the output lexicon variety *combined with* a degree of word deafness. Thus, unlike anomic patients, neologistic jargonaphasics can never learn by monitoring their own speech which words cause difficulties and which do not, hence they can never learn that words which are proving hard to access are likely to be mispronounced. Consequently, neologistic jargonaphasics cannot learn to limit their vocabulary to those words they can reliably say correctly. This interpretation has been queried by Butterworth (1985) and Butterworth and Howard (1987). It would be proved wrong if a patient was reported whose speech was like RD's but whose comprehension of the spoken word was intact, especially if the patient was shown to be able to distinguish reliably between correct pronunciations of words and distortions of the sort he or she commonly produced.

Morphology in Neologistic Jargonaphasia

There is one final point to make about neologistic jargonaphasia. Plural words like *ropes, robes*, and *roses* can be split up into their "root morphemes" (*rope, robe*, and *rose*) and the plural morpheme -*s*. Now, if you listen carefully to the pronunciation of *ropes, robes*, and *roses* you will hear that the plural morpheme -*s* is pronounced differently in the three words—"s" in *ropes*, "z" in *robes*, and "iz" in *roses*. The pronunciation given to the plural depends on the phoneme preceding it. A similar thing happens with the past-tense morpheme -*ed*. Listen to the pronunciations of *talked, declared*, and *spouted* and you will hear the -*ed* pronounced "t" in *talked*, "d" in *declared*, and "id" in *spouted*. As with the plural -*s*, the pronunciation given to the past-tense morpheme depends on the phoneme preceding it. Morphemes like -*s* and -*ed* which never occur on their own but only attached to root morphemes like *rope* or *talk* are called bound morphemes or *inflections*. Other common English inflections are -*er* (as in *taller, fatter*), -*est* (as in *shortest, thinnest*), and -*ing* (as in *growing, expanding*).

The relevance of all this to neologistic jargonaphasia can be seen if we ask what happens when a neologistic jargonaphasic tries to say an inflected word. The answer appears to be that whereas the root morpheme may be distorted, the inflection never is. Thus in the scout passage presented earlier, RD says "cherching" for *chasing* with the root *chase* neologised but the *-ing* morpheme present and correct (cf. also "swi'ing" for *swinging*). Many similar examples can be found in the transcripts provided by Buckingham and Kertesz (1976) and Butterworth (1979). The next question is, when the root morpheme of a plural or past-tense target word is jargonised, what form does the inflection take—is it the form appropriate to the correct root morpheme or to the neologised version? For instance, if *declare* were distorted to "dislap", would the past tense come out "dislapd" with the "d" appropriate to "declared", or would it emerge as "dislapt" with the version of the past-tense morpheme appropriate to the preceding "p"? Several studies agree that the pronunciation of variable inflections like *-s* or *-ed* is adapted (or "accommodated") to fit the *neologised* form of the root (see Buckingham & Kertesz, 1976; Butterworth, 1979; Caplan, Kellar, & Locke, 1972; Garrett, 1982). Thus "declared" with a "d" would be neologised to "dislapt" with a "t", as "robes" with a "z" might be neologised to "rofes" with an "s".

Earlier, we interpreted neologisms as indicating problems in retrieving the phonemic forms of words from the speech output lexicon. The analysis of the fate of inflected forms would appear to permit an additional claim to be made, namely that what are retrieved from the speech output lexicon are uninflected root morphemes. Inflections are then added and accommodated appropriately. *Declares, declared*, and *declaring* do not have separate entries in the speech output lexicon but are assembled in the act of speaking from the root (declare) by the addition of the appropriate inflection. In the neologistic jargonaphasic patient, retrieval from the speech output lexicon is impaired but the processes which supply the inflections remain intact so that what emerges are neologisms with the root incorrect but the inflection correctly affixed and appropriately adapted.

This conclusion about how the *normal* system must be organised is congenial because it agrees with observations on slips of the tongue. One type of speech error normal people occasionally make involves the reversal of two root morphemes, as happened in the case of the speaker who intended to say "She slants her writing" but instead said "She writes her slanting". Here the roots *write* and *slant* have been reversed, but the inflections *-s* and *-ing* have remained true to their intended positions. Now, in speech, both *slant* and *write* end with a "t" so that the appropriate form of the *-s* (which here is a verb marker not a plural) is "s". Morpheme reversals have, however, been reported which both required and got adaptation of the inflection (see Garrett, 1975; 1980). Examples we have heard include normal speakers saying "the forks ('s') of a prong" for "the prongs ('z') of a fork", and "a catful of houses ('iz')" for "a houseful of cats ('s')".

These morpheme exchange errors confirm that root morphemes and inflections are represented separately at some point or points in the speech planning process. The fact that the inflections adapt to the reversed roots implies that the precise forms of inflections are chosen after the stage in planning at which the root morphemes reverse, and therefore that the phonemic forms of roots are retrieved from the speech output lexicon with inflections being added later. The resistance of inflections to distortion may arise because they are effectively very high-frequency items which, like "the", "an", or "is" can always be accessed correctly by neologistic jargonaphasics.

APHASIC AND NORMAL ERRORS IN WORD FINDING AND PRODUCTION

In both anomia and neologistic jargonaphasia there are disorders of word finding and production. In this section we hope to convince the reader that there is nothing exclusively aphasic about the difficulties and errors seen in these patients, or the other word-finding and production problems that have been reported in aphasics. Normal people experience occasional problems in retrieving or articulating words, and we shall focus on two types of problem in particular. The first, to which we have alluded already, is the involuntary and unintentional slip of the tongue. These take a variety of different forms and have been studied in some detail for the insights they can provide into normal speech production processes (see Cutler, 1982; Fromkin, 1973; 1980). We shall argue here that some types of aphasic error represent a heightened tendency to errors which normal people occasionally make as slips of the tongue.

The second type of normal difficulty to which we shall compare aphasic problems occurs when a normal speaker is having a temporary difficulty recalling a word in his or her vocabulary. Everyone is aware of being unable to remember a word from time to time and knows how galling it can be. On some occasions a few seconds' search is enough to retrieve the word, while on others it refuses to come but then "pops up" some minutes or even days later. Sometimes you feel as if you have almost got the word, only for it to fade again into the background. The mental experience in this state is a peculiar one well described by William James (1890) who called it a "gap in consciousness" and wrote that (p. 251):

It is a gap that is intensely active. A sort of wraith is in it, beckoning us in a given direction, making us at moments tingle with the sense of closeness, and then letting us sink back without the longed for term. If wrong names are proposed to us, this singularly definite gap acts immediately so as to negate them. They do not fit its mould.

Psychologists have studied these normal word-finding problems either by collecting naturally occurring instances, or provoking them by having normal speakers try to fit words to definitions or faces (e.g. Brown & McNeill, 1966; Reason & Lucas, 1984; Woodworth, 1938). In such "tip-of-the-tongue" states a speaker will sometimes report a "feeling of knowing" but be unable to generate any attempt at the word. Sometimes other words will be retrieved which resemble the target word in some way but which the speaker will usually know to be wrong. Finally, the sought-for word may be so close to the tip of the speaker's tongue that he or she can say what phoneme it begins with, tap out its number of syllables, or even generate close approximations to it. We shall argue that each of the degrees of closeness and type of error have counterparts among aphasic word-finding problems.

Before going on to argue our case in detail we should acknowledge that there is nothing original in our general claim for similarities between persistent aphasic difficulties and the occasional lapses of normal people. Sigmund Freud, the founder of psychoanalysis, was trained initially as a neurologist and his first published book was in fact a short monograph on aphasia (Freud, 1891). That book contains the germs of a number of ideas that reappeared later in psychoanalytic theory, such as the concept of regression, which first appeared as the now unpopular notion that brain injury might cause language skills to regress to the level of a young child. In *The psychopathology of everyday life* (1901) Freud applied psychoanalytic concepts to the interpretation of slips of the tongue, but in *On aphasia* (1891) it was the similarity between slips of the tongue and aphasic errors which interested him. Freud wrote that:

> the paraphasia [i.e. speech error] in aphasic patients does not differ from the incorrect use and the distortion of words which the healthy person can observe in himself in states of fatigue or divided attention or under the influence of disturbing affects—the kind of thing that frequently happens to our lecturers and causes the listener painful embarrassment.

More recently, Lenneberg (1960) asserted that, "some forms of aphasia are an abnormally augmented and sustained state which in transient conditions is not uncommon in persons without demonstrable pathology". Detailed comparisons between normal and aphasic errors can be found in Soderpalm (1979), Buckingham (1980), Garrett (1984), and Ellis (1985).

We shall begin by considering whether there exists in normal, intact people any transient equivalent of the word-finding problems of anomic aphasics.

Anomic and Normal Word-finding Difficulties

Anomic aphasics, it will be remembered, have great difficulties in word finding. If given an object to name they will recognise it and be able to indicate its use, but will often be unable to name it. They will, however, recognise the name when they hear it spoken. A patient described by Potts (1901):

> understood everything that was said to him and could converse fluently until he was required to name either a person, place or object.... For instance, he was unable to give the name of his married sister, who was with him, but knew when it was pronounced correctly. There was inability to name paper, a penholder, an ink-well and a watch, but he could tell at once what they were used for, and whether or not they were named correctly by another.... He also insisted that he knew the name but could not say it.

Over 100 years ago, Ogle (1867, p. 94) likened this to normal word-finding problems:

> Most of us know what it is to have the pictorial image of some familiar object in our mind, and yet be perfectly unable to call up its name. The idea is there, but the idea does not suggest the proper symbol. The moment, however, some other person uses the word in our presence it is at once perfectly recognised. Now a similar forgetfulness of words, but more extensive—a similar inability, that is, to translate ideas into symbols—constitutes one form of aphasia; a form which I will call Amnemonic [= anomic] aphasia.

We have noted how normal word-finding problems take different forms. The form which seems most closely equivalent to anomia occurs when a normal person reports a strong "feeling of knowing" a word but is unable to generate any sort of attempt at it. The word's meaning is fully known and it has an entry in the speech output lexicon (as demonstrated by the fact that the elusive word often is retrieved some time later). It appears then to be the retrieval process that is at fault. This, of course, is precisely the explanation offered earlier for anomics like EST whose aphasia was attributed to problems in activating entries for words within the speech output lexicon.

Semantic Errors in Normals and Aphasics

When a patient described briefly by Schuell (1950) was asked what he grew on his farm he replied: "way down on the farm—tree—26 acres of hay—oats—barley—*corn*! Twenty-six or seven acres of— hay—oats—about three or four acres of—timothy—*clover*! Oh yes, that's it, about four acres of clover, that's right." Schuell relates how the patient would shake his head and look distressed each time he said a word related in meaning to the word he sought but not the correct target word which, if it were eventually spoken, would be accompanied by "relaxation and a smile of satisfaction".

In the same paper, Schuell (1950) lists and classifies a large number of such *semantic errors* in aphasic speech, most of which occurred in object-naming tasks. Table 5.1 provides a sample of these errors. In a more recent paper, Rinnert and Whitaker (1973) also classify and discuss aphasic semantic errors (in reading as well as speech) and note how they are not restricted to one variety of aphasia but occur in patients with a variety of different speech disorders. Although we know of no reports of patients in whom semantic errors were the *only* aphasic symptom, 42% of the object-naming errors made by the patient reported by Nolan and Caramazza (1982) were related in meaning to the target word. We suggested earlier that semantic errors are characteristic of that form of anomia attributable to deficits at the semantic level.

TABLE 5.1
Semantic Errors in Aphasic Misnaming (from Schuell, 1950)

lion	→ "buffalo"	*sheep*	→ "goat"	*desk*	→ "sink"
comb	→ "hair"	*towel*	→ "wash"	*leaves*	→ "tree"
knife	→ "cut"	*coffee*	→ "sugar"	*dish*	→ "spoon"
strawberries	→ "figs"	*shirt*	→ "dress"	*gloves*	→ "arm"
thimble	→ "thread"	*lamp*	→ "bulb"	*razor*	→ "shave"
gun→ "bow and arrow"				*hammer*→ "screwdriver"	

Note: Target words are given to the left of the arrow, the patient's error to the right.

Normal people in a tip-of-the-tongue state will sometimes produce strings of words related in meaning to the target word which they nevertheless reject as incorrect. Thus, one person, in a study by Davies (1984), when given the definition of *wharf* said, "dock, jetty, no, oh no, I know it, berth, dock, oh no, no, I do know it but it's not gonna come". When provided with the word "wharf" the speaker immediately recognised it as the target. Another person given the definition of *utopia* said: "Oh, I know this one definitely. I first of all thought about nirvana... paradise, no it's not paradise, something to do with a state. If it comes it'll just come [long pause]. I'm thinking of aquarius so

I don't know if I do know it now. No, it's a place but not a real place, its a perfect place [long pause] . . . utopia!"

Semantic errors also occur as slips of the tongue when a normal speaker involuntarily says a word related in meaning to the intended word. Again, the speaker will often correct these spontaneously, and will certainly acknowledge the slip as an error if questioned. Examples from Fromkin (1973; 1980) include:

I really *like* to—*hate* to get up in the morning . . .

It's at the *bottom*—I mean—*top* of the stack of books . . .

This room is too damn *hot*—*cold* . . .

the *oral*—*written* part of the exam . . .

Three, five and eight are the worst years for *beer*—I mean *wine* . . .

There's a small *Chinese*—I mean *Japanese* restaurant . . .

Butterworth (1980) argued that semantic errors occur as slips of the tongue through inadvertent activation of the wrong entry within a semantically structured lexicon. The same locus has been proposed as the source of semantic errors in some anomic aphasics. Thus, semantic errors may occur as slips of the tongue as a result of a temporary aberration within the semantic system, damage to which in aphasics produces a chronic disposition to make semantic errors (and an inability to detect them *as* errors).

Real Word Errors of Normals and Aphasics that are Similar in Sound to the Target Word

Semantic errors are not the only variety of aphasic misnaming reported by Schuell (1950). Some of her patients made errors in which the error was a real word similar in sound to the target word. Examples include *goat* misnamed as "ghost", *spoon* as "spool", *fountain* as "mountain", *hook* as "book", *chain* as "chair", and *basket* as "gadget". Freud (1891) mentions aphasic errors in which "words of a similar sound are mistakenly used for each other", such as "butter" for *mutter*, or "campher" for *pamphlet*, and Luria (1974) claims that some of his Russian patients showed "a prevalence for phonetic [i.e. sound] similarity over semantic similarity" in their misnamings, citing errors such as "Kolkhoz" (collective farm) for *holost* (bachelor). Green (1969) calls these errors "phonic verbal paraphasias" and gives as an example a patient intending to say "I got the *words* right at the end of my *tongue*" and instead saying "I got the *nerves* right at the end of my *thumb*". Soderpalm (1979, pp. 83–86) provides some Swedish examples.

Buckingham (1980) has noted that it is difficult from the examples given in the literature to exclude positively the possibility that some patients make frequent phoneme substitutions which result fortuitously in real words on some occasions. Butterworth (1979) and Ellis et al. (1983) argue for the occurrence of just such random "jargon homophones" in their neologistic jargonaphasic patients. What is needed—and what we have been unable to find—are case reports of patients whose only similar-sound errors in speech or naming are real words. We would note, however, that normal people make similar-sound errors in word finding and slips of the tongue.

As slips of the tongue, similar-sounding real word slips are called "malapropisms" after a character called Mrs Malaprop in Sheridan's play *The Rivals*. She was an inveterate misuser of words, but in the speech error literature the term has come to be applied to involuntary slips which the speaker, unlike Mrs Malaprop, would acknowledge immediately to be wrong. Examples from Fay and Cutler (1977) include "trampolines" said instead of the intended word "tambourines", "inoculation" instead of "inauguration", "insect" instead of "index", and "ludicrous" instead of "lucrative".

When we are searching for a particular word, similar-sound errors also occur. For example, one subject in Davies' (1984) study given a definition appropriate to *necromancy* said "nepotism... no it's not that but it's like that". Other examples from normal subjects include "vixen" and "viscous" as attempts at *viscera*, "crochet" for *creche*, "rotary" for *rosary*, "sideboard" for *scabbard*, and "colon" for *kernel*. All these were proffered in response to definitions of the italicized words.

How might these similar-sound errors arise in aphasics and normals (as slips of the tongue and in word search)? One possibility is to postulate spreading activation within the speech output lexicon akin to that often held to occur within the semantic system (e.g. Anderson, 1976). The difference would be that whereas spreading activation within the semantic system occurs between the entries for words having similar meanings, within the speech output lexicon activation would spread from the entry for one word to the entries for others having similar *sounds*. Stemberger (1985) suggests that this mutual activation of similar-sounding words in the speech output lexicon is not direct, but occurs via nodes at the phoneme level. In his model, activation flows back up from the phoneme level to the output lexicon as well as flowing down from the lexicon to the phoneme level. Similar-sound errors in normals thus arise as a consequence of rapid two-way interaction between the speech output lexicon and the phoneme level. As Ellis (1985a) notes, similar-sound errors may thus represent a type of mistake which is, paradoxically, characteristic of two *intact* subsystems interacting in a fast and (normally) efficient manner. They may thus tend to disappear when one or other level is impaired, and may never occur as the sole or predominant error form in aphasia.

Neologisms

At first glance it seems unlikely that normal people would ever produce neologisms like those of patients EST or RD discussed above. We have, however, observed a neologistic type of response to be made by normals when searching for a word they temporarily are unable to retrieve. Sometimes a normal person will claim to know a defined word and will generate a series of attempts at it which resemble the target word in the way that so-called "target-related neologisms" resemble their targets. All the instances we have observed of this phenomenon to date have culminated in a full, correctly pronounced word. In one example quoted by Ellis et al. (1983), a normal subject was given the definition *A platform for public speaking* and said "past... pestul... peda... pedestal". Another subject's response to the same definition was "strow... strum... rostrum". To the definition *The part of a steeple where bells are hung* a subject responded "belfrum... belfry", whereas in response to *Wordblindness; difficulty in learning to read or spell* another said, "flexi... plexi... plexia... dyslexia".

Earlier we interpreted target-related neologisms in aphasics as symptomatic of impaired activation reaching the speech output lexicon, with the result that only partial information about the phonemic forms of many words can be retrieved. It would appear that this problem may again be a habitual and disabling exaggeration of a problem which occasionally afflicts the normal person caught in a tip-of-the-tongue state for a little-used word. Even in the case of anomics and neologistic jargonaphasics we have seen how the most frequently used words can usually still be retrieved in their entirety, suggesting that although the band of "infrequently used words" has expanded greatly for them, the most common still remain accessible.

PHONOLOGICAL PROBLEMS IN APHASICS AND NORMALS

Many aphasic patients who may show a variety of other language difficulties have, in addition, problems with sequencing and articulating the phonemes in words. Blumstein (1973) studied the phonemic errors of three groups of aphasics (designated Broca's, conduction, and Wernicke's) and could find no differences between them. All three groups made phoneme substitution errors such as saying "*keams*" for "*teams*" or "ti*n*e" for "ti*m*e", and also phoneme misordering errors which might involve the anticipation of phonemes (e.g. saying "*b*istory *b*ooks" for "*h*istory *b*ooks" or "roa*f* bee*f*" for "roa*s*t bee*f*"), their perseveration (e.g. saying "*f*ront p*r*age" for "*f*ront page"), or reversal (e.g. "*g*ed*r*ees" for "*d*e*g*rees"). Subsequent studies have reported differences in predispositions to different types of error but with considerable overlap between groups (e.g. Blumstein, Cooper, Goodglass, Statlender, & Gottlieb, 1980; Monoi, Fukusako, Itoh, & Sasanuma, 1983; see Kohn, 1988, for a review). In our view the use of *group* studies rather than selected single-case studies virtually ensures a blurring of real individual differences that may exist between patients.

All the types of phonemic error seen in aphasic patients also occur in normal people as slips of the tongue. Thus in the Appendix to Fromkin's (1973) book *Speech errors as linguistic evidence*, we can find examples of normal phoneme substitutions (e.g. "*b*agnificent" for "*m*agnificent"; "pho*l*etic" for "pho*n*etic"), anticipations (e.g. "*t*addle *t*ennis" for "*p*addle *t*ennis", or "cu*ff* of co*ff*ee" for "cu*p* of co*ff*ee"), and reversals (e.g. "u*v*i*n*ersity" for "u*n*i*v*ersity", or "*m*oggy *b*arsh" for "*b*oggy *m*arsh").

In addition to their superficial comparability, fine-grain analyses show more detailed resemblances between normal and aphasic phoneme errors. Details of these similarities are shown in Table 5.2. In normal speakers phoneme misordering errors are often referred to as "Spoonerisms" after William Spooner (1844–1930), who reputedly made large numbers of such errors. Lashley (1951) was impressed by the similarity between normal and aphasic errors and wrote: "In some types of aphasia the tendency to disordered arrangement of words is greatly increased.... Professor Spooner, after whom such slips are named, was probably suffering from a mild form of aphasia." Spooner's life and slips are discussed by Potter (1980), and further comparisons between normal and aphasic phoneme errors can be found in Soderpalm (1979) and Buckingham (1980). We would argue that although some differences between the two sorts of error may exist [for example, in the distance covered by items in movement errors (anticipations, perseverations, and reversals), or in the relative frequencies of the subtypes], there are sufficient similarities for us to regard them as both originating from malfunctions of processes in and around the phoneme level—transient malfunctions in normals, more permanent and more disabling in aphasics.

TABLE 5.2
Fine-grain Similarities between Normal and Aphasic Phoneme Misordering Errors
(see also Soderpalm, 1979; Buckingham, 1980)

1. The target phoneme and the error phoneme that replaces it tend to be articulatorily and acoustically similar.
   normals: Nooteboom (1967), MacKay (1970), Garrett (1975).
   aphasics: Green (1969), Lecours & Lhermitte (1969), Blumstein (1973), Martin & Rigrodsky (1974), Lecours (1975).

2. The target and error phoneme tend to share similar or identical preceding and/or following phonemes.
   normals: Nooteboom (1967).
   aphasics: Lecours & Lhermitte (1969).

3. The target and error phonemes tend to originate from similar positions in their respective syllables.
   normals: Nooteboom (1967), MacKay (1970).
   aphasics: Blumstein (1978), Buckingham, Whitaker, & Whitaker (1978).

4. Target and error phonemes tend to originate in content words rather than function words.
   normals: Garrett (1975).
   aphasics: Blumstein (1973).

5. Consonants and vowels do not interchange.
   normals: Fromkin (1971), Garrett (1975).
   aphasics: Fry (1959), Blumstein (1973).

6. Errors rarely result in sequences of phonemes that are not permitted in the speaker's language.
   normals: Wells (1951), Boomer & Laver (1968), Garrett (1975).
   aphasics: Blumstein (1978).

7. The probability of two phonemes being involved in a misordering error decreases as the separation between them increases.
   normals: Cohen (1966), Nooteboom (1967), MacKay (1970).
   aphasics: Lecours & Lhermitte (1969).

ARTICULATORY DISORDERS

In most of the aphasic phoneme errors just described the phonemes are articulated reasonably smoothly. There are, however, a final set of speech production aphasias in which articulation itself—that is, the co-ordination and control of the articulatory muscle groups—is impaired. Probably the fullest description of such a disorder was provided in a series of papers spanning 37 years by Alajouanine, Ombredane, and Durand (1939), Alajouanine, Pichot, and Durand (1949), and Lecours and Lhermitte (1976). The patient receiving this intensive study was a French–English bilingual man (E.Fr.) who suffered a stroke at the age of 63. A few months later his speech comprehension was perfectly normal, as were his ability to read and write, but his speech production was slow and laborious with syllables being forced out explosively. In a (translated) letter to his doctor written in January, 1948, E.Fr. observes:

> I can only talk syllabically because my articulation is sluggard [*paresseuse*]. It is no longer automatic but has to be commanded, directed. I have to think of the word I am going to utter, and of the way in which to utter it. If I want to say '*bonjour*', I can no longer do so out of habit; it is no longer automatic.... I must articulate each vowel, each consonant, in short each syllable.

Subsequently, studies of this "phonetic disintegration syndrome" (alternatively known as "pure anarthria" or "aphemia") by Shankweiler and Harris (1966), Lebrun, Buyssens, and Henneaux (1973), and Nebes (1975) leave no doubt that in pure cases all internal language functions can remain intact, and that patients may have internal access to the sounds of words (as illustrated by the ability to make rhyme judgements or tap out the number of syllables in words they cannot say), but they can no longer translate phonemic forms fluently into articulations.

Finally, patients whom traditional classification systems label as "Broca's aphasics" have articulatory problems combined with other, grammatical difficulties that we shall review in Chapter 9. Techniques including computer controlled X-ray microbeams have revealed defective articulatory timing in Broca's aphasics, suggesting that an impairment of articulatory programming accompanies the several other features of this "syndrome" (Kohn, 1988). We shall argue in Chapter 9 that because the several features of "Broca's aphasia" can dissociate one from another, it is not a useful category for cognitive neuropsychological analysis.

OVERVIEW

If you are to name an object you are looking at you must perceive it clearly, recognise and "comprehend" it for what it is, retrieve its name from memory, and articulate it correctly. A normal person may experience a temporary difficulty with any of these stages on a particular occasion. Thus, viewing an object from an unusual angle may create momentary problems in recognition, or a tip-of-the-tongue state may signal a temporary problem of name retrieval. Each of the stages in object recognition and naming may also be more seriously impaired as a consequence of brain injury, so that even an apparently simple process like object naming is subject to several different forms of impairment (Morton, 1985a; Ratcliff & Newcombe, 1982). We reviewed disorders of object perception and recognition in Chapter 2 and have covered name retrieval and production in this chapter. Central semantic processes impinge on both recognition and name production and have consequently intruded into both chapters.

For the cognitive neuropsychologist it is a useful exercise to discover whether or not the impairments seen in brain-injured patients can be explained in terms of exaggerations of tendencies to error seen in normal people. If they can, then one has gained a degree of support for the assumption of *subtractivity*, whereby it is assumed that entirely new cognitive processes do not arise following brain injury (see Chapter 1). We have spent a considerable amount of time in this chapter on similarities between normal and aphasic errors because we feel that disorders of word-finding are a case where exaggeration theory can best be sustained and where the subtractivity assumption can best be corroborated.

Object naming is, of course, only one aspect of the more general process of word retrieval and production which is, in turn, only one aspect of successful speech production. In normal speech, words are arranged into sentences to express particular thoughts, and the words in each sentence are given appropriate intonation and emphasis. Linguists use the term "syntax" to refer to the processes whereby words are ordered into sentences, and the term "prosody" to refer to the intonation, stress, timing, and rhythm of utterances. One of the first achievements of the cognitive neuropsychology of language was to highlight the dissociations that can occur between disorders of word finding and syntax (Caramazza & Berndt, 1978; Marin, Saffran, & Schwartz, 1976; Saffran 1982). As we have seen, "anomic" patients have word-finding problems yet they may show normal syntactic skills. In contrast, patients labelled as "agrammatic" may be able to retrieve words well but can no longer arrange them into grammatical sentences (see Chapter 9). This "double dissociation" shows that separate sets of cognitive modules must exist for word finding and syntax, and accordingly constrains any future model of speech production, whether the model is meant to apply to aphasic or normal speech. As we shall also see in Chapter 9, prosody is subject to its own range of impairments which dissociate from disorders of syntax and word finding, so future models must also allow for a third set of separate processes for the production of prosody. This is, of course, another illustration of cognitive neuropsychological analysis driving the theorist inexorably toward a *modular* view of the total human cognitive apparatus.

SUMMARY

Problems in spoken-word retrieval and production can arise at a number of different levels. In pure cases, one stage may be selectively impaired leaving the others intact, though many patients will have multiple problems affecting several levels.

Impairments at the semantic level may in certain cases affect word retrieval for some semantic categories more than others (e.g. patient MD whose naming problems were specific to fruit and vegetables). Other patients have more general semantic problems. These patients have comprehension as well as production difficulties, suggesting that the same semantic system is involved in both comprehension and production.

Other "anomic" patients (like EST) can show word-finding problems for words whose semantic representations appear to be intact (as demonstrated by intact comprehension of the meanings of those words). The features of these cases, including the greater problems with low-frequency than high-frequency words, may be explained in terms of problems activating entries for words in a speech output lexicon. In this respect the problems of these anomic patients resemble greatly exaggerated and habitual tip-of-the-tongue states where semantic errors and similar-sound errors also occur.

When EST could not fully retrieve a word he could often generate a close approximation to it. These occurred more often in tasks like object naming than in spontaneous speech where EST would avoid difficult words as much as possible. Approximation errors (alias target-related neologisms) occur much more commonly in the speech of patients termed "neologistic jargonaphasics" (like RD). Such patients have profound speech perception difficulties which may prevent them from monitoring their own speech and detecting their own errors. The underlying output impairment appears otherwise to be similar to that of anomic patients like EST, namely a frequency related impairment affecting the activation of words in the speech output lexicon. More specifically, it is root morphemes which are difficult to access: Inflections are retrieved and accommodated correctly to the root, suggesting that root morphemes and inflections may have separate entries in the speech output lexicon (a conclusion supported by analyses of normal slips of the tongue).

Impairments at or below the phoneme level are common in aphasics, but currently we lack the detailed case studies that would allow us to tease apart any different forms of impairment that may exist. Phoneme level errors of substitution and misordering bear a close resemblance to the phonemic slips of the tongue of normal speakers, suggesting an exacerbation in the aphasics of processes which are already somewhat error-prone in normal speakers. Low-level articulatory disorders occur in pure form in patients suffering from "phonetic disintegration" or "pure anarthria", and also occur as a component of the condition referred to as "Broca's aphasia".

FURTHER READING

Garrett, M. (1992). Disorders of lexical selection. *Cognition, 42,* 143–180. A review of word-finding problems from a psycholinguist whose work on speech errors helped to lay the groundwork for modern theories of speech production.

Harley, T.A. (1995). *The psychology of language.* Hove, UK: Erlbaum (UK) Taylor & Francis. Chapter 8 reviews models of normal word finding and some of the impairments to which it is susceptible.

Levelt, W.J.M. (1989). *Speaking: from intention to articulation.* Cambridge, Mass.: MIT Press. A wide-ranging, theoretical account of normal speech production that has influenced much of the recent work on naming disorders.

McCarthy, R.A. (Ed.) (1995). *Semantic knowledge and semantic representations.* Hove, UK: Erlbaum (UK) Taylor & Francis. A collection of papers on aspects of semantic breakdown, including its impact on naming.

McCarthy, R.A. & Warrington, E.K. (1990). *Cognitive neuropsychology: a clinical introduction.* San Diego: Academic Press. Chapter 7 reviews word retrieval.

Patterson, K.E. & Hodges, J.R. (1994). Disorders of semantic memory. In A. Baddeley, B. Wilson, & F. Watts (Eds.), *Handbook of memory disorders.* Hove, UK: Lawrence Erlbaum Associates Ltd. Discusses how the breakdown of semantic knowledge in dementia affects naming and other aspects of word recognition and production.

6 Recognising and Understanding Spoken Words

INTRODUCTION

Spoken language travels from speaker to hearer as a sound wave. That sound wave is an extremely rich source of information. Without ever seeing a speaker we can often deduce correctly that person's sex, region of origin (from their accent), emotional state (e.g. whether they are happy, sad, or angry), approximate age, and so on. If the speaker is someone known to us we may be able to identify him or her as an individual from their voice and way of talking. There is, of course, linguistic information encoded in the speech wave too. This includes information about individual words, but in addition the syntactic boundaries of sentences or clauses are often signalled by pauses or changes in voice pitch, and even the transition from one general topic to another may be marked in a similar way (Ellis & Beattie, 1986).

We shall, however, principally be concerned here with recognising spoken words and extracting their meaning. Imagine the simple case of recognising a single word, clearly articulated and spoken in isolation. Unless that word is a homophone (like *their* and *there, one* and *won*) its sound pattern will be unique to it. To identify the word a listener will need to have stored in memory all the sound patterns of words he or she knows, and be able to compare the pattern just heard with these stored patterns to find the best match. What we are proposing is another word store or lexicon, but this time one involved in the recognition rather than the production of spoken words. We shall call it the *auditory input lexicon*.

There are currently two views prevalent on how the auditory input lexicon might work. One theory proposes that the listener first identifies phonemes (individual speech sounds) in the acoustic wave, and then identifies the word from its constituent phonemes. According to this view individual entries in the auditory input lexicon would be activated by a prior set of phoneme recognisers (e.g. Rumelhart & McClelland, 1981). The second theory, advocated by Klatt (1979) and Marcus (1981) among others, holds that the input to the auditory word recognition system is a low-level, relatively unsegmented description of the speech waveform. While acknowledging that either (or neither) of these theories may turn out to be correct in the long run, we shall tentatively adopt the first as our working hypothesis.

We propose, in Fig. 6.1, that the first stage of auditory word recognition performed by an early *auditory analysis system* attempts to identify phonemes in the speech wave. The results of this analysis are transmitted to the auditory input lexicon where a match is sought against the stored characteristics of known words. If the match is a good one, the appropriate recognition unit in the auditory input lexicon will be activated. It, in turn, will then activate the representation of the meaning of the heard word in the semantic system—the same semantic system that initiates the word production process in speaking via the same speech output lexicon and phoneme level that were discussed in the previous chapter. The arrow between the auditory input lexicon and the semantic system is bidirectional. This allows the semantic system to exert an influence upon the level of activity in the word-units which, in turn, provides a mechanism whereby the semantic context in which a word occurs can affect its ease of identification (see below).

One way to repeat a heard word would be to activate its entry in the speech output lexicon, release the phonemic form, and articulate it. This would be to take a route straight through Fig. 6.1. However, normal people can also repeat aloud unfamiliar words or non-words like "fep" or "flootil", for which there will be no entry in either the auditory input lexicon or the speech output lexicon. In Fig. 6.1, therefore, we need a by-pass route from the acoustic analysis system to the phoneme level. The by-pass route *must* be used to repeat unfamiliar words or non-words. It *could* be used for real words (treating them as if they were non-words), but real words can also be repeated via the input and output lexicons.

Figure 6.1 thus provides three "routes" between hearing a word and saying it. The first route is through word meanings and the two lexicons; the second is provided by the direct link between the auditory analysis system and the phoneme level; and the third route is provided by the arrow linking the auditory input lexicon to the speech output lexicon. This would allow heard words to activate their entries in the speech output lexicons directly, without going via the representations of word

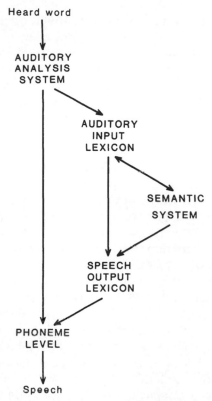

Heard word

AUDITORY
ANALYSIS
SYSTEM

AUDITORY
INPUT
LEXICON

SEMANTIC
SYSTEM

SPEECH
OUTPUT
LEXICON

PHONEME
LEVEL

Speech

FIG 6.1.   Simple functional model for the recognition, comprehension, and repetition of spoken words.

meanings in the semantic system. We will admit here and now that the evidence for such a route is weak. It is included because it allows us to explain in Chapter 7 how certain patients are able to write words to dictation without understanding the meanings of those words.

McCarthy and Warrington (1984) employed a model similar to Fig. 6.1 to explain two different patterns of repetition performance observed in three aphasic patients they studied. Patient ORF was able to repeat words considerably better than non-words of the same length (85% correct for words *vs*. 39% for non-words). Non-words can only be repeated via the link between auditory analysis and the phoneme level, whereas words can be repeated via any of the routes through Fig. 6.1. ORF's superiority for words over non-words suggests some impairment to the connection between the auditory analysis system and the phoneme level, with the routes via the lexicons and semantics assisting word repetition. These latter routes were not completely intact, however: ORF had word-finding problems in speech and naming, and his word repetition was not perfect, being affected by both word frequency and length (with more common, shorter words being repeated better than less common, longer words). Errors in both word and non-word repetition were phonemic distortions. Examples of his errors in word repetition include "fosh" for "wash", "acroldut" for "acrobat", and "kwokutrain" for "porcupine".

Further evidence for a role of the lexical-semantic routes in ORF's repetition came from the observation that he was assisted in repeating a word if it followed an incomplete priming sentence (e.g. The monster was...*hideous*). A second patient (RAN) of McCarthy and Warrington (1984) was similar to ORF, but the third patient (ART) showed a different pattern. ART's spontaneous speech was "halting and effortful", with many phonemic distortions ("paraphasias"). His repetition of words was good, however, at around 90% correct, and was unaffected by frequency or length. Furthermore, he was actually *worse* at repeating words when they followed incomplete priming sentences than when the words were presented in isolation.

McCarthy and Warrington (1984) argue that ART's repetition is mediated by the connection between the auditory analysis system and the phoneme level. Although ART's non-word repetition was not assessed, one would expect on this interpretation no difference between word and non-word repetition (assuming that the by-pass route is insensitive to the wordness of phoneme sequences and that advantages for words over non-words come from contributions from the lexicons and semantics).

Figure 6.1 links speech input to speech output and thus incorporates a model for auditory-vocal repetition. Our central concern in this chapter will, however, be with the recognition and understanding of spoken words, rather than with their simple repetition. We shall consider a number of aphasias in which the recognition and understanding of spoken words is impaired, aphasias known in the literature as pure word deafness, word meaning deafness, auditory phonological agnosia, and deep dysphasia.

PURE WORD DEAFNESS

The Pattern of Symptoms

Hemphill and Stengel (1940) reported the case of a 34-year-old labourer who suffered brain injury after falling from a bus. He could no longer repeat or understand speech addressed to him, and at first was thought to be deaf. This assumption was proved wrong, however, when audiometric testing showed him to be perfectly normal at hearing pure tones. He talked fluently with what are described as "no errors of grammar beyond what is common for his particular dialect and standard of education" [*sic*]. He read well with understanding and could write correctly with good spelling. He complained, however, that much of what he heard conveyed no meaning to him. In his own words: "I can hear you dead plain, but I cannot get what you say. The noises are not quite natural. I can hear but not understand."

Klein and Harper's (1956) patient, RC, showed a similar pattern. Following a stroke this 45-year-old Scottish sheep farmer's spontaneous speech returned almost to normal ("He made occasional slips in conversation, and in the naming of objects, but these mistakes became more and more sporadic"). His reading was "fluent and without mistakes", but he was quite unable to understand speech addressed to him. Audiometric testing showed normal hearing in his right ear with "moderate mixed deafness in the left ear". Though "he could hear everything, even a leaf falling", he said of listening to speech: "It sounds far away. You think you can catch it and it fades away... jumbled together like foreign folk speaking in the distance. You feel it should be louder but when anyone shouts it is still more confusing."

RC could repeat single vowel sounds correctly, but otherwise there was little or no similarity between what was said to him and his repetition. For example, he repeated "collaboration" as "setter", "God save the King" as "as in a mix", and "good morning" as "become". Interestingly, RC is reported as having been able to distinguish the voices of different people familiar to him, and able to say whether someone spoke with the accent of his own region, or from another part of Scotland, or "with a foreigner's accent" (it is not clear whether "foreigner" in this context included the English, though quite likely it did!).

These two patients approximate more or less closely to what is referred to in the neuropsychological literature as "pure word deafness". This involves impaired speech perception in the context of good speech production, reading, and writing (though RC had some spelling difficulties) and, importantly, intact perception of non-verbal environmental sounds. A historical review of cases given this designation is provided by Goldstein (1974); more recent and more detailed case studies can be found in Okada, Hanada, Hattori, and Shoyama (1963), Albert and Bear (1974), Denes and Semenza (1975), Saffran, Marin, and Yeni-Komshian (1976a), Shoumaker, Ajax, and Schenkenberg (1977), and Auerbach, Allard, Naeser, Alexander, and Albert (1982). In fact these cases vary in their purity—some, for example, have problems in the perception of melody, and Denes and Semenza's (1975) patient had difficulty with environmental sounds: What matters is that these associated deficits do not always accompany word deafness. Therefore, we can reasonably ignore them when looking at the possible causes of the *speech* perception problem.

The Psychological Nature of the Deficit

As noted earlier, these patients may have entirely normal perception of the sort of pure tones used in audiometric testing. The localisation of sounds in space was also normal in the patients of Okada et al. (1963), Denes and Semenza (1975), and Auerbach et al. (1982). Recognition of environmental sounds was good in all but the patients of Denes and Semenza (1975) and Auerbach et al. (1982). Clearly, then, we are not dealing with simple deafness in these cases.

Okada et al. (1963) seem to have been the first to make an important observation which others have replicated and discussed, namely that these patients sometimes understood a question or request if it was repeated *very slowly* two or three times. Albert and Bear's (1974) patient himself commented that "words come too quickly". Passage comprehension, though never very good, was reportedly better for this patient at a speech rate of 45 words per minute than 150 words per minute. In one experiment groups of three digits were spoken to him either rapidly with no pause between them or at a slower rate of one per 3 seconds. With the examiner's lips screened from view he identified 95% correctly at the slow rate but only 50% correctly at the faster rate. Auerbach et al.'s (1982) patient also commented that people's voices seemed fast and that it helped when they spoke more slowly.

A second clue as to the underlying cause of the deficit is given in reports of the differential ease with which these patients can identify spoken consonants and vowels. Denes and Semenza's (1975) patient was good at identifying single spoken vowels, but his performance became very poor if a consonant was added to the front of the vowel so that he had to identify a CV syllable. Auerbach et al.'s patient similarly was very good at identifying vowels but poor at consonants. In seeking to explain this discrepancy, Auerbach et al. (1982, p. 283) note that:

> When plotted on a frequency spectrogram, vowels are represented by steady state characteristic frequencies. In natural speech, vowel durations usually average 100 to 150 ms but may last as long as 400 ms. CV combinations with stop consonants such as ba, pa, da, ta, ga or ka all contain early rapid formant transitions. In these CV combinations, the vowels are characterised by steady state formants whereas the consonant is characterised by rapid frequency changes within the first 40 ms of onset of stimulus.

In order to identify and discriminate between spoken consonants you need to be able to make very fine temporal discriminations and track rapidly changing acoustic signals accurately (Miller, 1987). That, arguably, is what at least some word-deaf patients are no longer able to do.

Lateralisation and Modes of Perception

We shall have a little more to say about the nature of pure word deafness and strategies for overcoming it shortly, but it is worth noting at this point that this deficit provides one of the best illustrations of how cognitive neuropsychology can interface with that branch of neuropsychology concerned with the localisation of functions within different regions of the brain. Pure word deafness can follow from a single lesion in the temporal lobe of the left hemisphere, that half of the brain which controls many language functions in the majority of right-handed people. The left and right hemispheres receive their most important auditory inputs from the right and left ears respectively. Words are slightly but measurably better identified if presented to the right ear, and hence to the left hemisphere, than if presented to the left ear and hence to the right hemisphere. This right ear advantage is especially pronounced in the "dichotic listening" paradigm where pairs of words are presented simultaneously, one to each ear, through headphones (Bradshaw & Nettleton, 1983; Bryden, 1982). Where this ties in with pure word deafness is that steady-state vowels do *not* yield a right ear/left hemisphere advantage but are perceived equally well by either ear/hemisphere (Blumstein, Tartter, Michel, Hirsch, & Leiter, 1977; Shankweiler & Studdert-Kennedy, 1967). Most consonants cannot be presented in isolation, but as soon as one employs CV or CVC syllables in a dichotic listening test a right ear advantage emerges. This advantage accrues to the vowel segments of the syllables as well as to the consonants (Darwin, 1971; Godfrey, 1974; Haggard, 1971; Shankweiler & Studdert-Kennedy, 1967; Weiss and House, 1973). This may be because in natural syllables cues as to the identity of the vowel are not restricted to the medial portion, but are instead "smeared throughout the syllable" (Sergent, 1984). That is, the central vowel modifies and colours the consonants before and after it, so a component capable of the fine-grain analysis of consonants will gain additional information regarding the identity of the accompanying vowel.

Shankweiler and Studdert-Kennedy (1967) talk of two different "modes" of perception—a general *auditory* mode, and a speech-related *phonetic* mode. Both hemispheres, they argue, are capable of perceiving in the auditory mode, and the auditory mode is capable of processing steady-state vowels, so such vowels show no ear advantage in dichotic listening. The phonetic mode is, according to Shankweiler and Studdert-Kennedy, a unique possession of the human left hemisphere. This mode is necessary for the accurate perception of the rapidly changing acoustic signals that specify consonants, and so consonants display a right ear advantage. There are other lines of evidence for something like this distinction, for example in the patterns of auditory loss which accompany injury to one or other hemisphere (Oscar-Berman, Zurif, & Blumstein, 1975).

Albert and Bear (1974) presented digits through headphones to the left and right ears of their word-deaf patient. With "monaural presentation" (only one digit at a time to either the left ear or the right ear) performance was equally good with either ear. With "dichotic presentation", where the digits are simultaneously presented in pairs, one to each ear, left ear performance remained good, but right ear performance dropped to almost zero. Saffran et al. (1976a) obtained a similar pattern of "right ear extinction", under dichotic conditions from their patient using monosyllabic names like "Ben", "Chuck", or "Tom" (recall that the right ear is the one that shows the *advantage* in dichotic experiments with normal subjects). These authors argue that their digit and name stimuli can be discriminated reasonably well by the right hemisphere auditory system, and that under monaural presentation conditions stimuli to either ear can gain access to that component (there are, in fact, projections from both ears to both hemispheres, though the projections from each ear to the opposite hemisphere appear dominant). Under dichotic conditions the left ear/right hemisphere connection dominates and suppresses the right ear/right hemisphere connection. Stimuli presented to the right ear can no longer be processed by the injured left hemisphere, so the patient shows right ear extinction.

From the observations made so far it could be argued that the left hemisphere "phonetic" system damaged in word-deaf patients is *only* involved in speech processing. This would be in line with arguments for a special "speech mode" of perception (Mann & Liberman, 1983; Repp, 1982). The case for a *speech-specific* mode of perception has not, however, found universal acceptance (e.g. Schouten, 1980). Two points are possibly relevant to the question of whether the component impaired in word-deaf patients is speech-specific. The first is the point we noted earlier, that these patients benefit greatly from a reduction in speech rate. Slowing speech down may bring the range of temporal discriminations necessary to distinguish consonants within the capabilities of the right hemisphere "auditory" component. That is, a reduction of speech rate by one-half or one-third may permit the right hemisphere auditory component to function as a phonetic one.

Secondly, studies by Albert and Bear (1974) and Auerbach et al. (1982) have shown deficits in word-deaf patients in the processing of rapidly changing *non-speech* stimuli. Normal subjects can distinguish two clicks as separate if there is a silence of just 2 or 3 ms between them. Below such separation the clicks "fuse" into a single percept. (Miller & Taylor, 1948; Patterson, Green, 1970). Albert and Bear's patient fused clicks separated by anything less than 15 ms, whereas Auerbach et al.'s patient required clicks to be separated by at least 30 ms before he could distinguish them. So rather than talking of a left hemisphere phonetic system and a right hemisphere auditory one, it might be better to think of the left hemisphere system as more efficient than the right, capable of finer discriminations to more rapidly changing acoustic patterns. The fact that the right hemisphere system can sustain a degree of speech perception may explain why bilateral lesions have often been thought necessary to cause complete (rather than partial) word deafness (Auerbach et al., 1982; Goldstein, 1974).

If the rapid processing deficit in word deafness extends to non-verbal clicks there may be nothing speech-specific about the impairment; word-deaf patients may no longer be able to analyse *any* rapidly changing acoustic signal. Nevertheless, in everyday life the class of sounds particularly affected by such an impairment are spoken consonants. Without such an ability you can still identify steady-state vowels and environmental noises like cows mooing or telephones ringing. You can also process information extractable from vowel quality in speech: As mentioned earlier, word-deaf patients are often capable of identifying the voices of familiar people, distinguishing male from female voices, and locating individuals geographically from their accent. Denes and Semenza's (1975) patient could distinguish Italian from English or German (which have distinctive vowel repertoires) but not from Latin (which has much the same vowel repertoire).

Finally, word deafness does not *have* to be pure. The spontaneous speech of Caramazza, Berndt, & Basili's (1983) patient, JS, was neologistic jargonaphasic, very like RD of Ellis, Miller, and Sin (1983) whom we discussed in Chapter 5. But JS's speech perception deficit, analysed in detail by Caramazza et al. (1983), corresponds closely to the picture seen in patients with pure word deafness. Thus the features of word deafness may co-exist with other language impairments in many more aphasics than show *pure* word deafness. In line with this suggestion, Lasky, Weidner, and Johnson (1976) and Tallal and Newcombe (1978) both found the speech perception of mixed groups of aphasic patients to be somewhat improved by slower rates of presentation (which we have seen to be a characteristic of pure word deafness).

Use of Lip Information

Returning to the cases of pure(ish) word deafness, several investigators have noted that the patients pay close attention to lip movements in an attempt to supplement their impoverished auditory/phonetic processing ability (Albert & Bear, 1974; Denes & Semenza, 1975; Saffran et al., 1976a). Auerbach et al.'s (1982) patient said: "If I go blind, I won't hear anything!" For Albert and Bear's patient the deterioration in digit identification brought about by fast rates of presentation was considerably lessened if the tester's lips were not concealed from view (rather than falling from 95 to 50% as it did with lips concealed, performance only declined from 98 to 80% with lips visible). This parallels closely the use normal listeners make of lip movement information when speech quality is poor. Cotton (1935) had a speaker sit in a sound-proof booth with glass windows. His speech was transmitted to an audience sat outside, but was distorted by removing high frequencies and adding a loud buzzing noise. With the lighting adjusted so as to make the speaker invisible to the audience, only an occasional word or two could be identified, but when the speaker was made visible his speech was understood without difficulty. Cotton concluded that "there is an important element of visual hearing in all normal individuals". Likewise, Sumby and Pollack (1954) showed that speech distorted by hissing "white" noise is more easily perceived if the speaker's lip and face movements can also be seen.

One might be tempted to suggest that the use made by normal listeners and word-deaf patients of lipread information is akin to having available a poorly written transcript of what is being said—it provides a useful but entirely separate source of information. The studies of McGurk and MacDonald (1976) and Summerfield (1979), however, suggest otherwise. They showed that lip movement information combines with speech wave information very early in the process of perception to determine what is actually *heard*. It is thus possible that lipread information in some genuine sense helps word-deaf patients *hear* better. Auerbach et al.'s (1982) patient may have been closer to the mark than he thought. Maybe if he did go blind he would not *hear* what people were saying.

Use of Context

In addition to making use of lip movement cues, patients with pure word deafness also seem able to use the linguistic context to aid comprehension. Okada et al. (1963) note that their patient fared quite well when asked a series of questions related to a single topic (e.g. "the weather"), but comprehension became suddenly much worse when the topic changed. Saffran et al. (1976a) describe a conversation in which their patient "gets completely lost each time the questioning shifts from his smoking habits to his work experience, to the circumstances of his early life, but is able to respond appropriately once he grasps the general topic of conversation". In an experimental follow-up of this observation Saffran et al. showed that the perception of lists of words was better when the words came from a small number of semantic categories (animals, vehicles, furniture, fruits), with the words in each category being grouped together, than when unrelated words were presented. Also words presented in sentences which provided contextual cues (e.g. "The boy sailed the BOAT") were better identified than the same words presented in isolation ("BOAT").

Like the use made of lipread information, this use of context, as Saffran et al. (1976a) note, is very similar to that made by normal subjects. Miller, Heise, and Lichten (1951) had subjects try to identify words in a background of white noise. Words in isolation were found to be much less identifiable than words in sentence contexts. Even normal "good quality" speech may need supplementing by context. Lieberman (1963) and Pollack and Pickett (1964) sliced single words out of passages of perfectly intelligible conversational speech and found that less than half of them were comprehensible when heard in isolation from their contexts. Marslen-Wilson and Tyler (1975; 1980) had normal subjects listen to passages of undegraded speech and press a button each time particular target words were heard. Reaction times were much shorter in passages of normal, coherent text than in passages with the word order scrambled, where listeners had to rely for word identification entirely on stimulus information and could make no use of context.

In sum, because of a left hemisphere deficit which appears to affect high-speed processing of acoustic signals, word-deaf patients form only a very poor percept of speech—one good enough to distinguish many vowels but few consonants. They supplement the speech wave by use of lip movement information and also by use of context. In both these respects the patients resemble normal people trying to extract information from a noisy signal. In terms of our model, the locus of the deficit is very clearly the auditory analysis system.

"WORD MEANING DEAFNESS"

The second variety of auditory word recognition disorder we shall discuss has been called "word meaning deafness". A young woman aged 26 years and living near Edinburgh, Scotland in the 1890s suffered a stroke 11 days after giving birth to her third child. After a few weeks of recovery she "volunteered statements, spoke spontaneously, asked questions... [and] seemed able to say almost everything she wished to say, [though] she occasionally made use of a wrong word". She "could read aloud anything which was placed before her" such as the sentence, "No issue of a medical journal would be complete at the present time without containing the latest development in this greatest medical experiment of all time." She understood short written sentences, though she seems to have had some problems understanding long sentences or connected text. She experienced great difficulty understanding speech addressed to her, though she was not deaf. As she said on one occasion: "Is it not a strange thing that I can hear the clock ticking and cannot hear you speak? Now let me think what that means."

Thus far the patient sounds like a case of pure word deafness, but what distinguished her from those patients is that she could repeat the spoken words and sentences she could not understand, and she could even write them down to dictation. When asked, "Do you like to come to Edinburgh?", she did not understand the question, but repeated it correctly and wrote down the words she had just repeated. Having written the question down she then understood it by reading it.

This case report comes from Bramwell (1897), writing in the distinguished medical journal *The Lancet*. Despite its age, Bramwell's report remains one of the best descriptions available of a rare condition referred to as "word-meaning deafness". Bramwell's paper has recently been reprinted with commentary (Ellis, 1984a). Other reports of similar patients masquerading under a variety of diagnostic labels can be found in Lichtheim (1885), Goldstein (1915), Symonds (1953), Yamadori and Albert (1973), Luria (1976), and Kohn and Friedman (1986).

Kohn and Friedman (1986) state that a demonstration of word-meaning deafness must meet two conditions. When a word is not understood auditorily:

1. The word must have undergone adequate acoustic analysis as evidenced by correct repetition.
2. The semantic representation of the word must be intact as evidenced by immediate comprehension of the word when presented in written form.

Two patients reported by Kohn and Friedman (1986) displayed word-meaning deafness in mild form. They could understand many spoken words but showed the symptoms of word-meaning deafness for words they did not understand. For example, when asked to point to named objects in a picture, patient HN identified 9 out of 12 without difficulty, but for "cup" said, "cup, cup, C-U-P, cup. What is it?" Eventually he wrote *cup*, read it aloud, said, "Oh, cup", and immediately pointed to the cup in the picture.

Allport and Funnell (1981) consider word-meaning deafness to be "of great theoretical significance" (see also Allport, 1983; 1984). Intact repetition of words and sentences implies an intact early stage of auditory analysis (the stage thought to be impaired in patients with pure word deafness). Intact reading comprehension and spontaneous speech imply an intact semantic system and speech output lexicon. One might be tempted then to argue for an impairment to the auditory input lexicon, but the intact writing to dictation (with subsequent but not immediate comprehension) casts doubt on this interpretation. An alternative account is that word-meaning deafness represents a complete or partial disconnection of the auditory input lexicon from the semantic system. Entries in the auditory input lexicon can still be activated, but they are sometimes unable to cause subsequent activation of the representations of word meanings in the semantic system (Ellis, 1984a). (N.B. We shall discuss the processes that might permit words that are not understood to be written to dictation in Chapter 7.) On this account, at least some patients with severe word meaning deafness should still perform well on an auditory lexical decision task requiring the discrimination of spoken words from non-words. To the best of our knowledge such a test has not yet been carried out.

AUDITORY PHONOLOGICAL AGNOSIA

Beauvois, Dérousné, and Bastard (1980) described a patient with a very unusual and circumscribed language problem. The patient, a 58-year-old man (JL), had entirely normal spontaneous speech except if exhausted or upset, when he had some word finding problems and made occasional paraphasias. His reading aloud was good, if a little slow, and his spontaneous writing was also well preserved. JL complained, however, of some difficulties understanding spoken language, especially with new, technical scientific terms or the new names of people or towns. He reported no difficulty with old, familiar terms and names.

On more formal testing it was discovered that JL's repetition and writing to dictation of real, familiar words was almost perfect, whereas repetition and writing to dictation of invented non-words was very poor. His problem cannot have been a peripheral one because he could perceive real words perfectly well, and performed faultlessly in an "auditory lexical decision task" where he had to judge whether heard items were real words or non-words. JL's problem was not in the pronunciation of non-words either, because he read 40 "long and difficult" non-words without mistake. We are left, therefore, to locate his problem "at the level of acoustic-phonemic conversion, or at the level of the transmission of heard phonemes to spoken phonemes". In terms of our working model (Fig. 6.1) the patient's symptoms are neatly explained if we assume damage to the by-pass route, which in normals can shunt the phonemic descriptions of unfamiliar words directly from the auditory analysis system to the phoneme level, from which they can be outputted. If this by-pass route is impaired in JL his only way of repeating speech will be via the input and output lexicons [as was the case for McCarthy and Warrington's (1984) patients ORF and RAN discussed earlier]. This mode will cope quite happily with familiar words but will baulk at non-words (including new scientific terms and the names of new people or places). In such situations its only strategy will be to respond to a non-word with the most similar-sounding real word—something that JL was, in fact, capable of doing.

CATEGORY-SPECIFIC ACCESS PROBLEMS

The patient described by Yamadori and Albert (1973) showed word-meaning deafness in the sense that he could repeat and spell words he failed to comprehend. He differed from other patients with word-meaning deafness, however, in that his comprehension problems were greater for some semantic categories than others. He had particular difficulty with body parts and the names of objects in the room. Thus, "when asked to point to a chair, the patient stood up, looked around the room, then sat down, spelling to himself 'C-H-A-I-R, C-H-A-I-R'. Crossing his arms on his chest, he finally said, 'I'll have to double check that word later. I don't know'." In contrast, he showed no difficulty in understanding the names of tools, utensils, or items of clothing. (We will discuss how such patients might derive the spellings of words they fail to comprehend in Chapter 7.)

This patient fails one of Kohn and Friedman's (1986) criteria for word-meaning deafness, however, because he showed a similar, though apparently milder, category-specific comprehension problem with written words. He was also anomic, which might lead one to suggest an impairment to the semantic representations themselves. His anomia, however, was *not* category-specific, extending equally across categories of words he could and could not comprehend. Tentatively, one might propose that this patient had a problem in activating semantic representations in certain domains from the auditory input lexicon, but a general, non-specific problem in activating entries in the speech output lexicon from the semantic system.

There are other reports in the literature of patients whose problems in comprehending spoken words are greater for some semantic categories than for others. Goodglass, Klein, Carey, and James (1966) reported several different dissociations between the categories of body parts, objects, actions, colours, letters, and numbers in a study of 135 mixed aphasic patients. Unfortunately, Goodglass et al. used only six items per category in their study, so it is hard to tell genuine dissociations from random noise in the data. More secure is Warrington and McCarthy's (1983) case, VER, who had particular problems comprehending the names of inanimate objects in the context of much better comprehension of food names, flowers, and animals, thus presenting an interesting contrast to Warrington and Shallice's (1984) patient, JBR, whose comprehension of living things was impaired (see Chapter 2). We know that VER's comprehension of written words was also impaired but not, unfortunately, whether it displayed any comparable category-specificity. The repetition of words that VER could not understand was reasonably good.

Warrington and McCarthy (1983) present two arguments to support their contention that VER's deficit was one of accessing intact semantic representations. First, VER's performance in a word-picture matching task was improved by allowing more time between items in the test. This is compatible with the notion of very slow accessing of semantics from the auditory input lexicon. Secondly, although VER's overall level of performance was reasonably stable from one testing session to the next, the particular items she succeeded or failed on varied considerably. That is, there was a high degree of inconsistency in her performance from one session to another. If a patient fails to comprehend a word on one occasion but comprehends it correctly on the next, there are grounds for arguing that the semantic representation of the word was present all along but was temporarily inaccessible on the first occasion (cf. Coughlan & Warrington, 1981; Warrington & Shallice, 1979). It should be noted, though, that all patients reported so far have also experienced anomic word-finding difficulties.

SEMANTIC ERRORS IN REPETITION: "DEEP DYSPHASIA"

In 1973 Marshall and Newcombe reported the existence of an acquired reading disorder which they called "deep dyslexia". We shall look at that disorder in greater detail in Chapter 8, but its most striking feature is the occurrence of semantic errors in reading aloud, for example reading the written word *thermos* as "flask", *postage* as "stamps", or *turtle* as "crocodile".

Auditory analogues of this syndrome have been reported recently, sometimes under the heading of "deep dysphasia" (Goldblum, 1979; 1981; Michel, 1979; Michel & Andreewsky, 1983; Morton, 1980b). These patients make semantic errors when they try to repeat spoken words aloud. Thus Michel and Andreewsky's patient repeated "balloon" as "kite", "red" as "yellow", and "independence" as "meaning" (N.B. these are translations from French). Semantic errors were also made in writing to dictation. It is reported that the patient was sometimes uncertain in his responding but on other occasions was convinced he had just repeated the target word correctly.

Clearly a number of things could be going on here. Spoken words might be activating the correct semantic representations which are then misnamed or, alternatively, the spoken words may only be activating approximate conceptual areas from which the patient chooses a likely word. This latter alternative more easily explains why, when the patient was asked to write "brain", he wrote *"heart, liver, lungs . . ."*, making it clear by mime, gesture and three dots after the written words that he was not sure of his answer. When asked to point to the correct body part he could only make a vague movement with his hand over his body. The patient did not make semantic errors when reading aloud or writing the names of pictures. If the above suggestion of faulty access to semantics from the auditory input lexicon is correct, then this last observation suggests separate access routes to semantics for written words and pictures.

The patient's oral repetition showed other features that are also reminiscent of a deep dyslexic's reading. He was better at repeating concrete nouns like "tree" or "pencil" than more abstract nouns like "union" or "hazard". He was poor at repeating grammatical function words like "neither" and "just", and apt too to omit or change inflections like the -*er* on "gardener" or the -*ing* on "writing". In addition, he was quite unable to repeat simple non-words, suggesting that, like the auditory phonological agnosic patient discussed earlier, he has lost the use of the non-lexical by-pass route. It may be that loss of a non-lexical route is a necessary condition for the occurrence of semantic errors in repetition, for if the route were present it should be capable of completely taking over the repetition function in a patient in whom the route via semantics is impaired.

The patient reported by Metz-Lutz and Dahl (1984) as a case of "pure word deafness" also made semantic errors in repetition and was poor at non-word repetition. This patient could identify non-verbal sounds correctly, identify melodies, tell whether a sentence was spoken in her native French or in a foreign tongue, and could distinguish statements, questions, commands, and negative sentences on the basis of intonation. Further proof of intact auditory and phonetic processing up to and including the auditory input lexicon is provided by her intact ability to distinguish spoken words from non-words. A likely account of "deep dysphasia", at least for some of these cases, is in terms of impaired access to detailed semantics from the auditory input lexicon combined with an impaired non-lexical, auditory-phonological by-pass route, and also perhaps a syntactic impairment (to account for the difficulty with function words and inflections). If a direct route exists between the auditory input lexicon and the speech output lexicon, then that route must also be impaired in patients who make semantic errors in repeating heard words.

OVERVIEW

If you are engaged in ordinary conversational interaction with someone, then the two most important sources of information are the person's voice and face. The voice conveys several different sorts of information including affective information regarding the speaker's emotional state, identity information regarding *who* is speaking, and verbal or phonetic information regarding the sounds and words being spoken. The same three sorts of information are also encoded in the visual information emanating from the moving face. Thus facial expressions convey affective information, the features of the face convey identity information (who the person is), and lip and other facial movements convey phonetic information about the sounds being spoken.

This chapter is concerned specifically with what might be termed phonetic voice processing (notably the recognition and comprehension of spoken words). Affective voice processing is discussed in Chapter 9, while all three aspects of face processing are reviewed in Chapter 4. This separation of modes of processing, which in normal life operate simultaneously and perhaps interactively, may seem typical of the academic penchant for endless subdivision, yet it is a separation which appears to be honoured in the brain. Each of the three modes of voice and face processing seems capable of being impaired independently of all the rest (Ellis, 1988a).

Patients with "pure word deafness" are impaired on phonetic voice processing yet, as far as one can glean from the case reports, can still identify speakers from voices and can still extract affective information. More convincingly, there is a condition known as "phonagnosia", in which patients are impaired at recognising individual voices while still being able to recognise the words they are saying (Van Lancker & Canter, 1982; Van Lancker, Cummings, Kreiman, & Dobkin, 1988), and another condition (to be discussed in Chapter 9) in which patients can again comprehend the verbal content of speech normally but can no longer deduce the speaker's affective state from the tone of voice. Interestingly, these last two disorders follow right hemisphere injury, whereas pure word deafness requires left hemisphere injury. The dissociations between impairments in the processing of facial identity, facial affect, and facial speech information were discussed in Chapter 4.

Therefore, as you sit conversing with an acquaintance at least six separate sets of cognitive modules are actively engaged in processing the six sorts of information just described. We say six *sets* because we know that phonetic voice processing at least requires a number of modules (Fig. 6.1) and that damage to these different speech modules results in different patterns of symptoms. In this chapter, we have discussed those patterns using a limited set of "syndrome"-type categories like "pure word deafness" and "deep dysphasia", but we suspect this is because disorders of auditory word recognition are as yet underinvestigated. We are confident that as more patients are studied in depth, these categories will first stretch and then disintegrate, leaving us to relate individual patients to theoretical models in the way we must now do for disorders of reading (see Chapter 8).

SUMMARY

Disorders of spoken word recognition dissociate from disorders of visual word recognition (Chapter 8), spoken word production (Chapter 5), lip reading (Chapter 4), voice recognition, and the processing of emotional tone-of-voice (Chapter 9). In fact, the evidence suggests that these disorders are all capable of dissociating one from another, implying the existence of separate cognitive subsystems or modules for each of these types of language processing.

Even disorders of spoken word recognition take different forms. In "pure word deafness" the patient can still read, write and speak well, and can hear and recognise non-speech sounds. Vowel perception is better than the perception of spoken consonants, suggesting an impairment of a (left hemisphere) phonetic system capable of the very fine temporal discriminations that consonant perception demands. Slowing speech down may aid comprehension by bringing the required rate of temporal discriminations within the range of the less specialised right hemisphere auditory analysis system. Patients with "pure word deafness" utilise lip movement cues to assist comprehension, and also make use of the content or topic of the conversation to facilitate word recognition.

Patients with "pure word deafness" cannot repeat spoken words any better than they can understand them. Patients with "word meaning deafness", in contrast, can repeat spoken words they still fail to understand. The patient may even be able to write the word he or she cannot comprehend, then recognise it by reading what has just been written (reading remains intact). The symptoms in these cases suggest a complete or partial disconnection of the auditory input lexicon which recognises heard words from the semantic system which comprehends them.

One case has been reported of a patient with "auditory phonological agnosia" who could understand and repeat spoken words but could not repeat invented non-words. This is interpretable as a disorder affecting a link between auditory analysis and an output phoneme level, a link whose normal purpose is to allow a child or adult to repeat a word he or she has never heard before. Separate impairments of lexical and sublexical routes for repetition are reported by McCarthy and Warrington (1984).

Whereas the comprehension problems of patients with "word meaning deafness" appear to affect all words equally, some patients have been reported with comprehension difficulties that are greater for some semantic categories than others. These may be semantic access disorders rather than impairments of the semantic representations themselves. Impairments in or around the semantic system are also implicated in so-called "deep dysphasia", where patients make semantic errors repeating spoken words.

FURTHER READING

Caplan, D. (1992). *Language: structure, processing and disorders*. Cambridge, Mass.: MIT Press. Chapter 2 reviews normal and impaired auditory word comprehension.

Ellis, A.W. (1984). Bramwell's (1897) case of word meaning deafness. *Cognitive Neuropsychology, 1*, 245–258. Reproduction of Bramwell's original case with an introduction discussing its relevance to current issues.

Franklin, S. (1989). Dissociations in auditory word comprehension: evidence from nine fluent aphasics. *Aphasiology, 3*, 189–207. Analysis of the different patterns of auditory comprehension disorder shown by a group of six patients.

Harley, T.A. (1995). *The psychology of language*. Hove, UK: Erlbaum (UK) Taylor & Francis. Chapter 2 provides a useful overview of models of normal auditory word recognition.

Howard, D. & Franklin, S. (1988). *Missing the meaning?* Cambridge, Mass.: MIT Press. Incredibly detailed and painstaking investigation of the auditory comprehension (and other) deficits of a single patient, MK.

McCarthy, R.A. & Warrington, E.K. (1990). *Cognitive neuropsychology: a clinical introduction*. San Diego: Academic Press. Chapter 6 reviews auditory word comprehension.

Schacter, D.L., McGlynn, S.M., Millberg, W.P., & Church, B.A. (1993). Spared priming despite impaired comprehension: Implicit memory in a case of word–meaning deafness. *Neuropsychology, 7*, 107–118. Applies the concepts of implicit processing to word meaning deafness.

7 Spelling and Writing

INTRODUCTION

Even the most prolific authors speak more than they write, and for the bulk of the population writing is far and away the least used of their language skills. To be aphasic is to labour under an enormous disadvantage in daily life, and even a specific reading problem can be a considerable handicap, but a specific writing difficulty is generally perceived by the patient as much less of a problem. Perhaps because of the marginal nature of writing as a linguistic skill it has, until recently, received very little attention from neuropsychologists (or, for that matter, from psycholinguists and cognitive psychologists).

In so far as traditional neuropsychologists seem to have thought about writing as a skill, they appear all to have believed it to be closely parasitic upon speech. Neuropsychologists have commonly proposed that in order to write a word you must first say it to yourself, then translate that internal string of sounds into a string of letters, and then write those letters (e.g. Déjerine, 1914; Luria, 1970). Luria (1970, pp. 323–324) expressed this view very clearly when he wrote that:

> Psychologically, the writing process involves several steps. The flow of speech is broken down into individual sounds. The phonemic significance of these sounds is identified and the phonemes represented by letters. Finally, the individual letters are integrated to produce the written word.

This view of writing may be termed a "phonic mediation theory", in that spelling is presumed to be mediated by the phonic (sound) forms of words. Recent advances in cognitive neuropsychology have, however, rendered this theory untenable. First, patients have been reported who can still spell words whose spoken forms they seem quite unable to retrieve from memory (e.g. Bub & Kertesz, 1982a; Caramazza, Berndt, & Basili, 1983; Ellis, Miller, & Sin, 1983; Levine, Calvanio, & Popovics, 1982). Secondly, Shallice (1981) has provided a detailed case study of a "phonological" dysgraphic patient who could no longer generate spellings from sounds but could still spell many familiar words.

SPELLING WITHOUT SOUND

Patient EB (Levine, Calvanio, & Popovics, 1982)

Patient EB reported by Levine, Calvanio, and Popovics (1982) was a 54-year-old engineer who was rendered totally speechless by a stroke. He made strong efforts to talk but "could only produce a few undifferentiated sounds after a great delay". His speech comprehension and reading comprehension by contrast are both described as "excellent but slow". Not only was EB mute, he also appeared to have no "inner speech"; that is, no capacity to generate the spoken forms of words internally.

This lack of inner speech showed itself when EB was given a target picture of an object and then asked to point to the picture in a further set of four whose name rhymed with the target. In an attempt to do this task EB would generate to himself the spellings of all the picture names to see if one had the same final letters as the target word. Thus if the target was a picture of a BEE and one of the set of four pictures to choose among was a TREE, EB could match the two successfully. He failed, however, if the rhyming pair were not spelled alike. Thus he failed to match the pictures BEAR and CHAIR, ROPE and SOAP, or KITE and LIGHT. Rhyme matching was equally impaired for visually dissimilar written word-forms: In such instances EB was "puzzled and insisted he could find no rhyme". He was also unable to match spoken and written non-words.

EB's ability to generate the written names of pictures to himself already implies that his writing was less impaired than his speech. In fact his writing is described as "highly successful", with only a mild and variable agrammatism. He wrote correctly the names of objects, actions, shapes, and colours, though he had an occasional difficulty on one naming test, writing STRING YARD BED for *hammock*, MOOSE RACK for *antlers*, and FIND WAY IN/OUT PUZZLE for a *maze*. Otherwise EB's spelling of real words was excellent and he was able to write extensive passages without assistance. The following is an extract from his attempt to write down his earliest memories after his stroke:

Gradually after what seemed days and days, got back enough strength to pull myself up and sit if I held on. I tilted off to the right and had a hard time maintaining my balance. The nurse and doctor and an orderly helped me up then... I got to another part of the hospital where there were two doctors asking me questions I couldn't answer. I was scared. Nobody would tell me what happened to me.

It must be remembered that EB could have *said* none of this—his speech was reduced to inarticulate sounds. Further, Levine and his colleagues were unable to uncover evidence that EB had *any* internal access to the sounds of the words he could write. There seems no way that his writing could have been based on inner speech and the assembling of spellings from sounds in the manner long advocated by neuropsychologists.

Patient MH (Bub & Kertesz, 1982a)

We have encountered Bub and Kertesz's (1982a) patient MH in Chapter 5 as a well-described case of anomia. MH's speech was fluent but typically anomic, being circumlocutory and virtually devoid of content words. She could name hardly any pictures of objects and was unable to select out pairs of objects having names that rhymed, appearing to have no inner knowledge of the sounds of these words. Despite this she could *write* the names of objects correctly. Thus in one test, although she could only name one of a set of 20 pictures, she wrote 15 of the names correctly. When she made a spelling error, whether in picture naming or writing to dictation, she did not produce the sort of "phonic" misspelling one would expect from someone who was assembling spellings on the basis of the sounds of words. When her errors were real words they were either morphologically related to the target word (e.g. ACQUIRE for *acquisition*; TESTIMONIAL for *testimony*) or were visually similar (e.g. ABYSS for *abase*; COMPREHENSION for *apprehension*). Other errors were incorrect attempts at words which show substantial knowledge of unpredictable aspects of the target's spelling (e.g. ORCHATRIA for *orchestra*; ARCHETACT for *architect*). Finally, particularly with low-frequency words like *philosophy* or *effusive*, MH was sometimes unable to offer any sort of attempt at the spelling.   Another relevant observation is that although MH could repeat non-words like "brod" or "rosk" reasonably well she was extremely poor at generating appropriate spellings for them. Now, non-words are just possible words one has never met before, and asking someone to spell dictated non-words provides a fairly pure test of that person's ability to spell the way traditional neuropsychologists (and others) thought we spell all words; that is by breaking them down into their component sounds, accessing the appropriate letter or letters for each sound, and assembling the resulting letter string into spelling. MH's inability to do this simple test suggests that the correct spellings of many real words she was able to produce were again not generated by the process of phonic mediation. The non-phonic nature of her spelling errors lends further weight to this claim.

Patients JS (Caramazza, Berndt, & Basili, 1983) and RD (Ellis, Miller, & Sin, 1983)

The previous patient, MH, was anomic, and simply blocked at words she was unable to say. Patients JS and RD were, in contrast, neologistic jargonaphasics, which means that their speech was full of distorted, incorrect attempts at words. In Chapter 5 it was argued that these patients had a deficit affecting their speech output lexicons which left them able to retrieve only partial phonemic information about many words in their vocabularies. They were obliged, then, to generate attempts at the pronunciations of words based on that partial information. Of more direct relevance to present concerns is the fact that both JS and RD were frequently able to spell correctly words they could not say correctly. For instance, when RD was asked to say and then write the names of a set of pictures, he called a penguin a "senstenz" but then immediately wrote its name correctly. Similarly, he called an elephant an "enelust... kenelton" and a screwdriver a "kistro", but wrote both names perfectly (Ellis et al., 1983).

If writing were based on inner pronunciation, then the spellings of patients like RD and JS would surely reproduce their mispronunciations, yet they do not. In fact, when these patients did make misspellings they resembled some of MH's errors in appearing to be based on substantial but incomplete information about the word's spelling. Examples from JS (Caramazza et al., 1983, table 11) include *octopus* misspelled as OPUSPUS, *harp* as HARB... HARF, and *antlers* as ARRTAL: Examples from RD (Ellis et al., 1983, table 9) include *zebra* as ZEBARE, *candle* as CALDLE, and *giraffe* as GARFARA. (N.B. These errors were *not* transcriptions by the patients of their neologistic mispronunciations).

The fact that JS and RD could spell many words they mispronounced provides further evidence against an obligatory phonic mediation theory of spelling. The converging neuropsychological analyses of EB, MH, JS, and RD are important, and we shall be returning to these patients shortly to draw further conclusions about human spelling processes, but each of these case studies was predated by the first neuropsychological case study to cast serious doubt on phonic mediation theories of spelling, namely Shallice's (1981b) description of a case of "phonological" dysgraphia in his patient PR.

"Phonological" Dysgraphia

Patient PR, described by Shallice (1981b), is particularly interesting because his dysgraphia might easily have passed unnoticed and even undetected had not its theoretical significance been appreciated. PR had been a computer salesman before suffering a left hemisphere stroke in his mid-50's. Initially he had the speech disturbance of a "conduction" aphasic (good comprehension, poor repetition, spontaneous speech replete with phonemic errors), but by the time his writing was tested he is described as having quite normal speech comprehension combined with fluent speech production with good word choice and only occasional paraphasic errors.

PR's reading is described as rapid and effortless and he performed at quite high levels on several reading tests. His spontaneous writing is said to have been laboured and slow because of slight motor problems and difficulties of formulation. Nevertheless, he was able to write correctly over 90% of a set of common words dictated to him. He found abstract and less common words more difficult, but even here he was writing 80% or more correctly. PR's errors were predominantly morphological (e.g. "navigation" written as NAVIGATOR; "defect" as DEFECTION) or structurally similar real words which often sounded like the target word (e.g. "custom" misspelled as CUSTARD; "plum" as THUMB; "quart" as CAUGHT).

Although PR made some spelling errors, his writing of most real words (with the exception of function words, which he found difficult) was good. This stood in marked contrast to his extremely poor writing of invented non-words. PR was able to create appropriate spellings for only 2 of 10 four-letter non-words like "spid", and none of 10 six-letter non-words like "felute". Indeed, although he could write individual letters to dictation when given their names (e.g. K for "kay"; H for "aitch") he could not write letters when given their sounds (e.g. K for "kuh"; H for "huh"). Now a failure to write non-words could obviously be due to a failure to perceive them, or perhaps an inability to say them. Neither of these explanations is applicable to PR who could repeat non-words aloud (and therefore could both hear and say them), and was even reasonably good at reading them aloud. When PR *did* manage to write a non-word correctly he often commented that he had used a real word as a mediator; for example he spelled "sim" as SYM via *symbol* and "jund" as JUND via *junta* and *junk*. This strategy sometimes led to errors as when, in his attempt to write "sult" via *assault* he wrote AULT, and when he wrote GN for "na" via *gnat*. That noted, it is PR's good spelling of real words in the context of his virtual inability to spell simple non-words that is crucial to the current argument.

THE GRAPHEMIC OUTPUT LEXICON

None of the patients EB, MH, JS, RD, and PR can have been assembling spellings piecemeal from sound, yet all showed considerably preserved writing ability. Their spellings must, therefore, have been produced by some process other than assembly from sound. It would appear that these patients retrieved (or attempted to retrieve) the spellings of familiar words from some internal long-term memory store whose function in writing is equivalent to that of the speech output lexicon held responsible in Chapter 5 for the retrieval of spoken word-forms in spontaneous speech. We shall refer to this proposed store of word spellings as the *graphemic output lexicon*; alternative names in the literature for the same concept are the graphic or graphemic output logogen system (Ellis, 1982; Morton, 1980a), the orthographic lexicon (Allport & Funnell, 1981; Allport, 1983), and the graphemic word production system (Ellis, 1984b).

The idea being proposed is that each time you learn the spelling of a new word, an entry for that spelling is stored in a discrete portion of your memory that we are calling the graphemic output lexicon. Every time you write that word subsequently, that representation in the graphemic output lexicon will be activated and will make the spelling available to you. The spelling need no longer be assembled from the sound of the word. Having postulated this system we can now begin to ask further questions about it, some of which we will be able to answer by reference to findings in cognitive neuropsychology. Such questions include: How is spelling information represented in the graphemic output lexicon? Is retrieval from that lexicon all-or-nothing, or can one sometimes have partial information available about a word's spelling? Is the graphemic output lexicon a distinct and separate word store from the speech output lexicon? What sort of input or inputs activate entries in the graphemic output lexicon? We shall take these questions one at a time.

The Representation of Information in the Graphemic Output Lexicon

We can imagine a possible system which represents the spellings of words in terms of, say, the sequence of muscular movements necessary to write the word. There are, however, fairly straightforward reasons for rejecting this as a model of the human graphemic output lexicon. The reason is the number of different ways we can "produce" a spelling. Within the handwriting mode, one can print a word in capitals, print it in lower case letters, or write it in cursive (connected) handwriting. Each of these styles has its own letter forms, for example F, f, and *f*, or B, b, and *b*, yet to know how to spell a word is to be able to spell it in any of these styles. Further, if you can spell a word you can also spell it aloud and perhaps type it too. Whatever is represented in and retrieved from the graphemic output lexicon is presumably some abstract "graphemic" description of a letter sequence which can then be outputted in each of these different ways (Ellis, 1982).

Neuropsychological support can be found for the proposal that what is retrieved from the graphemic output lexicon is an abstract graphemic code rather than, say, a motor program for letter execution. Rosati and de Bastiani (1979) reported the case of a 62-year-old, Italian farmer and ex-telegraphist with intact speech production, speech comprehension and reading, whose stroke resulted in a fairly pure agraphic disturbance. He could spell words aloud without error (de Bastiani, personal communication), but his attempts to write words were replete with omissions, repetitions and transpositions of letters and letter strokes. This patient's intact spelling aloud attests to his preserved ability to retrieve spellings from his graphemic output lexicon; his deficit must have lain in the selection, sequencing and execution of letter forms for handwriting. Other cases of "pure dysgraphia" with relatively isolated writing problems will be discussed later.

Retrieval from the Graphemic Output Lexicon

Patients JS (Caramazza et al., 1983) and RD (Ellis et al., 1983) were mentioned earlier as cases whose written naming was better than their spoken naming. They could write correctly many words which they mispronounced as neologisms when trying to say them. Nevertheless, spelling was not perfectly preserved in either case: Both produced errors which were interpreted earlier as being based on partial but incomplete knowledge of the correct spellings of words. For example, when RD was shown a picture of a pair of scissors he wrote SICESSE. This error is typical, firstly in that it was not a transcription of his neologistic attempt to say the word, and secondly because it demonstrates substantial knowledge of the idiosyncratic spelling of the word *scissors*. There has been a *c* in the English spelling of *scissors* only since it was put there by spelling "reformers" in the sixteenth century. Those men thought *scissors* was a descendent of the Latin word *scindere* (meaning to cleave) and, therefore, inserted a *c* in the spelling where no *c* had been before. As it happens, they were wrong—scissors is actually descended from the Latin *cædere* (to cut)—but the *c*, which is totally unpredictable from the pronunciation and has to be something you just have to know about the word, has stuck. And RD knew it should be there, just as JS knew that the second sound in *pyramid* is spelled with a *y* though he misspelled the word PYMINIA... PYMINAL... PYAMIAL. Errors demonstrating such "partial lexical knowledge" (Ellis, 1982) are quite common, and seem not to be tied to any particular form of aphasia or dysgraphia.

The Distinctness of the Graphemic Output Lexicon and the Speech Output Lexicon

One can envisage a possible model of word production in which the written and spoken forms of words are two outputs from a single internal word store or lexicon. We would seem, however, to have good neuropsychological grounds for rejecting this notion in favour of a model in which the word store for spoken forms (our speech output lexicon) and the word store for written forms (our graphemic output lexicon) are conceived of as separate and discrete lexicons. In Chapter 5 we followed Saffran (1982), Allport (1983), and others in interpreting certain anomic word-finding problems in speech production as due to a partial disconnection of the speech output lexicon from the semantic system. Now, if retrieving word-forms for speech and writing were but two aspects of the same system in operation, then a patient who experiences word-finding problems in speech should experience similar problems in spelling. We have already seen, however, that this is not always the case. Bub and Kertesz's (1982a) patient MH and Hier and Mohr's (1977) patient AF were severely anomic in speech but had much less severe problems of word finding for writing. This is not possible under a single output lexicon model, but is readily accounted for if the speech and graphemic output lexicons are separate word stores which can be impaired separately and disconnected both from each other and from the other components of the language system.

A further argument for the separability of the two word production systems can be derived from cases JS and RD (Caramazza et al., 1983; Ellis et al., 1983). In the previous section we interpreted their spelling errors as due to their ability on some occasions to retrieve only partial information from their graphemic output lexicons. The phonological errors in the speech of these two patients are susceptible to a similar interpretation—this time as attempts at spoken targets based on partial phonemic information. Now, if there were only one word production system, an impairment affecting it should hamper both speech and writing equally. Speech and writing *were* both affected in JS and RD, but speech more so than writing, and the neologistic errors made in speech were different from those made in writing. One could try to explain this particular pattern on a single output lexicon model were it not for the fact that JS and RD seem to be unusual in having better preserved writing than spelling. The normal pattern among such patients is for spelling to be more severely impaired than speech (Kertesz, 1979). Thus, when contrasted with the more usual pattern, JS and RD provide a "double dissociation" between impairments affecting the speech and graphemic output lexicons, which in turn implies that the two systems are separate components of the total language system. The question of whether we are right to propose distinct lexicons for input and output will be dealt with more fully in Chapter 8.

The Nature of the Input to the Graphemic Word Production System

Each entry in the graphemic output lexicon corresponds to the spelling of a familiar word. The question under consideration here is how are those entries accessed? What inputs from what other systems serve to activate them? One possibility is that they receive their activation from the corresponding units in the speech output lexicon. That is, in writing, we might first activate the semantic representation of a word, then activate its representation in the speech output lexicon, then transmit that activation through one-to-one connections between corresponding representations in the two output lexicons to the graphemic output lexicon. This proposal is an attractive one for at least three reasons. First, when writing we are usually aware of an "inner voice" saying the words as we write them. Thus, we do seem habitually to activate the spoken forms of words as we are activating their graphemic forms. Secondly, a form of involuntary slip of the pen, which most people will be aware of having made from time to time, is unintentionally writing a word which has the same sound, or a similar sound, to the desired target word. Examples from Hotopf (1980) include SCENE written unwittingly when the intended target word was *seen*, THEIR written for *there*, SOUGHT for *sort*, SURGE for *search*, and COULD for *good*. These slips are explicable if the sounds of words play a part in selecting their spellings from the graphemic output lexicon. Note that these slips are *not* due to spellings being incorrectly assembled from sounds, because the errors are always real words, whereas assembling spellings would often yield non-words such as SURCH for *search* (as happens in genuine spelling errors as opposed to slips of the pen), and also because the errors produced are sometimes themselves irregular spellings which would not be generated by phoneme–grapheme (sound-to-letter) conversion procedures (words like COULD and SCENE).

A third reason for believing that the sound of a word plays some part in retrieving spellings from the graphemic output lexicon is that some acquired dysgraphic patients produce among their errors real words which are similar in sound to the targets. Like the normal slips of the pen, these are sometimes themselves irregular spellings (which argues against their having been assembled from the sound of the target words) and, in the case of Shallice's (1981b) phonological dysgraphic patient PR, occurred in the context of an almost complete inability to assemble spellings from sounds. Examples of such errors from PR's writing to dictation include "plum" misspelled as THUMB, "chore" as SHORE, and "quart" as CAUGHT.

Thus there is good evidence for some involvement of the sound patterns of words in retrieving spellings from the graphemic output lexicon (cf. Morton, 1980a), but there are also grounds for doubting that phonology is the *only* source of input to that system. MH (Bub & Kertesz, 1982a) is once again relevant here. She could write correctly words whose sound forms she did know, which argues for a mode of retrieval from the graphemic word production system which does not depend exclusively upon activating phonemic forms in the speech output lexicon.

A similar conclusion is indicated from the pattern of symptoms found in another patient reported by Bub and Kertesz (1982b). The patient in question manifested the symptoms of an acquired dysgraphia sometimes called "deep" dysgraphia, which we shall now consider.

Semantic Errors in Writing: The Case of "Deep Dysgraphia"

In Chapter 5 we looked briefly at a condition sometimes called "deep dysphasia" in which patients make semantic errors when attempting to repeat heard words. "Deep dyslexia", where semantic errors are made in reading aloud, will be discussed in the next chapter. Some "deep dyslexics" have been reported to make semantic errors when trying to write words to dictation. For example, when Newcombe and Marshall's (1980a) patient GR was asked to write "star" he wrote *MOON*. Eleven out of 31 errors obtained in a writing-to-dictation task were either straightforward semantic errors of this sort or misspelled semantic errors [e.g. "cousin" spelt as NEPHIL (= nephew), or "parrot" as CANISTY (= canary)]. Saffran, Schwartz, and Marin (1976b) report two patients who made errors such as writing TIME for "hours" or ORCHID for "lilac", and Peuser (1978) describes similar errors as being produced by a German patient, but the most complete description of "deep dysgraphia" to date is that provided by Bub and Kertesz (1982b) for their patient JC.

JC was a 21-year-old woman who had suffered a left hemisphere stroke. Her speech was the halting, telegraphic speech of a Broca's aphasic. Her comprehension of single spoken words and yes/no questions was good, though she had problems with longer and more complex sentences (presumably the syntactic deficit characteristic of at least some "Broca's" aphasics—see Chapter 9). What is of greatest current concern, however, is JC's writing. When asked to write to dictation 20 concrete and 20 abstract nouns of roughly equal length and frequency of usage in English, she correctly wrote 17 out of 20 concrete nouns but only 9 out of 20 abstract nouns. Whether a word was regularly or irregularly spelled appeared not to influence JC's performance, but she was fairly poor at writing function words (only 6/20 correct despite the fact noted elsewhere that they are far and away the most common words in the language).

Many of JC's writing errors were semantic errors. For example she wrote "time" as CLOCK, "sky" as SUN, "desk" as CHAIR, but "chair" as TABLE! Her errors with function words were either omissions (i.e. "don't knows") or substitutions of other function words; for example "our" written as MY, and "they" as THEIR. JC was also very poor at writing non-words to dictation, managing only 5 out of 20 four-letter non-words and 0 out of 17 eight-letter non-words.

There are two other noteworthy aspects of JC's "deep" dysgraphia. The first is that unlike, say, Newcombe and Marshall's (1980a) patient GR, it was not accompanied by a deep dyslexia. JC did not make semantic errors when reading aloud; in fact her reading and understanding of single words was very good. Even her non-word reading was far better than her non-word spelling, though she had something of a tendency to read non-words as words, for example reading *dosh* as "gosh", and *cred* as "shred".

The second noteworthy aspect is that JC's deep dysgraphic symptoms had entirely disappeared 6 months after her stroke, when she no longer made semantic writing errors, was as good at spelling abstract nouns as concrete nouns, and even spelled non-words quite well. As Bub and Kertesz (1982b) note, this fact rules out any explanation of her earlier difficulties as due to any developmental difficulties existing in JC before her stroke. It also implies that her symptoms should be explained as having been due to processes becoming temporarily inaccessible or inefficient rather than being totally abolished.

How does JC's pattern of symptoms relate to our question concerning the nature of the inputs to the graphemic output lexicon? We have already argued for one input from the speech output lexicon, and could persist with that if we could provide a satisfactory account of JC's symptoms on such a model. This would necessitate proposing that JC's semantic errors are errors of spoken word retrieval which are then translated into semantic writing errors. There is, however, no evidence that JC was prone to making semantic errors in selecting words for speech. She did not make semantic errors in reading aloud, repeating heard words, or naming objects. Bub and Kertesz (1982b), like Morton (1980a) and Ellis (1982) propose that there is a second direct input from the semantic system to the graphemic output lexicon. It is presumably some impairment to this connection in JC that accounts for her semantic errors in writing and also for the superiority of concrete over abstract words in writing that was not shown in reading or repetition.

JC would appear, therefore, to provide cognitive neuropsychological evidence for a second, semantic input to the graphemic output lexicon. Ellis (1982; 1984b) suggests that occasional errors of this route in normals may be responsible for the small number of semantic slips of the pen (e.g. involuntarily writing SPEAKING for *reading* or LAST WEEK for *next week*) that have been reported by Ellis (1979b) and Hotopf (1987; 1983). Presumably, however, the fact that the desired entry in the graphemic output lexicon is specified from *two* sources, one from the semantic system and one from the speech output lexicon, helps reduce any intrinsic liability to error in the system.

A MODEL FOR SPELLING

What emerges from the foregoing discussion is a theory of writing which can be expressed diagrammatically as in Fig. 7.1. Much of the model (the upper, central, and lower-left portions) is a simple redrawing of the model for auditory word recognition and speech production that we developed in Chapters 5 and 6 (see Fig. 6.1, p. 145). The new elements, added to that model to incorporate a writing facility, are the graphemic output lexicon, the grapheme level, phoneme–grapheme conversion, plus their connections one to another and to the other components of the total system.

To summarise and recapitulate briefly, the auditory analysis system and the auditory input lexicon mediate the recognition of heard words and activate their meanings in the semantic system. To say a word, its entry in the semantic system is used to retrieve its pronunciation (phonemic form) from the speech output lexicon. To write a familiar word whose spelling is known, the entry for that word in the graphemic output lexicon is activated. This activation comes from the semantic system and also from the speech output lexicon. Semantic writing errors are errors in activation from the semantic system; similar-sound errors are errors in activation from the speech output lexicon. What is released from the graphemic output lexicon is a string of graphemes; that is, an abstract description of the letter sequence which can be output as print, handwriting, typing, oral spelling, or whatever.

We must not forget that skilled writers *can* assemble plausible attempts at the spellings of unfamiliar words using procedures for translating spoken (phonemic) forms into letter strings. We have argued that this mode of spelling is not, as some have proposed, the sole strategy for spelling any word, but there is no doubt that it exists as an optional strategy for creating spellings of words not stored in the graphemic output lexicon. We have represented this strategy as being mediated by phoneme–grapheme conversion processes linking the phoneme level to the grapheme

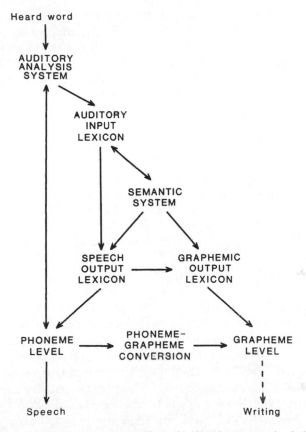

FIG. 7.1. Simple functional model for spelling, showing the proposed relations between auditory word recognition, speech production, and spelling.

level. In practice this single box must encompass a number of processes. To assemble a spelling the spoken form of a word must first be broken down into its phonemes (sounds). Each phoneme must then be replaced by the appropriate letter or letters, and the resultant letter string must be stored as it is being created. With a regular word there is a reasonable chance that the assembled attempt will be correct, but the vagaries of English spelling are such that many words are likely to be misspelled this way (Hatfield & Patterson, 1983). The resultant misspellings, diagnostic of the involvement of phoneme–grapheme conversion, will be misspellings which, when pronounced, sound like the target word (e.g. CASSEL for *castle*, or TAYBUL for *table*). Such misspellings are, of course, common in children who have yet to build up a large stock of entries in their graphemic output lexicons and so must resort to assembled spelling more often than a more practiced adult (Ellis, 1984b).

How does our model account for the patients we have already encountered in this chapter? Levine, et al.'s (1982) patient EB, who showed preserved writing in the context of completely abolished overt and inner speech, had presumably lost the use of his speech output lexicon and phoneme level but retained the use of the remaining language components including those used in writing familiar words.

Patient MH of Bub and Kertesz (1982a) was anomic in speech, indicating an impairment in activating entries in the speech output lexicon from the semantic system (cf. Chapter 5, pp. 116–124). She was less anomic in writing, implying less difficulty activating entries in the graphemic output lexicon. Some of MH's errors involved "partial lexical knowledge", where only part of the spelling can be retrieved from the graphemic output lexicon (e.g. writing ORCHATRIA for "orchestra"). MH was also unable to assemble spellings for non-words she could repeat correctly, implying impairment to the phoneme–grapheme conversion component.

Shallice's (1981b) "phonological" dysgraphic patient PR who could spell many real words correctly but very few non-words is also assumed to have suffered impairment to the phoneme–grapheme conversion system. Like "phonological" dysgraphics, "deep" dysgraphics have virtually inoperative phoneme–grapheme conversion and must rely entirely on whole-word retrieval from the graphemic output lexicon system. Indeed, two of the four "phonological" dysgraphics reported by Roeltgen, Sevush, and Heilman (1983) made some semantic errors, so it is not clear where the dividing line between these two putative "syndromes" should be drawn. As elsewhere, we shall interpret and draw conclusions from single patients rather than from "syndrome" categories of uncertain status.

We have argued earlier that an impairment to the route between the semantic system and the graphemic output lexicon must be present for semantic writing errors to occur in any numbers. It is also at least arguable that an impairment to phoneme–grapheme conversion is a necessary condition for the occurrence of semantic errors. For instance, it is hard to imagine that JC would have written CLOCK for "time" or CHAIR for "desk" if intact phoneme–grapheme conversion procedures could have treated "time" and "desk" as non-words and at least generated *t* as the only likely initial letter for "time" and *d* as the only likely initial letter for "desk". We are not arguing that this route prevents semantic errors in normals which might otherwise occur in large numbers, only that a phoneme–grapheme impairment must be present *as well as* a semantic transmission impairment before semantic writing errors will occur.

INTACT SPELLING IN "WORD MEANING DEAFNESS"

In Chapter 6 we encountered the phenomenon of "word meaning deafness", where patients can hear and repeat spoken words but may be unable to understand the words they hear. Of relevance to this chapter is the fact that at least some of these patients may also be able to write correctly the words they fail to understand. If their reading comprehension is intact they can then read what they have just written and so understand what has just been said to them. The example we quoted in Chapter 6 occurred when Bramwell (1897) asked such a patient: "Do you like to come to Edinburgh?" The patient failed to comprehend his question but wrote it down, read it, then replied appropriately (see Ellis, 1984a).

The spelling to dictation without comprehension displayed by these patients is not assembled by phoneme–grapheme conversion, because they do not make "phonic" errors and they spell irregular words correctly (Kohn & Friedman, 1986; Patterson, 1986). The spellings of the words they write without understanding must therefore be retrieved from the graphemic output lexicon. But what is the route from auditory input to writing output that permits such retrieval while by-passing the semantic system? Patterson (1986) proposes a route from the auditory input lexicon to the graphemic output lexicon via the speech output lexicon. The suggestion is that one-to-one connections between entries in the auditory input lexicon and the speech output lexicon allow heard words directly to activate their entries in the speech output lexicon. One-to-one connections of the sort we have already discussed between corresponding entries in the speech output lexicon and the graphemic output lexicon would then allow the spellings of the heard words to be retrieved using a route which is a lexical, whole-word route but which entirely by-passes the representations of word meanings in the semantic system. Although this proposal works, Patterson (1986) admits that the evidence favouring it over alternatives such as direct connections between entries in the auditory input lexicon and the graphemic output lexicon could be stronger.

ASSEMBLING SPELLINGS FROM SOUND: "SURFACE" DYSGRAPHIA

Beauvois and Dérousné (1981) described a French patient, RG, whose writing problems are almost the precise opposite to Shallice's patient PR. Whereas PR wrote words well but non-words very poorly, RG could produce plausible spellings for non-words with ease, but also wrote real words as if they were non-words. That is, he would produce a phonologically plausible spelling for each word, but the vagaries of French spelling meant that those spellings were often incorrect. For example, RG misspelled "habile" as ABILE and HABIL, "fauteuil" as FAUTEUI and FHOTEUIL, "rameau" as RAMO, and "copeau" as COPOT. French, like English, has so few words whose spellings can be predicted with confidence from their pronunciations that the successful speller really must store the spellings of familiar words in memory, not assemble them from sound. If you are a phonological speller of French or English your attempts are much more likely to be correct for regular words than irregular words. This was certainly true of RG who spelled correctly over 90% of regular, predictably-spelled words, but less than 40% of irregular words.

Like RG, Hatfield and Patterson's (1983) patient TP became a phonological speller after a stroke. Her picture is slightly more complex than RG's but perhaps even more informative as a consequence. Because TP's spelling was predominantly phonological she was more successful at spelling regular words than irregular words and many of her spelling errors were straightforwardly "phonic" (e.g. FLUD for "flood", LAF for "laugh", ANSER for "answer", and NEFFUE for "nephew"). The complications in the picture, which show that TP was not always spelling from sound alone, were:

1. She managed to spell correctly on at least one occasion quite a few irregular words, including COUGH, SIGN, AUNT, and ANSWER. This shows that she had not entirely lost the capacity for spelling from memory. (The same probably holds true for RG.)

2. Some of TP's misspellings clearly show partial knowledge of word-specific spellings. One cannot, as TP did, misspell "sword" as SWARD without retrieving from the graphemic output lexicon the fact that *sword* contains an unpronounced *w*, just as one cannot misspell "yacht" as YHAGHT without having retrieved the fact that there is a silent *h* and that the vowel letter is *a* not, as one would expect from the pronunciation, *o*. These errors show that TP could sometimes still retrieve some information about words she could not spell entirely correctly.

3. If a word TP was asked to write was a homophone she would sometimes produce the other member of the homophonic pair as an error, even when the context made it perfectly clear which meaning was meant. Thus she misspelled "sale" as SAIL, "hale" as HAIL, and "pane" as PAIN, though on other occasions she misspelled "hail" as HALE, "pain" as PANE and "plain" as PLANE. Of importance is the fact that sometimes the homophonic misspellings were themselves irregular spellings (e.g. "moan" misspelled as MOWN, "write" as RIGHT, and "sum" as SOME). We have proposed earlier that homophone errors arise from an input to the graphemic output lexicon from the speech output lexicon.

In terms of Fig. 7.1, TP clearly has an impaired graphemic output lexicon. She can no longer access the entries for many words that were undoubtedly once within her spelling vocabulary. There are some words, however, for which she can still retrieve partial information. If a word's spelling is completely inaccessible but has an alternative homophonic spelling, TP can still sometimes access the homophone. Failing that, her last resort is to assemble a plausible attempt at the word's spelling from its sound using her intact processes of phoneme–grapheme conversion.

The pattern shown by TP and RG of many phonic errors with poor spelling of irregular words has been given several different labels by different investigators, including "surface dysgraphia" (by analogy with "surface dyslexia"—see Chapter 8), "lexical" or "orthographic dysgraphia", and "phonological spelling". As we noted in Chapter 1, all this confusing terminology, based as it is in the desire to label syndromes, can be a positive hindrance. Our concern is with explaining patterns of disorders in individual patients in terms of impairment to one or more of the components of a model of normal cognitive processing, and within the framework of that approach all the patients we have just been discussing have impairments that affect the retrieval of the spellings of once-familiar words from the graphemic output lexicon. Because phoneme–grapheme conversion remains intact they can still spell many regular words correctly, can generate misspellings which sound like the target word, and can also generate plausible spellings for invented non-words.

A close inspection of the cases reported so far who show this pattern reveals that in none of them is retrieval from the graphemic output lexicon entirely abolished. All of them remain capable of spelling correctly at least a few highly irregular words. In three cases, the irregular words which remain accessible have been shown to be the more common (high-frequency) irregular words like *talk, noise*, or *head*. The cases in question are MW and JG of Goodman and Caramazza (1986a; 1986b; 1986c; Goodman-Schulman & Caramazza, 1987), and HG of Coltheart and Funnell (1987). We saw in our discussion in Chapter 6, how in some "anomic" and "neologistic jargonaphasic" patients, the retrieval of common (high-frequency) words may be spared when a lexicon (or access to it) is impaired. The retrieval of high-frequency words, both irregular and regular, seems to be similarly spared in these dysgraphic patients when an impairment in or around the graphemic output lexicon prevents the full and correct retrieval of less commonly used (low-frequency) words.

EXTERNALISING THE GRAPHEMIC CODE

Handwriting probably remains the most common way of expressing one's knowledge of spelling, but it is certainly not the only way. Typing, spelling aloud—even Morse code or arranging plastic letters—are alternative ways of tapping spelling skill. We shall assume that the same processes are involved in retrieving the spellings of familiar words or generating plausible spellings for unfamiliar words or non-words, whichever of these alternative modes of output is to be employed. That is, we shall assume that these different modes diverge after the grapheme level.

We shall concentrate here on disorders affecting handwriting at or below the grapheme level in patients whose spelling aloud, for example, remains well preserved. We should note, though, that the alternative output modes seem subject to their own disorders. Thus, Kinsbourne and Warrington (1965) report a patient whose oral spelling was more impaired than his written spelling. Critchley (1942) even reports acquired disorders of Morse and flag signalling in brain-injured naval signalmen.

Ellis (1982) proposed that at least two stages below the grapheme level should be identified in the production of handwriting. These stages are shown in Fig. 7.2. Each letter of the alphabet can take different forms which, following linguistic terminology, we may call "allographs". F, ⅎ , f and ꝑ are all allographs of the same grapheme which may co-exist in one person's handwriting, as B, b and ♭, or S, s and Ʂ may. In Ellis' model, then, the first step towards externalising a graphemic representation as handwriting involves the selection of the desired allographic form of each letter. This creates a representation at the *allograph level*.

For Ellis (1982) the allographic representation is a quasi-spatial description of the *shape* of each letter-form. The representation at the allographic level does not yet specify the sequence of *strokes* required to create a letter-form on paper. The sequence of strokes comprising a particular allograph is what Van Galen (1980) calls its *graphic motor pattern*. The final stage in Fig. 7.2 is therefore the retrieval or assembly of graphic motor patterns which will guide the movement of the pen in forming the handwriting.

Now a model such as this, however elegant, is only of use if it helps account for aspects of normal or impaired writing performance. Ellis (1982) sought to show how such a model could help account for different types of involuntary "slip of the pen" errors made by normal writers involving misorderings, omissions, additions, or malformations of letters. Here we shall attempt to show how such a model can help explain different types of acquired dysgraphia affecting the production of handwriting. These are what may be termed "peripheral" dysgraphias, because although writing output is impaired, central spelling knowledge appears

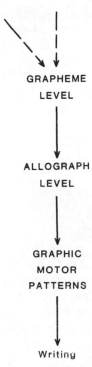

GRAPHEME
LEVEL

ALLOGRAPH
LEVEL

GRAPHIC
MOTOR
PATTERNS

Writing

FIG. 7.2. Processes "downstream" of the grapheme level required to explain the production of handwriting.

to be intact. We shall not attempt an exhaustive survey of the peripheral dysgraphias but will instead discuss selected dysgraphias which seem to affect different stages of planning from the grapheme level to actual writing.

PERIPHERAL DYSGRAPHIAS

Grapheme Level Impairment

Miceli, Silveri, and Caramazza (1985; 1987) describe the case of a 64-year-old lawyer, FV, with no detectable aphasia or dyslexia, whose writing was marred by frequent spelling errors. The errors consisted of additions, deletions, substitutions, and transpositions of letters. Spelling accuracy was unaffected by grammatical class, word frequency or imageability, but long words were less likely to be written correctly by FV than short ones. Although spelling was impaired, copying of written words was intact (even when a delay was introduced between presentation and response). Errors occurred with roughly equal probability across all word positions—initial letters were no better preserved than middle or end ones. Letters were well formed though the words were misspelled. Non-word spelling was also impaired, if anything slightly more than real word spelling, but the errors were of the same sort in both situations.

The deficit in FV must have been after the point at which the familiar word route via the graphemic output lexicon and the non-word route via phoneme–grapheme conversion come together; that is, at or below the grapheme level. Intact letter formation implies normal functioning at and below the level of graphic motor patterns. Miceli et al. (1985; 1987) locate the deficit in or around the grapheme level where abstract letter forms are stored and ordered. The complete preservation of other language skills, in particular reading, implies that the processes impaired in FV are specific to writing.

Allograph Level Impairment

Patient MW of Goodman and Caramazza (1986a; 1986b; 1986c) was mentioned in passing earlier in this chapter as one of those patients who could spell correctly high-frequency but not low-frequency irregular words. On that basis, a partial impairment affecting the retrieval of spellings from the graphemic output lexicon was suggested. However, MW's handwriting contained additional errors that were not seen in his spelling aloud. The errors in question were letter substitutions which caused him, for example, to miswrite "starve" as *starze*, "bump" as *bumd*, and "pierce" as *tierce*.

These letter substitutions also affected MW's attempts to write non-words, though not his attempts to spell them aloud. Thus, for "vand" he wrote *lond*, and for "reesh" he wrote *reech*. The errors, then, are arising at or below the level at which the mechanisms for writing familiar words and non-words converge; that is, at or below the grapheme level. The fact that letter substitutions were absent from MW's spelling aloud excludes the grapheme level as the locus of the impairment. Goodman and Caramazza (1986a; 1986b; 1986c) argue that the fact that MW's letters were correctly shaped, formed and executed also excludes the level of graphic motor patterns and conclude that "the allographic process for assigning the visual shape to a graphemic unit is impaired". So for words and non-words that MW could spell aloud correctly the grapheme level representation was intact and correct. However, that representation could no longer reliably guide the selection of letter shapes (allographs) for writing. Incorrect allographs were sometimes selected, with the result that MW substituted well-formed and well-executed but erroneous letters in the place of intended letters.

Impairment in Selecting Graphic Motor Patterns

A patient whose impairment lies at the level of assembling or retrieving graphic motor patterns should be able to spell aloud correctly, and should know the shapes of the letters required to write a word, but should not always know what sequence of pen movements will serve to create those letters on the page. A patient who seems to approximate this description has been described by Baxter and Warrington (1986). IDT's speech was fluent and his ability to spell words aloud was also normal, yet he was totally unable to write even common, three-letter words correctly. His writing errors, which extended to writing single letters of the alphabet, involved writing incorrect letters, incomplete letters, and forms which looked like fusions of two letters.

IDT's preserved spelling aloud implies an intact grapheme level, and his ability to describe the shapes of letters suggests that he could still activate letter forms at the allograph level. IDT could *copy* words and letters well and did not have more general apraxic disorders of motor planning or execution. Baxter and Warrington (1986, p. 374) conclude from this that IDT's difficulty "occurs at the level which specifies the motor sequences or 'graphic motor pattern'".

Impairment in Executing Graphic Motor Patterns: "Afferent" Dysgraphia

In the final type of "peripheral dysgraphia" we shall discuss, patients seem to get as far as knowing the sequence of movements (the graphic motor pattern) that would create the letters they wish to write, yet they have problems executing those movement sequences correctly. The peripheral dysgraphia in question is often referred to as either "spatial" dysgraphia (Hécaen & Marcie, 1974) or "afferent" dysgraphia (Lebrun, 1976; 1985). These patients usually show a tendency to write down the right-hand side of the page, difficulty maintaining a straight, horizontal writing line, and a tendency to either omit or duplicate letters and strokes in their writing. All of these features can be seen to a degree in the writing samples from patient VB of Ellis, Young, and Flude (1987b) shown in Figs 7.3 and 7.4. Figure 7.3 is a sample of her spontaneous writing done on a horizontally positioned sheet of paper. The tendency to leave a wide left margin and to write down the right-hand side of the page is clear. There is also a slight sloping of the lines, though this was not as pronounced a tendency in VB as in some other "afferent" dysgraphics.

Figure 7.4 shows the characteristic omissions and repetitions in both upper-case (capitals) and cursive handwriting. These errors tend to occur when the patient is attempting to write a sequence of similar or identical

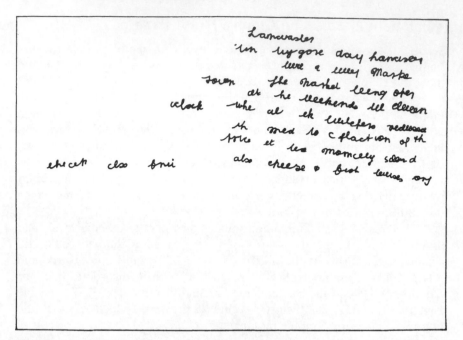

FIG. 7.3. Sample of the spontaneous handwriting of patient VB (from Ellis, Young, & Flude, 1987b).

letters or strokes. Thus doubled letters may be reduced to singles (goggles → gogles) or tripled (gallon → galllon), and strokes will be omitted or added from letters like m or w which contain repeated similar strokes.

As Lebrun (1976) and Ellis et al. (1987b) note, these omissions and repetitions of letters and strokes do not only occur in "afferent" dysgraphics like VB. They occur infrequently in the writing of normal people as involuntary "slips of the pen" (Ellis, 1979b; 1982), and their frequency can be greatly increased in normals by preventing sight of the writing hand and/or by requiring normal writers to perform an additional, secondary task such as counting or tapping with the left hand while writing (Smyth & Silvers, 1987). Ellis et al. (1987b) found that normal subjects writing without being able to see their writing hand, and simultaneously tapping with the fingers of their left hand, made as many errors in writing words to dictation as VB made under normal writing conditions. Furthermore, the normal subjects' errors were of the sort VB herself made— predominantly omissions and repetitions of letters and strokes. Examples of the errors made by the normal subjects are shown in Fig. 7.5.

Therefore, a normal subject writing while without sight of the writing hand and carrying out an additional task such as tapping or counting, effectively becomes an "afferent" dysgraphic. The difference, of course,

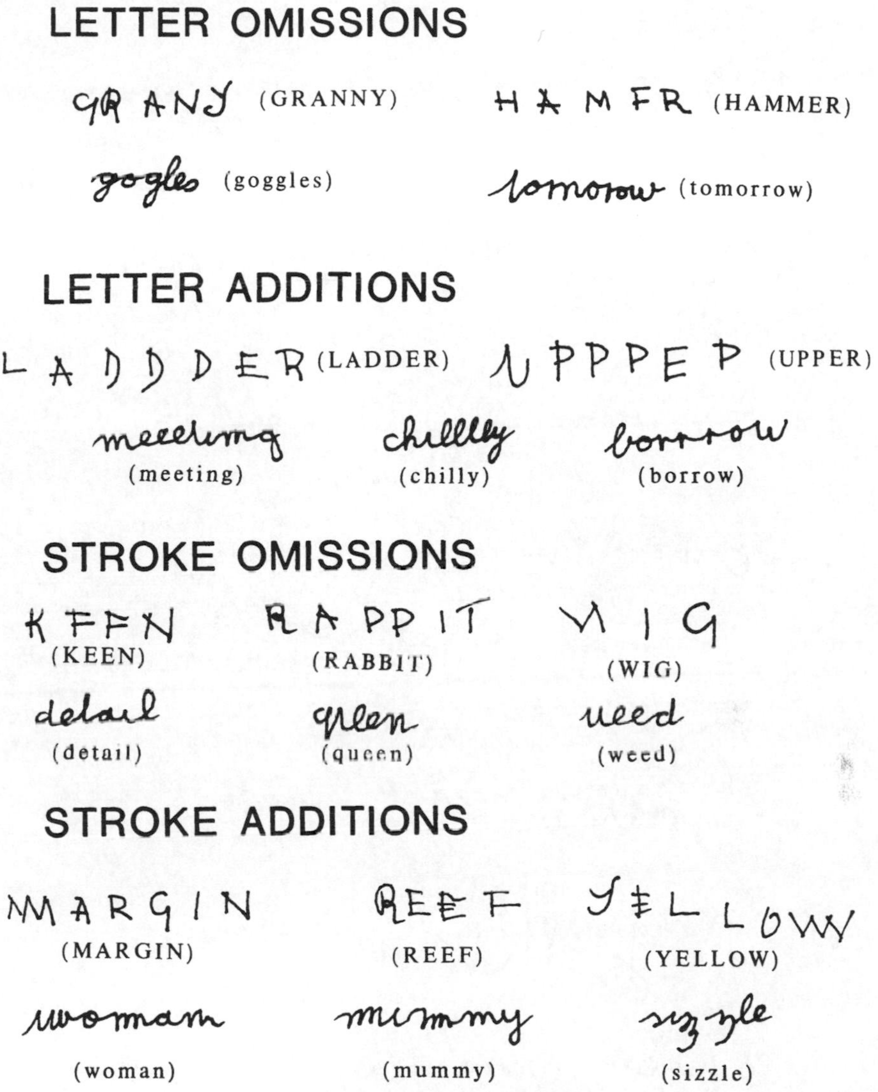

LETTER OMISSIONS

GRANY (GRANNY)   HAMFR (HAMMER)

gogles (goggles)   tomorow (tomorrow)

LETTER ADDITIONS

LADDDER (LADDER)   UPPPEP (UPPER)

meeeemg   chillly   borrrow
(meeting)   (chilly)   (borrow)

STROKE OMISSIONS

KFFN   RAPPIT   WIG
(KEEN)   (RABBIT)   (WIG)

detail   green   weed
(detail)   (queen)   (weed)

STROKE ADDITIONS

MARGIN   REEF   YELLOW
(MARGIN)   (REEF)   (YELLOW)

woman   mummy   sizzle
(woman)   (mummy)   (sizzle)

FIG. 7.4. Characteristic errors of patient VB (from Ellis, Young, & Flude, 1987b).

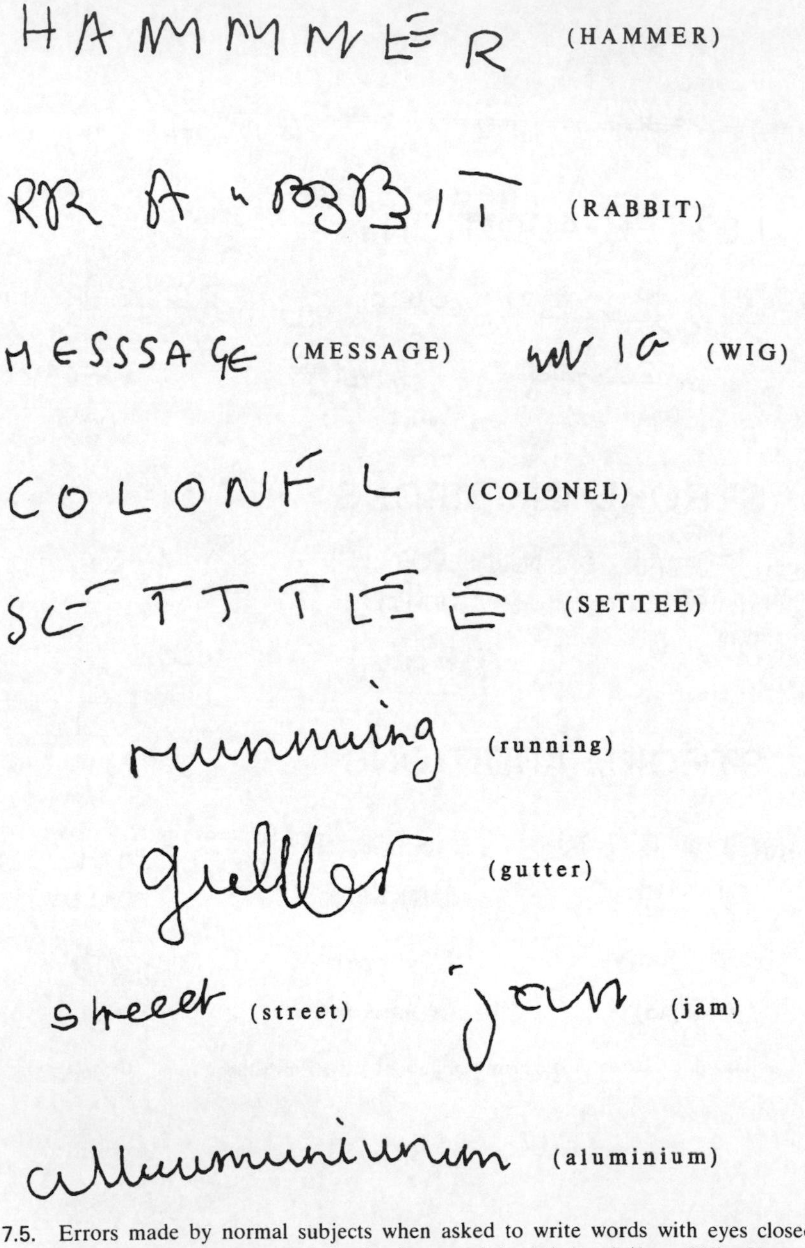

FIG. 7.5. Errors made by normal subjects when asked to write words with eyes closed while simultaneously tapping sequentially the fingers of the left hand (from Ellis, Young, & Flude, 1987b).

is that the truly dysgraphic patient makes these errors under normal writing conditions. How can this striking parallel be explained? Ellis et al. (1987b) suggested that normals become "afferent" dysgraphic when the experimental circumstances prevent them from monitoring and controlling their handwriting through the utilisation of visual feedback (sight of the hand and pen) and kinaesthetic feedback (the feeling of movement of fingers, wrist, and arm). Visual feedback is eliminated by obscuring the sight of the writing hand, and the addition of a secondary task interferes with the writer's ability to attend to kinaesthetic feedback.

Ellis et al. (1987b) showed that, unlike normal subjects, VB's writing was no more error-prone when she had her eyes closed than when she had her eyes open. She thus appears to have been permanently unable to use visual feedback to monitor for errors or help correct them. When, after she had closed her eyes, her forefinger was passively moved so as to form a letter, she was extremely poor at using kinaesthetic information to say what letter had been formed. And she could not distinguish reliably and correctly formed letters between incorrectly formed ones on the basis of kinaesthetic feedback. She thus seems to have also been permanently unable to use kinaesthesis for writing control.

In sum, writing is a complex perceptual-motor skill: Normal subjects use visual and kinaesthetic feedback at least some of the time to control their writing movements. When experimental conditions prevent normals from utilising those sources of feedback, normal writers make errors. Those errors are mostly omissions or repetitions of letters or strokes in sequences of similar items, and the errors may be interpreted as the consequence of a tendency to lose position in the middle of such sequences (Margolin, 1984). The brain injury suffered by "afferent" dysgraphics like VB may have robbed them of the ability to *attend* to visual and kinaesthetic feedback, so that they become permanently prone to errors at those points where close monitoring of writing movements is most needed.

OVERVIEW

If we define writing as a system of visual communication in which the written elements represent elements of the spoken language (words, syllables, or phonemes), then writing is less than 6000 years old. Only a tiny minority of the people who have ever lived have been able to read, and even fewer have been able to write. Accounts of the development of writing can be found in Gelb (1963), Gaur (1984), and Barton and Hamilton (in press).

The skill of writing is culturally transmitted from one generation to the next. The capacity to write is not one for which evolution can have equipped us with any genetically given modules, yet the cognitive neuropsychological evidence reviewed above suggests that writing processes in the skilled adult writer are as highly modularised as the speech-related processes discussed in Chapters 5 and 6. Thus a "surface dysgraphic" patient may lose the capacity to retrieve once-familiar spellings from some form of lexical store without losing the capacity to retrieve spoken word-forms, and without suffering amnesic memory retrieval problems. Similarly, a "phonological dysgraphic" patient may lose the capacity for phoneme–grapheme conversion required to generate plausible spellings for unfamiliar words or non-words without even losing the capacity for grapheme–phoneme conversion in reading (Beauvois and Dérousné, 1981).

The moral to be gleaned from this is that learning can create cognitive processes which are capable of becoming as highly modularised as genetically given modules. This conclusion contradicts Fodor's (1983) notion that modules must be genetically inherited, but the evidence for modularity is probably stronger for writing and reading (see Chapter 8) than for any other aspect of cognition (Ellis, 1987; Schwartz & Schwartz, 1984), so we must now allow that modules can be acquired as well as inherited.

The evidence for writing-specific disorders is stronger for what we have termed "central" dysgraphias than for "peripheral" dysgraphias. Writing is interesting because it begins as a linguistic process and ends as a perceptual-motor one. In the course of that transition the cognitive processes seem to become progressively less specific to writing. Thus "afferent dysgraphia" is probably the way that a general inattention to visual and kinaesthetic feedback affects handwriting, whereas other peripheral dysgraphias not covered here, such as mirror writing or the tiny "micrographic" handwriting of patients with Parkinsonism, similarly illustrate the effects of more general perceptual-motor impairments on handwriting.

SUMMARY

Acquired dysgraphias may be divided for convenience into "central dysgraphias" which affect the capacity to spell familiar or unfamiliar words in any output modality (handwriting, typing, oral spelling, etc.), and "peripheral dysgraphias" which may affect just one output modality, leaving the expression of spelling knowledge through the other modalities intact. But the cognitive neuropsychology of spelling and writing is not built solely upon patients in whom spelling and writing are impaired: patients in whom those skills are intact while other abilities are impaired can be equally important. For example, patients who can spell words correctly despite not having access to their correct spoken forms show that spellings of familiar words are not assembled by phoneme–grapheme conversion (a conclusion strengthened by "phonological dysgraphic" patients like PR—Shallice, 1981b). The spellings of familiar words must be capable of being retrieved as wholes from a graphemic output lexicon, and there must be ways of accessing that lexicon other than through the sound patterns of words.

Figure 7.1 proposes a graphemic output lexicon from which the spellings of familiar words are retrieved that is distinct from the speech output lexicon from which the spoken forms of words are retrieved. Spellings can be retrieved from the graphemic output lexicon using at least two inputs. One input comes direct from the semantic system and allows the meanings of words to activate their spellings without the intervention of sound forms. Disruption of this input is held responsible for semantic writing errors (e.g. time → CLOCK) seen in "deep dysgraphic" patients (and occasionally in normals).

A second input to the graphemic output lexicon comes from the speech output lexicon. Disruption of this input is held responsible for homophone (their → THERE) and similar-sound (plumb → THUMB) errors in which the errors are real, sometimes irregular words which would not be assembled by sublexical phoneme–grapheme conversion. Like semantic errors, these occur occasionally in normal writing as unintended slips of the pen, and at much higher frequencies in the writing of some acquired dysgraphic patients. "Visual" errors (e.g. custom → CUSTARD) may be explained in terms of interactive activation between the graphemic output lexicon and the grapheme level. Morphological errors of a sort that would imply separate representations of morphemes in the graphemic output lexicon have yet to be demonstrated convincingly.

Errors showing partial word-specific lexical knowledge occur in a wide range of qualitatively different acquired dysgraphic patients. They may affect less commonly used (low-frequency) words most, and show that the retrieval of spellings from the graphemic output lexicon is not an all-or-nothing thing. Errors of partial lexical knowledge in spelling may be the logical equivalents of the phonological approximation errors in the speech of some aphasic patients—errors interpretable in terms of partial retrieval of spoken word-forms from the speech output lexicon.

Sublexical phoneme–grapheme conversion of the sort required to assemble a plausible spelling for an unfamiliar word or non-word is represented in Fig. 7.1 in terms of a link between the phoneme level and the grapheme level. This conversion procedure is impaired in "phonological" dysgraphics, and preserved in "surface" dysgraphics for whom retrieval of words from the graphemic output lexicon is impaired. "Surface" dysgraphics are more successful at spelling regular than irregular words, to which they tend to make regularisation errors (e.g. misspelling "biscuit" as BISKET, or "nephew" as NEFFUE). Some theorists would probably prefer to think of lexical and sublexical spelling procedures as more closely intertwined than our model might suggest.

If a writer knows how a word is spelled, then he or she is equally capable of spelling it aloud, typing it (even if slowly), printing it in upper-case (capital) letters, or writing it in cursive handwriting. Because this variety of possible output modalities exists, we suggest that spellings are initially retrieved from the graphemic output lexicon or assembled by phoneme–grapheme conversion as abstract graphemic representations. Processes downstream of the grapheme level convert the graphemic representation progressively into more concrete forms ready for output. In Fig. 7.2 we propose that graphemes first activate particular spatial letter forms at the allograph level and that these then guide the retrieval or assembly of graphic motor patterns which will create the letter forms on paper. Different peripheral dysgraphias are interpretable as impairments affecting one or other of these stages.

FURTHER READING

Brown, G.D.A. & Ellis, N.C. (Eds.) (1994). *Handbook of spelling: theory, process and intervention.* Chichester: Wiley. Excellent survey of current thinking about spelling.

Caplan, D. (1992). Language: structure, processing and disorders. Cambridge, Mass.: MIT Press. Chapter 5 covers disorders of reading and writing.

Frith, U. (Ed.) (1980). *Cognitive processes in spelling.* London: Academic Press. A collection of papers that stimulated much of the more recent work on spelling.

McCarthy, R.A. & Warrington, E.K. (1990). *Cognitive neuropsychology: a clinical introduction.* San Diego: Academic Press. Chapter 11 reviews spelling and writing.

Parkin, A.J. (1996). *Explorations in cognitive neuropsychology.* Oxford: Blackwell. Chapter 8 reviews reading and writing disorders.

Shallice, T., Glasspool, D.W., & Houghton, G. (1995). Can neuropsychological evidence inform connectionist modelling? An analysis of spelling. *Language and Cognitive Processes, 10,* 195–225. Applies the connectionist approach to modelling the grapheme level.

8 Reading: And a Composite Model for Word Recognition and Production

INTRODUCTION AND A MODEL

Reading is subject to its own range of acquired disorders in just the same way as are writing, speech perception, and speech production. Disorders of reading consequent upon brain injury are called *acquired dyslexias*. The study of acquired dyslexias was one of the first areas to be investigated intensively from a cognitive neuropsychological perspective, and many qualitatively different forms of acquired dyslexia have been identified, each with different symptoms, different interpretations, and different implications for theories of normal reading. New varieties are still being reported, and our coverage here does not claim to be exhaustive. As in the two previous chapters we shall confine ourselves to disorders identifiable in the processing of single words, and shall defer disorders of the processing of sentences and connected text until Chapter 9. Recent reviews of cognitive neuropsychological investigations of the acquired dyslexias can be found in Coltheart (1981; 1986), Patterson (1981), Newcombe and Marshall (1981), and Ellis (1984b).

In Chapters 5 and 6 we gradually put together a model for the production and comprehension of spoken words, and for the production of written words, culminating in the model shown in Fig. 7.1 (p. 175). This chapter is concerned with reading rather than writing. In Fig. 8.1, the model we shall use in this chapter, processes specific to spelling and writing have been stripped off (for now) and replaced with processes specific to reading. As we shall see, a model for reading needs to preserve those processes which are also involved in speech comprehension and production.

Readers coming straight to this chapter will require a brief explanation of Fig. 8.1. The top left corner of the diagram is concerned with the recognition of spoken words. The auditory input lexicon contains representations of all the words that are familiar in their spoken (heard) forms. In order for a heard word to be identified its representation in the auditory input lexicon must be activated by the sound wave reaching the listeners' ears. The function of the acoustic analysis system is to transform that raw sound wave into a form to which the representations in the auditory input lexicon can respond. Representations of the *meanings* of words are contained within the semantic system. A heard word is only understood when the activation of its entry in the auditory input lexicon triggers the subsequent activation of that word's semantic (meaning) representation in the semantic system.

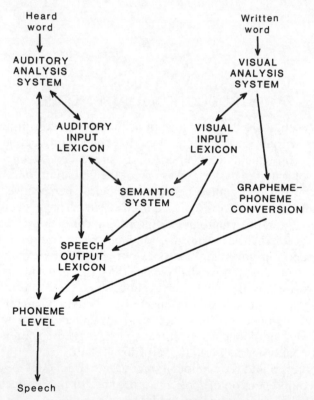

FIG. 8.1. Functional model for the recognition, comprehension and naming of written words in reading.

The lower portion of Fig. 8.1 is concerned with speech production. The speech output lexicon contains those representations of spoken words which are activated when a word is to be spoken (e.g. in spontaneous speech or object naming). Representations in the speech output lexicon are triggered when their meanings in the semantic system become active. This triggering serves, in turn, to activate the sequence of phonemes (distinctive speech sounds) at the phoneme level. Saying a word aloud then simply requires the activated string of phonemes to be articulated.

Words are not, however, always spoken out loud. They can also be "spoken" internally as "inner speech". This is represented in Fig. 8.1 by the arrow on the left-hand side of the diagram which cycles speech back from the phoneme level on the output side to the acoustic analysis system on the input side. Such a link allows a speaker to almost literally hear his or her own voice without anything being said aloud. There are additional advantages in having that connection two-way, thus providing a direct link from the acoustic analysis system to the phoneme level. One such advantage is that it provides a mechanism for repeating aloud words (or invented non-words) which we have never heard or spoken before and which cannot, therefore, have entries in either the auditory input lexicon or the speech output lexicon.

It may seem rather strange to open a chapter on reading with several paragraphs concerned with the comprehension and production of spoken words, but in the course of learning to read cognitive processes dealing with written words are grafted onto those processes we have just outlined which handle spoken words. And, as the chapter progresses, we shall see that although cognitive processes exist which are specific to reading and do not involve spoken word-forms, nevertheless, full, fluent reading also calls upon speech processes in a number of important ways.

Figure 8.1 introduces three new components which are specific to reading—a *visual analysis system*, a *visual input lexicon*, and a component labelled *grapheme–phoneme conversion*. A written word is typically a complex pattern of black lines on a white background. Meaning and sound are imposed by the reader. The function of the first reading component, the visual analysis system, is to identify the component letters of words and note their positions with the word. Identification here is a visual process; it does not involve naming the letters.

We assume that as written words become familiar to a reader, representations of those words are established in a visual input lexicon similar in function to, but separate from, the auditory input lexicon. Thus skilled readers who have learned to recognise many thousands of words "by sight" will have a representation for each word in their visual input lexicons, each representation being activated specifically by its own written word. The visual input lexicon receives its input from the letter recognisers in the visual analysis system and, in turn, activates stored representations of their meanings in the semantic system. For a skilled reader this is the usual route for understanding a familiar written word. Once a word has been comprehended the semantic system can activate the word's spoken form in the speech output lexicon (as in normal speech production), allowing the word to be read aloud. The speech output lexicon is the same component whose role in speech production and spelling has been discussed in Chapters 5 and 7. The route from print to speech via the visual input lexicon, the semantic system, and the speech output lexicon is probably the normal route for reading aloud connected text (see Ellis, 1984b, pp. 55–57).

There must, however, be at least one other route from print to pronunciation. *Pomelo* and *regelate* are both real words in the English language, but they are uncommon ones that most people will not have met before, and for which they are therefore unlikely to have representations in the visual input lexicon. Thanks to the (partially) alphabetic nature of the English spelling system we can, however, attempt a pronunciation for each one. That pronunciation is assembled by first identifying the letters (the job of the visual analysis system again), then converting those letters (or graphemes) into sounds (or phonemes). In our model, a component labelled *grapheme–phoneme conversion* is given the task of translating unfamiliar letter strings into phoneme strings. The input to grapheme–phoneme conversion is letters identified by the visual analysis system, whereas its output serves to activate phonemes at the phoneme level, from whence they can be articulated. We shall see later that there are a number of candidate theories of how unfamiliar letter strings are translated into sounds. For most of this chapter the term "grapheme–phoneme conversion" is meant to be neutral with respect to just how that translation is accomplished.

Grapheme–phoneme conversion is probably used only occasionally by skilled adult readers as the dominant route from print to sound (e.g. in reading an unfamiliar word for the first time), but the young or unskilled reader will encounter many words which are unfamiliar in their printed form and which must therefore be "sounded out" by grapheme–phoneme conversion. The point of doing this is that many words which are visually unfamiliar for the child or unskilled adult reader will be words he or she has *heard* before and whose meaning is known. Converting unfamiliar words into spoken form allows the possibility that they will be recognised auditorily where they were not recognised visually. This auditory recognition most probably involves activating the word's entry in the auditory input lexicon: This could be achieved either by saying the word aloud or by saying it internally using "inner speech".

In Fig. 8.1 an arrow connects the visual input lexicon which recognises familiar written words directly to the speech output lexicon which gives access to their pronunciations. The arrow therefore provides a pathway by which familiar written words may be identified and pronounced as wholes without (or in parallel to) activating their meanings. The justification and purpose of this third pathway from print to sound will be discussed later in this chapter.

Armed with our model we are now ready to survey the range of reading disorders which can occur as a result of injury to the brains of adults who were previously fully literate (the acquired dyslexias). Shallice and Warrington (1980) made a rough, but none the less useful distinction between "peripheral" and "central" acquired dyslexias. Peripheral dyslexias affect early stages in the visual analysis of letters and words, whereas central dyslexias affect deeper processes such as grapheme–phoneme conversion or semantic access. We shall begin our survey with the peripheral dyslexias.

PERIPHERAL DYSLEXIAS

"Neglect" Dyslexia

We have seen in Chapter 4 how brain injury can cause patients to neglect one side of the visual world. That neglect can extend to and affect reading. Kinsbourne and Warrington (1962) reported six patients who showed neglect of the left half of space. In reading they made visual errors which preserved the ends of words but were incorrect at the beginnings (e.g. reading *level* as "novel", *milk* as "chalk", *geography* as "autobiography", and *message* as "passage"). Four of the six patients had visual field defects that left them blind to the left half of the visual world ("left homonymous hemianopia"), but the reading disorder could not be attributed to this factor, first because the same neglect errors also occurred in two patients without blindness in the left visual field and, secondly, because neglect of the leftmost letters of words also occurred when words were presented entirely in the patients' intact right visual fields. Ellis, Flude, and Young (1987a) reported a detailed case study of a single patient, VB, who showed neglect dyslexia. When asked to read passages of text she often read only the right-hand half of each line, neglecting the left half. This tendency could be eliminated by the simple expedient of turning the page through 90° so that the lines of print now ran from bottom to top rather than from left to right.

When reading the right halves of lines of normal, horizontal print VB would misread some words. She made the same sorts of errors when given single printed words to read. With unlimited time to read each word she would misread about 8% of single words; with a time limit of around 2 seconds per word the error rate increased to around 15% of words. Some two-thirds of her errors were of the neglect type (e.g. misreading LOG as "dog", RIVER as "liver", or YELLOW as "pillow"). Other errors were either of a more general visual nature (e.g. misreading WHOM as "thumb", or CHOIR as "anchor"), or were errors in which she misread a word as a non-word (e.g. CABIN as "rabin"; GIRTH as "gorth").

The errors did not seem to be influenced by anything other than visual factors: VB freely produced errors like misreading HARDEN as "warden" where the target word and the error both sound different and belong to different grammatical classes. When VB misread a word she also misunderstood it. Thus when asked to read words and then define them, she misread RICE as "price... how much for a paper or something in a shop", and she misread LIQUID as a "kind of sea creature... squid". The errors seem therefore to happen in early visual processes before word recognition or comprehension occurs.

Although about 12% of VB's neglect errors involved the simple deletion of initial letters (e.g. CAGE misread as "age"; LEVER as "ever"), in the majority of neglect errors she substituted initial letters of the target words with other letters. This occurred even when she was given specially devised lists of words which could be misread by either deleting or substituting the initial letter. Thus she misread ELATE as "plate" not "late", PEACH as "beach" not "each", and JAUNT as "haunt" not "aunt". Furthermore, VB tended to substitute the same number of letters as she had neglected. Thus she would misread TOOL as "fool" with one letter in the error replacing one in the target word, but would very rarely misread, say, TOOL as "school", because that would involve replacing one target letter with three in the error.

Following Shallice (1981a), Ellis, Flude, and Young (1987a) argued that the impairment which led to VB's neglect dyslexic reading errors should be located within the visual analysis system. They proposed that two functions of that system are first to identify the component letters in a word and second to encode the positions of those letters in the word. The need to encode letter positions arises from the fact that the pairs of words may share the same letters and differ only in the positions of those letters (from ON and NO to ORCHESTRA and CARTHORSE). Given the word ELATE, the visual analysis system should therefore both identify each letter and mark it for its within-word position, generating a representation something like $E(1)$, $L(2)$, $A(3)$, $T(4)$, $E(5)$.

When VB neglected the initial letter of a word like ELATE, the *presence* of an initial letter was still reacted to because VB would tend to replace it with another letter rather than simply deleting it. This could happen if, as Ellis et al. (1987a) proposed, VB's neglect affected the encoding of letter identity more than the encoding of letter position. Neglecting the initial letter of ELATE would yield the representation $-(1)$, $L(2)$, $A(3)$, $T(4)$, $E(5)$. Such a representation would be more compatible with the entry in the visual input lexicon for PLATE than with the entry for LATE [which would require $L(1)$, $A(2)$, $T(3)$, $E(4)$]. Finally, Ellis et al. showed that VB's overall accuracy rate to single word targets (over 85%) was better than she could have achieved if she failed to encode the identity of the initial letter of *every* word she tried to read. It would seem that her problem compromised those processes which encoded the identity of the leftmost letters of words, with less or no effect on the processes which encode the position of letters within words.

Though neglect dyslexia, like visual neglect, usually affects elements on the left, a possible (though in some respects unclear) case of *right*-sided "neglect" dyslexia was presented by Warrington and Zangwill (1957). This patient made visual errors which preserved the beginnings of words but not their ends (e.g. reading *beware* as "because", *tongue* as "together", and *obtained* as "oblong"). Patient EA of Friedrich, Walker, and Posner (1985) also made visual errors affecting the ends of words. Some of these errors could be construed as "morphological" (e.g. *provide* misread as "providing"; *electrical* as "electricity"), but Friedrich et al. prefer to interpret these as visual errors which happen to involve the ends of words. The question of whether genuine morphological errors ever occur in acquired dyslexia will be returned to later in this chapter.

An important question concerns the relation of neglect dyslexia to other aspects of visual neglect (see Chapter 2). Ellis et al. (1987a) suggested that the errors found in neglect dyslexia arise when a more general visual neglect happens to compromise the reading process. On this hypothesis there is nothing about neglect dyslexia that is *specific* to reading. This straightforward position is, however, undermined by Costello and Warrington's (1987) report of a patient who misread the beginnings (i.e. the left side) of horizontal words but neglected the *right* side of external space in other tasks. This finding underscores the point discussed in Chapter 2 that there are probably a number of dissociable types of visual neglect.

Attentional Dyslexia

A different form of acquired peripheral dyslexia was reported by Shallice and Warrington (1977). Their two patients were first noticed because although they could read single whole words quite well they were very poor at naming the letters within those words. When these patients were required to identify particular letters in an array their errors tended to be one of the other letters present which the patient was supposed to ignore. So a patient asked to identify the central letter in the sequence BFXQL might say "F" or "L" instead of "X".

The inability of these two patients to ignore irrelevant letters became even clearer when they were asked to read a group of words presented together. Shown a card with WIN and FED on it one patient read them as "fin" and "fed". POT, BIG, and HUT were read as "but", "big", and "hut". In general, the errors involved the migration of letters (not phonemes) from one word into another, so that words the patient reported seeing were made up of letters from the target words combined with letters from other words on the card. Thus, "fin" is a combination of F from FED and -IN from WIN, and "but" is a combination of B from BIG, U from HUT, and T from POT, with all the letters preserving their within-word positions.

Interestingly, this is one of the class of symptoms found in neuropsychological patients which can also be observed in normal people under certain conditions. Allport (1977) showed groups of words very briefly to normal individuals and obtained a high proportion of letter migration errors (or "visual segmentation errors" as he called them). Shown briefly a card on which were written GLOVE and SPADE a normal person may claim to have *seen* the word GLADE (made up of the GL- from GLOVE and the -ADE of SPADE). These errors of normal readers have since been studied by Shallice and McGill (1978) and Mozer (1983). This work has shown for normals what Shallice and Warrington (1977) also found to be true of their patients, namely that letters tend to migrate from one position in a presented word to the corresponding position in the erroneously reported word. In addition, Mozer (1983) showed that migrations of letters into a particular word occur less often when the subject focusses attention on that word, a finding which lends support to Shallice and Warrington's (1977) choice of the term "attentional" dyslexia to describe their patients.

We have already talked of the need for the visual analysis system to identify letters *and* code them for their positions within words. To account for these migration errors we must now assign another responsibility to the visual analysis system. Written words are not normally encountered in isolation but in large numbers on a printed page. The visual analysis system must be able to group letters together as belonging to a particular word in a particular position on the page. That perceptual grouping can be sorely tested even under normal conditions, as in the following examples adapted from Wilkins (1910, cited by Woodworth, 1938):

Psychment

Departology

Ronan

Reagald

talder

powcum

Shakesbeth

Macpeare's

Very brief presentations disrupt this perceptual grouping in normal subjects, causing them to report having *seen* Psychology Department when the stimulus was Psychment Departology, or talcum powder when the stimulus was talder powcum. In "attentional" dyslexics the perceptual grouping is permanently disrupted through brain injury and extends to reading under normal conditions. One of Shallice and Warrington's (1977) patients spontaneously observed that "when reading a line of print it helped if he held a piece of paper over other parts of the page". This is precisely the sort of strategy one would recommend both to focus attention on the correct words and to prevent migrations from irrelevant words elsewhere on the page.

Letter-by-letter Reading

Patterson and Kay (1982) give a detailed analysis of the reading behaviour of four patients who showed a phenomenon called "letter-by-letter reading". When presented with a word these patients appeared able to identify it only after naming each letter either aloud or subvocally. Thus, shown *shepherd* a letter-by-letter reader would first name the letters in left-to-right order, and only then be able to name the whole word. Now, there is little in the letter *names* S(ess), H(aitch), E(ee), P(pee), H(aitch), E(ee), R(are), D(dee) to suggest the spoken word "shepherd", and letter-by-letter readers certainly do not proceed by in some way blending together phonemes derived from the letter names.

Some letter-by-letter readers [e.g. Warrington & Shallice's (1980) case, RAV] make few errors when identifying individual letters and will read almost any word successfully given sufficient time. Other patients, however, make rather a lot of errors when trying to identify letters. This, of course, leads to mistakes in identifying the word, for example naming the letters of *spade* as "S,H,A,D,E" then saying "shade" (Patterson & Kay, 1982).

Because such patients' reading proceeds letter-by-letter, the time taken to read a word increases as its length increases. Also, in those patients who are prone to letter misidentifications, the probability of failing to read a word correctly increases as its length increases. Word recognition in general can be a very slow process in letter-by-letter readers—from an average of 7.6 seconds for 3-letter words to 19.5 seconds for

9- or 10-letter words in the *fastest* of Patterson and Kay's (1982) four patients.

Letter-by-letter reading has a long history of study by neuropsychologists and neurologists from Déjerine (1892) onwards, but much of this work has concentrated on locating the anatomical site of the lesion(s) responsible for this dyslexia. Only recently with the work of Warrington and Shallice (1980), Patterson and Kay (1982) and others has a *cognitive* explanation of the disorder been sought.

There are really two questions to be answered if we are to explain letter-by-letter reading. The first is: What deficit(s) to which component(s) has impaired the normal capacity for identifying words as wholes? The second question is: What processes mediate the residual reading abilities of letter-by-letter readers? Regarding the first question, Warrington and Shallice (1980) propose that the deficit in letter-by-letter reading is in what they call the "word-form system" (indeed they dub letter-by-letter reading "word-form" dyslexia). In Warrington and Shallice's schema the word-form system is responsible for segmenting letter strings into recognisable units ranging in size from letters, through syllables and morphemes, to words. Thus it subsumes functions ascribed in our model (Fig. 8.1) to both the visual analysis system and the visual input lexicon. It would not, however, be too gross a violation of Warrington and Shallice's theory to say that, in terms of our model, they propose that letter-by-letter readers are no longer able to gain access to the visual input lexicon from print. They can still identify letters but can no longer activate recognition units in the visual input lexicon from the visual analysis system.

Warrington and Shallice (1980) answer our second question (how are the residual reading abilities sustained?) by proposing that letter-by-letter readers identify written words by some reverse operation of their intact spelling system. Apparently, it is a fact that all letter-by-letter readers who can still identify words correctly after naming their letters also have intact spelling capabilities. Further, two of Patterson and Kay's (1982) letter-by-letter readers were also dysgraphic, and their errors in letter-by-letter recognition mirrored the errors they made in spelling. One case in question was patient TP whom we encountered in Chapter 7 as a case of "surface" dysgraphia—that is, a patient who had lost the capacity to retrieve the spellings of many words from memory (i.e. from her graphemic output lexicon). TP had to resort to assembling plausible spellings from sounds, producing errors like NEFFUE for "nephew" and BISKET for "biscuit". Of relevance here is the fact that TP often made phonological reading errors after naming all the letters of a word correctly. For example, shown *head* she said, "H, E, A, D... heed"; similarly, *city* was read as "C, I, T, Y... kitty", and *ache* was read as "A, C, H, E... aych".

All of these errors are compatible with Warrington and Shallice's notion that letter-by-letter readers read via their spelling system which, in TP's case, is itself disordered (though Patterson and Kay discuss an alternative explanation whereby recognition is still mediated by the visual input lexicon). Much is left unspecified in Warrington and Shallice's account, such as *how* the spelling system is able to work in the reverse of its normal mode, and what role letter *names* play in the reading process, but the interpretation still has much to commend it. Perhaps if we knew more about how *normal* people can identify words they hear being spelled aloud (a curious and little-used skill), we might gain insights into the routes to word identification employed in letter-by-letter reading. A complicating factor is that there seem to be different causes of letter-by-letter reading.

We presented evidence in Chapter 4 to show that at least some prosopagnosic patients with face recognition disorders gain unconscious or "implicit" access to the identities of people whose faces feel utterly unfamiliar to the patient. A phenomenon which seems to be related to this type of observation may occur in some, but probably not all, letter-by-letter readers. Patient ML, studied by Shallice and Saffran (1986), read slowly in a letter-by-letter fashion. If asked to identify five- or six-letter words presented for 2 seconds each he could name very few of them correctly. He could, however, distinguish words from non-words with an accuracy significantly above chance at the same rate of presentation. In fact, his performance on non-words was, at 43%, around chance level, but he classified 87% of words correctly, being more accurate on common (high-frequency) words than on less common (low-frequency) words.

With 2-second presentation times ML could also classify words into semantic categories such as living things *vs.* non-living objects, or names of authors *vs.* names of politicians, at accuracy levels greater than chance, though again he could identify very few of the words explicitly. Shallice and Saffran (1986) propose that ML's route to semantics through the "word-form system" is impaired but not totally abolished. It can sustain levels of performance on lexical decision and semantic categorization tasks which are better than chance, though far from normal, but it cannot sustain explicit word identification. For that ML must resort to a letter-by-letter reading strategy. The letter-by-letter readers studied by Patterson and Kay (1982), however, showed no sign of any capability for "implicit" lexical decision or semantic categorisation and would be assumed on this account to have incurred more complete damage to the normal route to word meanings via the visual input lexicon than was incurred by ML.

"Visual" Dyslexia

One of the most influential papers in the revival of cognitive neuropsychology was undoubtedly that of Marshall and Newcombe (1973). They reported analyses of six patients who showed three different patterns of acquired reading disorder. The first pattern they called "visual" dyslexia (see also Newcombe & Marshall, 1981). The errors made by these patients take the form of misidentifying one word as another, visually similar one—for example, reading *lend* as "land", *easel* as "aerial", *arrangement* as "argument", or *calm* as "claim". An earlier and very pure case was reported by Casey and Ettlinger (1960).

Marshall and Newcombe (1973) emphasise the "essential normality" of these errors, pointing out that, like the letter segmentation errors mentioned earlier, they can occur in normal readers when words are glimpsed briefly (e.g. Cowie, 1985; Vernon, 1929). "Visual" dyslexics may have difficultes at the level of the visual analysis system. Alternatively, we may be dealing with a problem internal to the visual input lexicon, whereby the correct input in terms of positionally coded letters sometimes triggers the wrong representation. As yet we lack the sort of detailed, experimental case studies that might help tease apart alternative explanations of the characteristic errors of "visual" dyslexics.

Visual dyslexia lies on the borderline between the peripheral and the central acquired dyslexias. The remainder of the acquired dyslexias we shall cover belong clearly in the category of central dyslexias. The first group of central acquired dyslexias we shall look at all involve patients who have an impairment of the normal reading route via the visual input lexicon, semantic system, and speech output lexicon. They still have some capacity for reading aloud though, and by examining their performance we can learn something about the range of alternative routes from print to pronunciation.

READING WITHOUT MEANING?

Patient WLP, described by Schwartz, Saffran, and Marin (1980a), was a 62-year-old woman who suffered from a progressive senile dementia which severely impaired her ability to produce or comprehend either spoken or written language. We have already mentioned her in Chapter 2, where we discussed her preserved ability to mime the use of objects that she could not otherwise identify. In one task WLP was shown the written *name* of an animal, then was required to point to the appropriate picture from a set of four. Her selections were totally random, but she was nevertheless able to read animal names aloud with very few errors. In another task WLP was given a stack of index cards, upon each of which was written the name of a single animal, colour, or body part. She was required to read each word aloud, then place it on one of three piles according to its semantic category. WLP performed this task reasonably well for common names like *horse, red,* or *finger,* but her sorting of less common names like *giraffe, magenta,* or *china* was poor. However, she could still read aloud the words she could not categorise, including irregular words like *leopard, beige,* and *thumb.*

In simple reading tests she read correctly on at least some occasions irregular words such as *blood, climb, come, sugar, wan,* and *gone.* Because they are irregular, the pronunciations of words like these cannot be assembled piecemeal by grapheme–phoneme conversion; they must be recognised as wholes and pronounced as wholes. In terms of our model these words must be identified by the visual input lexicon, and their pronunciations must be retrieved from the speech output lexicon. WLP's performance on semantic memory tasks was very poor (Schwartz, Marin, & Saffran, 1979), and her comments attest her lack of understanding of the words she could still read aloud ("hyena... hyena... what in the heck is that").

Schwartz et al. (1980a) conclude that there is another route from print to sound which takes the form of direct, whole-word connections between corresponding representations in the visual input lexicon and in the speech output lexicon. These connections would thus link together the units in the visual input lexicon which identify *blood, climb, come,* etc. as familiar written words with the units in the speech output lexicon which store (or provide access to) the pronunciations of those words.

This proposal is reminiscent of the argument advanced in Chapter 7 that intact writing to dictation without comprehension in "word meaning deafness" might imply direct connections between corresponding units in the auditory input lexicon and the graphemic output lexicon. We noted alternative explanations in that instance, including the possibility that semantic units mediate the transfer from input to output although the patient cannot act upon the products of semantic processing in the manner required to indicate comprehension in a category-sorting or other task. The same reservations might apply here. Nebes, Martin, and Horn (1984) studied a group of patients with Alzheimer's disease (a form of dementia). As compared with a group of normal elderly patients, the demented patients were poor at generating animal names to request, and their recall of words in a memory test was not aided by cues as to the categories from which the words were drawn. The patients were, however, reason-ably good at reading words aloud (as WLP was). Importantly, Nebes et al. (1984) were able to show that they read words aloud faster if they had just read a word related in meaning to the word they were currently being asked to read. The priming effect shown by the demented patients was comparable in magnitude to that shown by the normals. Thus, although

Nebes et al.'s patients showed little conscious understanding of written words, they nevertheless read words like BREAD aloud more quickly if they had just read BUTTER than if they had just read WINDOW. This priming of word naming suggests that what we might be seeing in dementia is a disconnection of the recognition system from awareness, similar to the disconnection that can be seen in some prosopagnosic patients (see pp. 96–101). It thus becomes important to determine whether the priming effect arises in the semantic system itself, or at the input lexicon level. If it is established that demented patients continue to access semantic representations of which the patient has no conscious awareness, then cases like WLP would not provide evidence for direct connections between entries in the visual input lexicon and entries in the speech output lexicon.

That said, the proposal of such direct connections has been widely accepted, and has been incorporated into various influential models of reading (e.g. Morton & Patterson, 1980; Newcombe & Marshall, 1981). In addition, Warren and Morton (1982) have argued that a direct, word-specific route from print to sound may help explain an otherwise puzzling difference between words and pictures in the way they are processed by normal people. In an experiment by Potter and Faulconer (1975) normal subjects were required to classify words or pictures as living or non-living as quickly as possible or, alternatively, to name the words or pictures as quickly as possible. In the classification task pictures were responded to faster than words, but the reverse was true in the naming task, where words were named faster than pictures. Warren and Morton (1982) propose that pictures access the semantic system faster than do words, and so can be classified faster, but that when it comes to naming, the presence of the direct route between the visual input lexicon and the speech output lexicon allows words to be named rapidly, whereas pictures must activate their production units via semantics, which is presumed to be a slower process. Further neuropsychological evidence compatible with the notion of a "direct route" from print to sound will be discussed below.

"SURFACE" DYSLEXIA

Patient WLP, whom we described in the previous section, managed to read many irregular words correctly, but she also showed a tendency, particularly in the later stages of her illness, to break words down and pronounce them in a piecemeal fashion (the way you would if you were trying to pronounce a word you had never seen before). Thus on one occasion WLP pronounced *bury* as "burey" (to rhyme with "fury") though she read it correctly on two other occasions. Similarly, she twice read *deny* as "denny", read *pint* to rhyme with "hint", and pronounced the *w* when reading *sword*.

A patient similar in many respects to WLP was reported by Shallice, Warrington, and McCarthy (1983). This patient (HTR) also suffered from a progressive dementing illness, but she showed an even greater tendency to break words down and assemble a pronunciation as if the words were entirely unfamiliar. Her use of this strategy meant that she was more likely to read regular words aloud correctly than irregular words, and her errors were predominantly "regularisations"; that is, errors caused by treating irregular words as if they were regular (e.g. pronouncing *gauge* as "gorge", *trough* as "truff", *come* as "kome", and *quay* as "kway"). The retention in HTR of a capacity for grapheme–phoneme conversion when whole-word reading began to deteriorate would explain why she continued to be able to read aloud non-words like *wull* or *pild* at a time when she could no longer read correctly many once-familiar real words.

This switch from pronouncing familiar words as wholes to assembling pronunciations piecemeal following brain injury was first discussed in detail by Marshall and Newcombe (1973), who gave it the name of "surface" dyslexia. Marshall and Newcombe's patients JC and ST showed a tendency towards regularisation errors on irregular or ambiguously-spelled words, but they differed from WLP and HTR in certain ways. First of all, they did not have a semantic impairment. Provided they could pronounce a word correctly they could understand it and say what it meant. If their misreading of an irregular word was a word in its own right they would understand and define the word in accordance with their mispronunciation. Thus JC read *listen* as "liston" and commented, "that's the boxer" (this being in the heyday of the American heavyweight Sonny Liston). Similarly, he misread *begin* as "beggin" and then added, "collecting money".

Even though JC and ST were obliged to treat formerly familiar words as unfamiliar and pronounce them as one would an unfamiliar word or non-word, their grasp of grapheme–phoneme conversion also seems to have been impaired to a degree. Thus they often failed to apply the "rule of e" whereby a final *e* in a word like *bite* lengthens the preceding vowel, and so pronounced *bike* as "bik" and *describe* as "describ". Additionally, JC and ST made some visual errors like those of patients we have discussed earlier in this chapter, for example reading *reign* as "region" and *bargain* as "barge".

In terms of our model, JC and ST appear to have suffered impairments to the visual input lexicon and/or its connections to the semantic system. Some words could still be recognised as wholes by the visual input lexicon (hence some irregular words could still be read), but many words were now read by grapheme–phoneme conversion (which was itself mildly impaired). Reliance on grapheme–phoneme conversion produces a patient who is more successful at reading regular words than irregular words, since regular words are by definition words whose pronunciations would be correctly derived by the application of spelling–sound correspondences. Thus when JC was tested on two different sets of regular and irregular words, he read 40 of 80 and 27 of 50 regular words correctly as compared with only 27 of 80 and 14 of 50 irregular words (Newcombe & Marshall, 1984).

The Locus of the Impairment in Cases of "Surface" Dyslexia

In "surface" dyslexia, then, some impairment to the whole-word routes between print and pronunciation causes the patient to rely to a considerable extent on the "sublexical" route, involving what we have called grapheme–phoneme conversion. Effectively, the "surface" dyslexic treats the majority of words he or she is shown as if they were entirely new and unfamiliar, sounding them out, and pronouncing them in piecemeal fashion. The patient has problems with irregular words which, by definition, resist this reading strategy and the errors made tend to be "regularisations" in which words are pronounced as they look rather than being given their conventional pronunciations.

Inspection of Fig. 8.1 will reveal that reliance on grapheme–phoneme conversion will only come about if neither the route from the visual input lexicon to the speech output lexicon via the semantic system nor the direct route between the two lexicons can sustain whole-word recognition and pronunciation. Further inspection of Fig. 8.1 will also reveal that damage at a number of different loci in the model could force a reliance on grapheme–phoneme conversion. In a given patient, the symptoms which accompany the problems with irregular words and the regularisation errors should help us to decide where the impairment(s) lies.

"Surface" dyslexia could arise through damage to the visual input lexicon itself. Words would be unable to contact their representations in that lexicon and so would be unable to activate their meanings as wholes. The auditory input lexicon, semantic system, and speech output lexicon would remain intact, so the patient should have no problems in auditory word recognition and comprehension, should not experience naming problems in speech, and should comprehend those written words that can be pronounced correctly. One patient who seems to fit this description reasonably accurately is JC, the "surface" dyslexic already mentioned who has been described in a series of papers by Marshall and Newcombe (1973; Newcombe & Marshall, 1975; 1981; 1984; see also Holmes, 1973; 1978). JC has good comprehension of spoken words, indicative of an intact auditory input lexicon and semantic system. He also has fluent speech production with only slight word-finding difficulties on low-frequency words. These slight difficulties cannot be held responsible for his "surface" dyslexia because he fails to read many words he can use with ease in his spontaneous speech. A disorder in or around the visual input lexicon seems indicated by JC's symptoms. That diagnosis is reinforced by the fact that as well as making regularisation and other errors of grapheme–phoneme conversion, JC also made frequent visual errors where one word was misread as another (e.g. *apron* misread as "open"; *direction* as "decision"; *precise* as "precious"). In contrast to the laborious grapheme–phoneme errors, these visual errors were typically produced rapidly, though often acknowledged later to be incorrect (Holmes, 1973).

A different locus of impairment is indicated in "surface" dyslexic patients like HTR (Shallice, Warrington, & McCarthy, 1983) described above, or like MP (Bub, Cancelliere, & Kertesz, 1985) and KT (McCarthy & Warrington, 1986). These patients have impaired semantic systems with concomitant difficulties comprehending both spoken and written words, along with "anomic" word-finding problems in spontaneous speech (see pp. 116–119). Each of these patients showed good non-word reading and read highly regular words aloud well, though they often did not understand them.

Bub et al. (1985) carried out an instructive *post-hoc* analysis of their patient MP's ability to read aloud regular and irregular words of different word frequencies. The results are shown in Fig. 8.2. As can be seen, MP's problems with irregular words were only acute when they were of low frequency (i.e. relatively uncommon words). Common, high-frequency irregular words were read with around 80% accuracy.

Bub et al. (1985) also carried out a test in which MP was shown cards on which were printed an irregular word that she had mispronounced consistently on previous occasions (e.g. *leopard*) and a non-word modelled on an irregular word (e.g. *rubtle*). MP's task was to indicate which was the real word. She was able to do this reasonably well (82% correct), suggesting to Bub et al. that the representations of those irregular words she could not read aloud correctly were still present in the visual input lexicon and still able to sustain reasonable performance in this lexical decision task. MP's better reading of high-frequency rather than low-frequency irregular words is attributed by Bub et al. to stronger direct links between corresponding representations in the visual input lexicon and speech output lexicon for frequently encountered words. They suggest that even in normals whole-word reading via the direct, non-semantic route between the visual input and speech output lexicons may become inherently less efficient as word frequency decreases.

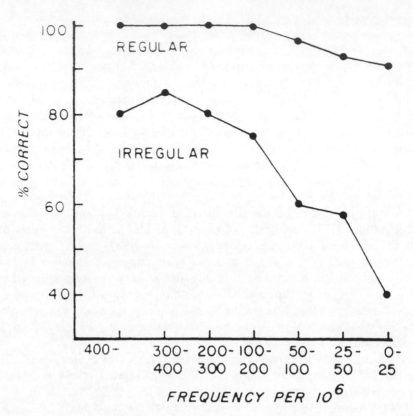

FIG. 8.2.   Effects of word frequency and orthographic regularity on the reading accuracy of patient MP. (Reproduced with permission from Bub, Cancelliere, & Kertesz, 1985.)

So far, then, we have encountered "surface" dyslexia as a consequence of impairment to the visual input lexicon and as a consequence of impairment to the semantic system. Figure 8.1 also permits "surface" dyslexia to arise, however, as a result of an impairment in or around the speech output lexicon. Whole-word reading aloud would be handicapped in such a patient because of difficulties in accessing the pronunciations of words as wholes from the speech output lexicon. The intact visual input lexicon and semantic system would ensure that all familiar written words were recognised and understood, but if the patient was required to read aloud, then those words whose pronunciations could no longer be retrieved from the speech output lexicon would have to have candidate pronunciations assembled by grapheme–phoneme conversion, with concomitant difficulties with irregular words and regularisation errors.

Patient MK (Howard & Franklin, 1987) fits this pattern reasonably well. He read regular words aloud better than irregular words, and the majority of his errors were regularisations. However, in a lexical decision task where he was required to distinguish real words from invented non-words he performed at 97.5% accuracy, and made no more errors to irregular words than to regular words. Similarly, when his task was to define words he was shown, rather than to read them aloud, he performed equally well on both regular and irregular words.

MK's ability to identify irregular words as words in the lexical decision task implies intact representations of these words in the visual input lexicon, and his ability to define them as well as he defines regular words implies that their semantic representations are being activated normally. Yet when required to read words aloud he seems to rely heavily on sublexical grapheme–phoneme conversion (hence the regular word advantage and regularisation errors). This suggests that his problems in reading words aloud lies at the stage of retrieving their spoken word-forms as wholes from the speech output lexicon. Other "surface" dyslexics whose problems appear to lie at this stage are described by Kremin (1985), Goldblum (1985), and Kay and Patterson (1985; see also Kay & Ellis, 1987).

We have thus seen that impairment at three different loci (at least) can force a reliance upon sublexical grapheme–phoneme conversion in reading aloud. It is a moot point whether the similarities between these patients (regularity effect in reading aloud and regularisation errors) outweigh their differences sufficiently to make it worth uniting them into a category called "surface dyslexia" (Coltheart & Funnell, 1987). The problem is exacerbated when patients are presented as "surface" dyslexics who show no regularity effect and very few regularisation errors (e.g. Margolin, Marcel, & Carlson, 1985), or when patients shift by imperceptible degrees from being whole-word non-semantic readers to being "surface" dyslexics (e.g. Shallice, Warrington, & McCarthy, 1983). As stated elsewhere in this book, our preferred solution to this dilemma is to avoid syndrome categories except as convenient shorthands and to relate each patient individually to an explicit theoretical model, treating each case as a separate test of that model. The differing reasons why each of the patients described in this section must lean on grapheme–phoneme conversion when reading aloud are explicable in terms of our model, and the question of whether they rightly belong together in a category called "surface dyslexia" is for present purposes of secondary importance.

READING VIA MEANING

From patients who are often unable to read aloud via semantics and must read via alternative routes we now turn to patients in whom it is those alternative routes that are impaired. This second group of central dyslexias involves patients whose brain injury has restricted them to reading via meanings, though in some even that route is affected.

"Phonological" Dyslexia

The first of this group of central dyslexias that we shall consider is of interest because it was only detected after it had been predicted by a cognitive theory. It has very direct and immediate implications for theories of normal reading processes. "Phonological" dyslexia was first reported by Beauvois and Dérousné (1979). Their French patient, RG, was a 64-year-old man whose ability to read real, familiar words was greatly superior to his ability to read invented non-words. Thus in one test he read 40 five- to nine-letter words without making any errors, but managed to read only 4 of 40 four- or five-letter non-words. His errors to non-words were either failed attempts at grapheme–phoneme conversion or visual errors rather like those of the "visual" dyslexics discussed above.

Shallice and Warrington (1980), Patterson (1982), and Funnell (1983) reported subsequent cases of "phonological" dyslexia in English-speaking patients. Patterson's (1982) patient AM was a 62-year-old former supervisor in a printing firm who had only minor problems with speech production and good auditory comprehension. His comprehension and reading aloud of single content words was good, but his reading aloud of non-words was poor. In one session of testing he successfully read aloud 95% of a list of content words, including fairly uncommon words like *decree* and *phrase*, but he managed to read only 8% of a list of non-words correctly. His errors mostly took the form of reading a non-word as a visually similar real word, for example reading *soof* as "soot", and *klack* as "slack, black, flock".

AM made some derivational errors reading real words (e.g. reading *applaud* as "applause", and *sole* as "absolve") and had difficulties with function words, but neither of these occurred in Funnell's (1983) patient WB. This patient had, however, the same difficulty as AM with non-words which he too tended to misread as visually similar real words (e.g. *cobe* read as "comb", *ploon* as "spoon"). Funnell carried out further tests to try to diagnose more closely the nature of WB's problem with unfamiliar non-words. WB was able to segment spoken words into syllables and to isolate the initial phoneme from a spoken word. He could also segment written words into further words on request (e.g. divide *inside* into "in" and "side", or *father* into "fat" and "her"), and could find the hidden word in a written non-word (e.g. *for* in *alforsut*). He did not, however, segment non-words like *tugant* or *pigham* spontaneously into their component real words in order to read them aloud, and had considerable difficulty applying this strategy when encouraged to do so.

Funnell (1983) proposed that WB first inspected a letter string for wordness. If it was a word it could be comprehended and pronounced as a whole via the visual input lexicon. If it was not a word he was at a loss, because he could no longer draw upon grapheme–phoneme conversion procedures. His competence with visual and phonological segmentation suggests that the processes at either side of grapheme–phoneme conversion were reasonably well preserved, but that the *translation* of a letter string into a phoneme string could no longer be effected.

The theoretical implications of WB's dyslexia are clear. He cannot apply grapheme phoneme conversion procedures to letter strings he has never seen before, yet a letter string which forms a familiar word can be read aloud with comparative ease. Therefore, the processes for pronouncing known words must be separable from those for pronouncing unknown words. Also, access to the meaning of familiar words cannot normally be preceded by a process of piecemeal grapheme–phoneme translation as had been proposed as an account of skilled reading by Meyer and Schvaneveldt (1971), Gough (1972), and others.

Finally, we might note that assembling a pronunciation for an unfamiliar letter string is likely to involve more than one psychological process (Coltheart, 1986). The first process might involve a graphemic segmentation of the letter strings into groups which will map onto single phonemes or syllables (e.g. *THACHIPHORE* into TH – A – CH – I – PH – O(R)E). The second stage might be the actual translation of those segments into a string of phonemes, whereas the third might be the "blending together" of the phonemes into an articulated pronunciation. Funnell's (1983) patient WB may primarily have suffered damage to the second, translation stage, whereas other "phonological" dyslexics may be identified whose primary difficulty lies at one of the other stages. Thus the same set of surface symptoms can, as all clinicians know, arise from different underlying deficits. We must be careful not to assume too readily that patients showing the same symptoms necessarily have the same underlying functional impairment.

"Semantic Access" Dyslexia

Patient AR, reported by Warrington and Shallice (1979), had difficulty naming seen objects though he could name them from descriptions. His reading aloud of single words was reduced to only 30–50% correct, though his spelling to dictation was much better. Of special interest here is what AR could do with words he could not read aloud. Shown the word *beaver* AR said: "could be an animal, I have no idea which one". Shown *cereal* he said: "It is something you eat." He then added: "It seems as if I am almost there, but it seems as if I can't go over the last little bit and finally grasp it."

More detailed testing by Warrington and Shallice (1979) confirmed the impression that AR grasped much, though not all, of the meaning of words he could not read aloud. Thus he could usually categorise correctly a word he could not read aloud as being an animal, or a part of the body, or a foodstuff, etc. Sometimes a semantic prompt helped him name the word. Thus having failed initially to read *pyramid*, he read it correctly after being given the clue "Egypt".

Warrington and Shallice (1979) interpret AR's difficulty as lying between the visual input lexicon and the semantic system (see also Shallice, 1981a). That is, AR could activate the correct representation in the visual input lexicon but often could not negotiate successfully the next step to activating the precise semantic entry. He could usually access the broad area however, providing enough information to succeed in categorisation tasks. Verbal prompts presumably activated the same semantic areas even more from a different access route, helping to form the connection between visual input lexicon and semantic entries. An alternative possibility is that AR's semantic representations were being fully activated, but that his problem lay in gaining *conscious access* to word meanings. We have seen earlier in this chapter how some demented patients may continue to show semantic priming while no longer being consciously aware of the meanings of words they are reading (Nebes, Martin, & Horn, 1984).

As a final point we note that AR had much less difficulty accessing the meanings of heard words. Other patients discussed in Chapter 6 have problems accessing the meanings of heard words but not of seen words. Whatever interpretation is placed upon such access problems, this dissociation supports our policy of regarding the visual and auditory input lexicons as separate components having separate access routes to the semantic system.

"Deep" Dyslexia

Recent interest in the reading disorder known as "deep" dyslexia stems again from the work of Marshall and Newcombe (1966; 1973), but earlier patients in the literature have, with hindsight, been diagnosed retrospectively as cases of "deep" dyslexia (Coltheart, 1980a; Marshall & Newcombe, 1980). The symptom of deep dyslexia which has probably caused most interest is the *semantic error*. A semantic error occurs when a patient reads aloud a printed word as another word similar in meaning. Examples taken from the Appendix to Coltheart, Patterson, and Marshall (1980) are *tandem* read as "cycle", *cost* read as "money", *deed* as "solicitors", *decay* as "rubbish", and *city* as "town".

Patients who make semantic errors in reading also show a number of other characteristics which typically co-occur with the semantic errors and are often considered as defining features of deep dyslexia (Coltheart, 1980a).

These features include:

1. Greater success at reading aloud concrete, imageable words like *butter* or *windmill* than abstract words like *grief* or *wish*, and greater success with content words in general (nouns, verbs, and adjectives) than function words like *was* or *quite*. Errors to function words tend to be other function words (e.g. *was* read as "with", *if* as "yet", *quite* as "perhaps").
2. Frequent visual errors such as misreading *signal* as "single", *decree* as "degree", or *charter* as "garters".
3. "Morphological" (or "derivational") errors such as misreading *edition* as "editor" or *courage* as "courageous".
4. Visual-then-semantic errors, as when a patient misreads *sympathy* as "orchestra", presumably by a visual error to *sympathy* producing the intermediate "symphony" which a semantic error transmuted into "orchestra" (Marshall & Newcombe, 1966). Other likely examples from Patterson (Appendix to Coltheart, Patterson, & Marshall, 1980) include *charter* read as "map" (via *chart*?), *favour* as "taste" (via *flavour*?), and *pivot* as "airplane" (via *pilot*?).
5. Very poor reading of non-words.

What are we to make of this cluster of co-occurring features (including the semantic errors)? At the time of writing there are two main schools of thought regarding deep dyslexia. The first school, exemplified by Morton and Patterson (1980), Newcombe and Marshall (1980a; 1980b), and Shallice and Warrington (1980), takes the same attitude to deep dyslexia that we have taken here to the other acquired dyslexias; that is, it seeks to explain deep dyslexia as the reading performance of a damaged, normal reading system. The alternative school of thought, exemplified by Coltheart (1980b; 1983), Saffran, Bogyo, Schwartz, and Marin (1980a), and Zaidel and Peters (1981), draws attention to the extensive left cerebral hemisphere damage suffered by deep dyslexic patients and suggests that many of the characteristics of deep dyslexia may reflect the involvement of the patient's intact right hemisphere using its limited reading powers. We shall inspect this "right hemisphere hypothesis" of deep dyslexia more closely a little later, but will begin with an examination of the "impaired normal system hypothesis".

First, what is the role in deep dyslexia of the almost total inability to read unfamiliar words or non-words aloud? All investigators agree in construing this inability as an impairment (usually severe) to the processes involved in grapheme–phoneme conversion. Newcombe and Marshall (1980a; 1980b) have, however, gone one step further in suggesting, albeit tentatively, that an impairment to grapheme–phoneme conversion may be *sufficient* to cause semantic errors. They argue that reading via semantics may be a procedure that is inherently prone to semantic errors which are prevented from occurring when normal people read single words aloud by the error-checking function of grapheme–phoneme conversion. Thus a normal reader would never, according to Newcombe and Marshall, read *tandem* as "cycle", because the phoneme level would be receiving a candidate pronunciation via grapheme–phoneme conversion, which would be so different from "cycle" as to inhibit the possible production of "cycle" as a response.

This hypothesis is not without its attractions—semantic errors *have* been observed in normal rapid reading where the speed of reading might be thought to impede grapheme–phoneme conversion (e.g. Morton, 1964)—but it also has its problems. One objection is that "phonological" dyslexics are also poor at reading non-words, yet they make few or no semantic errors (though "phonological" dyslexics are typically not *as* poor at non-word reading as the "deep" dyslexic patients who make semantic errors). A weaker version of the Newcombe and Marshall hypothesis might propose that grapheme–phoneme conversion impairment is a *necessary* condition for the occurrence of semantic errors if not a *sufficient* one. Semantic errors should not occur in a patient with a reasonable capacity for grapheme–phoneme conversion (i.e. a reasonable ability to read non-words aloud). We might note at this point that deep dyslexics must also have an impairment to the whole-word route mediated by the connections between the visual input lexicon and the speech output lexicon. It is only because both this route *and* the route via grapheme–phoneme conversion are inoperative that the patient must read via the semantic route.

Those authors who wish to subscribe to the "impaired normal system" approach, but who do not believe that all of the deep dyslexic symptoms can be blamed on loss of the non-semantic routes, usually propose an additional impairment somewhere around the semantic system. Unfortunately, most of the case studies of deep dyslexics have concentrated solely on reading and have not assessed semantic competence in other areas. If the semantic system is impaired in deep dyslexics, then they should have problems with auditory word comprehension (e.g. of abstract words), and might make semantic errors in other tasks. In one of the few case studies to assess competence more widely, Nolan and Caramazza (1982) found that their patient made semantic errors not only in reading aloud, but also in picture naming (e.g. misnaming a sofa as a "chair"). A central semantic impairment might also ultimately explain the better reading of concrete than abstract words by deep dyslexics, a feature which is presumably due to some difference in the semantic representations of those words.

There is some evidence that the precise nature of the central deficit may vary between patients. Patient GR of Newcombe and Marshall (1980a) made semantic errors when shown a written word and then asked to point to the correct picture in a set which included the correct item plus other, semantically related objects. Thus, if shown the word *fork*, GR might fail to point to the picture of a fork and point instead to the picture of a knife. In contrast, patients PW and DE (Patterson, 1978; 1979; Morton & Patterson, 1980) would make semantic errors in reading aloud but not in word-picture matching (Patterson & Besner, 1984). These and other differences suggest that GR has difficulty accessing precise semantic representations of words from print and sometimes accesses the wrong meanings, whereas PW and DE can access the meanings of the words they are asked to read but make errors when trying to activate the correct representations in the speech output lexicon. This distinction between "input" and "output" forms of "deep" dyslexia was first proposed by Shallice and Warrington (1980).

Morphological Errors

The defining list of symptoms of deep dyslexia includes the presence of so-called morphological errors, such as misreading *angling* as "angler", *worker* as "working", or *salty* as "salt" (Patterson, 1980). These errors are not confined to deep dyslexics, having been observed in several other types of acquired dyslexic patient, but there are problems in how they should be interpreted. For some theorists, the existence of morphological errors in acquired dyslexia supports accounts of normal word recognition which propose that written words are decomposed into their component morphemes before they access the visual input lexicon (e.g. Taft, 1985). By this account, dyslexics who make morphological errors can decompose words into their component morphemes, separating *angling* into *angl-* + *ing*, *worker* into *work-* + *er*, and *salty* into *salt-* + *y*, but have problems with the "bound" morphemes *-ing*, *-er*, and *-y*, and tend to omit or substitute them in reading aloud, resulting in morphological errors (see Caramazza, Miceli, Silveri, & Laudanna, 1985; Job & Sartori, 1984).

Unfortunately, all acquired dyslexic patients so far reported who make morphological errors also make visual errors, semantic errors, or both, and morphological errors are open to alternative construal as either visual or semantic errors. Thus one cannot be confident that a patient who misreads *edition* as "editor" is making a morphological error when that same patient also misreads *gravel* as "grave" and *pupil* as "puppy". Funnell (1987) found that the morphological errors of the two patients she studied were influenced by the variables of word frequency and imageability in precisely the same way as their non-morphological errors, leading Funnell to conclude that the study of morphological errors "has turned out to be a study of a type of visual error in which an embedded word in the stimulus is produced as oral reading response".

Similarly, doubts can be cast over the evidence from experiments on normal subjects that is used to support the notion of obligatory morphological decomposition in visual word recognition (Henderson, 1985). At the time of writing the issue is, however, still being debated strongly, so a firm conclusion one way or the other would be unwise.

Deep Dyslexia and the Right Hemisphere

Returning to the explanation of deep dyslexia, a quite different approach was proposed by Coltheart (1980b; 1983) in his "right hemisphere hypothesis". The hypothesis proposes that word recognition is mediated by a visual input lexicon in the deep dyslexic patient's right hemisphere, though word pronunciations still come from the speech output lexicon in the left hemisphere. Coltheart seeks to support this view by comparing deep dyslexic reading (1) to the capacities claimed for the right hemispheres of "split-brain" patients (whose two cerebral hemispheres have been surgically separated in an operation to relieve epilepsy); (2) to the residual language skills of the few patients whose entire left hemispheres have been surgically removed; and (3) to the capacities of the normal right hemisphere as revealed through experiments on normal subjects in which words are presented briefly to the left or right of a fixation spot (a technique which, for purely anatomical reasons, projects information initially to one or other of the cerebral hemispheres—see Beaumont, 1982; Young, 1982).

Some support can be gained for the right hemisphere hypothesis by making these comparisons. Deep dyslexics cannot read non-words, and neither can the right hemispheres of split-brain patients (Zaidel & Peters, 1981) or normal subjects (Young, Ellis, & Bion, 1984). With normal subjects, abstract words have sometimes been found to lead to a greater right visual half-field (left hemisphere) advantage than concrete words, which is compatible with the suggestion that, whereas all recognition of abstract words is performed by the left hemisphere, the right hemisphere can contribute to the recognition of concrete words (e.g. Bradshaw & Gates, 1978; Day, 1977; Ellis & Shepherd, 1974; Hines, 1976, 1977; Young & Ellis, 1985). Also, two split brain patients studied by Zaidel (1982) made semantic errors when selecting pictures to match printed words, and a patient studied by Gott (1973) made some semantic reading errors after removal of her left hemisphere. The parallels with the semantic errors of deep dyslexic patients are obvious.

Despite these positive lines of comparison, some serious problems for the right hemisphere hypothesis have been raised by Marshall and Patterson (1983) and Patterson and Besner (1984). First, the reading performance of the two deep dyslexics studied by Patterson and Besner (1984) was substantially superior to that of the right hemispheres of any split-brain patients yet reported. Secondly, there has been discussion about whether the few intensively studied split-brain patients are exceptional in the extent of their right hemisphere language capacities (possibly due to early left hemisphere damage). Gazzaniga (1983), for instance, maintains that only 5 of the 44 split-brain patients studied to date have any genuine right hemisphere language. Thirdly, several of the studies which have looked for differences between the two visual half-fields (and hence the two cerebral hemispheres) of normal people in their capacity to identify concrete rather than abstract words have failed to find any difference (see Lambert, 1982; Patterson & Besner, 1984; Young, 1987b for reviews). When differences have been found, they are always such as to imply greater left hemisphere superiority for abstract words, but because this finding is not made consistently it would be unwise to draw firm conclusions from these experiments at present.

The debate as to how deep dyslexia should be interpreted is clearly not over yet. Its resolution is, however, of some importance to cognitive neuropsychology. If what we see in deep dyslexia is the word recognition and comprehension skills of the right hemispheres of normal people (or even a minority of normal people), then we must begin to ask what role, if any, that secondary reading system plays in the normal reading process. It could be that the secondary system is *suppressed* in normal, intact individuals and hence only becomes evident after brain injury (Landis, Regard, Graves, & Goodglass, 1983) but this would leave us to ask with Marshall and Patterson (1983) "How plausible is it that one part of the normal... brain should inhibit the performance of another part which is committed (albeit less effectively perhaps) to the same functions? What principle of biological engineering could demand such organisation?" In sum, why develop a right hemisphere reading system only to suppress it?

Additionally, a main aim of cognitive neuropsychology is to be able to draw inferences and conclusions from the performance of brain-injured patients to models and theories of *normal* cognitive processes. If what we see in deep dyslexia is the performance of a secondary, and possibly inessential, right hemisphere reading system, then we are unlikely to be able to draw any conclusions from deep dyslexia about the nature of the normal, dominant (left hemisphere) reading system. Only if deep dyslexia reflects the reading capacities of a damaged normal system (as proposed by the first school of thought we reviewed) will it have much to teach us about the properties of that normal system.

READING AND SPEECH PROCESSES

Access to Semantics Without Access to Sound

We have argued from the reported cases of "phonological" and "deep" dyslexia that graphcmc–phoneme conversion processes do not necessarily, or even ordinarily, intervene in extracting the meaning from a printed word (see Coltheart, 1980c). Other patients permit us to go one step further to the conclusion that single written words can be understood without the reader's having any idea of how the word sounds.

One line of evidence comes from neologistic jargonaphasic patients like JS (Caramazza, Berndt, & Basili, 1983) and RD (Ellis, Miller, & Sin, 1983). We first came across these patients in Chapter 5 where we noted how their spontaneous speech is full of distorted approximations to target words ("neologisms"). These distortions also characterised their attempts at reading aloud. Thus JS read *both* as "blukts", *bible* as "mowbl", and *butterfly* as "bowdlfley". Similarly, RD read *biscuit* as "biskyut", *despite* as "rediyvist", and *whether* as "geishta". What matters here, however, is that the inability of JS and RD to pronounce many written words correctly did not prevent them from understanding those words. After RD had read *grief* as "preevd" he added, "one is sad". Shown *depth*, he said, "seft... it's very deep down", and to *chaos* he said, "kwost... people all muddled up... out of order... chost". RD could sort written words into categories (e.g. animals *vs*. musical instruments) despite being able to pronounce very few of them correctly, could judge whether pairs of words had similar or different meanings, and could sort sentences into those like *He sat reading a paper* which made sense, and those like *Passing overhead was a kitchen* which were nonsensical (Ellis et al., 1983). Likewise, JS, despite an ability to read aloud which was if anything worse than RD's, could sort written words from non-words and could reject as nonsensical sentences like *The barber captured the razor* (Caramazza et al., 1983).

Levine, Calvanio, and Popovics' (1982) patient EB was discussed in the previous chapter because he retained the capacity to write despite loss of any access to, or apparent knowledge of, the sounds of words. He could not tell which two of a set of four words sounded the same, or rhymed (a deficit also observed in JS), and tended to choose the pair which looked most alike irrespective of their sounds. His understanding of what he read was, however, apparently intact. He read only slowly, but obtained close to maximum scores on a range of tests of reading comprehension.

Patients like JS, RD, and EB can understand written words despite having little or no access to the sounds of those words. They therefore lend support to the theory that there is a route from print to meaning for familiar words which does not involve the sound of the word in any way. In our model, that route is represented by the direct visual access to semantics that is provided by the visual input lexicon. If a letter string corresponds to a known word it will activate the representation for that word in the visual input lexicon. Activation will then pass directly to the representation of the word's meaning in the semantic system along a route in which sound plays no part.

Inner Speech and Reading

We have said that print can access meanings without any involvement of the sounds of words. And yet in normal reading most people are aware of an "inner voice" saying the words as they are read. Does that inner voice have no role to play? Before trying to answer that question we must first ask how inner speech is generated. The voice in the head pronounces irregular words as happily as it pronounces regular words. That simple observation is sufficient to establish that the inner voice we hear is not relaying the products of the grapheme–phoneme conversion route. Additionally, the inner voice assigns the correct pronunciation to a word like *tear* whose pronunciation depends on which of its two meanings is implied (*Her dress had a tear in it* vs. *Her eye had a tear in it*). This suggests that the inner voice speaks words *after* they have been understood, a proposal which is endorsed by the fact that words in inner speech carry the appropriate emphasis and intonation.

In our model, inner speech is represented by the loop back from the phoneme level below the speech output lexicon to the acoustic analysis system and thence to the auditory input lexicon. Familiar written words are recognised via the visual input lexicon, understood by the semantic system, and pronounced by the speech output lexicon. Those pronunciations can then be recycled from the phoneme level as inner speech, allowing the words to be "heard" as well as seen. Familiar words will then be recognised again, this time by the auditory input lexicon, and their semantic representations will receive a fresh boost. Detailing the procedure in this way makes the whole sequence of operations sound slow and ponderous, but in fact it is probably very rapid and fairly automatic (Jakimik, Cole, & Rudnicky, 1985; Rollins & Hendricks, 1980).

So what happens if a patient has lost the capacity for inner speech? Do any penalties accrue to reading comprehension? There are hints in the neuropsychological literature that there may be some penalties, and these hints converge to some extent with the results of experiments in which normal subjects have been asked to read without benefit of inner speech. It will be recalled that patient JS (Caramazza et al., 1983) produced many distorted neologisms in attempting to read aloud, but could nevertheless perform various semantic judgements on written words and sentences. His performance deteriorated badly, however, when success was made contingent upon the processing of syntactic cues such as word order. He could reliably select a picture to match *The block is under the pyramid*, provided that the other pictures depicted balls under pyramids, say, or blocks beside pyramids. If, however, one of the pictures was of a pyramid under a block he was very likely to select it erroneously. JS understood *pyramid, block*, and *under* as individual words, and provided that comprehension was sufficient to solve the task he was all right. But when he had to use the *order* of the words in the sentence to determine which object was under which other object his performance declined markedly. Similarly, he could reject semantically anomalous sentences like *The barber captured the razor* as ill-formed, but he could not reject a syntactically anomalous sentence like *The girl will dressing the doll* as unacceptable in English. Caramazza et al. (1983) propose on the basis of these observations that phonological information is necessary to provide access to the internal machinery which utilises sentence structure in the service of better text comprehension. A patient with rather similar problems confined to understanding reversible sentences was reported by Caramazza, Basili, Koller, and Berndt (1981). In neither of these cases, however, was the problem shown to be specific to reading and absent from the comprehension of spoken sentences.

Patient MV, reported by Bub, Black, Howell, and Kertesz (1987), could detect both semantic and syntactic (word order) anomalies in spoken sentences. With written sentences, however, she could detect semantic anomalies but not syntactic ones. Thus she would reject a written sentence like *The bird flew up the book* (semantically anomalous) as unacceptable, but not *They gave me ride a home* (syntactically anomalous), though she *could* reject the latter sentence perfectly well if she heard it rather than read it. Analysis of MV's performance on a variety of other tasks suggested that she had an impairment which prevented the silent recycling of phonemic representations as inner speech. Her grammatical deficit specific to reading is precisely what one would predict if Caramazza et al.'s theory is correct.

Finally, the converging evidence from normals that we alluded to earlier comes from experiments like those of Kleiman (1981), Baddeley and Lewis (1981), and Levy (1981). In these experiments normal individuals are required to perform various judgements on written sentences while simultaneously saying something irrelevant such as a string of digits or "the-the-the". The aim of the irrelevant articulation is to inhibit inner speech during reading. The results of these experiments suggest that concurrent articulation impairs the capacity of normal readers to detect syntactic anomalies more than it impairs their ability to detect semantic anomalies.

Thus, single written words can be understood without their sound-patterns having to be evoked first. But the direct link from the visual input lexicon to the semantic system does not appear to engage those syntactic processes necessary for the grammatical analysis of sentences one is reading. Those processes appear to operate upon a speech-based code, so that written sentences which are to undergo syntactic analysis must first be converted into spoken form and then recycled back to auditory comprehension processes. As stated earlier, however, the conversion of print to sound in the normal reading of text is a whole-word, semantically mediated process which does not depend upon sublexical grapheme–phoneme conversion.

OVERVIEW: A COMPOSITE MODEL FOR WORD RECOGNITION AND PRODUCTION

The model for reading used in this chapter (Fig. 8.1) shares components in common with the model for spoken word production in Chapter 5 (Fig. 5.2, p. 116), with the model for spoken word comprehension in Chapter 6 (Fig. 6.1., p. 145), and with the model for spelling and writing in Chapter 7 (Figs 7.1 and 7.2, pp. 175 and 181). Each of those models, however, only drew upon the components necessary for the particular skill under consideration.

Figure 8.3 shows the composite model which emerges if those four separate models are fused together, while Table 8.1 represents an extensive commentary on the composite model, summarising the role of each module and some of the connections, and the symptoms which arise when those components and connections are damaged. We would point out that every one of the modules in Fig. 8.3 can be justified with reference to evidence from both normal subjects and brain-injured patients. Similarly, all the connections are empirically motivated: We have kept the links between modules down to the bare minimum necessary to account for the available evidence.

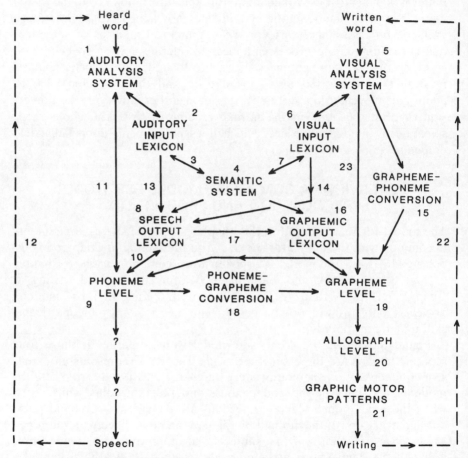

FIG. 8.3. Composite model for the recognition and production of spoken and written words (see Table 8.1 for an explanation of each numbered component and connection).

TABLE 8.1
A Summary of the Functions of all the Components and Some of the Connections in
Fig. 8.3, with a Mention of the Disorders which may Arise through Impairment

1. The function of the auditory analysis system is to extract individual speech sounds (possibly phonemes, though there are other candidates) from the speech wave. It does this despite differences in accent, voice, speech rate, etc. and so must have the flexibility to cope with these variations. It must also cope with the fact that speech is often heard against a substantial level of background noise.

The acoustic analysis system may be impaired selectively in some patients with "pure word deafness" (pp. 146–153) who have difficulties understanding and repeating heard words though they can still speak, read, and write normally. They still hear speech, and may be able to identify vowels but not consonants (which require the analysis of rapidly changing acoustic signals). Speech comprehension may be aided by lipreading cues, by context, and by slowing the speech to a rate which may allow the less efficient acoustic analysis system of the right hemisphere to sustain phonetic perception.

2. The function of the auditory input lexicon is to recognise familiar spoken words. It simply signals that a word has been heard before—knowing what the word means requires subsequent activation of its semantic representation in the semantic system.

Selective impairment of the auditory input lexicon would result in a patient who could no longer recognise many or all spoken words but could repeat them correctly using the by-pass route from the acoustic analysis system to the phoneme level. Intact repetition distinguishes this impairment from "pure word deafness" (see 1 above). Speech production should be intact as should most aspects of reading (though not the ability to comprehend misspelled pseudohomophones like "phoks" or "neffue") and most aspects of writing (though the patient should tend to misspell dictated homophones like *peak* and *pique* when these are not understood). Certain patients with "word meaning deafness" (pp. 153–155) may fit this description (though see 3 below).

3. The link between the auditory input lexicon and the semantic system allows heard words which have been recognised as familiar to access their meanings in the semantic system. Selective impairment to this connection will result in a patient who can distinguish heard words from non-words (auditory lexical decision), and can repeat both words and non-words, but fails to understand many words. This failure of auditory word comprehension need not be accompanied by any problems in understanding familiar written words, nor any problems with speech production.

Some patients with "word meaning deafness" who can still write to dictation irregular words they cannot understand may fit this description (pp. 153–155 and p. 177). Impairment of 3 is also seen in patients with "semantic access dysphasia", which may be specific to certain categories of words (pp. 156–158).

4. The semantic system is the (grossly underspecified) component in which word meanings are represented. It corresponds to the "semantic memory" component of many cognitive theories of memory. According to some theorists, the semantic system should be divided into a verbal semantic system where word meanings are represented and a non-verbal semantic system in which such things as one's knowledge of objects and people is stored.

Several different neuropsychological conditions may include semantic system impairments. Among these are dementia, category-specific impairments which compromise equally the production and comprehension of both spoken and written words, "deep dysphasia" where semantic errors are made in auditory-vocal repetition (pp. 157–158), and "deep dyslexia" in which both semantic errors in reading aloud and the characteristic imageability effect

(Continued)

TABLE 8.1
(Continued)

(better reading of concrete than abstract words) have been attributed to semantic system impairments (pp. 212–217).

5. The visual analysis system has three functions: (1) to identify letters in written words (or non-words or letter strings); (2) to encode each letter for its position within its word; and (3) to group perceptually those letters which belong together as part of the same word. One or other of these functions may be disturbed in patients with certain "peripheral" acquired dyslexias. Thus patients with "neglect dyslexia" may fail to identify letters at one end of a word (pp. 195–197), whereas "attentional dyslexics" may have problems with perceptual groupings which result in errors which incorporate letters from two or more words present in the visual field (pp. 197–199).

Normally the visual analysis system can identify several letters simultaneously and in parallel (hence word length has little effect on the recognition of familiar words). On one theory of "letter-by-letter reading" (pp. 199–201) letter identification has been reduced to a serial process with only one letter at a time being transmitted from the visual analysis system to the visual input lexicon (Patterson & Kay, 1982). An alternative theory (Warrington & Shallice, 1980) holds that transmission of information from the visual analysis system to the visual input lexicon is completely severed, so that letter information must be transmitted instead along connection 22 to the spelling system which effects recognition in a slow and laborious manner (possibly back up through the graphemic output lexicon to the semantic system, though this is *highly* speculative).

6. The function of the visual input lexicon in reading is analogous to that of the auditory input lexicon in speech perception. It identifies strings of letters which form familiar written words. It can respond to an unfamiliar word (or non-word) by declaring it unfamiliar, by allowing it to activate the representation of a visual similar real word (hence perhaps allowing a patient to respond "table" to the non-word *toble*), or possibly by initiating an attempt at pronunciation based on analogy with familiar words. The visual input lexicon indicates that a word has been seen before, but if the word is to be understood it must activate its semantic representation in the semantic system (4), and if it is to be pronounced correctly it must activate its spoken form in the speech output lexicon (8).

Impairment to the visual input lexicon may account for visual errors such as misreading *arrangement* as "argument", or *calm* as "clam". These are the predominant error forms in "visual" dyslexia (p. 202), but accompany other symptoms in many other forms of acquired dyslexia.

7. The link between the visual input lexicon and the semantic system allows written words which have been recognised as familiar to access their meanings in the semantic system (4). Selective impairments to this connection will result in a patient who can distinguish written words from non-words (visual lexical decision) but fails to understand many written words, or understands them only slowly and incompletely. Auditory word comprehension, speaking, and writing could remain intact. Patients with "semantic access dyslexia" may approximate to this description (pp. 211–212).

8. The function of the speech output lexicon is to make the spoken form of a word available to a speaker. In speech production this will occur in response to activation from the semantic system; in reading it may occur through a combination of input from the semantic system and more direct connections from the visual intput lexicon (see 14 below).

Evidence from both normal subjects and brain-injured patients suggests that ease of activating entries for words in the speech output lexicon is a function of word frequency, with

(Continued)

TABLE 8.1
(Continued)

commonly used (high-frequency) words being easier to access than less commonly used (low-frequency) words. This pattern may be seen in "anomic" aphasics with word-finding problems for words whose meanings they have full awareness of (pp. 119–124). Such patients may only be able to retrieve reliably high-frequency words, though for less common words they may show partial access, generating approximations to words which can also be seen in normal subjects caught in tip-of-the-tongue states. These neologistic approximations may occur frequently in the speech of patients with "neologistic jargonaphasia", a condition in which word retrieval is also frequency-related (pp. 124–129). Target-related neologisms (phonological approximations) also show that retrieval of word-forms from the speech output lexicon is not an all-or-nothing affair.

9. At the phoneme level are represented individual distinctive speech sounds. These could be positionally coded, as letters are thought to be in the visual analysis system. The phoneme level receives inputs from three different sources. The first is the auditory analysis system. This provides a mechanism for the auditory-vocal repetition of both familiar and unfamiliar words (or non-words)—see 11 below. The second input is from the speech output lexicon: phonemes may be activated in the course of spontaneous speech production or reading aloud or semantically mediated repetition or object naming, and so on. Thirdly, the phoneme level may be activated by grapheme–phoneme conversion when unfamiliar words or non-words are being read aloud (see 15 below).

The phoneme level guides speech production through as yet unspecified processes which end in the articulation of speech sounds. The phoneme level can also guide "sublexical" or "assembled" spelling of words whose spellings are not represented in the graphemic output lexicon (see 16 and 17 below).

Slips of the tongue made by normal speakers involving substitution or misordering of phonemes may be attributed to errors at the phoneme level. One hallmark of such errors seems to be that they involve the replacement of phonemes by other phonetically similar phonemes (e.g. replacement of /b/ by /p/, or /g/ by /k/—see Ellis, 1979a; 1980). Errors arising at this level may also be seen in the speech of some Broca's aphasics and possibly some "conduction" aphasics.

10. The two-way arrow connecting the speech output lexicon to the phoneme level is meant to represent the notion that the lexicon and the phoneme level exist in a state of mutual, interactive activation. This means that as an entry in the speech output lexicon is activating its phonemes at the phoneme level, so activation is fed back up to the speech output lexicon in a form of positive feedback. The normal function of this interactive activation is to hasten the selection of entries in the lexicon and the activation of phonemes at the phoneme level, but it may occasionally err, resulting in the production of errors known as malapropisms, where a word similar to an intended target word is spoken by mistake. These word substitution errors are quite common in normal slips of the tongue and may also occur in aphasic patients. It may also be possible to invoke this interactive activation in order to account for certain spelling errors of normals and acquired dysgraphics in which a real word misspelling is produced which is similar or identical in sound to the intended word. This can be done if we postulate a direct link between corresponding entries in the speech output lexicon and the graphemic output lexicon (16; see also pp. 171–172).

11. Both normal speakers and many aphasic patients are able to repeat aloud unfamiliar words or invented non-words for which there will be no entries in the auditory input lexicon or speech output lexicon. This means that we must postulate a route from input to output

(Continued)

TABLE 8.1
(Continued)

which does not go through the two lexicons: This is provided in the model by the direct link between the auditory analysis system and the phoneme level. Although repetition of unfamiliar words is relatively uncommon in adulthood, it is a necessity which must arise very commonly in childhood where children repeat words they have not heard before in order to question adults about their meaning. In this respect, non-lexical repetition is more important in childhood than in adulthood, as may be non-lexical reading (see 15 below). The provision of a direct link between the auditory analysis system and the phoneme level provides a mechanism whereby unfamiliar words may be repeated without comprehension or recognition. This route is impaired in certain aphasic patients, e.g. "auditory phonological agnosics" and "deep dysphasics", whose repetition of non-words is much worse than their repetition of words.

The link between the auditory analysis system and the phoneme level is represented as a two-way link. This means that activation of phonemes at the phoneme level can be fed back to the auditory analysis system. This could provide a mechanism for what we experience in everyday life as "inner speech", where we appear to hear our own silent speech internally. This inner process of generating what is effectively an acoustic image from a phoneme level representation may also be important in the silent comprehension of written words which have been read aloud using grapheme–phoneme conversion, as when a child reads silently an unfamiliar written word, recognises its sound form as one which has been heard before, and understands the word.

12. As an alternative to the internal feedback from phonemes to the auditory analysis system afforded by 11 above, one may speak a word aloud and monitor one's own speech output by external feedback. The inability to monitor one's own speech and detect one's own errors may be a contributing factor in certain forms of aphasia. Thus it is suggested in Chapter 5 that "neologistic jargonaphasics" may freely produce large numbers of errors in their speech precisely because an accompanying speech perception disorder prevents them from detecting their own errors and therefore from knowing that their own speech is replete with mispronunciations.

13. A direct connection between an auditory input lexicon and a speech output lexicon appears in several models, including the logogen model (e.g. Morton & Patterson, 1980). The evidence for its existence is slim, however, and its presence makes models with separate input and output lexicons harder to distinguish empirically from models with a single input–output lexicon for spoken words (e.g. Allport & Funnell, 1981).

The main argument in favour of this connection is the fact that it helps complete a whole-word route from auditory input to written output that by-passes the semantic system (auditory analysis system to auditory input lexicon to speech output lexicon to graphemic output lexicon to writing or oral spelling). Such a route seems necessary to explain the ability of some patients with "word meaning deafness" to spell to dictation irregular words they appear not to understand (see p. 177). Better evidence for such a connection would be provided by a patient who could repeat words but not non-words without understanding the words he could repeat correctly.

It is a measure of the incomplete development of models such as Fig. 8.3 that we do not feel the need for a comparable connection between the visual input lexicon and the graphemic output lexicon.

14. Patients have been reported who can read aloud irregular words correctly without appearing to understand what those words mean. This has been taken to imply the existence

(Continued)

TABLE 8.1
(Continued)

of a whole-word route from the visual input lexicon to the speech output lexicon, by-passing the semantic system. Unlike route 13, this route is also supported by evidence from normal, intact subjects who are able to read aloud familiar, irregular words faster than they can perform any form of semantic categorisation upon those words. This finding is compatible with the notion that the retrieval of the pronunciation of a word following its recognition by the visual input lexicon can operate simultaneously and in parallel with the retrieval of the word's meaning from the semantic system.

15. Normal readers can read aloud unfamiliar words or non-words which they have never seen before. Hence we must incorporate into our models a route from letter recognition to speech output which does not depend on words being recognised as familiar by the visual input lexicon. One option is to postulate a distinct sublexical route by which unfamiliar words or non-words can be read aloud through a process of dividing a word up into letters or letter groups and translating those visual units into corresponding phoneme strings. This route would be relatively little used by skilled adult readers, but used extensively by children, for whom far fewer words are represented as wholes in the visual input lexicon, or by unskilled adult readers.

Some aspect of grapheme–phoneme conversion is impaired in "phonological dyslexics" who can read aloud real words much better than they can read aloud unfamiliar words or non-words. Grapheme–phoneme conversion is also severely impaired in "deep dyslexics".

On pp. 203–233 we acknowledge the existence of alternative theoretical accounts of how we might read aloud unfamiliar words, including accounts which would effectively merge grapheme–phoneme conversion with the whole-word route (14), which connects the visual input lexicon with the speech output lexicon.

16. The function of the graphemic output lexicon is to store the spellings of familiar words and make them available in the process of writing. It is particularly important for a language like English that spellings should be retrieved as wholes from memory, because of the presence in the language of so many words with irregular, unpredictable spellings. Words can be retrieved from the graphemic output lexicon in response to input from three different sources—the semantic system, the auditory input lexicon, and the speech output lexicon. We have discussed in 10 above the fact that an input from the speech output lexicon may allow us to explain certain types of spelling errors in which words are produced which are similar in sound to the intended word. An input from the semantic system may allow explanation of semantic errors in writing, both as made occasionally by normal subjects and as made in large numbers by "deep dysgraphics". Retrieval of spellings from the graphemic output lexicon is not all-or-nothing: We can see both in normal subjects and in a variety of acquired dysgraphic patients the occurrence of errors which incorporate unpredictable elements of a word's spelling, while nevertheless being incorrect. Arguably, such errors result from incomplete activation of entries in the graphemic output lexicon.

17. The reasons for including a connection between entries in the speech output lexicon and the graphemic output lexicon are discussed in Chapter 7 (pp. 170–172). They include the fact that normal writers will produce involuntary "slips of the pen" occasionally, where an intended word is miswritten as another real word which is identical or similar in sound to it (e.g. writing *scene* for *seen*, or *surge* for *search*). Some dysgraphics produce similar errors at higher frequencies.

The connection also plays a part in explaining how some "word deaf" patients may be able to write to dictation irregular words they do not understand (see 13 above).

(Continued)

TABLE 8.1
(Continued)

18. Skilled writers can devise plausible spellings for unfamiliar words or invented non-words. In English this is a hazardous enterprise given the variability and unreliability of sound-to-spelling correspondences in English. The ability to generate spellings for unfamiliar words is explained in the model in terms of a system of phoneme–grapheme conversion connecting representations at the phoneme level to representations at the grapheme level (i.e. a system for mapping sounds onto spellings).

The hallmark of phoneme–grapheme conversion is the occurrence of "regularisation" errors which sound like the intended target word (e.g. misspelling biscuit as "biskit"). Such errors are seen in large numbers in the spelling of "surface dysgraphic" patients in whom the process of whole-word retrieval from a graphemic output lexicon is impaired. Conversely, phoneme–grapheme conversion is itself impaired in "phonological dysgraphic" patients whose spelling of familiar real words is much better than their spelling of unfamiliar words or non-words.

19. At the grapheme level are somewhat abstract representations of each of the letters used in English. These representations are abstract because it is assumed that the upper- and lower-case versions of a letter will be represented by a single entry at the grapheme level. Selection of particular letter forms and particular modes of spelling output (handwriting, typing, spelling aloud, etc.) is made downstream of the grapheme level.

The grapheme level receives three inputs—one from the visual analysis system permitting words to be copied directly from print, a second from phoneme–grapheme conversion, and a third from the graphemic output lexicon. Certain slips of the pen made by normal writers may be attributed to errors at the grapheme level, as may the more frequent errors of some "peripheral" dysgraphic patients (pp. 181–182).

20 and 21. At the allograph level letters are represented in spatial form. Each grapheme has at least two allographic variants—its upper- and lower-case form. At the level of graphic motor patterns the letters are represented as the movements necessary to create particular allographs. Certain letter-level slips of the pen in normal subjects, and also certain forms of "peripheral" dysgraphia, may be interpreted in terms of problems arising at the allograph level or the level of graphic motor patterns (pp. 182–187).

22. This link from writing back to the visual analysis system represents the external feedback which can be gained by reading one's own writing. Patients with "afferent" dysgraphia appear not to attend sufficiently to external visual feedback, as they also fail to attend sufficiently to internal kinaesthetic feedback. As a result, they make characteristic errors involving repetitions or omissions of strokes or letters in sequences of similar items. The same sorts of errors can be induced in normal subjects by depriving them of visual feedback (e.g. having them write with eyes closed), and these errors may reach levels in normal subjects comparable to those seen in "afferent dysgraphics" if the removal of visual feedback is combined with a secondary task such as tapping or counting while the person is trying to write. The secondary task probably interferes with attention to kinaesthetic feedback in normal subjects (see pp. 183–187).

23. The provision of a direct connection between the visual analysis system and the grapheme level allows words or non-words to be copied without being recognised or understood. The copying in question is not slavishly pictorial, but involves copying of the stimulus material in the subject's own handwriting. Making the connection between the

(Continued)

TABLE 8.1
(Continued)

visual analysis system and the grapheme level two-way provides a mechanism whereby subjects might image visually words retrieved from the graphemic output lexicon or assembled by phoneme–grapheme conversion. This internal feedback would be analogous to the internal feedback from the phoneme level to the auditory analysis system (see 11 above).

Note: Some of the arrows connecting components are two-way, whereas others are shown as unidirectional. The conservative rule we have followed is only to show a connection as two-way if we have *evidence* that two components can exert a *mutual* influence on one another. Thus, two-way arrows connect the auditory and visual analysis systems to the auditory and visual input lexicons as a device for explaining the "top-down" word-superiority effect, whereby phonemes and letters are perceived more rapidly and more accurately in words than in non-words. Similarly, the semantic system has bidirectional connections to the auditory and visual input lexicons to explain semantic priming and other "context effects" (see McClelland, 1987, for a review of such interactive phenomena in language processing). In contrast, there are grounds for believing that grapheme–phoneme conversion is a one-way translation process distinct from phoneme–grapheme conversion. Other connections shown as one-way may, in reality, be two-way connections allowing interactive activation between components.

Part of the apparent complexity of Fig. 8.3 derives from the need to display it in two dimensions—even imagining elements 13, 14, and 15 sitting above or below the plane of the page helps resolve some of the confusion of crossing lines. An alternative riposte to allegations of Byzantine complexity is to note that the composite model is probably a gross over-simplification. Some of the modules proposed will almost certainly need to be subdivided further: The semantic system, for example, covers a multitude of representations and operations, and the visual analysis system carries more weight than a single module should be expected to. Like the models of the late nineteenth-century "diagram makers" mentioned in Chapter 1, Fig. 8.3 is also severely limited in as much as it only addresses the comprehension and production of single spoken or written words. As the next chapter will show, several more modules need to be postulated when we contemplate the comprehension and production of phrases, sentences, and larger linguistic segments. Finally, Fig. 8.3 relates exclusively to verbal processes, yet language processes must interface with perceptual processes such as those involved in object and face recognition discussed in Chapters 2 and 4. The ultimate model of cognition must show how modules mediating those skills tie in with verbal modules, and the reader may care to play around with possible fusions of Fig. 8.3 and Figs 2.1 and 4.1.

Another obvious point is that a model like Fig. 8.3 is only half a theory. The missing half is the specification of how each module works and how it communicates with the other modules to which it is connected. This is the half that was missing from the nineteenth-century diagrams and one of the causes of dissatisfaction with them. The modern diagram maker is rather better off in this regard because the development of computational concepts has provided a vocabulary for talking about the possible internal workings of modules. Thus we now possess theories, some of them implemented in computer simulations, of the possible mechanics of the auditory input lexicon (e.g. McClelland & Elman, 1985; Klatt, 1979; Marslen-Wilson, 1984), the visual input lexicon (e.g. Brown, 1987; McClelland & Rumelhart, 1981; Morton, 1979), the speech output lexicon (e.g. Dell, 1986; Stemberger, 1985), and so on.

Experience teaches us that some people find diagrams like Fig. 8.3 more congenial than others. That is a fact about individual preferences, not about scientific merit. If we are to take the modularity hypothesis seriously, however, and if we are to continue to use diagrams as expository devices, then we had better get used to models like Fig. 8.3.

We shall close this chapter by commenting briefly on two somewhat controversial features of Fig. 8.3—our separation of grapheme–phoneme conversion from the whole-word route from print to sound (represented in Fig. 8.3 by the direct link 14 between the visual input lexicon and the speech output lexicon), and our separation of input from output lexicons.

Grapheme–Phoneme Conversion

In Fig. 8.3 there are two routes from print to sound by which written words can be read aloud without involving the representations of the meanings of those words in the semantic system. The first route is provided by the provision of direct links between corresponding representations in the visual input lexicon and the speech output lexicon (arrow 14 in Fig. 8.3). This route allows familiar written words (i.e. words with entries in the visual input lexicon) to activate directly their pronunciations in the speech output lexicon while their meanings are being activated simultaneously in the semantic system.

The second route is provided by the grapheme–phoneme conversion system (15). It maps letters or letter groups identified by the visual analysis system onto phonemes or phoneme groups at the phoneme level. It provides a mechanism by which pronunciations can be derived in a piecemeal fashion for unfamiliar written words or for invented non-words. According to traditional (i.e. 5 or 6 years old at the time of writing) formulations of grapheme–phoneme conversion, it will yield the correct pronunciation if the word being read aloud is one with regular spelling–sound correspondences, but irregular words will be pronounced as if they were regular (i.e. "regularised").

When these two routes are combined with the route from the visual input lexicon through the semantic system to the speech output lexicon we end up with a total of three routes from print to sound. Some theorists are happy with this (e.g. Howard & Franklin, 1987; Patterson & Morton, 1985), but others wish to reduce the three to two by combining the whole-word non-semantic route with sub-word grapheme–phoneme conversion. This issue is discussed further by Henderson (1985), Humphreys and Evett (1985), Kay (1985), and Patterson and Coltheart (1987).

There is some empirical support for such a move. If grapheme–phoneme conversion were a separate module then it should, by Fodor's (1983) logic, be autonomous and insulated from activities within the whole-word route. It is not, however. Kay and Marcel (1981) showed that the pronunciation given to a non-word by normal readers can be influenced by the real words they have seen recently. Specifically, the pronunciation given to a non-word like NOUCH embedded in a mixed list of words and non-words is influenced by whether the subject has recently read COUCH or TOUCH. Now COUCH and TOUCH are familiar real words which should be recognised by the visual input lexicon and whose pronunciations should be accessed via the direct links to the speech output lexicon. All this should have no effect whatsoever on the grapheme–phoneme conversion system, and in particular that system should be unaffected by the pronunciation given to the irregular word TOUCH. Yet it *is* affected, because reading TOUCH biases subjects towards a different pronunciation of NOUCH than they would otherwise have given.

There are various ways that theories can respond to this sort of evidence. Kay and Marcel (1981) followed Glushko (1979) in arguing that unfamiliar words and non-words are not read aloud by a separate grapheme–phoneme conversion system at all, but are pronounced by a process of *analogy* with familiar words. In terms of our model, a mechanism for reading aloud non-words (or unfamiliar words) by analogy might begin by allowing a non-word to activate entries in the visual input lexicon through resemblance between the non-word and familiar, known words.

For the non-word NOUCH, this set might include words of similar length beginning NO- (e.g. NOISY, NONE, NORMAL) and words ending in -OUCH (e.g. COUCH, POUCH, TOUCH). All those entries would transmit activation to their corresponding entries in the speech output lexicon causing activation of the nodes at the phoneme level for all those words. Eventually the phonemes which win out should be the ones activated by the greatest number of resemblances between the non-word being read and familiar, known words. For NOUCH an initial /n/ would obviously be selected. Because more words ending in -OUCH are pronounced as in COUCH than as in TOUCH, NOUCH would normally be pronounced to rhyme with COUCH, particularly if COUCH or a similar word had been read recently (assuming that words read recently retain a certain primacy). If, however, TOUCH has been seen recently, that may be enough to bias the pronunciation of NOUCH towards a rhyme with TOUCH—precisely the result obtained by Kay and Marcel (1981).

Not all theorists are enamoured with that sort of analogy model. Some have sought to maintain a separate grapheme–phoneme conversion system, but have modified that system to incorporate alternative letter–sound correspondences and to permit some biassing of correspondences by recently encountered familiar words (e.g. Patterson & Morton, 1985).

A third, radical alternative has been proposed by Shallice, Warrington, and McCarthy (1983) and Shallice and McCarthy (1985). In terms of our model they would effectively merge the visual analysis system and visual input lexicon into a visual "word-form" system containing units representing everything from single letters through letter groups and morphemes to whole words. These units would link up to corresponding units in a phonological "word-form" system created by merging the speech output lexicon and the phonemic level. Familiar words would be read aloud by connections between word-sized units in the two word-form systems, and unfamiliar words or non-words by connections between units for letters and letter groups in the two systems. Biassing and analogy effects are explained in terms of interaction between different sized units in the two word-form systems.

At this point the reader might well be asking whether cognitive neuropsychology could not arbitrate between these alternatives, particularly through a consideration of "phonological" dyslexics whose reading of familiar words is much better than their reading of non-words, and "surface" dyslexics who read non-words well but irregular words poorly, and indeed read aloud many once-familiar words as if they were non-words (making regularisation errors to irregular words in the process). There is a double dissociation between whole-word and subword (or "sublexical") reading here, but double dissociations are between tasks, not postulated modules. This double dissociation is between whole-word reading and piecemeal, "assembled" reading (Patterson, 1982). As such, it shows that there are cognitive processes involved in whole-word reading that are not involved in piecemeal reading, and vice versa. But as Patterson and Coltheart (1987) observe, when all of the types of theory outlined above are inspected closely, processes can be found within them which are specific to piecemeal reading which could be impaired in "phonological" dyslexics, and processes are found which are specific to whole-word reading which could be impaired in (some) "surface" dyslexics.

None of the theories is overly embarrassed by the simple fact of a dissociation between whole-word and piecemeal reading. It could be that when the theories are spelled out in detail or implemented as computer models, then differences will emerge in the precise manner in which each would expect the different sorts of reading to break down. At the time of writing such detailed, implemented models are just beginning to emerge (e.g. Brown, 1987; Sejnowski & Rosenberg, 1986), but the predictions for neuropsychological breakdown are yet to be made and tested. It is already apparent, however, that as greater specificity is demanded and achieved, so the boundaries between "dual-route" models, "analogy" models, and "multiple levels" models begin to blur and dissolve. It seems quite likely that if we ever create a model capable of explaining all the relevant experimental and neuropsychological data it will incorporate aspects of all three types of model.

It would be foolhardy of us to back one type of theory of print-to-sound translation over another with the present state of knowledge. We shall content ourselves with having alerted the reader to the fact that our inclusion in Figs 8.1 and 8.3 of a distinct module named "grapheme–phoneme conversion" is done in the knowledge that such a step is controversial and quite possibly unwise.

Input and Output Lexicons

Another feature of Fig. 8.3 which posterity might well judge unwise is its separation of input from output lexicons. Virtually all theorists nowadays wish to distinguish between phonological lexical systems dealing with spoken words and orthographic lexical systems dealing with written words, but not everyone wishes to make the further division into input lexicons handling word recognition and output lexicons handling word production.

Allport and Funnell have argued in a series of papers that the available experimental and neuropsychological evidence can be handled by a model which has one phonological lexicon handling both the recognition and production of spoken words, and one orthographic lexicon handling both the recognition and production of written words (Allport, 1983; 1984; Allport and Funnell, 1981). Their model can be represented diagrammatically as in Fig. 8.4. Morton (1984) has observed that a similar rivalry between models having two or four word "centres" existed among the nineteenth-century diagram makers.

In more recent times, cognitive neuropsychological arguments in favour of a single orthographic lexicon have been advanced by Coltheart and Funnell (1987). They studied a patient HG who was mildly "surface dyslexic" and mildly "surface dysgraphic". In fact, he read irregular words aloud quite well if the lists he was given contained only real words,

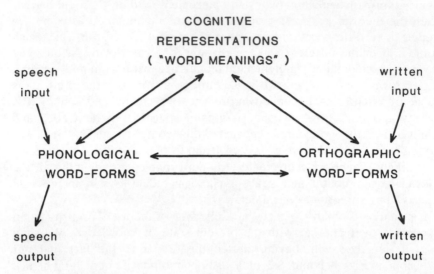

FIG. 8.4.   Functional model for the recognition and production of spoken and written words incorporating one phonological and one orthographic lexicon (after Allport & Funnell, 1981).

but if they contained a sprinkling of non-words then he began to make some "regularisation" errors to less common (low-frequency) irregular words; for example, misreading *quay* as "kway", *suede* as "sood", and *colonel* as "kollonel". It seemed as if he failed to recognise these as real words in lists of mixed words and non-words and instead read them aloud using grapheme–phoneme conversion (or analogies, or whatever).

In spelling to dictation he made similar regularisation errors to less common words; for example, misspelling "moan" as *mone* and "blew" as *bloo*. Now, as Coltheart and Funnell (1987) note, HG's particular brand of "surface" dyslexia implies a mild impairment of access of a visual lexicon involved in recognising written words in reading, whereas his "surface" dysgraphia implies a mild impairment of retrieval from an orthographic lexicon involved in producing written words in spelling and writing. If that visual lexicon and orthographic lexicon are one and the same module—a dual-purpose input–output lexicon of the sort proposed by Allport and Funnell (1981)—then the words he has slight problems reading should be the same words as the ones he has problems spelling. Testing this prediction is not quite as easy as it would appear at first glance, because HG's reading and spelling were both affected by word frequency, so one would expect some overlap between sets of words read and spelled successfully or unsuccessfully. When Coltheart and Funnell tested HG's spelling of words he could or could not read reliably they found a remarkably close association between spelling and reading: His spelling performance was better for words he read perfectly than for words he read imperfectly, even when the confounding factor of word frequency was taken into account. On the basis of this finding, Coltheart and Funnell (1987) elected to support the single orthographic lexicon view, while acknowledging the problems involved in using consistency measures to discriminate between one and two lexicon theories.

Set against Coltheart and Funnell (1987) is Campbell's (1987b) argument for separate visual input and graphemic output lexicons. Campbell's starting point is that many normal people misspell some words *consistently*, despite the fact that they see the correct spelling time and again in the course of their reading. One of us drove to Dunfermline nearly every month for 3 years, passing (and using) many road signs, but persisted in writing letters and reports on his visits to Dunfermline. Campbell investigated this phenomenon in two student subjects, JM and RM, both of whom had experienced reading and spelling problems as children and continued to spell rather poorly as adults. Some of their misspellings were consistent from one attempt to the next (e.g. misspelling *talking* as *torking, logical* as *logicle*, and *guarantee* as *garentee*). JM and RM were shown lists of mixed words and non-words where some of the non-words were in fact their own consistent misspellings. On other occasions the correct spellings of those words were presented. The task was one of "lexical decision" with JM and RM being required to decide whether each letter string they read was a word or a non-word.

JM and RM proved to be quite good (around 90%) at judging the correctly spelled words to be words in English. They were poor, however, at rejecting their own consistent misspellings as non-words. In fact they were at chance on this decision (RM 43% correct; JM 48% correct). They were better, though not particularly good (around 75%), at rejecting misspellings generated by the experimenter which they themselves did not make.

Campbell (1987b) maintains that these findings are more easily explained by a model which postulates separate reading (input) and spelling (output) lexicons. She argues that their spelling lexicons (our graphemic output lexicon) only contain their misspellings of words they consistently spell incorrectly, hence those misspellings are all they can generate in writing. Their reading lexicons (our visual input lexicon) will contain the correct spellings, acquired through reading, but are also likely to contain their consistent misspellings, acquired by reading their own written material. The lexical decision task effectively asks whether a letter string is represented in the visual input lexicon: If it is, then it can be assumed to be a real word. But because at least some of JM and RM's consistent misspellings are also represented in their visual input lexicons they are apt to be falsely accepted as real words in English.

As far as reading and spelling are concerned, then, both single and separate lexicon models have their adherents and it is hard to arbitrate between them on current evidence. The situation is similar regarding the issue of one or two lexicons for spoken word recognition and production. If the two alternatives are equally viable, then the scientific principles of parsimony (simplicity) should lead us to prefer single lexicon models. There is, however, at least one observation in the neuropsychological literature which seems more readily explicable in terms of separate auditory input and speech output lexicons, and that is the phenomenon of semantic errors in the repetition attempts of "deep" dysphasics (see pp. 157–158).

Asked simply to repeat the word "crocus", a "deep" dysphasic might say "daffodil". Such repetition is clearly semantically mediated. On a two-lexicon model like Fig. 8.3, this would mean that the more direct route for repetition (11) between the auditory analysis system and the phoneme level is impaired (hence deep dysphasics should be poor at repeating non-words which have no entry in the auditory input lexicon, which they are). Repetition is therefore obliged to proceed via the auditory input lexicon, the semantic system, and the speech output lexicon. Semantic errors would be attributed to an additional impairment in or around the semantic system.

On a one-lexicon model like Fig. 8.4, even where repetition is lexically mediated it can proceed *straight through* the phonological lexicon because the representations in that lexicon which recognise spoken words are also the representations which guide their production. For a semantic error to occur in repetition a representation in the lexicon would have to be activated yet not itself mediate repetition. Rather it would have to transmit activation only up to the (impaired) semantic system which would transmit activation back down to the phonological lexicon, but this time to the entry for a different word of similar meaning which the patient then says.

We are not saying that single-lexicon models could not explain semantic errors in repetition, just that their explanations seem strained in comparison with the accounts which fall readily out of two-lexicon models (Howard & Franklin, 1987). As with the debate over the number of routes from print to sound, the debate over the required number of lexicons is not one we see any sense in taking sides on at present. The interested reader is referred to Monsell (1985) for a review of the scarcely less equivocal evidence to be derived from the experimental cognitive literature.

SUMMARY OF THE COGNITIVE
NEUROPSYCHOLOGY OF READING

The acquired dyslexias may be divided for convenience into peripheral and central dyslexias. Peripheral dyslexias affect early visual processes by which letters are recognised, coded for position and grouped into words. "Neglect dyslexic" patients like VB omit or, more often, substitute letters at the beginnings of words. In VB's case these errors usually involved substituting the correct number of letters, suggesting that her neglect may have affected the encoding of letter identities more than letter positions. Patients with "attentional" dyslexia erroneously combine letters from words simultaneously present on the page. The letters typically retain their within-word positions, suggesting that the impairment may affect the processes which perceptually group letters which belong together as part of the same word. "Letter-by-letter readers" can no longer identify the letters of a word simultaneously and in parallel, and can only identify a word after identifying each letter separately. Warrington and Shallice's (1980) theory proposes that the visual input lexicon which normally recognises familiar words can no longer be accessed and that word recognition is mediated by some form of reversed use of the patients' intact spelling systems.

Central dyslexias affect word recognition, comprehension and naming processes, and/or processes dealing with unfamiliar words or non-words. Patients such as WLP who can read aloud irregular words they fail to understand may provide evidence for word-specific links between corresponding entries in the visual input lexicon and the speech output lexicon.

"Surface" dyslexics rely to a considerable extent on grapheme–phoneme correspondences to read aloud once-familiar words. Accordingly, they read regular words more successfully than irregular words, which they are apt to "regularise". Detailed investigations of single cases show that a number of different impairments can generate these symptoms, including impairment of the visual input lexicon, the semantic system, and the speech output lexicon. The symptoms which accompany the regularity effect and regularisation errors distinguish between these different loci of impairment. It is a moot point whether such different patients belong together in the same "syndrome" category.

The precise nature of the inability to read aloud unfamiliar words or non-words, sometimes termed "phonological" dyslexia, may also vary from patient to patient. These patients show clearly, however, that the recognition of familiar words is not dependent on the availability of low-level grapheme–phoneme conversion procedures.

Problems of a more semantic nature are seen in "semantic access" dyslexics who are unable to gain full, conscious access to word meanings. Semantic problems also occur in "deep" dyslexics in the form of semantic errors and problems reading abstract words. Typically, these patients also make visual errors and are poor at reading non-words, but there are signs that some or all of these symptoms may dissociate. One prevalent view explains "deep" dyslexia in terms of impairment to components of the normal (left hemisphere) reading system; another in terms of the reading capabilities of the right cerebral hemisphere.

Finally, although access to word meanings is possible without the words' sounds, patients who have problems accessing the sound patterns of words may also have problems utilising the grammatical structure of sentences to assist comprehension. It is not yet clear to what extent this is linked to an impairment of auditory-verbal short-term memory.

FURTHER READING

Caplan, D. (1992). *Language: structure, processing and disorders*. Cambridge, Mass.: MIT Press. Chapter 5 covers disorders of reading and writing.

McCarthy, R.A. & Warrington, E.K. (1990). *Cognitive neuropsychology: a clinical introduction*. San Diego: Academic Press. Chapter 10 covers reading and acquired dyslexia.

Parkin, A.J. (1996). *Explorations in cognitive neuropsychology*. Oxford: Blackwell. Chapter 8 reviews reading and writing disorders.

Patterson, K.E., Vargha-Khadem, F., & Polkey, C.E. (1989). Reading with one hemisphere. *Brain*, *112*, 39–63. Support for the right hemisphere hypothesis of deep dyslexia.

Plaut, D.C. & Shallice, T. (1994). *Connectionist modelling in cognitive neuropsychology: a case study*. Hove, UK: Lawrence Erlbaum Associates Ltd. Simulates several aspects of deep dyslexia by lesioning a connectionist model of normal, semantically-mediated reading.

VIDEOS

Two videos in the series edited by E. Funnell & G.W. Humphreys: *Teaching programmes in cognitive neuropsychology* (Hove, UK: Lawrence Erlbaum Associates Ltd.) illustrate varieties of acquired dyslexia. They are *Words and sentences: phonological dyslexia case study* and *Reading for meaning: a case study of deep dyslexia*.

9 Further Language and Communication Processes

INTRODUCTION

Language use and its impairments have always occupied a central position within cognitive neuropsychology. We have already discussed work on writing, reading, and the production and comprehension of spoken words, and yet we still have aspects of language to cover. In this chapter we shall begin by discussing briefly the conceptual language disorder known as "semantic jargon". We shall then examine the instructive history of the putative syndrome of "Broca's aphasia" or "agrammatism" which, as we shall see, turns out not to be a syndrome at all (in the sense of being a coherent set of symptoms arising from a single functional impairment) but is instead a cluster of often associated but separable deficits, each requiring a separate explanation. We shall then review a range of language-related disorders, several of which are said to follow injury to the *right* cerebral hemisphere (rather than, as is more normal in the case of language disorders, following left hemisphere injury). Towards the end of the chapter we shall examine briefly disorders of gesture and sign language, ending with a consideration of the nature of language as viewed through the eyes of a cognitive neuropsychologist.

SEMANTIC JARGON

The term "jargon aphasia" is used to refer to speech production which is fluent but very difficult to extract any coherent message from. Butterworth (1985) argues that this term is too vague and all-embracing, covering as it does a range of aphasias for which we would want to provide quite different explanations. Thus, so-called "neologistic jargonaphasia" which we reviewed in Chapter 5 seems to result from a word-finding difficulty in combination with a severe speech comprehension deficit. The patient produces fluent speech, but many words are distorted to the extent that the listener may have great difficulty working out what the patient is trying to say. Such patients may have clear communicative intentions, but those intentions become jargonised in the act of translation into speech (Ellis, Miller, & Sin, 1983).

When looked at closely, the fluent but incoherent speech of patients producing "semantic jargon" is very different from the speech of "neologistic jargonaphasics", in that "semantic jargon" is composed only of real words whereas "neologistic jargon" includes many non-words (often phonological approximations to target words). "Semantic jargon" and "neologistic jargon" are different too from the long strings of meaningless sounds seen in some cases of "phonemic jargon" (Perecman & Brown, 1981). Asked about the job he formerly held (a draughtsman; Kinsbourne & Warrington, 1963, case 2), a "semantic jargonaphasic" said:

> My job was... original... him... concerned with... particulars... of... so that I could tell them exactly what to take, and, where to... take it from... so that I could get away to the... gestures of the conditions of one side... which would give me particular items or discussion according to that...

Similar fluent and reasonably grammatical but semantically opaque speech can be seen in the following extract from case 1 of Brown (1981):

> And I said, this is wrong, I'm going out and doing things and getting ukeleles taken every time and I think I'm doing wrong because I'm supposed to take everything down from the top so that we do four flashes of four volumes before we get down low...

Patients who produce semantic jargon can be fully oriented for time and place, may behave generally in an organised, coherent way, and may perform well on non-verbal tests of intelligence (Kinsbourne & Warrington, 1963). Comprehension impairments seem always to be present, but although these impairments may be orthodox linguistic ones in many patients with semantic jargon, they may take a more subtle form in others. Case 1 of Kinsbourne and Warrington (1963) could obey quite complex commands such as: "When I tap on the table touch the top of your head and put out your tongue." He could also rearrange jumbled words into meaningful sentences like "We started for the country on an early train." When recorded samples of his own jargon spoken by an experimenter were played back to him for comment he rejected them as incomprehensible and in bad English, but when his own speech was played back to him he declared it to be comprehensible and in good English. In general, he appeared entirely unaware of his speech defect and denied that anything was amiss (a form of "anosognosia"—denial of illness).

If we take as a simple example of speech production the situation of describing a real or pictured scene, then we can distinguish three broad stages (Ellis & Beattie, 1986). First the speaker must comprehend the scene in the sense of recognising the components and understanding their relations one to another. Secondly, that understanding must be formulated into a conceptual message in which certain components of the scene and certain relations or actions are selected and arranged coherently. Thirdly, linguistic processes such as syntax and word retrieval must convert the message into a verbal utterance to be spoken or written. At the moment we lack the sort of detailed case reports of patients with semantic jargon that would allow us to locate the deficit with any great confidence, or even assert that the impairment is the same in all cases. That said, the good general orientation and intact non-verbal intelligence of Kinsbourne and Warrington's two cases suggests that the root cause of semantic jargon does not lie in any failure to comprehend the physical world or to have a coherent understanding of it. Similarly, semantic jargon is often grammatically fluent and well articulated in a way that may argue against a straightforwardly linguistic deficit.

What *may* be impaired in patients showing semantic jargon is the capacity to translate a general understanding into the sort of structured, propositional message that can serve as *input* to linguistic processes. The ability of Kinsbourne and Warrington's case 1 to understand the speech of others implies that such a deficit can be unidirectional, affecting production but not comprehension. The presence of *some sort* of comprehension deficit may be important, however (even if it is just a denial that one's *own* speech is impaired), because the willingness of these patients to produce copious quantities of semantic jargon is presumably related to an inability (or unwillingness?) to monitor their own output and detect its incoherence. Because they do not realise that they are talking gibberish they continue to produce it in large quantities.

THE SAGA OF "BROCA'S APHASIA" AND "AGRAMMATISM"

Goodglass and Geschwind (1976) defined Broca's aphasia as a syndrome "marked by effortful, distorted articulation, reduced speech output, and agrammatic syntax but sparing of auditory comprehension. Writing is usually impaired commensurately with speech, but reading is only mildly disturbed." The term "agrammatism" refers to "the dropping out of connective words, auxiliaries, and inflections so that grammar may, in extreme cases, be reduced to rudimentary form—the juxtaposition of one- or two-word sentences" (Goodglass, 1976, pp. 237–239).

"Connective" words and "auxiliaries" in that description are what we have elsewhere called "function words"—words like *and, the, by, through, to*, and *except*, whose presence in a sentence plays an important role in conveying the sentence structure, and hence in communicating the relationships between the "content words" of the sentence, particularly the nouns and verbs. "Inflections", for our purposes, are such as the past tense -*ed* in *walked*, the plural -*s* in *dogs*, and the -*est* in *quickest*; affixes which cannot stand alone but which the grammar demands to be added to words in certain sentence roles.

The effect of omitting function words and inflections is to reduce the resulting speech to strings of words which are often described as "telegraphic" because of their resemblance to the pared-down language of telegrams, where function words and inflections may be omitted to save money. This quality of agrammatic speech is illustrated in the following extract from Goodglass (1976) of the speech of a patient who is trying to explain that he has returned to the hospital to have work done on his gums:

> Ah... Monday... ah, Dad and Paul Haney [*referring to himself by his full name*] and Dad... hospital. Two... ah, doctors..., and ah... thirty minutes... and yes... ah... hospital. And, er, Wednesday... nine o'clock. And er Thursday, ten o'clock... doctors. Two doctors... and ah... teeth. Yeah,... fine.

When asked to relate the events in a film, a patient described by Luria (1970) says:

> "Ah! Policeman... ah... I know!... cashier!... money... ah! cigarettes... I know... this guy... beer... moustache....

Historically, there was an important spate of work done on aphasic patients of this sort between about 1900 and 1925, mostly in Germany and published in German (e.g. Bonhöffer, 1902; Heibronner, 1906; Isserlin, 1922; Kleist, 1916). Unfortunately, many of the insights gleaned by these aphasiologists were lost and have ended up being rediscovered independently in more recent times (Howard, 1985a; 1985b). These early studies were often intensive investigations of single patients, but research on "Broca's aphasia" or "agrammatism" has tended to be dominated more recently by studies in which the performance of *groups* of agrammatic aphasics on one or more tasks is compared with the performance of normal subjects, or other types of aphasics, or both. Reviews of this work can be found in Caramazza and Berndt (1978), Berndt and Caramazza (1980), Kean (1985), and Howard (1985a). Our treatment of agrammatism will lean heavily on Howard's (1985a) excellent review. We shall begin by summarising some of the findings of the group studies before going on to reflect on some of their problems and shortcomings.

Group Studies of "Agrammatism"

1. Function Words and Inflections. Patients whose speech is "agrammatic" do not omit *all* function words and inflections, only some. Group studies have shown that this omission or retention is not random but is influenced by a number of factors. Some function words and inflections seem intrinsically more prone to omission than others (De Villiers, 1974). Thus Goodglass and Hunt (1958) found twice as many omissions of the inflectional ending -*s* when it occurred as a possessive marker (as in *Dick's*) than when it occurred as a plural marker (as in *bricks*). Gleason, Goodglass, Green, Ackerman, and Hyde (1975) found the plural -*s* and the present participle -*ing* (as in *wishing, kicking*) to be less likely to be omitted than the past tense -*ed* (as in *wished, kicked*). Goodglass and Berko (1960) found the plural -*s* less likely to be omitted when it is expressed as a syllable (as in *horses*) than when it is non-syllabic (as in *goats* or *cows*), and Goodglass, Fodor, and Schulhoff (1967) found more omissions of function words if they were at the beginnings of sentences and/or unstressed than if they occurred within sentences and/or were stressed (sentence position effects have also been found by Gleason et al., 1975, and by Wales & Kinsella, 1981). Friederici (1982) found German prepositions (the equivalents of English function words like *at*, *on*, or *through*) to be more likely to be omitted when their role in a sentence was purely grammatical than when the preposition conveyed referential meaning.

2. Content Words. Although the problems with function words and inflections are usually regarded as prototypical features of agrammatism, the problems experienced by agrammatic patients may not be solely confined to those elements. Myerson and Goodglass (1972) and others have noted that verbs are relatively infrequent in agrammatic speech and often occur in the -*ing* form. Saffran, Schwartz, and Marin (1980b) have suggested that these may be "nounified" verbs which serve to name actions as nouns name things, and cite in evidence sentences like "She is bookening (reading) it" and "The baby bottleing" (is drinking from a bottle). Even nouns may cause problems for agrammatic aphasics: Myerson and Goodglass (1972) found a strong bias towards use of nouns referring to concrete rather than abstract entities, with names of people and places predominating.

3. Sentence Structure. If the use of function words and inflections were the only problem for agrammatic aphasics, then it should be possible to take samples of their speech and recreate straightforwardly their target sentences by adding the missing function words and inflections. It is not. As Howard (1985a) observes: "... on the whole, the content words do not form sentences stripped of their grammatical structures".

Saffran, Schwartz, and Marin (1980c) showed that agrammatic aphasics have problems indicating grammatical relations that are signalled by the order or arrangement of nouns in sentences. Their descriptions of pictures were reasonably good as far as the positioning of nouns was concerned when the pictures showed animate objects as the actors in sentences and inanimate objects as the recipients of the actions (e.g. "The boy pulling a wagon"). But when both the actor and the recipient were animate (e.g. a picture of a horse kicking a cow), the patients chose the wrong noun to initiate the sentence on 35% of occasions. They understood the picture and knew who was doing what to whom, but their ability to use the conventions of English syntax (sentence structure) to express that knowledge seemed impaired.

If agrammatic problems were confined to function words and inflections, then sequences of content words like *large white house* or *give friend dollar* should create no difficulties for them. Yet, as Gleason et al. (1975) showed, agrammatic aphasics find such sequences (Adjective–Adjective–Noun and Verb–Indirect Object–Direct Object) very hard to produce. Like Saffran et al.'s (1980c) observations on word order, this suggests a sentence construction problem over and above the difficulties with function words and inflections.

4. Comprehension. The description of Broca's aphasia given by Goodglass and Geschwind (1976) included agrammatic syntax but also reported "sparing of auditory comprehension". It is not hard to see how the view that language comprehension is spared could come about, for in ordinary clinical or social interactions these patients typically struggle to express themselves in speech yet seem to understand what is said to them without difficulty. Careful testing can show, however, that they often do have language comprehension problems, though these are much less debilitating or obvious in everyday life than are their output difficulties.

Caramazza and Zurif (1976) required their Broca's aphasic subjects to select from a set of alternative pictures the one which matched a sentence they heard. The Broca's aphasics were found to have particular difficulty with sentences whose correct comprehension required the analysis and use of sentence structure. Given the sentence "The man that the woman is hugging is happy", the patients' responses indicated that they knew it to be about a man and a woman, that someone was being hugged, and that someone was happy, but because they could not make use of the sentence structure they could not choose reliably between a picture of a man hugging a woman and a picture of a woman hugging a man. The patients had little difficulty with sentences like "The bicycle that the boy is holding is broken", where the sentence can be interpreted correctly from the content words alone (bicycle... boy... hold... broken), but given an anomalous sentence like "The dog that the man is biting is black", where the grammatical structure of the sentence forces an unusual interpretation, the patients often chose the picture depicting the more likely scenario (i.e. a dog biting a man rather than a man biting a dog). Similarly, Schwartz, Saffran, and Marin (1980b) found agrammatic (alias Broca's) aphasics to have great difficulty interpreting sentences like "The square is above the circle" or "The dancer applauds the clown", where there is nothing in the meanings of the words to help one decide who is above whom or who is applauding whom: Sentence structure must be used to make that decision.

"Agrammatic" aphasics understand the words they hear, then, and very often the meanings of the individual words are enough to guide a correct construal of what the speaker is saying. Consequently, their speech comprehension appears to be relatively intact. Only when correct comprehension is made to depend crucially on cues contained in the sentence structure are their characteristic impairments revealed. We should emphasise, though, that this is a summary of the *average* "agrammatic" aphasic as revealed by the averaged performance of groups of subjects. We shall now see that some patients reveal exceptions to these generalisations.

Dissociations within "Agrammatism"

When agrammatic aphasics are treated as a group, problems with sentence construction and problems with sentence comprehension are seen to accompany the tendency to omit function words and inflections. If we were to treat these all as aspects of one aphasic syndrome then we might be tempted to try to account for them all in terms of a single underlying deficit. Several such attempts have indeed been made (e.g. Berndt and Caramazza, 1980; Kean, 1977, 1979), but their viability has been undermined by the growing evidence that patients may show some of these symptoms without showing the others. If the various features shown to hold for agrammatic aphasics as a group can nevertheless also be shown to be dissociable, with each symptom capable of occurring without the rest, then it would seem more plausible to conclude that what we have is a cluster of deficits which tend to co-occur but which are nevertheless separable and require separate explanations.

1. Dissociation between Agrammatism (Omission of Function Words

and Inflections) and the Sentence Construction Deficit in Speech Produc-
tion. One of the many pitfalls lying in wait for the unwary venturer into
this particular literature is a certain inconsistency in the use of the word
"agrammatism". Some authors reserve the term for a particular *symptom—*
the tendency to omit function words and inflections. Others, however,
want it to be the label for a *syndrome*, so that when additional sentence
production or comprehension problems are found to be typically present in patients who omit function words and inflections, the term
"agrammatism" is expanded to encompass those impairments. We shall
adopt the former approach, so that "agrammatism" for us will be a
specific problem (the tendency to omit function words and inflections)
which is capable of being dissociated from other difficulties which may
often accompany it.

Tissot, Mounin, and Lhermitte (1973) argued that different patterns
of speech production impairment could be discerned among "agrammatic" aphasics. One pattern involves classic "telegraphic" speech, with
omissions of function words and inflections but with correct word order
and therefore reasonably comprehensible speech. In a second pattern,
in contrast, language is "reduced to a chaos of words" with disturbed
word order and consequently incomprehensible speech.

Subsequent studies which have contrasted individual aphasic patterns
have shown that the "syntactic" problem with word order and the
"morphological" problem with function words and inflections can indeed
be dissociated. Saffran et al. (1980b) described a patient who made
frequent and appropriate use of function words and inflections but who
could still not arrange words into grammatical sentences. When trying
to describe a picture of a girl giving flowers to her teacher she said:
"Girl... wants to... flowers... flowers and wants to... the
woman... wants to... the girl wants to... the flowers and the
woman." Describing a picture of a woman kissing a man, she said: "The
kiss... the lady kissed... the lady is... the lady and the man
and the lady... kissing." This patient cannot construct grammatical sentences, yet her speech is full of function words and inflections;
that is, she shows the sentence construction deficit without agrammatism. Simil ar cases have been reported since by Berndt (1987) and Parisi
(1987).

A case showing Tissot et al.'s (1973) converse pattern, with severe
agrammatism but only a mild sentence construction difficulty, was reported by Miceli, Mazzucchi, Menn, and Goodglass (1983). This patient
(their case 2) omitted function words but tended to use incorrect inflections
rather than omitting them. This seems to be characteristic of agrammatism
in languages like Italian and Hebrew which are heavily inflected and in
which, unlike English, words may not have an uninflected form capable

of standing alone (cf. Grodzinsky, 1984). Apart from the severe agrammatism, sentence construction was only mildly impaired in Miceli et al.'s case 2. This contrasted sharply with their case 1, who was much more like Saffran et al.'s (1980b) patient, showing only mild agrammatism in the context of a severe sentence construction deficit.

Miceli et al. (1983) conclude from their two contrasting cases that the sentence construction deficit and the impairment responsible for agrammatism are two separate problems whose degree of severity can vary independently in different patients. Accordingly, they echo Schwartz et al.'s (1980b, p. 235) view that "the constructional and morphological aspects... are dissociable... [and] reflect impairments to separate stages in the production process".

2. Dissociation between Production and Comprehension Impairments. If patients who have constructional or morphological impairments in speech production could be shown invariably to have comparable problems comprehending sentence structure or morphology (e.g. use of function words and inflections) then we would be tempted strongly to posit central syntactic and morphological components, damage to which causes corresponding problems in production and comprehension. Thus, a belief that syntactic problems with sentence structure always co-occurred led Berndt and Caramazza (1980) to argue for a single, central syntactic component whose impairment caused parallel problems in production and comprehension.

We have already seen that comprehension problems commonly co occur with production problems, so that groups of patients classified as Broca's aphasics or agrammatics on the basis of their speech production show group deficits on comprehension tests, but is that co-occurrence invariable or can patients be found with impairment of production not comprehension, or vice versa?

In Schwartz et al.'s (1980b) study of comprehension in patients whose speech output was agrammatic only one of five patients was able to score above chance consistently, and that was the patient whose speech production was *most severely* impaired. Kolk, Van Grunsven, and Keyser (1985) and Berndt (1987) report two patients whose speech production is severely agrammatic but who performed at or near normal levels on comprehension tests.

It seems likely, then, that some patients may show agrammatic speech production in the presence of intact sentence comprehension, but does the reverse occur? Are there patients whose sentence comprehension is marred by problems with function words and inflections, or problems utilising word order cues, but whose speech production is normal? Two obstacles are encountered in trying to answer this question. The first is that patients with normal speech production would never get classified as "Broca's" or "agrammatic" aphasics, because spontaneous speech is given priority in making such a diagnosis. The second problem is that the comprehension deficits we are looking for may need special tests to detect them and they may not reveal themselves in normal conversational exchanges.

It has often been noted that the comprehension of patients called "conduction" aphasics (whose speech production may include phonemic errors but is certainly not agrammatic) is very similar to the comprehension of many agrammatic aphasics (e.g. Caramazza & Zurif, 1976; Heilman & Scholes, 1976). Howard (1985a) suggests that the conduction aphasic patient MC of Caramazza, Basili, Koller, and Berndt (1981) may fit the description of agrammatic comprehension without agrammatic production. MC's speech was described as "relatively normal", with no tendency to omit function words or inflections and with good control of word order. In sentence comprehension he was, however, very poor at the sort of reversible sentences that often (but not always) cause problems for patients with agrammatic production (sentences like *The cat is being chased by the dog*). However, although MC *may* fit the bill as a patient with agrammatic (or asyntactic) comprehension without comparable problems in production, Caramazza and Berndt (1985) note that MC also had a very restricted repetition span, and suggest that "conduction aphasics" like MC (whose essential symptom is poor repetition in the context of better preserved comprehension and production) may show asyntactic comprehension because they have an impairment to an auditory-verbal short-term memory store which serves as a point of entry to syntactic comprehension processes.

In conclusion, although the status of putative cases of impaired comprehension with intact production may be uncertain, the opposite dissociation of impaired, agrammatic production with intact comprehension seems secure. Parisi (1987) argues that the computational processes required to assemble grammatical sentences are unlikely to be able simply to reverse their direction of operation in order to contribute to sentence comprehension, which will need its own dedicated syntactic processes. Accordingly, Parisi maintains that we should *expect* to discover the sorts of dissociations between production and comprehension impairments that are currently being documented.

"Agrammatism": Some Morals

So where does this all leave "agrammatism", and us? The conclusion drawn by many cognitive neuropsychologists is that the saga of agrammatism is a salutory lesson in how *not* to do cognitive neuropsychology (cf. Badecker & Caramazza, 1985; 1986; Berndt, 1987; Caramazza & Berndt,

1985; Goodglass & Menn, 1985; Howard, 1985a). The initial mistake, these commentators argue, was to take as the object of investigation a "syndrome" which consisted of a cluster of associated but nevertheless dissociable symptoms. That mistake was compounded when the "syndrome" was then studied by presenting tasks to *groups* of subjects. Theories were developed on the basis of group average scores which concealed potentially important individual differences between members of the groups.

Any group of mixed "Broca's aphasics" *will* score below normal on tests of word order in production, tests of syntax in comprehension, and so on, because there is no denying that these impairments are *associated* in such a way that a patient who has one impairment will *tend* to have the others. But the presence of exceptions to that generality shows that the observed frequent co-occurrence is not the result of one underlying functional deficit. More likely the association is attributable to there being several separate functions which happen to be dependent for their successful execution on adjacent regions of cerebral cortex. An injury to the brain which impairs one of those functions will thus tend to impair the others because brain injuries such as strokes are usually crude and undiscriminating, but the occasional patient with impairment to some of these functions but not others will reveal them for the separate and autonomous processes that they are.

In summarising an extensive and insightful review of agrammatism Howard (1985a, pp. 26–27) concludes that:

> Agrammatism has become *reified*: instead of the subject of study being the syntactic problems of aphasic patients, it becomes the "syndrome" of agrammatism. The patients become simply exemplars of the syndrome which is *assumed* to exist.... [This] assumption is faulty. There is sufficient evidence to show that there are a variety of qualitatively different patterns of... impairment. Seen in this light, all the present theories of agrammatism, subtle and sophisticated as they are, are no longer relevant: they are attempts to explain something that may not even exist.

Work so far may thus have revealed several separate language impairments which cognitive neuropsychologists will need to explain:

1. A morphological impairment which creates problems when using function words and inflections in speech production ("agrammatism").
2. A syntactic problem with speech production which shows itself (in English at least) as an inability to order nouns correctly around the verb in a sentence.
3. An impairment affecting the utilisation of sentence structure information in language comprehension.
4. A fourth dissociation is implied by Parisi's (1987) contrast between

patients who have problems with function words and not inflections (e.g. his patients COA and GJ) and patients who have problems with inflections and not function words (e.g. patient AS).

Once the distinctness of these various symptoms has been acknowledged it may be possible to reinterpret some of the earlier group studies as studies of patients who, though they may have been heterogeneous with respect to their other symptoms, mostly showed one or other of these impairments. What is now inadmissible are theories which seek to explain these dissociable symptoms in terms of a single underlying impairment.

Stemberger (1984) makes use of group data to develop his account of the agrammatic tendency to omit function words and inflections in their speech output. Stemberger begins by observing differences in the types of "slip of the tongue" that most commonly affect function words and content words in the speech errors of normal, healthy adults. One interesting difference is that whereas slips of the tongue commonly involve the unintended substitution of one content word for another (e.g. "You'll find the ice-cream in the oven"—intended word, fridge), content words are rarely simply omitted from the intended sentence. Omissions of function words, in contrast, are relatively common ("You wouldn't have to worry that... *about* that"), as are omissions of inflections ("He relax when you go away"—intended word, relaxes). Stemberger notes the similarities between normal speech errors involving function words and inflections, and characteristic agrammatic errors (e.g. the predominance of omissions over substitutions, and the fact that when substitutions of function words do occur they almost always involve the replacement of one function word by another). These similarities are interpreted within an "interactive activation" theory (which we shall not explore here) as suggesting that what we may be seeing in agrammatism is an *exaggeration* of a tendency to error which is already seen in normal people (just as we proposed in Chapter 5 that the word-finding difficulties of some "anomic" aphasics may represent an exaggerated form of the normal "tip-of-the-tongue" state).

Stemberger's (1984) theory may help us explain the omissions of function words and inflections in speech output, but cannot explain the syntactic problem with word order (nor should it be asked to, because the two symptoms are separate and dissociable). It is also not clear how it might explain the dissociation between problems with inflections and function words reported by Parisi (1987). With regard to the syntactic deficit, Schwartz, Linebarger, and Saffran (1985) note that patients with word-order problems *understand* the pictures they are asked to describe, and are thus aware at a conceptual level who is doing what to whom. In other words, comprehension of thematic roles like agent (or performer) of an action and recipient of the action are preserved. What is lost according to Schwartz et al. (1985) is the capacity to *map* those conceptual or thematic roles onto syntactic categories like the subject or object of the verb. As yet, the "mapping hypothesis" lacks detail, but it at least provides a framework to guide future investigation.

"AUTOMATIC" OR "NON-PROPOSITIONAL" SPEECH

Yamadori, Osui, Masuhara, and Okubo (1977) tested 24 right-handed patients with Broca's aphasia for the ability to sing, and discovered that 21 produced good melody and that 12 of these could also produce the lyrics well. Five of the patients whose lyrics were fluent were rated simultaneously as severe Broca's aphasics. Case TO was so aphasic that she could say only her name and a few greetings, yet she sang a song from *The Sound of Music* both excellently and fluently. We have seen a patient ourselves whose spontaneous speech was effectively limited to "Yes" and "No" but who would launch at the drop of a hat into a fluent rendition of the hymn "I am so glad that Jesus loves me".

Song lyrics are not the only bits of language that can be preserved in otherwise very severe aphasics. Zollinger (1935) reports the case of a woman whose entire left cerebral hemisphere had to be removed because of an extensive tumour. During the 17 days that she lived she was severely aphasic, but a few hours after the operation she could say "all right". "Yes" and "no" were added the next day, then "thank you", "sleep", and "please". Smith's (1966) patient also underwent removal of the left cerebral hemisphere and was also severely aphasic. He did, however, utter a range of expletives and short emotional phrases (e.g. "Goddamit!"), and in the fifth month of his operation he showed sudden recall of whole songs (e.g. "Home on the range", and "My counry 'tis of thee"). Other cases are reviewed by Searleman (1983), Code (1987), and Van Lancker (1987).

Jackson (1874) grouped singing, swearing, idioms, cliches, phrases like "thank you" and "good morning", and serial speech such as counting or reciting the days of the week together as *automatic* or *non-propositional* speech. Most normal speech is propositional in the sense that it is made up of sentences assembled *de novo* to express particular thoughts. Non-propositional speech, in contrast, comes "ready-made", so that one can say "Have a nice day" or "Know what I mean" with very little conceptual or semantic contribution.

Hughlings Jackson believed that only the left hemisphere is normally capable of propositional speech, but that both hemispheres can produce non-propositional speech, with the right hemisphere possibly being dominant for such automatic language use. Thus, "the right hemisphere is the one for the most automatic use of words, and the left the one in which automatic use of words merges into voluntary use of words—into speech" (Jackson, 1874, pp. 81–82). Larsen, Skinhoj, and Lassen's (1978) observation of increased blood flow in the right cerebral hemisphere during serial counting is compatible with right hemisphere dominance for automatic speech, though until such time as a case is reported of *loss* of automatic speech following right hemisphere injury it is probably safest to assume that both cerebral hemispheres can produce this sort of speech.

The notion that propositional language can be impaired or lost completely, leaving only automatic or non-propositional speech, is not without its problems. First, there is apparently considerable variation in the amount of "automatic" speech retained by global aphasic patients or patients whose left hemispheres have been removed, suggesting the possibility of individual variation in the normal population in the extent of right hemisphere speech. Secondly, although the distinction between propositional and non-propositional or automatic speech has some intuitive appeal, the distinction has never been defined rigorously within either linguistics or psychology (though, see Van Lancker, 1987). The danger then becomes one of circularity—global aphasics and left hemispherectomy patients have preserved automatic speech, and automatic speech is what is preserved in global aphasics and left hemispherectomy patients. That said, there are examples of speech produced by such cases which could never be classed plausibly as "automatic" or "non-propositional". For example, when Smith's (1966) hemispherectomy patient was asked, "Is it snowing outside?", he replied, "What do you think I am? A mind reader?" That was said, however, 6 months after his operation, and there are hints throughout these reports of genuine acquisition (rather than retention) of propositional language by the right hemisphere following left hemisphere removal.

The situation regarding automatic speech is thus somewhat unclear, but there are clues scattered throughout the literature to suggest that the cognitive processes required to count to ten, say "Have a nice day", or sing the lyrics of "Home on the range", may be separate from the cognitive processes operating when we convert newly-formed ideas into novel utterances.

PROSODY

When a sentence is spoken it acquires aspects and features over and above those it possesses when written down. Those features exist by virtue of the *way* the sentence is spoken. By altering the way we say the same sentence we can change it from a simple statement to a question and then to a command:

You're going out tonight. (statement)
You're going out tonight? (question)
You're going out tonight! (command)

These changes are brought about by changing what linguists refer to as the *prosody* of the sentence, where the term "prosody" covers such things as the emphasis given to certain syllables or words (e.g. contrasting GREENhouse with green HOUSE), the rise and fall of voice pitch (intonation), and the distribution of pauses in the sentence. We can also change our tone of voice in order to say the same sentence in a happy, sad, puzzled, angry, or disbelieving way. This emotive use of tone of voice (and other cues) has been termed *affective prosody*.

Although the bulk of research on language disorders has dealt with such things as word and sentence meanings, syntax, and word retrieval, a growing body of work is showing that prosody is subject to its own range of disorders. And whereas conventional aphasias usually follow injury to the left cerebral hemisphere (Kertesz, 1983), disorders of prosody may often follow injury to the *right* cerebral hemisphere.

The idea that the right hemisphere might play an important role in the expression and interpretation of emotion has a long history (Mills, 1912), though current interest in prosodic impairment stems from the work of Heilman, Scholes, and Watson (1975). This work tended to focus at first on "affective" prosody; that is, the use of tone of voice and other cues to convey emotional states. Heilman et al. found that right hemisphere injured patients could respond well to the content of sentences they heard, but performed at chance levels when required to judge from the speaker's tone of voice whether the speaker was happy, sad, angry, or indifferent. Similarly, Tucker, Watson, and Heilman (1977) reported right hemisphere injured patients who were quite unable to discriminate or repeat an "affective" tone of voice. Both these studies, however, reported averaged data from groups of patients. Potentially important individual differences are often lost in such averaging procedures, and subsequent investigations using more of a case study methodology have indeed revealed a number of qualitatively different patterns of prosodic impairment.

Ross and Mesulam (1979) provided two case reports of patients with impaired affective prosody following right hemisphere injury. Case 1 was a teacher who, on returning to work, experienced difficulty in maintaining classroom discipline. She had formerly relied to a considerable extent on tone of voice to do this, but now she had an "unmodulated, monotonous voice that was devoid of inflections and colouring". Although her comprehension of affective tone of voice was not tested formally, she reported no difficulties in perceiving other people's emotional states from their tone of voice. Case 2 also experienced "marked difficulty in modulating the tone of his voice to match the mood he wanted to impart to the listener", though he reported feeling emotions inwardly.

The possibility raised by Ross and Mesulam's (1979) case 1, that production and comprehension of affective tone of voice can be independently impaired, was assessed by Ross (1981). Ross examined the spontaneous use of affective tone of voice, the repetition of sentences in different tones of voice, and the identification of emotional state (happy, sad, angry, surprised, etc.) from tone of voice. The different patterns of intact and impaired processing of affective prosody obtained by Ross (in admittedly clinical rather than experimental testing) are shown in Table 9.1

Ross's (1981) work conveys the important message that disturbances of prosody take more than one qualitatively different form, even when only the processing of *affective* prosody is considered (see also Ross, Harney, deLacoste-Utamsing, & Purdy, 1981). Weintraub, Mesulam, and Kramer (1981) showed that right hemisphere injured patients can also show deficits (as a *group*) in more linguistic uses of prosody. These included distinguishing compound nouns by stress (GREENhouse *vs.* green HOUSE), discriminating between pairs of sentences differing only in stress or intonation, repeating sentences with varied stress or intonation, and adjusting sentence stress for contrastive emphasis (e.g. the question "Who walked to the store?" requires the answer "The MAN walked

TABLE 9.1

Patterns of Impairment and Preservation in the Spontaneous Use, Repetition, and Identification (Comprehension) of Affective Prosody, and in the Identification of Emotional from Facial Expressions and Gestures (from Ross, 1981)

Patient	Spontaneous Use	Repetition	Identification/ Comprehension	Interpretation of Facial Expressions and Gestures
1	×	×	√	√
2	×	×	√	√
3	×	×	√	√
4	√	×	×	×
5	×	×	×	×
6	×	√	√	√
7	×	√	√	√
8	√	√	×	n.a.
9	×	×/√	×	×
10	×	×	×	√

Note: √ = intact; × = impaired; ×/√ = slightly impaired; n.a. = not assessed.

to the store", with MAN stressed, while the question "Did the man walk to the store or to the station?" requires the answer "The man walked to the STATION", with the stress on STATION.)

Heilman, Bowers, Speedie, and Coslett (1984) pointed out that because Weintraub et al. (1981) had not included a group of *left* hemisphere injured patients they could not prove that the right hemisphere was any more important than the left for the processing of linguistic ("non-affective") prosody. When Heilman et al. (1984) ran a study comparing left hemisphere injured patients, right hemisphere injured patients, and normal controls, they found the right hemisphere group to be more impaired than the left hemisphere group on processing affective prosody, but no difference between the groups on processing linguistic prosody. Both groups were impaired relative to the normal controls on both types of prosody. Emmorey (1987) found the capacity to make the linguistic-prosodic distinction between compound nouns like "GREENhouse" and noun phrases like "green HOUSE" to be impaired by left but not right hemisphere injury.

There are thus questions to be resolved regarding which hemisphere is specialised for which aspects of prosodic processing. Of more relevance to present concerns, though, is evidence from these studies that impairments in the identification of affective and linguistic prosody are indeed dissociable. The task used by Heilman et al. (1984) required patients to listen to speech which had been acoustically filtered in a way which rendered the words unintelligible, while having little effect on tone of voice and prosody. Filtered sentences were spoken as statements, questions, or commands (linguistic prosody) or in a happy, sad, or angry tone of voice (affective prosody). When linguistic prosody was being assessed patients identified the sentence type by pointing to a full stop, question mark, or exclamation mark; for affective prosody they pointed to a happy face, sad face, or angry face. Fortunately, Heilman et al. (1984) provide individual results for each of their patients, and from these we can see that some patients performed better on affective prosody than linguistic prosody (e.g. *Patient L4*: 70% *vs.* 36%; *Patient L5*: 90% *vs.* 53%), while others performed worse (e.g. *Patient R1*: 30% *vs.* 70%; *Patient R4*: 46% *vs.* 83%).

Thus the "comprehension" of linguistic prosody appears to be dissociable from the "comprehension" of affective prosody, which we already know to be dissociable from the repetition and production of affective prosody.

To date research has focussed on establishing the existence of prosodic disorders and on the involvement of the two cerebral hemispheres in prosodic use. From the viewpoint of cognitive neuropsychology, what we now need are explicit information-processing theories of how prosody is produced and comprehended and how it ties in with systems for processing language and other channels of emotional expression. If prosody is anything like other aspects of language, then when we try to develop such models and use them to explain the problems of particular patients, we shall find that prosody is subject to a multitude of impairments and that simple distinctions between affective and linguistic prosody, or between comprehension, production, and repetition, are nowhere near rich enough to capture that diversity. For example, Monrad-Krohn's (1947) case of "dysprosody or altered 'melody of language'" was a Norwegian woman who, following a *left* hemisphere stroke, spoke with a mild agrammatism, and also with an altered intonation which made listeners think she was German. Prosody had not been lost but changed, with unusual emphases and pitch variations suggesting a foreign accent.

"HIGH-LEVEL" LANGUAGE DISORDERS

In this section we turn to a collection of language or language-related disorders which may have little in common with each other except that they are rather "high-level" (often being on the border between language and more general thinking and reasoning) and that, like prosodic disorders, they often follow *right* hemisphere injury rather than the left hemisphere injury we normally associate with language disorders. Indeed, the disorders we shall now review have often been discovered by investigators looking for deficits in right hemisphere injured patients (see Gardner, Brownell, Wapner, & Michelow, 1983, and Searleman, 1983, for reviews).

Two papers published in 1962 by Critchley and by Eisenson pointed to high-level language problems in patients with right hemisphere injuries. Eisenson (1962) reported difficulties on sentence-completion tasks, particularly where abstract concepts were involved, while Critchley (1962) commented upon problems in word finding with frequent resort to circumlocution, difficulties learning novel linguistic material, and severe problems with creative literary work.

Caramazza, Gordon, Zurif, and DeLuca (1976) found that patients with right hemisphere injury can experience difficulties solving verbal problems of the sort: "If John is taller than Bill, who is shorter?" Caramazza et al. (1976) suggest that people may often use imagery to help solve such problems and argue that right hemisphere injury may create problems in the use of visual imagery. Similarly, Hier and Kaplan (1980) found that right hemisphere injured patients performed worse than normal control subjects on spatial reasoning tasks, but qualified this by noting that the deficit occurred in only some of their patients, not others.

Winner and Gardner (1977) found group impairments in patients with right hemisphere injuries on another aspect of "high-level" language comprehension, namely the metaphorical interpretation of sentences. In this study, patients were asked to indicate which of four pictures best matched a metaphorical sentence like *Sometimes you have to give someone a hand*. Winner and Gardner found a tendency among right hemisphere injured patients to select pictures which depicted a literal rather than metaphorical interpretation of the sentence (e.g. a picture of a person offering someone a hand on a tray). Normal control subjects and left hemisphere injured patients rarely selected such literal pictures. Similar tendencies among right hemisphere injured patients towards literal inter- pretations rather than conventional ones have also been found for the interpretation of proverbs like *Don't cry over spilt milk* (Hier & Kaplan, 1980) and idioms like *break the ice* or *kick the bucket* (Myers & Linebaugh, 1981). Swinney and Cutler (1979) and Glass (1983) have suggested on the basis of experimental work with normal subjects that the literal and the figurative meanings of idioms may be computed simultaneously and in parallel. The results just mentioned imply that whereas the left hemisphere may be able to derive a literal interpretation satisfactorily, deriving the figurative meaning may require the additional help of an intact right hemisphere.

Another area where abnormalities have been reported in patients with right hemisphere injuries who are not aphasic by normal criteria is the interpretation and appreciation of verbal humour (Brownell, Michel, Powelson, & Gardner, 1983; see also Gardner, Ling, Flamm, & Silver- man, 1975). In the study by Brownell et al. (1983), subjects heard incomplete jokes and were asked to select the best finishing punchline from a set of alternatives offered. The right hemisphere injured patients could reject sad or neutral "punchlines" as inappropriate, but were as likely to select a "punchline" which was simply bizarre or odd as one which was genuinely humorous. Brownell et al. suggest that these patients are still sensitive to incongruity or incoherence between the "body" of a joke and the punchline, but lack an appreciation of humorous relations. Gardner et al. (1975) found a similar lack of awareness of humour in right hemisphere injured patients' responses to pictorial cartoons, so what we are dealing with here is probably a deficit in the appreciation of humour which affects language comprehension (understanding verbal jokes), but is not specific to it.

Several of the aforementioned features can be seen operating in harness with other features to impair the story recall of right hemisphere injured patients in the study by Gardner et al. (1983). The patients were told a fable-like story which they were asked to retell in their own words. Although, again, none of the patients was aphasic in the conventional sense of that word, their attempts at retelling showed that their story comprehension was not normal. They were more inclined than normal subjects to recall parts of the story verbatim rather than recoding them into their own words. They accepted and rationalised bizarre elements in the story without expressing the amusement these elements elicited in normals, and they had problems comprehending emotions attributed to characters in the tale. They also tended to misorder the elements of the story, producing as a result a less cohesive narrative. Finally, they were deficient in their ability to abstract the moral of the story from the particulars of the plot.

Summarising his own observations on language disorders following right hemisphere injury, Eisenson (1962, p. 53) wrote that, "the right cerebral hemisphere might be involved with super- or extra-ordinary language function, particularly as this function calls upon the need of the individual to deal with relatively abstract established language formulations, to which he must adjust". Many years later it is hard to generate any more precise characterisation of the language deficits shown by groups of right hemisphere injured patients. Once again, a major problem is that the studies have all been *group studies* and have rarely reported data from individual subjects. Thus, although we know that the prototypical patient with language problems following right hemisphere injury will *tend* to have problems completing abstract sentences, problems learning novel material, problems with certain logical tasks, problems interpreting metaphors, proverbs and idioms, problems appreciating verbal humour, problems ordering the elements of a narrative story, and so on, we do not know which of these problems *necessarily* co-occur, and which can be dissociated.

One can believe that a single cognitive deficit could underlie the problems with, say, interpreting metaphors, proverbs, and idioms. At a pinch one might even believe that the same deficit could cause difficulties in extracting the moral of a story (going beyond the literal message). But it is harder to conceive of a cognitive process or component, damage to which would cause these problems *and* problems with verbal humour or ordering the elements of a story. What we badly need before we can do proper cognitive neuropsychology is to know which of these impairments (and here one could throw in the prosodic impairments too) can be dissociated from which of the others, and which apparently co-occur. When we have such data we can begin to speculate about the precise nature of the "high-level" language processing components which reside in the right cerebral hemisphere, and we can begin to relate the impairments of right hemisphere injured patients to information-processing models.

GESTURES AND SIGN LANGUAGE

Language is an important mode of human communication, but it is by no means the only one. In normal life communication is a rich, interwoven blend of speech, facial expressions, body postures, gestures, etc. (Ellis & Beattie, 1986). In deaf people gesture has been developed to the level of a full-blown language (Klima & Bellugi, 1979). In this section we shall explore two of these channels of communication—gesture and sign language—from the cognitive neuropsychological perspective.

Gestures

By "gestures" we mean such things as waving goodbye, nodding the head in agreement, shrugging the shoulders to mean "I don't know", or giving a thumbs-up sign to mean "that's OK" or "Good luck". Gestures like these are symbolic combinations of movements and meanings that are as arbitrary as the connections between words like "dog" and "table" and the objects those words denote. Gestures are acquired like words, as part of the social process of learning to communicate with others (Lock, 1980).

If you were approaching gestures from a naive cognitive neuropsychological direction there are a number of questions it might occur to you to ask. Can the capacity to communicate by gesture occur in isolation, separated from other linguistic or motor disorders? Do aphasics also have problems communicating gesturally, and if they do, are those gestural problems in some way a mirror of their speech difficulties? And so on. Unfortunately, only some of these questions have been addressed by what little research has been done on gestural disorders (see Feyereisen & Seron, 1982a, 1982b; Nespoulos, Perron, & Lecours, 1986; Peterson & Kirshner, 1981).

We do not know, for example, whether brain injury can rob you of the ability to communicate gesturally while leaving speech production, the production of facial expressions, and general movement control intact. Disorders of movements are known as *apraxias*. Within that broad category various subtypes may be identified (Lecours, Nespoulos, Desaulniers, 1986; Roy, 1982). Difficulty with gestures would traditionally be classed under the heading of "ideational apraxia", but that category encompasses *any* difficulty in formulating and executing action plans, and so extends to cover difficulties making cups of coffee as well as difficulties giving a thumbs-up sign appropriately. The fact that clinicians and researchers have not felt the need to subdivide ideational apraxia further *may* mean that gestures do not dissociate from other complex movements, but as we have already seen several times, when viewed under the cognitive neuropsychological microscope, traditional neuropsychological categories often turn out to be heterogeneous clusters of symptoms which commonly co-occur but which can dissociate in key patients. Thus it is quite possible that specific impairments of gestural communication will be discovered once their theoretical significance is appreciated.

The question of whether aphasics also have gestural impairments has received rather more attention. This has often taken the form of assessing the severity of the speech disorder on a linear scale from mild to severe, assessing the severity of the gestural disorder on a similar scale, and then looking to see if the two sets of scores correlate in such a way that more severe aphasia tends to be associated with more severe gestural impairment. Several studies have found a significant association (e.g. De Renzi, Motti, & Nichelli, 1980; Kadish, 1978; Pickett, 1974) though Goodglass and Kaplan (1963) failed to find any such association. Peterson and Kirshner (1981) suggest that an association is found when the sample includes patients with very severe "global" aphasia, but that if the patient sample includes only mild and moderate aphasics then there is no correlation of the aphasia with severity of gestural impairment.

For the cognitive neuropsychologist such evidence is not easy to interpret. First, significant correlations within a group of subjects can conceal the occasional individual who may retain good gestural ability while being severely aphasic (or vice versa). Reports that some severe aphasics can benefit from being taught simple gestural communication systems reinforce this possibility (e.g. Glass, Gazzaniga, & Premack, 1973; Heilman, Rothi, Campanella, & Wolfson, 1979). Secondly, symptoms can co-occur for anatomical rather than cognitive-neuropsychological reasons (a point discussed in Chapter 1 and repeated many times throughout this book). The left cerebral hemisphere is specialised in most people for most aspects of speech production and comprehension, but it is also specialised for the planning and execution of complex motor movements and sequences (Kimura & Archibald, 1974). Impairment to those motor functions is highly likely to affect gestural communication. Therefore, on purely anatomical grounds, even if speech and gesture were entirely separate psychologically, we might expect small lesions of the left hemisphere to cause mild aphasic and mild gestural disorders, whereas large lesions would typically cause severe aphasic and severe gestural disorders, hence the observed correlation when severe aphasics are included in the test group. (N.B. If speech and gesture *are* distinct, then small lesions might affect one function more than the other, depending on the precise site of the injury. This potential for separate impairment might explain the lack of correlation among milder aphasics.)

Ranking patients on a linear scale from mildly to severely aphasic also loses much potentially valuable information because the middle range could be occupied by a truly heterogeneous mixture of anomic aphasics, agrammatic aphasics, jargon aphasics, and so on. It is of more interest to see how gestural communication is affected, if at all, in aphasic patients of different types. Butterworth, Swallow, and Grimston (1981) examined the spontaneous gestures of a "neologistic jargonaphasic" patient, KC, whose speech was littered with distorted approximations to words (neologisms). They found KC's gesturing to be normal, to be associated with content words (nouns, verbs, and adjectives), and to occur during hesitation pauses in his speech. They interpret these observations as compatible with the view that patients like KC have a word-finding difficulty similar to that of some anomic aphasics where they know the meaning they want to convey and can express that meaning gesturally, but can no longer retrieve the correct spoken word-forms to match many of the meanings (see Butterworth, 1979, and pp. 124–129).

Cicone, Wapner, Foldi, Zurif, and Gardner (1979) compared the gestures of two agrammatic "Broca's" aphasics, two "Wernicke's" aphasics with spontaneous speech which was fluent but semantically empty with many neologisms, and four normal control patients. In terms of the total amount of gesturing the two Wernicke's aphasics produced most, the normals produced an intermediate amount, and the two Broca's aphasics produced least. However, although the Wernicke's aphasics produced copious gestures, they were relatively uninformative. There was a lot of attempted pantomiming which failed to convey the patient's intended meaning to observers, but a marked absence of conventional gestures (nods, shrugs, thumbs-ups, etc.). In contrast, although the Broca's aphasics produced relatively few gestures, those they did use were clear and informative, and included a proportion of conventional gestures which was, in fact, higher than the proportion used by the normal subjects.

Cicone et al.'s (1979) observations are compatible with the view that Broca's aphasics have clear communicative intentions and know the meanings they wish to convey, but their attempts to express their intentions in speech are handicapped by the syntactic, morphological, and articulatory impairments which, as we have seen, commonly (though not invariably) co-occur in these patients. Many Wernicke's aphasics, on the other hand, may have high-level problems with message formulation which prevent the assembling of a clear communicative message. The lack of a clear communicative intention reveals itself in both unfocussed, incoherent speech and unfocussed, incoherent gesturing.

The evidence such as it is would seem to suggest, then, that initially we formulate communicative messages in a form which is essentially non- or pre-linguistic. If the message is a fairly simple one, it can be equally well conveyed in words or in gestures: We can nod our heads or say

"Yes", shrug our shoulders or say "I don't know", give a thumbs-up sign or say "That's good". If, however, the message is a more complex propositional one, then it is far easier to convey in speech than in gesture (it would be well-nigh impossible, for example, to convey the meaning of this sentence gesturally). Some Wernicke's aphasics may be impaired in the creation of communicative messages and so are impaired in communicating both gesturally and verbally. For Broca's aphasics, though, the impairments may lie entirely within the language system so that gestural communication, limited though it is, can remain intact.

Sign Language

In the sign language of the deaf, gestural communication has evolved to the status of a full language capable of all the intricacies and nuances of any spoken language. The "words" of sign language are individual gestures which can stand for both concrete and abstract concepts, whereas sentence structure is expressed in the spatial and temporal relations between these words (Klima & Bellugi, 1979). Sign language is different from "finger spelling" (sometimes called "dactylology"), where different hand positions represent different letters of the English alphabet. Finger spelling allows a deaf person to spell out a name or other word for which no standard sign exists, and may be intermixed with sign language proper in everyday communication among the deaf.

That sign language, like spoken language, is predominantly a left hemisphere specialisation is shown by the fact that disorders of sign language use typically follow injury to the left rather than the right cerebral hemisphere (Burr, 1905; Lebrun & Leleux, 1986; Marshall, 1986). Also, signing is much more impaired following temporary anaesthetisation of the left hemisphere by intracarotid injection of sodium amobarbital than following anaesthetisation of the right hemisphere (Homan, Criswell, Wada, & Ross, 1982). We have noted, however, that the planning and execution of complex motor acts is also a left hemisphere specialisation. The question has been asked, therefore, whether disorders of sign language are truly linguistic aphasias or are apraxic disorders of movement (Kimura, 1981). Two lines of evidence suggest that the "sign aphasias" are linguistic rather than apraxic. The first is that although one would expect on anatomical grounds (see above) that many deaf patients suffering from sign aphasia after left hemisphere injury would also be apraxic, nevertheless cases have been reported who have sign aphasia without apraxia (Poizner, Bellugi, & Iragui, 1984). Secondly, sign aphasias come in different varieties which more closely resemble varieties of spoken language aphasia than they resemble varieties of apraxia. That said, the differences between, say, spoken American English and American Sign Language (Ameslan) are such that one should not expect *too* close a correspondence between speech and sign aphasias.

As yet only a small number of cases of sign aphasia have been reported (Lebrun & Leleux, 1986). Following a series of left hemisphere strokes, Leischner's (1943) patient produced many concatenations of signs which did not make sense or were ill-formed, and he had great difficulty understanding the signing of others. The spontaneous signing of Underwood and Paulson's (1981) sign aphasic was marred by sign-finding errors, substitutions and jargon, but in an interesting parallel with the preservation of "automatic speech" in some speaking aphasics, this patient could count from 1 to 10 and recite the Lord's Prayer fluently in sign language.

Three contrasting cases of sign aphasia (PD, KL, and GD) have been described in a series of papers by Kimura, Battison, and Lubert (1976), Chiarello, Knight, and Mandel (1982), Bellugi, Poizner, and Klima (1983), and Poizner et al. (1984). Patient PD was an 81-year-old man who had been deaf since the age of 5 and who developed a sign aphasia following a left hemisphere stroke. His signing remained fluent with good "phrasing", but he made semantic and grammatical errors in his selection and use of signs. Examples of semantic errors are using the sign for DAUGHTER instead of WIFE, QUIT instead of DEPART, and BED instead of CHAIR. The grammatical errors are harder to explain without going into the details of sign language, but Bellugi et al. (1983) give as examples PD using an inflected sign meaning "walk for a while" instead of the simple uninflected sign WALK, and using an illegal sign combination which would translate as something like "always brillianting" instead of the simpler BRILLIANT. Other grammatical difficulties and a mild comprehension impairment were also seen in PD.

Patient KL, a 67-year-old woman who had been deaf since the age of 6 months, also continued to sign fluently after a left hemisphere stroke, though paralysis of her right hand meant that she could only sign with her left hand. Like PD, her phrase length and temporal phrasing were normal, but KL's signing errors were different. First, she used pronouns freely (the sign equivalents of "she", "it", "they", etc.) but often failed to specify what they referred to. Secondly, she made errors in the formation of signs involving incorrect handshapes, movements, and locations. For example, the sign ENJOY should be made with a circular movement but was made instead with an up-and-down movement, and the sign SEE was made at the chin instead of at the cheek location. KL's comprehension of signing was severely impaired.

The third patient, GD, was the most severely aphasic patient, being reduced to single sign utterances which were mostly nouns and verbs. GD's single signs were produced effortfully and were always in the simple, uninflected form. Despite the severe output impairment GD's comprehension of signing was only mildly impaired.

As the investigators of these patients note, there are parallels between their sign aphasias and certain aphasias of spoken language. Thus GD's signing resembles that of some "Broca's" or "agrammatic" aphasics, whereas KL's signing has similarities to that of some "Wernicke's" aphasics. More importantly, the differences between GD, KL, and PD are linguistic not motoric.

Users of sign language tend, obviously, to be deaf, and the speech of the profoundly deaf may not be fluent or easy to understand (though they may read the language of their native country well). As a consequence, although it would be interesting to know whether injury to the brain of someone fluent in both signed and spoken languages necessarily affected both forms of language, few opportunities to tackle that issue arise.

Meckler, Mack, and Bennett (1979) report the consequences of brain injury to the hearing son of deaf parents. The patient became globally aphasic with severely impaired comprehension and production of speech, and his comprehension and use of sign language was also severely impaired. Reider's (1941) similar case was more impaired in his use of speech than his use of sign. Cases like these are hard to interpret, however. We have seen that both sign language and spoken language are largely left hemisphere specialisations. Global aphasia only occurs after quite extensive left hemisphere injury (Kertesz, 1979), and such extensive injury is almost bound to affect sign language as well if signed and spoken language occupy the same cerebral hemisphere. The notion of intra-hemispheric sharing is supported by Damasio, Bellugi, Damasio, Poizner, and Van Gilder's (1986) report of how anaesthetising the left hemisphere of a hearing interpreter of sign language produced a temporary aphasia for both spoken English and American Sign Language. Removing part of the patient's right temporal lobe to relieve debilitating seizures had no effect on either signed or spoken language.

Finally, Hamanaka and Ohashi (1974) report the effects of brain injury in a hearing Japanese businessman whose wife was deaf and mute. This woman communicated by means of a sign language used by Japanese Geisha girls "to preserve professional secrecy in the guest room". The sign language employed a gesture for each of the 45 basic syllables of spoken Japanese, and the businessman used this sign language to communicate with his wife. After brain injury the man displayed mild word-finding problems in speaking which were more severe for nouns than for verbs, but no agrammatism, jargon, articulation problems or comprehension deficits. His use of sign language was more impaired, but there are hints of parallels between his signing problems and his word-finding problems in speaking. Briefly, some syllable-signs are derived from gestures which mime an object whose name (a noun) begins with that syllable, whereas others are derived from gestures which mime an action whose name (a verb) begins with that syllable [thus the sign for "ma" involves pointing to the eyebrow (-*mayuge*, a noun), whereas the sign for "ta" involves clapping (-*tataku*, a verb)]. Just as this patient found verbs easier to retrieve in speaking than nouns, so he found signs based on verbs easier to remember than signs based on nouns.

An acquired disorder of Geisha sign language in a Japanese patient may sound about as abstruse as it would be possible to get in cognitive neuropsychology, but it is the only case we know of in which aphasic disorders of speech and signing may be compared within an individual. In this patient the two disorders have interesting similarities, but we should avoid concluding prematurely that such similarities will always exist. The relationship between Geisha sign language and spoken Japanese is much closer than that between, say, American Sign Language and spoken American English, so it is more plausible to argue that they might share cognitive processes. Also, this patient learned his sign language late rather than having been bilingual from early childhood. This too could contribute to greater dependence between the two languages.

OVERVIEW

We have now devoted the best part of five chapters to the cognitive neuropsychology of language. In part this simply reflects the central position that aphasias, dyslexias, and dysgraphias have occupied in the development of cognitive neuropsychology. But such a position would not have arisen were there not such a bewildering variety of qualitatively distinct, yet interpretable and informative, forms of acquired language disorder. We have covered many such disorders in what has by no means been an exhaustive review. The question arises, what general view of human language is implied by the sheer existence of so many different patterns of reading, writing, and speech disorder?

The answer to this question that many cognitive neuropsychologists would subscribe to asserts that language is not a single, unified human faculty; rather speech production, speech comprehension, writing, and reading are capabilities which arise out of the co-ordinated activity of many language-sustaining cognitive processes or "modules".

We have discussed many such modules in this and the preceding chapters: modules for identifying phonemes in the sound wave, for recognising spoken words, for identifying letters in print, for recognising written words, for processing word meanings, sentence structure and prosody, for retrieving spoken and written word-forms in speech and spelling, for co-ordinating the output of phonemes in speaking and the output of letters in writing, and so on. If each of these processes is handled by a separate module (cognitive subsystem), and if each module is capable of being impaired independently of the others, then we can understand how the number of possible distinct patterns of language disorder can become very large. On top of this we must admit the possibility of symptom-patterns arising through complete or partial *disconnection* of intact modules, the possibility that certain modules may be impaired in two or more different ways, and the possibility that certain symptoms may only arise when a particular *combination* of modules is damaged.

Of course we must recognise that patients in whom a single module or connection is damaged will be uncommon: The grossness of most brain injuries will ensure that most patients' symptoms will reflect damage to several different cognitive subsystems. The particular sets damaged in different patients will vary, causing widespread individual differences which are likely to undermine any attempt to group patients into small numbers of homogeneous "syndromes". Patient groupings of one sort or another may be useful for certain purposes (e.g. for determining the probable site of damage, or for designing and evaluating therapies), but the best groupings for one purpose may not be the best for another, and they are unlikely to be easily sanctified by reference to cognitive neuropsychology. As we have said throughout this book, the cognitive neuropsychologist need only be concerned with how the patterns of symptoms displayed by particular patients relate to theories of the normal operation of cognitive processes. Attempts to group patients into syndromes for the purposes of cognitive neuropsychological analysis have thus far only resulted in confusion.

Our everyday use of spoken and written language is made possible by many independent but interacting cognitive components, each handling its own aspect of language use. Normally we are happy for these components to operate entirely automatically, so that all we have to do is formulate ideas and speech follows, or move our eyes along a line of text and understanding follows. In everyday life the existence and operation of these components is only brought to our attention when they malfunction temporarily (as, for example, when we find ourselves caught in a tip-of-the-tongue state). But the implications are never so forcibly driven home as when we contemplate how it is possible for a brain-injured person to have lost the capacity to make use of sentence structure in language understanding while still grasping the meanings of the individual words, or to be unable to write satisfactorily while still being able to talk and read normally.

More generally, a patient may show multiple and severe language problems whereas perception, orientation, thinking, reasoning, memory, and so on may remain intact (though needing, of course, to be tapped non-verbally). Once again, these claims are not best evaluated by comparing groups of aphasic patients with groups of normals (Allport, 1983). For example, group studies have sometimes found average performance on non-verbal tests of reasoning and "intelligence" to be lower in aphasics than normals (e.g. Bay, 1962; Kertesz & McCabe, 1975). Other studies, however, have failed to find any difference, and have failed to find within the aphasic group any correlation between performance on intelligence tests and severity of the language disorder (e.g. Basso, DeRenzi, Faglioni, Scotti, & Spinnler, 1973; Corkin, 1979). Equally important are the few published reports of patients with severe language impairments whose non-verbal intelligence remains high (e.g. Van Harskamp, 1974; Welman & Lanser, 1974; Zangwill, 1964; see also Allport, 1983).

There are clearly many non-linguistic cognitive processes which can continue to function normally even when most of the language modules have been damaged. Impairment to the non-linguistic modules gives rise, of course, to disorders of perception, orientation, thinking, action, memory, and so on, some of which are discussed in Chapters 2 to 4 and Chapter 10 of this book. Those non-linguistic disorders can occur in patients whose language use remains perfectly normal. As a final point we might note that the distinction between linguistic and non-linguistic cognitive modules may not always be easy to draw. Is an impairment in the ability to judge tone-of-voice a linguistic or a non-linguistic impairment? Are impairments in comprehending metaphors or logical sentences exclusively linguistic or do they extend to areas of non-linguistic functioning? And what are we to conclude if patients with certain forms of semantic impairment have problems organising gestural as well as verbal communication, or if patients with impaired phonetic perception are always impaired at the processing of other rapidly-changing, non-verbal acoustic stimuli?

From an evolutionary point of view language is a relatively recent arrival on the scene, and those language-sustaining cognitive modules which are part of our biological endowment are recent acquisitions. Evolution often prefers to adapt old capabilities to serve new purposes rather than to develop completely new ones (Gould, 1980; 1983), so we should not be surprised if, for example, a module for phonetic perception has been adapted from an older and more general capability for processing rapidly-changing acoustic signals, or if processes for handling word meanings also continue to involve themselves in the comprehension or production of arbitrary, symbolic gestures. Nor should we be surprised if we flounder in our attempts to draw hard-and-fast distinctions between language disorders (aphasias) and other forms of cognitive impairment.

SUMMARY

Disorders of speech processing other than those affecting word production and recognition (see Chapters 5 and 6) take many different forms. We have speculated that high-level conceptual impairment may cause the fluent but semantically empty speech of patients with "semantic jargon-aphasia". Patients with so-called "Broca's aphasia" commonly show distorted articulation, impaired use of word order, and "agrammatism" (the omission or substitution of grammatical function words and inflections). Case studies have shown these commonly associated symptoms to be dissociable, and have shown syntactic problems in sentence production to dissociate from problems in comprehension. "Broca's aphasia" is probably best regarded as a collection of symptoms which tend to co-occur for anatomical rather than functional or cognitive reasons.

Nevertheless, some patients with severe aphasias may show preservation of automatic or non-propositional speech (e.g. use of everyday phrases and idioms; reciting the days of the week, or well-learned poems or song lyrics). The right cerebral hemisphere may have some advantage for producing this sort of speech. More conclusive evidence has been reported for a right hemisphere superiority for the comprehension and production of prosody, and a number of different forms of "aprosodia" have been reported following right hemisphere injury. Impairments of affective prosody are dissociable from impairments of linguistic prosody. Other language-related impairments which have been observed to follow right hemisphere injury include solving spatial reasoning problems, interpreting metaphors, proverbs and idioms, and appreciating verbal humour.

Gestural communication is often impaired in aphasic patients, and may mirror the high-level message formulation problems of some "Wernicke's" aphasics. In other aphasic patients, however, gestural communication may be preserved.

Impairments of sign language in the deaf take several different forms which in some ways resemble varieties of spoken-language aphasia. The few reports of aphasias in individuals fluent in both spoken language and sign language do not clarify the nature of the interdependence of the interrelationship between them, but show the linguistic aspects of both forms of language to be left hemisphere specialisations.

FURTHER READING

Caplan, D. (1992). *Language: structure, processing and disorders*. Cambridge, Mass.: MIT Press. Strong on "higher level" language disorders.

Harley, T.A. (1995). *The psychology of language: from data to theory*. Hove, UK: Erlbaum (UK) Taylor & Francis. Discusses both normal and aphasic sentence comprehension and production.

Lesser, R. & Milroy, L. (1993). *Linguistics and aphasia*. London: Longman. Psycholinguistic and pragmatic aspects of aphasia.

McCarthy, R.A. & Warrington, E.K. (1990). *Cognitive neuropsychology: a clinical introduction*. San Diego: Academic Press. Chapters 8 and 9 review sentence comprehension and production.

10 Memory

INTRODUCTION

Imagine that you are visiting someone in hospital and that you are attempting to hold a conversation. The patient . . .

> gives the impression of a person in complete possession of his faculties; he reasons about everything perfectly well, draws correct deductions from given premises, makes witty remarks, plays chess or a game of cards, in a word, comports himself as a mentally sound person. Only after a long conversation with the patient, [you] may note that at times he utterly confuses events and that he remembers absolutely nothing of what goes on around him: he does not remember whether he had his dinner, whether he was out of bed. On occasion the patient forgets what happened to him just an instant ago: you came in, conversed with him, and stepped out for one minute; then you come in again and the patient has absolutely no recollection that you had already been with him. [The patient] may read the same page over and over again sometimes for hours, because [he is] absolutely unable to remember what [he has] read. In conversation [he] may repeat the same thing 20 times, remaining wholly unaware that [he] is repeating the same thing.

This description of *amnesia* (loss of memory) is taken from Korsakoff's classic paper written in 1889 (see Victor & Yakovlev, 1955). Korsakoff was not the first to observe and comment upon memory loss (see Levin, Peters, & Hulkonen, 1983; Schacter & Tulving, 1982), but the present-day tradition of research into amnesia can be traced back to his pioneering work. Reviews of more recent work can be found in Stern (1981), Cermak (1982), Hirst (1982), Meudell and Mayes (1982), Squire (1982, 1987), Squire and Cohen (1984), and Parkin (1987).

The cognitive neuropsychologist looks at amnesia with a view to attempting to explain memory disorders in terms of impairment to aspects of the normal process of learning and remembering, and with a view to asking what the observed patterns of impairment can tell us about the nature of normal, intact memory processes. There are a number of important questions that must be answered in attempting such an analysis of amnesia, notably the question of whether amnesics are all alike, or whether there are significant individual differences of the sort we know to exist among aphasics, agnosics, acquired dyslexics, etc. Such individual differences are arguably easier to discover by carrying out intensive single-case studies than by, for example, comparing groups of amnesics with groups of normals on particular tasks. Unfortunately, from our perspective, there have only been a few detailed case studies in this area, but from those that have been done, and from those studies which compare groups of amnesics of different aetiologies, we can begin to trace the outlines of a plausible cognitive neuropsychology of memory.

FUNDAMENTALS OF MEMORY

The Greek philosopher Plato, in his *Theaetetus*, likened memory to an aviary. Acquiring a new memory is, he said, like adding a new bird to the collection in the aviary, whereas recalling the memory is like catching that same bird for inspection. As Marshall and Fryer (1978) observe in the course of a comparison of old and more recent models of memory, Plato's aviary model enables one to draw an important distinction between storage and recall. A bird (event or item of knowledge) may be in the aviary (memory store), but at a particular instant it may evade capture (recall), though you may succeed in capturing it later (the familiar experience of recalling something which you had earlier been unable to remember).

The metaphor provides several potential reasons why an experienced event may fail to be remembered at some later date. It may be that the bird was never captured and placed in the aviary in the first place (i.e. no representation of the event was ever established in memory). The bird may die in captivity and so be missing when looked for later (i.e. the memory trace of the event may be destroyed in storage). Alternatively, as mentioned above, the bird may be one of thousands in a large aviary and you may be unable to recapture it when you wish to (a recall or retrieval failure).

We may for convenience label these three potential causes of memory failure, a failure of *registration*, a failure of *retention*, and a failure of *retrieval*. Although theories of memory abound, and vary considerably in their particulars, most incorporate these fundamental 3 R's which are logically necessary. It is not difficult to realise that the pattern of an amnesia based on registration failure would be different from, say, a pattern based on retrieval failure. We can sketch out the profile that we would expect each to generate, then survey the literature for reports of patients whose symptoms fit the expected profile.

REGISTRATION AMNESIA?

Suppose a person was suddenly afflicted with a selective inability to establish (register) new memory traces. What would the symptoms be? Memory for events experienced before the onset of the illness should be normal, because retention and retrieval are presumed to be intact, but the patient should have difficulties remembering anything that has happened since the onset of the illness. In terms of a distinction commonly made in the amnesia literature, the patient should show an *anterograde amnesia* (difficulty recalling events that occurred after the onset of the illness) but no *retrograde amnesia* (no difficulty recalling events that occurred before the onset of the illness). The anterograde amnesia could be complete if the registration deficit was a total one, or partial if the deficit was milder.

Has a selective anterograde amnesia indicative of a registration deficit been reported? Liepmann (1910) reported a patient who suffered brain injury in 1870 during the Franco-Prussian war. Apparently, he could remember much of his life before the injury but virtually nothing since. In fact, the last thing he could remember was being a student before he entered the army. Having no memory for anything since, he imagined that he still was a student, and that his parents, who had died many years ago, were still alive. The patient had been an accomplished mathematician and chess player, and retained these skills despite his amnesia.

Syz (1937) reported the case of a man of 45 who fell backwards on his head while shovelling snow from the roof of the factory where he worked. The man suffered a complete, though fortunately only temporary, loss of memory for events since the accident. He could recall details of his life before the accident and retained his knowledge of geography, astronomy, biblical history, etc. He could define words, differentiate between words of similar meaning, and showed no evidence of a perceptual disorder or agnosia. Memory for new events, however, seemed to fade rapidly. Syz (1937, p. 363) comments how, "when performing, for instance, a somewhat involved calculation... he would forget the initial problem before having arrived at the solution. Similarly, in describing pictures that had been shown to him, the impressions would 'fade away' or 'evaporate', as he said, while he was engaged in the process of description."

On 11 March, two months after his accident on 11 January, he remarked: "It should be the 12th of January... but there is something wrong, it is almost spring outside. I saw my wife the last time—if I am to say it as I feel it—yesterday, Friday, on the day of the accident. But when I think it over, I realise that something must have happened in between" (p. 359).

His rapid forgetting was made apparent on his daughter's visits. He "greets her joyfully, kisses her and asks whether she had heard of the accident. The daughter, after a brief conversation, leaves the room and returns after two minutes. The greeting is repeated, he kisses her as before. The patient is very much surprised that the daughter knows everything about the accident.... His daughter leaves the room again, we talk about her for four minutes, when she reenters. [The] patient is emotionally moved again and a similar greeting as before takes place.... [The patient] forgot completely in two minutes that he had seen his daughter and there was no evidence of recall on the second and third repetition" (pp. 361–363).

In time this patient's disorder improved and his memory returned to normal. By 1936, "There are no difficulties with his memory, he only notices that there is a certain difficulty in retaining new names." An attempt was made to find out what the patient recalled of his illness. He remembered the different people who had been in his environment during his stay at the hospital, also that he had suffered from marked headaches, but, he said, "there is a hole. I have tried to fill it out but in vain, so I gave it up" (p. 371).

HM

Perhaps the best known and most intensively studied case of amnesia in recent decades has been patient HM. This man, in his mid-20s, had suffered from major epileptic seizures for many years. In an attempt to relieve these, HM underwent an operation in 1953 involving bilateral resection of the medial portions of the temporal lobes, with partial removal also of the hippocampus and amygdala on each side (midbrain structures now thought to be important in mediating memory processes; Scoville & Milner, 1957). The operation was successful in relieving the seizures, but it left HM with a permanent and profound amnesia.

HM can retain and remember very little of what has happened to him since the operation (an anterograde amnesia). Scoville and Milner (1957, p. 14) state that "he will do the same jigsaw puzzles day after day", and will "read the same magazines over and over again without finding their contents familiar. This patient has even eaten luncheon in front of one of us... without being able to name, a mere half-hour later, a single item of food he had eaten; in fact, he could not remember having eaten luncheon at all." HM describes his situation as "like waking from a dream" and once remarked: "Every day is alone in itself, whatever enjoyment I've had, and whatever sorrow I've had" (Milner, Corkin, & Teuber, 1968, p. 217). Milner et al. (1968, p. 217) comment that, "His experience seems to be that of a person who is just becoming aware of his surroundings without fully comprehending the situation, because he does not remember what went before".

Scoville and Milner (1957) found HM's early memories to be "apparently vivid and intact" and comment upon how, in conversation, he refers constantly to the events of his boyhood. This suggests the lack of a retrograde amnesia, and Marslen-Wilson and Teuber (1975) did indeed find that HM performed at normal levels at recognising photographs of the faces of people who were well known before 1953. There is, however, some loss of memory for events in the years before his operation (Corkin, 1984). He was unable, for example, to remember the death of a favourite uncle 3 years before the operation, and could not remember his time in hospital before his operation.

If HM's recall of events before his operation is not totally intact, then his anterograde amnesia for events since is not absolutely complete either. Marslen-Wilson and Teuber (1975) found him able to recognise 20% of a set of faces of people who had risen to prominence since his operation in 1953, including Elvis Presley, astronaut John Glenn, and Russian president Nikita Khrushchev. In another testing session he identified correctly the face of Kennedy on a coin and recalled such post-operation news events as the death of Pope John XXIII (Milner et al., 1968).

Thus HM shows a degree of retrograde amnesia for events before his operation and some recollection of events since. His retrograde amnesia extends back for several years, but is considerably milder than his profound anterograde amnesia. HM thus corresponds fairly well, though by no means perfectly, to our conception of a "pure" registration amnesic.

NA

NA's injury "resulted from a mock duel with another serviceman, when a miniature fencing foil entered the patient's right nostril and punctured the base of the brain, after taking an obliquely upward course, slightly to the left" (Teuber, Milner, & Vaughan, 1968). NA was born in 1938 and the injury occurred in 1960. When tested by Kaushall, Zetin, and

Squire (1981) he could remember little of what had happened to him since the accident and could also remember little of the 6 months prior to the accident. He was intelligent though (I.Q. = 124), and his recall for events before 1960 was normal (Cohen & Squire, 1981; Squire & Slater, 1978).

Possibly because he only has normal recall for things that happened over 20 years ago, NA gives the impression of living behind the times. He continues to wear his hair in a 1950s crew cut and uses anachronistic phrases. On one occasion he reports having kept himself awake during a 2-hour neurological procedure by thinking of Betty Grable.

NA's memory problems affect his everyday life in many ways. Social relations are difficult because he often cannot remember people from one meeting to the next. He does not enjoy television as he might because he cannot retain the narrative across a commercial break. Cooking is also hard because he cannot keep track of the sequence of steps required by a recipe. The reason why he does not use many external memory aids such as notes is perhaps illustrated by the occasion when, at a testing session, "he repeatedly tried to recall a question that he had wanted to ask. He finally searched his pockets, and found a written note: 'Ask Dr. Squire if my memory is getting better'" (Kaushall et al., 1981, p. 385).

Of some potential theoretical interest is the fact that NA's amnesia is measurably more severe for verbal than for non-verbal material. Teuber et al. (1968) devised a test in which subjects were shown a sequence of items in which some items occurred more than once. The subject's task was to say "Yes" if an item had been seen before, "No" if it had not. In one test the items were meaningless geometrical figures; in a second test they were meaningless syllables or words. Whereas a group of normal control subjects were better at detecting recurring syllables or words than nonsense figures, NA showed the opposite pattern, being better at figures than syllables or words. Thus NA's memory problem affected his verbal recall more than his non-verbal recall. That said, it should be noted that NA performed worse than the normal controls on both tests, so his deficit was not restricted to verbal material.

The four patients we have discussed so far [the Liepmann (1910) case, the Syz (1937) case, HM, and NA] all broadly fit our criteria for "registration" amnesia—impaired acquisition of new memories in the context of good recollection of old ones. Patient BY reported in depth by Winocur, Oxbury, Roberts, Agnetti, and Davis (1984) provides a fifth case. We shall discuss later precisely what form or forms the registration problem seen in these patients might take, and will also discuss the significance of various observations we have made but not commented upon. First, however, we shall review cases of amnesia in which a retrieval impairment seems to play a part.

RETRIEVAL DEFICITS IN AMNESIA?

Despite their differences, the cases described above conform tolerably well to our notion of registration amnesia. We now wish to see if there exist patients interpretable as cases of retrieval amnesia. What would such a case be like? Suppose a patient became suddenly unable to retrieve items from memory, though registration and retention remained intact. Unlike registration amnesia, this deficit would affect old and new memories alike. The patient would be equally unable to remember things learned or experienced before the onset of the illness (retrograde amnesia) and things learned or experienced after the onset (anterograde amnesia).

There is a problem here in that it would not seem possible with such a case to show that registration of memories continued intact, though the memories were no longer accessible. We could only know that registration had continued intact if the patient were eventually to *recover* from the amnesia. If this happened, then all the memory traces of events that happened during the illness should become available, and the patient should be able to remember incidents that happened during the illness as well as before and after. We have been unable to locate such a patient in the literature, so cannot put forward a clear and indisputable case of pure retrieval amnesia. There are, however, cases in which retrieval difficulties undoubtedly form a part of the picture.

The Dana (1894) Case

The very first volume of the prestigious scientific journal *Psychological Review* contains a report by Dana of a case of amnesia following accidental poisoning by domestic gas (carbon monoxide). The patient was a 24-year-old man who

> was quiet and sane in every way.... He dressed himself neatly and with his usual attention to his toilet, understanding apparently the use of various articles of dress. He showed by his conversation at once that he did not know who he was or where he was, and that his conscious memory of everything connected with his past life was gone.... Everything had to be explained to him, such as the qualities and uses of the horse and cow and of the various articles about the house (Dana, 1894, p. 572).

This amnesia was, fortunately, of quite short duration. One morning, about 3 months after the attack,

> he woke up and found his memory restored. He remembered distinctly the events of three months ago: his visit to his *fiancee*, his supper at the club afterwards, his journey home, his shutting his bedroom door and getting into bed. His memory stopped there. He did not recall a thing that had

occurred between times [the gas leak had occurred after he had fallen asleep]. He knew all his family at once and was plainly just the same man as before. But the three months was an entire blank to him. Next day he came to see me [Professor Dana], but he did not know me (I had never seen him before his accident). Not a thing connected with the three months could be recalled. It was so much taken entirely out of his existence (p. 575).

This case is explicable if we argue that during the 3-month period of the amnesia there was a virtual cessation of both registration *and* retrieval. The patient could neither lay down memories for the events occurring around him nor retrieve past memories. When the illness abated both functions returned. He could now retrieve memory traces as normal, and so could remember everything up to the onset of the illness, but because no traces had been registered during the illness there were no memory traces of that period to retrieve. It really was so much taken entirely out of his existence. Other cases of "transient global amnesia" whose symptoms suggest a similar interpretation are reviewed by Whitty (1977), and a case study provided by Gordon and Marin (1979) is also interpreted as a retrieval impairment combined with a registration (or consolidation) impairment.

Traumatic Amnesia

The Dana (1894) case discussed earlier showed a temporary retrograde amnesia resolving to leave just a limited gap in memory. Similar patterns have been reported following blows to the head or other "closed head injuries". For example, a young man reported by Russell (1935) suffered a closed head injury in August, 1933. A week after the accident he was able to converse sensibly but was under the impression that the date was February, 1922 and that he was a schoolboy. Three weeks after the injury he returned to the village where he had lived for the past 2 years but it seemed entirely unfamiliar to him. Gradually, however, his memory for the missing period returned until, eventually, he was able to remember everything to within a few minutes of the accident. Russell and Nathan (1946) present a whole series of similar cases.

The phenomenon of "shrinking retrograde amnesia", where the patient gradually recovers access to old memories, must be reflecting a loss then recovery of retrieval functions. A temporary retrieval impairment gives the only intelligible explanation of a patient's ability to recall an event at time $t1$ before the injury, inability to recall the event at time $t2$ shortly after the injury, and recovered recall ability at time $t3$ when the retrograde amnesia has resolved (Benson & Geschwind, 1967). Williams and Zangwill (1952) studied the form of the recovery from retrograde amnesia and reported how memories originally return as isolated and disconnected "islands". The first memory to return is often for some quite trivial event which occurred some 15–30 minutes before the accident. This recollection can seem hazy, impersonal and "curiously remote" (Whitty & Zangwill, 1977). Other memories re-emerge gradually, often in no particular order, and have to be placed in sequence by the patient until eventually recall of the patient's entire past life is more or less completely re-established. It is common, however, for memory of the accident and the few minutes leading up to it to be lost forever.

In addition to the shrinking retrograde amnesia, head injury often leaves an anterograde or post-traumatic amnesia, so that when the patient is recovered he or she may be unable to remember what happened in the first hours or days after the accident though they were conscious at the time. Fisher's (1966) patient was unconscious for a few seconds at most after falling off her chair and banging her head, and her initial retrograde amnesia cleared almost completely, but she could later remember nothing about the events of the 10 hours following the accident. Similarly, footballers who have been concussed may play on in the game but later remember little or nothing of what happened after the injury (Yarnell & Lynch, 1973).

Once again there would appear to be a combination of registration and retrieval deficits at work in these traumatic amnesias. The retrieval deficit affects the patient's ability to recall events from before the accident but resolves in time. The registration deficit also resolves, but leaves a hole in the patient's memory for the period of its duration. A similar combination of reversible retrograde and anterograde amnesias is seen in cases of "transient global amnesia", a well recognised clinical entity whose organic basis is still unclear (e.g. Evans, 1966; Gordon & Marin, 1979; Shuttleworth & Wise, 1973).

Retrograde Amnesia in Huntington's Disease

Huntington's Disease is a genetically transmitted dementing disorder characterised by involuntary, erratic muscle movements and progressive mental deterioration. Moderately advanced patients show impaired recall of past events. This was demonstrated by Albert, Butters, and Brandt (1981a) using a test which assessed recall and recognition of people and events which had been prominent between 1920 and 1975. The patients with Huntington's Disease were impaired on memory for all decades equally. This contrasts with, for example, patients with alcoholic Korsakoff amnesia whose memory for remote decades is less impaired than their memory for more recent decades.

As Albert (1984) observes, impaired memory for people and events from many years before the onset of the disease is incompatible with an explanation solely in terms of a learning (registration) disorder. It could, however, be accounted for by the proposal that patients with Huntington's Disease are impaired in their ability to *retrieve* old memories. That said, these patients also have a severe anterograde amnesia, so it is impossible to know for certain that the retrieval impairment is not accompanied by a registration impairment in the way we have seen to hold true for transient global amnesia and traumatic amnesia. Nevertheless, these cases and others in which amnesia of sudden onset includes a retrograde component (e.g. Cermak, 1976; Rose & Symonds, 1960; Williams & Smith, 1954) show that retrieval processes are capable of being impaired in amnesia. Given the problems of memory retrieval we all experience from time to time, it would be very surprising if those problems could not be exacerbated and magnified in at least some forms of amnesia.

ALCOHOLIC KORSAKOFF AMNESIA

Cases of amnesia due to sudden injury or illness are comparatively rare. A much more common cause of memory disorders is alcoholism, or rather, a deficiency of the vitamin thiamine which appears to accompany prolonged alcohol abuse and which causes damage to several thalamic and hypothalamic structures surrounding the third ventricle of the brain, possibly including the dorsomedial nucleus of the thalamus and the mamillary bodies (Butters, 1984). Amnesia resulting from prolonged alcohol abuse is commonly referred to as "Korsakoff's syndrome" and most amnesics studied experimentally have been of this sort. Unfortunately, there are a number of respects in which from a cognitive neuropsychological perspective they are less ideal than cases where amnesia results from injury or sudden illness. For example, the memory problems of an alcoholic may develop slowly, and the patient may have been experiencing difficulties for many years before he or she is finally admitted to hospital (Goodwin, Crane, & Guze, 1969). This gradual onset makes it difficult to make the conventional distinction between problems in recalling events that occurred before the onset of the amnesia (retrograde amnesia) and problems recalling events that occurred after onset (anterograde amnesia).

Also, the brain damage in Korsakoff syndrome patients is by no means clearly delimited. Although the damage which follows vitamin deficiency includes those structures like the hippocampus and amygdala, whose intactness appears vital for normal memory functions, it also commonly extends to other parts of the brain, notably the frontal lobes (Squire, 1982). Thus it can be very difficult to determine whether a particular symptom displayed by alcoholic Korsakoff patients is due to their amnesia or to cognitive deficits created by frontal lobe or other brain damage.

Perhaps because of these difficulties agreement has proved much harder to achieve for Korsakoff amnesia than for the amnesia of patients like HM and NA. Whereas a registration account of Korsakoff amnesia has many proponents, so has the notion that the fundamental problem is one of memory retrieval, but it is with registration theories that we shall begin.

Registration Theories of Korsakoff Amnesia

Since the earliest days of enquiry into Korsakoff amnesia there has existed a school of thought which ascribed the disorder to a problem of registration rather than one of recall. Müller and Pilzecker (1900) supported this view, as did Bonhöffer (1901), Burnham (1904), Gregor (1909), Moll (1915), and Bernard (1951), among others. Talland (1965) provides a valuable historical review. We should note that the amnesic patients studied by early advocates of both registration and recall deficits were not all amnesic as a consequence of chronic alcoholism. The expectation among most theorists was that all amnesias would have the same explanation, but it is possible that investigators were led in different directions through studying patients who were themselves different one from another.

While a considerable number of investigators have converged upon some form of registration deficit as a possible cause of amnesia, they have rather diverged again when it came to specifying in a little more detail what precise form that registration defect might take. Many suggestions have been made, but few have received any lasting favour. For example, Craik and Lockhart (1972) proposed a theory of normal learning and remembering which distinguished between "shallow" and "deep" encoding of to-be-remembered material. Roughly speaking, "shallow" encoding focusses upon the physical form of a stimulus (e.g. the appearance of a written word) whereas "deep" encoding focusses on its meaning. Many experiments have shown deep encoding to produce better long-term recall in normals than shallow encoding, but amnesics do not always show such a benefit (e.g. Cermak & Reale, 1978). Cermak and Butters (1973) suggested that a failure to encode experiences to a deep level might lead to the poor recall of past experiences seen in amnesia.

There are several problems, however, with this particular registration account of amnesia. First, as Rozin (1976) pointed out, amnesics can often hold intelligent and intelligible conversations about the here and now. That would not be possible if they do not routinely process words they hear in a "deep" way for their meanings. Secondly, Meudell, Mayes, and Neary (1980a) showed that amnesic recognition memory is better for funny strip cartoons than for unfunny ones. This again would not be possible if the amnesics were not processing the cartoons "deeply" for their "point"—the source of their humour.

Squire (1982) points out that while Korsakoff amnesics may fail to benefit from instructions to encode stimuli deeply, patient NA and patients suffering memory problems as a result of electroconvulsive therapy treatment do show benefits (Wetzel & Squire, 1980). Squire suggests that the failure of Korsakoff amnesics to exhibit rich encoding may be more a reflection of cognitive deficits produced by the frontal lobe damage commonly seen in alcoholic Korsakoff patients than a reflection of their core amnesia.

Retrieval Theories of Korsakoff Amnesia

Over the years numerous theorists have suggested that an impairment of retrieval from long-term memory may lie at the heart of Korsakoff amnesia (e.g. Colella, 1894; Grünthal, 1923, 1924; Schneider, 1912, 1928; Warrington & Weiskrantz, 1970, 1973). We shall start by reviewing briefly some of the lines of evidence which have been held to support a retrieval explanation before evaluating the theory.

First, amnesics sometimes recall incidents they are usually unable to remember, showing that the memory traces for those events were present in their brains even when they were unable to recall them. Coriat (1906, 1907) reports memories being recovered in dreams or "states of abstraction", and Gillespie (1937) is among those who have claimed recovery of amnesic memories under hypnosis. Amnesics not under hypnosis may produce rambling "confabulatory" accounts of their former lives containing much that is fabricated, but also occasional true recollections (Buerger-Prinz & Kaila, 1930/1951; Lewis, 1961; Moll, 1915).

Secondly, if a Korsakoff amnesic is given the same list of items to memorise on two or more occasions, the patient will show "savings" on the second and subsequent learnings, even though he or she will have no conscious recollection of the first learning episode. This was first demonstrated by Brodmann (1902, 1904) and has been confirmed by subsequent investigators (see Lewis, 1961; Talland, 1965; Williams, 1953).

Related to this is the observation that Korsakoff amnesics benefit from prompts or cues presented at the time of recall (Lidz, 1942; Williams, 1953). Warrington and Weiskrantz have reported the beneficial effects of retrieval cues on the performance of amnesic patients in an extensive series of studies. For example, Warrington and Weiskrantz (1970) gave word lists to amnesic and normal subjects to learn. With free and unprompted recall the amnesics managed only 33% correct to the normals' 60% correct. When, however, the first three letters of each word were provided as cues, amnesic performance rose to 60%, and it was statistically indistinguishable from the 66% correct obtained by the normal subjects. Warrington and Weiskrantz (1968) demonstrated that cueing by parts of previously seen line drawings improved performance in Korsakoff amnesics. Mayes, Meudell, and Neary (1978) again found cueing to improve amnesic recall (this time of word lists), but cueing was not enough to bring the amnesics to the level of the normal subjects.

Another argument for a retrieval theory is based on the contrast between the performance of Korsakoff amnesics on tests of recall and their performance on tests of recognition. In a recall paradigm the patient is shown a set of stimuli (e.g. words or pictures) and is later asked to recall the items in the set. In a recognition paradigm the patient is again shown a set of stimuli to memorise, but is later tested by being shown a fresh set of stimuli, some of which were in the original memory set whereas others are new. The patient must judge which items in the test set are old (i.e. were in the memory set) and which are new. Whereas the recall performance of Korsakoff amnesics is very poor, their performance on recognition tests can be very much better, sometimes rivalling that of normal subjects (e.g. Hirst, Johnson, Kim, Phelps, Risse, & Volpe, 1986; Huppert & Piercy, 1976, 1977, 1978; Mayer-Gross, 1943; Starr & Phillips, 1970; Woods & Piercy, 1974; Zubin, 1948).

It is clear that all of the above observations [and others reviewed by Knight & Wooles (1980) and Meudell & Mayes (1982)] are *compatible* with a retrieval deficit account of Korsakoff amnesia. It is reasonable to propose that if Korsakoff amnesics experience difficulty accessing memory traces they might show occasional, rare successes, might benefit from repetition and retrieval practice and so show the "savings" effect, might be aided by cues to assist the recall process, and might perform well in recognition memory tasks which arguably reduce the load upon retrieval operations. However, it can also be argued that poor *registration* of memories could produce exactly the same picture. Memories which are weak or faint as a result of poor registration might still occasionally be recovered in dreams, states of distraction, under hypnosis, or with the aid of cues. Janis (1950) found that amnesics could sometimes recover "lost" memories if they were allowed to "work on" them, but precisely the same is true of normals. For example, Williams and Hollan (1981) asked four subjects who had left high school between 4 and 19 years previously to recall the names of their former classmates over several sessions and found that names continued to be retrieved even after 10 hours of searching and recollecting.

Similarly, the recovery of memories which are weak due to poor registration could show better recognition than recall, and could be aided by cueing in both amnesics and normals. As Squire (1982, p. 249) observes: "The critical issue is not whether performance can be improved at all by such techniques but whether they disproportionately improve the performance of amnesic patients, or are simply effective ways to elicit information from all subjects alike". Schacter and Tulving (1982, p. 9) call this the *rule of differential effects*, arguing that:

> The effect of an experimental manipulation must be greater for amnesics than control subjects before deficits in the memory performance of amnesics can be attributed to corresponding underlying processes. It does not matter how dramatically a particular treatment... affects the operation of a given memory process in a group of amnesics. One can only entertain the hypothesis that amnesia reflects a deficit in a particular process when it can be shown that the memory performance of an appropriate control group is not affected or is affected less markedly, by the same treatment.

In order to ascertain whether the law of differential effects holds, we must look at the results of experiments which have compared the performance of normals and Korsakoff amnesics on memory tasks.

Comparing Normal and Amnesic Memory

Imagine carrying out an experiment to look at the effectiveness of retrieval cues at aiding normal and amnesic recall. Suppose you decide to teach a list of 12 words to each subject, going over them repeatedly until each normal person or amnesic patient can repeat all 12 correctly on two successive attempts. You then wait a few hours and retest each subject. Without prompts or cues the normals manage an average of nine correct but the amnesics only manage three correct. You then supply retrieval prompts (e.g. the first letter of each word, or the category to which it belongs). The normals show a 22% improvement from 9 to 11 correct, but the amnesics leap from 3 to 10 correct (a 230% improvement). Have you satisfied Schacter and Tulving's law of differential effects? After all, the amnesics *have* benefited more than the normals from your retrieval cues.

The problem with an experiment like this (which is similar in design to many of those in the literature) is that an initial, uncued score of 3 out of 12 provides much more room for improvement than a score of 9 out of 12. Potentially, from 3 out of 12 you can achieve a 300% improvement, whereas from 9 out of 12 the most you could achieve is a 33.3% improvement. A fairer comparison would be one in which the *uncued* recall rates of the normals and amnesics are equated (Knight & Wooles, 1980). One way to achieve this is to test the normal subjects after a much longer interval. In the imaginary experiment above we might find that the uncued recall of normal subjects would drop to 3 out of 12 if several days were allowed to elapse between learning and test. The question is, if cues were then provided, would the normal performance still improve by only 22% to an average of 3.66 correct (a differential effect), or would it show an improvement to around 10 out of 12, comparable with the amnesics (no differential effect)?

The strategy of testing normals at longer retention intervals, when their performance level has dropped to around that shown by amnesics at short retention intervals, has been employed by Woods and Piercy (1974), Squire, Wetzel, and Slater (1978), and in an extensive series of studies by Meudell, Mayes and their collaborators (see Mayes & Meudell, 1984; Meudell & Mayes, 1982 for reviews). The general finding of these studies has been that normal, weak memories are in many respects indistinguishable from Korsakoff amnesics' memories. For example, Woods and Piercy (1974) and Squire et al. (1978) found comparable effects of initial letter cueing of word recall in Korsakoff amnesics and normals when the normals were tested at longer retention intervals than the amnesics. Mayes and Meudell (1981) replicated this finding and also noted that for both amnesics and normals, words recalled with the aid of initial letter cues felt unfamiliar, like guesses. In a study of normal and amnesic recognition of famous voices, Meudell et al. (1980b) again found comparable effects of retrieval cues in amnesics and normals when the normals were tested at longer retention intervals.

In sum, there would appear to be no evidence for the law of differential effects as applied to the effects of retrieval cues on amnesia and normal recall. Retrieval cues do not differentially aid amnesic recall, so the fact that amnesics benefit from recall cues cannot be taken as support for the theory that the fundamental deficit in Korsakoff amnesia is a retrieval deficit. In fact, the existence of parallels between amnesic performance and normal weak memories cannot in itself be taken to support any particular theory of the amnesic deficit. Meudell and Mayes (1982, p. 227) comment: "...we believe that an amnesic's memory shortly after learning is probably similar to that of a normal person's after a considerable degree of forgetting. Of course, in the absence of further data, this claim does not discriminate between acquisition [*registration*], storage and retrieval failure explanations of amnesia since normal people could forget for any one of these reasons."

Retrograde Amnesia in Korsakoff Amnesics

If Korsakoff amnesia had a sudden onset, then evidence for a retrograde amnesia for events that happened well before the amnesia began would point clearly to a retrieval deficit in these patients. There is no doubt that Korsakoff patients *do* show retrograde amnesia for several decades before they became clinically amnesic. A striking feature of this retrograde amnesia is that it is *temporally graded*, with memory for more recent time periods being more severely disrupted than memory for earlier time periods. As compared with normal control subjects, Korsakoff amnesics show much less of a decrement in memory for events that occurred 30 or 40 years ago than for events that occurred 10 or 15 years ago. This pattern has been shown to characterise Korsakoff amnesic memory for events from different decades (e.g. Cohen & Squire, 1981; Seltzer & Benson, 1974) and memory for the faces and voices of people who achieved fame or notoriety in different decades (Albert, Butters, & Brandt, 1981b; Albert, Butters, & Levin, 1979; Marslen-Wilson & Teuber, 1975; Meudell, Northen, Snowden, & Neary, 1980).

All this would count as good evidence for a retrieval deficit *if* the memory problems of Korsakoff amnesics had a sudden onset, but they almost certainly do not. Learning difficulties have been demonstrated in alcoholics who are not (yet) clinically amnesic (Parker & Noble, 1977; Ryan, Butters, & Montgomery, 1980), and non-amnesic alcoholics have nevertheless been shown to have the same pattern of better memory for old than for recent decades that Korsakoff amnesics show (Albert, Butters, & Brandt, 1981b; Brandt, Butters, Ryan, & Bayog, 1983; Butters & Albert, 1982; Cohen & Squire, 1981). There is thus the possibility that patients who end up as Korsakoff amnesics have in fact suffered from *registration* difficulties for several decades (ever since they became alcoholic) and that their poor memory for recent decades is due to the fact that as the decades passed they became increasingly impaired at registering new events and people (even assuming that chronic alcoholics pay the same attention to the world about them as do normal people, which is also questionable).

Butters (1984) and Butters and Cermak (1986) have sought to resolve this issue through a rather remarkable case study of an eminent scientist and university professor (PZ) who developed alcoholic Korsakoff amnesia at the age of 65. As a scientist he had published many papers and books in the course of a career spanning 40 years or more, including an extensive autobiography published 2 years before he became clinically amnesic. PZ showed the registration impairments on new learning tasks that one would expect to see in a Korsakoff amnesic, and he also showed a temporally graded retrograde amnesia for famous people from different decades. Using his publications and autobiography, Butters and Cermak were able to assess PZ's memory for scientists who had once been well known to him, and for people, events and works which featured prominently in his autobiography. PZ proved to have precisely the same pattern of temporally graded retrograde amnesia for this personal material as he had for people from the public domain.

Butters and Cermak (1986, p. 270) comment that "there can be little doubt that his [PZ's] severe retrograde amnesia developed acutely with the onset of his amnesic disorder". He did not deteriorate by imperceptible degrees into a full-blown amnesia, but became clinically amnesic fairly suddenly after previously functioning reasonably well. The amnesia extended back to cover material he once had good command of, implying a genuine retrieval problem in at least this case. However, Butters and Cermak (1986) also note that PZ had a history of alcohol abuse going back for 35 years, and admit that during those years he may have suffered a progressive deterioration in his capacity to register new memories. Butters and Cermak do not question the contribution of a registration deficit to PZ's final amnesia (they are *not* advocating a retrieval theory as the complete explanation), but they do believe that their data show clear evidence for a retrieval impairment superimposed upon the registration impairment.

Korsakoff Amnesia: A Summary

We have spent quite some time on alcoholic Korsakoff amnesia, reflecting in part the extent to which research on amnesia has focussed upon this form of memory disorder. As a result of our survey we may draw some tentative conclusions. First, it seems unlikely that the pattern of impairments can be *fully* explained in terms of a retrieval deficit. Much of the evidence that has been adduced to support such an account is at least as compatible with the theory that a registration impairment is a major causal factor in Korsakoff amnesia. That registration deficit probably begins early on in the patient's life and builds up gradually over the years, resulting in a progressive decline in the ability to learn new information.

Butters and Cermark's work on patient PZ seems to establish, however, that a retrieval component constitutes part of the full-blown Korsakoff amnesia. We saw earlier in this chapter that patients with Huntington's Disease may also develop a retrograde amnesia, but in their case it is "flat", being equally severe for distant and recent memories. The retrograde amnesia of the Korsakoff amnesic, in contrast, is temporally graded. Albert (1984) and Butters (1984) propose a two-factor theory according to which the temporally graded retrograde amnesia may be the result of an essentially uniform retrieval deficit *superimposed* upon a longstanding and progressive registration impairment. The older memories of the Korsakoff amnesic were well established and consolidated at the time and are thus more likely to be accessible after the onset of the retrieval impairment than are the more recent memories, weakly established and poorly consolidated after years of alcohol abuse.

This two-factor theory of Korsakoff amnesia would explain why, typically, amnesics perform worse than normals even on remote memories. It also has the potential of reconciling Korsakoff amnesia with other forms of memory disorder in which either the registration impairment or the retrieval impairment predominate. As we shall see in the next section, the registration impairment of Korsakoff amnesics seems comparable with that of amnesics like NA whose retrieval functions are intact.

We should insert a note of caution, though, before moving on. We have been talking about "Korsakoff amnesics" as if they were all alike, rather in contrast to the emphasis on heterogeneity in the rest of the book. Baddeley and Wilson (1986) examined the extent to which personal memories could be evoked in amnesic patients by cue words like *letter* or *find*. Unlike most Korsakoff amnesics, their two patients (AB and MO'C) appeared to have normal access to personal memories when tested in this way, arguing against a retrieval deficit (at least for autobiographical episodes). As Baddeley and Wilson note, Zola-Morgan, Cohen, and Squire (1983) also found relatively normal autobiographical memories in their Korsakoff patients. Thus, whereas all Korsakoff amnesics probably share the registration deficit, the extent and severity of the retrieval impairment may vary considerably from patient to patient, and perhaps also with the type of memory being tested. In the words of Baddeley and Wilson (1986, p. 235), this "serves to emphasise a general point in neuropsychology, namely that common aetiology [*i.e. physical cause of illness*] does not guarantee equivalent cognitive dysfunction". Equally, distinct aetiology does not guarantee distinct cognitive dysfunction.

TWO FORMS OF REGISTRATION DEFICIT?

An inability to establish new, lasting memory traces is thought by many theorists to underlie several, if not all, forms of amnesia. This impairment may be accompanied in some cases by an additional retrieval deficit. It has been suggested, however, that the precise nature of the registration deficit may differ between types of amnesic patient. In particular, some amnesics may show abnormally fast forgetting of learned material whereas others may forget at a normal rate.

Huppert and Piercy (1979) claimed that patient HM showed abnormally fast forgetting. HM studied a sequence of pictures for 16 seconds each. With this exposure duration for each item he could perform at something over 70% correct on a recognition memory test after a retention interval of 10 minutes. Normal control subjects could achieve a similar performance level after 10 minutes given only 1 second exposure to each picture. Huppert and Piercy (1979) then retested the recognition memory of both HM and the control subjects after retention intervals of 1 and 7 days.

HM's performance was seen to decline more rapidly than the performance of the normal controls, suggesting to Huppert and Piercy that HM's rate of forgetting was abnormally fast.

This conclusion has, however, been criticised by Squire and Cohen (1984). They note that HM's level of performance after the 10-minute interval was only just within the normal range and that the evidence for faster forgetting in HM comes largely from the fact that his performance after the 7-day retention interval fell to chance. Between 10 minutes and 1 day the decline in HM's recognition memory performance roughly parallelled that of the controls. In a subsequent study of HM's recognition memory, Freed, Corkin, and Cohen (1984) failed to find any evidence of abnormally rapid forgetting.

Clearer evidence for fast forgetting comes in a study by Squire (1981) of the recognition memory performance of patients who had recently undergone electroconvulsive therapy (ECT) as a treatment for psychiatric disorders. It has been known for some time that memory problems can follow ECT (Miller & Marlin, 1979). Using a picture memory test similar to that of Huppert and Piercy (1979), Squire (1981) showed that patients receiving ECT could achieve comparable (in fact, rather better) performance than control subjects when the patients studied the pictures for 8 seconds per item and the normals for 1 second per item. Over the next 32 hours, however, the recognition memory performance of the ECT patients declined much more rapidly than the controls.

Thus patients who have recently received ECT show abnormally rapid forgetting. In contrast, both alcoholic Korsakoff amnesics and patient NA seem to show normal rates of forgetting once material has been learned to a criterion level. Huppert and Piercy (1978) established comparable levels of recognition memory performance for pictures in Korsakoff amnesics and normal controls after a 10-minute retention interval by allowing the amnesics 4 seconds study time per picture as compared to 1 second per picture for the normals. With comparability of performance after a relatively short delay thus established, recognition memory at 1- and 7-day intervals was found not to differ for the two groups, while remaining above chance at both intervals. Similar results for picture memory were obtained by Squire (1981) and Kopelman (1985) when comparing Korsakoff amnesics and controls, and by Squire (1981) when comparing patient NA and controls.

Although none of these studies addresses the question of what forgetting *is*, or how it arises, it is not hard to accept that abnormally fast forgetting might contribute to the memory problems of ECT patients. The normal forgetting rates of NA and Korsakoff amnesics imply, however, that if one is committed to some form of registration impairment in these cases, then one seems constrained to suggest, as Squire and

Cohen (1984) do, that NA and Korsakoff amnesics are slower to *establish* memory traces—slower, in other words, to learn. Once traces have been established, however, their fate is the same as that of normal memories of comparable strength.

It would be neat and tidy if we could assert that NA and Korsakoff amnesics show slow learning but normal forgetting, whereas ECT patients (and possibly HM) show normal learning but fast forgetting. Unfortunately, for such an elegant theory, the data clearly show that in addition to forgetting faster than normals, ECT patients and HM also *learn* more slowly. In both cases the initial study periods required to achieve criterial performance after 10-minute delays are much longer than are required by normal controls. That said, it may be unreasonable to suggest that normal learning rates could ever accompany abnormally fast forgetting, because forgetting is presumably something which is going on while you are learning the items, not just something which starts to happen after the items have been learned. Forgetting also presumably occurs during the initial 10-minute retention intervals in the above-mentioned studies, so that patients with abnormally fast forgetting would need to learn the items *better* than the controls in the study phase in order to show comparable retention after 10 minutes. (If one could introduce into both the study and retention phases of these experiments a secondary task for the normal subjects which increased their forgetting to a rate comparable with that of the fast-forgetting ECT patients, then one might find that the normals required study times as long as the patients to achieve equal recognition memory performance after the 10-minute retention interval.)

It has been suggested that the registration deficit in at least some amnesics should be interpreted as a difficulty in *consolidating* memory traces—a failure perhaps of a biochemical process which "fixes" newly-formed memory traces. (e.g. Milner, 1966; Squire, Cohen, & Nadel, 1984). McClelland and Rumelhart (1986) offer an account of how such a failure of consolidation could be construed which is both quasi-neurochemical and implemented as a computational model. Following earlier advocates of consolidation theories, McClelland and Rumelhart note how this theory can explain an otherwise puzzling phenomenon, namely the brief retrograde amnesia for events that occurred some months or even a year or two before the onset of the amnesia in patients whose amnesia began *suddenly*. We noted earlier, for example, how HM's memory for events before his operation is generally good but shows some weaknesses for some years before the operation. Similarly, patients with traumatic amnesia often remain permanently unable to recall events leading up to their head injury, even when their memories have otherwise returned to normal.

These observations are explicable if we assume that the consolidation of memory traces is a process which continues for some time, and if we also assume that if consolidation is disrupted, traces for experiences not completely fixed tend to decay and be lost. Depending on how severe the impairment of consolidation is, and how soon (if ever) the process resumes, then we would *expect* a limited retrograde amnesia in patients whose deficit is essentially one of memory registration (consolidation being part of the registration process).

WHAT CAN SURVIVE AMNESIA, AND WHY?

We opened this chapter with Korsakoff's (1889) description of a typical encounter with an amnesic patient. It is worth repeating the first part of that description. Korsakoff observes how the patient "...gives the impression of a person in complete possession of his faculties; he reasons about everything perfectly well, draws correct deductions from given premises, makes witty remarks, plays chess or a game of cards, in a word, comports himself as a mentally sound person" (Victor & Yakovlev, 1955, p. 398). Liepmann's (1910) patient remained an accomplished mathematician and chess player despite his amnesia; Syz's (1937) patient retained his knowledge of geography, astronomy, biblical history, etc.; HM could still do jigsaw puzzles, though he did the same ones day after day. It is obvious that many aspects of cognitive performance can survive despite the presence of a dense amnesia. The question is, is there any logic to the pattern of loss and retention, and if there is, can it shed any light on either the nature of amnesia or the organisation of normal cognitive processes? In the sections that follow we shall evaluate and discuss claims that auditory–verbal short-term memory, semantic memory, skills and perceptual learning may escape impairment in cases of amnesia.

Auditory–Verbal Short-term Memory

If a string of random letters or digits is read out at a pace of about one per second and you are required to repeat the string back in the correct order, then most normal people can repeat between six and eight items before they begin to make mistakes (Miller, 1956). Wechsler (1917) showed that Korsakoff amnesics were as good as normals at immediate recall of digit strings, a result later replicated by Drachman and Arbit (1966) and Butters and Cermak (1980). The amnesic patients HM and NA have also been shown to have normal immediate recall to digits and letters (Teuber, Milner, & Vaughan, 1968; Wickelgren, 1968).

From a cognitive neuropsychological perspective it would be interesting even if only *some* amnesics showed normal immediate recall in the context of deficient long-term recall; the fact that the great majority do is particularly impressive, especially when coupled with reports of patients who show the reverse pattern—impaired immediate recall with normal long-term recall. Warrington and Shallice (1969) provided a detailed case report of a patient, KF, whose digit span was reduced from the normal 6–8 to a maximum of 2. Immediate recall of letters and word strings was comparably impaired. In contrast to this very poor immediate recall, KF's cued recognition memory and his learning of word-pairs were within the normal range, as was his learning of a list of 10 words.

In the late 1960s it was popular to attribute immediate recall to a "short-term memory" (STM) store whose capacity limitations were revealed through limits on digit span, etc. It was thought that perceived stimuli had to pass through STM on their way into long-term memory (LTM) (e.g. Atkinson & Shiffrin. 1968; Waugh & Norman, 1965). But if this were true, then damage to STM should also impair the entry of information into LTM, yet KF's learning rate seemed normal. Shallice and Warrington (1970) proposed that STM and LTM exist as parallel memory stores, so that each can be impaired without affecting the functioning of the other.

Two later studies of KF helped delineate more closely the nature of the impairment of his short-term memory capabilities. Warrington and Shallice (1972) showed that his short-term forgetting of auditory letters and digits was much faster than his forgetting of visual stimuli. Also, with visual presentation, KF did not make the errors involving the substitution of similar-sounding items (e.g. B for P, F for S) that are made by normals and which he himself made with auditory presentation. Warrington and Shallice (1972) argued that KF employed a form of visual storage whenever possible and that his visual (as opposed to auditory) short-term storage capabilities were intact. Later, Shallice and Warrington (1974) showed that KF's deficit was restricted to verbal materials like letters, digits and words, and that his immediate recall of meaningful sounds such as cats mewing or telephones ringing was normal. The short-term store impaired in KF was thus auditory rather than visual, and within the auditory modality verbal rather than non-verbal, hence Shallice and Warrington's final designation of it as the "auditory–verbal short-term store".

There is an obvious parallel between the finding that KF showed impaired short-term yet intact long-term memory for verbal materials and the demonstration of patients with impaired short-term yet intact long-term memory for spatial locations made by De Renzi and his colleagues (De Renzi & Nichelli, 1975; De Renzi et al., 1977a) and discussed in Chapter 3 (pp. 81–84). It is also, however, clear that impairments of auditory–verbal short-term memory and impairments affecting short-term memory for spatial locations are dissociable (De Renzi & Nichelli, 1975), and a number of different types of short-term memory impairment are beginning to be identified. Baddeley and his colleagues have been particularly successful in this enterprise (e.g. Baddeley & Wilson, 1985; Vallar & Baddeley, 1984a, 1984b) and have been able to relate their findings to Baddeley's (1983, 1986) conception that short-term storage involves a working memory system in which a central executive interacts with a number of interrelated subsystems.

Semantic Memory

At the same time that cognitive psychologists were proposing, in the late 1960s and early 1970s, that short-term memory was not a single store, it was also suggested that there might exist more than one type of long-term memory. Influential among these proposals was the theory put forward by Tulving (1972). Tulving drew a distinction between two different sorts of memory. The first are autobiographical memories for episodes in your own past life, as when you think back and recollect some event or occasion in which you participated. Tulving called these *episodic memories*; they are personal memories which are dated in time and located in space— you know when these episodes happened and where. The second type of memories are for items of information you have acquired repeatedly over the years—what the capital of France is; what *reluctant* means; whether pigs have wings. What distinguishes these *semantic memories* from episodic memories is that you are commonly unable to recall where and when you acquired a typical piece of semantic information.

Kinsbourne and Wood (1975) were the first to suggest that we might see in amnesia an impairment to episodic memory with preserved semantic memory. Amnesics, they observed, have difficulty retaining and recollecting incidents and events that have happened to them (episodic memory) yet perform well on tests of factual knowledge or on tests which tap their understanding of word meanings (semantic memory). This observation is undoubtedly a valid one for many amnesics. We have already noted preserved factual knowledge in the cases discussed above. Grünthall (1923, 1924) showed amnesic word associations to be normal, and Baddeley and Warrington (1973) found amnesics to be unimpaired at generating instances from semantic categories such as animals or fruit. A distinction between memories similar to Tulving's (1972) was, in fact, made by Gillespie (1937, p. 749) who argued that

> the kind of remembering involved in saying "I visited Paris in 1925" is different from what is implied in saying "Waterloo was fought in 1815". Both are acts of remembering, but that latter is much simpler than the former. It is an example of the so-called "mechanical" type of memory, as compared with the personal type of remembering. That continuity of

personal identity and memory are separate phenomena is shown by clinical cases in which mechanical memory, when tested, is found to be intact but the recollection of everyday events in the patient's life... is missing.

The distinction between episodic/personal memory and scmantic/mechanical memory is an intuitively appealing one, and if neuropsychological evidence were genuinely to support it then that would be a major contribution. We have already discussed impairments that do seem to affect semantic memory in Chapters 2, 5, and 6, and noted that these can be category-specific. But there are two objections to the theory of impaired episodic memory with intact semantic memory in amnesia which seriously call into question its usefulness as an explanation of amnesic loss and retention. First, many different sorts of "knowledge" can be preserved in amnesia, from biblical knowledge, through knowledge of how to play the piano, to knowledge of how to dress oneself. Tulving (1983), like Parkin (1982), sought to extend the concept of semantic memory to encompass many or all of these aspects of preserved performance. This brought the rebuke from Baddeley (1984a, p. 239) that Tulving "simply labels tasks which amnesics can perform as semantic and then concludes that their semantic memory performance is intact". If the distinction is to be productive, then this circularity must be removed, possibly by restoring the concept of semantic memory back to its original delineation concerning factual knowledge and knowledge of the meanings of words and objects.

The more damaging objection arises from the belief discussed earlier that registration deficits of one form or another comprise a major part of many or all amnesic disorders. In Korsakoff amnesics the deficit may have been building up over many years, but as we have seen, memories for episodes in the patient's early life are usually preserved. The significance of this point is that most of the information assessed in tests of semantic memory is information that is normally acquired in the first 20 years or so of life. One can argue therefore that what we commonly see in amnesia is the relative preservation of memory traces laid down in early life before the onset of any registration deficit, traces which include most of the patients' knowledge of words and the world as well as individual autobiographical episodes (we note, however, that the existence of dissociable category-specific deficits demonstrates that age of acquisition will not be a useful explanatory construct for cases in which semantic memories are themselves impaired; our point is only that it may explain the relative preservation of semantic memory in certain forms of amnesia).

For the episodic/semantic distinction to prove useful as an explanation of amnesia it would be necessary to show that whereas the acquisition of episodic memories is impaired in amnesic patients, the acquisition of semantic information remains intact. This would not seem to be the case. As Baddeley (1984a, 1984b) notes, amnesics do not seem to update their semantic memories, "frequently being quite unaware of who is the current prime minister or president, where they themselves are, or what is going on in the world about them. They have great difficulty in learning the names of new people, and in finding their way about using anything other than previously learned routes" (Baddeley, 1984a, p. 239).

Gabrieli, Cohen, and Corkin (1983) tried to teach HM the meanings of eight new words. Despite repeating the items 115 times per day for 10 days, HM showed virtually no learning when tested with alternative definitions, synonyms or sentence frames that used the words. Cermak and O'Connor (1983) studied a patient (SS) with a profound anterograde amnesia following an encephalitic illness. He was formerly a pioneer in the field of laser technology and could still discourse knowledgeably on the topic. Cermak and O'Connor (1983) decided, however, to test SS's acquisition of new semantic information about lasers by giving him an article to read about a new laser discovery. He read it and explained its contents as he went along, showing that he could use his existing knowledge to help grasp the new points, but a few moments afterwards he could neither recall the new points nor recognise them when presented by the experimenter. Repeated attempts to teach him new information failed completely.

In the course of their paper Cermak and O'Connor (1983) also make an important point about autobiographical memory. They argue that you can have two sorts of memories about your own past. The first are genuine recollections in which you seem to be able to re-experience a scene or event. The second are facts you know to be true about your past though you cannot remember them personally. Certain things you did or said as a child may, for example, have become part of your family "lore" and may crop up from time to time in family conversations. You may know about these "episodes" though they do not form part of your episodic memory in Tulving's (1972, 1983) sense. Cermak and O'Connor (1983) felt that SS's autobiographical memories were primarily of this last sort rather than true recollections. One might argue on this basis that SS is an exceptional amnesic and that evidence from SS should not be given too great weight when evaluating the relevance to most amnesics of the episodic/semantic distinction. That said, evidence that any form of amnesic patient can register and retain semantic information at normal levels while being unable to register and retain episodic information is lacking (Baddeley, 1984, 1984b; Damasio, Eslinger, Damasio, Van Hoesen, & Cornell, 1985; Squire & Cohen, 1984), yet it is upon such evidence that the relevance of the distinction must depend.

Skills

Another capacity which has been held to remain intact in amnesic patients is "skills"—things like piano playing, carving wood, or playing golf. The same point applies here as to semantic memory: Do amnesics merely retain skills acquired before the onset of their memory problems, or do they retain also the capacity to acquire new skills at normal rates? There is no doubt that old skills can be preserved, as for example the piano-playing skills of Dana's (1894) patient, or the golfing skills of Schacter's (1983) case.

There is also ample documentation of amnesics acquiring new skills. The patient reported by Dunn (1845) learned dressmaking but had to be reminded each morning of her unfinished work as well as her ability to carry it out. Dana's (1894) patient learned billiards and carving, NA has developed model-building skills since his accident (Teuber et al., 1968), and the amnesic patient of Starr and Phillips (1970) learned new piano pieces. What matters crucially, however, is whether they can acquire new skills *at normal rates*. On this the evidence is mixed. HM showed progressive improvement in his performance on tasks like tracing a pattern in a mirror, learning a tactile "finger maze", and tracking a moving target on a "pursuit rotor", but when his performance was compared with that of normals his rate of learning was found to be markedly inferior (Corkin, 1965, 1968). The patients studied by Cermak, Lewis, Butters, and Goodglass (1973) and Cermak and O'Connor (1983) were also slower than normals at learning finger mazes but these authors point out that normals often assist themselves in this task by memorising a series of verbal instructions about the required sequence of turns; something that amnesics would, of course, have great difficulty in doing.

There is no denying that amnesic patients may be capable of learning very sophisticated new skills. Glisky, Schacter, and Tulving (1986) taught four patients with amnesia following traumatic head injuries to manipulate information on a computer screen, to write, edit and execute simple computer programs, and to store and retrieve information on computer disks. They were all capable of learning to some degree, but their rate of learning was slower than that of normals, and the nature of their learning seemed different from that of the normals. In particular, they were thrown by questions about their skill which did not use the same phrases as the materials from which they had learned, and they failed to generalise their learning to tasks similar but slightly different from those they had mastered. In other words, their learning seemed more inflexible and specific than that of normal subjects.

Considering the emphasis placed by some theorists upon claims of amnesics' preserved capacity for learning perceptual-motor skills, the number of studies reporting this finding is surprisingly small. Such studies must incorporate an appropriate "control group" of normals and must find the rate of amnesic acquisition of the skill to be at normal levels. Cermak et al. (1973) compared nine alcoholic Korsakoff amnesics and nine controls on a finger maze task and on the "pursuit rotor" (an apparatus requiring the subject to track a metal target moving on a turntable with a stylus). As mentioned earlier, the amnesics were slower than the normals at learning the finger maze, but they acquired the pursuit rotor skill at the same rate as the normals. Brooks and Baddeley (1976) replicated this observation and also showed normal rates of learning of jigsaw completions in their amnesics. Cohen and Squire (1980) and Martone, Butters, Payne, Becker, and Sax (1984) found normal rates of learning of the skill of reading mirror-reversed print in Korsakoff amnesics, though their retention of the content of what they read was worse than normal controls.

Finally, Cohen (1984) has claimed that a group of amnesics which included HM could learn how to solve a puzzle known as the "Tower of Hanoi" at a rate comparable to that of normal subjects. The Tower of Hanoi game requires the player to transfer a set of rings one at a time from one peg to another in the minimum possible number of moves. The amnesics improved across four training sessions as much as the normals did, and showed comparable generalisation to a slightly different version of the puzzle. HM showed savings on the task even a year later when he would, of course, have been able to recall little or nothing of the earlier training sessions. In contrast to Cohen's (1984) finding, however, the amnesic patient of Beatty, Salmon, Bernstein, Martone, Lyon, and Butters (1987) was slower than normals at learning the Tower of Hanoi puzzle, so although we may be able to claim that some amnesics show normal learning of this problem-solving skill, we cannot claim that they all do, and we do not yet know what distinguishes those who do from those who do not. From our perspective, though, the observation of normal learning in some amnesics is the crucial one.

More studies are needed in order to delineate what sorts of skills can be acquired at normal rates by what sorts of amnesics, because the few existing studies are currently bearing a considerable theoretical burden. It is also by no means obvious that skills as diverse as mirror reading, jigsaw puzzle solving, and computer programming form a sensible grouping for psychological analysis. Neither is it clear where to draw the line between the skills just reviewed and the more perceptual forms of learning we come to next, which, apparently, may also proceed normally in amnesics.

Perceptual Learning (Repetition Priming)

Confusion commonly arises in the memory literature due to the fact that the word "recognition" is used by cognitive psychologists in at least two different ways. An experimenter can present a stimulus such as a familiar word to a subject, initially for a very brief time and then for progressively longer, until the subject identifies the stimulus. The experimenter can then claim to have measured the presentation time necessary for that subject to "recognise" that stimulus. Used in this sense, to recognise the word PENCIL is to know that that string of letters is familiar and to know what meaning to assign to it. Most amnesic patients do not appear to have any problems recognising in this perceptual sense—they continue to recognise objects and words for what they are and use them appropriately.

The second sense in which cognitive psychologists use the word "recognise" has to do with recognition *memory*. In a typical recognition memory experiment a subject is first shown a list of items to memorise. After an interval the subject is shown a second, "test" list of items and is required to indicate which were in the original memory list and which were not. Here "recognising" a word means identifying it as having been encountered on a particular previous occasion. It is not hard to see that this sense of the word "recognition" is different from the first one. Suppose, for example, the word PENCIL occurred in the second, test list but not in the original memory list. A subject encountering PENCIL should recognise it in our first sense (i.e. acknowledge it to be a familiar word with a known meaning) but ought not to recognise it in our second sense (i.e. should not claim that it was in the memory list).

We now know that the processes mediating these two forms of recognition are different in part, and evidence from amnesic patients has been important in establishing this. It has been known for some time that if you read a word now you will identify it more rapidly and more accurately several minutes or hours later than if you had not had the recent encounter. This phenomenon is known as "repetition priming" (e.g. Neisser, 1954; Winnick & Daniel, 1970). The important point is that "recognition" (in the sense of perceptual identification) can be primed in this way without the subject "recognising" (in the memory sense) that the word being identified now is one he or she identified some time ago. This line of research has developed out of the pioneering studies by Warrington and Weiskrantz (1968, 1970).

Cermak, Talbot, Chandler, and Wolbarst (1985), for instance, required amnesic patients first of all to read aloud a list of concrete nouns presented one at a time for 5 seconds each, then to perform two subsequent tests involving the words. One was a perceptual identification test where words from the memory list, mixed in with new "filler" words, were presented initially for very brief exposures and then for progressively longer times until they were identified correctly. In the second test words from the memory list were again mixed with new filler words, but this time the patient had to say for each word whether or not it had been in the memory list (i.e. a standard recognition memory test). The memory task was presented either before or after the perceptual identification task. Their results showed that whereas amnesic recognition memory performance declined dramatically to well below the level shown by a control group of non-amnesic alcoholics if the memory test occurred after the perceptual identification task, the amount of perceptual priming observed was independent of the presence or absence of an intermediate recognition memory task and remained at a level comparable to that shown by non-amnesic control subjects.

Similar results have been obtained in studies investigating priming in the "fragment completion" task. Here subjects are supplied with fragments of words and are required to supply the missing letters so as to complete the word (e.g. completing P-NC-- as PENCIL, or -IN--W as WINDOW). Performance on this task can be primed in normals by recent experience with the full written forms of the words which later appear as fragments (Tulving, Schacter, & Stark, 1982).

Graf, Squire, and Mandler (1984) gave normals and amnesics word lists to study. They were later tested in one of four ways—free recall of the words, cued recall (the cue being the initial three letters of the words), recognition memory, and fragment completion. The amnesic patients were impaired relative to the normals on the free recall, cued recall and recognition memory tests, but their completion of word fragments was primed as much as the normals and the priming declined with time at the same rate as for the normals. A neat twist in this experiment is that the fragments used in the fragment completion test were the same initial three letters of words as were used as cues in the cued recall test. So if the word MARKET occurred in the study list the amnesics were more likely to complete MAR- as MARKET than if they had not been primed with that word, and this tendency was as strong as for normal subjects, but the amnesics were far poorer than the normals at using MAR- as a cue to *remember* that MARKET had actually occurred in the study list.

The crucial difference between fragment completion and cued recall is that there is no requirement in the fragment completion task to *remember overtly* that the completion word occurred in the study list. Subjects are simply instructed to complete the fragment with the first word that comes to mind. Priming in other tasks which do not require the amnesic to recognise that the primed word has recently been encountered has been demonstrated by Jacoby and Witherspoon (1982), Moscovitch (1982), and Graf, Shimamura, and Squire (1985)—see Shimamura (1986) and Schacter (1987) for reviews. A similar form of perceptual learning without explicit remembering may underlie the demonstration by Johnson, Kim, and Risse (1985) that amnesic patients came to prefer Korean melodies which they heard repeatedly over new ones, even though they could not reliably discriminate old from new.

How can the Pattern of Preservation and Loss in Amnesia best be Explained?

Auditory–verbal short-term memory, the acquisition of certain perceptual-motor skills, and some forms of perceptual priming all seem to be preserved in at least some amnesic patients. Considerable effort has gone into trying to explain why these aspects of amnesic performance can be preserved when other memory functions are so severely impaired.

A common approach is to posit more than one memory system and to argue that whereas certain memory systems are impaired in amnesia, others are preserved. We have already encountered one example of this approach in the proposal that immediate recall of strings of letters, digits or words is mediated by a separate auditory–verbal short-term memory system which is preserved in most amnesics though it may be impaired in other neurological patients (e.g. Shallice, 1979b; Warrington, 1979). Although this suggestion may go some of the way towards explaining the amnesic pattern, there is obviously much that it cannot handle, notably findings of intact perceptual-motor skill acquisition and repetition priming. To explain these, theorists have often gone a step further and proposed distinct *long-term* memory systems.

The problems of attempting to capture the amnesic pattern in terms of Tulving's (1972, 1983) episodic-semantic distinction have already been discussed. Cohen and Squire (1980) suggested that the amnesic pattern might yield to a different distinction, between *procedural* knowledge (or "knowing how") and *declarative* knowledge (or "knowing that"). The idea is that some of our knowledge, including that mobilised in the performance of perceptual-motor skills, involves rules and procedures which run fairly automatically when activated by appropriate inputs or commands. This procedural knowledge is held to be preserved in amnesic patients. Other types of knowledge are more item- or data-based. These include both episodic and semantic knowledge which depend on the encoding, storage, and explicit retrieval of distinct events or facts. The storage and/or retrieval of this "declarative" type of knowledge is held to be impaired in amnesics (see Cohen, 1984; Squire, 1982; Squire & Cohen, 1984, for further discussion).

The procedural/declarative (or "knowing how"/"knowing that") distinction has a venerable history in philosophy (e.g. Ryle, 1949), psychology (e.g. Bergson, 1896; Bruner, 1969), and computer science (e.g. Winograd, 1975), but its extension to amnesia is not without its difficulties. Auditory–verbal short-term storage is not obviously procedural, so the distinction may only apply once such short-term memory systems have been fractionated off from systems mediating longer-term storage. Also, it is not at all clear that priming of perceptual recognition depends on rules and procedures. It may instead depend on priming of the stored representations of the appearance of stimuli (e.g. Ellis, Young, Flude, and Hay, 1987c; McClelland & Rumelhart, 1985). These perceptual memories may be separate again from other sorts of long-term storage (Tulving, 1984).

A rather different approach to the amnesic pattern has been adopted by Jacoby (1984) and Schacter (1985, 1987). On this approach, preservation and loss is explained not in terms of distinct stores or distinct types of knowledge, but in terms of the manner in which knowledge is tapped. Jacoby (1984) argues against the notion of separate memory stores and for a distinction between "incidental" and "intentional" retrieval of information from long-term memory. Amnesics fare well, Jacoby argues, on tasks where past experiences can exert effects of an incidental nature on present performance. Perceptual priming is a clear example: The amnesic is simply required to respond to the present stimulus (e.g. complete a word fragment or identify a letter string), but the fact that the stimulus has been encountered recently facilitates performance, even though the patient cannot remember the previous encounter.

A similar distinction, but this time between "explicit" and "implicit" remembering, has been proposed by Schacter (1985) as relevant to explaining the amnesic pattern. Amnesics, he suggests, can demonstrate learning and recall when not required to remember explicitly what they have learned. Conventional memory testing procedures, he argues, demand that we know we have remembered something—they test memory explicitly. Perceptual-motor skills and perceptual priming do not require explicit recall of what was learned or when, but can still show implicit learning in the form of facilitation of test performance without conscious recollection. Strong evidence in favour of this view comes from Graf et al.'s (1984) study (see p. 299), in which amnesic performance matched that of normal subjects on fragment completion (which does not require remembering the previous encounter with the word, and is thus an implicit test) but was below normal when fragments of the words had to be used as an explicit cue to remembering the previously seen words. Furthermore, these types of implicit learning can be shown in normals to be also independent of conscious recollection of the learning episode (see Schacter, 1987, for a review). Put simply, the implicit/explicit distinction may relate to whether or not we are *aware of remembering* something. Schacter, McAndrews, and Moscovitch (1988) thus point to parallels between amnesia and other types of disorder, including blindsight (see Chapter 3) and prosopagnosia (Chapter 4) in which patients retain capacities that can be shown to be remarkably preserved, yet fail to know that this is the case. These disorders, Schacter et al. (1988) argue, can be considered to involve *specific forms of loss of awareness*.

Jacoby's (1984) intentional/incidental and Schacter's (1985) explicit/implicit accounts represent a considerable step forward in understanding amnesia, but they are not without their difficulties. The preservation of auditory–verbal short-term memory is not easily encompassed within either of these frameworks, because immediate recall of digit or letter strings is surely both intentional and explicit. That preservation seems better accounted for by a separate stores model, in which case some hybrid of separate stores and modes-of-testing accounts would be needed by any final theory. In addition, the notion that priming and skill learning are preserved in amnesics because testing is incidental or implicit in those tasks currently exists largely as an alternative account to the theory that they are preserved because they are mediated by separate memory systems. Neither account has yet emerged as clearly superior to the other. Finally, believers in the incidental/intentional or implicit/explicit account have currently shown that amnesics can show perceptual priming without conscious recollection, and also that they can be primed by word associations, both old and new (Schacter, 1985, 1987). It has *not* yet been established, as it needs to be, that implicit or incidental testing procedures can reveal the presence in amnesic memory of connected episodes or life events of which they have no conscious recollection.

Commenting on research on amnesia, Morton (1985b, p. 285) observes that, "The pattern of amnesic loss seems to make intuitive sense but every attempt to grasp it formally has failed." Both the multiple stores and modes-of-testing approach seem at times to get tantalisingly close to a really good explanation of amnesic preservation and loss, yet problems remain for each. That said, it is clearly the view of many investigators that exploring processes whose operation remains intact in amnesics despite their memory impairment is one of the most promising research fronts at present. We would not dissent from that view.

OVERVIEW

Although the study of amnesia has engaged more people for a longer time than the study of, say, acquired dyslexia, most commentators feel that progress in the cognitive neuropsychology of memory has been less certain than in an area like reading: We seem neither to have such good explanations of the disorders themselves nor such firm conclusions to draw about the normal state from the analysis of its impairments.

A serious problem is that from the very outset of amnesia research, theorists have tended to think in terms of the "amnesic syndrome", believing that all amnesias would yield to a single explanation, and have treated all amnesic patients as alike and interchangeable. Consequently, the typical research project on amnesia has involved comparing a group of amnesics and a group of normals on one or more tests and reporting only the average scores for the groups. This procedure is, of course, quite different from the single-case methodology that has been dominant and productive in other areas of cognitive neuropsychology, and the averaging across normals and amnesics will obscure any important individual differences in both groups.

This tactic seems to us strange even when one simply compares and contrasts the few single-case studies that *have* been published over the decades. For it to continue now would be bizarre in the extreme when one considers that in every other domain of cognition—visual perception, object recognition, spatial representation, reading, writing, speaking, etc.—heterogeneity of impairments has proved to be the norm. In all of these domains brain injury gives rise to a wide variety of patterns of impairment whose differences one from another are of immense theoretical significance. How odd it would be if long-term memory was the single exception to this rule.

A further point worth making is that many of the cognitive disorders we have dealt with elsewhere in this book can be construed as memory disorders of a sort different from the classical amnesic patient. The anomic aphasic patient, for example, appears to have lost conscious access to the representations in memory of the spoken forms of many words (see pp. 116–124). The patient with "surface" dysgraphia has similarly lost conscious access to the representations in memory of the spellings of many words (see pp. 177–179). Recognition problems covering objects (agnosia), faces (prosopagnosia), or words ("surface" dyslexia; letter-by-letter reading; word meaning deafness) can similarly be considered to involve material-specific forms of memory impairment, causing those stimuli to be no longer recognised. Patients with certain acquired dysgraphias appear to have forgotten the shapes of letters or how to form them (pp. 180–187).

These and other disorders, like the "semantic memory" impairments discussed in Chapters 2, 5, and 6, can stand alongside orthodox amnesia as types of memory disorder, and their omission from most treatments of memory disorders may be one reason why memory has seemed to be only subject to a small number of impairments. That said, there are suggestions in the literature that additional forms of amnesia may exist and await detailed cognitive investigation. For example, the 59-year-old patient reported by Andrews, Poser, and Kessler (1982) "came to" after a blackout and found himself unable to remember anything of the last 40 years though he could recall events from before that time. He could remember nothing of his own personal history for the blank period, did not recognise his house, family or friends, and could not remember how to use modern appliances like televisions, microwave ovens, or showers. He identified Charles Chaplin, Fred Astaire, Jean Harlow, and President Roosevelt from pictures but failed to recognise Orson Welles, Marilyn Monroe, President Johnson, or Snoopy.

The sudden onset of amnesia in a patient with no history of alcohol abuse suggests a retrieval disorder, but any simple retrieval disorder would be expected to affect memory for events experienced after the illness, as well as memory for events before the illness. According to Andrews et al. (1982), however, this did not happen: The patient retained and remembered experiences and facts from after his illness well (though unfortunately his retention of new material was not assessed formally). At the clinical level at least this patient appeared to have an isolated retrograde amnesia. Other similar cases have been reported by Roman-Campos, Poser, and Wood (1980) and Goldberg, Antin, Bilder, Gerstman, Hughes, and Mattis (1981; see also Goldberg & Bilder, 1985; Goldberg, Hughes, Mattis, & Antin, 1982).

Isolated retrograde amnesia does not yield to a simple registration/ consolidation or retrieval explanation. Andrews et al.'s (1982) patient could retrieve some knowledge of the missing 40 years in dreams, under hypnosis, or following injection with the drug amytal IV, indicating that the memory traces may have been disrupted or weakened rather than lost completely. It may be that these patients suffer a sudden disruption to all stored memory traces—episodic, semantic, and procedural—a disruption which does not affect the processes of registration and retrieval themselves.

In sum, there are many different neuropsychological conditions relevant to cognitive theories of memory. Memories of some type are crucial to everything we do. Trying to base a cognitive neuropsychology of memory solely on amnesia as traditionally construed could be like trying to base a cognitive neuropsychology of reading solely on a "syndrome" like "surface" dyslexia (the difficulty being confounded by the fact that neither amnesia nor surface dyslexia is a unitary, homogeneous disorder). It is legitimate to take a particular form of memory disorder as your object of investigation, but the theorist interested in the wider issue of inferring how normal memory works from the disorders to which it is prone may need to embrace a wider range of disorders than have conventionally been considered.

Progress may also be hastened by a deeper consideration of what memory is *for*. The psychological study of memory has too often been founded upon the results of laboratory tasks which have few, if any, counterparts in everyday experience. Under such conditions memory can appear severely limited and inaccurate. But the memory systems we now enjoy have evolved over millions of years for specific purposes, though like all specialised systems they can be made to look limited if tested on tasks for which they were not developed (a finely engineered racing car looks limited if you try to drive it across a field). Whenever a set of tasks appears to display our cognitive apparatus in a poor light it is more likely that the tasks are maladapted than that our cognitive systems are.

In recent years cognitive psychologists have shown an increasing willingness to step outside the laboratory in order to examine the cognitive system at work in everyday life (e.g. Harris & Morris, 1984; Neisser, 1982). One realisation which follows from such an exercise is that memory is as much about the future as it is about the past. Memory helps us to use our past experiences in order to better evaluate our present situation and better decide what to do next. We also store in our memories the plans for future actions. The amnesic patient NA found cooking difficult because he could no more retain a sequence of planned actions in memory than a sequence of past events (Kaushall et al., 1981), but so-called "prospective memory" (i.e. memory for future plans) has not been investigated systematically in amnesia. The sustained and reflective observation of the problems of amnesics in everyday life could pay substantial dividends in terms of increased understanding of both normal and impaired memory (cf. Schacter, 1983).

SUMMARY

If an event or piece of information is to be recalled at a later date, then three (possibly related) processes seem to be almost logically necessary. The event or item must be *registered* in memory, must be *retained* in memory, and must be capable of being *retrieved* from memory. Registration impairment causes an inability to form new memory traces, though old ones which comfortably preceded the onset of the amnesia should still be capable of recall (i.e. the patient shows anterograde but not retrograde amnesia). This pattern has been reported several times, including patients HM and NA. Retrieval deficits affect the recall of both old and new memories (anterograde and retrograde amnesia). Such deficits have never been demonstrated convincingly in the absence of registration impairment, but occur alongside a registration deficit in cases of transient global amnesia, traumatic amnesia, and Huntington's disease.

Both registration and retrieval impairments have been proposed as the sole cause of the memory impairments seen in alcoholic Korsakoff amnesics. Registration impairments are certainly present in these cases. The retrograde amnesia which would demonstrate a retrieval impairment is often hard to establish because of the gradual onset of the disease, though Butters (1984) and Butters and Cermak (1986) argue for a retrograde amnesia in their patient PZ.

The nature of the registration impairment may vary among amnesics. Patients with amnesia following electroconvulsive therapy forget abnormally rapidly, whereas patient NA and alcoholic Korsakoff amnesics forget at normal rates but only learn very slowly.

General cognitive and intellectual powers can survive the onset of amnesia, as can certain sorts of "memories". These include auditory–verbal short-term memory, some motor skills, and the sort of perceptual learning revealed in "repetition priming". It is important when claims of preserved types of memory are being made to show clearly that the learning of new material is intact as well as the recall of old material. This has *not* been established for semantic memories. Two broadly different views exist about why some sorts of "memory" may be preserved in some amnesic patients. One view asserts that only performance requiring explicit, conscious, intentional recall is impaired whereas performance which only requires implicit, incidental learning is preserved. The second view asserts that those sorts of memory which are preserved rely on distinct, unimpaired memory systems. Evidence for domain-specific losses of memory for spoken words, spellings, faces, objects, geographical knowledge, etc., certainly establish the existence of memory systems distinct from those damaged in amnesic patients.

FURTHER READING

De Renzi, E., Liotti, M., & Nichelli, P. (1987). Semantic amnesia with preservation of autobiographic memory. A case report. *Cortex, 23,* 575–597. Seminal description of a person with preserved autobiographical memory in the context of profound loss of semantic memory.

Greene, J.D.W. & Hodges, J.R. (1996). Identification of famous faces and famous names in early Alzheimer's disease. Relationship to anterograde episodic and general semantic memory. *Brain, 119,* 111–128. How breakdowns of person recognition relate to more general failures of episodic and semantic memory.

Hanley, J.R. & Young, A.W. (1994). The cognitive neuropsychology of memory. In P.E. Morris & M.M. Gruneberg (Eds.), *Theoretical aspects of memory* (pp. 238–272). London: Routledge. Looks at a range of memory impairments from a cognitive neuropsychological perspective.

Parkin, A.J. & Leng, N.R.C. (1993). *Neuropsychology of the amnesic syndrome.* Hove, UK: Erlbaum. Textbook based around discussion of the classical amnesic syndrome.

Schacter, D.L. (1992). Implicit knowledge: new perspectives on unconscious processes. *Proceedings of the National Academy of Science, USA, 89,* 11113–11117. Examines the relation between studies of implicit memory and other studies of non-conscious processes.

Squire, L.R., Haist, F., & Shimamura, A.P. (1989). The neurology of memory: quantitative assessment of retrograde amnesia in two groups of amnesic patients. *Journal of Neuroscience, 9,* 828–839. More on temporal gradients in retrograde amnesia.

References

Abadi, R. V., Kulikowski, J. J., & Meudell, P. (1981). Visual performance in a case of visual agnosia. In M. V. Van Hof & G. Mohn (Eds), *Functional recovery from brain damage*. Amsterdam: Elsevier.

Alajouanine, T., Ombredane, A., & Durand, M. (1939). *Le syndrome de désintégration phonétique dans l'aphasie*. Paris: Masson and Cie.

Alajouanine, T., Pichot, P., & Durand, M. (1949). Dissociations des altérations phonétiques avec conservation relative de la langue ancienne dans un cas d'anarthrie pure chez un sujet francais bilingue. *Éncephale, 28*, 245–246.

Alajouanine, T., Lhermitte, F., Ledoux, F., Renaud, D., & Vignolo, L. A. (1964). Les composants phonémiques et sémantiques de la jargon aphasie. *Revue Neurologique, 110*, 5–20.

Albert, M. L. (1973). A simple test of visual neglect. *Neurology, 23*, 658–664.

Albert, M. L., & Bear, D. (1974). Time to understand: A case study of word deafness with reference to the role of time in auditory comprehension. *Brain, 97*, 373–384.

Albert, M. L. Reches, A., & Silverberg, R. (1975). Associative visual agnosia without alexia. *Neurology, 25*, 322–326.

Albert, M. S. (1984). Implications of different patterns of remote memory loss for the concept of consolidation. In H. Weingartner & E. S. Parker (Eds), *Memory consolidation*. Hillsdale, N. J.: Lawrence Erlbaum Associates Inc.

Albert, M. S., Butters, N., & Levin, J. (1979). Temporal gradients in the retrograde amnesia of patients with alcoholic Korsakoff's Disease. *Archives of Neurology, 36*, 211–216.

Albert, M. S., Butters, N., & Brandt, J. (1981a). Development of remote memory loss in patients with Huntington's Disease. *Journal of Clinical Neuropsychology, 3*, 1–12.

Albert, M. S., Butters, N., & Brandt, J. (1981b). Patterns of remote memory in amnesic and demented patients. *Archives of Neurology, 38*, 495–500.

Alexander, M. P., Stuss, D. T., & Benson, D. F. (1979). Capgras syndrome: A reduplicative phenomenon. *Neurology, 29*, 334–339.

Allport, D. A. (1977). On knowing the meaning of words we are unable to report: The effects of visual masking. In S. Dornic (Ed.), *Attention and Performance VI*. Hillsdale, N. J.: Lawrence Erlbaum Associates Inc.

Allport, D. A. (1983). Language and cognition. In R. Harris (Ed.), *Approaches to language*. Oxford: Pergamon Press.

Allport, D. A. (1984). Speech production and comprehension: One lexicon or two? In W. Prinz & A. F. Sanders (Eds), *Cognition and motor processes*. Berlin: Springer-Verlag.

Allport, D. A. & Funnell, E. (1981). Components of the mental lexicon. *Philosophical Transactions of the Royal Society* (London), *B295*, 397–410.

Allport, D. A., Antonis, B., & Reynolds, P. (1972). On the division of attention: A disproof of the single channel hypothesis. *Quarterly Journal of Experimental Psychology*, *24*, 225–235.

Anderson, J. R. (1976). *Language, memory and thought*. Hillsdale, N. J.: Lawrence Erlbaum Associates Inc.

Andrews, E., Poser, C. M., & Kessler, M. (1982). Retrograde amnesia for forty years. *Cortex*, *18*, 441–458.

Assal, G., Favre, C., & Anderes, J. P. (1984). Non-reconnaissance d'animaux familiers chez un paysan: zooagnosie ou prosopagnosie pour les animaux. *Revue Neurologique*, *140*, 580–584.

Atkinson, R. C. & Shiffrin, R. M. (1968). Human memory: A proposed system and its control processes. In K. W. Spence & J. T. Spence (Eds), *The psychology of learning and motivation*, Vol. 2. London: Academic Press.

Auerbach, S. H., Allard, T., Naeser, M., Alexander, M. P., & Albert, M. L. (1982). Pure word deafness: An analysis of a case with bilateral lesions and a defect at the prephonemic level. *Brain*, *105*, 271–300.

Baddeley, A. D. (1983). Working memory. *Philosophical Transactions of the Royal Society* (London), *B302*, 311–324.

Baddeley, A. D. (1984a). Neuropsychological evidence and the semantic/episodic distinction. *Behavioral and Brain Sciences*, *7*, 238–239.

Baddeley, A. D. (1984b). The fractionation of human memory. *Psychological Medicine*, *14*, 259–264.

Baddeley, A. D. (1986). *Working memory*. Oxford: Oxford University Press.

Baddeley, A. D. & Lewis, V. (1981). Inner active processes in reading: The innner voice, the inner ear, and the inner eye. In A. M. Lesgold & C. A. Perfetti (Eds), *Interactive processes in reading*. Hillsdale, N. J.: Lawrence Erlbaum Associates Inc.

Baddeley, A. D. & Lieberman, K. (1980). Spatial working memory. In R. S. Nickerson (Ed.), *Attention and Performance VIII*. Hillsdale, N. J.: Lawrence Erlbaum Associates Inc.

Baddeley, A. D. & Warrington, E. K. (1973). Memory coding and amnesia. *Neuropsychologia*, *11*, 159–165.

Baddeley, A. D. & Wilson, B. (1985). Phonological coding and short-term memory in patients without speech. *Journal of Memory and Language*, *24*, 490–502.

Baddeley, A. D. & Wilson, B. (1986). Amnesia, autobiographical memory, and confabulation. In D. C. Rubin (Ed.), *Autobiographical memory*. Cambridge: Cambridge University Press.

Badecker, W. & Caramazza, A. (1985). On considerations of method and theory governing the use of clinical categories in neurolinguistics and cognitive neuropsychology: The case against agrammatism. *Cognition*, *20*, 97–125.

Badecker, W. & Caramazza, A. (1986). A final brief in the case against agrammatism. *Cognition*, *24*, 277–282.

Bálint, R. (1909). Die Seelenlähmung des Schauens, optische Ataxie, räumliche Störung der Aufmerksamkeit. *Monatsschrift für Psychiatrie und Neurologie*, *25*, 51–81.

Barbur, J. L., Ruddock, K. H., & Waterfield, V. A. (1980). Human visual responses in the absence of the geniculo-calcarine projection. *Brain*, *103*, 905–928.

Barton, D. & Hamilton, M. E. (in press). Social and cognitive factors in the historical development of writing. In A. Lock & C. Peters (Eds), *Handbook of human symbolic evolution*. Oxford: Oxford University Press.

Basso, A., De Renzi, E., Faglioni, P., Scotti, G., & Spinnler, H. (1973). Neuropsychological evidence for the existence of cerebral areas critical to the performance of intelligence tests. *Brain, 96,* 715–728.

Bauer, R. M. (1984). Autonomic recognition of names and faces in prosopagnosia: A neuropsychological application of the guilty knowledge test. *Neuropsychologia, 22,* 457–469.

Baxter, D. M. & Warrington, E. K. (1986). Ideational agraphia: A single case study. *Journal of Neurology, Neurosurgery and Psychiatry, 49,* 369–374.

Bay, E. (1962). Aphasia and non-verbal disorders of language. *Brain, 85,* 411–426.

Beattie, G. W. & Butterworth, B. (1979). Contextual probability and word frequency as determinants of pauses and errors in spontaneous speech. *Language and Speech, 22,* 201–211.

Beatty, W. W., Salmon, D. P., Bernstein, N., Martone, M., Lyon, L., & Butters, N. (1987). Procedural learning in a patient with amnesia due to hypoxia. *Brain and Cognition, 6,* 386–402.

Beaumont, J. G. (Ed.) (1982). *Divided visual field studies of cerebral organisation.* London: Academic Press.

Beauvois, M.-F. (1982). Optic aphasia: a process of interaction between vision and language. *Proceedings of the Royal Society* (London), *B298,* 35–47.

Beauvois, M.-F. & Dérousné, J. (1979). Phonological alexia: Three dissociations. *Journal of Neurology, Neurosurgery and Psychiatry, 42,* 1115–1124.

Beauvois, M.-F. & Dérousné, J. (1981). Lexical or orthographic dysgraphia. *Brain, 104,* 21–50.

Beauvois, M.-F. & Saillant, B. (1985). Optic aphasia for colours and colour agnosia: A distinction between visual and visuo-verbal impairments in the processing of colours. *Cognitive Neuropsychology, 2,* 1–48.

Beauvois, M.-F., Dérousné, J., & Bastard, V. (1980). Auditory parallel to phonological alexia. Paper presented at the Third European Conference of the International Neuropsychological Society, Chianciano, Italy, June 1980.

Bellugi, U., Poizner, H., & Klima, E. S. (1983). Brain organization for language: Clues from sign aphasia. *Human Neurobiology, 2,* 155–170.

Benson, D. F. (1979). Neurologic correlates of anomia. In H. Whitaker & H. A. Whitaker (Eds), *Studies in neurolinguistics,* Vol. 4. New York: Academic Press.

Benson, D. F. & Geschwind, N. (1967). Shrinking retrograde amnesia. *Journal of Neurology, Neurosurgery and Psychiatry, 30,* 539–544.

Benson, D. F. & Greenberg, J. P. (1969). Visual form agnosia: A specific defect in visual discrimination. *Archives of Neurology, 20,* 82–89.

Benson, D. F., Gardner, H., & Meadows, J. C. (1976). Reduplicative paramnesia. *Neurology, 26,* 147–151.

Benton, A. L. (1979). Visuoperceptive, visuospatial, and visuoconstructive disorders. In K. M. Heilman & E. Valenstein (Eds), *Clinical neuropsychology.* New York: Oxford University Press.

Benton, A. L. (1980). The neuropsychology of facial recognition. *American Psychologist, 35,* 176–186.

Benton, A. L. (1982). Spatial thinking in neurological patients: Historical aspects. In M. Potegal (Ed.), *Spatial abilities: Development and physiological foundations.* New York: Academic Press.

Benton, A. L. & Van Allen, M. W. (1972). Prosopagnosia and facial discrimination. *Journal of the Neurological Sciences, 15,* 167–172.

Bergson, H. (1896). *Matière et mémoire*. Paris: Alcan. (Translated as *Matter and memory*. London: Allen, 1911.)

Bernard, P. (1951). Essai psycho-pathologique sur le comportement dans le syndrome de Korsakoff. *La Raison, 2*, 93–101.

Berndt, R. S. (1987). Symptom co-occurrence and dissociation in the interpretation of agrammatism. In M. Coltheart, G. Sartori, & R. Job (Eds), *The cognitive neuropsychology of language*. London: Lawrence Erlbaum Associates Ltd.

Berndt, R. S. & Caramazza, A. (1980). A redefinition of the syndrome of Broca's aphasia: Implications for a neuropsychological model of language. *Applied Psycholinguistics, 1*, 225–278.

Bisiach, E. (1988). Language without thought. In L. Weiskrantz (Ed.), *Thought without language*. Oxford: Oxford University Press.

Bisiach, E. & Luzzatti, C. (1978). Unilateral neglect of representational space. *Cortex, 14*, 129–133.

Bisiach, E., Luzzatti, C., & Perani, D. (1979). Unilateral neglect, representational schema and consciousness. *Brain, 102*, 609–618.

Bisiach, E., Capitani, E., Luzzatti, C., & Perani, D. (1981). Brain and conscious representation of reality. *Neuropsychologia, 19*, 543–552.

Bisiach, E., Cornacchia, L., Sterzi, R., & Vallar, G. (1984). Disorders of perceived auditory lateralization after lesions of the right hemisphere. *Brain, 107*, 37–52.

Bisiach, E., Perani, D., Vallar, G., & Berti, A. (1986a). Unilateral neglect: Personal and extra-personal. *Neuropsychologia, 24*, 759–767.

Bisiach, E., Vallar, G., Perani, D., Papagno, C., & Berti, A. (1986b). Unawareness of disease following lesions of the right hemisphere: Anosognosia for hemiplegia and anosognosia for hemianopia. *Neuropsychologia, 24*, 471–482.

Blanc-Garin, J. (1986). Faces and non-faces in prosopagnosic patients. In H. D. Ellis, M. A. Jeeves, F. Newcombe, & A. Young (Eds), *Aspects of face processing*. Dordrecht: Martinus Nijhoff.

Blumstein, S. (1973). *A phonological investigation of aphasic speech*. The Hague: Mouton.

Blumstein, S. E. (1978). Segment structure and the syllable in aphasia. In A. Bell & J. B. Hooper (Eds), *Syllables and segments*. Amsterdam: North-Holland.

Blumstein, S. E., Cooper, W. E., Goodglass, H., Statlender, S., & Gottlieb, J. (1980). Production deficits in aphasia: A voice-onset time analysis. *Brain and Language, 9*, 153–170.

Blumstein, S. L., Tartter, V. C., Michel, D., Hirsch, B., & Leiter, E. (1977). The role of distinctive features in the dichotic listening perception of vowels. *Brain and Language, 4*, 508–520.

Bodamer, J. (1947). Die Prosop-Agnosie. *Archiv für Psychiatrie und Nervenkrankheiten, 179*, 6–53.

Bonhöffer, K. (1901). *Die akuten Geisteskrankheiten der Gewohnheitstrinker*. Jena: Fischer.

Bonhöffer, K. (1902). Zur Kenntis der Rückbildung motorische Aphasien. *Mitteilungen aus den Grenzbieten der Medizin und Chirurgie, 10*, 203–224.

Boomer, D. S. & Laver, J.D.M.H. (1968). Slips of the tongue. *British Journal of Disorders of Communication, 3*, 2–12. (Reprinted in V. A. Fromkin (Ed.) (1973). *Speech errors as linguistic evidence*. The Hague: Mouton.)

Bornstein, B (1963). Prosopagnosia. In L. Halpern (Ed.), *Problems of dynamic neurology*. Jerusalem: Hadassah Medical School.

Bornstein, B., Sroka, M., & Munitz, H. (1969). Prosopagnosia with animal face agnosia. *Cortex, 5*, 164–169.

Bowers, D. & Heilman, K. (1984). Dissociation between the processing of affective and nonaffective faces: A case study. *Journal of Clinical Neuropsychology, 6*, 367–379.

Bradshaw, J. L. & Gates, E. A. (1978).   Visual field differences in verbal tasks: Effects of task familiarity and sex of subject. *Brain and Language, 5,* 166–187.

Bradshaw, J. L. & Nettleton, N. C. (1983).   *Human cerebral asymmetry.* Englewood Cliffs, N. J.: Prentice-Hall.

Brain, Lord (1964).   Statement of the problem. In A. V. S. De Reuck & M. O'Connor (Eds), *Ciba foundation symposium on disorders of language.* London: Churchill.

Brain, W. R. (1941).   Visual disorientation with special reference to lesions of the right cerebral hemisphere. *Brain, 64,* 244–272.

Bramwell, B. (1897).   Illustrative cases of aphasia. *The Lancet, i,* 1256–1259. (Reprinted in *Cognitive Neuropsychology,* 1984, *1,* 245–258.)

Brandt, J., Butters, N., Ryan, C., & Bayog, R. (1983).   Cognitive loss and recovery in chronic alcohol abusers. *Archives of General Psychiatry, 40,* 435–442.

Brodmann, K. (1902).   Experimenteller und Klinischer Beitrag zur Psychopathologie der polyneuritischen Psychose. I. *Journal der Psychologie und Neurologie, 1,* 225–247.

Brodmann, K. (1904).   Experimenteller und klinischer Beitrag zur Psychopathologie der polyneuritischen Psychose. II. *Journal der Psychologie und Neurologie, 3,* 1–48.

Brooks, N. & Baddeley, A. D. (1976).   What can amnesic patients learn? *Neuropsychologia, 14,* 111–122.

Brown, G. D. A. (1987).   Resolving inconsistency: A computational model of word naming. *Journal of Memory and Language, 26,* 1–23.

Brown, J. W. (1981).   Case reports of semantic jargon. In J. W. Brown (Ed.), *Jargonaphasia.* New York: Academic Press.

Brown, R. & McNeill, D. (1966).   The "tip of the tongue" phenomenon. *Journal of Verbal Learning and Verbal Behavior, 5,* 325–337.

Brownell, H. H., Michel, D., Powerson, J., & Gardner, H. (1983).   Surprise but not coherence: Sensitivity to verbal humor in right-hemisphere patients. *Brain and Language, 18,* 20–27.

Bruce, V. (1988).   *Recognising faces.* London: Lawrence Erlbaum Associates Ltd.

Bruce, V. & Young, A. W. (1986).   Understanding face recognition. *British Journal of Psychology, 77,* 305–327.

Bruner, J. S. (1969).   Modalities of memory. In G. A. Talland & N. C. Waugh (Eds), *The pathology of memory.* New York: Academic Press.

Bruyer, R., Laterre, C., Seron, X., Feyereisen, P., Strypstein, E., Pierrard, E., & Rectem, D. (1983).   A case of prosopagnosia with some preserved covert remembrance of familiar faces. *Brain and Cognition, 2,* 257–284.

Bryden, M. P. (1982).   *Laterality: Functional asymmetry in the intact brain.* New York: Academic Press.

Bub, D. & Kertesz, A. (1982a).   Evidence for lexicographic processing in a patient with preserved written over oral single word naming. *Brain, 105,* 697–717.

Bub, D. & Kertesz, A. (1982b).   Deep agraphia. *Brain and Language, 17,* 146–165.

Bub, D., Cancelliere, A., & Kertesz, A. (1985).   Whole-word and analytic translation of spelling to sound in a non-semantic reader. In K. E. Patterson, J. C. Marshall, & M. Coltheart (Eds), *Surface dyslexia: Neuropsychological and cognitive studies of phonological reading.* London: Lawrence Erlbaum Associates Ltd.

Bub, D., Black, S., Howell, J., & Kertesz, A. (1987).   Speech output processes and reading. In M. Coltheart, G. Sartori, & R. Job (Eds), *The cognitive neuropsychology of language.* London: Lawrence Erlbaum Associates Ltd.

Buckingham, H. W. (1977).   The conductive theory and neologistic jargon. *Language and Speech, 20,* 174–184.

Buckingham, H. W. (1980).   On correlating aphasic errors with slips of the tongue. *Applied Psycholinguistics, 1,* 199–220.

Buckingham, H. W. & Kertesz, A. (1976). *Neologistic jargonaphasia.* Amsterdam: Swets and Zeitlinger B. V.

Buckingham, H. W., Whitaker, H., & Whitaker, H. A. (1978). Alliteration and assonance in neologistic jargonaphasia. *Cortex, 14,* 365–380.

Buerger-Prinz, H. & Kaila, M. (1930). Über die Struktur des amnestischen Symptomenkomplexes. *Zeitschrift für Neurologie und Psychiatrie, 124,* 553–595. (Translated in D. Rapaport (Ed.), *Organization and pathology of thought.* New York: Columbia University Press, 1951.)

Burnham, W. H. (1904). Retroactive amnesia: illustrative cases and a tentative explanation. *American Journal of Psychology, 14,* 118–132.

Burr, C. (1905). Loss of the sign language in a deaf mute from cerebral tumor and softening. *New York Medical Journal, 81,* 1106–1108.

Butters, N. (1984). Alcoholic Korsakoff's syndrome: an update. *Seminars in Neurology, 4,* 226–244.

Butters, N. & Albert, M. L. (1982). Processes underlying failures to recall remote events. In L. S. Cermak (Ed.), *Human memory and amnesia.* Hillsdale, N. J.: Lawrence Erlbaum Associates Inc.

Butters, N. & Cermak, L. S. (1980). *Alcoholic Korsakoff's syndrome: An information-processing approach.* New York: Academic Press.

Butters, N. & Cermak, L. S. (1986). A case study of the forgetting of autobiographical knowledge: implications for the study of retrograde amnesia. In D. C. Rubin (Ed.), *Autobiographical memory.* Cambridge: Cambridge University Press.

Butterworth, B. (1979). Hesitation and the production of verbal paraphasias and neologisms in jargon aphasia. *Brain and Language, 8,* 133–161.

Butterworth, B. (1980). Constraints on models of language production. In B. Butterworth (Ed.), *Language production,* Vol. 1. London: Academic Press.

Butterworth, B. (1985). Jargon aphasia: processes and strategies. In S. Newman and R. Epstein (Eds), *Current perspectives in dysphasia.* Edinburgh: Churchill Livingstone.

Butterworth, B. & Howard, D. (1987). Paragrammatisms. *Cognition, 26,* 1–37.

Butterworth, B., Swallow, J., & Grimston, M. (1981). Gestures and lexical processes in jargonaphasia. In J. W. Brown (Ed.), *Jargonaphasia.* New York: Academic Press.

Butterworth, B., Howard, D., & McLoughlin, P. (1984). The semantic deficit in aphasia: The relationship between semantic errors in auditory comprehension and picture naming. *Neuropsychologia, 22,* 409–426.

Campbell, R. (1987a). Cognitive neuropsychology. In G. Claxton (Ed.), *New directions in cognition.* London: Routledge and Kegan Paul.

Campbell, R. (1987b). One or two lexicons for reading and writing words; can misspellings shed any light. *Cognitive Neuropsychology, 4.* 487–499

Campbell, R., Landis, T., & Regard, M. (1986). Face recognition and lipreading: A neurological dissociation. *Brain, 109,* 509–521.

Campion, J. (1987). Apperceptive agnosia: The specification and description of constructs. In G. W. Humphreys & M. J. Riddoch (Eds), *Visual object processing.* London: Lawrence Erlbaum Associates Ltd.

Campion, J. & Latto, R. (1985). Apperceptive agnosia due to carbon poisoning. An interpretation based on critical band masking from disseminated lesions. *Behavioural Brain Research, 15,* 227–240.

Campion, J., Latto, R., & Smith, Y. M. (1983). Is blindsight an effect of scattered light, spared cortex, and near-threshold vision? *Behavioral and Brain Sciences, 6,* 423–486.

Capgras, J. & Reboul-Lachaux, J. (1923). L'illusion des "soisies" dans un délire systématisé chronique. *Bulletin de la Société Clinique de Médecine Mentale, 1,* 6–16.

Caplan, B. (1985). Stimulus effects in unilateral neglect. *Cortex, 21*, 69–80.

Caplan, D. (1981). On the cerebral localization of linguistic functions: Logical and empirical issues surrounding deficit analysis and function localization. *Brain and Language, 14*, 120–137.

Caplan, D., Kellar, L., & Locke, S. (1972). Inflection of neologisms in aphasia. *Brain, 95*, 169–172.

Caramazza, A. (1984). The logic of neuropsychological research and the problem of patient classification in aphasia. *Brain and Language, 21*, 9–20.

Caramazza, A. (1986). On drawing inferences about the structure of normal cognitive systems from the analysis of patterns of impaired performance: The case for single-patient studies. *Brain and Cognition, 5*, 41–66.

Caramazza, A. & Berndt, R. S. (1978). Semantic and syntactic processes in aphasia: A review of the literature. *Psychological Bulletin, 85*, 898–918.

Caramazza, A. & Berndt, R. S. (1985). A multi-component deficit view of agrammatic Broca's aphasia. In M. L. Kean (Ed.), *Agrammatism*. Orlando: Academic Press.

Caramazza, A. & Zurif, E. B. (1976). Dissociation of algorithmic and heuristic processes in language comprehension: Evidence from aphasia. *Brain and Language, 3*, 572–582.

Caramazza, A., Gordon, J., Zurif, E. B., & DeLuca, D. (1976). Right-hemispheric damage and verbal problem solving behavior. *Brain and Language, 3*, 41–46.

Caramazza, A., Basili, A. G., Koller, J. J., & Berndt, R. S. (1981). An investigation of repetition and language processing in a case of conduction aphasia. *Brain and Language, 14*, 235–275.

Caramazza, A., Berndt, R. S., & Basili, A. G. (1983). The selective impairment of phonological processing: A case study. *Brain and Language, 18*, 128–174.

Caramazza, A., Miceli, G., Silveri, M. C., & Laudanna, A. (1985). Reading mechanisms and the organisation of the lexicon: Evidence from acquired dyslexia. *Cognitive Neuropsychology, 2*, 81–114.

Casey, T. & Ettlinger, G. (1960). The occasional 'Independence' of dyslexia and dysgraphia from dysphasia. *Journal of Neurology, Neurosurgery and psychiatry, 23*, 228–236.

Cermak, L. S. (1976). The encoding capacity of a patient with amnesia due to encephalitis. *Neuropsychologia, 14*, 311–326.

Cermak, L. (1982). *Human memory and amnesia*. Hillsdale, N. J.: Lawrence Erlbaum Associates Inc.

Cermak, L. & Butters, N. (1973). Information processing deficits of alcoholic Korsakoff patients. *Quarterly Journal of Studies of Alcohol, 34*, 1110–1132.

Cermak, L. S. & O'Connor, M. (1983). The anterograde and retrograde retrieval ability of a patient with amnesia due to encephalitis. *Neuropsychologia, 21*, 213–234.

Cermak, L. S. & Reale, L. (1978). Depth of processing and retention of words by alcoholic Korsakoff patients. *Journal of Experimental Psychology: Human Learning and Memory, 4*, 165–174.

Cermak, L. S., Lewis, R., Butters, N., & Goodglass, H. (1973). Role of verbal mediation in performance of motor tasks by Korsakoff patients. *Perceptual and Motor Skills, 37*, 259–262.

Cermak, L. S., Talbot, N., Chandler, K., & Wolbarst, L. R. (1985). The perceptual priming phenomenon in amnesia. *Neuropsychologia, 23*, 615–622.

Charcot, J. M. (1883). Un cas de suppression brusque et isolée de la vision mentale des signes et des objetse (forms et couleurs). *Le Progres Medicale, 88*, 568–571.

Chedru, F. (1976). Space representation in unilateral spatial neglect. *Journal of Neurology, Neurosurgery and Psychiatry, 39*, 1057–1061.

Chiarello, C., Knight, R., & Mandel, M. (1982). Aphasia in a prelingually deaf woman. *Brain, 105*, 29–52.

Cicone, M., Wapner, E., Foldi, N., Zurif, E. B., & Gardner, H. (1979). The relation between gesture and language in aphasic communication. *Brain and Language, 8,* 324–349.

Code, C. (1987). *Language, aphasia and the right hemisphere.* Chichester: John Wiley.

Cohen, A. (1966). Errors of speech and their implications for understanding the strategy of language users. *Zeitschrift für Phonetik, 21,* 177–181. (Reprinted in V. A. Fromkin (Ed.) (1973). *Speech errors as linguistic evidence.* The Hague: Mouton.)

Cohen, G. & Faulkner, D. (1986). Memory for proper names: Age differences in retrieval. *British Journal of Developmental Psychology, 4,* 187–197.

Cohen, N. J. (1984). Preserved learning capacity in amnesia: Evidence for multiple memory systems. In L. R. Squire & N. Butters (Eds), *Neuropsychology of memory.* New York: Guilford Press.

Cohen, N. J. & Squire, L. R. (1980). Preserved learning and retention of pattern-analyzing skill in amnesia: Dissociation of knowing how and knowing that. *Science, 210,* 207–210.

Cohen, N. J. & Squire, L. R. (1981). Retrograde amnesia and remote memory impairment. *Neuropsychologia, 19,* 337–356.

Cole, M., Schutta, H. S., & Warrington, E. K. (1962). Visual disorientation in homonymous half-fields. *Neurology, 12,* 257–263.

Colella, R. (1894). La psicosi polyneuritica. *Annales de Neurologie, 12,* 1–66, 151–225, 449–521.

Coltheart, M. (1980a). Deep dyslexia: A review of the syndrome. In M. Coltheart, K. E. Patterson, & J. C. Marshall (Eds), *Deep dyslexia.* London: Routledge and Kegan Paul.

Coltheart, M. (1980b). Deep dyslexia: A right hemisphere hypothesis. In M. Coltheart, K. E. Patterson, & J. C. Marshall (Eds), *Deep dyslexia.* London: Routledge and Kegan Paul.

Coltheart, M. (1980c). Reading, phonological recoding, and deep dyslexia. In M. Coltheart, K. E. Patterson, & J. C. Marshall (Eds), *Deep dyslexia.* London: Routledge and Kegan Paul.

Coltheart, M. (1981). Disorders of reading and their implications for models of normal reading. *Visible Language, 15,* 245–286.

Coltheart, M. (1983). The right hemisphere and disorders of reading. In A. W. Young (Ed.), *Functions of the right cerebral hemisphere.* London: Academic Press.

Coltheart, M. (1986). Cognitive neuropsychology. In M. Posner & O. S. M. Marin (Eds), *Attention and Performance, XI.* Hillsdale, N. J.: Lawrence Erlbaum Associates Inc.

Coltheart, M. & Funnell, E. (1987). Reading and writing: One lexicon or two? In D. A. Allport, D. G. MacKay, W. Prinz, & E. Scheerer (Eds), *Language perception and production: Shared mechanisms in listening, reading and writing.* London: Academic Press.

Coltheart, M., Patterson, K. E., & Marshall, J. C. (Eds) (1980). *Deep dyslexia.* London: Routledge and Kegan Paul.

Coltheart, M., Sartori, G., & Job, R. (1987). *The cognitive neuropsychology of language.* London: Lawrence Erlbaum Associates Ltd.

Coriat, I. H. (1906). The experimental synthesis of the dissociated memories in alcoholic amnesia. *Journal of Abnormal Psychology, 1,* 109–122.

Coriat, I. H. (1907). The Lowell case of amnesia. *Journal of Abnormal Psychology, 2,* 93–111.

Corkin, S. (1965). Tactually-guided maze learning in man: Effects of unilateral cortical excisions and bilateral hippocampal lesions. *Neuropsychologia, 3,* 339–351.

Corkin, S. (1968). Acquisition of motor skill after bilateral medial temporal-lobe excision. *Neuropsychologia, 6,* 255–265.

Corkin, S. (1979). Hidden-figures test performance: Lasting effects of unilateral penetrating head injury and transient effects of bilateral cingulotomy. *Neuropsychologia, 17,* 585–605.

Corkin, S. (1984).   Lasting consequences of bilateral medial temporal lobectomy: Clinical course and experimental findings in H. M. *Seminars in Neurology, 4,* 249–259.

Costello, A. de L. & Warrington, E. K. (1987).   The dissociation of visuospatial neglect and neglect dyslexia. *Journal of Neurology, Neurosurgery and Psychiatry, 50,* 1110–1116.

Cotton, J. (1935).   Normal "visual hearing". *Science, 82,* 592–593.

Coughlan, A. D. & Warrington, E. K. (1978).   Word comprehension and word retrieval in patients with localised cerebral lesions. *Brain, 101,* 163–185.

Coughlan, A. D. & Warrington, E. K. (1981).   The impairment of verbal semantic memory: A single case study. *Journal of Neurology, Neurosurgery and Psychiatry, 44,* 1079–1083.

Cowey, A. (1982).   Sensory and non-sensory visual disorders in man and monkey. *Philosophical Transactions of the Royal Society* (London), *B298,* 3–13.

Cowey, A. (1985).   Aspects of cortical organization related to selective attention and selective impairments of visual perception: A tutorial review. In M. I. Posner & O. S. M. Marin (Eds), *Attention and performance, XI.* New Jersey: Lawrence Erlbaum Associates Inc.

Cowie, R. (1985).   Reading errors as clues to the nature of reading. In A. W. Ellis (Ed.), *Progress in the psychology of language,* Vol. 1. London: Lawrence Erlbaum Associates Ltd.

Craik, F. I. M. & Lockhart, R. S. (1972).   Levels of processing: A framework for memory research. *Journal of Verbal Learning and Verbal Behavior, 11,* 671–684.

Craik, K. (1943).   *The nature of explanation.* Cambridge: Cambridge University Press.

Critchley, M. (1942).   Aphasic disorders of signalling (constitutional and acquired) occurring in naval signalmen. *Journal of the Mount Sinai Hospital* (New York), *9,* 363–375.

Critchley, M. (1962).   Speech and speech-loss in relation to the duality of the brain. In V. Mountcastle (Ed.), *Interhemispheric relations and cerebral dominance.* Baltimore: Johns Hopkins University Press.

Cutler, A. (Ed.) (1982).   *Slips of the tongue.* The Hague: Mouton.

Damasio, A. R. (1985).   Disorders of complex visual processing: Agnosias, achromatopsia, Balint's syndrome, and related difficulties of orientation and construction. In M. M. Mesulam (Ed.), *Principles of behavioral neurology.* Philadelphia: F. A. Davis.

Damasio, A. R. & Benton, A. L. (1979).   Impairment of hand movements under visual guidance. *Neurology, 29,* 170–178.

Damasio, A. R., Damasio, H., & Van Hoesen, G. W. (1982).   Prosopagnosia: Anatomic basis and behavioral mechanisms. *Neurology, 32,* 331–341.

Damasio, A. R., Eslinger, P. J., Damasio, H., Van Hoesen, G. W., & Cornell, S. (1985).   Multimodal amnesic syndrome following bilateral temporal and basal forebrain damage. *Archives of Neurology, 42,* 252–259.

Damasio, A., Bellugi, U., Damasio, H., Poizner, H., & Van Gilder, J. (1986).   Sign language aphasia during left hemisphere amytal injection. *Nature, 332,* 363–365.

Dana, C. L. (1894).   The study of a case of amnesia or "double consciousness". *Psychological Review, 1,* 570–580.

Darwin, C. J. (1971).   Ear differences in the recall of fricatives and vowels. *Quarterly Journal of Experimental Psychology, 23,* 46–62.

Davidoff, J. B. & Ostergaard, A. L. (1984).   Colour anomia resulting from weakened short-term colour memory. *Brain, 107,* 415–431.

Davies, L. (1984).   *Word-finding difficulties: An information processing approach.* Unpublished undergraduate dissertation, Department of Psychology, University of Lancaster.

Day, J. (1977).   Right-hemisphere language processing in normal right-handers. *Journal of Experimental Psychology: Human Perception and Performance, 3,* 518–528.

De Haan, E. H. F., Young, A., & Newcombe, F. (1987a).   Face recognition without awareness. *Cognitive Neuropsychology, 4,* 385–415.

De Haan, E. H. F., Young, A., & Newcombe, F. (1987b).   Faces interfere with name classification in a prosopagnosic patient. *Cortex, 23,* 309–316.

Déjerine, J. (1892).   Contribution à l'étude anatomo-pathologique et clinique des differentes variétés de cécité verbale. *Compte Rendu Hebdomadaire des Séances et Memoires de la Société de Biologie, 4,* 61–90.

Déjerine, J. (1914).   *Sémiologie des affections du systeme nerveux.* Paris: Masson.

Dell, G. S. (1986).   A spreading-activation theory of retrieval in sentence production. *Psychological Review, 93,* 283–321.

Denes, G. & Semenza, C. (1975).   Auditory modality-specific anomia: Evidence from a case study of pure word deafness. *Cortex, 11,* 401–411.

De Renzi, E. (1982a).   *Disorders of space exploration and cognition.* Chichester: Wiley.

De Renzi, E. (1982b).   Memory disorders following focal neocortical damage. *Philosophical Transactions of the Royal Society* (London), *B298,* 73–83.

De Renzi, E. (1986).   Current issues in prosopagnosia. In H. D. Ellis, M. A. Jeeves, F. Newcombe, & A. Young (Eds), *Aspects of face processing.* Dordrecht: Martinus Nijhoff.

De Renzi, E., & Nichelli, P. (1975).   Verbal and non-verbal short-term memory impairments following hemispheric damage. *Cortex, 11,* 341–354.

De Renzi, E. & Spinnler, H. (1966).   Visual recognition in patients with unilateral cerebral disease. *Journal of Nervous and Mental Disease, 142,* 515–525.

De Renzi, E., Scotti, G., & Spinnler, H. (1969).   Perceptual and associative disorders of visual recognition. *Neurology, 19,* 634–642.

De Renzi, E., Faglioni, P., Scotti, G., & Spinnler, H. (1972).   Impairment in associating colour to form, concomitant with aphasia. *Brain, 95,* 293–304.

De Renzi, E., Faglioni, P., & Previdi, P. (1977a).   Spatial memory and hemispheric locus of lesion. *Cortex, 13,* 424–433.

De Renzi, E., Faglioni, P., & Villa, P. (1977b).   Topographical amnesia. *Journal of Neurology, Neurosurgery, and Psychiatry, 49,* 498–505.

De Renzi, E., Motti, F., & Nichelli, P. (1980).   Imitating gestures: A quantitative approach to ideomotor apraxia. *Archives of Neurology, 37,* 6–10.

De Villiers, J. (1974).   Quantitative aspects of agrammatism in aphasia. *Cortex, 10,* 36–54.

Drachman, D. A. & Arbit, J. (1966).   Memory and the hippocampal complex. *Archives of Neurology, 15,* 52–61.

Duncan, J. (1986).   Disorganisation of behaviour after frontal lobe damage. *Cognitive Neuropsychology, 3,* 271–290.

Dunn, R. (1845).   Case of suspension of the mental faculties of the powers of speech and special senses. *Lancet, ii,* 536–538 and 588–590.

Efron, R. (1968).   What is perception? In R. S. Cohen & M. W. Wartofsky (Eds), *Boston studies in the philosophy of science, 4.* Dordrecht: Reidel.

Eisenson, J. (1962).   Language and intellectual modifications associated with right cerebral damage. *Language and Speech, 5,* 49–53.

Ellis, A. W. (1979a).   Speech production and short-term memory. In J. Morton & J. C. Marshall (Eds), *Psycholinguistics series,* Vol. 2. London: Elek; and Cambridge, Mass.: MIT Press.

Ellis, A. W. (1979b).   Slips of the pen. *Visible Language, 13,* 265–282.

Ellis, A. W. (1980).   Errors in speech and short-term memory: The effects of phonemic similarity and syllable position. *Journal of Verbal Learning and Verbal Behavior, 19,* 624–634.

Ellis, A. W. (1982).   Spelling and writing (and reading and speaking). In A. W. Ellis (Ed.), *Normality and pathology in cognitive functions.* London: Academic Press.

Ellis, A. W. (1983).   Syndromes, slips and structures. *Bulletin of the British Psychological Society, 36,* 372–374.

Ellis, A. W. (1984a).   Introduction to Bramwell's (1897) case of word meaning deafness. *Cognitive Neuropsychology, 1,* 245–258.

Ellis, A. W. (1984b).   *Reading, writing and dyslexia: A cognitive analysis.* London: Lawrence Erlbaum Associates Ltd.

Ellis, A. W. (1985a).   The production of spoken words: A cognitive neuropsychological perspective. In A. W. Ellis (Ed.), *Progress in the psychology of language,* Vol. 2. London: Lawrence Erlbaum Associates Ltd.

Ellis, A. W. (1985b).   The cognitive neuropsychology of developmental (and acquired) dyslexia: A critical survey. *Cognitive Neuropsychology, 2,* 169–205.

Ellis, A. W. (1987).   Intimations of modularity, or, The modularity of mind. In M. Coltheart, G, Sartori, & R. Job (Eds), *The cognitive neuropsychology of language.* London: Lawrence Erlbaum Associates Ltd.

Ellis, A. W. (1988).   Neurocognitive processing of faces and voices. In A. W. Young & H. D. Ellis (Eds), *Handbook of research on face processing.* Amsterdam: North-Holland.

Ellis, A. W. & Beattie, G. (1986).   *The psychology of language and communication.* London: Lawrence Erlbaum Associates Ltd., and New York: The Guilford Press.

Ellis, A. W., Miller, D., & Sin, G. (1983).   Wernicke's aphasia and normal language processing: A case study in cognitive neuropsychology. *Cognition, 15,* 111–144.

Ellis, A. W., Flude, B. M., & Young, A. W. (1987a).   "Neglect dyslexia" and the early visual processing of letters in words. *Cognitive Neuropsychology, 4,* 439–464.

Ellis, A. W., Young, A. W., & Flude, B. M. (1987b).   "Afferent dysgraphia" and the role of feedback in the motor control of handwriting   *Cognitive Neuropsychology, 4,* 465–486.

Ellis, A. W., Young, A. W., Flude, B. M., & Hay, D.C. (1987c).   Repetition priming of face recognition. *Quarterly Journal of Experimental Psychology, 39A,* 193 210.

Fllis, H. D. (1986a).   Processes underlying face recognition. In R. Bruyer (Ed.), *The neuropsychology of face perception and facial expression.* Hillsdale, N. J.: Lawrence Erlbaum Associates Inc.

Ellis, H. D. (1986b).   Disorders of face recognition. In K. Poeck, H. J. Freund, & H. Gänshirt (Eds), *Neurology: Proceedings of the 13th World Congress of Neurology.* Berlin: Springer-Verlag.

Ellis, H. D. & Shepherd, J. W. (1974).   Recognition of abstract and concrete words presented in left and right visual fields. *Journal of Experimental Psychology, 103,* 1035–1036.

Emmorey, K. D. (1987).   The neurological substrates for prosodic aspects of speech. *Brain and Language, 30,* 305–320.

Etcoff, N. L. (1985).   The neuropsychology of emotional expression. In G. Goldstein & R. E. Tarter (Eds), *Advances in clinical neuropsychology,* Vol. 3. New York: Plenum.

Ettlinger, G. (1956).   Sensory deficits in visual agnosia. *Journal of Neurology, Neurosurgery and Psychiatry, 19,* 297–307.

Evans, J. J. (1966).   Transient loss of memory: An organic mental syndrome. *Brain, 89,* 539–548.

Eysenck, M. (1984).   *Handbook of cognitive psychology.* London: Lawrence Erlbaum Associates Ltd.

Fay, D. & Cutler, A. (1977).   Malaproprisms and the structure of the mental lexicon. *Linguistic Inquiry, 8,* 505–520.

Ferro, J. M. & Santos, M. E. (1984).   Associative visual agnosia: A case study. *Cortex, 20,* 121–134.

Feyereisen, P. & Seron, X. (1982a).   Nonverbal communication and aphasia: A review. I. Comprehension. *Brain and Language, 16,* 191–212.

Feyereisen, P. & Seron, X. (1982b). Nonverbal communication and aphasia: A review. II. Expression. *Brain and Language, 16,* 213–236.

Fisher, C. M. (1966). Concussion amnesia. *Neurology, 16,* 826–830.

Fodor, J. (1983). *The modularity of mind.* Cambridge, Mass.: MIT Press.

Fodor, J. A. (1985). Précis of "the modularity of mind" (with commentaries). *The Behavioral and Brain Sciences, 8,* 1–42.

Francis, W. N. & Kucera, H. (1982). *Frequency analysis of English usage: Lexicon and grammar.* Boston: Houghton Mifflin.

Franz, S. I. (1930). The relations of aphasia. *Journal of Genetic Psychology, 3,* 401–411.

Freed, D. M., Corkin, S., & Cohen, N. J. (1984). Rate of forgetting in H. M.: A reanalysis. *Society for Neuroscience Abstracts, 10,* 383.

Freud, A. (1891). *On aphasia.* (Translated by E. Stengel. London: Imago, 1935.)

Freud, S. (1901). *The psychopathology of everyday life.* Harmondsworth: Penguin, 1975.

Freund, C. S. (1889). Ueber optische Aphasie und Seelenblindheit. *Archiv für Psychiatrie und Nervenkrankheiten, 20,* 276–297, 371–416.

Friederici, A. D. (1982). Syntactic and semantic processes in aphasic deficits: The availability of prepositions. *Brain and Language, 15,* 249–258.

Friedrich, F. J., Walker, J. A., & Posner, M. I. (1985). Effects of parietal lesions on visual matching: Implications for reading errors. *Cognitive Neuropsychology, 2,* 253–264.

Frith, U. (Ed.) (1980). *Cognitive processes in spelling.* London: Academic Press.

Fromkin, V. A. (1971). The non-anomalous nature of anomalous utterances. *Language, 47,* 27–52.

Fromkin, V. A. (Ed.) (1973). *Speech errors as linguistic evidence.* The Hague: Mouton.

Fromkin, V. A. (Ed.) (1980). *Errors in linguistic performance: Slips of the tongue, ear, pen and hand.* New York: Academic Press.

Fry, D. B. (1959). Phonemic substitutions in an aphasic patient. *Language and Speech, 2,* 52–61.

Funnell, E. (1983). Phonological processes in reading: New evidence from acquired dysgraphia. *British Journal of Psychology, 74,* 159–180.

Funnell, E. (1987). Morphological errors in acquired dyslexia: A case of mistaken identity. *Quarterly Journal of Experimental Psychology, 39A,* 497–538.

Gabrieli, J. D. E., Cohen, N. J., & Corkin, S. (1983). The acquisition of lexical and semantic knowledge in amnesia. *Society for Neuroscience Abstracts, 9,* 238.

Gainotti, G. (1976). The relationship between semantic impairment in comprehension and naming in aphasic patients. *British Journal of Disorders of Communication, 11,* 57–61.

Gainotti, G., Miceli, G., Caltagirone, C., Silveri, M. C., & Masullo, C. (1981). Selective semantic-lexical impairment of language comprehension in right-brain-damaged patients. *Brain and Language, 13,* 201–211.

Gardner, H., Ling, P. K., Flamm, L., & Silverman, J. (1975). Comprehension and appreciation of humorous material following brain damage. *Brain, 98,* 399–412.

Gardner, H., Brownell, H. H., Wapner, W., & Michelow, D. (1983). Missing the point: The role of the right hemisphere in the processing of complex linguistic materials. In E. Perecman (Ed.), *Cognitive processes in the right hemisphere.* New York: Academic Press.

Garner, W. R., Hake, H. W., & Eriksen, C. W. (1956). Operationalism and the concept of perception. *Psychological Review, 63,* 149–159.

Garrett, M. F. (1975). The analysis of sentence production. In G. H. Bower (Ed.), *The psychology of learning and motivation,* Vol. 9. New York: Academic Press.

Garrett, M. F. (1980). Levels of processing in sentence production. In B. Butterworth (Ed.), *Language production, Vol. 1: Speech and talk.* London: Academic Press.

Garrett, M. F. (1982). Production of speech: Observations from normal and pathological language use. In A. W. Ellis (Ed.), *Normality and pathology in cognitive functions.* London: Academic Press.

Garrett, M. F. (1984). The organization of processing structure for language production: Applications to aphasic speech. In D. Caplan, A. R. Lecours, & A. Smith (Eds), *Biological perspectives on language.* Cambridge, Mass.: MIT Press.

Gaur, A. (1984). *A history of writing.* London: The British Library.

Gazzaniga, M. S. (1983). Right hemisphere language following brain bisection; a 20 year perspective. *American Psychologist, 38,* 525–537.

Gelb, I. J. (1963). *A study of writing.* Chicago: Chicago University Press.

Geschwind, N. (1965a). Disconnexion syndromes in animals and man: I. *Brain, 88,* 237–294.

Geschwind, N. (1965b). Disconnexion syndromes in animals and man: II. *Brain, 88,* 585–644.

Geschwind, N. (1982). Disorders of attention: A frontier in neuropsychology. *Philosophical Transactions of the Royal Society* (London), *B298,* 173–185.

Geschwind, N. & Fusillo, M. (1966). Color-naming defects in association with alexia. *Archives of Neurology, 15,* 137–146.

Gillespie, R. D. (1937). Amnesia. *Archives of Neurology and Psychiatry, 37,* 748–764.

Glass, A. L. (1983). The comprehension of idioms. *Journal of Psycholinguistic Research, 12,* 429–442.

Glass, A., Gazzaniga, M., & Premack, D. (1973). Artificial language training in global aphasics. *Neuropsychologia, 11,* 95–103.

Gleason, J. B., Goodglass, H., Green, E., Ackerman, N., & Hyde, M. (1975). The retrieval of syntax in Broca's aphasia. *Brain and Language, 2,* 451–471.

Glisky, E. L., Schacter, D. L., & Tulving, E. (1986). Computer learning by memory-impaired patients: Acquisition and retention of complex knowledge. *Neuropsychologia, 24,* 313–328.

Glushko, R. J. (1979). The organization and activation of orthographic knowledge in reading aloud. *Journal of Experimental Psychology: Human Perception and Performance, 5,* 674–691.

Godfrey, J. J. (1974). Perceptual difficulty and the right ear advantage for vowels. *Brain and Language, 1,* 323–335.

Goldberg, E. & Bilder, R. M. (1985). Neuropsychological perspectives: Retrograde amnesia and executive deficits. In L. Poon (Ed.), *Handbook of clinical memory assessment in older adults.* Washington, D. C.: American Psychiatric Association.

Goldberg, E., Antin, S. P., Bilder, R. M., Gerstman, L. J., Hughes, J. E. O., & Mattis, S. (1981). Retrograde amnesia: Possible role of mesencephalic reticular activation in long-term memory. *Science, 213,* 1392–1394.

Goldberg, E., Hughes, J. E. O., Mattis, S., & Antin, S. P. (1982). Isolated retrograde amnesia: Different etiologies, same mechanisms? *Cortex, 18,* 459–462.

Goldblum, M. C. (1979). Auditory analogue of deep dyslexia. In O. Creutzfeldt, H. Scheich, & C. Schreiner (Eds), *Hearing mechanisms and speech.* (Experimental brain research, Supplementum 2.) Berlin: Springer-Verlag.

Goldblum, M. C. (1981). Un équivalent de la dyslexie profonde dans la modalité auditive. In *Études Neurolinguistiques* (Numéro special de la Revue Grammatica) 7 (1), 157–77. (Services des Publications de l'Université de Toulouse—Le Mirail.)

Goldblum, M. C. (1985). Word comprehension in surface dyslexia. In K. E. Patterson, J. C. Marshall, & M.Coltheart (Eds), *Surface dyslexia: Neuropsychological and cognitive studies of phonological reading.* London: Lawrence Erlbaum Associates Ltd.

Goldstein, K. (1915). *Die Transkortikale Aphasien.* Jena: Gustav Fischer.

Goldstein, M. N. (1974). Auditory agnosia for speech ("pure word deafness"): A historical review with current implications. *Brain and Language, 1,* 195–204.

Goodglass, H. (1976). Agrammatism. In H. Whitaker & H. A. Whitaker (Eds), *Studies in neurolinguistics,* Vol. 1. New York: Academic Press.

Goodglass, H. & Berko, J. (1960). Aphasia and inflectional morphology in English. *Journal of Speech and Hearing Research, 3,* 257–267.

Goodglass, H. & Geschwind, N. (1976). Language disorders (aphasia). In E. C. Carterette & M. Friedman (Eds), *Handbook of perception,* Vol. 7. New York: Academic Press.

Goodglass, H. & Hunt, J. (1958). Grammatical complexity and aphasic speech. *Word, 14,* 197–207.

Goodglass, H. & Kaplan, E. (1963). Disturbance of gesture and pantomime in aphasia. *Brain, 86,* 703–720.

Goodglass, H. & Kaplan, E. (1972). *Assessment of aphasia and related disorders.* Philadelphia: Lea and Febinger.

Goodglass, H. & Menn, L. (1985). Is agrammatism a unitary phenomenon? In M.-L. Kean (Ed.), *Agrammatism.* Orlando: Academic Press.

Goodglass, H., Klein, B., Carey, P., & James, K. J. (1966). Specific semantic word categories in aphasia. *Cortex, 2,* 74–89.

Goodglass, H., Fodor, I. G., & Schulhoff, C. (1967). Prosodic factors in grammar: Evidence from aphasia. *Journal of Speech and Hearing Research, 10,* 5–20.

Goodman, R. A. & Caramazza, A. (1986a). Dissociation of spelling errors in written and oral spelling: The role of allographic conversion in writing. *Cognitive Neuropsychology, 3,* 179–206.

Goodman, R. A. & Caramazza, A. (1986b). Phonologically plausible errors: Implications for a model of the phoneme–grapheme conversion mechanism in the spelling process. In G. Augst (Ed.), *New trends in graphemics and orthography.* Berlin: Walter de Gruyter.

Goodman, R. A. & Caramazza, A. (1986c). Aspects of the spelling process: Evidence from a case of acquired dysgraphia. *Language and Cognitive Processes, 1,* 1–34.

Goodman-Schulman, R. A. & Caramazza, A. (1987). Patterns of dysgraphia and the nonlexical spelling process. *Cortex, 23,* 143–148.

Goodwin, D. W., Crane, J. B., & Guze, S. B. (1969). Phenomenological aspects of the alcoholic "blackout". *British Journal of Psychiatry, 115,* 1033–1038.

Gordon, B. & Marin, O. S. M. (1979). Transient global amnesia: An extensive case report. *Journal of Neurology, Neurosurgery and Psychiatry, 42,* 572–575.

Gott, P. S. (1973). Language after dominant hemispherectomy. *Journal of Neurology, Neurosurgery and Psychiatry, 36,* 1082–1088.

Gough P. B. (1972). One second of reading. In J. F. Kavanagh & I. G. Mattingly (Eds), *Language by ear and by eye.* Cambridge, Mass.: MIT Press.

Gould, S. J. (1980). *The panda's thumb.* New York: W. W. Norton; and Harmondsworth: Pelican.

Gould, S. J. (1983). *Hen's teeth and horse's toes.* New York: W. W. Norton; and Harmondsworth: Pelican.

Graf, P., Squire, L. R., & Mandler, G. (1984). The information that amnesic patients do not forget. *Journal of Experimental Psychology: Learning, Memory and Cognition, 10,* 164–178.

Graf, P., Shimamura, A. P., & Squire, L. R. (1985). Priming across modalities and priming across category labels: Extending the domain of preserved function in amnesia. *Journal of Experimental Psychology: Learning, Memory and Cognition, 11,* 386–396.

Green, E. (1969). Phonological and grammatical aspects of jargon in an aphasic patient: A case study. *Language and Speech, 12,* 103–118.

Greenblatt, S. H. (1973). Alexia without agraphia or hemianopsia: Anatomical analysis of an autopsied case. *Brain, 96,* 307–316.

Gregor, A. (1909). Beiträge zur Psychopathologie des Gedächtnisses. *Monatschrift für Psychiatrie und Neurologie, 25,* 218–255, 330–386.

Grodzinsky, Y. (1984). The syntactic characterisation of agrammatism. *Cognition, 16,* 99–120.

Grünthal, E. (1923). Zur Kenntnis de Psychopathologie des Korsakowschen Symptomenkom plexes. *Monatschrift fur Psychiatrie und Neurologie, 53,* 85–132.

Grünthal, E. (1924). Uber das Symptom der Einstellungstorung bei exogenen Psychosen. *Zeitschrift für Neurologie und Psychiatrie, 92,* 255–266.

Haggard, M. P. (1971). Encoding and the REA for speech signals. *Quarterly Journal of Experimental Psychology, 23,* 34–45.

Hamanaka, T. & Ohashi, H. (1974). "Aphasia" in pantomimic sign language. *Studia Phonologica, 8,* 23–35.

Hamsher, K. de S. & Roberts, R. J. (1985). Memory for recent U.S. Presidents in patients with cerebral disease. *Journal of Clinical and Experimental Neuropsychology, 7,* 1–13.

Harris, J. E. & Morris, P. E. (Eds) (1984). *Everyday memory, actions and absent-mindedness.* London: Academic Press.

Hart, J., Berndt, R. S., & Caramazza, A. (1985). Category-specific naming deficit following cerebral infarction. *Nature, 316,* 439–440.

Hatfield, F. M. & Patterson, K. E. (1983). Phonological spelling. *Quarterly Journal of Experimental Psychology, 35A,* 451–468.

Hay, D. C. & Young, A. W. (1982). The human face. In A. W. Ellis (Ed.), *Normality and pathology in cognitive functions.* London: Academic Press.

Hécaen, H. (1981). The neuropsychology of face recognition. In G. Davies, H. Ellis, & J. Shephered (Eds), *Perceiving and remembering faces.* New York: Academic Press.

Hécaen, H. & Angelergues, R. (1962). Agnosia for faces (prosopagnosia). *Archives of Neurology, 7,* 92–100.

Hécaen, H. & Marcie, P. (1974). Disorders of written language following right hemisphere lesions. In S. J. Dimond & J. G. Beaumont (Eds), *Hemisphere function in the human brain.* London: Elek.

Hécaen, H., Goldblum, M. C., Masure, M. C., & Ramier, A. M. (1974). Une nouvelle observation d'agnosie d'objet. Deficit de l'association ou de la categorisation, specifique de la modalité visuelle? *Neuropsychologia, 12,* 447–464.

Heeschen, C. (1985). Agrammatism versus Paragrammatism: A fictitious opposition. In M.-L. Kean (Ed.), *Agrammatism.* Orlando: Academic Press.

Heilbronner, K. (1906). Ueber Agrammatismus und die Storung der Innere Sprache. *Archiv für Psychiatrie und Nervenkrankheiten, 75,* 332–416.

Heilman, K. M. (1979). Neglect and related disorders. In K. M. Heilman & E. Valenstein (Eds), *Clinical neuropsychology.* New York: Oxford University Press.

Heilman, K. M. & Scholes, R. J. (1976). The nature of comprehension errors in Broca's, conduction, and Wernicke's aphasias. *Cortex, 12,* 258–265.

Heilman, K. M. & Watson, R. T. (1978). Changes in the symptoms of neglect induced by changing task strategy. *Archives of Neurology, 35,* 47–49.

Heilman, K. M., Scholes, R. J., & Watson, R. T. (1975). Auditory affective agnosia. *Journal of Neurology, Neurosurgery and Psychiatry, 38,* 69–72.

Heilman, K. M., Rothi, L., Campanella, D., & Wolfson, S. (1979). Wernicke's and global aphasia without alexia. *Archives of Neurology, 36,* 129–133.

Heilman, K. M., Bowers, D., Speedie, L., & Coslett, H. B. (1984). Comprehension of affective and nonaffective prosody. *Neurology, 34,* 917–921.

Hemphil, R. E. & Stengel, E. (1940). A study on pure word deafness. *Journal of Neurology, Neurosurgery and Psychiatry, 3,* 251–262.

Henderson, L. (1985). The psychology of morphemes. In A. W. Ellis (Ed.), *Progress in the psychology of language*, Vol. 1. London: Lawrence Erlbaum Associates Ltd.

Heywood, C. A., Wilson, B., & Cowey, A. (1987). A case study of cortical colour "blindness" with relatively intact achromatic discrimination. *Journal of Neurology, Neurosurgery and Psychiatry, 50*, 22–29.

Hier, D. B. & Kaplan, J. (1980). Verbal comprehension deficits after right hemisphere damage. *Applied Psycholinguistics, 1*, 279–294.

Hier, D. B. & Mohr, J. P. (1977). Incongruous oral and written naming: Evidence for a subdivision of the syndrome of Wernicke's aphasia. *Brain and Language, 4*, 115–126.

Hines, D. (1976). Recognition of verbs, abstract nouns and concrete nouns from the left and right visual half-fields. *Neuropsychologia, 14*, 211–216.

Hines, D. (1977). Differences in tachistoscopic recognition between abstract and concrete words as a function of visual half-field and frequency. *Cortex, 13*, 66–73.

Hirst, W. (1982). The amnesic syndrome: Descriptions and explanations. *Psychological Bulletin, 91*, 435–460.

Hirst, W., Johnson, M. K., Kim, J. K., Phelps, E. A., Risse, G., & Volpe, B. (1986). Recognition and recall in amnesics. *Journal of Experimental Psychology: Learning, Memory and Cognition, 12*, 445–516.

Holmes, G. (1918). Disturbances of visual orientation. *British Journal of Ophthalmology, 2*, 449–468, 506–615.

Holmes, G. (1919). Disturbances of visual space perception. *British Medical Journal, 2*, 230–233.

Holmes, G. & Horrax, G. (1919). Disturbances of spatial orientation and visual attention, with loss of stereoscopic vision. *Archives of Neurology and Psychiatry, 1*, 385–407.

Holmes, J. M. (1973). *Dyslexia: A neurolinguistic study of traumatic and developmental disorders of reading.* Unpublished Ph.D. thesis, University of Edinburgh.

Holmes, J. M. (1978). "Regression" and reading breakdown. In A. Caramazza & E. B. Zurif (Eds), *Language acquisition and language breakdown: Parallels and divergences.* Baltimore: Johns Hopkins University Press.

Homan, R. W., Criswell, E., Wada, J. A., & Ross, E. D. (1982). Hemispheric contributions to manual communication (signing and finger spelling). *Neurology, 32*, 1020–1023.

Hotopf, W. H. N. (1980). Slips of the pen. In U. Frith (Ed.), *Cognitive processes in spelling.* London: Academic Press.

Hotopf, W. H. N. (1983). Lexical slips of the pen and tongue: What they tell us about language production. In B. Butterworth (Ed.), *Language production*, Vol. 2. London: Academic Press.

Howard, D. (1985a). Agrammatism. In S. Newman & R. Epstein (Eds), *Current perspectives in dysphasia.* Edinburgh: Churchill Livingstone.

Howard, D. (1985b). Introduction to "On agrammatism" (*Über Agrammatismus*) by Max Isserlin, 1922. *Cognitive Neuropsychology, 4*, 303–307.

Howard, D. & Franklin, S. (1987). Three ways for understanding written words, and their use in two contrasting cases of surface dyslexia. In D. A. Allport, D. MacKay, W. Prinz, & E. Scheerer (Eds), *Language perception and production: Common processes in listening, speaking, reading and writing.* London: Academic Press.

Howard, D. & Hatfield, F. M. (1987). *Aphasia therapy.* London: Lawrence Erlbaum Associates Ltd.

Howard, D. & Orchard-Lisle, V. (1984). On the origin of semantic errors in naming: Evidence from the case of a global aphasic. *Cognitive Neuropsychology, 1*, 163–190.

Humphreys, G. W. & Evett, L. J. (1985). Are there independent lexical and nonlexical routes in reading? An evaluation of the dual route theory of reading. *The Behavioral and Brain Sciences, 8*, 689–740.

Humphreys, G. W. & Riddoch, M. J. (1984). Routes to object constancy: Implications from neurological impairments of object constancy. *Quarterly Journal of Experimental Psychology, 36A,* 385–415.

Humphreys, G. W. & Riddoch, M. J. (1985). Authors' correction to "Routes to object constancy". *Quarterly Journal of Experimental Psychology, 37A,* 493–495.

Humphreys, G. W. & Riddoch, M. J. (1987a). *To see but not to see: A case study of visual agnosia.* London: Lawrence Erlbaum Associates Ltd.

Humphreys, G. W. & Riddoch, M. J. (1987b). The fractionation of visual agnosia. In G. W. Humphreys & M. J. Riddoch (Eds), *Visual object processing.* London: Lawrence Erlbaum Associates Ltd.

Huppert, F. A. & Piercy, M. (1976). Recognition memory in amnesic patients: Effect of temporal context and familiarity of material. *Cortex, 12,* 3–20.

Huppert, F. A. & Piercy M. (1977). Recognition memory in amnesic patients: A defect of acquisition? *Neuropsychologia, 15,* 643–653.

Huppert, F. A. & Piercy, M. (1978). Dissociation between learning and remembering in organic amnesia. *Nature, 275,* 317–318.

Huppert, F. A. & Piercy, M. (1979). Normal and abnormal forgetting in organic amnesia: Effect of locus of lesion. *Cortex, 15,* 385–390.

Isserlin, M. (1922). Über Agrammatismus. *Zeitschrift für die Gesamte Neurologie und Psychiatrie, 75,* 332–410. (Translated with Introduction by D. Howard in *Cognitive Neuropsychology,* 1985, *2,* 303–345.)

Jackson, J. H. (1874). On the nature of the duality of the brain. *Medical Press and Circular, 1,* 19–43. (Reprinted in J. Taylor (Ed.), *Selected writings of J. H. Jackson,* Vol. 2. New York: Basic Books, 1958.)

Jacoby, L. L. (1984). Incidental versus intentional retrieval: Remembering and awareness as separate issues. In L. R. Squire & N. Butters (Eds), *Neuropsychology of memory.* New York: Guilford Press.

Jacoby, L. L. & Witherspoon, D. (1982). Remembering without awareness. *Canadian Journal of Psychology, 36,* 300–324.

Jakimik, J., Cole, R. A., & Rudnicky, A. I. (1985). Sound and spelling in spoken word recognition. *Journal of Memory and Language, 24,* 165–178.

James, W. (1980). *The principles of psychology.* New York: Holt.

Janis, I. (1950). Psychological effects of electroconvulsive treatments I. Post-treatment amnesias. *Journal of Nervous and Mental Disease, 111,* 359–382.

Joanette, Y., Keller, E., & Lecours, A. R. (1980). Sequences of phonemic approximations in aphasia. *Brain and Language, 11,* 30–44.

Job, R. & Sartori, G. (1984). Morphological decomposition: Evidence from crossed phonological dyslexia. *Quarterly Journal of Experimental Psychology, 36A,* 435–458.

Johnson, M. K., Kim, J. K., & Risse, G. (1985). Do alcoholic Korsakoff's syndrome patients acquire affective reactions? *Journal of Experimental Psychology: Learning, Memory and Cognition, 11,* 22–36.

Jones, G. V. (1983). On double dissociation of function. *Neuropsychologia, 21,* 397–400.

Joseph, A. B. (1986). Focal central nervous system abnormalities in patients with misidentification syndromes. *Bibliotheca Psychiatrica, 164,* 68–79.

Kadish, J. (1978). A neuropsychological approach to the study of gesture and pantomime in aphasia. *South African Journal of Communication Disorders, 25,* 102–117.

Kaushall, P. I., Zetin, M., & Squire, L. R. (1981). A psychosocial study of chronic, circumscribed amnesia. *Journal of Nervous and Mental Disease, 169,* 383–389.

Kay, J. (1985). Mechanisms of oral reading: A critical appraisal of cognitive models. In A. W. Ellis (Ed.), *Progress in the psychology of language,* Vol. 2. London: Lawrence Erlbaum Associates Ltd.

Kay, J. & Ellis, A. W. (1987).   A cognitive neuropsychological case study of anomia: Implications for psychological models of word retrieval. *Brain, 110,* 613–629.

Kay, J. & Marcel, T. (1981).   One process not two in reading aloud: Lexical analogies do the work of nonlexical rules. *Quarterly Journal of Experimental Psychology, 33A,* 397–413.

Kay, J. & Patterson, K. E. (1985).   Routes to meaning in surface dyslexia. In K. E. Patterson, J. C. Marshall, & M. Coltheart (Eds), *Surface dyslexia: Neuropsychological and cognitive analyses of phonological reading.* London: Lawrence Erlbaum Associates Ltd.

Kean, M.-L. (1977).   The linguistic interpretation of aphasia syndromes: Agrammatism in Broca's aphasia, an example. *Cognition, 5,* 9–46.

Kean, M.-L. (1979).   Agrammatism, a phonological deficit. *Cognition, 7,* 69–83.

Kean, M.-L. (Ed.) (1985).   *Agrammatism.* New York: Academic Press.

Keller, E. & Gopnik, M. (Eds) (1987).   *Motor and sensory processes of language.* Hillsdale, N. J.: Lawrence Erlbaum Associates.

Kertesz, A. (1979).   *Aphasia and associated disorders: Taxonomy, localization and recovery.* New York: Grune and Stratton.

Kertesz, A. (Ed.) (1983).   *Localization in neuropsychology.* New York: Academic Press.

Kertesz, A. & McCabe, P. (1975).   Intelligence and aphasia. *Brain and Language, 2,* 387–395.

Kimura, D. (1981).   Neural mechanisms in manual signing. *Sign Language Studies, 33,* 291–312.

Kimura, D. & Archibald, Y. (1974).   Motor functions of the left hemisphere. *Brain, 97,* 333–350.

Kimura, D., Battison, R., & Lubert, B. (1976).   Impairment of nonlinguistic hand movements in a deaf aphasic. *Brain and Language, 3,* 566–571.

Kinsbourne, M. & Warrington, E. K. (1962).   A variety of reading disability associated with right hemisphere lesions. *Journal of Neurology, Neurosurgery and Psychiatry, 25,* 339–344.

Kinsbourne, M. & Warrington, E. K. (1963).   Jargon aphasia. *Neuropsychologia, 1,* 27–37.

Kinsbourne, M. & Warrington, E. K. (1964).   Observations on colour agnosia. *Journal of Neurology, Neurosurgery and Psychiatry, 27,* 296–299.

Kinsbourne, M. & Warrington, E. K. (1965).   A case showing selectively impaired oral spelling. *Journal of Neurology, Neurosurgery and Psychiatry, 28,* 563–566.

Kinsbourne, M. & Wood, F. (1975).   Short-term memory processes and the amnesic syndrome. In D. Deutsch & J. A. Deutsch (Eds), *Short-term memory.* New York: Academic Press.

Klatt, D. H. (1979).   Speech perception: A model of acoustic-phonetic analysis and lexical access. *Journal of Phonetics, 7,* 279–312.

Kleiman, G. M. (1981).   Speech recoding in reading. *Journal of Verbal Learning and Verbal Behavior, 14,* 323–339.

Klein, R. & Harper, J. (1956).   The problem of agnosia in the light of a case of pure word deafness. *Journal of Mental Science, 102,* 112–120.

Kleist, K. (1916).   Über Leitungsafasie und grammatische Störungen. *Monatschrift für Psychiatrie und Neurologie, 16,* 118–121.

Klima, E. S. & Bellugi, U. (1979).   *The signs of language.* Cambridge, Mass.: Harvard University Press.

Knight, R. G. & Wooles, I. M. (1980).   Experimental investigation of chronic organic amnesia: A review. *Psychological Bulletin, 88,* 753–771.

Kohn, S. E. (1987).   Phonological production deficits in aphasia. In H. Whitaker (Ed.), *Phonological processes and brain mechanisms.* New York: Springer-Verlag.

Kohn, S. E. & Friedman, R. B. (1986).   Word-meaning deafness: A phonological-semantic dissociation. *Cognitive Neuropsychology, 3,* 291–308.

Kolb, B. & Whishaw, I. Q. (1985).   *Fundamentals of human neuropsychology.* New York: Freeman.

Kolk, H. H. J., Van Grunsven, M. J. F., & Keyser, A. (1985).   On parallelism between production and comprehension in agrammatism. In M.-L. Kean (Ed.), *Agrammatism.* Orlando: Academic Press.

Kopelman, M. D. (1985).   Rates of forgetting in Alzheimer-type dementia and Korsakoff's syndrome. *Neuropsychologia, 23,* 623–638.

Korsakoff, S. S. (1889).   Über eine besondere Form psychischer Störung, Kombiniert mit multiplen Neuritis. *Archiv für Psychiatrie und Nervenkrankheiten, 21,* 669–704. (Translated by M. Victor & P. I. Yakovlev in *Neurology,* 1955, 5, 394–406.)

Kremin, H. (1985).   Routes and strategies in surface dyslexia and dysgraphia. In K. E. Patterson, J. C. Marshall, & M. Coltheart (Eds), *Surface dyslexia: Neuropsychological and cognitive studies of phonological reading.* London: Lawrence Erlbaum Associates Ltd.

Kuhl, P. K. & Meltzoff, A. N. (1982).   The bimodal perception of speech in infancy. *Science, 218,* 1138–1144.

Kurucz, J. & Feldmar, G. (1979).   Prosopo-affective agnosia as a symptom of cerebral organic disease. *Journal of the American Geriatrics Society, 27,* 225–230.

Kurucz, J., Feldmar, G., & Werner, W. (1979).   Prosopo-affective agnosia associated with chronic organic brain syndrome. *Journal of the American Geriatrics Society, 27,* 91–95.

Lakatos, I. (1974).   Falsification and the methodology of scientific research programmes. In I. Lakatos & A. Musgrave (Eds), *Criticism and the growth of knowledge.* Cambridge: Cambridge University Press.

Lambert, A. J. (1982).   Right hemisphere language ability: 2. Evidence from normal subjects. *Current Psychological Reviews, 2,* 139–152.

Landis, T., Regard, M., Graves, R., & Goodglass, H. (1983).   Semantic paralexia: A release of right hemispheric function from left hemispheric control? *Neuropsychologia, 21,* 359–364.

Landis, T., Cummings, J. L., Benson, D. F., & Palmer, E. P. (1986).   Loss of topographic familiarity: An environmental agnosia. *Archives of Neurology, 43,* 132–136.

Larsen, B., Skinhoj, E., & Lassen, N. A. (1978).   Variations in regional cortical blood flow in the right and left hemispheres during automatic speech. *Brain, 101,* 193–209.

Lashley, K. S. (1941).   Coalescence of neurology and psychology. *Proceedings of the American Philosophical Society, 84,* 461–470.

Lashley, K. S. (1951).   The problem of serial order in behavior. In L. A. Jeffress (Ed.), *Cerebral mechanisms in behavior.* New York: Wiley.

Lasky, E. Z., Weidner, W. E., & Johnson, J. P. (1976).   Influence of linguistic complexity, rate of presentation, and interphrase pause time on auditory-verbal comprehension of adult aphasic patients. *Brain and Language, 3,* 386–395.

Lebrun, Y. (1976).   Neurolinguistic models of language and speech. In H. Whitaker & H. A. Whitaker (Eds), *Studies in neurolinguistics,* Vol. 1. New York: Academic Press.

Lebrun, Y. (1985).   Disturbances of written language and associated abilities following damage to the right hemisphere. *Applied Psycholinguistics, 6,* 231–260.

Lebrun, Y. & Leleux, C. (1986).   Central communication disorders in deaf signers. In J.-L. Nespoulous, P. Perron, & A. R. Lecours (Eds), *The biological foundations of gestures: Motor and semiotic aspects.* Hillsdale, N. J.: Lawrence Erlbaum Associates Inc.

Lebrun, Y. & Rubio, S. (1972).   Reduplications et omissions graphiques chez des patients attients d'une lésion hémisphérique droite. *Neuropsychologia, 10,* 249–251.

Lebrun, Y., Buyssens, E., & Henneaux, J. (1973).   Phonetic aspects of anarthria. *Cortex*, *9*, 126–135.

Lebrun, Y., Lessinnes, A., De Vresse, L., & Leleux, C. (1985).   Dysprosody and the non-dominant hemisphere. *Language Sciences*, *7*, 41–52.

Lecours, A. R. (1975).   Methods for the description of aphasic transformations of language. In E. H. Lenneberg & E. Lenneberg (Eds), *Foundations of language development*, Vol. 2. New York: Academic Press.

Lecours, A. R. & Lhermitte, F. (1969).   Phonemic paraphasias: Linguistic structures and tentative hypotheses. *Cortex*, *5*, 193–228.

Lecours, A. R. & Lhermitte, F. (1976).   The "pure form" of the phonetic disintegration syndrome (pure anarthria): Anatomico-clinical report of a historical case. *Brain and Language*, *3*, 88–113.

Lecours, A. R., Nespoulous, J.-L., & Desaulniers, P. (1986).   Standard teaching on apraxia. In J.-L. Nespoulous, P. Perron, & A. R. Lecours (Eds), *The biological foundations of gestures: Motor and semiotic aspects*. Hillsdale, N. J.: Lawrence Erlbaum Associates Ltd.

Lecours, A. R., Osborn, E., Travis, L., Rouillon, F., & Lavallee-Huynh, G. (1980).   Jargons. In J. W. Brown (Ed.), *Jargonaphasia*. New York: Academic Press.

Lecours, A. R., Travis, L., & Osborn, E. (1980).   Glossolalia as a manifestation of Wernicke's aphasia: A comparison to glossolalia in schizophasia and in procession. In O. Höök & M. Taylor-Sarno (Eds), *Aphasia: Concepts of analysis and management*. Stockholm: Almquist & Wiksell.

Leech, G., Deuchar, M., & Hoogenraad, R. (1982).   *English grammar for today*. London: The Macmillan Press.

Lehiste, I. (1973).   Phonetic disambiguation of syntactic ambiguity. *Glossa*, *7*, 107–122.

Lehiste, I. (1979).   Perception of sentence and paragraph boundaries. In B. Lindblom & S. Ohman (Eds), *Frontiers of speech communication research*. New York: Academic Press.

Lehiste, I., & Wang, W. (1977).   Perception of sentence and paragraph boundaries with and without information. In W. Dressler & R. Pfeiffer (Eds), *Phonologica, 1976*. Innsbruck: Institut für Sprachwissenschaft der Universitat Innsbruck.

Lehmann, W. P. (1973).   *Historical linguistics* (2nd ed.). New York: Holt, Rinehart and Winston.

Leischner, A. (1943).   Die Aphasie der Taubstummen. *Archiv für Psychiatrie und Nervenkrankheiten*, *115*, 469–548.

Lenneberg, E. H. (1960).   A review of "Speech and brain mechanisms" by W. Penfield and L. Roberts. *Language*, *36*, 97–112.

Lesser, R. (1978).   *Linguistic investigation of aphasia*. London: Edward Arnold.

Levin, H. S., Peters, B. H., & Hulkonen, D. A. (1983).   Early concepts of anterograde and retrograde amnesia. *Cortex*, *19*, 427–440.

Levine, D. N. (1978).   Prosopagnosia and visual object agnosia: A behavioral study. *Brain and Language*, *5*, 341–365.

Levine, D. N., Calvanio, R., & Popovics, A. (1982).   Language in the absence of inner speech. *Neuropsychologia*, *20*, 391–409.

Levine, D. N., Warach, J., & Farah, M. (1985).   Two visual systems in mental imagery: Dissociation of "what" and "where" in imagery disorders due to bilateral posterior cerebral lesions. *Neurology*, *35*, 1010–1018.

Levy, B. A. (1981).   Interactive processing during reading. In A. M. Lesgold & C. A. Perfetti (Eds), *Interactive processes in reading*. Hillsdale, N. J.: Lawrence Erlbaum Associates Inc.

Lewis, A. (1961).   Amnesic syndromes. *Proceedings of the Royal Society of Medicine*, *54*, 955–961.

Lewis, S. W. (1987).   Brain imaging in a case of Capgras' syndrome. *British Journal of Psychiatry, 150*, 117–121.

Lhermitte, F. & Beauvois, M.-F. (1973).   A visual-speech disconnexion syndrome: Report of a case with optic aphasia, agnosic alexia and colour agnosia. *Brain, 97*, 695–714.

Lichtheim, L. (1885).   On aphasia. *Brain, 7*, 433–484.

Lidz, T. (1942).   The amnesic syndrome. *Archives of Neurology and Psychiatry, 47*, 588–605.

Lieberman, P. (1963).   Some effects of semantic and grammatical context on the production and perception of speech. *Language and Speech, 6*, 172–187.

Liepmann, H. (1910).   Beitrag zur Kenntnis des amnestischen Symptomenkomplexes. *Neurologie Zeitblatt, 29*, 1147–1161.

Lissauer, H. (1890).   Ein Fall von Seelenblindheit nebst einem Beitrage zur Theorie derselben. *Archiv für Psychiatrie und Nervenkrankheiten, 21*, 222–270.

Lock, A. (1980).   *The guided reinvention of language.* London: Academic Press.

Luria, A. R. (1970).   *Traumatic aphasia.* The Hague: Mouton.

Luria, A. R. (1974).   Language and brain: Towards the basic problems of neurolinguistics. *Brain and Language, 1*, 1–14.

Luria, A. R. (1976).   *Basic problems in neurolinguistics.* The Hague: Mouton.

MacCallum, W. A. G. (1973).   Capgras symptoms with an organic basis. *British Journal of Psychiatry, 123*, 639–642.

McCarthy, R. & Warrington, E. K. (1984).   A two-route model of speech production. *Brain, 107*, 463–485.

McCarthy, R. & Warrington, E. K. (1986).   Visual associative agnosia: A clinico-anatomical study of a single case. *Journal of Neurology, Neurosurgery and Psychiatry, 49*, 1233–1240.

McClelland, J. L. (1987).   The case for interactionism in language processing. In M. Coltheart (Ed.), *Attention and Performance XII: The psychology of reading.* London: Lawrence Erlbaum Associates Ltd.

McClelland, J. L. & Elman, J. L. (1986).   The TRACE model of speech perception. *Cognitive Psychology, 18*, 1–86.

McClelland, J. L. & Rumelhart, D. E. (1981).   An interactive activation model of context effects in letter perception: Part 1. An account of basic findings. *Psychological Review, 88*, 375–407.

McClelland, J. L. & Rumelhart, D. E. (1985).   Distributed memory and the representation of general and specific information. *Journal of Experimental Psychology: General, 114*, 159–188.

McClelland, J. L. & Rumelhart, D. E. (1986).   Amnesia and distributed memory. In J. L. McClelland & D. E. Rumelhart (Eds), *Parallel distributed processing: Explorations in the microstructure of cognition, Vol. 2: Psychological and biological models.* Cambridge, Mass: MIT Press.

McGurk, H. & MacDonald, J. (1976).   Hearing lips and seeing voices. *Nature, 264*, 746–748.

MacKain, K. S., Studdert-Kennedy, M., Spieker, S., & Stern D. (1983).   Infant intermodal speech perception is a left hemisphere function. *Science, 219*, 1347–1349.

MacKay, D. G. (1970).   Spoonerisms: The structure of errors in the serial order of speech. *Neuropsychologia, 8*, 323–350. (Reprinted in V. A. Fromkin (Ed.) (1973), *Speech errors as linguistic evidence.* The Hague: Mouton.)

McKenna, P. & Warrington, E. K. (1980).   Testing for nominal dysphasia. *Journal of Neurology, Neurosurgery, and Psychiatry, 43*, 781–788.

McWeeny, K. H., Young, A. W., Hay, D. C., & Ellis, A. W. (1987).   Putting names to faces. *British Journal of Psychology, 78*, 143–149.

Mack, J. L. & Boller, F. (1977).   Associative visual agnosia and its related deficits: The role of the minor hemisphere in assigning meaning to visual perceptions. *Neuropsychologia, 15,* 345–349.

Malone, D. R., Morris, H. H., Kay, M. C., & Levin, H. S. (1982). Prosopagnosia: A double dissociation between the recognition of familiar and unfamiliar faces. *Journal of Neurology, Neurosurgery, and Psychiatry, 45,* 820–822.

Mann, V. A. & Liberman, A. M. (1983). Some differences between phonetic and auditory modes of perception. *Cognition, 14,* 211–235.

Marcel, A. J. (1983). Conscious and unconscious perception: An approach to the relations between phenomenal experience and perceptual processes. *Cognitive Psychology, 15,* 238–300.

Marcie, P. (1983). Writing disorders associated with focal cortical lesions. In M. Martlew (Ed.), *The psychology of written language: Developmental and educational perspectives.* Chichester: J. Wiley.

Marcus, S. M. (1981). ERIS—context-sensitive coding in speech perception. *Journal of Phonetics, 9,* 197–220.

Margolin, D. I. (1984). The neuropsychology of writing and spelling: Semantic, phonological, motor and perceptual processes. *Quarterly Journal of Experimental Psychology, 36A,* 459–489.

Margolin, D. I., Marcel, A. J., & Carlson, N. R. (1985). Common mechanisms in dysnomia and post-semantic surface dyslexia. In K. E. Patterson, J. C. Marshall, & M. Coltheart (Eds), *Surface dyslexia: Neuropsychological and cognitive processes in phonological reading.* London: Lawrence Erlbaum Associates Ltd.

Marin, O. S. M., Saffran, E. M., & Schwartz, M. F. (1976). Dissociations of language in aphasia: Implications for normal function. *Annals of the New York Academy of Sciences, 280,* 868–884.

Marr, D. (1976). Early processing of visual information. *Philosophical Transactions of the Royal Society* (London), *B275,* 483–524.

Marr, D. (1980). Visual information processing: The structure and creation of visual representations. *Philosophical Transactions of the Royal Society* (London), *B290,* 199–218.

Marr, D. (1982). *Vision.* San Francisco: W. H. Freeman.

Marr, D. & Nishihara, K. (1978). Representation and recognition of the spatial organization of three-dimensional shapes. *Philosophical Transactions of the Royal Society* (London), *B200,* 269–294.

Marshall, J. C. (1979). Disorders in the expression of language. In J. Morton & J. C. Marshall (Eds), *Psycholinguistics series,* Vol. 1. London: Elek; and Cambridge, Mass.: MIT Press.

Marshall, J. C. (1982). What is a symptom-complex? In M. Arbib, D. Caplan, & J. C. Marshall (Eds), *Neural models of language processes.* New York: Academic Press.

Marshall, J. C. (1986). Signs of language in the brain. *Nature, 322,* 307–308.

Marshall, J. C. (1987). The cultural and biological context of written languages: Their acquisition, deployment, and breakdown. In J. R. Beech & A. M. Colley (Eds), *Cognitive approaches to reading.* Chichester: John Wiley.

Marshall, J. C. & Fryer, D. M. (1978). Speak, Memory! An introduction to some historic studies of remembering and forgetting. In M. M. Gruneberg & P. E. Morris (Eds), *Aspects of memory.* London: Methuen.

Marshall, J. C. & Newcombe, F. (1966). Syntactic and semantic errors in paralexia. *Neuropsychologia, 4,* 169–176.

Marshall, J. C. & Newcombe, F. (1973). Patterns of paralexia: A psycholinguistic approach. *Journal of Psycholinguistic Research, 2,* 175–199.

Marshall, J. C. & Newcombe, F. (1980). The conceptual status of deep dyslexia: An historical perspective. In M. Coltheart, K. E. Patterson, & J. C. Marshall (Eds), *Deep dyslexia*. London: Routlege and Kegan Paul.

Marshall, J. C. & Patterson, K. E. (1983). Semantic paralexia and the wrong hemisphere: A note on Landis, Regard, Graves and Goodglass (1983). *Neuropsychologia, 21*, 425–427.

Marslen-Wilson, W. D. (1984). Function and process in spoken word recognition—A tutorial review. In H. Bouma & D. B. Bouwhuis (Eds), *Attention and Performance, X: Control of language processes*. London: Lawrence Erlbaum Associates Ltd.

Marslen-Wilson, W. D. & Teuber, H.-L. (1975). Memory for remote events in anterograde amnesia: Recognition of public figures from news photographs. *Neuropsychologia, 13*, 347–352.

Marslen-Wilson, W. D. & Tyler, L. K. (1975). Processing structure of sentence perception. *Nature, 257*, 784–786.

Marslen-Wilson, W. D. & Tyler, L. K. (1980). The temporal structure of spoken language understanding. *Cognition, 8*, 1–71.

Martin, A. D. & Rigrodsky, S. (1974). An investigation of phonological impairment in aphasia, Part 2: Distinctive feature analysis of phonemic commutation errors in aphasia. *Cortex, 10*, 329–346.

Martone, M., Butters, N., Payne, M., Becker, J. T., & Sax, D. S. (1984). Dissociations between skill learning and verbal recognition in amnesia and dementia. *Archives of Neurology, 41*, 965–970.

Mayer-Gross, W. (1943). Memory defects after ECT. *Lancet, ii*, 603.

Mayes, A. R. & Meudell, P. R. (1981). How similar is the effect of cueing in amnesics and in normal subjects following forgetting? *Cortex, 17*, 113–124.

Mayes, A. R. & Meudell, P. R. (1984). Problems and prospects for research on amnesia In L. R. Squire & N. Butters (Eds), *Neuropsychology of memory*. New York: Guilford Press.

Mayes, A. R., Meudell, P. R., & Neary, D. (1978). Must amnesia be caused by either encoding or retrieval disorders? In M. M. Gruneberg, P. E. Morris, & R. N. Sykes (Eds), *Practical aspects of memory*. London: Academic Press.

Meadows, J. C. (1974a). The anatomical basis of prosopagnosia. *Journal of Neurology, Neurosurgery, and Psychiatry, 37*, 489–501.

Meadows, J. C. (1974b). Disturbed perception of colours associated with localized cerebral lesions. *Brain, 97*, 615–632.

Meckler, R. J., Mack, J. L., & Bennett, R. (1979). Sign language aphasia in a non-deaf-mute. *Neurology, 29*, 1037–1040.

Metz-Lutz, M.-N. & Dahl, E. (1984). Analysis of word comprehension in a case of pure word-deafness. *Brain and Language, 23*, 13–25.

Meudell, P. R. & Mayes, A. R. (1982). Normal and abnormal forgetting: Some comments on the human amnesic syndrome. In A. W. Ellis (Ed.), *Normality and pathology in cognitive functions*. London: Academic Press.

Meudell, P. R., Mayes, A. & Neary, D. (1980a). Orienting task effects on the recognition of humorous pictures in amnesic and normal subjects. *Journal of Clinical Neuropsychology, 2*, 75–88.

Meudell, P. R., Northen, B., Snowden, J. S., & Neary, D. (1980b). Long-term memory for famous voices in amnesic and normal subjects. *Neuropsychologia, 18*, 133–139.

Meyer, D. E. & Schvaneveldt, R. W. (1971). Facilitation in recognizing pairs of words: Evidence of a dependence between retrieval operations. *Journal of Experimental Psychology, 90*, 227–234.

Miceli, G., Mazzucchi, A., Menn, L., & Goodglass, H. (1983). Contrasting cases of Italian agrammatic aphasia without comprehension disorder. *Brain and Language, 19*, 65–97.

Miceli, G., Silveri, C., & Caramazza, A. (1985). Cognitive analysis of a case of pure dysgraphia. *Brain and Language, 25,* 187–212.

Miceli, G., Silveri, C., & Caramazza, A. (1987). The role of the phoneme-to-grapheme conversion system and of the graphemic output buffer in writing: Evidence from an Italian case of pure dysgraphia. In M. Coltheart, G. Sartori, & R. Job (Eds), *The cognitive neuropsychology of language.* London: Lawrence Erlbaum Associates Ltd.

Michel, F. (1979). Preservation du language ecrit malgré un deficit majeur du language oral. *Le Lyon Medicale, 241,* 141–149.

Michel, F. & Andreewsky, E. (1983). Deep dysphasia: An analogue of deep dyslexia in the auditory modality. *Brain and Language, 18,* 212–223.

Milberg, W. & Blumstein, S. E. (1981). Lexical decision and aphasia: Evidence for semantic processing. *Brain and Language, 14,* 371–385.

Miller, D. & Ellis, A. W. (1987). Speech and writing errors in "neologistic jargon-aphasia": A lexical activation hypothesis. In M. Coltheart, G. Sartori, & R. Job (Eds), *The cognitive neuropsychology of language.* London: Lawrence Erlbaum Associates Ltd.

Miller, G. A. (1956). The magic number seven, plus or minus two: Some limits on our capacity for processing information. *Psychological Review, 63,* 81–93.

Miller, G. A. & Taylor, J. (1948). Perception of repeated bursts of noise. *Journal of the Acoustical Society of America, 20,* 171–182.

Miller, J. L. (1987). Rate-dependent processing in speech perception. In A. W. Ellis (Ed.), *Progress in the psychology of language,* Vol. 3. London: Lawrence Erlbaum Associates Ltd.

Miller, J. L., & Marlin, N. A. (1979). Amnesia following electroconvulsive shock. In J. F. Kihlstrom & F. J. Evans (Eds), *Functional disorders of memory.* Hillsdale, N. J.: Lawrence Erlbaum Associates Inc.

Mills, C. K. (1912). The cerebral mechanism of emotional expression. *Transactions of the College of Physicians of Philadelphia, 34,* 147–185.

Milner, B. (1966). Amnesia following operation on the temporal lobes. In C. W. M. Whitty & O. L. Zangwill (Eds), *Amnesia.* London: Butterworths.

Milner, B., Corkin, S., & Teuber, H.-L. (1968). Further analysis of the hippocampal amnesia syndrome: 14 year follow-up study of H.M. *Neuropsychologia, 6,* 215–234.

Mohr, J. P., Leicester, J., Stoddard, L. T., & Sidman, M. (1971). Right hemianopia with memory and colour deficits in circumscribed left posterior cerebral artery territory infarction. *Neurology, 21,* 1104–1113.

Moll, J. M. (1915). The "Amnestic" or "Korsakow's" syndrome with alcoholic aetiology: an analysis of thirty cases. *Journal of Mental Science, 61,* 424–443.

Mollon, J. D. (1982). Colour vision and colour blindness. In H. D. Barlow & J. D. Mollon (Eds), *The senses.* Cambridge: Cambridge University Press.

Mollon, J. D., Newcombe, F., Polden, P. G., & Ratcliff, G. (1980). On the presence of three cone mechanisms in a case of total achromatopsia. In G. Verriest (Ed.), *Colour vision deficiences, V.* Bristol: Hilger.

Monoi, H., Fukusako, Y., Itoh, M., & Sasanuma, S. (1983). Speech sound errors in patients with conduction and Broca's aphasia. *Brain and Language, 20,* 175–194.

Monrad-Krohn, G. H. (1947). Dysprosody or altered "melody of language". *Brain, 70,* 405–415.

Monsell, S. (1985). Repetition and the lexicon. In A. W. Ellis (Ed.), *Progress in the psychology of language,* Vol. 2. London: Lawrence Erlbaum Associates Ltd.

Morrow, L., Ratcliff, G., & Johnston, C. S. (1985). Externalising spatial knowledge in patients with right hemisphere lesions. *Cognitive Neuropsychology, 2,* 265–273.

Morton, J. (1964). A model for continuous language behaviour. *Language and Speech, 7,* 40–70.

Morton, J. (1979).   Facilitation in word recognition: Experiments causing change in the logogen model. In P. A. Kolers, M. Wrolstad, & H. Bouma (Eds), *Processing of visible language,* Vol. 1. New York: Plenum.

Morton, J. (1980a).   The logogen model and orthographic structure. In U. Frith (Ed.), *Cognitive processes in spelling.* London: Academic Press.

Morton, J. (1980h)   An analogue of deep dyslexia in the auditory modality. In M. Coltheart, K. E. Patterson, & J. C. Marshall (Eds), *Deep dyslexia.* London: Routledge and Kegan Paul.

Morton, J. (1981).   The status of information processing models of language. *Philosophical Transactions of the Royal Society* (London), *B295,* 387–396. (Also published in H. C. Longuet-Higgins, J. Lyons, & D. E. Broadbent (Eds), *The psychological mechanisms of language.* London: The Royal Society and the British Academy, 1981.)

Morton, J. (1984).   Brain-based and non-brain-based models of language. In D. Caplan, A. R. Lecours, & A. Smith (Eds), *Biological perspectives on language.* Cambridge, Mass.: MIT Press.

Morton, J. (1985a).   Naming. In S. Newman & R. Epstein (Eds), *Current perspectives in dysphasia.* Edinburgh: Churchill Livingstone.

Morton, J. (1985b).   The problem with amnesia: The problem with human memory. *Cognitive Neuropsychology, 2,* 281–290.

Morton, J. & Patterson, K. E. (1980).   A new attempt at an interpretation, or, an attempt at a new interpretation. In M. Coltheart, K. E. Patterson, & J. C. Marshall (Eds), *Deep dyslexia.* London: Routledge and Kegan Paul.

Moscovitch, M. (1982).   Multiple dissociations of function in amnesia. In I. S. Cermak (Ed.), *Human memory and amnesia.* Hillsdale, N. J.: Lawrence Erlbaum Associates Inc.

Mozer, M. C. (1983).   Letter migration in word perception. *Journal of Experimental Psychology: Human Perception and Performance, 9,* 531–546.

Müller, G. E. & Pilzecker, A. (1900)   Experimentelle Beiträge zur Lehre vom Gedächtnis. *Zeitschrift für Psychologie, Ergänzungsband, 1,* 1–300.

Myers, P. S. & Linebaugh, C. W. (1981).   Comprehension of idiomatic expressions by right-hemisphere-damaged adults. In R. H. Brookshire (Ed.), *Clinical aphasiology: Conference proceedings.* Minneapolis: BRK Publishers.

Myerson, R. & Goodglass, H. (1972).   Transformational grammars of three agrammatic patients. *Language and Speech, 15,* 40–50.

Nebes, R. D. (1975).   The nature of internal speech in a patient with aphemia. *Brain and Language, 2,* 489–497.

Nebes, R. D., Martin, D. C., & Horn, L. C. (1984).   Sparing of semantic memory in Alzheimer's disease. *Journal of Abnormal Psychology, 93,* 321–330.

Neisser, U. (1954).   An experimental distinction between perceptual process and verbal response. *Journal of Experimental Psychology, 47,* 399–402.

Neisser, U. (1982).   *Memory observed.* San Fransisco: W. H. Freeman.

Nespoulous, J.-L., Perron, P., & Lecours, A. R. (1986).   *The biological foundations of gestures: Motor and semiotic aspects.* Hillsdale, N. J.: Lawrence Erlbaum Associates Inc.

Newcombe, F. (1969).   *Missile wounds of the brain: A study of psychological deficits.* Oxford: Oxford University Press.

Newcombe, F. (1974).   Selective deficits after focal cerebral injury. In S. J. Dimond & J. G. Beaumont (Eds), *Hemisphere function in the human brain.* London: Elek.

Newcombe, F. (1979).   The processing of visual information in prosopagnosia and acquired dyslexia: Functional versus physiological interpretation. In D. J. Oborne, M. M. Gruneberg, & J. R. Eiser (Eds), *Research in psychology and medicine,* Vol. 1. London: Academic Press.

Newcombe, F. & Marshall, J. C. (1975).   Traumatic dyslexia: Localization and linguistics. In K. J. Zulch, O. Creutzfeldt, & G. C. Galbraith (Eds), *Cerebral localization*. Berlin: Springer-Verlag.

Newcombe, F. & Marshall, J. C. (1980a).   Response monitoring and response blocking in deep dyslexia. In M. Coltheart, K. E. Patterson, & J. C. Marshall (Eds), *Deep dyslexia*. London: Routledge and Kegan Paul.

Newcombe, F. & Marshall, J. C. (1980b).   Transcoding and lexical stabilization in deep dyslexia. In M. Coltheart, K. E. Patterson, & J. C. Marshall (Eds), *Deep dyslexia*. London: Routledge and Kegan Paul.

Newcombe, F. & Marshall, J. C. (1981).   On psycholinguistic classifications of the acquired dyslexias. *Bulletin of the Orton Society, 31,* 29–46.

Newcombe, F. & Marshall, J. C. (1984).   Varieties of acquired dyslexia: A linguistic approach. *Seminars in Neurology, 4,* 181–195.

Newcombe, F. & Ratcliff, G. (1974).   Agnosia: A disorder of object recognition. In F. Michel & B. Schott (Eds), *Les syndromes de disconnexion calleuse chez l'homme*. Lyon: Colloque International de Lyon.

Newcombe, F. & Russell, W. R. (1969).   Dissociated visual perceptual and spatial deficits in focal lesions of the right hemisphere. *Journal of Neurology, Neurosurgery and Psychiatry, 32,* 73–81.

Newcombe, F., Ratcliff, G., & Damasio, H. (1987).   Dissociable visual and spatial impairments following right posterior cerebral lesions: Clinical, neuropsychological and anatomical evidence. *Neuropsychologia, 25,* 149–161.

Newman, S. & Epstein, R. (Eds) (1985).   *Current perspectives in dysphasia*. Edinburgh: Churchill Livingstone.

Nolan, K. A. & Caramazza, A. (1982).   Modality-independent impairments in word processing in a deep dyslexic patient. *Brain and Language, 16,* 237–264.

Nooteboom, S. G. (1967).   Some regularities in phonemic speech errors. Institut voor Perceptie Onderzoek, Eindhoven, *Annual Progress Report*, No. 2, 65–70.

Ogden, J. A. (1985).   Autotopagnosia: Occurrence in a patient without nominal aphasia and with an intact ability to point to parts of animals and objects. *Brain, 108,* 1009–1022.

Ogle, W. (1867).   Aphasia and agraphia. *St. George's Hospital Reports, 2,* 83–122.

Okada, S., Hanada, M., Hattori, H., & Shoyama, T. (1963).   A case of pure word-deafness. *Studia Phonologica, 3,* 58–65.

Oldfield, R. C. & Wingfield, A. (1965).   Response latencies in naming objects. *Quarterly Journal of Experimental Psychology, 17,* 273–281.

Oppenheimer, D. R. & Newcombe, F. (1978).   Clinical and anatomical findings in a case of auditory agnosia. *Archives of Neurology, 35,* 712–719.

Oscar-Berman, N., Zurif, E. B., & Blumstein, S. (1975).   Effects of unilateral brain damage on the processing of speech sounds. *Brain and Language, 2,* 345–355.

Oxbury, J. M., Oxbury, S. M., & Humphrey, N. K. (1969).   Varieties of colour anomia. *Brain, 92,* 847–860.

Paillard, J., Michel, F., & Stelmach, G. (1983).   Localization without content: A tactile analogue of "blind sight". *Archives of Neurology, 40,* 548–551.

Pallis, C. A. (1955).   Impaired identification of faces and places with agnosia for colours. *Journal of Neurology, Neurosurgery and Psychiatry, 18,* 218–224.

Parisi, D. (1987).   Grammatical disturbances of speech production. In M. Coltheart, G. Sartori, & R. Job (Eds), *The cognitive neuropsychology of language*. London: Lawrence Erlbaum Associates Ltd.

Parker, E. & Noble, E. (1977).   Alcohol consumption and cognitive functioning in social drinkers. *Journal of Studies on Alcohol, 38,* 1224–1232.

Parkin, A. J. (1982).   Residual learning capability in organic amnesia. *Cortex, 18,* 417–440.

Parkin, A. J. (1987). *Memory and amnesia.* Oxford: Basil Blackwell.

Patterson, J. H. & Green, D. M. (1970). Discrimination of transient signals having identical energy spectra. *Journal of the Acoustical Society of America, 20,* 171–182.

Patterson, M. B. & Mack, J. L. (1985). Neuropsychological analysis of a case of reduplicative paramnesia. *Journal of Clinical and Experimental Neuropsychology, 7,* 111–121.

Patterson, K. E. (1978). Phonemic dyslexia: Errors of meaning and the meaning of errors. *Quarterly Journal of Experimental Psychology, 30,* 587–601.

Patterson, K. E. (1979). What's right with "deep" dyslexics. *Brain and Language, 8,* 111–129.

Patterson, K. E. (1980). Derivational errors. In M. Coltheart, K. E. Patterson, & J. C. Marshall (Eds), *Deep dyslexia.* London: Routledge and Kegan Paul.

Patterson, K. E. (1981). Neuropsychological approaches to the study of reading. *British Journal of Psychology, 72,* 151–174.

Patterson, K. E. (1982). The relation between reading and phonological coding: Further neuropsychological observations. In A. W. Ellis (Ed.), *Normality and pathology in cognitive functions.* London: Academic Press.

Patterson, K. E. (1986). Lexical but non-semantic spelling? *Cognitive Neuropsychology, 3,* 341–367.

Patterson, K. E. (1988). Acquired disorders of spelling. In G. Denes, C. Semenza, P. Bisiacchi, & E. Andreewsky (Eds), *Perspectives in cognitive neuropsychology.* London: Lawrence Erlbaum Associates Ltd.

Patterson, K. E. & Besner, D. (1984). Is the right hemisphere literate? *Cognitive Neuropsychology, 1,* 315–341.

Patterson, K. E. & Coltheart, V. (1987). Phonological processes in reading: A tutorial review. In M. Coltheart (Ed.), *Attention and Performance, XII: The psychology of reading.* London: Lawrence Erlbaum Associates Ltd.

Patterson, K. & Kay, J. (1982). Letter-by-letter reading: Psychological descriptions of a neurological syndrome. *Quarterly Journal of Experimental Psychology, 34A,* 411–441.

Patterson, K. E. & Morton, J. (1985). From orthography to phonology: An attempt at an old interpretation. In K. E. Patterson, J. C. Marshall, & M. Coltheart (Eds), *Surface dyslexia: Neuropsychological and cognitive studies of phonological reading.* London: Lawrence Erlbaum Associates Ltd.

Patterson, K. E., Marshall, J. C., & Coltheart, M. (1985). *Surface dyslexia: Neuropsychological and cognitive studies of phonological reading.* London: Lawrence Erlbaum Associates Ltd.

Perecman, E. & Brown, J. W. (1981). Semantic jargon: A case report. In J. W. Brown (Ed.) *Jargonaphasia.* New York: Academic Press.

Perenin, M. T. (1978). Visual function within the hemianopic field following early cerebral hemidecortication in man, II: Pattern discrimination. *Neuropsychologia, 16,* 696–708.

Perenin, M. T. & Jeannerod, M. (1978). Visual function within the hemianopic field following early hemidecortication in man, I: Spatial localization. *Neuropsychologia, 16,* 1–13.

Peterson, L. N. & Kirshner, H. S. (1981). Gestural impairment and gestural ability in aphasia: A review. *Brain and Language, 14,* 333–348.

Peuser, G. (1978). *Aphasie.* Munchen: Wilhelm Fink Verlag.

Pickett, L. (1974). An assessment of gestural and pantomime deficit in aphasic patients. *Acta Symbolica, 5,* 69–86.

Poeck, K. (1983). What do we mean by "aphasic syndromes"? A neurologist's view. *Brain and Language, 20,* 79–89.

Poizner, H., Bellugi, U., & Iragui, V. (1984). Apraxia and aphasia for a visual-gestural language. *American Journal of Physiology: Regulative, Integrative and Comparative Physiology, 246,* R868–R883.

Pollack, I. & Pickett, J. M. (1964). The intelligibility of excerpts from fluent speech: Auditory versus structural context. *Language and Speech, 6,* 151–165.

Pöppel, E., Held, R., & Frost, D. (1973). Residual visual function after brain wounds involving the central visual pathways in man. *Nature, 243,* 295–296.

Posner, M. I. (1980). Orienting of attention. *Quarterly Journal of Experimental Psychology, 32,* 3–25.

Posner, M. I., Cohen, Y., & Rafal, R. D. (1982). Neural systems control of spatial orienting. *Philosophical Transactions of the Royal Society* (London), *B298,* 187–198.

Posner, M. I., Walker, J. A., Friedrich, F. J., & Rafal, R. D. (1984). Effects of parietal injury on covert orienting of visual attention. *Journal of Neuroscience, 4,* 1863–1874.

Posner, M. I., Rafal, R. D., Choate, L. S., & Vaughan, J. (1985). Inhibition of return: Neural basis and function. *Cognitive Neuropsychology, 2,* 211–228.

Potter, J. M. (1980). What was the matter with Dr. Spooner? In V. A. Fromkin (Ed.), *Errors in linguistic performance: Slips of the tongue, ear, pen and hand.* New York: Academic Press.

Potter, M. C. & Faulconer, B. A. (1975). Time to understand pictures and words. *Nature* (London), *253,* 437–438.

Potts, C. S. (1901). A case of transient motor aphasia, complete anomia, nearly complete agraphia and word blindness occurring in a left-handed man; with special reference to the existence of a naming center. *Journal of the American Medical Association, 36,* 1239–1241.

Ratcliff, G. (1979). Spatial thought, mental rotation and the right cerebral hemisphere. *Neuropsychologia, 17,* 49–54.

Ratcliff, G. (1982). Disturbances of spatial orientation associated with cerebral lesions. In M. Potegal (Ed.), *Spatial abilities: Development and physiological foundations.* New York: Academic Press.

Ratcliff, G. & Cowey, A. (1979). Disturbances of visual perception following cerebral lesions. In D. J. Oborne, M. M. Gruneberg, & J. R. Eiser (Eds), *Research in psychology and medicine.* New York: Academic Press.

Ratcliff, G. & Davies-Jones, G. A. B. (1972). Defective visual localization in focal brain wounds. *Brain, 95,* 49–60.

Ratcliff, G. & Newcombe, F. (1973). Spatial orientation in man: Effects of left, right, and bilateral posterior cerebral lesions. *Journal of Neurology, Neurosurgery, and Psychiatry, 36,* 448–454.

Ratcliff, G. & Newcombe, F. (1982). Object recognition: Some deductions from the clinical evidence. In A. W. Ellis (Ed.), *Normality and pathology in cognitive functions.* London: Academic Press.

Reason, J. T. & Lucas, D. (1984). Using cognitive diaries to investigate naturally occurring memory blocks. In J. Harris & P. E. Morris (Eds), *Everyday memory, actions and absentmindedness.* London: Academic Press.

Reider, N. (1941). A note on the influence of early training on the development of aphasic manifestations. *Bulletin of the Menninger Clinic, 5,* 1–4.

Repp, B. H. (1982). Phonetic trading relations and context affects: New experimental evidence for a speech mode of perception. *Psychological Bulletin, 92,* 81–110.

Riddoch, G. (1917). Dissociation of visual perceptions due to occipital injuries, with especial reference to appreciation of movement. *Brain, 40,* 15–57.

Riddoch, G. (1935). Visual disorientation in homonymous half-fields. *Brain, 58,* 376–382.

Riddoch, M. J. & Humphreys, G. W. (1983). The effect of cueing on unilateral neglect. *Neuropsychologia, 21,* 589–599.

Riddoch, M. J. & Humphreys, G. W. (1987a). A case of integrative visual agnosia. *Brain*, *110*, 1431–1462

Riddoch, M. J. & Humphreys, G. W. (1987b). Visual object processing in optic aphasia: A case of semantic access agnosia. *Cognitive Neuropsychology, 4*, 131–185.

Rinnert, C. & Whitaker, H. A. (1973). Semantic confusions by aphasic patients. *Cortex, 9*, 56–81.

Rochford, G. & Williams, M. (1965). Studies in the development and breakdown of the use of names. I. The relationship between nominal dysphasia and the acquisition of vocabulary in childhood. *Journal of Neurology, Neurosurgery and Psychiatry, 25*, 222–227.

Roeltgen, D. P., Sevush, S., & Heilman, K. M. (1983). Phonological agraphia: Writing by the lexical-semantic route. *Neurology, 33*, 755–765.

Rollins, H. A. & Hendricks, R. (1980). Processing of words presented simultaneously to eye and ear. *Journal of Experimental Psychology: Human Perception and Performance, 6*, 99–109.

Roman-Campos, G., Poser, C. M., & Wood, F. B. (1980). Persistent retrograde memory deficit after transient global amnesia. *Cortex, 16*, 509–518.

Rosati, G. & Bastiani, P. de (1979). Pure agraphia: A discrete form of aphasia. *Journal of Neurology, Neurosurgery and Psychiatry, 42*, 266–269.

Rosch, E. (1978). Principles of categorization. In E. Rosch & B. B. Lloyd (Eds), *Cognition and categorization*. Hillsdale, N. J.: Lawrence Erlbaum Associates Inc.

Rosch, E., Mervis, C. B., Gray, W. D., Johnson, D. M., & Boyes-Braem, P. (1976). Basic objects in natural categories. *Cognitive Psychology, 8*, 382–439.

Rose, F. C. & Symonds, C. P. (1960). Persistent memory defect following encephalitis. *Brain, 83*, 195–212.

Ross, E. D. (1981). The aprosodias. *Archives of Neurology, 38*, 561–569.

Ross, E. D., Harney, J. H., de Lacoste-Utamsing, C., & Purdy, P. D. (1981). How the brain integrates affective and propositional language into a unified behavioral function. *Archives of Neurology, 38*, 745–748.

Ross, E. G. & Mesulam, M.-M. (1979). Dominant language functions of the right hemisphere? *Archives of Neurology, 36*, 144–148.

Roy, E. A. (1982). Action and performance. In A. W. Ellis (Ed.), *Normality and pathology in cognitive functions*. London: Academic Press.

Rozin, P. (1976). The psychobiological approach to human memory. In M. R. Rosensweig & E. L. Bennett (Eds), *Neural mechanisms of learning and memory*. Cambridge, Mass.: MIT Press.

Rubens, A. B. (1979). Agnosia. In K. M. Heilman & E. Valenstein (Eds), *Clinical neuropsychology*. New York: Oxford University Press.

Rubens, A. B. & Benson, D. F. (1971). Associative visual agnosia. *Archives of Neurology, 24*, 305–316.

Rumelhart, D. E. & McClelland, J. L. (1981). Interactive processing through spreading activation. In A. M. Lesgold & C. A. Perfetti (Eds), *Interactive processes in reading*. Hillsdale, N. J.: Lawrence Erlbaum Associates Inc.

Russell, W. R. (1935). The after-effects of head injury. *Edinburgh Medical Journal, 41*, 129–144.

Russell, W. R. & Nathan, P. W. (1946). Traumatic amnesia. *Brain, 69*, 280–300.

Ryan, C., Butters, N., & Montgomery, L. (1980). Memory deficits in chronic alcoholics: Continuities between the intact alcoholic and the alcoholic Korsakoff patient. In H. Begleiter (Ed.), *Advances in experimental medicine and biology: Biological effects of alcohol*, Vol. 126. New York: Plenum Press.

Ryle, G. (1949). *The concept of mind*. London: Hutchinson.

Saffran, E. M. (1982). Neuropsychological approaches to the study of language. *British Journal of Psychology, 73*, 317–337.

Saffran, E. M., Marin, O. S. M., & Yeni-Komshian, G. H. (1976a). An analysis of speech perception in word deafness. *Brain and Language, 3*, 209–228.

Saffran, E. M., Schwartz, M. F., & Marin, O. S. M. (1976b). Semantic mechanisms in paralexia. *Brain and Language, 3*, 255 265.

Saffran, E. M., Bogyo, L. C., Schwartz, M. F., & Marin, O. S. M. (1980a). Does deep dyslexia reflect right-hemisphere reading? In M. Coltheart, K. E. Patterson, & J. C. Marshall (Eds), *Deep dyslexia*. London: Routledge and Kegan Paul.

Saffran, E. M., Schwartz, M. F., & Marin, O. S. M. (1980b). Evidence from aphasia: Isolating the components of a production model. In B. Butterworth (Ed.), *Language production*, Vol. 1. London: Academic Press.

Saffran, E. M., Schwartz, M. F., & Marin, O. S. M. (1980c). The word order problem in agrammatism, II. Production. *Brain and Language, 10*, 249–262.

Sanders, H. I. & Warrington, E. K. (1971). Memory for remote events in amnesic patients. *Brain, 94*, 661–668.

Schacter, D. L. (1983). Amnesia observed: Remembering and forgetting in a natural environment. *Journal of Abnormal Psychology, 92*, 236–242.

Schacter, D. L. (1985). Multiple forms of memory in humans and animals. In N. M. Weinberger, J. L. McCaugh, & G. Lynch (Eds), *Memory systems of the brain*. New York: The Guilford Press.

Schacter, D. L. (1987). Implicit memory: History and current status. *Journal of Experimental Psychology: Learning, Memory and Cognition, 13*, 501–518.

Schacter, D. L. & Tulving, E. (1982). Amnesia and memory research. In L. S. Cermak (Ed.), *Human memory and amnesia*. Hillsdale, N. J: Lawrence Erlbaum Associates Inc.

Schacter, D. L., McAndrews, M. P., & Moscovitch, M. (1988). Access to consciousness: Dissociations between implicit and explicit knowledge in neuropsychological syndromes. In L. Weiskrantz (Ed.), *Thought without language*. Oxford: Oxford University Press.

Schneider, K. (1912). Über einige klinisch-pathologischen Untersuchungsmethoden und ihre Ergebnisse. Zugleich ein Beitrag zur Psychopathologie der Korsakowschen Psychose. *Zeitschrift für Neurologie und Psychiatrie, 8*, 553–616.

Schneider, K. (1928). Die Störungen des Gedächtnisses. In O. Bumke (Ed.), *Handbuch der Geisteskrankheiten*, Vol. 1. Berlin: Springer.

Schouten, M. E. H. (1980). The case against a speech mode of perception. *Acta Psychologica, 44*, 71–98.

Schuell, H. (1950). Paraphasia and paralexia. *Journal of Speech and Hearing Disorders, 15*, 291–306.

Schwartz, M. F. & Schwartz, B. (1984). In defence of organology. *Cognitive Neuropsychology, 1*, 25–42.

Schwartz, M. F., Marin, O. S. M., & Saffran, E. M. (1979). Dissociations of language function in dementia: A case study. *Brain and Language, 7*, 277–306.

Schwartz, M. F., Saffran, E. M., & Marin, O. S. M. (1980a). Fractionating the reading process in dementia: Evidence for word-specific print-to-sound associations. In M. Coltheart, K. E. Patterson, & J. C. Marshall (Eds), *Deep dyslexia*. London: Routledge and Kegan Paul.

Schwartz, M. F., Saffran, E. M., & Marin, O. S. M. (1980b). The word order problem in agrammatism, I. Comprehension. *Brain and Language, 10*, 249–262.

Schwartz, M. F., Linebarger, M. C., & Saffran, E. M. (1985). The status of the syntactic deficit theory of agrammatism. In M.-L. Kean (Ed.), *Agrammatism*. Orlando: Academic Press.

Scoville, W. B. & Milner, B. (1957). Loss of recent memory after bilateral hippocampal lesions. *Journal of Neurology, Neurosurgery and Psychiatry, 20*, 11–21.

Searleman, A. (1983). Language capabilities of the right hemisphere. In A. W. Young (Ed.), *Functions of the right cerebral hemisphere*. London: Academic Press.

Sejnowski, T. J. & Rosenberg, C. R. (1986). Parallel networks that learn to pronounce English text. *Complex Systems, 1*, 145–168.

Seltzer, B. & Benson, D. F. (1974). The temporal pattern of retrograde amnesia in Korsakoff's disease. *Neurology, 24*, 527–530.

Semmes, J., Weinstein, S., Ghent, L., & Teuber, H.-L. (1963). Correlates of impaired orientation in personal and extrapersonal space. *Brain, 86*, 747–772.

Sergent, J. (1984). Processing of visually presented vowels in cerebral hemispheres. *Brain and Language, 21*, 136–146.

Seymour, P. H. K. (1979). *Human visual cognition*. West Drayton: Collier MacMillan.

Shallice, T. (1979a). Case-study approach in neuropsychological research. *Journal of Clinical Neuropsychology, 1*, 183–211.

Shallice, T. (1979b). Neuropsychological research and the fractionation of memory systems. In L. G. Nilsson (Ed.), *Perspectives in memory research*. Hillsdale, N. J.: Lawrence Erlbaum Associates Inc.

Shallice, T. (1981a). Neurological impairment of cognitive processes. *British Medical Bulletin, 37*, 187–192.

Shallice, T. (1981b). Phonological agraphia and the lexical route in writing. *Brain, 104*, 413–429.

Shallice, T. (1982). Specific impairments of planning. *Philosophical Transactions of the Royal Society* (London), *B298*, 199–209. (Reprinted in D. E. Broadbent & L. Weiskrantz (Eds), *The neuropsychology of cognitive function*. London: The Royal Society.)

Shallice, T. (1984). More functionally isolable subsystems but fewer "modules"? *Cognition, 17*, 243–252.

Shallice, T. & Jackson, M. (1988). Lissauer on agnosia. *Cognitive Neuropsychology, 5*, 153–192.

Shallice, T. & McCarthy, R. (1985). Phonological reading: From patterns of impairment to possible procedures. In K. E. Patterson, J. C. Marshall, & M. Coltheart (Eds), *Surface dyslexia: Neuropsychological and cognitive studies of phonological reading*. London: Lawrence Erlbaum Associates Ltd.

Shallice, T. & McGill, J. (1978). The origins of mixed errors. In J. Requin (Ed.), *Attention and Performance, XII*. Hillsdale, N. J.: Lawrence Erlbaum Associates Inc.

Shallice, T. & Saffran, E. (1986). Lexical processing in the absence of explicit word identification: Evidence from a letter-by-letter reader. *Cognitive Neuropsychology, 3*, 429–458.

Shallice, T. & Warrington, E. K. (1970). Independent functioning of verbal memory stores: A neuropsychological study. *Quarterly Journal of Experimental Psychology, 22*, 261–273.

Shallice, T. & Warrington, E. K. (1974). The dissociation between short-term retention of meaningful sounds and verbal material. *Neuropsychologia, 12*, 553–555.

Shallice, T. & Warrington, E. K. (1977). The possible role of selective attention in acquired dyslexia. *Neuropsychologia, 15*, 31–41.

Shallice, T. & Warrington, E. K. (1980). Single and multiple component central dyslexic syndromes. In M. Coltheart, K. E., Patterson, & J. C. Marshall (Eds), *Deep dyslexia*. London: Routledge and Kegan Paul.

Shallice, T., Warrington, E. K., & McCarthy, R. (1983). Reading without semantics. *Quarterly Journal of Experimental Psychology, 35A*, 111–138.

Shallice, T., McLeod, P., & Lewis, K. (1985). Isolating cognitive modules with the dual-task paradigm: Are speech perception and production separate processes? *Quarterly Journal of Experimental Psychology, 37A*, 507–532.

Shankweiler, D. & Harris, K. S. (1966).   An experimental approach to the problem of articulation in aphasia. *Cortex, 2,* 277–292.

Shankweiler, D. & Studdert-Kennedy, M. (1967).   Identification of consonants and vowels presented to left and right ears. *Quarterly Journal of Experimental Psychology, 19,* 59–63.

Shimamura, A. P. (1986).   Priming effects in amnesia: Evidence for a dissociable memory function. *Quarterly Journal of Experimental Psychology, 38A,* 619–644.

Shoumaker, R. D., Ajax, E. J., & Schenkenberg, T. (1977).   Pure word deafness (auditory verbal agnosia). *Diseases of the Nervous System, 38,* 293–299.

Shraberg, D. & Weitzel, W. D. (1979).   Prosopagnosia and the Capgras syndrome. *Journal of Clinical Psychiatry, 40,* 313–316.

Shuttleworth, E. C. & Wise, G. R. (1973).   Transient global amnesia due to arterial embolism. *Archives of Neurology, 29,* 340–342.

Smith, A. (1966).   Speech and other functions after left (dominant) hemispherectomy. *Journal of Neurology, Neurosurgery and Psychiatry, 29,* 467–471.

Smith, S. & Holmes, G. (1916).   A case of bilateral motor apraxia with disturbance of visual orientation. *British Medical Journal, 1,* 437–441.

Smyth, M. M. & Silvers, G. (1987).   Function of vision in the control of handwriting. *Acta Psychologica, 65,* 47–64.

Smyth, M. M., Morris, P. E., Levy, P., & Ellis, A. W. (1987).   *Cognition in action.* London: Lawrence Erlbaum Associates Ltd.

Snodgrass, J. G. & Vanderwart, M. (1980).   A standardised set of 260 pictures: Norms for name agreement, image agreement, familiarity and visual complexity. *Journal of Experimental Psychology: Human Perception and Performance, 6,* 174–215.

Soderpalm, E. (1979).   *Speech errors in normal and pathological speech.* (Travaux de l'Institut de Linguistique de Lund, XIV.) Malmo: CWK Gleerup.

Squire, L. R. (1981).   Two forms of human amnesia: An analysis of forgetting. *Journal of Neuroscience, 1,* 635–640.

Squire, L. R. (1982).   The neuropsychology of human memory. *Annual Review of Neuroscience, 5,* 241–273.

Squire, L. R. (1987).   *Memory and brain.* New York: Oxford University Press.

Squire, L. R. & Cohen, N. J. (1984).   Human memory and amnesia. In G. Lynch, J. L. McGaugh, & N. M. Weinberger (Eds), *Neurobiology of learning and memory.* New York: The Guilford Press.

Squire, L. R. & Slater, P. C. (1978).   Anterograde and retrograde memory impairment in chronic amnesia. *Neuropsychologia, 16,* 313–322.

Squire, L. R., Wetzel, C. D., & Slater, P. C. (1978).   Anterograde amnesia following ECT: An analysis of the beneficial effects of partial information. *Neuropsychologia, 16,* 339–348.

Squire, L. R., Cohen, N. J., & Nadel, L. (1984).   The medial temporal region and memory consolidation: A new hypothesis. In H. Weingartner & E. S. Parker (Eds), *Memory consolidation.* Hillsdale, N. J.: Lawrence Erlbaum Associates Inc.

Starr, A. & Phillips, L. (1970).   Verbal and motor memory in the amnesic syndrome. *Neuropsychologia, 8,* 75–88.

Stemberger, J. P. (1984).   Structural errors in normal and agrammatic speech. *Cognitive Neuropsychology, 1,* 281–314.

Stemberger, J. P. (1985).   An interactive activation model of language production. In A. W. Ellis (Ed.), *Progress in the psychology of language,* Vol. 1. London: Lawrence Erlbaum Associates Ltd.

Stern, L. D. (1981).   A review of theories of human amnesia. *Memory and Cognition, 9,* 247–262.

Studdert-Kennedy, M. (1983).   On learning to speak. *Human Neurobiology, 2,* 191–195.

Sumby, W. H. & Pollack, I. (1954).   Visual contribution to speech intelligibility in noise. *Journal of the Acoustical Society of America, 26,* 212–215.

Summerfield, Q. (1979).   Use of visual information for phonetic perception. *Phonetica, 36,* 314–331.

Swinney, D. A. & Cutler, A. (1979).   The access and processing of idiomatic expressions. *Journal of Verbal Learning and Verbal Behavior, 18,* 523–534.

Symonds, C. (1953).   Aphasia. *Journal of Neurology, Neurosurgery and Psychiatry, 16,* 1–6.

Syz, H. (1937).   Recovery from loss of mnemonic retention after head trauma. *Journal of General Psychology, 17,* 355–387.

Taft, M. (1985).   The decoding of words in lexical access: A review of the morphographic approach. In D. Besner, T. G. Waller, & G. E. MacKinnon (Eds), *Reading research: Advances in theory and practice,* Vol. 5. New York: Academic Press.

Tallal, P. & Newcombe, F. (1978).   Impairment of auditory perception and language comprehension in dysphasia. *Brain and Language, 5,* 13–24.

Talland, G. (1965).   *Deranged memory.* New York: Academic Press.

Taylor, A. & Warrington, E. K. (1971).   Visual agnosia: A single case report. *Cortex, 7,* 152–161.

Teuber, H.-L. (1955).   Physiological psychology. *Annual Review of Psychology, 6,* 267–296.

Teuber, H.-L., Milner, B., & Vaughan, H. G. (1968).   Persistent anterograde amnesia after stab wound of the basal brain. *Neuropsychologia, 6,* 267–282.

Tiberghien, G. & Clerc, I. (1986).   The cognitive locus of prosopagnosia. In R. Bruyer (Ed.), *The neuropsychology of face perception and facial expression.* Hillsdale, N. J.: Lawrence Erlbaum Associates Inc.

Tissot, R., Mounin, G., & Lhermitte, F. (1973).   *L'agrammatisme.* Paris: Dessart.

Tranel, D. & Damasio, A. R. (1985).   Knowledge without awareness: An autonomic index of facial recognition by prosopagnosics. *Science, 228,* 1453–1454.

Tucker, D. M., Watson, R. T., & Heilman, K. M. (1977).   Discrimination and evocation of affectively intoned speech in patients with right parietal disease. *Neurology, 27,* 947–950.

Tulving, E. (1972).   Episodic and semantic memory. In E. Tulving & W. Donaldson (Eds), *Organization of memory.* New York: Academic Press.

Tulving, E. (1983).   *Elements of episodic memory.* Oxford: Oxford University Press.

Tulving, E. (1984).   Multiple learning and memory systems. In K. M. J. Lagerspetz & P. Niemi (Eds), *Psychology in the 1990's.* Amsterdam: Elsevier Science.

Tulving, E., Schacter, D. L., & Stark, H. A. (1982).   Priming effects in word-fragment completion are independent of recognition memory. *Journal of Experimental Psychology: Learning, Memory and Cognition, 8,* 352–373.

Tzavaras, A., Luaute, J. P., & Bidault, E. (1986).   Face recognition dysfunction and delusional misidentification syndromes (D.M.S.). In H. D. Ellis, M. A. Jeeves, F. Newcombe, & A. Young (Eds), *Aspects of face processing.* Dordrecht: Martinus Nijhoff.

Underwood, J. & Paulson, C. (1981).   Aphasia and congenital deafness: A case study. *Brain and Language, 12,* 285–291.

Ungerleider, L. G. & Mishkin, M. (1982).   Two cortical visual systems. In D. J. Ingle, M. A. Goodale, & R. J. W. Mansfield (Eds), *Analysis of visual behavior.* Cambridge, Mass.: MIT Press.

Vallar, G. & Baddeley, A. (1984a).   Fractionation of working memory: Neuropsychological evidence for a phonological short-term store. *Journal of Verbal Learning and Verbal Behavior, 23,* 151–162.

Vallar, G. & Baddeley, A. (1984b).   Phonological short-term store, phonological processing and sentence comprehension: A neuropsychological case study. *Cognitive Neuropsychology, 1,* 121–141.

Van Galen, G. P. (1980). Handwriting and drawing: A two-stage model of complex motor behaviour. In G. Stelmach & J. Requin (Eds), *Tutorials in motor behaviour*. Amsterdam: North-Holland.

Van Harskamp, F. (1974). Some considerations concerning the utility of intelligence tests in aphasic patients. In Y. Lebrun & R. Hoops (Eds), *Intelligence and aphasia*. Amsterdam: Swets and Zeitlinger.

Van Lancker, D. (1987). Nonpropositional speech: Neurolinguistic studies. In A. W. Ellis (Ed.), *Progress in the psychology of language*, Vol. 3. London: Lawrence Erlbaum Associates Ltd.

Van Lancker, D. & Canter, G. J. (1982). Impairment of voice and face recognition in patients with hemispheric damage. *Brain and Cognition, 1*, 185–195.

Van Lancker, D., Cummings, J. L., Kreiman, J., & Dobkin, B. H. (1988). Phonagnosia: A dissociation between familiar and unfamiliar voices. *Cortex, 24*.

Van Zomeren, A. H. & Deelman, B. G. (1978). Long term recovery of visual reaction time after closed head injury. *Journal of Neurology, Neurosurgery and Psychiatry, 41*, 452–457.

Vernon, M. D. (1929). *The errors made in reading*. Medical Research Council Special Report Series, No 130. London: HMSO.

Victor, M. & Yakovlev, P. I. (1955). S. S. Korsakoff's psychic disorder in conjunction with peripheral neuritis. *Neurology, 5*, 394–406.

Vignolo, L. A. (1982). Auditory agnosia. *Philosophical Transactions of the Royal Society* (London), *B298*, 49–57.

Volpe, B. T., LeDoux, J. E., & Gazzaniga, M. S. (1979). Information processing of visual stimuli in an "extinguished" field. *Nature, 282*, 722–724.

Wales, R. & Kinsella, G. (1981). Syntactic effects in sentence completion by Broca's aphasics. *Brain and Language, 13*, 301–307.

Warren, C. & Morton, J. (1982). The effects of priming on picture recognition. *British Journal of Psychology, 73*, 117–129.

Warrington, E. K. (1975). The selective impairment of semantic memory. *Quarterly Journal of Experimental Psychology, 27*, 635–657.

Warrington, E. K. (1979). Neuropsychological evidence for multiple memory systems. In *Brain and mind*. Ciba Foundation Symposium 69 (New series). Amsterdam: Excerpta Medica.

Warrington, E. K. (1982). Neuropsychological studies of object recognition. *Philosophical Transactions of the Royal Society* (London), *B298*, 15–33.

Warrington, E. K. (1987). Visual deficits associated with occipital lobe lesions in man. In C. Chagass, R. Gattass, & C. Gross (Eds), *Pontificae Academia Scientarium Scripta Varia, 54*, 247–261.

Warrington, E. K. & James, M. (1967a). Disorders of visual perception in patients with localized cerebral lesions. *Neuropsychologia, 5*, 253–266.

Warrington, E. K. & James, M. (1967b). An experimental investigation of facial recognition in patients with unilateral cerebral lesions. *Cortex, 3*, 317–326.

Warrington, E. K. & McCarthy, R. (1983). Category specific access dysphasia. *Brain, 106*, 859–878.

Warrington, E. K. & Shallice, T. (1969). The selective impairment of auditory verbal short-term memory. *Brain, 92*, 885–896.

Warrington, E. K. & Shallice, T. (1972). Neuropsychological evidence of visual storage in short-term memory tasks. *Quarterly Journal of Experimental Psychology, 24*, 30–40.

Warrington, E. K. & Shallice, T. (1979). Semantic access dyslexia. *Brain, 102*, 43–63.

Warrington, E. K. & Shallice, T. (1980). Word-form dyslexia. *Brain, 30*, 99–112.

Warrington, E. K. & Shallice, T. (1984).   Category-specific semantic impairments. *Brain*, *107*, 829–854.

Warrington, E. K. & Taylor, A. M. (1973).   The contribution of the right parietal lobe to object recognition. *Cortex*, *9*, 152–164.

Warrington, E. K. & Taylor, A. M. (1978).   Two categorical stages of object recognition. *Perception*, *7*, 695–705.

Warrington, E. K. & Weiskrantz, L. (1968).   New method of testing long-term retention with special reference to amnesic patients. *Nature*, *277*, 972–974.

Warrington, E. K. & Weiskrantz, L. (1970).   Organizational aspects of memory in amnesic patients. *Neuropsychologia*, *9*, 67–71.

Warrington, E. K. & Weiskrantz, L. (1973).   An analysis of short-term and long-term memory defects in man. In J. A. Deutsch (Ed.), *The physiological basis of memory*. New York: Academic Press.

Warrington, E. K. & Zangwill, O. L. (1957).   A study of dyslexia. *Journal of Neurology, Neurosurgery and Psychiatry*, *20*, 208–215.

Waugh, N. C. & Norman, D. A. (1965).   Primary memory. *Psychological Review*, *72*, 89–104.

Wechsler, D. (1917).   A study of retention in Korsakoff psychosis. *Psychiatric Bulletin of the New York State Hospital*, *2*, 403–451.

Weintraub, S., Mesulam, M. M., & Kramer, L. (1981).   Disturbances in prosody: A right-hemisphere contribution. *Archives of Neurology*, *38*, 742–744.

Weiskrantz, L. (1968).   Treatments, inferences, and brain functions. In L. Weiskrantz (Ed.), *Analysis of behavioural change*. New York: Harper and Row.

Weiskrantz, L. (1980).   Varieties of residual experience. *Quarterly Journal of Experimental Psychology*, *32*, 365–386.

Weiskrantz, L. (1986).   *Blindsight: A case study and implications.* Oxford Psychology Series, 12. Oxford: Oxford University Press.

Weiskrantz, L., Warrington, E. K., Sanders, M. D., & Marshall, J. (1974).   Visual capacity of the hemianopic field following a restricted occipital ablation. *Brain*, *97*, 709–728.

Weiss, M. & House, A. (1973).   Perception of dichotically presented vowels. *Journal of the Acoustical Society of America*, *53*, 51–58.

Wells, R. (1951).   Predicting slips of the tongue. *Yale Scientific Magazine*, December 1951. (Reprinted in V. A. Fromkin (Ed.), 1973. *Speech errors as linguistic evidence*. The Hague: Mouton.)

Welman, A. & Lanser, J. (1974).   Intelligence or intellectual tests in aphasic patients. In Y. Lebrun & R. Hoops (Eds), *Intelligence and aphasia*. Amsterdam: Swets and Zeitlinger.

Wernicke, C. (1874).   *Der Aphasische Symptomencomplex*. Breslau: Cohn and Weigart. (Translated in G. H. Eggert. *Wernicke's works on aphasia*. The Hague: Mouton, 1977.)

Weston, M. J. & Whitlock, F. A. (1971).   The Capgras syndrome following head injury. *British Journal of Psychiatry*, *119*, 25–31.

Wetzel, C. D. & Squire, L. R. (1980).   Encoding in anterograde amnesia. *Neuropsychologia*, *18*, 177–184.

Whiteley, A. M. & Warrington, E. K. (1977).   Selective impairment of topographical memory: A single case study. *Journal of Neurology, Neurosurgery and Psychiatry*, *41*, 575–578.

Whitty, C. W. M. (1977).   Transient global amnesia. In C. W. M. Whitty & O. L. Zangwill (Eds), *Amnesia* (2nd edn). London: Butterworths.

Whitty, C. W. M. & Zangwill, O. L. (1977).   Traumatic amnesia. In C. W. M. Whitty & O. L. Zangwill (Eds), *Amnesia* (2nd edn). London: Butterworths.

Wickelgren, W. A. (1968).   Sparing of short-term memory in an amnesic patient: Implications for strength theory of memory. *Neuropsychologia*, *6*, 235–244.

Wilbrand, H. (1892). Ein Fall von Seelenblindheit und Hemianopie mit Sectionsbefund. *Deutscher Zeitschrift für Nervenkrankheiten, 2,* 361–387.

Wilcox, J. & Waziri, R. (1983). The Capgras symptom and nondominant cerebral dysfunction. *Journal of Clinical Psychiatry, 44,* 70–72.

Williams, M. (1953). Investigations of amnesic defects by progressive prompting. *Journal of Neurology, Neurosurgery and Psychiatry, 16,* 14–18.

Williams, M. & Smith, H. V. (1954). Mental disturbances in tuberculous meningitis. *Journal of Neurology, Neurosurgery and Psychiatry, 17,* 173–182.

Williams, M. & Zangwill, O. L. (1952). Memory defects after head injury. *Journal of Neurology, Neurosurgery and Psychiatry, 15,* 54–58.

Williams, M. D. & Hollan, J. S. (1981). The process of retrieval from very long-term memory. *Cognitive Science, 5,* 87–119.

Wingfield, A. (1968). Effects of frequency on identification and naming of objects. *American Journal of Psychology, 81,* 226–234.

Winner, E. & Gardner, H. (1977). The comprehension of metaphor in brain-damaged patients. *Brain, 100,* 717–729.

Winnick, W. A. & Daniel, S. A. (1970). Two kinds of response priming in tachistoscopic recognition. *Journal of Experimental Psychology, 84,* 74–81.

Winocur, G., Oxbury, S., Roberts, R., Agnetti, V., & Davis, C. (1984). Amnesia in a patient with bilateral lesions to the thalamus. *Neuropsychologia, 22,* 123–143.

Winograd, T. (1975). Understanding natural language. In D. Bobrow & A. Collins (Eds), *Representation and understanding.* New York: Academic Press.

Woods, R. T. & Piercy, M. (1974). A similarity between amnesic memory and normal forgetting. *Neuropsychologia, 12,* 437–445.

Woodworth, R. S. (1938). *Experimental psychology.* New York: Holt, Rinehart and Winston.

Yamadori, A, & Albert, M. L. (1973). Word category aphasia. *Cortex, 9,* 83–89.

Yamadori, A., Osumi, Y., Masuhara, S., & Okubo, M. (1977). Preservation of singing in Broca's aphasia. *Journal of Neurology, Neurosurgery and Psychiatry, 40,* 221–224.

Yarnell, P. R. & Lynch, S. (1973). The "ding": Amnesic states in football trauma. *Neurology, 23,* 196–197.

Yealland, L. R. (1916). Case of gunshot wound involving visual centre, with visual disorientation. *Proceedings of the Royal Society of Medicine, 9,* 97–99.

Young, A. W. (1982). Methodological and theoretical bases of visual hemifield studies. In J. G. Beaumont (Ed.), *Divided visual field studies of cerebral organisation.* London: Academic Press.

Young, A. W. (1987). Cerebral hemisphere differences in reading. In J. R. Beech & A. M. Colley (Eds), *Cognitive approaches to reading.* Chichester: Wiley.

Young, A. W. (1988). Functional organisation of visual recognition. In L. Weiskrantz (Ed.), *Thought without language.* Oxford: Oxford University Press.

Young, A. W. & De Haan, E. H. F. (1988). Boundaries of covert recognition in prosopagnosia. *Cognitive Neuropsychology, 5.*

Young, A. W. & Deregowski, J. B. (1981). Learning to see the impossible. *Perception, 10,* 91–105.

Young, A. W. & Ellis, A. W. (1985). Different methods of lexical access for words presented in the left and right visual hemifields. *Brain and Language, 24,* 326–358.

Young, A. W. & Ellis, H. D. (1988). Childhood prosopagnosia. *Brain and Cognition.*

Young, A. W. & Ratcliff, G. (1983). Visuospatial abilities of the right hemisphere. In A. W. Young (Ed.), *Functions of the right cerebral hemisphere.* London: Academic Press.

Young, A. W., Ellis, A. W., & Bion, P. J. (1984). Left hemisphere superiority for pronounceable nonwords, but not for unpronounceable letter strings. *Brain and Language, 22,* 14–25.

Young, A. W., Hay, D. C., & Ellis, A. W. (1985a). The faces that launched a thousand slips: Everyday difficulties and errors in recognizing people. *British Journal of Psychology, 76,* 495–523.

Young, A. W., Hay, D. C., McWeeny, K. H., Flude, B. M., & Ellis, A. W. (1985b). Matching familiar and unfamiliar faces on internal and external features. *Perception, 14,* 737–746.

Young, A. W., Ellis, A. W., Flude, B. M., McWeeny, K. H., & Hay, D. C. (1986). Face-name interference. *Journal of Experimental Psychology: Human Perception and Performance, 12,* 466–475.

Zaidel, E. (1982). Reading by the disconnected right hemisphere: An aphasiological perspective. In Y. Zotterman (Ed.), *Dyslexia: Neuronal, cognitive and linguistic aspects.* Oxford: Pergamon Press.

Zaidel, E. & Peters. A. M. (1981). Phonological encoding and idiographic reading by the disconnected right hemisphere: Two case studies. *Brain and Language, 14,* 205–234.

Zangwill, O. L. (1964). Intelligence in aphasia. In A. De Reuck & M. O'Connor (Eds), *Disorders of language.* London: Churchill.

Zeki, S. (1978). Functional specialization in the visual cortex of the rhesus monkey. *Nature, 274,* 423–428.

Zihl, J., Von Cramon, D., & Mai, N. (1983). Selective disturbance of movement vision after bilateral brain damage. *Brain, 106,* 313–340.

Zola-Morgan, S., Cohen, N. J., & Squire, L. R. (1983). Recall of remote episodic memory in amnesia. *Neuropsychologia, 21,* 487–500.

Zollinger, R. (1935). Removal of left hemisphere: Report of a case. *Archives of Neurology and Psychiatry, 34,* 1055–1064.

Zubin, J. (1948). Memory functioning in patients treated with electric shock therapy. *Journal of Personality, 17,* 33–41.

Zurif, E. B., Caramazza, A., Myerson, R., & Galvin, J. (1974). Semantic feature representations for normal and aphasic language. *Brain and Language, 1,* 167–187.

Readings on Cognitive Neuropsychology

Chapter 1   What is Cognitive Neuropsychology?

Newcombe, F. & Marshall, J.C. (1988). Idealisation meets psychometrics: the case for the right groups and the right individuals. *Cognitive Neuropsychology*, 5, 549–564.

Chapter 1 introduces many of the underlying principles and assumptions of cognitive neuropsychology. As in any new area of scientific inquiry, these continue to be discussed and modified. The reading reprinted to accompany Chapter 1 gives a particularly well-balanced discussion of the issues concerning when group studies or single case studies are most effectively employed, and the types of inference that can be drawn from each. To do this, it expands a number of themes discussed in Chapter 1, including the usefulness (or otherwise) of syndrome categories, and the interpretation of associations and dissociations.

The methods used in cognitive neuropsychology continue to be highly eclectic; there as yet is no single right way to carry out a cognitive neuropsychological study (we suspect there never will be such a prescription). Instead, one has to make best use of all the sources of information available. These sources include neurological information, which often forms a useful background pointing toward likely types of impairment, and which can help in narrowing down the possible causes of a person's problems. We do not make a great deal of use of such information here, because saying that a person has a medial temporal lobe lesion does not *explain* what is wrong with his or her memory; it simply makes some form of memory impairment likely. However, we agree with much of Shallice's (1988) critique of what he calls ultra-cognitive neuropsychology—a doctrine that holds (among other things) that lesion locations and other neurological information are irrelevant. In our view, neurological information is highly relevant, but not to be confused with a cognitive neuropsychological account, which requires a different level of analysis (albeit one that we anticipate may eventually be mapped onto the underlying neurology). At the neurological level, one might say that a person's memory is impaired because they have suffered damage to peri-rhinal cortex, or to the hippocampus. As cognitive neuropsychologists, though, we also want to know whether the memory deficit reflects a failure to create new memories, problems in retrieving them, or any of the other issues discussed extensively in Chapter 10.

This point is especially important because of the rapid advances that are taking place in brain imaging, which allow us to investigate the normal brain in operation, through measuring blood flow in different regions and other physiological indices. The most sophisticated of such studies offer an exciting interplay between neuroscience, cognitive psychology, and neuropsychology, making it possible to begin to relate the kinds of models described in this book to their underlying neurophysiology (Petersen, Fox, Posner, Mintun, & Raichle, 1988). In doing this, we must not forget that the effectiveness of such mappings depends ultimately on the quality of each component; it needs good neurophysiology *and* good psychology.

The value of linking psychological and neurophysiological levels of analyses can also be clearly seen in one of the readings we selected to accompany Chapter 3 (Goodale & Milner, 1992), which shows how findings concerning impairments of visual and motor performance after brain injury can be related to knowledge of separate visual processing streams in the cerebral cortex. Again, this is not a one-way mapping in which understanding the brain-injured person's problems is simply reduced to understanding the neuro-physiology. Instead, Goodale and Milner (1992) show that the types of impairment observed after brain injury allow more precise specification of the functions subserved by these different cortical processing streams.

The notion of cortical processing streams provides one way of bridging the gap between our knowledge of the brain's anatomical organisation and the relatively "modular" deficits that can be observed after brain injury. In particular, it may help in accounting for the paradoxical finding that highly selective impairments sometimes follow quite diffuse cerebral damage. For example, category-specific impairments of semantic memory are often noted after encephalitis (see Chapter 2), and more general semantic memory impairments have been found in the context of neurodegenerative disease (Hodges, Patterson, Oxbury, & Funnell, 1992; Hodges, Patterson, & Tyler, 1994).

Neurodegenerative diseases are of course particularly distressing because, unlike after a stroke or head injury, there is little possibility of improvement. They therefore require exceptional sensitivity on the part of researchers if unacceptable burdens are not to be placed on patients and their families who may already be under exceptional stress. When properly done, though, such studies can also provide a useful indirect means of help and support.

Investigating the course of the breakdown of cognitive abilities in neuro-degenerative diseases turns out to be very informative scientifically. For example, Hodges et al. (1994) studied loss of semantic memory longitudinally across two years in patient PP. During this time, PP's ability to recognise everyday objects and to understand or produce basic vocabulary underwent a profound deterioration, yet many of her other cognitive abilities showed little or no decline. As Hodges et al. (1994) show, such differential patterns of loss can have important implications for understanding what is and what is not modularly organised in the brain, and which modules are dependent for their successful operation on the integrity of which others.

The research agenda of Hodges and his colleagues is also of particular methodological interest, because they are beginning to explore what one can learn from the patterns of association of deficits found in neurodegenerative diseases, as well as the more usually studied dissociations. This forms part of a wider trend to think very carefully about associations and dissociations, and how best to interpret them, seeded by a very thorough discussion in Shallice (1988).

Two other particularly significant recent developments require comment in their own right; these are connectionism and rehabilitation. In line with our advocacy of an eclectic approach, we see these as enhancing the range of techniques that can be used in trying to arrive at a better understanding.

Connectionism has been the more widely trumpeted development, and has had considerable impact on psychology as well as cognitive neuropsychology. The key ideas are introduced by Patterson (1990), in one of the readings chosen to accompany Chapter 8. Connectionist models (often called "neural nets" in the research literature—though in our view this label should be regarded as a metaphor) consist of large numbers of simple processing elements (units) that are connected one to another via excitatory or inhibitory links in various possible ways. A typical organisation might be to create several "pools" of units, some (or all) of which correspond to specific levels of representation. Surprisingly complex (and nontrivial) patterns of interaction can be created in such networks (McClelland & Rumelhart, 1988), allowing the possibility of determining how well these simulate known aspects of human behaviour. For cognitive neuropsychology, it then becomes possible to explore the changes resulting from damage to a network thought to provide a reasonable simulation of normal performance, to see how these damaged networks compare to the performances of people with brain injuries. Some impressive results have already been achieved (Plaut & Shallice, 1993a, b).

The value of connectionist models is that, like any computer simulation, nothing can be left vague or unspecified. This can provide a very useful degree of discipline. The danger, though, is one of being misled (even mesmerised) into taking something that merely mimics some aspect of human performance for the real thing (Young, 1994). The connectionist genie is potentially very powerful, and now decidedly out of the lamp, but we have much to learn about how to make him obey the true spirit of our commands.

Finally, a few words about rehabilitation. It is a natural wish to try to repay some of the generosity of brain-injured people who give their time to carry out what can often be uninteresting research tasks. An obvious way to do this is by exploring whether or not the knowledge obtained can be used to underpin theoretically driven rehabilitation techniques. In fact, the prospects for this are at present fairly mixed, but readings we have selected to accompany Chapter 8 (Patterson, 1994), Chapter 9 (Mitchum, Haendiges, & Berndt, 1995), and Chapter 10 (Wilson, Baddeley, Evans, & Shiel, 1994) show that some progress is being made. Even so, it is clear that even when they are demonstrably effective, such therapies can only form part of a rounded approach to rehabilitation (Wilson & Patterson, 1990). What cognitive neuropsychologically oriented attempts at rehabilitation are also achieving, though, is to add another important source of evidence about the nature of a person's impairment after brain injury; to some extent, therapies can form tests of theories.

REFERENCES

Goodale, M.A. & Milner, A.D. (1992). Separate visual pathways for perception and action. *Trends in Neurosciences*, *15*, 20–25.

Hodges, J.R., Patterson, K., Oxbury, S., & Funnell, E. (1992). Semantic dementia: progressive fluent aphasia with temporal lobe atrophy. *Brain*, *115*, 1783–1806.

Hodges, J.R., Patterson, K., & Tyler, L.K. (1994). Loss of semantic memory: implications for the modularity of mind. *Cognitive Neuropsychology*, *11*, 505–542.

McClelland, J.L. & Rumelhart, D.E. (1988). *Explorations in parallel distributed processing*. Cambridge, Mass.: Bradford Books.

Mitchum, C.C., Haendiges, A.N., & Berndt, R.S. (1995). Treatment of thematic mapping in sentence comprehension: implications for normal processing. *Cognitive Neuropsychology*, *12*, 503–547.

Patterson, K.E. (1990). Alexia and neural nets. *Japanese Journal of Neuropsychology*, *6*, 90–99.

Patterson, K. (1994). Reading, writing, and rehabilitation: a reckoning. In M.J. Riddoch & G.W. Humphreys (Eds.), *Cognitive neuropsychology and cognitive rehabilitation* (pp. 425–447). Hove, UK: Lawrence Erlbaum Associates Ltd.

Petersen, S.E., Fox, P.T., Posner, M.I., Mintun, M., & Raichle, M.E. (1988). Positron emission tomographic studies of the cortical anatomy of single-word processing. *Nature*, *331*, 585–589.

Plaut, D.C. & Shallice, T. (1993a). Deep dyslexia: a case study of connectionist neuropsychology. *Cognitive Neuropsychology*, *10*, 377–500.

Plaut, D.C. & Shallice, T. (1993b). Perseverative and semantic influences on visual object naming errors in optic aphasia: a connectionist account. *Journal of Cognitive Neuroscience*, *5*, 89–117.

Shallice, T. (1988). *From neuropsychology to mental structure*. Cambridge: Cambridge University Press.

Wilson, B. & Patterson, K. (1990). Rehabilitation for cognitive impairment: does cognitive psychology apply? *Applied Cognitive Psychology*, *4*, 247–260.

Wilson, B.A., Baddeley, A., Evans, J., & Shiel, A. (1994). Errorless learning in the rehabilitation of memory impaired people. *Neuropsychological Rehabilitation*, *4*, 307–326.

Young, A.W. (1994). What counts as local? Commentary on M.J. Farah, 'Neuropsychological inference with an interactive brain: a critique of the "locality" assumption'. *Behavioral and Brain Sciences*, *17*, 88–89.

Idealisation Meets Psychometrics: The Case for the Right Groups and the Right Individuals

Freda Newcombe and John C. Marshall

The Radcliffe Infirmary, Oxford, U.K.

We consider some of the methodological issues involved in using data from brain-damaged individuals in support (or disproof) of claims about the structure of normal cognition. More specifically, we address whether single cases or group studies provide a more reliable and valid source of relevant information. We conclude that the dichotomy is itself misconceived if approached from a purely methodological stance, and that selection of a particular group (or individual) must be based upon the precise nature of the theoretical claims under consideration. The status of "minority effects" in group studies is determined, we argue, by whether they arise from biological variation in fixed functional architecture or from "strategic" variation *within* a common architecture.

INTRODUCTION

Arguments about the respective merits of single-case and group studies have been rumbling around the neuropsychological community for some time now (Caramazza, 1984; Marshall, 1982; Marshall & Newcombe, 1984; Schwartz, 1984; Shallice, 1979). Indeed, glimmerings of recognition that there are important questions lurking here go back at least to the 1920s when single-case studies, no matter how well-conducted, first began to be described as "merely anecdotal". Two primary factors were perhaps responsible for this swing of the pendulum away from the single-case studies that fuelled theoretical progress in the "heroic" decades of Broca (1865), Wernicke (1874), Lissauer (1889), and Liepmann (1900). Initially, the 1st World War sadly provided appropriate material for group studies—large numbers of previously healthy young men who sustained relatively focal brain damage due to penetrating missile injury (Marie, 1926; Poppelreuter, 1917); secondly, there has been sustained growth in the numbers of psychologists who examine patients with organic disorders of cognitive functioning (Weisenberg & McBride, 1935). Experimental psychologists, raised on a diet of latin squares and agricultural statistics and with ready access to a totally homogeneous population of college sophomores, might well be underwhelmed by single cases.

Despite the problem's extensive provenance there nonetheless seems to have been relatively little "frank and open" discussion of the issues at stake. Hence, whatever one's reaction to the validity of Caramazza's recent claims, it can only be productive to have such sharp methodological statements brought out for airing (Caramazza, 1986; Caramazza and McCloskey, 1988). We are not, however, convinced that the set of arguments under discussion is best summarised as case studies *versus* group studies. Accordingly, the moral that we shall stress is *not* "Thou shalt not commit group-studies", but rather the much more positive injunction "Thou shalt seriously consider what hypotheses thy data could logically speak to". This latter standpoint will eventually lead us to conclude that there are a number of important issues that can best (or perhaps even *only*) be addressed by group studies (in some sense of that multiply-ambiguous term). But first, we will consider, along with Caramazza (1986), some potentially misleading consequences of group-study methodology.

SYNDROMES: OR BETWEEN THE DEVIL AND THE DEEP BLUE SEA

Much of the force behind Caramazza's condemnation of group studies arises from his attack on the assumption of (patient) homogeneity (Caramazza, 1986) in settings where every experienced examiner knows that variability is the norm. Consider a very broadly defined group—the set of all aphasic patients (examined), where aphasia is defined as *any* impairment of *any* language function. From the mean performance of these n patients on m tasks, would one expect to be able to draw any conclusions about "the structure of normal cognitive processes" (Caramazza, 1986)? Very likely not: there may be many good uses for such data as, say, the group's mean score on an object-naming test is 22/36, but those uses do not include the theoretical understanding of normal cognition.

Perhaps a more tightly defined group would help; a traditional aphasic syndrome, for example? The initial problem that arises here is that there are (at least) two mutually incompatible accounts of the nature of a syndrome. The first, fixed-syndrome definition is outlined by Strub and Geschwind (1983, p. 317) in the course of their analysis of the Gerstmann syndrome: "The essence of a medical syndrome is that a collection of signs or symptoms, when all present, indicate the presence of a specific disease". Now, one can, of course, list *by fiat* the necessary and sufficient conditions for application of a particular syndrome-label, but such definitions must themselves be justified. In behavioural neurology, that justification has traditionally been anatomic—the syndrome points to pathology of a particular cerebral locus. This line of argument, however, leads Strub and Geschwind (1983, p. 318) to argue that: "a syndrome is most useful as a diagnostic tool precisely when the elements usually are not found together". One can admittedly see the point of this kind of definition for anatomo-clinical purposes, but what are the implications for group studies based upon such syndromes? Given patients grouped together by virtue of all showing *n* symptoms which *rarely co-occur* in an unselected series, will that group be homogeneous with respect to symptom *n + 1*? Will the *mean* of the group's performance on task *m + 1* be a valid datum for or against any claim about the structure of normal cognition? There seems to be no good reason to *assume* a positive answer to either question, and we are left with Caramazza's observation that relevant homogeneity of patient samples can only be assessed after the fact (i.e. by empirical inspection of the data). Worse, on the Strub and Geschwind analysis, the very definition of a syndrome pulls in a direction that is diametrically opposed to the discovery of *functional* relationships between the behavioural phenomena of preserved and impaired cognitive mechanisms: the signs are " . . . usually not found together".

Consider now an alternative, "variable" definition of syndromes. Benson (1979, p. 57) claims: "Medical syndromes do not exist as fixed, consistent entities . . . variability, inexactness and incompleteness are commonplace". On Benson's analysis, an aphasic syndrome can be thought of "as a set of family relationships akin to Wittgensteinian analyses of the concept of a game" (Marshall, 1982). Although no individual symptom or fixed set of features is criterial, variable subsets of features do provide grounds for inference to underlying pathology. Such inference is, however, actuarial, not deductive. As Benson (1979, p. 58) writes: " . . . the syndrome is the collection of symptoms suggesting the location or type of pathology, not the invariable result of pathology involving a given site". Such a definition is perhaps more realistic than that proposed by Strub and Geschwind (1983), but can provide little comfort for the pursuit of traditional group studies. Groups formed on the basis of Wittgensteinian, "polytypic" (Schwartz, 1984) criteria are not even homogeneous with respect to their *inclusion* characteristics. What then is the likelihood that they *will* be homogeneous with respect to any further features that were not included in the initial actuarial checklist? Albert, Goodglass, Helm, Rubens, and Alexander (1981) also stress patient variability *within* a taxonomic class, but reverse the pathology-behaviour relationship. Where Benson (1979) notes that pathology to a given site does not always provoke a particular symptom-complex, Albert et al. (1981, p. 53) observe that the occurrence of a particular behaviourally defined syndrome does not invariably imply "a specific lesion location".

We seem thus to be caught in the following dilemma. If groups are formed on the basis of Strub and Geschwind's analysis of syndromes, the population will, by definition, be homogeneous with respect to its fixed set of criterial features, but the group will be unrepresentative of patients who manifest any of the individual features. If groups are formed on the basis of Benson's definition, the population will not be homogeneous on any "pre-hoc" grounds. In neither case are there rational grounds for expecting groups so-formed to provide on other tasks homogeneous data suitable for theory construction.

Two conclusions seem to follow:

1.   Syndromes (and their names) should be retained *solely* as " . . . convenient short expressions whereby one medical practitioner can convey to another a lengthy but standard message" (Holladay & Poole, 1979). The information conveyed may be constant for limited periods only: "Since the name of a disease is a code-word for a lengthy message whose detailed content is changing continuously, it follows that such a name is of limited applicability outside the time and place to which it belongs" (Holladay & Poole, 1979).

2.   In the absence of specific valid arguments to the contrary, it is safer to map data from individual patients directly onto structural models of cognitive functioning, rather than to do so via the intermediate step of grouping patients into syndromes. Unless the assumption of homogeneity is *known* to be met, the use of groups can only increase the "noise" in the data. The practise of averaging should be constrained by the form of the underlying distribution of scores. But the demonstration of "majority effects" (Caplan, 1988) in ill-defined, highly-variable populations should not constrain the limits of our ambition in cognitive neuropsychology.

It may nonetheless turn out that the arguments so far advanced are not against groups per se but are rather disguised attacks on the *particular* groups that have traditionally been employed. The question may not be "Why do you need a group?" but rather "Why this group?"

NORMAL GROUPS AND PATHOLOGICAL INDIVIDUALS

Neuropsychological studies based upon syndromes clearly grew out of a medical model in which a syndrome is the manifestation of an underlying disease process. Yet this model, Strub and Geschwind (1983) not withstanding, may not be the most appropriate foundation for cognitive neuropsychology. As Kinnear Wilson (1926, p. 3) points out:

> Aphasia is not a disease, but a symptom. Like all symptoms, it is the expression of departure from a normal state, the external manifestation of disorder of function of a mechanism. When we speak of different types of aphasia, we

do not refer to different varieties of a particular morbid entity or disease, but to certain groups of symptoms, all of which are disturbances of the function of speech.

The first group that we need to consider, then, is people in "a normal state".

One can assume, as part of the intuitive definition of humankind, that all normal adults will, for example: be able to hold a (fairly) sensible conversation about their interests; recognise by sight common objects in their environment; find their way from home to the workplace; recognise the faces of family and friends; remember what they ate for lunch; execute a learnt sequence of simple actions . . . etc., etc. (Some small percentage of people without brain-damage detectable by current technology may admittedly *not* have these competences . . . but they manifest the "developmental" form of whatever they would be suffering from if acquired brain damage *was* the cause of the impairment. We shall return to this issue latter.)

When a person subsequent, say, to cerebro-vascular accident, is manifestly unable to perform such tasks we do not worry overmuch about testing a group of normal subjects to see if our patient really is impaired in one or more cognitive domains. For such simple tasks, one assumes a ceiling effect in normals and a standard deviation of essentially zero. The patient is confidently labelled (for convenience) as suffering from aphasia, visual agnosia, topographical agnosia, prosopagnosia, amnesia, or apraxia.

Historically, single-case studies have played a major role in driving theoretical advance in neuropsychology in the restricted circumstances outlined here: namely, where a patient's performance on one task (or a small group of tasks) was so deviant (qualitatively or quantitatively) that the issue of pre-morbid competence simply did not arise. Human autobiographical memory is highly variable, but HM's deficit is not within that range (Milner, 1958); the ability to draw varies from your and my efforts to the skill of the young Picasso, but none of us when asked to draw or copy a daisy will systematically leave out the entire left-hand side (Paterson & Zangwill, 1944); literate people differ in reading speed and comprehension of complex texts, but do not read the single word *sick* as "ill" (Marshall & Newcombe, 1966).

Yet in the course of further investigating these deficits, either in the original extreme cases or in other "milder" cases, we may well want to employ tasks (and scoring procedures) that do not have such an obvious ceiling—we may, for example, want to know the patient's digit span, the number of trials he takes to learn a ten choice-point visuo-tactile maze, how many Mooney-faces he can recognise, how quickly he can name an octopus . . . At this point a normal control group is clearly required. That group will be matched to the patient for factors that one has reason to believe may correlate with quantitative peformance (age, sex, education, handedness . . .). The mean performance of the control group is our best guess as to the level of functioning of some "idealised" normal human brain. But what is "normal"? Here we would support the line of argument in Bogen (1985, p. 30):

> What I think "normal" in this context means depends upon the knowledge that most of us bear scars on the brain. When babies are born, their heads are often moulded out of shape. They look funny, most of them. Some of them look a little blue, too. And we all fall on our heads when we're little. So it is easy to see why almost everybody has scars on the brain. For most of us it doesn't make too much difference—it depends on the size of the scar, the location, the orientation, and so on. What the word "normal" refers to is the fact that when we have a fairly sizeable group (say, an n of 30 or so) the scars are in different places, so it all washes out in the statistics.

The functioning of the "normal" brain, then, is best described by the mean performance of n "real" brains, each one of which is *slightly* abnormal. It is against this "idealised" brain that we judge the abilities of our single patient . . . a patient whose performance on task X may be 1 or 2 S.D.s below "normal". So far, so good. But given that normal people differ along the dimension measured, how do we know that our patient did not fall well below the mean *pre-morbidly*? Short of the patient having been tested in the pre-morbid state, we can, of course, never be sure. We can, however, increase our confidence that the deficit is consequent upon brain injury in adult life. One might do so by testing a *group* of patients with (roughly) comparable cerebral damage. As Bogen (1985) writes, the situation with a group of randomly scarred brains is quite different from "a situation in which one has only five or six people, all of whom have had a right temporal lobectomy. There, the lesion in the brain, in this case the temporal lobectomy, is the major variable in the equation." If the majority of the patient sample (or the mean performance of the group) is found to differ significantly from the normal control group (or perhaps from another patient group, all of whom had lesions outside the temporal lobe), then one may justifiably feel more secure in asserting that the first patient's deficit did not pre-date the lesion that brought him to our attention. We seem, then, to have a set of conditions under which group studies are valid, where they can, indeed, provide information that is not usually available in single-case studies. But if groups based *directly* upon lesion site are legitimate for this purpose, why should groups based upon syndromes (which are *correlated* with lesion site, albeit far from perfectly) not be equally legitimate?

For the most part, either group *will* be appropriate, because it is in precisely these circumstances that a "majority effect" (a statistically significant difference between the normal and the pathological groups, even with "exceptions") is tolerable. The "absolute" homogeneity of the pathological group is not requisite, because the relevant inference is simply that *at least* one member of the group has a small but demonstrably abnormal impairment. Nonetheless, choosing the appropriate pathological group is not theoretically neutral; the decision must be motivated.

For example: the decision to employ (directly) an anatomically defined patient group implies that the locus and limits of the anatomic area selected can be defended. It is not always clear that gross analysis by lobes can be so defended (see, for example, Newcombe, Ratcliff, & Damasio, 1987, for observations on the complexity of the anatomical structures that may mediate quite simple visual and spatial tasks). When more restricted locales are employed (Broca's area or Wernicke's area, for example), it is well known that there is controversy over exactly where these regions are (Bogen & Bogen, 1976; Lecours, Basso, Moraschini, & Nespoulous, 1984). As Albert et al. (1981) write: " . . . Broca's and Wernicke's areas are anatomical conventions with no clearly agreed upon boundaries". Further problems are raised when the correlation between infarction of "Broca's area" and "Broca's aphasia" is far from perfect (Mazzocchi & Vignolo, 1979; Mohr et al., 1978).

The same points thus hold with even greater strength when pathological groups are based upon syndromes as indirect indicators of lesion site. Polytypic syndromes do predict areas of damage, albeit with numerous counter-examples (Basso, Lecours, Moraschini, & Vanier, 1985; Poeck, de Bleser, & Keyserlingk, 1984). When genuine biological variation in brain anatomy is combined with the "man-made" variability of polytypic syndromes, the least one can say is that an explicit justification should always be given for *any* grouping of patients. That justification may differ consequent upon whether our observations concern an association or a dissociation of symptoms. It should also be borne in mind that the "natural kinds" of behavioural neurology may not be co-extensive with the "natural kinds" of cognitive neuropsychology (see Fodor, 1974).

VARIATION IN ASSOCIATION AND DISSOCIATION

Natural kinds in behavioural neurology have often been based upon the geometry of cerebral vascularisation and the anatomical contiguity of *functionally* distinct areas (Poeck, 1983). When behavioural syndromes are predicated upon such contiguity, the features that constitute the syndrome will fractionate, as in the Gerstmann syndrome (Strub & Geschwind, 1983). In these conditions one would clearly be mistaken if one attempted to unify the deficits *psychologically* as manifestations of some single underlying functional component (Marshall, 1982; 1986). Anatomical contiguity or partial overlap is a sufficient explanation for the observed association (Brain, 1964), although there may be further *psychological* consequences to be drawn from the fact that the pertinent anatomical locales *are* contiguous; that is, the contiguity may reflect efficient biological engineering. It may also be the case that when the individual symptoms of the syndrome do occur in isolation (or in other combinations) they are subtly different from their occurrence as part of the syndrome. This possibility is best investigated by detailed case-by-case studies. The former hypothesis of anatomical contiguity requires group study, but the group will be selected in the manner that Caramazza (1986) demands; it will be chosen precisely because each and every member meets the fixed definition of, say, Gerstmann's syndrome. Consistency of lesion site (subject, no doubt, to some individual anatomic variation) can then be looked for. The issue of what other *behavioural* symptoms the group may (or may not) have in common is irrelevant. The research strategy here clearly involves continued transfer of information between single-case studies and group studies. But if the situation is as we have described, the conclusion would be that the Gerstmann-syndrome is not a natural kind in cognitive neuropsychology. Groups formed on this basis would not therefore be mandatory for further investigation of finger agnosia, right-left disorientation, agraphia, and acalculia, the defining features of the syndrome (Strub & Geschwind, 1983).

It is nonetheless reasonable to claim that if *association* of symptoms is at stake, little beyond the impetus to further investigation will be obtained from a single case; in either a normal or a brain-damaged individual any association could occur by chance in populations where the two "traits" were uncorrelated. Transparently, groups are required, but which ones? Equally clearly, the answer depends upon the hypothesis under consideration. Functionally pertinent association is present when X "feeds" Y, Y "feeds" X, or some other factor A underlies performance on both X and Y. The relevant groups can then be selected for X or Y (or A when the investigator has some decent guess as to what A is) and the question of theoretically pertinent homogeneity is assured. Assume the study is performed (on either a normal or a "pathological" population) and gives a reasonable but far from perfect correlation, say +0.70. Some of the residual variance (51%) can no doubt be easily "explained away" by the standard arguments about the "noise" attendant upon any empirical measurements (including the subject/patient simply "trying harder" in one set of testing conditions than another). The real problem arises when the "trend" is obvious enough but a small group of subjects/patients fall far outside the regression line. Assume that they do so reliably—split-half reliability and test-retest reliability is high for those individuals. What now?

Well, one can, as Caplan (1988) claims usually happens with "normal psychology", simply ignore them. But this is to ignore the fact that they do seem to be genuine counter-examples to what purports to be a universal generalisation. One can indeed erect a theoretical edifice on the basis of the "majority effect", but this is no excuse for not exploring a potentially important example of real psychobiological variation. The particular example Caplan (1988) cites comes from an experiment by Waters and Seidenberg (1985). Three (normal) subjects out of 28 *failed* to show a regularity effect on the speed of reading low-frequency words.

If those data points are reliable, one could advance a suggestion or two. Since 10% of the subject population is a not inconsiderable proportion, one should either show how the performance of those subjects is consistent with a universal reading model, or one should perforce construct a "minority-model" in addition to the "majority-model". If the latter alternative was required, then it would be obligatory to exclude the data of these three subjects from entering into the construction of the majority model; their reaction times are "noise" which distorts the numerical value of the regularity effect which will (eventually) enter into genuinely quantitative models of cognitive functioning. In this particular instance we suspect that a new "minority-model" will not be required; the standard triple-route model (Patterson, Marshall, & Coltheart, 1985) provides ample scope for individual variation in the efficiency of lexical and extra-lexical routes (that is, of procedures that address and assemble phonology). Furthermore, we already know that there is substantial (quantitative) "Chinese" versus "Phoenician" variation in normal (adult) readers (Baron & Strawson, 1976), such that an occasional "normal" subject would have been confidently labelled as suffering from "phonological dyslexia" had there been any indication of brain damage (Campbell & Butterworth, 1985).

Nonetheless, the logic of "minority effects" seems clear enough, and is applicable to both normal and pathological populations. There are three main categories into which reliable minority effects in properly conducted investigations may fall.

1.   The theory within the domain of which the majority effect falls permits *principled* variation such that defined classes of minority effects are actually predicted by the theory. Multi-route theories of reading and writing have precisely such a structure.

For example: "all normal people", after adequate exposure to an alphabetically written language, acquire the ability to read aloud words (with regular and irregular spellings) and nonwords (which, by definition, have regular spellings). Campbell and Butterworth (1985) have reported a case in which a highly literate subject who could read aloud such words as *placebo* or *idyll* without hesitation experienced "great difficulty in reading the simplest nonwords, like *bant*, sometimes failing to offer any pronunciation for them". The subject of this single-case report was a young woman of 21, with a verbal I.Q. of 123, and who obtained a second-class honours degree in psychology at London University. There was no known history of neurological disease or trauma. This woman is "statistically" abnormal in the sense that *most* children with a congenital impairment of the sub-lexical reading route would be predicted to have a "reading impairment" for *words* (Temple & Marshall, 1983; Seymour & MacGregor, 1984). Nonetheless, the structure of triple-route reading models (Patterson, Marshall, & Coltheart, 1985) allows for the possibility that a developmental inferiority of the sub-lexical route could be overcome by superiority in the efficiency of either or both of the lexical routes.

2. Some minority effects may be explained away by virtue of "compensatory strategies", strategies whereby the subject/patient is, in some sense, performing a different set of operations from those specified in the relevant (majority) theory. The cross-cueing strategies adopted by some split-brain patients (Gordon, 1974) would be one illustration of the maxim that there is more than one way to scramble an egg. More generally, the notion of a "task" is susceptible to decomposition. Cognitive theory is concerned with the structure of how tasks are performed. Thus the observation that some subjects/patients can find their way around by (often verbalised) "land-marks" would not constitute evidence against the validity of an association between two components or aspects of topographical memory (e.g. spatial orientation and visuo-spatial memory) when such landmarks could not be employed (Whitty & Newcombe, 1973). The overall point is clear: minority effects due to compensatory strategies should revert to majority effects when the experimenter precludes the adoption of the compensatory strategy.

3. The minority effect may reflect a genuine, biological difference between different members of the human species (and hence require a different theory from the one appropriate to the majority effect). The following case should perhaps be considered in this light: "all normal people" manifest some degree of visual persistence (Haber, 1983) and have stereoscopic vision. One technique for the investigation of stereopsis involves the use of Julesz random-dot stereograms in which a subset of elements in one array (the figure) is laterally shifted with respect to the other. If the two arrays are presented with a temporal separation of 150msec (or greater) the figure cannot be detected. Stromeyer and Psotka (1970) have reported a case in which with million-dot stereograms, the array seen with one eye could be fused with an array seen by the other eye four hours later; with arrays that only (sic!) contained ten-thousand elements, the arrays could be fused at intervals of three days. The subject of this single-case report was a young woman of 23, a teacher at Harvard and a skilled artist. Her performance could hardly be regarded as falling at the extreme limits of the capacity of a majority-effect mechanism. Her ability is clearly so extreme that one must at very least consider the hypothesis that her visual memory

was mediated by a mechanism which simply does not exist in the vast majority of "normal" humankind.

Imagine that one tested ten "normal" subjects, one of whom was this young woman, on the stereogram task. And then took the *mean* interval as the descriptive statistic that characterised normal visual persistence! Conclusion: persistence = 25,920,135msec (when the "true" value is *circa* 150msec). True, no investigator in his or her right mind would make a blunder quite so egregious as this. But we may be making similar mistakes, albeit on a smaller scale, if we ignore the possibility that minority effects may arise from (qualitatively) minority brains.

We have, of course, chosen an example where it is unlikely that this young woman was merely employing a universal cognitive system in ways that were strategically different from the majority use (Caplan, 1987). It would seem far-fetched to imagine that practice and the deployment of super-efficient "strategies" could boost your or my visual memory to such heights. We appear to be dealing here with fixed functional architecture (Pylyshyn, 1984) rather than strategic programming. One would accordingly distinguish such phenomena from (many) cases of prodigious mental calculation. Here it would seem that a comparatively slight superiority in short-term memory, combined with "brute-force" memorisation of number facts and learnt knowledge of fancy algorithms, can conspire to produce phenotypic performance that far outstrips the (statistically) normal (Hunter, 1968). But there is probably no call to postulate a "genotypically" distinct functional architecture.

Leaving such cases aside, however, any attack upon the status of "black swans" as counterexamples to a universal generalisation must be justified. That is, one must advance both argument and data to show that the purported disproof of a functional relationship is not valid. Merely asserting that theory can be built upon majority effects will not suffice in populations of either normal or brain-damaged individuals.

We can now turn the question on its head and ask what weight a dissociation can bear in an individual case. In a properly investigated case, the dissociation is obviously an "existence-proof" that there is no necessary and sufficient universal association between symptoms (phenomena) X and Y. Further investigation, and generalisation to a group, will depend upon the investigator's theory of the dissociation (or minority effect). If the dissociation (or minority effect) is permitted by the majority theory (based upon association), then the question becomes: why does a minority (of subjects/patients) take the (statistically) nonpreferred "path" through the (multi-component) universal model? In the absence of a well-worked-out theory of individual variation, one would probably indulge in associative and dissociative fishing expeditions. One would look for other aspects of behaviour or symptomatology that the minority group ($n \geqslant 1$) did not share with the majority group; when the minority group was $n > 1$, common characteristics other than the ones that initially defined the group could be sought.

When the dissociation or minority effect is due to strategic adaptation, experimental manipulation is required. The effect previously found in a minority of cases should generalise to the majority when that majority is specifically enjoined or taught to use the adaptation that was spontaneously employed by the minority.

When one suspects that a dissociative minority effect reflects real biological variation in cognitively impenetrable domains (Pylyshyn, 1984), one hopes that further investigation comparing the individual (minority) case with the (theoretically homogeneous) majority cases will reveal more precisely what the variation consists in. Search for further cases of the minority effect will be guided by associated characteristics of the first case that are not held in common with the majority effect subjects/patients.

Are there examples where we need to know reasonably accurately the percentage of subjects/patients who show a minority effect (and must hence perform a group study)? One such example concerns the language-competence of the normal right hemisphere, where "normal" means "typical". Information about this competence, its range and variability, could bear upon the following issues: when sodium amytal testing reveals that residual aphasic speech (in right handers) is frequently abolished after left-sided injection (see Code, 1987), should this fact be taken to indicate that a majority of (clinically) normal brains possess some (limited) capacity for right-hemisphere speech? If some of the error types seen in "deep dyslexia" arise when a subsidiary reading-system in the right hemisphere is released from the inhibitory control of the left hemisphere (see Marshall & Patterson, 1985; Patterson & Besner, 1984; and Zaidel, 1985, for conflicting views on the validity of this claim), are the right hemispheres of patients who manifest these errors *representative* of the prototypical normal brain?

The *typicality* of such phenomena obviously bears upon the role that these data play in the construction of "majority-effect" models, granted that various types and degrees of bilateral speech representation and "crossed dominace" can be found in a minority of patients (Annett, 1985). The most striking controversy that (in part) turns upon the statistics of right-hemisphere competence for language concerns commissurotomy patients. Many investigators who have studied this population believe that the right-hemisphere linguistic capacity demonstrated in a small group of such patients is representative of the functioning of the normal right hemisphere (see Zaidel, 1985). But Gazzaniga (1983) claims that only a very small percentage of commissurotomy patients display any right-hemisphere language competence. Indeed, by Gazzaniga's account the proportion is so small that it would be unwise to incorporate the data from these patients into any model of the cognitive functioning of the normal, "typical" brain. We make no comment here upon the truth of Gazzaniga's claim (see Myers, 1984) or upon any other problems associated with the interpretation of commissurotomy data (see Bogen, 1985). We simply note that there are occasions when the typicality of an effect does indeed bear upon the theoretical deployment of that effect. One case of right-hemisphere language obviously demonstrates the biological possibility of right-hemisphere language, but the detailed fractionation of such competence will not necessarily contribute to the analysis of the *modal* model.

Finally, we return to more general anatomical considerations. As previously noted, association of symptoms can arise from anatomical contiguity of the damaged areas. One black swan (with dissociated symptoms) or two black swans (with double dissociation) will not *necessarily* show that a majority association is psychologically spurious. The escape clause of strategic adaptation can always be invoked; or it may be that the dissociated case really is a biological "mutant". But a series of black swans with lesions subtly different from those found in the majority association would give grounds for acute suspicion. Likewise, when a theory that is plausible *on other grounds* predicts a dissociation, one may accept just one actual case of empirical dissociation as adequate proof and dismiss on the grounds of anatomical contiguity *all* other cases of association. In such instances, it is the minority effect in the data that becomes the "majority effect" in the theory. As we have previously argued (Marshall & Newcombe, 1984): "The theoretical significance (in the nonstatistical sense) of a clinical datum is not logically linked to the number of patients in whom that datum can be observed".

CONCLUSION

We have attempted to support the general position outlined by Caramazza and McCloskey (1988) and yet preserve some territory where group studies may play a valid, heuristic role in the development of neuropsychological theory, or where they are essential checks upon the abnormality of small (but theoretically significant) effects. We have also attempted to dispute the implication of some of Caplan's (1988) arguments—namely, that majority effects can "automatically" be employed in the construction of theories of normal cognition. We would, however, agree that it may be important to know in what proportion of subjects/patients a particular effect is found; this knowledge about groups and subgroups could play a substantial role in determining the course of further behavioural inquiry and be pertinent to the (eventual) construction of genetic and epigenetic models of *neuro-psychology*.

Nonetheless, there are groups and groups. To measure the mean performance of a heterogeneous group of patients is one thing; to look for a correlation between two variables over a population of individuals is another; to inquire what proportion of people (or men, or women, or right-handers or left-handers . . .) have crossed-dominance for language is yet another. To revert to our introduction: there's nothing wrong with group studies that cannot be cured by thinking about how and why we employ them. And likewise with single-case studies. If cognitive neuro-psychology is to attain the status of a mature science we must not allow methodological issues to be divorced from the theoretical claims upon which they bear.

Revised manuscript received 3 September 1987

REFERENCES

Albert, M. L., Goodglass, H., Helm, N. A., Rubens, A. B., & Alexander, M. P. (1981). *Clinical aspects of dysphasia*. New York: Springer.

Annett, M. (1985). *Left, right, hand and brain: The right shift theory*. London: Lawrence Erlbaum Associates Ltd.

Baron, J. & Strawson, C. (1976). Use of orthographic and word-specific knowledge in reading words aloud. *Journal of Experimental Psychology: Human Perception and Performance*, 2, 386–393.

Basso, A., Lecours, A. R., Moraschini, S., & Vanier, M. (1985). Anatomoclinical correlations of the aphasias as defined through computerised tomography: Exceptions. *Brain and Language, 26*, 201–229.

Benson, D. F. (1979). *Aphasia, alexia, and agraphia*. New York: Churchill Livingstone.

Bogen, J. E. (1985). The dual brain: Some historical and methodological aspects. In D. F. Benson & E. Zaidel (Eds.), *The dual brain*. New York: The Guilford Press, 27–43.

Bogen, J. E. & Bogen, G. M. (1976). Wernicke's region—where is it? *Annals of the New York Academy of Sciences, 280*, 834–843.

Brain, W. R. (1964). Statement of the problem. In A. V. S. de Reuck & M. O'Connor (Eds.), *Disorders of language*. London: Churchill, 5–13.

Broca, P. (1865). Sur le siège de la faculté du language articulé. *Bulletin de la Société d'Anthropologie, 6*, 337–393.

Campbell, R. & Butterworth, B. (1985). Phonological dyslexia and dysgraphia in a highly literate subject: A developmental case with associated deficits of phonemic processing and awareness. *Quarterly Journal of Experimental Psychology, 37A*, 435–475.

Caplan, D. (1988). On the role of group studies in neuropsychological and pathopsychological research. *Cognitive Neuropsychology, 5*, 535–548.

Caramazza, A. (1984). The logic of neuropsychological research and the problem of patient classification in aphasia. *Brain and Language, 21*, 9–20.

Caramazza, A. (1986). On drawing inferences about the structure of normal cognitive systems from the analysis of patterns of impaired performance: The case for single-patient studies. *Brain and Cognition, 5*, 41–46.

Caramazza, A. & McCloskey, M. (1988). The case for single-patient studies. *Cognitive Neuropsychology*, 5, 517–528.

Code, C. (1987). *Language, aphasia and the right hemisphere*. New York: Wiley.

Fodor, J. A. (1974). Special sciences. *Synthese*, 28, 77–115.

Gazzaniga, M. S. (1983). Right hemisphere language following brain bisection: A 20-year perspective. *American Psychologist*, 38, 525–537.

Gordon, H. W. (1974). Olfaction and cerebral separation. In M. Kinsbourne & W. L. Smith (Eds.), *Hemispheric disconnection and cerebral function*. Springfield, Illinois: C. C. Thomas, 137–154.

Haber, R. N. (1983). The impending demise of the icon: A critique of the concept of iconic storage in visual information processing. *The Behavioural and Brain Sciences*, 6, 1–11.

Holladay, A. J. & Poole, J. C. F. (1979). Thucydides and the plague of Athens. *Classical Quarterly*, 29, 282–300.

Hunter, I. M. L. (1968). Mental calculation. In P. C. Wason & P. N. Johnson-Laird (Eds.), *Thinking and reasoning*. Harmondsworth: Penguin Books Ltd., 341–351.

Lecours, A. R., Basso, A., Moraschini, S., & Nespoulous, J.-L. (1984). Where is the speech area, and who has seen it? In D. Caplan, A. R. Lecours, & A. Smith (Eds.), *Biological perspectives on language*. Cambridge, Mass.: M.I.T. Press, 220–246.

Liepmann, H. (1900). Das Krankheitsbild der Apraxie ("Motorischen Asymbolie"). *Monatsschrift für Psychiatrie und Neurologie*, 8, 15–44, 102–132, 181–197.

Lissauer, H. (1889). Ein Fall von Seelenblindheit nebst einem Beitrag zue Theorie derselben. *Archiv für Psychiatrie*, 21, 222–270.

Marie, P. (1926). *Travaux et memoires*. Paris: Masson.

Marshall, J. C. (1982). What is a symptom-complex? In M. A. Arbib, D. Caplan, & J. C. Marshall (Eds.), *Neural models of language processes*. New York: Academic Press, 389–409.

Marshall, J. C. (1986). The description and interpretation of aphasic language disorder. *Neuropsychologia*, 24, 5–24.

Marshall, J. C. & Newcombe, F. (1966). Syntactic and semantic errors in paralexia. *Neuropsychologia*, 4, 169–176.

Marshall, J. C. & Newcombe, F. (1984). Putative problems and pure progress in neuropsychological single-case studies. *Journal of Clinical Neuropsychology*, 6, 65–70.

Marshall, J. C. & Patterson, K. E. (1985). Left is still left for semantic paralexias: A reply to Jones and Martin (1985). *Neuropsychologia*, 23, 689–690.

Mazzocchi, F. & Vignolo, L. A. (1979). Localisation of lesions in aphasia: Clinical CT-scan correlations in stroke patients. *Cortex*, 15, 627–654.

Milner, B. (1958). Psychological defects produced by temporal lobe excision. *Research Publications of the Association for Research in Nervous and Mental Disease*, 36, 244–257.

Mohr, J. P., Pessin, M. S., Finkelstein, S., Funkenstein, H. H., Duncan, G. W., & Davis, K. R. (1978). Broca aphasia: Pathological and clinical. *Neurology*, 28, 311–324.

Myers, J. J. (1984). Right hemisphere language: Science or fiction? *American Psychologist*, 39, 315–320.

Newcombe, F., Ratcliff, G., & Damasio, H. (1987). Dissociable visual and spatial impairments following right posterior cerebral lesions: Clinical, neuropsychological, and anatomical evidence. *Neuropsychologia*, 25, 149–161.

Paterson, A. & Zangwill, O. L. (1944). Disorders of space perception associated with lesions of the right cerebral hemisphere. *Brain*, 67, 331–358.

Patterson, K. E. & Besner, D. (1984). Is the right hemisphere literate? *Cognitive Neuropsychology*, 1, 315–341.

Patterson, K. E., Marshall, J. C., & Coltheart, M. (Eds.) (1985). *Surface dyslexia: Neuropsychological and cognitive studies of phonological reading*. London: Lawrence Erlbaum Associates Ltd.

Poeck, K. (1983). What do we mean by "aphasic syndromes"? A neurologist's view. *Brain and Language, 20,* 79–89.

Poeck, K., Bleser, R. de, & Keyserlingk, D. G. von (1984). Computed tomographic localisation of standard aphasic syndromes. In F. C. Rose (Ed.), *Progress in aphasiology.* New York: Raven Press, 71–89.

Poppelreuter, W. (1917). *Die psychischen Schädigungen durch Kopfschuss im Kriege 1914–1916.* Leipzig: Voss.

Pylyshyn, Z. W. (1984). *Computation and cognition: Toward a foundation for cognitive science.* Cambridge, Mass.: M.I.T. Press.

Schwartz, M. F. (1984). What the classical aphasia categories can't do for us, and why. *Brain and Language, 21,* 3–8.

Seymour, P. H. K. & MacGregor, C. J. (1984). Developmental dyslexia: A cognitive experimental analysis of phonological, morphemic, and visual impairments. *Cognitive Neuropsychology, 1,* 43–82.

Shallice, T. (1979). Case study approach in neuropsychological research. *Journal of Clinical Neuropsychology, 1,* 183–211.

Stromeyer, C. F. & Psotka, J. (1970). The detailed texture of eidetic images. *Nature, 225,* 346–349.

Strub, R. L. & Geschwind, N. (1983). Localisation in Gerstmann syndrome. In A. Kertesz (Ed.), *Localisation in neuropsychology.* New York: Academic Press, 295–321.

Temple, C. M. & Marshall, J. C. (1983). A case study of developmental phonological dyslexia. *British Journal of Psychology, 74,* 517–533.

Waters, G. & Seidenberg, M. (1985). Spelling-sound effects in reading: Time-course and decision critera. *Memory and Cognition, 13,* 557–572.

Weisenburg, T. H. & McBride, K. E. (1935). *Aphasia: A clinical and psychological study.* New York: Commonwealth Fund.

Wernicke, C. (1874). *Der aphasische Symptomenkomplex.* Breslau: Cohn & Weigart.

Whitty, C. W. M. & Newcombe, F. (1973). R. C. Oldfield's study of visual and topographic disturbances in a right occipito-parietal lesion of 30 years duration. *Neuropsychologia, 11,* 471–475.

Wilson, S. A. K. (1926). *Aphasia.* London: Kegan Paul, Trench, & Trubner.

Zaidel, E. (1985). Language in the right hemisphere. In D. F. Benson & E. Zaidel (Eds.), *The dual brain.* New York: The Guilford Press, 205–231.

Chapter 2   Object Recognition

Farah, M.J. (1991). Patterns of co-occurrence among the associative agnosias: implications for visual object representation. *Cognitive Neuropsychology, 8*, 1–19.

Chapter 2 shows how we can use evidence from impairments of object recognition to develop a model outlining different components involved in this ability. A particularly important distinction is between the *visual* representation of its appearance needed to recognise a familiar object, and *semantic* representations of its functional properties accessible from any input domain (vision, touch, sound).

This type of model is widely used, but demarcating and accounting for category-specific deficits has become an important issue. This applies to both visual and semantic representations.

Chapter 2 does not discuss the issue of category-specific *visual* representations, tending instead to assume that a distinct type of representation will be needed for the task of object recognition as compared to other forms of everyday visual recognition, such as word recognition or face recognition. This assumption is explored in detail in the reading we have chosen (Farah, 1991), which both introduces a particularly neat hypothesis and makes an important methodological point.

Farah (1991) was interested in the question of whether different neural systems might be needed to recognise words, faces, and everyday objects. To this end, she reviewed the literature on neuropsychological impairments of face, word, and object recognition, examining the different patterns of deficit that have been reported. This literature search showed that whereas people with brain injuries have been found to lose the ability to recognise words yet remain able to recognise objects and faces, or to lose the ability to recognise faces while remaining able to recognise objects and words, there were at the time no convincing cases in which object recognition was compromised without impairment of either face recognition or word recognition.

As Farah (1991) pointed out, this suggests that, rather than there being three separate recognition systems for objects, words and, faces, the brain may make use of two underlying systems; one that is particularly appropriate for words but is also needed for some objects, and one that is particularly appropriate for faces but is also needed for some objects, as shown in Fig. 2.9. A plausible account would be that one system might be needed to represent stimuli (such as faces) that are not readily identifiable from their constituent parts (most eyes, noses, mouths are hard to recognise as isolated fragments) and hence are usually treated holistically, while another system represents stimuli that are readily decomposable into simpler nameable parts used to identify them (e.g. words into letters). A mild impairment of the whole-based encoding system could then lead to impaired face recognition only, as faces are the stimuli that

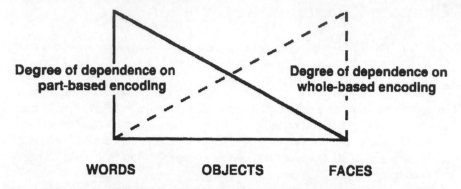

FIG. 2.9. Farah's (1991) hypothesis that the brain uses two structural encoding systems. Part-based encoding is particularly appropriate for words but is also needed for some objects. Whole-based encoding is particularly appropriate for faces but is also needed for some objects.

place the greatest demands on this form of recognition, but more severe impairments would begin to compromise recognition of at least some objects. Similarly, mild impairment of the part-based encoding system would initially affect word recognition only, and then increasingly severe impairments would start to involve objects.

The methodological moral is that it is unwise to base claims of three distinct forms of representation (in this case, for words, objects, and faces) on the existence of pairwise dissociations; instead, all three putative abilities need to be investigated simultaneously. This point is, we believe, entirely correct, and it has implications for many areas of the discipline.

The fate of Farah's (1991) specific hypothesis of two representational systems is at present looking less sanguine. Although attractive and ingenious, her view clearly predicts that certain patterns of deficit should never occur; the main prediction is that impaired recognition of objects with intact recognition of both words and faces cannot happen. Its ability to be falsified if cases like this were to come to light is, of course, part of what makes this such a good scientific hypothesis. Unfortunately for Farah's (1991) hypothesis, though, at least one such case has recently been described, and investigated in detail (Rumiati, Humphreys, Riddoch, & Bateman, 1994). We must therefore be cautious about its long-term survival. The less parsimonious account that the brain creates separate representations of objects, words, and faces may well prove to be correct.

There are in any case other phenomena that show that the whole- versus part-based encoding hypothesis cannot be more than itself a part of the overall picture. Bruce and Humphreys (1994) point out the importance of the properties the visual system is able to exploit to achieve recognition of different types of stimuli. A good deal of work suggests that identification of objects at a basic level depends on edge-coding, whereas face recognition depends more on the representation of surface properties, such as texture and shading. However, when the demands of object recognition are made more similar to those of face recognition, then there appear to be some similarities in the perceptual representations used for objects and faces.

Another example of the possible limitations of Farah's account can be taken from studies of face perception, where it has been known for some time that brain injury may compromise different aspects of face processing (see Chapter 4). Observations of dissociable impairments affecting different aspects of face processing suggest that the brain analyses some of the different social signals we can get from the face independently from each other. In particular, the literature suggests that recognition of emotion and recognition of identity are carried out independently (Young, Newcombe, de Haan, Small, & Hay, 1993).

The importance of this claim lies in the fact that these different social signals (identity, expression, etc.) can be read from a common physical stimulus (the face). As far as we know, some degree of whole-based encoding is needed both for recognition of a face's identity and for recognition of its expression, yet deficits affecting these abilities can dissociate from each other. This implies that Farah's (1991) emphasis on physical properties of the visual stimulus is incomplete, and we need to give at least as much importance to the social purposes for which different types of information are used.

Turning to the issue of category-specific *semantic* representations, Chapter 2 introduces evidence pointing toward differences between impairments affecting the semantic representations of living and non-living things. We followed Warrington and Shallice (1984) in suggesting that this might reflect different organisation of semantic systems for things that have significance in terms of the way we use them (many non-living things such as tools, or household objects) and things that we know primarily through vision (many living things including birds, insects, flowers, and plants). Farah and McClelland (1991) have shown how a simple version of such a scheme can be implemented as a computer simulation that can mimic observed patterns of category-specific deficit when damaged.

However, recent reports have shown that apparent category-specific deficits affecting living things can disappear when care is taken to control item familiarity (Funnell & Sheridan, 1992) or the combined effects of word frequency, concept familiarity, and visual complexity (Stewart, Parkin, & Hunkin, 1992). This raises the possibility that such findings are artifactual, i.e. unintended consequences of not controlling such factors. These demonstrations show that, as in all areas of cognitive neuropsychology, great care needs to be taken to rule out possible alternative interpretations of one's findings. Importantly, though, studies that do control thoroughly for these factors have still found category-specific deficits for living things in other cases (Farah, Meyer, & McMullen, 1996; Young, Newcombe, Hellawell, & de Haan, 1989), showing that this type of artifact is unlikely to provide a universally convincing account.

REFERENCES

Bruce, V. & Humphreys, G.W. (1994). Recognizing objects and faces. *Visual Cognition, 1*, 141–180.

Farah, M.J. (1991). Patterns of co-occurrence among the associative agnosias: implications for visual object representation. *Cognitive Neuropsychology, 8*, 1–19.

Farah, M.J. & McClelland, J.L. (1991). A computational model of semantic memory impairment: modality specificity and emergent category specificity. *Journal of Experimental Psychology: General, 120*, 339–357.

Farah, M.J., Meyer, M.M., & McMullen, P.A. (1996). The living/nonliving dissociation is not an artifact: giving an a priori implausible hypothesis a strong test. *Cognitive Neuropsychology, 13*, 137–154.

Funnell, E. & Sheridan, J. (1992). Categories of knowledge? Unfamiliar aspects of living and nonliving things. *Cognitive Neuropsychology, 9*, 135–153.

Rumiati, R.I., Humphreys, G.W., Riddoch, M.J., & Bateman, A. (1994). Visual object agnosia without prosopagnosia or alexia: evidence for hierarchical theories of visual recognition. *Visual Cognition, 1*, 181–225.

Stewart, F., Parkin, A.J., & Hunkin, N.M. (1992). Naming impairments following recovery from herpes simplex encephalitis: category-specific? *Quarterly Journal of Experimental Psychology, 44A*, 261–284.

Warrington, E.K. & Shallice, T. (1984). Category specific semantic impairments. *Brain, 107*, 829–854.

Young, A.W., Newcombe, F., de Haan, E.H.F., Small, M., & Hay, D.C. (1993). Face perception after brain injury: selective impairments affecting identity and expression. *Brain, 116*, 941–959.

Young, A.W., Newcombe, F., Hellawell, D., & de Haan, E.H.F. (1989). Implicit access to semantic information. *Brain and Cognition, 11*, 186–209.

Patterns of Co-occurrence Among the Associative Agnosias: Implications for Visual Object Representation

Martha J. Farah

Carnegie-Mellon University, Pittsburgh, U.S.A.

The patterns of co-occurrence among associative agnosia for faces, words and other objects are analysed and found to be consistent with the existence of two, rather than three, underlying visual recognition capacities. Different degrees and combinations of damage to these two capacities can account for the five different combinations of word, face, and object agnosia that are found, as well as for the apparent absence of two particular combinations. A tentative interpretation of the two inferred visual recognition capacities is offered, in terms of the idea of structural representations.

INTRODUCTION

"Visual agnosia" is an impairment in the recognition of visual stimuli, despite intact elementary perceptual abilities such as acuity and brightness discrimination. Following Lissauer (1988/1890), two main types of agnosia have been distinguished: "apperceptive agnosia", in which the recognition difficulty is caused by faulty perception (at levels of perceptual processing beyond those elementary sensory processes just mentioned), and "associative agnosia", in which perception seems virtually normal, and the recognition difficulty is therefore thought to originate in the process of "associating" a normal percept with its meaning.

Associative agnosia is itself a heterogeneous category, within which some subdivision seems necessary (Farah, 1990; Humphreys & Riddoch, 1987). For example, cases of generalised loss of semantic knowledge, not

---

This research was supported by O.N.R. contract N0014-89-J3016, N.I.H. grant NS23458, and N.I.H. R.C.D.A. K04NS10405. I would like to thank Tim Shallice, Andy Young, and an anonymous reviewer for their insightful comments and criticisms of an earlier version of this paper.

confined to the visual modality, have been labelled associative agnosics, as have cases of visual modality-specific anomia (also called "optic aphasia"). For purposes of the present analysis, the relevant sense of "associative agnosia" will be those cases of visual modality-specific recognition impairment in which perception seems roughly normal. In this respect, the classical criteria for diagnosing associative agnosia will be used. However, although I will use the same *extension* of the term "associative agnosia" as most other writers (i.e. those cases of agnosia in which perception seems roughly normal), I will diverge from them in suggesting that a subtle perceptual impairment underlies the object recognition difficulties. Although associative agnosics are able to describe the appearance of the objects they cannot recognise and copy drawings of them, consistent with the criterion of intact perception, recent investigations of such patients have revealed subtle perceptual impairments not apparent in describing objects or copying drawings (e.g. Levine & Calvanio, 1989; Ratcliff & Newcombe, 1982; Riddoch & Humphreys, 1987), which seem to reflect an inability to see the whole of an object simultaneously. In retrospect, even the good descriptions and copies produced by associative agnosics are probably accomplished using abnormal strategies to compensate for this perceptual impairment: these strategies are typically characterised as "slavish" and "piecemeal". Therefore, the line between associative and apperceptive agnosia is less clear than was once thought, and probably reflects a difference in the *level* of perceptual processing that has been impaired, rather than the presence versus absence of perceptual impairments. In the present article, it will be assumed that an impairment in the high-level (i.e. relatively late, abstract) perceptual representation of shape underlies associative agnosia (see Farah, 1990; Chapter 5, for supporting arguments). This assumption is declared at the outset mainly for the sake of terminological simplicity, so that the questions and conclusions of the article can be phrased in terms of the perceptual representations underlying object recognition. However, the analysis to be presented here does not depend upon this assumption. If one prefers the hypothesis that a loss of stored visual memories underlies associative agnosia, and that the perceptual impairments are coincidental and not causal of the recognition impairment, then the questions and conclusions can be re-phrased in terms of the organisation of stored visual memories.

The scope of associative agnosia varies somewhat from case to case, affecting the recognition of different types of stimuli to different degrees. The goal of this article is to use this variability as a source of information about the types of high-level perceptual representations that normally underlie visual recognition. By studying the patterns of association and dissociation among different forms of associative agnosia, we can make inferences about the organisation of normal visual object representation.

Within certain boundary conditions (see Shallice, 1988; Chapter 10), a dissociation between the recognition of two categories of visual stimulus implies that they rely on different underlying representational capacities. A reliable association between abilities is consistent with the hypotheses that they rely in common capacities, although it is also consistent with neuroanatomic proximity of functionally distinct processes such that lesions affecting one process will affect the other.

DISSOCIATIONS AMONG FACE, OBJECT, AND WORD RECOGNITION

One well-known dissociation within the associative agnosias is between face recognition and the recognition of other kinds of visual stimuli. In prosopagnosia, the recognition of faces appears to be disproportionately impaired, relative to the recognition of other types of stimuli.[1] There are cases of prosopagnosia in which the recognition of other objects is only mildly, if at all, affected. Perhaps the best example of this is the patient described by DeRenzi (1986b). His Case 4 (1986b, p. 246) was sufficiently prosopagnosic that "the identification of relatives and close friends constituted an insurmountable problem if he could not rely upon their voices". Nevertheless, he was able (1986b, p. 249) to distinguish among subtly different objects: "He was requested to identify his own electric razor, wallet, glasses, and neckties, when each of them was presented together with 6 to 10 objects of the same category, chosen so as to have physical resemblance with the target. He was also asked to write a sentence on a cardboard, and then to identify his own handwriting from nine samples of the same sentence written by other persons. Finally, he was required to identify the photograph of a Siamese cat from photographs of other cats, and to sort out 20 Italian coins from 20 foreign coins. On all of these tasks he performed unhesitatingly and correctly. It must be added that on inquiry both the patient and his wife had denied that he had ever shown any problem in the identification of personal objects. He easily recognised his car in parking lots". Although other tests, including tachistoscopic stimulus presentations, might have shown *some* impairment in the recogni-

---

[1]A similar dissociation may exist among the apperceptive agnosias, corresponding to "apperceptive prosopagnosia", in which perception of faces is grossly abnormal, despite relative preservation of the perception of other types of stimuli. Such cases cannot reliably match or describe faces, even by a slow and slavish strategy, and often report that faces appear distorted. It is difficult to determine whether this impairment differs only in degree, or in kind, from that of associative prosopagnosics. However, for purposes of the present analysis, I will follow others in assuming that the apperceptive and associative forms of prosopagnosia differ in kind (presumably in the level of visual representation affected), and confine the analysis to the associative form of the disorder.

tion of nonface objects, De Renzi's data provide at least a lower bound on how selective face recognition impairments can be, and they do demonstrate an impressively large degree of selectivity.

There are also cases in which the recognition of certain objects other than faces is obviously disturbed. Animals comprise one such class of objects. For example, Shuttleworth, Syring, and Allen's (1982) Case 2 was able to recognise only 2 out of 12 colour photographs of common animals, making flagrant errors such as calling geese "fish" because of the surrounding water. The patients studied by Boudouresques, Poncet, Cherif, and Balzamo (1979), Damasio, Damasio, and Van Hoesen (1982), Gomori and Hawryluk (1984), Lhermitte, Chain, Escourelle, Ducarne, and Pillon (1972), Lhermitte and Pillon (1975), and Pallis (1955) all showed similar problems of varying degree in recognising the species depicted in animal pictures. Prosopagnosics have also been noted to have specific problems recognising plants (Boudouresques et al., 1979; Gomori & Hawryluk, 1984; Whiteley & Warrington, 1977, Case 1) and even man-made stimuli such as buildings and public monuments (Assal, Favre, & Anderes, 1984; Bornstein & Kidron, 1959; Boudouresques et al., 1979; Gomori & Hawryluk, 1984; Lhermitte et al., 1972; Lhermitte & Pillon, 1975; Pallis, 1964; Shuttleworth et al., Case 2), makes of automobile (Boudouresques et al., 1979; Damasio et al., 1982; Gomori & Hawryluk, 1984; Lhermitte et al., 1972; Lhermitte & Pillon, 1975; Newcombe, 1979; Shuttleworth et al., 1982, Case 2) and articles of clothing (Damasio et al., 1982; Shuttleworth et al., 1982, Case 2). Food is another category of stimuli with which prosopagnosics may experience difficulty. Damasio et al. (1982, p. 338) say of their Case 1 that she "would confuse foodstuffs and required help in her cooking. To select articles from the shelves in the supermarket, she had to read every label, whereas before the mere shape and size of containers would permit the correct choice". Despite these impairments, the preserved ability of prosopagnosics to recognise a variety of other objects makes it inappropriate to categorise them as across-the-board associative object agnosics. The latter type of patient is profoundly impaired at recognising all types of visual stimuli, including common objects and printed words, as well as faces.

There are also patients who are more impaired at recognising a variety of different objects than they are at recognising faces (e.g. Feinberg, Gonzalez-Rothi, & Heilman, 1986; McCarthy & Warrington, 1986). For example, McCarthy and Warrington's patient failed to recognise any of the objects in the Graded Difficulty Naming test or the Oldfield Pictures test, and reported difficulties in everyday life suggestive of object recognition impairment. Nevertheless, he performed at a level characterised as "satisfactory" by the authors on a test of famous faces recognition. Thus, we cannot account for the dissociability of face recognition from the recognition of other objects in prosopagnosia by hypothesising that they require the same underlying mechanisms but that face recognition merely taxes these mechanisms more heavily. There is a double dissociation between face and object recognition, and this implies that they rely on a least partially distinct capacities.

A second double dissociation had been observed between the recognition of printed words and other visual stimuli. The relevant form of reading impairment is, of course, "pure alexia", in which all other forms of language-related processing (including spoken language comprehension and written language production) are preserved. Thus, in contrast to the majority of reading impairments studied by cognitive neuropsychologists, pure alexia appears to result from damage to some aspect of visual pattern recognition, and not to language processed per se. Accordingly, it is sometimes called "agnosic alexia".[2] Most patients with pure alexia are not agnosic for objects other then printed words. In addition, there are a number of associative agnosic patients who are not alexic (e.g. Albert, Reches, & Silverberg, 1975; Bauer, 1982; Gomori & Hawryluk, 1984; Ratcliff & Newcombe, 1982). For example, the case described by Gomori and Hawryluk (1984) was impaired at recognising a variety of common objects as well as the faces of his family and friends. In contrast, he was able to read easily, even when interfering lines had been drawn across the printed words.

The dissociability of both face and written word recognition from object recognition would seem to imply that there are three corresponding types of visual recognition ability, needed for recognising faces, common objects, and words. However, this predicts that all combinations of word, face, and object recognition impairments should occur. If there are certain combinations that do not occur, then this suggests that the relation between underlying visual capacities on the one hand and manifest recognition impairments on the other may be more complex than a simple one-to-one mapping. In fact, the patterns of association and dissociation among impairments of face, object, and word recognition suggest that the

---

[2]In the present analysis, I am considering pure alexia to be an associative rather than an apperceptive agnosia. Consistent with the perceptual abilities of associative agnosics described earlier, pure alexics generally perform well on perceptual tests such as matching, but only by adopting a slow, piecemeal strategy (e.g. Levine & Calvanio, 1978). There are several reports of perceptual impairment when appropriate visual tests are administered (e.g. Farah & Wallace, in press; Friedman & Alexander, 1984; Kinsbourne & Warrington, 1962; Levine & Calvanio, 1978), although, as with other types of associative agnosia, these are not normally apparent to clinical observation. It should also be mentioned that the syndrome of pure alexia could conceivably result from a variety of different underlying impairments, some of a visual-agnostic nature and others affecting memory representations or access to memory representations.

underlying visual capacities have a two-part, rather than a three-part, structure, and that different degrees and combinations of the two basic capacities underlie the range of associative agnosic phenomena.

Before presenting the patterns of association and dissociation that support the two-part organisation, I will sketch out an hypothesis about visual object recognition according to which there are two types of visual representational capacity. This hypothesis is speculative. Nevertheless, having a specific interpretation for the two kinds of visual capacity will facilitate discussion of the data, and for this reason the hypothesis will be presented first.

A TENTATIVE HYPOTHESIS: STRUCTURAL DESCRIPTIONS AND ASSOCIATIVE AGNOSIA

Most cognitive psychologists and computer scientists studying vision favour some form or other of "structural description" for the representations of shape underlying object recognition (Pinker, 1985). A structural description is a very general term referring to visual representations of shape that are composed of parts and the spatial relations among the parts. The parts may be relatively simple or complex enough to be considered objects in their own right. Even without knowing what kinds of parts the visual system uses in decomposing shapes, it is probably correct to assume that some objects will be decomposed into more parts, and hence more elementary parts, than others. Some objects may not be decomposed at all, but recognised as a single unit, all of a piece.

If we assume that our ability to know whether a single part has come from a particular object is roughly indicative of whether that part is explicitly represented in our structural description of the object, then we can hazard some guesses about which objects are recognised via decomposition into simpler parts and which are recognised with little or no decomposition. Face recognition seems to be a likely candidate for the latter type of process. We are not apt to know whether an isolated facial feature came from a particular face or not: we could know Jim's face very well but not be able to say whether or not a fragment of a photograph showing only the nose was from a photograph of Jim. The fact that most face-selective cells in the primate visual system respond to whole faces, and do not respond to individual components presented in isolation nor to the full set of features presented in an altered spatial arrangement (e.g. Desimone, Albright, Gross, & Bruce, 1984), is also supportive of the idea that faces are recognised "all of a piece" rather than by decomposition into simpler parts. This is not inconsistent with the fact that we can direct our attention to the "parts" of a face such as the nose or eyes, and recognise them as such. The claim being made here is that such parts are not automatically represented, as parts, in the representations normally used by our visual system in recognising faces.

Other types of stimuli, such as animals, share this property with faces, although to lesser extent. For example it is difficult to know whether an ear or a tail viewed in isolation came from a particular animal; a cat's ear looks much like a horse's ear. In contrast, we can often make accurate guesses about the sources of other relatively simple object parts: a key from a typewriter keyboard, a doorknob, the sharpened end of a pencil lead. This is consistent with the idea that our representations of these objects include these parts, explicitly represented as parts. Printed words are the clearest case of objects that are decomposed into simpler part units: there is no doubt whether the letter "c" does or doesn't come from the word "cat".

Among the many abilities that we must possess if we do indeed represent objects using structural descriptions are the following: first, the ability to represent the parts themselves, including quite complex parts for objects that undergo little or no shape decomposition. (For an object such as a face, which by hypothesis undergoes little or no decomposition, the "part" may be the whole object.) Second, the ability to represent multiple parts, especially for objects that undergo decomposition into many parts. The conjecture being offered here that impairments in these two abilities underlie the range of associative agnosic phenomena. In other words, associative agnosia can be understood in terms of difficulty representing complex parts or difficulty representing numerous parts, or some combination of the two.

According to this account, if the representation of parts is only mildly impaired then most objects will be recognised, and only those objects that undergo little or no decomposition into parts, and whose parts are therefore relatively complex, will be affected. This corresponds to prosopagnosia. If the representation of parts is more severely impaired, then the recognition deficit will extend to more objects, and only objects with the simplest parts will be recognised. This corresponds to object agnosia with prosopagnosia but without alexia. If the ability to represent parts is intact, but the ability to represent multiple parts is impaired, then most objects will be recognised. The only objects that will be affected will be those that undergo decomposition into many parts, and for which multiple parts must be represented before recognition can occur. This corresponds to alexia, and is consistent with the letter-by-letter reading strategy adopted by many of these patients, in which only one letter at a time is recognised. If the impairment in this ability is severe enough such that even a moderate number of parts cannot be represented rapidly and accurately, then the recognition of objects other than words will be affected as well. However, even in this case faces should not be affected, as they do not require the representation of multiple separate parts. This corresponds to agnosia with alexia but without prosopagnosia. If both abilities are impaired, then the recognition of all objects will be affected. This corresponds to "across-the-board" agnosia, that is, object agnosia with alexia and prosopagnosia.

TWO CAPACITIES UNDERLYING VISUAL OBJECT RECOGNITION?

How can this hypothesis, that two main types of representational capacity underlie the range of associative agnosias, be tested? The hypothesis makes two predictions which would enable it to be falsified. It would be falsified by a case of object agnosia without either prosopagnosia or alexia. It would also be falsified by a case of prosopagnosia and alexia that does not have *some* degree of object agnosia.[3] Table 1 shows a set of 99 case reports that were used to test these predictions. The table is comprised of all adult cases of associative visual agnosia reported in English or French since 1966 listed in the "Medline" periodical database, along with assorted cases from earlier articles and from book chapters.[4] Most of these cases include information about recognition of real or depicted faces, objects, and printed words, and this information is also listed in Table 1, along with a brief description of lesion localisation. Cases of pure alexia without any other agnosic features are too numerous to list, and are not relevant to testing the hypothesis as they do not have the potential to falsify it.

Table 2 shows the distribution of cases among the seven possible patterns of agnosia discussed earlier, along with an eighth category for cases with incomplete information. The different possible patterns do not occur with equal frequency. In particular, the two patterns that cannot be accommodated within the present two-capacity account occur only once each, and in each of these cases there is some inconsistency in the way these cases are described such that one description conforms to a predicted

---

[3]This prediction is weaker than the first one, in that it requires some assumptions about the relative severity of the different impairments. Very mild impairments in each of two kinds of representational capacity could conceivably lead to mild prosopagnosia and alexia with no easily detectable impairment in object recognition. I would like to thank an anonymous reviewer for pointing this out.

[4]Some cases published as cases of associative agnosia seem, in fact, to be cases of optic aphasia, by some or all of the following criteria (see Farah, 1990): their recognition of stimuli when tested nonverbally was significantly better than when tested verbally, their ability to recognise a stimulus was relatively insensitive to the visual quality of the stimulus, and their misidentifications tended to be either semantically related to the correct response or perseverations of previous responses, rather than visual confusions. These cases, which are not included in Table 1, are: Ferro & Santos (1984), Morin, Rivrain, Eustache, Lambert, & Courtheoux (1984), Mouren, Tatossian, Trupheme, Guidicelli, & Fresco (1967), and Rouzaud, Dumas, Degiovanni, Larmande, Ployet, & Laffont (1978). However, even if these cases were included they would not change the conclusions to be reported.

TABLE 1

Case	Lesion Localisation	Faces	Objects	Words
Aimard et al. (1981) #4	R temp.	×		?
Albert et al. (1979)	Bilat. temp.-occ.	×	×	
Aptman et al. (1977)[a]	Bilat. occip.	×	×	×
Assal (1969)	R par.-occ.	×		
Assal et al. (1984)	Bilat. temp.-occ.	×		
Bauer (1982) (also Bauer & Trobe, 1984; Bauer, 1984)	Bilat. temp.-occ.	×	×	
Bauer & Verfaellie (1988)	Bilat. temp.-occ.	×	×	×
Benke (1988)	L par.-occ.	×	×	×
Benton & Van Allen (1972)	?	×	?	
Beyn & Knyazeva (1962)	Bilat. occ.	×	×	?
Bornstein & Kidron (1959)[b]	R par.-occ.	×		
Bornstein et al. (1969)	R posterior	×	?	
Boudouresques et al. (1972)	L occip.	?	×	×
Boudouresques et al. (1979)	R temp.-par.	×	×	
Bruyer et al. (1983)	Bilat. occip.	×		
Cambier et al. (1980)	Bilat. temp.-occ.	×	×	×
Cohn et al. (1974) (also Cohn et al., 1977)	Bilat. temp.-occ.	×		
Cole & Perez-Cruet (1964)	?	×	×	
Damasio et al. (1982) #1	Bilat. temp.-occ.	×	×	
Damasio et al. (1982) #2	Bilat. temp.-occ.	×	×	×
Damasio et al. (1982) #3[c]	Bilat. temp.-occ.	×		×
Davidoff & Wilson (1985)	?	×	×	×
De Haan et al. (1987) (also Young & De Haan, 1988)	?	×	×	
DeRenzi (1986b) #1	R temp.-occ.	×	?	?
DeRenzi (1986b) #2	R temp.-occ.	×	?	?
Duara et al. (1975)	Bilat. occip.	×	×	
Dumont et al. (1981)[d,e]	L temp.-occ.; R par.-occ.		×	×
Feinberg et al. (1986)	L temp.-occ.		×	×
Gallois et al. (1988)[f]	L occip.		×	×
Gloning et al. (1970)	Bilat. temp.-occ.	×		
Gloning et al. (1970), App.	?	×	×	×
Glowic & Violon (1981)	Bilat. temp.-occ.	×		
Gomori & Hawryluk (1984)	Bilat. temp.-occ.	×	×	
Guard et al. (1981)[g]	L temp.-occ.; R temp.	×	×	×
Hécaen & Ajuriaguerra (1956)[h]	L occip.		×	×
Hécaen et al. (1974)	L occip.		×	×
Karpov et al. (1979) #1	Bilat. occip.	×	×	×
Karpov et al. (1979) #2	R occip.	×	×	×
Karpov et al. (1979) #3	L occip.		×	×
Karpov et al. (1979) #4	L occip.		×	×
Karpov et al. (1979) #5[i]	Bilat. occip.		×	
Kawahata & Nagata (1989)	Bilat. temp.-occ.	×	×	×

(Continued)

TABLE 1
(Continued)

Case	Lesion Localisation	Faces	Objects	Words
Kay & Levin (1982) #1	Bilat. temp.-occ.; R par.	×		
Kay & Levin (1982) #2	Bilat. occip.	×		
Kay & Levin (1982) #3	R posterior	×		?
Kumar et al. (1986) #1	R temp.-occ.	×		
Kumar et al. (1986) #2	R temp.-occ.	×		?
Landis et al. (1986) #1	R temp.-occ.	×		
Landis et al. (1986) #2	R temp.-occ.	×	?	
Landis et al. (1986) #3	R temp.-occ.	×	?	?
Landis et al. (1986) #4	R par.-occ.	×	?	
Landis et al. (1986) #5	R par.-temp.-occ.	×	?	
Landis et al. (1986) #6	R par.-occ.	×		?
Landis et al. (1988)	L par.-occ.; R temp.-occ; R frontal	×	×	
Larrabee et al. (1985) #1[j]	L occip.; R frontal		×	×
Levine (1978)	R occip.	×	×	
Levine & Calvanio (1989)	Bilat. temp.-occ.; R front.	×	×	
Levin & Peters (1976)	?	×	?	
Lhermitte et al. (1969) #1	L temp.-occ.; R temp.	×	×	×
Lhermitte et al. (1972)	L temp.; R temp.-occ	×	×	×
Lhermitte et al. (1973)[k]	L posterior	×	×	×
Lhermitte & Pillon (1975)	R temp.-occ.	×		
Mack & Boller (1977)	L par.-occ.; R occ.	×	×	
Macrae & Trolle (1956)	Bilat.	×	×	×
Malone et al. (1982) #2	Bilat. par.-occ.	×		
Marks & De Vito (1987) #1	Bilat. temp.-occ.	×	×	×
Marks & De Vito (1987) #2[l]	R temp.-par.-occ.		×	×
Marx et al. (1970)	Bilat. posterior	×		
McCarthy & Warrington (1986)	L temp.-occ.		×	×
Mendez (1988) #1	?		×	×
Mendez (1988) #2	Bilat. occip.		×	×
Michel et al. (1986)	R temp.-occ.	×		
Nardelli et al. (1982) #1	Bilat. temp.-occ.	×		
Nardelli et al. (1982) #2	Bilat. temp.-occ.	×	×	?
Nardelli et al. (1982) #3	Bilat. temp.-occ.	×		
Nardelli et al. (1982) #4	Bilat. occ.	×		
Newcombe & Ratcliff (1974) #1	?	×	×	
Newcombe & Ratcliff (1974) #2 (also Ratcliff & Newcombe, 1982)	Bilat. par.-temp.-occ.	×	×	
Noel & Meyers (1971) #1	Bilat. par.-occ.		×	×
Noel & Meyers (1971) #2	L posterior		×	×
Orgogozo et al. (1972) #2	L occip.		×	×
Pallis (1955)	Bilat. occip.	×		
Pillon et al. (1981)[m]	L temp.-par.-occ.		×	×
Raizada & Raizada (1972)	?	?	×	?

(Continued)

TABLE 1
(Continued)

Case	Lesion Localisation	Faces	Objects	Words
Renault et al. (1989)	R temp.-occ.	×		?
Riddoch & Humphreys (1987) (also Humphreys & Riddoch, 1987a)	Bilat. temp.-occ.	×	×	×
Rondot et al. (1967)	Bilat. temp.-occ.	×		
Rubens & Benson (1971) (also Benson et al., 1974)	Bilat. temp.-occ.	×	×	×
Shuttleworth et al. (1982) #1	Bilat. temp.-occ.	×	×	×
Shuttleworth et al. (1982) #2	R temp.-occ.; L post.	×	×	×
Striano et al. (1981)	Bilat. temp.-par.-occ.	×	×	
Taylor & Warrington (1971)	?	×	×	×
Tranel & Damasio (1988) #1 (also Tranel et al., 1988)	Bilat. temp.-occ.	×		
Tranel & Damasio (1988) #2 (also Tranel et al., 1988)	Bilat. occip.	×		
Tranel & Damasio (1988) #3 (also Tranel et al., 1988)	L temp.; R temp. occ.	×		
Tzavaras et al. (1973)[n]	L temp.	×		
Whiteley & Warrington (1977) #1	Bilat. occip.	×		
Whiteley & Warrington (1977) #2	R occip.	×		
Whiteley & Warrington (1977) #3	R occip.	×		

Cases of Associative Agnosia, Showing Lesion Localisation and Profile of Recognition Abilities. The Ability to Recognise Real or Depicted Faces and Objects, and Printed Words, is Indicated by an "x" (Impaired), a "?" (Unknown) or a Blank (Intact).

[a] Patient was left-handed.
[b] Possibility of bilateral damage noted.
[c] Patient was termed prosopagnosic and alexic, but authors note recognition difficulties with cars and articles of clothing.
[d] Right parietal-occipital lesion old and asymptomatic.
[e] Report mentions "prosopagnosia", but face recognition problems are exclusively anterograde and secondary to amnesia.
[f] Patient was described as agnosic for objects and anomic for faces (i.e. not prosopagnosic).
[g] Some signs of optic aphasia superimposed on associative agnosia.
[h] Some signs of optic aphasia superimposed on associative agnosia.
[i] The two references to this case in the text of the article refer to him as nonagnosic; however, the table of cases lists a "slight object agnosia" among his neurological characteristics.
[j] Three months postonset, when she was classified as "associative".
[k] Authors remark that face recognition least affected.
[l] Patient was ambidextrous.
[m] Some signs of optic aphasia superimposed on associative agnosia.
[n] Patient was left-handed.

381

TABLE 2

Possible Patterns of Agnosia, their Interpretation in Terms of the Two Kinds of Pattern Recognition Ability Postulated here, and the Number of Cases Conforming to Each Pattern.

Pattern of Agnosia	Interpretation	No. of Cases
Prosopagnosia without object agnosia or alexia	Mild-moderate impairment in representation of complex parts	27
Prosopagnosia and object agnosia without alexia	Severe impairment in representation of complex parts	15
Alexia without object agnosia or prosopagnosia	Mild-moderate impairment in representation of numerous parts	not included in search
Object agnosia and alexia without prosopagnosia	Severe impairment in representation of numerous parts	16
Prosopagnosia, object agnosia alexia	Impairment in representation of complex parts and numerous parts	22
Object agnosia without prosopagnosia or alexia	No interpretation possible	1?
Prosopagnosia and alexia without object agnosia	No interpretation possible[a]	1?
Missing information about recognition for one or more of the categories face, object, and word		17

[a]See footnote 3 regarding limitations on this assumption.

pattern and the other violates it. Case 5 of Karpov, Meerson, and Tonko-nough (1979) is described in their table of cases as having a "slight object agnosia" with no prosopagnosia or alexia. However, this case was also referred to twice in the text of the article as nonagnosic. Case 3 of Damasio et al. (1982) was described by the authors as prosopagnosic and alexic, with no other neuropsychological impairments. However, Case 3 is also described as handicapped in everyday life by his inability to recognise items such as clothing and cars, suggesting that there was some degree of object agnosia. Of the remaining 97 cases, none fails to conform to one of the 5 predicted patterns. In 9 of the 17 cases with missing information, the potential exists to disconfirm the present account. For example, the brief report of Raizada and Raizada (1972) mentions object agnosia but gives no information about the patient's reading and face recognition abilities. If it were the case that both of these were intact, then the present account would be disconfirmed.

The neuropathology in these cases is also at least weakly supportive of the division being proposed here. Prosopagnosia generally follows bilateral lesions, although some nonautopsied cases appear to have unilateral right hemisphere lesions. Given that agnosia without alexia is interpreted as a more severe case of the same impairment that underlies prosopagnosia, then patients with agnosia without alexia should have either bilateral or unilateral right lesions. Of the 15 cases reviewed here, 3 lacked localising information, 2 had unilateral right hemisphere lesions affecting the visual areas of the brain, and 10 had bilateral lesions affecting the visual areas of the brain, mostly affecting the temporo-occipital regions. Two additional cases may be relevant as there were reported to be face and object recognition problems and no mention of reading problems. One patient had bilateral temporo-occipital lesions (Nardelli et al., 1982; Case 2) and one had bilateral occipital lesions (Beyn & Knyazeva, 1962).

Given that pure alexia follows left posterior lesions, and that agnosia without prosopagnosia is interpreted as a more severe case of the same impairment that underlies pure alexia, it is then to be expected that cases of object agnosia without prosopagnosia would have left hemisphere lesions. Of the 16 cases reviewed here, one lacked localising information, 10 had unilateral left hemisphere lesions affecting the visual areas of the brain (occipital lobe and neighbouring parts of the temporal and parietal lobe), one had a unilateral right temporo-occipital lesion, and 4 had bilateral lesions. The case of unilateral right hemisphere damage was ambidextrous and had a left-handed brother (Marks & De Vito, 1987; Case 2). One of the bilateral cases involved an old, asymptomatic right hemisphere lesion in the parieto-occipital area (Dumont, Griggio, Dupont, & Jacquy, 1981). In another bilateral case (Larrabee et al., 1985) the right hemisphere lesion was in the frontal lobe, and hence unlikely to be related to the patient's visual recognition difficulties. A seventeenth case may also be relevant, as there were reading and object recognition difficulties but no mention of face recognition difficulties (Boudouresques, Poncet, Sebahoun, & Alicherif, 1972). The patient had a left occipital lesion.

Finally, given the lesion sites associated with prosopagnosia and alexia, cases of across-the-board agnosia would be expected to have bilateral damage. Of the 22 cases of impaired face, object, and word recognition, 3 lacked localising information, 16 had bilateral lesions affecting the visual areas of the brain (mostly temporo-occipital), one had a unilateral right posterior lesion, and 2 had unilateral left posterior lesions.

CONCLUSIONS

The patterns of co-occurrence among associative object agnosia, prosopagnosia, and pure alexia can put constraints on the organisation of visual object recognition. Although disorders of object, face, and word recognition are all pair-wise dissociable, consistent with three underlying representational capacities, the occurrence of only certain three-way combinations and not others suggests that two kinds of representational capacity underlie recognition of these three kinds of stimuli.

What might these representational capacities be? The available data do not provide many clues. The hypothesis offered here, of a capacity for representing complex parts and a capacity for representing numerous parts, is admittedly speculative. There are other ways that the distinctions among the recognition processes required for object, face, and word recognition have been described, and some of these could be adapted to provide alternative interpretations of the two capacities identified here. For example, Levine and Calvanio (1989) suggest that the relation between different kinds of visual stimuli and language may determine how these different stimuli are recognised, as well as determining the role of the left hemisphere in recognition. They distinguish between agnosia for stimuli with nameable and non-nameable parts, associating the former with alexia and the latter with prosopagnosia. To the extent that objects will have some nameable parts and some non-nameable parts, their account may also be extendable to the range of agnosias reviewed here. Corballis (1989) proposes that the left hemisphere is specialised for part-based represent-ations in language, imagery, and object recognition, which he conjectures are evolutionarily recent representations. Therefore, in his framework the distinction between the two representational capacities could be phrased in terms of evolutionarily newer versus older recognition mechanisms. Diamond and Carey (1986) offer a proposal for the difference between face and object recognition, according to which the locations of parts of faces are represented relative to their prototypical pcations ("second order spatial relations") whereas for other objects the locations of parts are merely represented relative to each other ('first order spatial relations"). Although this framework is not currently equipped to account for dissoci-ations between word and object recognition, it does serve as another illustration of the wide range of ways in which the visual representations required for recognising different types of stimuli might differ.

Further research is required to determine the best interpretation of the two representational capacities identified in the present analysis. Although the hypothesis that the associative agnosias can be explained in terms of impairment in the representation of complex parts, numerous parts, or both is consistent with the available data, other interpretations are also possible. In contrast, what can be concluded with relative certainty is that just two underlying representational capacities are sufficient. Further-more, the pattern of neuropathology in these cases seems to respect the two-part organisation being proposed here.

Manuscript received 12 October 1989
Revised manuscript received 18 April 1990

REFERENCES

Aimard, G., Vighetto, A., Confavreux, C., & Devic, M. (1981). La désorientation spatiale. *Revue Neurologique, 137*, 97–111.

Albert, M. L., Reches, A., & Silverberg, R. (1975). Associative visual agnosia without alexia. *Neurology, 25*, 322–326.

Albert, M. L., Soffer, D., Silverberg, R., & Reches, A. (1979). The anatomic basis of visual agnosia. *Neurology, 29*, 876–879.

Aptman, M., Levin, H., & Senelick, R. C. (1977). Alexia without agraphia in a left-handed patient with prosopagnosia. *Neurology, 27*, 533–537.

Assal, G. (1969). Régression des troubles de la réconnaissance des physionomes et de la mémoire topographique chez un malade opéré d'un hématome intracérébral parieto-temporal droit. *Revue Neurologique, 121*, 184–185.

Assal, G., Favre, C., & Anderes, J. (1984). Nonrecognition of familiar animals by a farmer: Zooagnosia or prosopagnosia for animals. *Revue Neurologique, 140*, 580–584.

Bauer, R. M. (1982). Visual hypoemotionality as a symptom of visual-limbic disconnection in man. *Archives of Neurology, 39*, 702–708.

Bauer, R. M.. (1984). Autonomic recognition of names and faces in prosopagnosia: A neuropsychological application of the guilty knowledge test. *Neuropsychologia, 22*, 457–469.

Bauer, R. M. & Trobe, J. D. (1984). Visual memory and perceptual impairments in prosopagnosia. *Journal of Clinical Neuro-opthalmology, 4*, 39–46.

Bauer, R. M. & Verfaellie, M. (1988). Electrodermal discrimination of familiar but not unfamiliar faces in prosopagnosia. *Brain and Cognition, 8*, 240–252.

Beauvois, M.-F. (1982). Optic aphasia: A process of interaction between vision and language. *Philosophical Transactions of the Royal Society, London, B298*, 35–47.

Benke, T. (1988). Visual agnosia and amnesia from a left unilateral lesion. *European Neurology, 28*, 236–239.

Benson, D. F., Segarra, J., & Albert, M. L. (1974). Visual agnosia-prosopagnosia: A clinicopathologic correlation. *Archives of Neurology, 30*, 307–310.

Benton, A. L. & Van Allen, M. W. (1972). Prosopagnosia and facial discrimination. *Journal of Neurological Sciences, 15*, 167–172.

Beyn, E. S. & Knyazeva, G. R. (1962). The problem of prosopagnosia. *Journal of Neurology, Neurosurgery, and Psychiatry, 25*, 154–158.

Bornstein, B. (1963). Prosopagnosia. In L. Halpern (Ed.), *Problems of dynamic neurology*. Jerusalem: Hadassah Medical Organisation, 283–318.

Bornstein, B. & Kidron, D. P. (1959). Prosopagnosia. *Journal of Neurology, Neurosurgery, and Psychiatry, 22*, 124–131.

Bornstein, B., Sroka, H., & Munitz, H. (1969). Prosopagnosia with animal face agnosia. *Cortex, 5*, 164–169.

Boudouresques, J., Poncet, M., Cherif, A., & Balzamo, M. (1979). L'agnosie de visages: un témoin de la désorganisation fonctionnelle d'un certain type de connaissance des éléments du monde extérieur. *Bulletin de l'Academie Nationale de Medicine, 163*, 695–702.

Boudouresques, J., Poncet, M., Sebahoun, M., & Alicherif, A. (1972). Two cases of alexia without agraphia with disorders of colour and image naming. *Bulletin de l'Academie Nationale de Medicine, 44*, 297–303.

Brown, J. W. (1972). *Aphasia, apraxia, and agnosia: Clinical and theoretical aspects*, Springfield, Illinois: Charles C. Thomas.

Bruyer, R., Laterre, C., Seron, X., Feyereisne, P., Strypstein, E., Pierrard, E., & Rectem, D. (1983). A case of prosopagnosia with some preserved covert remembrance of familiar faces. *Brain and Cognition, 2*, 257–284.

Cambier, J., Masson, M., Elghozi, D., Henin, D., & Viader, F. (1980). Visual agnosia without right hemianopia in a right-handed patient. *Revue Neurologique*, *136*, 727–740.

Cohn, R., Neumann, M. A., & Wood, D. H. (1977). Prosopagnosia: A clinicopathological study. *Annals of Neurology*, *1*, 177–182.

Cole, M. & Perez-Cruet, J. (1964). Prosopagnosia. *Neuropsychologia*, *2*, 237–246.

Corballis, M. C. (1989). Laterality and human evolution. *Psychological Review*, *96*, 492–505.

Damasio, A. R. & Damasio, H. (1983). The anatomic basis of pure alexia. *Neurology*, *33*, 1573–1583.

Damasio, A. R., Damasio, H., & Van Hoesen, G. W. (1982). Prosopagnosia: Anatomic basis and behavioural mechanisms. *Neurology*, *32*, 331–341.

Davidoff, J. & Wilson, B. (1985). A case of visual agnosia showing a disorder of pre-semantic vision classification. *Cortex*, *21*, 121–134.

De Haan, E. H. F., Young, A., & Newcombe, F. (1987). Faces interfere with name classification in a prosopagnosic patient. *Cortex*, *23*, 309–316.

DeRenzi, E. (1986a). Prosopagnosia in two patients with C.T.-scan evidence of damage confined to the right hemisphere. *Neuropsychologia*, *24*, 385–389.

DeRenzi, E. (1986b). Current issues in prosopagnosia. In H. D. Ellis, M. A. Jeeves, F. Newcombe, & A. Young (Eds.), *Aspects of face processing*. Dordrecht: Martinus Nijhoff.

Desimone, R., Albright, T. D., Gross, C. D., & Bruce, C. (1984). Stimulus-selective responses of inferior temporal neurons in the macaque. *Journal of Neuroscience*, *4*, 2051–2062.

Diamond, R. & Carey, S. (1986). Why faces are and are not special: An effect of expertise. *Journal of Experimental Psychology: General*, *115*, 107–117.

Duara, R., Phatak, P. G., & Wadia, N. H. (1975). Prosopagnosia and associated disorders. *Neurology India*, *23*, 149–155.

Dumont, I., Griggio, A., Dupont, H., & Jacquy, J. (1981). A propos d'un cas d'agnosie visuelle avec prosopagnosie et agnosie des coleurs. *Acta Psychiatrica Belgica*, *81*, 25–45.

Farah, M. J. (1990). *Visual agnosia: Disorders of object recognition and what they tell us about normal vision*. Cambridge: M.I.T. Press.

Farah, M. J. & Wallace, M. A. (in press). Pure alexia as a visual impairment: A reconsideration. *Cognitive Neuropsychology*.

Feinberg, T. E., Gonzalez-Rothi, L. J., & Heilman, K. M. (1986). Multimodal agnosia after unilateral left hemisphere lesion. *Neurology*, *36*, 864–867.

Ferro, J. M. & Santos, M. E. (1984). Associative visual agnosia: A case study. *Cortex*, *20*, 121–134.

Friedman, R. B. & Alexander, M. P. (1984). Pictures, images, and pure alexia: A case study. *Cognitive Neuropsychology*, *1*, 9–23.

Gallois, P., Ovelacq, P., Hautecoeur, P., & Dereux, J. F. (1988). Disconnexion et réconnaissance des visages. *Revue Neurologique*, *144*, 113–119.

Gloning, I., Gloning, K., Jellinger, K., & Quatember, R. (1970). A case of prosopagnosia with necropsy findings. *Neuropsychologia*, *8*, 199–204.

Glowic, C. & Violon, A. (1981). Un cas de prosopagnosie régressive. *Acta Neurologica Belgica*, *81*, 86–97.

Gomori, A. J. & Hawryluk, G. A. (1984). Visual agnosia without alexia. *Neurologica*, *34*, 947–950.

Guard, O., Graule, A., Spautz, J. M., & Dumas, R. (1981). Anomie fabulante par agnosie visuelle et tactile au cours d'une démence arteriopathique. *L'Encephale*, *7*, 275–291.

Hécaen, H. & de Ajuriaguerra, J. (1956). Agnosie visuelle pour les objets inanimés par lesion unilaterale gauche. *Revue Neurologique*, *94*, 222–233.

Hécaen, H., Goldblum, M. C., Masure, M. C., & Ramier, A. M. (1974). A new case of object agnosia. A deficit in association or categorisation specific for the visual modality. *Neuropsychologia*, *12*, 447–464.

Humphreys, G. W. & Riddoch, M. J. (1987). *To see but not to see: A case study of visual agnosia.* Hillsdale, N.J.: Lawrence Erlbaum Associates Inc.

Karpov, B. A., Meerson, Y. A., & Tonkonough, I. M. (1979). On some peculiarities of the visuomotor system in visual agnosia. *Neuropsychologia, 17*, 281–294.

Kawahata, N. & Nagata, K. (1989). A case of associative visual agnosia: Neuropsychological findings and theoretical considerations. *Journal of Clinical and Experimental Neuropsychology, 11*, 645–664.

Kay, M. C. & Levin, H. S. (1982). Prosopagnosia. *American Journal of Opthamology, 94*, 75–80.

Kinsbourne, M. & Warrington, E. K. (1962). A disorder of simultaneous form perception. *Brain, 85*, 461–486.

Kumar, N., Verma, A., Maheshwari, M. C., & Kumar, B. R. (1986). Prosopagnosia (a report of two cases). *Journal of the Association of Physicians of India, 34*, 733–735.

Landis, T., Cummings, J. L., Christen, L., Bogen, J. E., & Imhof, H. (1986). Are unilateral right posterior cerebral lesions sufficient to cause prosopagnosia? Clinical and radiological findings in six additional patients. *Cortex, 22*, 243–252.

Landis, T., Regard, M., Bliestle, A., & Kleihues, P. (1988). Prosopagnosia and agnosia for noncanonical views. *Brain, 111*, 1287–1297.

Larrabee, G. J., Levin, H. S., Huff, F. J., Kay, M. C., & Guinto, F. C. (1985). Visual agnosia contrasted with visual-verbal disconnection. *Neuropsychologia, 23*, 1–12.

Levine, D. N. (1978). Prosopagnosia and visual object agnosia: A behavioural study. *Neuropsychologia, 5*, 341–365.

Levine, D. N. & Calvanio, R. (1978). A study of the visual defect in verbal alexia-simultanagnosia. *Brain, 101*, 65–81.

Levine, D. & Calvanio, R. (1989). Prosopagnosia: A defect in visual configural processing. *Brain and Cognition, 10*, 149–170.

Levin, H. S. & Peters, B. H. (1976). Neuropsychological testing following head injuries: Prosopagnosia without visual field defect. *Diseases of the Nervous System, 37*, 68–71.

Lhermitte, F., Chain, F., Aron-Rosa, D., Leblanc, M., & Souty, O. (1969). Enregistrement des mouvements du regard dans un cas d'agnosie visuelle et dans un cas de désorientation spatiale. *Revue Neurologique, 121*, 121–137.

Lhermitte, J., Chain, F., Escourolle, R., Ducarne, B., & Pillon, B. (1972). Etude anatomo-clinque d'un cas de prosopagnosie. *Revue Neurologique, 126*, 329–346.

Lhermitte, F., Chedru, F., & Chain, F. (1973). A propos d'un case d'agnosie visuelle. *Revue Neurologique, 128*, 301–322.

Lhermitte, F. & Pillon, B. (1975). La prosopagnosie. Role de l'hemisphère droit dans la perception visuelle. *Revue Neurologique, 131*, 791–812.

Lissauer, H. (1890). Ein fall von seelenblindheit nebst einem Beitrage zur Theori derselben. *Archiv fur Psychiatrie und Nervenkrankheiten, 21*, 222–270.

Mack, J. L. & Boller, F. (1977). Associative visual agnosia and its related deficits: The role of the minor hemisphere in assigning meaning to visual perceptions. *Neuropsychologia, 15*, 345–349.

Macrae, D. & Trolle, E. (1956). The defect of function in visual agnosia. *Brain, 79*, 94–110.

Malone, D. R., Morris, H. H., Kay, M. C., & Levin, S. H. (1982). Prosopagnosia: A double dissociation between the recognition of familiar and unfamiliar faces. *Journal of Neurology, Neurosurgery, and Psychiatry, 45*, 820–822.

Marks, R. L. & De Vito, T. (1987). Alexia without agraphia and associated disorders: Importance of recognition in the rehabilitation setting. *Archives of Physical Medicine and Rehabilitation, 68*, 239–243.

Marx, P., Boquet, J., Luce, R., & Farbos, J. P. (1970). Spatial agnosia and agnosia of physiogomies, sequelae of cortical blindness. *Bulletin des Societes d'Opthalmologie, Vol. 70*.

McCarthy, R. A. & Warrington, E. K. (1986). Visual associative agnosia: A clinico-anatomical study of a single case. *Journal of Neurology, Neurosurgery, and Psychiatry*, *49*, 1233–1240.

Mendez, M. F. (1988). Visuoperceptual function in visual agnosia. *Neurology*, *38*, 1754–1759.

Michel, F., Perenin, M. T., & Sieroff, E. (1986). Prosopagnosie sans hémianopsie après lesion unilaterale occipito-temporale droite. *Revue Neurologique*, *142*, 545–549.

Morin, P., Rivrain, Y., Eustache, F., Lambert, J., & Courtheoux, P. (1984). Agnosi visuelle et agnosie tactile. *Revue Neurologique*, *140*, 271–277.

Mouren, P., Tatossian, A., Trupheme, R., Giudicelli, S., & Fresco, R. (1967). L'alexie par déconnection visuo-verbale (Geschwind): A propos d'un cas de cecité verbale pure sans agraphie avec troubles de la denomination des coleurs, des nombres et des images. *Encephale*, *56*, 112–137.

Nardelli, E., Buonanno, F., Coccia, G., Fiaschi, H., Terzian, H., & Rizzuto, N. (1982). Prosopagnosia: Report of four cases. *European Neurology*, *21*, 289–297.

Newcombe, F. (1979). The processing of visual information in prosopagnosia and acquired dyslexia: Functional versus physiological interpretation. In D. J. Oborne, M. M. Grune-berg, & J. R. Eiser (Eds.), *Research in psychology and medicine*. London: Academic Press.

Newcombe, F. & Ratcliff, G. (1974). Agnosia: A disorder of object recognition. In F. Michel & B. Schott (Eds.), *Les syndromes de disconnexion calleuse chez l'homme*. Lyon: Colloque International.

Noel, G. & Meyers, C. (1971). Two cases of visual agnosia with achromatoagnosia. *Acta Neurologica Belgica*, *71*, 173–184.

Orgogozo, J. M., Pere, J. J., & Strube, E. (1979). Alexie sans agraphie, "agnosie" des couleurs et atteinte de l'hémichamp visual droit: Un syndrome de l'artère cérébrale postérieure. *Semaines des Hopitaux de Paris*, *55*, 1389–1394.

Pallis, C. A. (1955). Impaired identification of faces and places with agnosia for colours. *Journal of Neurology, Neurosurgery, and Psychiatry*, *18*, 218–224.

Pillon, B., Signoret, J. L., & Lhermitte, F. (1981). Agnosie visuelle associative: Role de l'hemisphere gauche dans la perception visuelle. *Revue Neurologique*, *137*, 831–842.

Pinker, S. (1985). Visual cognition: An introduction. In S. Pinker (Ed.), *Visual cognition*. Cambridge: M.I.T. Press.

Raizada, V. N. & Raizada, I. N. (1972). Visual agnosia. *Neurology India*, *20*, 181–182.

Ratcliff, G. & Newcombe, F. (1982). Object recognition: Some deductions from the clinical evidence. In A. W. Ellis (Ed.), *Normality and pathology in cognitive functions*. New York: Academic Press.

Renault, B., Signoret, J. L., Debruille, B., Breton, F., & Bolgert, F. (1989). Brain potentials reveal covert facial recognition in prosopagnosia. *Neuropsychologia*, *27*, 905–912.

Riddoch, M. J. & Humphreys, G. W. (1987). A case of integrative visual agnosia. *Brain*, *110*, 1431–1462.

Rondot, P., Tzavaras, A., & Garcin, R. (1967). Sur un cas de prosopagnosie persistant depuis quinze ans. *Revue Neurologique*, *117*, 424–428.

Ross, E. D. (1980). Sensory-specific and fractional disorders of recent memory in man: I: Isolated loss of visual recent memory. *Archives of Neurology*, *37*, 193–200.

Rouzaud, M., Ribadeau, J. L., Degiovanni, E., Larmande, P., Ployet, M. J., & Laffont, F. (1978). Troubles associatifs visuels (agnosie et syndrome de dysconnexion); atteinte auditive d'origine ischemique. *Revue Otoneuroopthalmologique*, *50*, 365–382.

Rubens, A. B. & Benson, D. F. (1971). Associative visual agnosia. *Archives of Neurology*, *24*, 305–316.

Shallice, T. (1988). *From neuropsychology to mental structure*. New York: Cambridge University Press.

Shuttleworth, E. C., Syring, V., & Allen, N. (1982). Further observations on the nature of prosopagnosia. *Brain and Cognition*, *1*, 302–332.

Striano, S., Grossi, D., Chiacchio, & Fels, A. (1981). Bilateral lesion of the occipital lobes. *Acta Neurologica (Napoli)*, *36*, 690–694.

Taylor, A. M. & Warrington, E. K. (1971). Visual agnosia: A single case report. *Cortex*, *7*, 152–161.

Tranel, D. & Damasio, A. R. (1988). Nonconscious face recognition in patients with face agnosia. *Behavioural Brain Research*, *30*, 235–249.

Tranel, D., Damasio, A. R., & Damasio, H. (1988). Intact recognition of facial expression, gender, and age in patients with impaired recognition of face identity. *Neurology*, *38*, 690–696.

Tzavaras, A., Merienne, L., & Masure, M. C. (1973). Prosopagnosie, amnesie et troubles du langage par lesion temporale gauche chez un sujet Gaucher. *Encephale*, *62*, 382–394.

Whiteley, A. M. & Warrington, E. K. (1977). Prosopagnosia: A clinical, psychological, and anatomical study of three patients. *Journal of Neurology, Neurosurgery, and Psychiatry*, *40*, 395–403.

Young, A. & De Haan, E. H. F. (1988). Boundaries of covert recognition in prosopagnosia. *Cognitive Neuropsychology*, *5*, 317–336.

Chapter 3   Visual and Spatial Abilities

Goodale, M.A. & Milner, A.D. (1992). Separate visual pathways for perception and action. *Trends in Neurosciences, 15,* 20–25.
Hanley, J.R., Young, A.W., & Pearson, N. (1991). Impairment of the visuo-spatial sketch pad. *Quarterly Journal of Experimental Psychology, 43A,* 101–125.

We have always been a little unhappy about Chapter 3, which reviews a wide range of studies of visual and spatial abilities, but does not succeed in developing any overall theoretical position. A sophisticated theory has now been offered by Milner, Goodale, and their colleagues. This is outlined in one of our chosen readings (Goodale & Milner, 1992), and dealt with at length in an impressive book (Milner & Goodale, 1996).

What Goodale and Milner (1992) achieve is to set the study of spatial perception firmly in the context of neurophysiological understanding of visual pathways specialised for the control of action. They argue that much of the brain is devoted to the control of action, for which specialised systems have evolved. The purpose of perceptual systems is to create representations of external events that can permit effective action in the world that an organism inhabits. As human beings, we often want a degree of flexibility in our responses to a complex environment. But flexibility of response requires sophisticated representations of events, which take precious time to compute. Consider the favourite textbook comparison to the frog, whose retinal outputs include bug detectors that allow it to make very fast responses to flies. Our own visual system is much less specialised at the retinal level, allowing increased flexibility of response, but at the cost of loss of speed. One way of solving the competing demands of the need for flexibility in some circumstances and speed in others is to allow most actions to run off under automatic, non-conscious control, and to involve mechanisms that can allow greater choice only when these are needed. This is a particularly convenient solution for the nervous system, in which many actions (like breathing) can be safely left under "automatic pilot" much of the time, and only require occasional conscious intervention (e.g. if you are about to put your head underwater). It is doubly convenient because nervous systems must evolve, and one way to do this is to add extra levels of control to mechanisms that are already sufficient for many purposes. Such points have been recognised for many years both in neuropsychology (Hughlings Jackson, 1884; Luria, 1973) and in experimental psychology (Baars, 1988; Shiffrin & Schneider, 1977). They come as no surprise to non-psychologists, who often note that the performance of skilled actions is disrupted rather than facilitated if one attends to them too carefully.

Milner, Goodale, and their colleagues have provided compelling demonstrations of the force of this general position. They have made a very thorough investigation of the dissociation of action from conscious perception in a case of visual form agnosia (Goodale, Milner, Jakobson, & Carey, 1991; Milner et al., 1991).

In visual form agnosia (see Chapter 2, pp. 34–35), there is a severe visual recognition impairment in the context of defective processing of basic properties involved in shape perception (Benson & Greenberg, 1969; Sparr, Jay, Drislane, & Venna, 1991). Milner et al.'s (1991) patient, DF, was severely impaired when she was asked to judge the orientation of a slot by manually rotating a visible matching slot to the same inclination. Yet when DF was asked to put her hand into the slot, she immediately positioned it correctly. Other studies showed that DF shaped her fingers appropriately for the size of an object she was about to pick up, even though her ability to make overt size judgements was poor (Goodale & Milner, 1992; Goodale et al., 1991). In both examples, DF was able to *do* something with a visual stimulus, yet proved poor at *judging* the relevant perceptual qualities. Perception for action was preserved, even though perception for conscious reflection was severely impaired.

Goodale and Milner (1992) point out that cases like DF, who can make accurate movements directed at objects she does not seem to be "seeing" at all well, contrast with other cases involving bilateral parietal damage in which actions on the world are very defective even though shape processing and visual recognition are intact. They propose that such differences are "largely a reflection of the specific transformations of input required by perception and action", and that functional modularity in vision "extends from input right through to output" (Goodale & Milner, 1992).

This point may well be important for understanding unilateral neglect (Chapter 2, pp. 76–81). Recent findings have strongly supported our contention (Chapter 2, pp. 80–81) that there can be different forms of unilateral neglect. Bisiach (1994) has reviewed evidence pointing to a relative differentiation of perceptual from premotor forms of unilateral neglect. A particularly impressive example comes from the work of Tegnér and Levander (1991), who used the simple but ingenious expedient of asking neglect patients to perform a crossing-out task (such as that shown in Fig. 3.1, p. 76) while viewing what they were doing via a mirror. The mirror, of course, reverses the left and right positions of the items in the task. The effect of this was to reveal two different patterns of performance. Ten of 14 patients who showed left neglect without the mirror crossed out the lines that were apparently to their right (but actually on the left) when viewing them in the mirror. To do this, they had to make leftward hand movements, so their problem seemed primarily to do with neglecting the left side of a perceptually based left–right dimension. The other four patients did the opposite; they cancelled the stimuli that were apparently to their left (but actually on the right) when viewing them in the mirror. These four people therefore seemed to have difficulty making leftward movements.

Differences have also been noted between object-based and spatial neglect. Humphreys and Riddoch (1994) report two cases for whom neglect affected opposite sides of a visual display when items were coded as parts of a single perceptual object or as separate perceptual objects. They argue that this shows that visual selection operates differently when one is selecting part of an individual object from when one is selecting part of a display with multiple objects.

An important point about Milner and Goodale's work is that they have demonstrated that it is *only certain types of action* that are preserved for DF. Her accurate responses involve well-practised everyday movements that can be run off without conscious control (putting your hand into something), whereas the inaccurate responses arise in tasks that need continual conscious intervention (judging whether or not two orientations are the same, and how to reduce any difference between them). Milner and Goodale (1996) show how such observations might be extended to provide an account of other dissociations of vision and awareness, including blindsight.

Further important observations on the relation between perceptual mechanisms and experience have arisen from work on achromatopsia. In Chapter 2 we noted that although achromatopsic patients experience the world in shades of grey, work with case MS had shown that he retained certain responses to light wavelength even though he could not match, sort, or name colours (Mollon, Newcombe, Polden, & Ratcliff, 1980). These findings have been confirmed and extended in subsequent work.

Heywood, Cowey, and Newcombe (1991) measured the sensitivity to light of different wavelengths for MS. In this test, MS described all the stimuli he saw as "dim white" or "grey", despite the differences in wavelength. Similarly, other work established that MS could not match or name colours, and he performed at random when asked to arrange colour patches by hue. However, although MS showed a general overall loss of sensitivity, Heywood et al. (1991) found that the wavelengths he could see best were none the less the same as for a normal observer. Such differences in sensitivity across wavelength are known to derive from opponent cone mechanisms involved in colour processing; thus this result demonstrated the presence of opponent cone mechanisms despite MS's complete loss of colour experience.

Loss of part of our normal visual experience after brain injury can therefore be highly selective; in this case for colour, which was no longer seen by MS even though much of the mechanism for dealing with wavelengths by opponent channels continued to function. Further work with MS produced many more demonstrations of this, including the important finding that he could still use differences in wavelength to extract information about shape (Heywood, Cowey, & Newcombe, 1994).

Our second reading (Hanley, Young, & Pearson, 1991) shows the value of a very different theoretical approach, based on Baddeley's (1986) working memory model. The work also brings together topics that recur in Chapter 4 (memory for faces) and Chapters 8 and 10 (short-term memory). After treatment for an aneurysm of the right middle cerebral artery, ELD was found to be poor at learning new visuo-spatial material, including new faces and new routes (Hanley, Pearson, & Young, 1990). In terms of Baddeley's (1986) model, such a pattern would be expected after damage to the visuo-spatial sketch pad component of working memory. From this theoretical observation, Hanley   et al. (1991) were able to derive and test several predictions concerning ELD's performance of short-term memory tasks. Impressively, her performance was much as would be predicted by Baddeley's model.

REFERENCES

Baars, B.J. (1988). *A cognitive theory of consciousness.* Cambridge: Cambridge University Press.

Baddeley, A. (1986). *Working memory.* Oxford: Oxford University Press.

Benson, D.F. & Greenberg, J.P. (1969). Visual form agnosia: a specific defect in visual discrimination. *Archives of Neurology, 20,* 82–89.

Bisiach, E. (1994). Perception and action in space representation: evidence from unilateral neglect. In G. d'Ydewalle, P. Eelen, & P. Bertelson (Eds.), *International perspectives on psychological science: Vol. 2, The state of the art* (pp. 51–66). Hove, UK: Lawrence Erlbaum Associates Ltd.

Goodale, M.A. & Milner, A.D. (1992). Separate visual pathways for perception and action. *Trends in Neurosciences, 15,* 20–25.

Goodale, M.A., Milner, A.D., Jakobson, L.S., & Carey, D.P. (1991). A neurological dissociation between perceiving objects and grasping them. *Nature, 349,* 154–156.

Hanley, J.R., Pearson, N., & Young, A.W. (1990). Impaired memory for new visual forms. *Brain, 113,* 1131–1148.

Hanley, J.R., Young, A.W., & Pearson, N. (1991). Impairment of the visuo-spatial sketch pad. *Quarterly Journal of Experimental Psychology, 43A,* 101–125.

Heywood, C.A., Cowey, A., & Newcombe, F. (1991). Chromatic discrimination in a cortically colour blind observer. *European Journal of Neuroscience, 3,* 802–812.

Heywood, C.A., Cowey, A., & Newcombe, F. (1994). On the role of parvocellular (P) and magnocellular (M) pathways in cerebral achromatopsia. *Brain, 117,* 245–254.

Hughlings Jackson, J. (1884). Evolution and dissolution of the nervous system: Croonian Lectures delivered at the Royal College of Physicians, March 1884. In J. Taylor (Ed.), *Selected writings of John Hughlings Jackson* (Vol. 2, pp. 45–75). London: Staples Press.

Humphreys, G.W., & Riddoch, M.J. (1994). Attention to within-object and between-object spatial representations: multiple sites for visual selection. *Cognitive Neuropsychology, 11,* 207–241.

Luria, A.R. (1973). *The working brain: an introduction to neuropsychology.* Harmondsworth, UK: Penguin.

Milner, A.D. & Goodale, M.A. (1996). *The visual brain in action.* Oxford Psychology Series, 27. Oxford: Oxford University Press.

Milner, A.D., Perrett, D.I., Johnston, R.S., Benson, P.J., Jordan, T.R., Heeley, D.W., Bettucci, D., Mortara, F., Mutani, R., Terazzi, E., & Davidson, D.L.W. (1991). Perception and action in 'visual form agnosia'. *Brain, 114,* 405–428.

Mollon, J.D., Newcombe, F., Polden, P.G., & Ratcliff, G. (1980). On the presence of three cone mechanisms in a case of total achromatopsia. In G. Verriest (Ed.), *Colour vision deficiencies* (Vol. V, pp. 130–135). Bristol: Hilger.

Shiffrin, R.M. & Schneider, W. (1977). Controlled and automatic human information processing: II. Perceptual learning, automatic attending, and a general theory. *Psychological Review, 84,* 127–190.

Sparr, S.A., Jay, M., Drislane, F.W., & Venna, N. (1991). A historic case of visual agnosia revisited after 40 years. *Brain, 114*, 789–800.

Tegnér, R. & Levander, M. (1991). Through a looking glass. A new technique to demonstrate directional hypokinesia in unilateral neglect. *Brain, 114*, 1943–1951.

Separate Visual Pathways for Perception and Action

Melvyn A. Goodale
University of Western Ontario, London, Ontario, Canada
A. David Milner
University of St. Andrews, UK

Accumulating neuropsychological, electrophysiological and behavioural evidence suggests that the neural substrates of visual perception may be quite distinct from those underlying the visual control of actions. In other words, the set of object descriptions that permit identification and recognition may be computed independently of the set of descriptions that allow an observer to shape the hand appropriately to pick up an object. We propose that the ventral stream of projections from the striate cortex to the inferotemporal cortex plays the major role in the perceptual identification of objects, while the dorsal stream projecting from the striate cortex to the posterior parietal region mediates the required sensorimotor transformations for visually guided actions directed at such objects.

In an influential article that appeared in *Science* in 1969, Schneider[1] postulated an anatomical separation between the visual coding of the location of a stimulus and the identification of that stimulus. He attributed the coding of the location to the ancient retinotectal pathway, and the identification of the stimulus to the newer geniculostriate system; this distinction represented a significant departure from earlier monolithic descriptions of visual function. However, the notion of 'localization' failed to distinguish between the many different patterns of behaviour that vary with the spatial location of visual stimuli, only some of which turn out to rely on tectal mechanisms.[2-4] Nevertheless, even though Schneider's original proposal is no longer generally accepted, his distinction between object identification and spatial localization, between 'what' and 'where', has persisted in visual neuroscience.

TWO CORTICAL VISUAL SYSTEMS

In 1982, for example, Ungerleider and Mishkin[5] concluded that 'appreciation of an object's qualities and of its spatial location depends on the processing of different kinds of visual information in the inferior temporal and posterior parietal cortex, respectively.' They marshalled evidence from a number of electrophysiological, anatomical and behavioural studies suggesting that these two areas receive independent sets of projections from the striate cortex. They distinguished between a 'ventral stream' of projections that eventually reaches the inferotemporal cortex, and a 'dorsal stream' that terminates finally in the posterior parietal region. The proposed functions of these two streams were inferred largely from behavioural evidence derived from lesion studies. They noted that monkeys with lesions of the inferotemporal cortex were profoundly impaired in visual pattern discrimination and recognition,[6] but less impaired in solving 'landmark' tasks, in which the location of a visual cue determines which of two alternative locations is rewarded. Quite the opposite pattern of results was observed in monkeys with posterior parietal lesions.[7-9]

So, according to Ungerleider and Mishkin's 1982 version of the model of two visual systems, the inferotemporal lesions disrupted circuitry specialized for identifying objects, while the posterior parietal lesions interfered with neural mechanisms underlying spatial perception. Thus, within the visual domain, they made much the same functional distinction between identification and localization as Schneider, but mapped it onto the diverging ventral and dorsal streams of output from the striate cortex. Since 1982, there has been an explosion of information about the anatomy and electrophysiology of cortical visual areas[10,11] and, indeed, the connectional anatomy among these various areas largely confirms the existence of the two broad 'streams' of projections proposed by Ungerleider and Mishkin (see Fig. 1).[12,13]

It has recently been suggested[14] that these two streams can be traced back to the two main cytological subdivisions of retinal ganglion cells: one of these two subdivisions terminates selectively in the parvocellular layer, while the other terminates in the magnocellular layer of the lateral geniculate nucleus (LGN).[14-16] Certainly, these 'parvo' and 'magno' subdivisions remain relatively segregated at the level of the primary visual cortex (V1) and in the adjacent visual area V2. They also appear to predominate, respectively, the innervation of area V4 and the middle temporal area (MT), which in turn provide the major visual inputs to the inferotemporal and posterior parietal cortex, respectively. However, it is becoming increasingly clear that the separation between magno and parvo information in the cortex is not as distinct as initially thought. For example, there is recent evidence for a parvo input into a subset of MT neurones[17] as well as for a large contribution from the magno pathway to V4 neurones[18] and to the 'blobs' in V1 (Ref. 19). In short, it now appears that the dorsal and the ventral streams each receive inputs from both the magno and the parvo pathways.

TWO VISUOMOTOR SYSTEMS: 'WHAT' VERSUS 'HOW'

Our alternative perspective on modularity in the cortical visual system is to place less emphasis on input distinctions (e.g. object location versus object

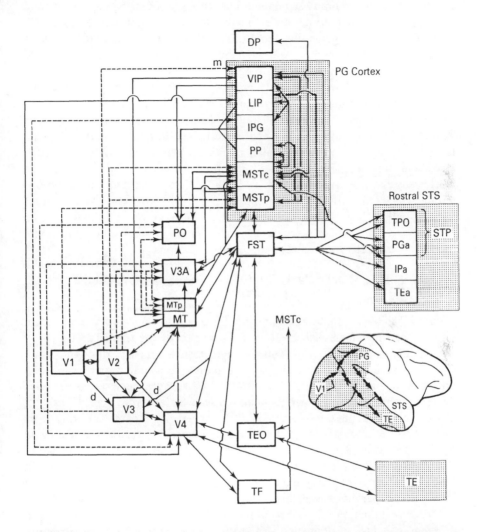

FIG. 1. The 1982 version of Ungerleider and Mishkin's[5] model of two visual systems is illustrated in the small diagram of the monkey brain inset into the larger box diagram. In the original model, V1 is shown sending a dorsal stream of projections to the posterior parietal cortex (PG), and a ventral stream of projections to the inferotemporal cortex (TE). The box diagram illustrates one of the most recent versions of the interconnectivity of the visual cortical areas, showing that they can still be broadly segregated into dorsal and ventral streams. However, there is crosstalk between the different areas in the two streams and there may be a third branch of processing projecting into the rostral superior temporal sulcus (STS) that is intimately connnected with both the dorsal and ventral streams. This is illustrated in both the brain and box diagrams. Thus, the proposed segregation of input that characterized the dorsal and ventral streams in the original model is not nearly as clear cut as once was thought (Modified, with permission, from Ref. 11.)

qualities) and to take more account of output requirements.[20,21] It seems plausible from a functional standpoint that separate processing modules would have evolved to mediate the different uses to which vision can be put. This principle is already generally accepted in relation to 'automatic' types of behaviour such as saccadic eye movements,[22] and it is possible that it could be extended to other systems for a range of behavioural skills such as visually guided reaching and grasping, in which close coordination is required between movements of the fingers, hands, upper limbs, head and eyes.

It is also our contention that the inputs and transformations required by these skilled visuomotor acts differ in important respects from those leading to what is generally understood as 'visual perception'. Indeed, as has been argued elsewhere, the functional modules supporting perceptual experience of the world may have evolved much more recently than those controlling actions within it.[21] In this article, it is proposed that this distinction ('what' versus 'how')—rather than the distinction between object vision and spatial vision ('what' versus 'where')—captures more appropriately the functional dichotomy between the ventral and dorsal projections.

DISSOCIATION BETWEEN PREHENSION AND APPREHENSION

Neuropsychological studies of patients with damage to one projection system but not the other have also been cited in support of the model proposed by Ungerleider and Mishkin.[5,23] Patients with visual agnosia following brain damage that includes, for example, the occipitotemporal region, are often unable to recognize or describe common objects, faces, pictures, or abstract designs, even though they can navigate through the everyday world—at least at a local level—with considerable skill.[24] Conversely, patients suffering from optic ataxia following damage to the posterior parietal region are unable to reach accurately towards visual targets that they have no difficulty recognising.[25] Such observations certainly appear to provide support in humans for an occipitotemporal system mediating object vision but not spatial vision, and a parietal system mediating spatial vision but not object vision.

Closer examination of the behaviour of such patients, however, leads to a different conclusion. Patients with optic ataxia not only have difficulty reaching in the right direction, but also in positioning their fingers or adjusting the orientation of their hand when reaching toward an object that can be oriented at different angles.[25] Such patients may also have trouble adjusting their grasp to reflect the size of the object they are asked to pick up.

Visually guided grasping was recently studied in a patient who had recovered from Balint's syndrome, in which bilateral parietal damage causes profound disorders of spatial attention, gaze and visually guided reaching.[26] While this patient had no difficulty in recognizing line drawings of common objects, her ability to pick up such objects remained quite impaired. For example, when she reached out for a small wooden block that varied in size from trial to trial there was little relationship between the magnitude of the aperture between her index finger and thumb and the size of the block as the movement unfolded. Not only did she fail to show normal scaling of the grasping movement; she also made a large number of adjustments in her grasp as she closed in on the object—adjustments rarely observed in normal subjects. Such studies suggest that damage to the parietal lobe can impair the ability of patients to use information about the size, shape and orientation of an object to control the hand and fingers during a grasping movement, even though this same information can still be used to identify and describe the objects. Clearly, a 'disorder of spatial vision' fails to capture this range of visuomotor impairments.

There are, of course, other kinds of visuospatial disorders, many of which are associated with parietal lobe damage, while others are associated with temporal lobe lesions.[27,28] Unfortunately, we lack detailed analyses of the possible specificity of most such disorders: in many, the deficit may be restricted to particular behavioural tasks. For example, a recently described patient with a parietal injury performed poorly on a task in which visual guidance was needed to learn the correct route through a small ten-choice maze by moving a hand-held stylus.[23] However, he was quite unimpaired on a locomotor maze task in which he was required to move his whole body through space when working from a two-dimensional visual plan. Moreover, he had no difficulty in recalling a complex geometrical pattern, or in carrying out a task involving short-term spatial memory.[29] Such dissociations between performance on different 'spatial' tasks show that after parietal damage spatial information may still be processed quite well for some purposes, but not for others. Of course, the fact that visuospatial deficits can be fractionated in humans does not exclude combinations of such impairments occurring after large lesions, nor would it exclude possible selective input disorders occurring after smaller deafferentation lesions close to where the dorsal stream begins.

Complications also arise on the opposite side of the equation (i.e. in relation to the ventral stream), when the behaviour of patients with visual agnosia is studied in detail. The visual behaviour of one patient (DF) who developed a profound visual-form agnosia following carbon monoxide poisoning was recently studied. Although MRI revealed diffuse brain damage consistent with anoxia, most of the damage in the cortical visual areas was evident in areas 18 and 19, with area 17 apparently remaining largely intact. Despite her profound inability to recognize the size, shape and orientation of visual objects, DF showed strikingly accurate guidance of hand and finger movements directed at the very same objects.[30,31.] Thus, when she was presented with a pair of rectangular blocks of the same or different dimensions, she was unable to distinguish between them. When she was asked to indicate the width of a single block by means of her index finger and thumb, her matches bore no relationship to the dimensions of the object and showed considerable trial to trial variability (Fig. 2A). However, when she was asked simply to reach out and pick up the block, the aperture between her index finger and thumb changed systematically with the width of the object, just as in normal subjects (Fig. 2B). In other words, DF scaled her grip to the dimensions of the objects she was about to pick up, even though she appeared to be unable to 'perceive' those dimensions.

A similar dissociation was seen in her responses to the orientation of stimuli. Thus, when presented with a large slot that could be placed in one of a number of different orientations, she showed great difficulty in indicating the

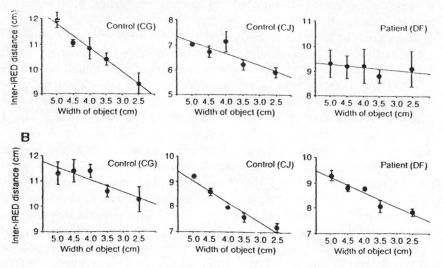

FIG. 2.   In both (A) the manual matching task and (B) the grasping task five white plaques (each with an overall area of 25 cm² on the top surface, but with dimensions ranging from 5 × 5 cm to 2.5 × 10 cm) were presented, one at a time, at a viewing distance of approximately 45 cm. Diodes emitting infrared light (IREDs) were attached to the tips of the index finger and thumb of the right hand and were tracked with two infrared-sensitive cameras and stored on a WATSMART computer (Northern Digital Inc, Waterloo, Canada). The three-dimensional position of the IREDs and the changing distance between them were later reconstructed off line. (A) In the manual matching task, DF and two control subjects were instructed to indicate the width of each plaque over a series of randomly ordered trials by separating the index finger and thumb of their right hand. In DF, unlike the controls (CG and CJ), the aperture between the finger and thumb was not systematically related to the width of the target. DF also showed considerable trial to trial variability. (B) In contrast, when they were instructed to reach out and pick up each plaque, DF's performance was indistinguishable from that of the control subjects. The maximum aperture between the index finger and thumb, which was achieved well before contact, was systematically related to the width of the plaques in both DF and the two control subjects. In interpreting all these graphs, it is the slope of the function that is important rather than the absolute values plotted, since the placement of the IREDs and the size of the hand and fingers varied somewhat from subject to subject. Bars represent means ± SE. (Modified, with permission, from Ref. 31.)

orientation either verbally or manually (i.e. by rotating her hand or a hand-held card). Nevertheless, she was as good as normal subjects at reaching out and placing her hand or the card into the slot, turning her hand appropriately from the very onset of the movement.[30,31]

These disparate neuropsychological observations lead us to propose that the visual projection system to the human parietal cortex provides action-relevant information about the structural characteristics and orientation of objects, and not just about their position. On the other hand, projections to the temporal lobe may furnish our visual perceptual experience, and it is these that we postulate to be severely damaged in DF.

DORSAL AND VENTRAL SYSTEMS IN THE MONKEY

How well do electrophysiological studies of the two projection systems in the visual cortex of the monkey support the distinction we are making? While any correlations between human neuropsychology and monkey neurophysiology should only be made with caution, it is likely that humans share many features of visual processing with our primate relatives—particularly with the Old World monkeys in which most of the electrophysiology has been carried out. Furthermore, lesion studies of the two projection systems in the monkey should show parallels with the results of work done on human patients.

It was noted earlier that although there are differences in the major retinal origins of inputs to the dorsal and ventral systems in the monkey brain, there is subsequently a good deal of pooling of information. Moreover, there are convergent similarities in what is extracted within the two systems. For example, both orientation and disparity selectivity are present in neurones in both the magno and parvo systems within cortical areas V1 and V2 (Ref. 15).

Nevertheless, there are special features in the properties of individual neurones in the posterior parietal cortex (and in its major input areas V3A and MT) that are not found in the ventral system. The most striking feature of neurones in the posterior parietal region is not their spatial selectivity (indeed, like those of inferotemporal cells, their receptive fields are typically large), but rather the fact that their responses depend greatly on the concurrent behaviour of the animal with respect to the stimulus. Separate subsets of cells in the posterior parietal cortex have been shown to be implicated in visual fixation, pursuit and saccadic eye movements, eye–hand coordination, and visually guided reaching movements.[32] Many cells in the posterior parietal region have gaze-dependent responses; i.e. where the animal is looking determines the response amplitude of the cell (although not the retinal location of its receptive field).[33] In reviewing these studies, Andersen[32] emphasizes that most neurones in this area 'exhibit both sensory-related and movement-related activity'. In a particularly interesting recent development, Taira et al.[34] have shown that some parietal cells are sensitive to those visual qualities of an object that determine the posture of the hand and fingers during a grasping movement. They studied neurones selectively associated with hand movements made by the monkey in reaching and picking up solid objects. Many of these cells were selective for the visual appearance of the object that was to be manipulated, including its size and in several cases its orientation.

The posterior parietal cortex may receive such form information from one or both of the areas V3 or V4, both of which project to area MT.[35] Other visual inputs pass through area MT and the adjacent medial superior temporal (MST) area, both of which contain cells variously selective for object motion in different directions, including rotation and motion in depth.[32] Thus, the posterior parietal cortex appears to receive the necessary inputs for continually updating the monkey's knowledge of the disposition and structural qualities of objects in its three-dimensional ego-space. Also, many motion-sensitive cells in the posterior parietal cortex itself appear to be well suited for the visual monitoring of limb position during reaching behaviour;[36] in contrast, motion-sensitive cells in the temporal lobe have been reported not to respond to such self-produced visual motion.[37] As for the output pathways, the posterior parietal region is strongly linked with those pre-motor regions of the frontal cortex directly implicated in ocular control,[33,38] reaching movements of the limb,[39] and grasping actions of the hand and fingers.[39]

Thus, the parietal cortex is strategically placed to serve a mediating role in the visual guidance and integration of prehensile and other skilled actions (see Ref. 40 for a detailed account of this argument). The results of behavioural analyses of monkeys with posterior parietal damage support this further. Like patients with optic ataxia, such animals fail to reach correctly for visual targets,[41] and they also have difficulty in shaping and orienting their hands when attempting to retrieve food.[42,43] Their reaching impairment is, therefore, one symptom of a wider visuomotor disorder, and most of the deficits that have been reported on 'maze' tasks following posterior parietal damage may also be visuomotor in nature.[9,40]

Nonetheless, neurones in the dorsal stream do not show the high-resolution selectivity characteristic of neurones in the inferotemporal cortex, which are strikingly sensitive to form, pattern and colour.[10] In this and in neighbouring temporal lobe areas, some cells respond selectively to faces, to hands, or to the appearance of particular actions in others.[44] Therefore, it is unsurprising that monkeys with inferotemporal lesions have profound deficits in visual recognition; however, as noted by Pribram,[45] they remain highly adept at the visually demanding skill of catching flies!

A further peculiarity of many visual cells in the temporal cortex is that they continue to maintain their selective responsiveness over a wide range of size, colour, optical and viewpoint transformations of the object.[44,46] Such cells, far from providing the momentary information necessary for guiding action, specifically ignore such changing details. Consistent with this, behavioural studies have shown that by lesioning the inferotemporal cortex (but not the posterior parietal cortex), a monkey is less able to generalize its recognition of three-dimensional shape across viewing conditions.[47,48]

VISUAL AND ATTENTIONAL REQUIREMENTS FOR PERCEPTION AND ACTION

As DeYoe and Van Essen[15] have suggested, 'parietal and temporal lobes could both be involved in shape analysis but associated with different computational strategies.' For the purposes of identification, learning and distal (e.g. social) transactions, visual coding often (though not always)[44,46] needs to be 'object-centred'; i.e. constancies of shape, size, colour, lightness, and location need to be maintained across different viewing conditions. The above evidence from behavioural and physiological studies supports the view that the ventral stream of processing plays an important role in the computation of such object-specific descriptions. In contrast, *action* upon the object requires that the location of the object and its particular disposition and motion with respect to the observer is encoded. For this purpose, coding of shape would need to be largely 'viewer-centred',[49] with the egocentric coordinates of the surface of the object or its contours being computed each time the action occurs. We predict that shape-encoding cells in the dorsal system should predominantly have this property. Nevertheless, certain constancies, such as size, would be necessary for accurate scaling of grasp aperture, and it might therefore be expected that the visual properties of the manipulation cells found by Taira et al.[34] in the posterior parietal region would have this property.

It is often suggested that the neuronal properties of the posterior parietal cortex qualify it as the prime mediator of visuospatial attention.[50] Certainly, many cells (e.g. in area 7a) are modulated by switches of attention to different parts of the visual field.[51] (Indeed, the 'landmark' disorder that follows posterior parietal damage in monkeys may be primarily due to a failure to attend or orient rather than a failure to localize[9,40,52]). However, it is now known that attentional modulation occurs in neurones in many parts of the cortex, including area V4 and the inferotemporal region within the ventral stream.[53,54] This might explain the occurrence of landmark deficits after inferotemporal as well as posterior parietal damage.[7,8]

In general terms, attention needs to be switched to particular locations and objects whenever they are the targets either for intended action[51,55] or for identification.[54] In either case, this selection seems typically to be spatially based. Thus, human subjects performing manual aiming movements have a predilection to attend to visual stimuli that occur within the 'action space' of the hand.[56] In this instance the attentional facilitation might be mediated by mechanisms within the dorsal projection system; in other instances it is probably mediated by the ventral system. Indeed, the focus of lesions causing the human attentional disorder of 'unilateral neglect' is parietotemporal (unlike the superior parietal focus for optic ataxia[25]), as is the focus for object constancy impairments.[57] We conclude that spatial attention is physiologically non-unitary,[55] and may be as much associated with the ventral system as with the dorsal.

A SPECULATION ABOUT AWARENESS

The evidence from the brain-damaged patient DF described earlier suggests that the two cortical pathways may be differentiated with respect to their access to consciousness. DF certainly appears to have no conscious perception of the orientation or dimensions of objects, although she can pick them up with remarkable adeptness. It may be that information can be processed in the dorsal system without reaching consciousness, and that this prevents interference with the perceptual constancies intrinsic to many operations within the ventral system that do result in awareness. Intrusions of viewer-centred information could disrupt the continuity of object identities across changing viewpoints and illumination conditions.

If this argument is correct, then there should be occasions when normal subjects are unaware of changes in the visual array to which their motor system is expertly adjusting. An example of such a dissociation has been reported in a study on eye–hand coordination during visually guided aiming.[58] Subjects were unable to report, even in forced-choice testing, whether or not a target had changed position during a saccadic eye movement, although correction saccades and manual aiming movements directed at the target showed near-perfect adjustments for the unpredictable target shift. In other words, an illusory perceptual constancy of target position was maintained in the face of large amendments in visuomotor control. In another recent example, it has been reported that the compelling illusion of slowed motion of a moving coloured object that is experienced at equiluminance does not prevent accurate ocular pursuit under the same conditions (see Ref. to Lisberger and Movshon, cited in Ref. 59). Such observations may illustrate the independent functioning of the ventral and dorsal systems in normal humans.

We do not, however, wish to claim that the division of labour we are proposing is an absolute one. In particular, the above suggestion does not imply that visual inputs are necessarily blocked from awareness during visuomotor acts, although that may be a useful option to have available. Rather, we assume that the two systems will often be simultaneously activated (with somewhat different visual information), thereby providing visual experience during skilled action. Indeed, the two systems appear to engage in direct crosstalk; for example, the posterior parietal and inferotemporal cortex themselves interconnect[33,60] and both in turn project to areas in the superior temporal sulcus.[11-13] There, cells that are highly form selective lie close to others that have motion specificity,[44] thus providing scope for cooperation between the two systems (see Fig. 1). In addition, there are many polysensory neurons in these areas so that not only visual but also cross-modal interaction between these networks may be possible. This may provide some of the integration needed for the essential unity and cohesion of most of our perceptual experience and behaviour, although overall control of awareness may ultimately be the responsibility of superordinate structures in the frontal cortex.[61] Nevertheless, it is feasible to maintain the hypothesis that a *necessary condition* for conscious visual experience is that the ventral system be activated.

CONCLUDING REMARKS

Despite the interactions between the dorsal and ventral systems, the converging lines of evidence reviewed above indicate that each stream uses visual information about objects and events in the world in different ways. These differences are largely a reflection of the specific transformations of input required by perception and action. Functional modularity in cortical visual systems, we believe, extends from input right through to output.

SELECTED REFERENCES

1. Schneider, G.E. (1969). *Science. 163*, 895–902.
2. Ingle, D.J. (1982). In *Analysis of Visual Behavior* (Ingle, D.J., Goodale, M.A. & Mansfield, R.J.W., eds), pp. 67–109, MIT Press.
3. Goodale, M.A. & Murison, R. (1975). *Brain Res. 88*, 243–255.
4. Goodale, M.A. & Milner, A.D. (1982). In *Analysis of Visual Behavior* (Ingle D.J., Goodale, M.A. & Mansfield. R.J.W., eds), pp. 263–299, MIT Press.
5. Ungerleider, L.G. & Mishkin, M. (1982). In *Analysis of Visual Behavior* (Ingle D.J., Goodale, M.A. & Mansfield, R.J.W., eds), pp. 549–586, MIT Press.
6. Gross, C.G. (1973). *Prog. Physiol. Psychol. 5*, 77–123.
7. Pohl, W. (1973). *J. Comp. Physiol. Psychol. 82*, 227–239.
8. Ungerleider, L.G. & Brody, B.A. (1977). *Exp. Neurol. 56*, 265–280.
9. Milner, A.D., Ockleford, E.M. & Dewar, W. (1977). *Cortex, 13*, 350–360.
10. Desimone, R. & Ungerleider, L.G. (1989). In *Handbook of Neuropsychology*, Vol. 2 (Boller, F., & Grafman. J., eds), pp. 267–299, Elsevier.
11. Boussaoud D., Ungerleider, LG. & Desimone, R. (1990). *J. Comp. Neurol. 296*, 462–495.
12. Morel, A. & Bullier, J. (1990). *Visual Neurosci. 4*, 555–578.
13. Baizer, J.S., Ungerleider, L.G. & Desimone, R. (1991). *J. Neurosci. 11*, 168–190.
14. Livingstone, M. & Hubel, D. (1988). *Science 240*, 740–749.
15. DeYoe, E.A. & Van Essen, D.C. (1988). *Trends Neurosci. 11*, 219–226.
16. Schiller, P.H. & Logothetis, N.K. (1990). *Trends Neurosci. 13*, 392-398.
17. Maunsell, J.H.R., Nealy, T.A. & De Priest, D.D. (1990). *J. Neurosci. 10*, 3323–3334.
18. Nealey, T.A. & Maunsell, J.H.R. (1991). *Invest. Ophthalmol. Visual Sci. 32* (Suppl.) 1117.
19. Ferrera, V.P., Nealey, T.A. & Maunsell, J.H.R. (1991). *Invest. Ophthalmol. Visual Sci. 32* (Suppl.) 1117.
20. Goodale, M.A. (1983). In *Behavioral Approaches to Brain Research* (Robinson, T.E., ed.); pp. 41–61, Oxford University Press.

21. Goodale, M.A. (1988). In *Computational Processes in Human Vision: An Interdisciplinary Perspective* (Pylyshyn, Z., ed.), pp. 262–285, Ablex.
22. Sparks, D.L. & May, L.E. (1990). *Annu. Rev. Neurosci. 13*, 309–336.
23. Newcombe, F., Ratcliff, G. & Damasio, H. (1987). *Neuropsychologia 25*, 149–161.
24. Farah, M. (1990). *Visual Agnosia*, MIT Press.
25. Perenin, M-T. & Vighetto, A. (1988). *Brain 111*, 643–674.
26. Jakobson, L.S., Archibald, Y.M., Carey, D. & Goodale, M.A. (1991). *Neuropsychologia 29*, 803–809.
27. Milner, B. (1965). *Neuropsychologia 3*, 317–338.
28. Smith, M.L. & Milner, B. (1989). *Neuropsychologia 27*, 71–81.
29. Ettlinger, G. (1990). *Cortex 26*, 319–341.
30. Milner, A.D. *et al.* (1991). *Brain 114*, 405–428.
31. Goodale, M.A., Milner, A.D., Jakobson, L.S. & Carey, D.P. (1991). *Nature 349*, 154–156.
32. Andersen, R.A. (1987). In *Higher Functions of the Brain, Part 2 (The Nervous System, Vol. V. Handbook of Physiology, Section 1)* (Mountcastle, V.B., Plum, F. & Geiger, S.R., eds), pp. 483–518, American Physiological Association.
33. Andersen, R.A., Asanuma, C., Essick, G. & Siegel, R.M. (1990). *J. Comp. Neurol. 296*, 65–113.
34. Taira, M., Mine, S., Georgopoulos, A.P., Murata, A. & Sakata, H. (1990). *Exp. Brain Res. 83*, 29–36.
35. Felleman, D.J., & Van Essen, D.C. (1987). *J. Neurophysiol. 57*, 889–920.
36. Mountcastle, V.B., Motter, B.C., Steinmetz M.A. & Duffy C.J. (1984). In *Dynamic Aspects of Neocortical Function* (Edelman, G.M., Gall, W.E. & Cowan, W.M., eds), pp. 159–193, Wiley.
37. Perrett, D.I., Mistlin, A.J., Harries M.H. & Chitty, A.J. (1990). In *Vision and Action: The Control of Grasping* (Goodale, M.A., ed.), pp. 163–180, Ablex.
38. Cavada, C. & Goldman-Rakic, P.S. (1989). *J. Comp. Neurol. 287*, 422–445.
39. Gentilucci, M. & Rizzolatti, G. (1990). In *Vision and Action: The Control of Grasping* (Goodale, M.A., ed.), pp. 147–162, Ablex.
40. Milner, A.D. & Goodale, M.A. *Prog. Brain Res.* (in press).
41. Bates, J.A.V. & Ettlinger, G. (1960). *Arch. Neurol. 3*, 177–192.
42. Faugier-Grimaud, S., Frenois, C. & Stein, D.G. (1978). *Neuropsychologia 16*, 151–168.
43. Haaxma, R. & Kuypers, H.G.J.M. (1975). *Brain 98*, 239–260.
44. Perrett, D.I., Mistlin, A.J. & Chitty, A.J. (1987). *Trends Neurosci. 10*, 358–364.
45. Pribram, K.H. (1967). In *Brain Function and Learning* (Lindsley, D.B. and Lumsdaine, A.A., eds), pp. 79–122, University of California Press.
46. Perrett, D.I. *et al.* (1991). *Exp. Brain Res. 86*, 159–173.
47. Humphrey, N.K. & Weiskrantz, L. (1969). *Quart. J. Exp. Psychol. 21*, 225–238.
48. Weiskrantz, L. & Saunders, R.C. (1984). *Brain 107*, 1033–1072.
49. Marr, D. (1982). *Vision*, Freeman.
50. Goldberg, M.E. & Colby, C.L. (1989). In *Handbook of Neuropsychology* (Vol. 2) (Boller, F., & Grafman, J., eds), p. 301–315, Elsevier.
51. Bushnell, M.C., Goldberg, M.E. & Robinson, D.L. (1981). *J. Neurophysiol. 46*, 755–772.
52. Lawler, K.A. & Cowey, A. (1987). *Exp. Brain Res. 65*, 695–698.
53. Fischer, B. & Boch, R. (1981). *Exp. Brain Res. 44*, 129–137.
54. Moran, J. & Desimone, R. (1985). *Science 229*, 782–784.
55. Rizzolatti, G., Gentilucci, M. & Matelli, M. (1985). In *Attention and Performance XI* (Posner, M.I. & Marin, O.S.M., eds), pp. 251–265, Erlbaum.
56. Tipper, S., Lortie, C. & Baylis, G. *J. Exp. Psychol. Human Percept. Perform.* (in press).
57. Warrington, E.K. & Taylor, A.M. (1973). *Cortex 9*, 152–164.
58. Goodale, M.A., Pelisson, D. & Prablanc, C. (1986). *Nature 320*, 748–750.
59. Sejnowski, T.J. (1991). *Nature 352*, 669–670.

60. Cavada, C. & Goldman-Rakic, P.S. (1989). *J. Comp. Neurol. 287*, 393–421.
61. Posner, M.I. & Rothbart, M.K. (1991). In *The Neuropsychology of Consciousness* (Milner, A.D & Rugg, M.D., eds), pp. 91–111, Academic Press.

Impairment of the Visuo-spatial Sketch Pad

J. Richard Hanley

University of Liverpool, U.K.

Andrew W. Young

University of Durham, U.K.

Norma A. Pearson

Manchester Royal Infirmary, U.K.

A case study is presented of a female patient, ELD, who has difficulty in the immediate recall of short sequences of visuo-spatial material following a right-hemisphere aneurysm. Despite poor performance on tasks such as the Brooks Matrix and the Corsi Blocks, ELD is good at the immediate serial recall of letters even when presentation modality is visual and shows effects of phonological similarity and articulatory suppression. This pattern of performance represents a double dissociation from that which has been observed with the short-term memory patient PV (Vallar & Baddeley, 1984), who is extremely poor at serial recall of verbal material but shows no visual memory impairment. It is argued that ELD has an impairment to the visuo-spatial component of working memory (Baddeley, 1986) in the absence of any phonological loop deficit. Further investigation reveals that ELD performs poorly on mental rotation tasks and finds it difficult to use imagery mnemonics, but has no difficulty in retrieving visuo-spatial information from long-term memory so long as it was learnt before her illness.

According to the model of working memory put forward by Baddeley (1986, 1990), temporary storage of information within the cognitive system depends on two separate slave systems, the visuo-spatial sketch pad and the phono-

We thank Freda Newcombe, Edward de Haan, and Brenda Flude for their assistance in making tests available to us. In particular we would like to acknowledge the assistance of Clive Skilbeck in enabling us to make contact with the patient described here, and Alan Baddeley for encouraging us to carry out a study of this kind. Rick Hanley and Andy Young are supported by ESRC grant R000231922

logical loop. The sketch pad is responsible for the storage of visuo-spatial information over brief periods and also plays a key role in the generation and manipulation of mental images. The phonological loop is responsible for the temporary storage of verbal information; items are held within a phonological store of limited duration but can be maintained within the store via the process of articulation. Both storage systems are in direct contact with a central executive system. The central executive is considered to be mainly responsible for co-ordinating activity within the cognitive system, but it can also devote some of its limited capacity to increasing the amount of information that can be held in the two slave systems.

Some of the most powerful evidence for the existence of a separate phonological loop system comes from the study of brain-injured patients with short-term memory impairments, first described by Warrington and Shallice (1969). As a result of their brain injuries, these patients are severely impaired at the immediate serial recall of short sequences of letters or words. Digit span may be as low as one item, but there is often no sign of any other major cognitive impairment. Vallar and Baddeley (1984) have made a detailed investigation of the serial recall performance of an Italian woman, PV, whose immediate memory problems followed a left hemisphere stroke. A key finding was that she showed particularly poor recall when the to-be-learned material was presented in the auditory modality. In addition, PV showed no phonological similarity effect when stimuli were presented in the visual modality. As she had no articulatory problems, it was concluded that PV had suffered an impairment to the phonological store. As a consequence, it was argued that she did not use the phonological loop when material was presented visually and suffered correspondingly when auditory presentation made this unavoidable.

A different pattern of impairment was reported by Morris (1984) in patients suffering from Alzheimer's disease. These patients were also poor at serial recall (relative to age-matched controls) but showed every sign of using the phonological loop. Thus they showed effects of phonological similarity when material was presented visually and performed better when stimuli were of short rather than long spoken duration. Morris argued that the phonological loop was working normally in these patients, but that the central executive was unable to make a normal contribution to the system when list length increased.

So far, however, no patients have been reported with an impairment to the visuo-spatial sketch pad, despite the fact that the working memory model clearly predicts that such patients should exist. Recently, we have had the opportunity of studying a patient who finds it extremely difficult to learn new faces and routes following a right-hemisphere aneurysm sustained in 1985 (Hanley, Pearson, & Young, 1990). The present study provides a detailed investigation of her short-term memory capacities and of her ability to use mental imagery. The results reveal a dissociation between short-term memory for verbal and visuo-spatial material of a kind not previously reported. We demonstrate that this can be considered to reflect impairment of the visuo-spatial sketch-pad.

A SINGLE CASE STUDY: ELD

Case Details

ELD is a right-handed woman who was born in 1936. She left school at 18 with seven "O-levels" and one "A-level". She worked throughout her adult life until, in September 1985, she suffered a middle cerebral artery aneurysm in the right hemisphere. This led to a sub-arachnoid haematoma in the Sylvian Fissure subfrontally, which was confirmed by a CT scan the following month. ELD underwent an operation to clip the aneurysm and was released from hospital in November 1985, having made a rapid clinical recovery.

Neuropsychological Testing

Clinical testing since the time of her illness has revealed that ELD does not suffer from any major general cognitive deficits. Her performance on the Wisconsin card sorting test, a task that is considered to be sensitive to frontal lobe damage, is normal. Her WAIS Verbal IQ is 119 and her Performance IQ is 100. Her Wechsler Memory quotient is 100, which suggests that she does not suffer from a global amnesia. There is, however, a striking discrepancy between her ability to remember new verbal information and her ability to learn new visual information. The most recent administration of the Warrington (1985) Recognition Memory test revealed a score of 49/50 on the test for words but a score of only 29/50 on the unfamiliar faces test. Both ELD's level of performance on recognition memory for faces, and the discrepancy between the words and faces scores, were well outside the normal range. Subsequent testing has revealed that she is as poor at remembering unfamiliar objects as unfamiliar faces (Hanley et al., 1990).

Visual Memory

This pattern of poor performance on "non-verbal" recognition memory tests is consistent with ELD's spontaneous complaints. She states that she finds it very difficult to recognize the faces of people that she has met since her illness. This includes personal acquaintances and people she sees in the mass media. On formal tests using photographs of celebrities, ELD's recognition performance was very impaired relative to controls for faces that have become famous since 1985, but was as good as controls for faces that were famous before 1980. Her ability to recognize the *names* of the people who have become famous since 1985, however, was quite normal.

Other aspects of visual recognition are also normal. ELD immediately identified each of 36 line drawings from the Snodgrass and Vanderwart (1980) set and was also able to distinguish normal from anomalous line drawings of objects and animals without difficulty (see Riddoch & Humphreys, 1987). She can recognize photographs of objects taken from unusual as well as prototypical views. There is no evidence of acquired dyslexia or visual neglect. She is also proficient at matching unfamiliar faces and judging their facial expression. Reaction time studies have confirmed that she can identify familiar faces and objects as quickly and as accurately as control subjects. Data for ELD and control subjects for most of these tasks are given by Hanley et al. (1990).

Spatial Memory

ELD's other main source of spontaneous complaint relates to spatial memory. She lives in a part of the city with which she was not familiar before her illness and has great difficulty in finding the way back to her new flat when she goes out alone. She says that she cannot remember new routes and must rely on familiar landmarks (e.g. a church) to work out where she is. If she leaves the room when she is at her day-centre, she will often return to the wrong seat, much to her friends' amusement. She is also unable to remember her way around new houses that she visits. As is the case with her visual memory problems, these spatial memory difficulties seem to occur only with locations with which she was unfamiliar before her illness. She claims to be well oriented in her parents' house and in her sister's house, both of which she knew before 1985. Similarly, when given a map of England and asked to mark the location of 15 major cities, she performed at the same level as control subjects.

ELD appears, therefore, to be suffering from what Ross (1980) has referred to as "loss of recent visual memory"—that is, a severe difficulty in learning new visuo-spatial material in the absence of retrograde impairment or verbal memory deficit. Further details of her ability to remember faces, objects and words is given by Hanley et al. (1990). The experiments reported below investigate whether she also experiences corresponding difficulties on tasks associated with short-term memory and mental imagery.

EXPERIMENT 1:
THE BROOKS MATRIX

The task used most extensively by Baddeley and his colleagues (Baddeley, Grant, Wight, & Thomson, 1975; Baddeley & Lieberman, 1980) to investigate the visuo-spatial sketch-pad was devised by Brooks (1967). The subject is asked to repeat back a series of eight sentences in their order of presentation. In one condition the sentences describe the location of numbers relative to one another in a 4 × 4 matrix, and the subject is told to store them by forming a mental image of the numbers within the matrix. This image, they are told, can then be used to reconstruct the sentences at recall. In the other ("nonsense") condition, the numbers are replaced by irrelevant words and the sentences must be stored by verbal rather than spatial coding. Strong evidence that separate systems are involved in the storage of the two types of material was provided by Baddeley et al. (1975). They showed that if pursuit rotor tracking was used as a secondary task, it interfered significantly with recall of the spatial material but had no effect on the recall of the nonsense material.

Method

In a preliminary study based on Baddeley et al. (1975, Expt. 2), we compared ELD's performance on the two types of material by giving her five spatial sequences with eight sentences per sequence, and five nonsense sequences with five sentences per sequence. Sequences of this length were chosen because Baddeley et al. showed that their subjects were able to recall sequences of eight sentences in the spatial condition at approximately the same level of performance as sequences of five sentences in the nonsense condition. In contrast to Baddeley et al.'s subjects, ELD performed much better with the nonsense material, getting two of the five sequences correct and making only 5 errors in total. With the spatial material, however, she made 20 errors and got none of the sequences correct.

As a result of this pattern of performance, we decided to examine her recall of spatial material in greater detail by starting with short sequences and gradually increasing list length. Following three practice lists, ELD was given three lists that contained three sentences each, then three lists that comprised four sentences each, and so on up to three lists with eight sentences per list. Performance was compared with that of five age- and sex-matched control subjects of similar educational background. All the controls were women aged between 40 and 62 years who had left school at either 15 or 18 years of age. None of them had a degree.

Results and Discussion

The results of Experiment 1 are summarized in Table 1. It can be seen that ELD's performance on this task is very poor, and that the total number of errors she makes across all the lists is more than 2.5 standard deviations above the number made by controls. ELD can cope with sequences containing five sentences but starts to make many errors as soon as the sequence gets any longer. Controls, on the other hand, can maintain a reasonable level of performance even with eight sentences per sequence. As a result of ELD's

TABLE 1
ELD's Performance on the Brooks Matrix Task

		Number of Errors						
		Controls						
Sequence Length	ELD	1	2	3	4	5	Mean	SD
3	0	1	0	0	0	0	0.2	0.45
4	0	0	0	0	0	0	0	0
5	0	0	0	0	4	0	0.8	1.79
6	6	0	0	0	3	0	0.6	1.34
7	8	1	9	0	7	0	3.4	4.28
8	13	5	6	4	2	1	3.6	2.07
Total errors across all lists	27	7	15	4	16	1	8.6	6.66

		Number of Sequences Correct (max = 3)						
		Controls						
Sequence Length	ELD	1	2	3	4	5	Mean	SD
3	3	2	3	3	3	3	2.8	0.45
4	3	3	3	3	3	3	3.0	0
5	3	3	3	3	2	3	2.8	0.45
6	0	3	3	3	1	3	2.6	0.89
7	0	2	0	3	1	3	1.8	1.30
8	0	1	1	2	1	2	1.4	0.55
Total correct	9	14	13	17	11	17	14.4	2.61

performance on this task, we decided to examine her ability to recall sequences of other types of visuo-spatial material. In Experiment 2, we used the Corsi Blocks (e.g. De Renzi, Faglioni, & Previdi, 1977), which provide a rather different way of investigating short-term memory for spatial information.

EXPERIMENT 2: CORSI BLOCKS

Method

A board, on which are glued nine randomly located wooden blocks, is placed between the subject and the experimenter. The experimenter taps a series of blocks one at a time, in a pre-determined order, and the subject must reproduce the sequence as soon as the experimenter has finished. As in Experiment 1, performance was tested by gradually increasing list length. Length went up from one block per sequence to as high as seven blocks per sequence. Ten sequences were presented at each length, subject to the constraint that if a subject got the first five sequences correct, then she went straight on to the next sequence length. If a subject made errors on the first five sequences at any length, then testing was terminated. This was because pilot work revealed that repeated failure on this task caused distress to some control subjects. This was not the case with ELD, however, and she received six-item sequences, despite having failed with five items, in order to confirm that she continued to get zero correct. ELD's performance on this task was compared with six age- and sex-matched controls.

Results and Discussion

The results of Experiment 2 are summarized in Table 2. It can be seen that, once more, performance by ELD becomes poor relative to the control subjects as list length is increased. In fact, ELD's level of performance is very similar to the level achieved by a comparable group of right-hemisphere patients tested by De Renzi et al. (1977), whose performance was also well below that of controls. In addition, ELD's performance is much worse than that of the short-term memory patient PV, who performs normally with Corsi Blocks (Basso, Spinnler, Vallar, & Zanobio, 1982). ELD's performance with Corsi Blocks has also been tested on a separate occasion, with virtually identical results.

The impairment to spatial short-term memory observed with the Brooks matrix appears to have been confirmed by ELD's performance with the Corsi Blocks. Experiment 3 investigated immediate memory for faces, to discover

TABLE 2
The proportion of sequences recalled correctly on the Corsi Blocks Task

| Sequence Length | ELD | Control Subjects | | | | | | | |
		1	2	3	4	5	6	Mean	SD
1	1.00	1.00	1.00	1.00	1.00	1.00	1.00	1.00	0
2	1.00	1.00	1.00	1.00	1.00	1.00	1.00	1.00	0
3	1.00	1.00	1.00	1.00	1.00	1.00	1.00	1.00	0
4	0.70	1.00	0.80	1.00	1.00	1.00	0.90	0.95	0.08
5	0	0.60	0.60	1.00	0.60	0.80	0.60	0.70	0.17
6	0	0.30	0	0.90	0	0.70	0.30	0.37	0.37
7	—	0	—	0.30	—	0.50	0	0.13	0.22

whether performance would be impaired with visual as well as with spatial material.

EXPERIMENT 3:
SHORT-TERM MEMORY FOR FACES

Method

In this experiment, subjects were presented with 18 sequences of faces. Each sequence comprised four different unfamiliar male faces. Each face appeared only once throughout the experiment. The four faces in each sequence were matched for age and expression. Faces were presented one at a time on $3\frac{1}{2} \times 5$-in. photographs, for 3 sec each. As soon as subjects had seen the fourth photograph, copies of all four target photographs were shown simultaneously in a 2×2 matrix, and the subject had to indicate the order in which they had originally been presented. The next sequence commenced immediately afterwards. ELD's performance was compared with that of seven age- and sex-matched controls.

Results and Discussion

The results of Experiment 3 are presented in Table 3. Once more, ELD's performance is poor relative to controls. This is most noticeable at Serial

TABLE 3
ELD's Performance on the Short-Term Memory Task for Faces

	Serial Position				Total Correct	Sequences Correct
	1	2	3	4		
Max.	18	18	18	18	72	18
ELD	11	11	10	9	41	6
Controls:						
1	17	14	13	15	59	11
2	11	11	9	14	45	7
3	17	17	16	15	65	15
4	10	12	11	14	47	8
5	14	14	13	15	56	12
6	17	18	18	17	70	17
7	15	11	12	15	53	10
Mean	14.43	13.86	13.14	15.00	56.43	11.43
SD	2.94	2.80	3.02	1.00	9.09	3.60

Position 4, where her score is several standard deviations below that of controls. It is also interesting to note that whereas controls show signs of improvement on the last item in the list, ELD's performance gets slightly worse—i.e. she shows no visual recency effect.

Taken together, then, the results of Experiments 1–3 show that ELD suffers from a deficit in remembering short sequences of visual and spatial stimuli immediately after they have been presented. Such a pattern of performance is consistent with an impairment to the visuo-spatial sketch pad component of working memory (Baddeley, 1986). Experiment 4 examined whether these problems are specific to visuo-spatial material, or whether they also encompass short-term memory for verbal material.

EXPERIMENT 4:
THE PHONOLOGICAL LOOP

Experiment 4 examined serial recall of short sequences of letters. We examined the effects of three different variables: presentation modality, articulatory suppression, and phonological similarity. In normal subjects, phonological similarity is known to interfere with serial recall of verbal material even when the lists are presented visually (Conrad & Hull, 1964). By contrast, the short-term memory patient PV shows no phonological similarity effect with visual presentation (Vallar & Baddeley, 1984), nor does she show any effects of articulatory suppression. Vallar and Baddeley also showed that PV performs much worse when stimuli are presented in the auditory modality. If ELD shows a similar pattern to PV, then it will be clear that she suffers from an impairment to the phonological loop system as well as to the visuo-spatial sketch pad.

The use of articulatory suppression with visual presentation made it possible to investigate one further issue. It is believed that articulatory suppression cuts visually presented material off from the phonological loop system (Baddeley & Hitch, 1974), and the subject must therefore rely on some form of visual coding. If ELD was to perform well under these conditions, it would follow that visual coding of verbal stimuli does not make use of the visuo-spatial sketch pad.

Method

Phonological similarity was manipulated by comparing recall of the acoustically similar set of letters *B C D G P T V* with the dissimilar set *H J L R S Y Z* (see Hull, 1973, for details of the confusability of the two sets). In the auditory condition, list length gradually increased from two items per list to seven items per list. Half of the six lists at each length comprised acoustically similar letters, sampled without replacement, and half comprised acoustically different letters. Stimuli were spoken at the rate of one every 1.5 sec to subjects, who then had to repeat back the lists in their order of presentation.

The test which used visual presentation took place a few minutes after presentation of the final auditory list. The letters were presented to the subjects on white index cards. In all other respects, the procedure was identical to that used with auditory presentation.

The test that investigated the effects of articulatory suppression took place during a separate session. It used items from the acoustically dissimilar set of letters, which were presented to the subject on index cards. On half the lists of each length, the subjects had to articulate the word "the" repeatedly during both presentation and recall of the lists. Subjects wrote down their responses. In all other respects, the procedure was identical to that reported above. In all the tests, performance was compared with that of five age- and sex-matched controls.

TABLE 4

The Effect of Phonological Similarity with Auditory Presentation

	ELD		Control Subjects			
Sequence Length	Error Rate	Number of Sequences Correct	Error Rate[a]		Number of Sequences Correct[a]	
Phonologically Different						
2	0	3	0	(0)	3.0	(0)
3	0	3	0	(0)	3.0	(0)
4	0	3	0.03	(0.08)	2.8	(0.45)
5	0	3	0.05	(0.07)	2.6	(0.55)
6	0	3	0.22	(0.17)	1.4	(1.34)
7	0.14	1	0.48	(0.14)	0.6	(0.55)
Mean	0.04	2.7	0.18	(0.03)	2.2	(1.10)
Phonologically Similar						
2	0	3	0	(0)	3.0	(0)
3	0	3	0.07	(0.10)	2.6	(0.55)
4	0.08	2	0.17	(0.13)	2.0	(0.71)
5	0.33	1	0.44	(0.11)	0.6	(0.55)
6	0.42	0	0.47	(0.18)	0.2	(0.45)
7	0.71	0	0.66	(0.15)	0	(0)
Mean	0.36	1.5	0.39	(0.07)	1.4	(1.28)

[a] SD in parentheses.

TABLE 5
The Effect of Phonological Similarity with Visual Presentation

Sequence Length	ELD		Control Subjects			
	Error Rate	Number of Sequences Correct	Error Rate[a]		Number of Sequences Correct[a]	
Phonologically Different						
2	0	3	0	(0)	3.0	(0)
3	0	3	0	(0)	3.0	(0)
4	0	3	0.02	(0.04)	2.8	(0.45)
5	0	3	0.07	(0.09)	2.4	(0.89)
6	0.06	2	0.27	(0.15)	1.0	(0.71)
7	0.43	1	0.41	(0.27)	0.6	(0.89)
Mean	0.12	2.5	0.19	(0.08)	2.1	(1.14)
Phonologically Similar						
2	0	3	0	(0)	3.0	(0)
3	0	3	0	(0)	3.0	(0)
4	0	3	0.17	(0.20)	2.2	(0.84)
5	0.23	1	0.05	(0.07)	2.6	(0.55)
6	0.78	0	0.24	(0.11)	1.2	(0.45)
7	0.43	1	0.35	(0.19)	0.8	(0.84)
Mean	0.35	1.8	0.18	(0.06)	2.1	(1.01)

[a] *SD* in parentheses.

Results and Discussion

The effects of phonological similarity on serial recall following both visual and auditory presentation are summarized in Tables 4 and 5. The first thing to note is ELD's excellent overall level of performance relative to controls in both modalities. This is in striking contrast to her poor recall of visuo-spatial material reported earlier. In addition, unlike the short-term memory patient PV (Vallar & Baddeley, 1984), ELD shows a strong phonological similarity effect, regardless of presentation modality. Consequently, it is clear that ELD does not suffer from an impairment to the phonological loop system. It is also interesting to note that the control subjects do not show a phonological similarity effect with visual presentation. This is most surprising given the number of times this effect has been replicated previously, and we are unable to offer a satisfactory explanation.

ELD's performance under articulatory suppression is presented in Table 6. It can be seen that, once again, her performance is at least as good as

TABLE 6
The Effect of Articulatory Suppression with Visual Presentation

	ELD		Control Subjects			
Sequence Length	Error Rate	Number of Sequences Correct	Error Rate[a]		Number of Sequences Correct[a]	
No Articulatory Suppression						
2	0	3	0	(0)	3.0	(0)
3	0	3	0	(0)	3.0	(0)
4	0	3	0.07	(0.09)	2.6	(0.55)
5	0.13	2	0.17	(0.18)	1.8	(0.84)
6	0	3	0.22	(0.12)	1.2	(0.84)
7	0.14	1	0.31	(0.14)	0.8	(0.84)
Mean	0.06	2.5	0.17	(0.10)	2.1	(1.05)
Articulatory Suppression						
2	0	3	0	(0)	3.0	(0)
3	0	3	0.22	(0.31)	2.0	(1.41)
4	0.25	1	0.42	(0.19)	0.8	(0.84)
5	0.40	1	0.40	(0.12)	0.4	(0.55)
6	0.44	0	0.78	(0.18)	0	(0)
7	0.43	0	0.77	(0.19)	0	(0)
Mean	0.32	1.3	0.53	(0.13)	1.0	(1.30)

[a] SD in parentheses.

that of controls, and like the controls, ELD performs much worse when forced to articulate an irrelevant word throughout the experiment. As the phonological loop cannot be used under articulatory suppression with visual presentation, ELD's good performance suggests that she is not overly reliant on phonological rather than visual coding in recalling verbal material. It follows from this that the sketch pad is probably not used in verbal memory span tasks with visual presentation, even when articulation is suppressed. Instead, we would speculate that visual coding of verbal material in these circumstances probably relies on temporary activation of some form of lexical representation. It is important to note that the control subjects found this task very difficult—the overall error rate was over 50%, and only a third of the sequences were repeated correctly. This means that ELD's good performance cannot be explained in terms of this simply being an easier task than those employed in Experiments 1–3.

It is clear from these findings that ELD's impairment to the visuo-spatial sketch pad is not accompanied by any corresponding phonological loop deficit. The pattern of performance that she shows in serial recall is quite different from that of PV (Vallar & Baddeley, 1984) and therefore strongly supports the view that separate systems are responsible for the temporary storage of verbal and visuo-spatial material. The remaining experiments investigate whether the impairment to the sketch-pad also leads to difficulties on tasks that are generally considered to rely on mental imagery.

EXPERIMENT 5:
IMAGERY MNEMONICS

It is well known that the use of imagery instructions significantly improves recall of lists of words and paired associates (e.g. Bower, 1972; Paivio, 1971). Baddeley and Lieberman (1980) provided evidence that the visuo-spatial sketch-pad plays a key role in this process, by showing that pursuit-rotor tracking significantly reduced the recall performance of subjects who had been given imagery instructions, but had no detrimental effect when subjects were given instructions to learn by rote rehearsal. If the sketch-pad is involved in learning words via mental imagery, then ELD should fail to show the benefit of imagery instructions.

Method

ELD was given four lists of paired associates to learn. She was told that at testing she would be given the first member of each pair and would be asked to provide the word that went with it. Each list contained 10 pairs of concrete nouns, matched for frequency across lists. Items were paired together in such a way as to avoid any obvious pre-experimental association. On the first list, ELD was told to learn the pairs by repeating them over and over again to herself. On the second list she was told to attempt to integrate the two members of each pair by forming an image in which the two words were interacting in some way. She was given the example of the pair *MONKEY–CIGAR* and was told that an appropriate image might feature a monkey smoking a cigar. She gave every indication of understanding the instructions clearly. Pairs were presented at the rate of one every 8 sec, to allow adequate time for the formation of images. The third list asked for rote learning once more, and the fourth list again requested the use of imagery.

Results and Discussion

ELD performed poorly on this task. She produced only 2/10 correct responses on List 1, and 1/10 correct responses on the other three lists. This made a total of 2/20 under imagery instructions and 3/20 under repetition instructions. When asked whether she had used imagery, she replied that "the pictures wouldn't come". To check whether the inability to benefit from imagery instructions would generalize to other encoding instructions, the experiment was repeated some weeks later with the imagery instructions being replaced by a semantic task (cf. Craik & Lockhart, 1972). The instructions told ELD to think of things that the two words in each pair had in common until the next pair was presented. She produced 2/20 (1/10 and 1/10, respectively) correct responses under repetition instructions, and 7/20 (4/10 and 3/10, respectively) correct responses with semantic instructions. A chi-square test revealed that the effect of semantic instructions leads to a marginally significant increase in recall relative to repetition instructions ($\chi^2 = 3.58, p = 0.058$). Although performance is still not good, it would appear that ELD can probably derive benefit from other types of instruction, even though she cannot use imagery mnemonics.

The results support the view that the visuo-spatial sketch-pad plays a key role in enabling one to make mental images interact in novel ways. It is also interesting to note ELD's generally poor performance at learning unrelated paired associates; the control subjects we have tested generally perform at ceiling. This contrasts sharply with ELD's excellent recognition memory for verbal material, reported by Hanley et al. (1990). This suggests that functionally distinct mechanisms might be involved in recall and recognition of words in secondary memory tasks.

One possible reason for this might be that as recall relies more heavily on subject initiated retrieval processes than recognition (e.g. Jacoby, Craik, & Begg, 1979), ELD's recall problems reflect a retrieval impairment in the absence of any impairment of the decision process that is often assumed to be involved in recognition memory tasks. Alternatively, ELD's poor recall performance may reflect the fact that recall is generally a more difficult task than recognition. It would therefore be interesting to discover in future studies whether the excellent recognition memory for verbal material shown by patients like ELD persists when the task is made more difficult by, for instance, increasing the delay between learning and test.

EXPERIMENT 6:
MENTAL ROTATION

Mental rotation tasks require the matching of visual stimuli that are presented at different angles of orientation. It is generally accepted that these tasks provide some of the most persuasive evidence that mental imagery plays an important functional role in cognition (e.g. Shepard, 1978, 1984). If the imagery account is true, then mental rotation must involve the maintenance and manipulation of visuo-spatial representations in some form of "visual buffer" (Kosslyn, 1980). The visuo-spatial sketch-pad would appear to have the appropriate attributes to carry out this role. If this is so, then it would be expected that ELD will have severe difficulties on tests of mental rotation.

Method

ELD was given two different standard tests of mental rotation. One of these was Thurstone and Jeffrey's (1956) "Flags" test, and the other was based on Shepard and Metzler's (1971) test of three-dimensional form rotation. In the latter task, the subject is given a booklet with a typical Shepard and Metzler form on the left of each page and is asked to decide which two out of four forms to its right represent the same form when viewed from a different perspective, and which represent a different shape. Several different angles of rotation are employed, and some of the forms are rotated in the picture plane and some in depth. A total of 20 trials are used, preceded by 3 practice trials in which subjects are corrected if they make an error. Subjects are allowed as long as they like to make each decision.

In the "Flags" test, the subject is shown a picture of a black-and-white flag on the left of the page and has to indicate which of six flags to the right are genuine rotations of the standard flag, and which are rotations of the opposite side of the standard flag. Subjects are given 5 min to make as many decisions as they can.

Results and Discussion

ELD's performance on these tasks was compared with that of male control subjects aged 55–65 years, tested at the Radcliffe Infirmary in Oxford, U.K. On the 3D form rotation test, ELD was correct on only 3/20 trials, whereas the controls had a mean score of 14.6/20 ($N = 25$, $SD = 5.4$). On the Flags test, ELD was correct on 37 trials and wrong on 11 trials, whereas controls were correct on 51.7 trials ($N = 21$, $SD = 14.2$) and incorrect on 4.3 ($SD = 4.2$).

ELD's performance is thus clearly very poor on these tasks. She appears to find it extremely difficult to manipulate mental images of two- and three-dimensional objects, just as one might expect in someone with a visuo-spatial sketch-pad deficit. In Kosslyn's (1980) terms, this would correspond with an impairment to the visual buffer. The final experiment investigated whether such an impairment would lead to difficulties in retrieving visuo-spatial information already stored in long-term memory.

EXPERIMENT 7:
RETRIEVAL OF VISUO-SPATIAL INFORMATION FROM
LONG-TERM MEMORY

The imagery tasks on which ELD performs badly (Brooks matrix, mental rotation, imagery mnemonics) all require the manipulation within a temporary storage system of visuo-spatial representations generated from an external source. This may well involve quite different mechanisms from those involved in the *retrieval* of visuo-spatial information from long-term memory. For instance Farah, Hammond, Levine, and Calvanio (1988) have recently described a patient who can perform the Brooks matrix task and the Shepard and Metzler 3D rotation task very well but is unable to answer questions about the colour and relative size of familiar objects and whether animals have long or short tails. Our final experiment, therefore, examined ELD's performance on a variety of tasks that require the retrieval of visuo-spatial information from long-term memory. All the tests except the "Faces of Celebrities Test" were based on those used by Farah et al. (1988).

Method

Full details of all the stimuli used in this experiment can be found in the Appendix.

Colour.   Twenty-five objects and animals were selected that have characteristic colours but are not verbally associated with the colour. The names of the objects and animals were read to subjects one at a time, and they were asked to state the appropriate colour. Examples of items in the list are *golf ball, motorway sign, sheep.*

Size Comparison.   The names of 16 pairs of objects were presented, and the subject had to decide which was the bigger of the two. Examples of pairs used in the experiment are *ping-pong ball* or *grape, LP record* or *saucer, cheque book* or *cigarete packet, toothbrush* or *banana.*

Animals' Tails.   The names of 20 animals were read to subjects who had to decide whether each animal had a long or a short tail. Once again, verbal associations were avoided as far as possible. Animals in the list included *kangaroo, wolf, lion* (long tails) and *goat, deer, rhino* (short tails).

Country Shapes.   On each trial, the name of a target country was read out, followed by two further countries. Subjects had to decide which of this pair most closely resembled the shape of the target country. Seven triads were used in all. Examples are *Portugal: Chile* or *Denmark; Italy: India* or *Mexico.*

City Locations.   Procedure was similar to that for country shapes, except that subjects had to decide which British city was closest to the target city. Examples are *Liverpool: Leeds* or *Manchester; Nottingham: Northampton* or *Derby.*

Faces of Celebrities.   Subjects were read a target famous name followed by two other famous names and had to decide which of these two people's faces most closely resembled that of the target. Examples are *Charlie Chaplin: Adolf Hitler* or *Winston Churchill; Nigel Lawson: Geoffrey Howe* or *Leon Brittan.*

Results and Discussion

ELD's performance, together with that of age- and sex-matched control subjects, is presented in Table 7. It can be seen that she performs well on all six tasks relative to controls. Her ability to retrieve visuo-spatial information from long-term memory is clearly unimpaired, despite her problems with mental rotation tasks and tasks such as the Brooks matrix.

This pattern of performance makes a striking contrast with that which Farah et al. (1988) observed with their patient LH. LH is good at tasks such as the Brooks matrix and mental rotation but is severely impaired on tasks such as Animals' Tails and Size Comparison, which require retrieval of visual information from long-term memory. Perhaps the most obvious interpretation of these results is that the sketch-pad plays a role in encoding and manipulating new visuo-spatial information but is not involved in the retrieval of old information from long-term memory. Further analysis of this issue is presented in the General Discussion.

TABLE 7
ELD's performance in Experiment 7

	Colour	Size Comparison	Animal's Tails	Country Shape	City Location	Faces of Celebrities
Max.	25	16	20	7	15	20
ELD	25	16	17	6	11	19
Controls	24.3	16.0	16.8	4.7	10.3	16.3
SD	0.8	0	1.0	2.5	1.8	3.2

GENERAL DISCUSSION

The main implications of this study are discussed under four headings. These concern the dissociation between the phonological loop and the visuo-spatial sketch-pad, the dissociation between anterograde and retrograde components of mental imagery, the role of the sketch-pad in retrieving information stored in long-term memory, and the role of the sketch-pad in learning new information.

A Dissociation Between the Phonological Loop and the Visuo-Spatial Sketch-Pad

ELD has great difficulty in remembering short sequences of visuo-spatial material but is unimpaired when the stimuli comprise letters of the alphabet. We therefore conclude that she suffers from an impairment to the visuo-spatial component of the working memory system (Baddeley, 1986) that is not accompanied by a corresponding phonological loop deficit. Her case thus provides a double dissociation with short-term memory patients such as PV (Vallar & Baddeley, 1984) who show the opposite pattern of impairment and strongly supports the view that there are separate verbal and visuo-spatial short-term memory systems.

A Dissociation Between Anterograde and Retrograde Components of Mental Imagery

ELD's poor performance on tasks such as the Brooks (1967) matrix and Shepard and Metzler's (1971) 3D mental rotation test is not accompanied by poor performance on several other tasks, which involve retrieval of visual information from long-term memory (Experiment 7). This pattern is very different from that observed with the patient LH. According to Farah et al. (1988), LH suffers a visual but not a spatial imagery deficit. Consequently, this raises the question of whether ELD shows impaired spatial imagery in the context of preserved visual imagery.

In an important series of recent articles, Farah and her colleagues have argued that a distinction should be drawn between *visual* and *spatial* components of mental imagery (Farah, 1988; Farah et al., 1988; Levine, Warach, & Farah, 1985). This distinction is analogous to the idea that there might be two functionally and anatomically discrete visual systems operating in *perception* (Ungerleider & Mishkin, 1982).

Ungerleider and Mishkin have shown that one cortical visual system involves inferior temporal cortex and is responsible for identifying an object, whereas the other involves parietal cortex and is responsible for locating an object's position in space. This concept of "two cortical visual systems" is supported by the contrasting effects of parietal and temporal lesions on object perception in monkeys (Ungerleider & Mishkin, 1982) and by the dissociable visual and spatial impairments that can follow human brain injury (Newcombe, Ratcliff, & Damasio, 1987). For instance, patients with parieto-occipital lesions can identify objects but appear to have difficulty in pointing to them (De Renzi, 1982), whilst certain types of agnosic patient appear to have essentially the opposite pattern of impairment (Bauer & Rubens, 1985).

In extending this distinction to the study of mental imagery, Farah et al. (1988) point to Baddeley and Lieberman's (1980) demonstration that performance of the Brooks matrix task can be more disrupted by a secondary task that contains a spatial component than by a secondary task that requires visual discriminations. Other results point to the functional role that an essentially visual attribute such as colour can have in a mental image.

It is the performance of LH, however, that provides some of the most compelling evidence for the visual imagery/spatial imagery distinction. Farah et al. (1988) argue that LH's good scores on tasks such as mental rotation, the Brooks matrix, locating the position of states in the United States, and his ability to describe familiar routes around the city suggest that spatial imagery is intact. Conversely, his poor performance on tests requiring retrieval of properties such as shape, colour, and relative size of objects suggests a visual imagery impairment.

ELD provides an interesting contrast with LH, performing well on many of the tasks that he finds difficult and failing at tasks on which he is unimpaired. However, we would wish to emphasize that ELD does *not* provide a double dissociation with LH; there are several reasons why ELD cannot be suffering from a spatial imagery deficit in the context of preserved visual imagery. For instance, ELD is as impaired at short-term memory for visual information (faces) as she is at short-term memory for spatial information (Brooks matrix). Moreover, in the Location of Cities task in Experiment 7, she performed as well as the control subjects at retrieving *spatial* information from long-term memory.

What ELD shows instead is a dissociation between imagery for material she has been exposed to *since* her illness and imagery for information acquired *before* her illness. Thus she is poor on the visuo-spatial short-term memory tasks because they involve the generation of *new* images, but is good on the tasks used in Experiment 7 because they require *retrieval* of representations laid down before she became ill in 1985. Consistent with this, ELD was good at the Faces of Celebrities test in Experiment 7, which requires imagery for faces that became famous before 1985. However, she is poor at recognizing people who have achieved prominence since 1985 (Hanley et al., 1990) and has correspondingly poor imagery for them. When questioned, for instance, she knew that Mikhail Gorbachev was the leader of the Soviet Union but stated that he was not balding; she knew that Madonna was a pop singer but did not know that she had fair hair; she stated that James Anderton was a well-known police chief of right-wing inclination and that Mike Gatting was a famous cricketer, but did not recall that either of them had beards. There is preserved visual imagery, therefore, *only* for people that ELD was familiar with before her illness in 1985. She shows a dissociation between preserved retrograde and impaired anterograde components of mental imagery ability.

An interpretation in terms of an anterograde imagery deficit is also consistent with ELD's spontaneous complaints regarding imagery. She states that she has difficulty in forming a mental picture of her new flat when she is out shopping and is trying to decide whether a piece of furniture or an ornament would look attractive in her living room. In addition, she will sometimes wake up in the middle of the night quite unable to bring to mind the layout of her bedroom in the darkness. On the other hand, she says that she *can* bring to mind the layout of the shop where she worked before her illness and the house that she was brought up in by her parents. Finally, she says that she has not had any dreams since the time of her illness but remembers dreaming frequently before 1985.

The Role of the Sketch-Pad in Retrieving Information Stored in Long-Term Memory

It is also important to consider further the implications of ELD's ability to access and retrieve visuo-spatial information about pre-morbidly familiar stimuli from long-term memory in Experiment 7, despite the proposed sketch-pad impairment. One possible explanation is that the sketch-pad is involved in processing incoming visuo-spatial information but is not involved in the retrieval of visuo-spatial information from long-term memory. Consistent with this interpretation, the short-term memory patient PV has no apparent difficulties in accessing familiar phonological information despite her articulatory loop impairment (Vallar & Baddeley, 1984). As ELD's lesion is in the right hemisphere, such a conclusion is also compatible with Farah's (1989) claim that the generation of images from long-term memory makes more demands of the left hemisphere than the right, whereas the spatial transformation of images has greater right-hemisphere involvement.

Nevertheless, such a conclusion raises the question as to how ELD is able to perform so well on tasks such as the animals' tails, the faces of celebrities task, and the country shape comparisons, which seem to involve both retrieval *and* detailed processing of visuo-spatial information stored in long-term memory. One possibility is that these tasks do not require an imagery buffer, and that the comparisons they involve are carried out within a propositional framework (cf. Pylyshyn, 1973). Such a suggestion is not inconsistent with a dissociation between visual and verbal memory systems.

As Anderson (1978) puts it, "One could propose that all information has a propositional form, but that propositions encoding visual information are stored in the right hemisphere and propositions encoding verbal in the left" (p. 271).

Alternatively, it might be the case that these tasks do make use of an imagery buffer, but a different buffer from that which is involved in the processing of incoming visuo-spatial information. This would be consistent with Riddoch's (1990) recent claim that there are two separate imagery buffers. One of these (the visual buffer) represents incoming visuo-spatial information, whereas the other (the imagery buffer) represents information generated from long-term visual memory. According to such a view, ELD would be seen as having an impairment of the visual *input* buffer at the same time as having a normal imagery buffer for previously learned information. However, it is not clear how such an account would handle ELD's poor performance on the imagery mnemonic task (Experiment 5) as it presumably involves the processing of old images.

The suggestion that there might be two separate imagery buffers is, of course, in conflict with the views of Kosslyn (1980) and Farah (1984), who argue for a single system. The only way of reconciling ELD's pattern of performance with this position would be to argue that the tasks that ELD finds difficult (e.g. mental rotation, imagery mnemonics, Brooks matrix, etc.) make more demands of the imagery buffer than do the tasks that ELD performs successfully (e.g. face comparison, animals' tails etc.). Logie (1989) has recently proposed that visual short-term memory comprises a passive visual store and an active visual rehearsal process. It may be the case that ELD can generate information into the visual store but starts to perform poorly whenever the task involves any manipulation or rehearsal of information that is held in that store. Such an account would mean that the tasks used in Experiment 7 either do not require image rehearsal or else require less rehearsal than do the tasks on which ELD is impaired. The issue cannot be resolved without further investigation of ELD, or related cases. The present findings serve simply to highlight its importance.

The Role of the Sketch-Pad in Learning New Information

In essence, our findings show that ELD's impairment on visual imagery tasks parallels her impairment in visual recognition tasks. In both cases, the use of anterograde but not retrograde visual memory is impaired. It is therefore tempting to argue that ELD's imagery and visual recognition problems all have a common cause in her visuo-spatial sketch-pad impairment. If the sketch-pad plays a role in transferring new information into long-term memory as well as maintaining it in short-term memory, then a sketch-pad impairment might well cause problems in learning new faces, objects, and routes.

In this respect, it is interesting to note that Baddeley, Papagno, and Vallar (1988) have shown that PV is extremely poor at learning new vocabulary and suggest that this is because the words could not be maintained within the phonological loop long enough for consolidation in long-term memory to take place.

If ELD's sketch-pad impairment prevents consolidation of visuo-spatial information in long-term memory, then it would obviously impair recognition of novel stimuli and lead to difficulties in bringing to mind visual or spatial detail about them. We are particularly impressed by the fact that ELD's sketch-pad impairment was predicted to us by Baddeley (personal communication) on the basis of our findings concerning her visual recognition impairment (Hanley et al., 1990). However, one always has to bear in mind that an inference based on a pattern of neuropsychological *association*, especially in a single case, is weak at best. Careful investigation of the performance of other patients with recent visual memory loss on tasks associated with the visuo-spatial sketch-pad may reveal whether this link is causal or coincidental.

REFERENCES

Anderson, J. R. (1978). Arguments concerning representations for mental imagery. *Psychological Review, 85*, 249–277.

Baddeley, A. D. (1986). *Working memory*. Oxford: Clarendon Press.

Baddeley, A. D. (1990). *Human memory: Theory and practice*. Hove: Lawrence Erlbaum Assoc. Ltd.

Baddeley, A. D., Grant, S., Wight, E., & Thomson, E. (1975). Imagery and visual working memory. In *Attention and performance* (Vol. 5). London: Academic Press.

Baddeley, A. D. & Hitch, G. (1974). Working memory. In G. H. Bower (Ed.) *The psychology of learning and motivation* (Vol. 8). New York: Academic Press.

Baddeley, A. D. & Lieberman, K. (1980). Spatial working memory. In *Attention and performance* (Vol. 8). Hillsdale, NJ: Lawrence Erlbaum Associates, Inc.

Baddeley, A. D., Papagno, C., & Vallar, G. (1988). When long-term learning depends on short-term storage. *Journal of Memory and Language, 27*, 586–595.

Basso, A., Spinnler, H., Vallar, G., & Zanobio, M. E. (1982). Left hemisphere damage and selective impairment of auditory verbal short-term memory. *Neuropsychologia, 20*, 263–274.

Bauer, R. M. & Rubens, A. B. (1985). Agnosia. In K. M. Heilman & E. Valenstein (Ed.), *Clinical psychology* (2nd ed.). New York: Oxford University Press.

Bower, G. H. (1972). Mental imagery and associative learning. In L. W. Gregg (Ed.), *Cognition in learning and memory*. New York: Wiley.

Brooks, L. R. (1967). The suppression of visualization by reading. *The Quarterly Journal of Experimental Psychology, 19*, 289–299.

Conrad, R. & Hull, A. J. (1964). Information, acoustic confusion and memory span. *British Journal of Psychology, 55*, 429–432.

Craik, F. I. M. & Lockhart, R. S. (1972). Levels of processing: A framework for memory research. *Journal of Verbal Learning and Verbal Behavior, 11*, 671–684.

De Renzi, E. (1982). *Disorders of space exploration and cognition.* New York: Wiley.
De Renzi, E., Faglioni, P., & Previdi, P. (1977). Spatial memory and hemispheric locus of lesion. *Cortex, 13,* 424–433.
Farah, M. J. (1984). The neurological basis of mental imagery: A componential analysis. *Cognition, 18,* 245–272.
Farah, M. J. (1988). Is visual imagery really visual? Overlooked evidence from neuropsychology. *Psychological Review, 95,* 307–317.
Farah, M. J. (1989). The neural basis of mental imagery. *Trends in Neurosciences, 12,* 395–399.
Farah, M. J., Hammond, K. L., Levine, D. N., & Calvanio, R. (1988). Visual and spatial mental imagery: Dissociable systems of representation. *Cognitive Psychology, 20,* 439–462.
Hanley, J. R., Pearson, N. A., & Young, A. W. (1990). Impaired memory for new visual forms. *Brain, 113,* 1131–1148.
Hull, A. J. (1973). A letter-digit matrix of auditory confusions. *British Journal of Psychology, 64,* 579–585.
Jacoby, L. L., Craik, F. I. M., & Begg, I. (1979). Effects of decision difficulty on recognition and recall. *Journal of Verbal Learning and Verbal Behavior, 18,* 585–600.
Kosslyn, S. M. (1980). *Image and mind.* Cambridge: Harvard University Press.
Levine, D. N., Warach, J., & Farah, M. J. (1985). Two visual systems in mental imagery: Dissociations of what and where in imagery disorders due to bilateral posterior cerebral lesions. *Neurology, 35,* 1010–1018.
Logie, R. H. (1989). Characteristics of visual short-term memory. *European Journal of Cognitive Psychology, 1,* 275–284.
Morris, R. (1984). Dementia and the functioning of the articulatory loop system. *Cognitive Neuropsychology, 1,* 143–159.
Newcombe, F., Ratcliff, G., & Damasio, H. (1987). Dissociable visual and spatial impairments following right posterior cerebral lesions: Clinical, neuropsychological and anatomical evidence. *Neuropsychologia, 25,* 149–161.
Paivio, A. (1971). *Imagery and verbal processes.* New York: Holt, Rinehart and Winston.
Pylyshyn, Z. W. (1973). What the mind's eye tells the mind's brain: A critique of mental imagery. *Psychological Bulletin, 80,* 1–24.
Riddoch, M. J. (1990). Loss of visual imagery: A generation deficit. *Cognitive Neuropsychology, 7,* 249–273.
Riddoch, M. J. & Humphreys, G. W. (1987). Visual object processing in optic aphasia: A case of semantic access agnosia. *Cognitive Neuropsychology, 4,* 131–185.
Ross, E. D. (1980) Sensory-specific and fractional disorders of recent memory in man. Isolated loss of visual recent memory. *Archives of Neurology, 37,* 193–200.
Shepard, R. N. (1978). The mental image. *American Psychologist, 33,* 125–137.
Shepard, R. N. (1984). Kinematics of perceiving, imagining, thinking, and dreaming. *Psychological Review, 91,* 417–447.
Shepard, R. N. & Metzler, J. (1971). Mental rotation of three-dimensional objects. *Science, 171,* 701–703.
Snodgrass, J. G. & Vanderwart, M. (1980). A standardized set of 260 pictures: norms for name agreement, image agreement, familiarity and visual complexity. *Journal of Experimental Psychology : Human Learning and Memory, 6,* 174–215.
Thurstone, T. G. & Jeffrey, T. E. (1956). *Flags. A test of spatial thinking.* Chicago: Industrial Relations Center.
Ungerleider, L. G. & Mishkin, M. (1982). Two cortical visual systems. In D. J. Ingle, M. A. Goodale, & R. J. W. Mansfield (Eds.), *Analysis of visual behavior* (pp. 549–586). Cambridge, MA: MIT Press.
Vallar, G. & Baddeley, A. D. (1984). Fractionation of working memory: Neuropsychological evidence for a phonological short-term store. *Journal of Verbal Learning and Verbal Behavior, 23,* 151–161.

SKETCH-PAD IMPAIRMENT

431

Warrington, E. K. (1985). *Recognition memory test*. Windsor: NFER-Nelson.
Warrington, E. W. & Shallice, T. (1969). The selective impairment of auditory verbal short-term memory. *Brain*, *92*, 885–896.

Manuscript received 24 May 1990

APPENDIX

The stimuli used in Experiment 7 were as follows:

Colour

What is the typical colour associated with:

postvan (red), carrot (red or orange), butter (yellow or white), salt (white), tree bark (brown), police uniform (blue), golf ball (white), motorway sign (blue), tarmac (black), dandelion (yellow), beer (brown), xmas tree (green), elephant (grey), cricket ball (red), tiger (yellow and black), buttercup (yellow), sheep (white), ladybird (red and black), fire engine (red), ambulance (white), pillar box (red), LP record (black), daffodil (yellow), flour (white), cauliflower (white).

Animal's Tails

Do these animals generally have short or long tails:

kangaroo (long), horse (long), rabbit (short), spaniel (short), elephant (long), sheep (short), lion (long), labrador (long), goat (short), rhino (short), mole (short), polar bear (short), giraffe (long), deer (short), badger (short), wolf (long), cow (long), hippo (short), camel (long), tiger (long).

Size Comparison

Which is the larger of these two objects:
(the correct answer is the first member of the pair).

sprout/peanut, date/sultana, box of matches/sugar cube, ping-pong ball/grape, pillow/sponge, tie/pencil, wine glass/thimble, banana/toothbrush, briefcase/hot-water bottle, toilet roll/egg cup, cheque book/cigarette packet, LP record/saucer, tea pot/light bulb, book/credit card, tea bag/engagement ring, 50 pence piece/postage stamp.

City Locations

Which of these two cities is closer to:
(the correct answer is the first member of the pair).

Liverpool: Manchester/Leeds, Exeter: Bristol/Dover, Glasgow: Edinburgh/Aberdeen, Cardiff: Swansea/Wrexham, Bradford: Durham/Newcastle, York: Hull/Sheffield, Blackpool: Preston/Bolton, Doncaster: Lincoln/Middlesbrough, Stoke: Chester/Cambridge, Southampton: Brighton/Plymouth, Dublin: Belfast/Londonderry, Nottingham: Derby/Northampton, Stirling: Dundee/Inverness, Oxford: Reading/Ipswich, Wolverhampton: Coventry/Norwich.

Country Shapes

Which of these two countries is closer in shape to:
(the correct answer is the first member of the pair).

Canada: Turkey/Norway, Argentina: Germany/Australia, Spain: Wales/Alaska, China: USA/
South Africa, Italy: Mexico/India, Portugal: Chile/Denmark, Brazil: France/Ireland.

Faces of Celebrities

Which of these two celebrities looks most like:
(the correct answer is the first member of the pair).

Cliff Richard: Mike Read/Noel Edmonds, John Wayne: Robert Mitchum/Charles Bronson,
Nigel Lawson: Leon Brittan/Geoffrey Howe, Dolly Parton: Diana Dors/Hattie Jacques, Emlyn
Hughes: Kenny Dalglish/Kevin Keegan, Charlie Chaplin: Adolf Hitler/Winston Churchill, Paul
McCartney: Tony Blackburn/Mick Jagger, Bobby Charlton: Norman Tebbit/Sean Connery,
Margaret Thatcher: June Whitfield/Pat Phoenix, David Bellamy: Dave Lee Travis/Roy Kin-
near, Eamonn Andrews: Bamber Gascoigne/Nicholas Parsons, Eric Sykes: Spike Milligan/
Harry Secombe, Willie Carson: Paul Daniels/Larry Grayson, Neil Kinnock: Val Doonican/
Frank Bough, David Essex: Paul Michael Glaser/Dennis Waterman, Elizabeth Taylor: Joan
Collins/Barbara Windsor, John Gielgud: Ralph Richardson/Charles Laughton, Sebastian Coe:
John Craven/Richard Briers, David Steel: Melvyn Bragg/Bruce Forsyth, Ernie Wise: Kenneth
Kendall/Ronnie Corbett.

Chapter 4   Face Processing

McNeil, J.E. & Warrington, E.K. (1993). Prosopagnosia: a face-specific disorder. *Quarterly Journal of Experimental Psychology, 46A*, 1–10.

The neuropsychology of face processing has attracted strong interest, driven in part by rapidly accumulating neurophysiological evidence of differential involvement of some brain regions in face perception (Gross & Sergent, 1992; Sergent & Signoret, 1992a). However, it seems that these specialised brain regions are not involved with the processing of faces to the exclusion of all other visual stimuli; cells that respond maximally to faces are interspersed with other cells having different functional properties (Gross & Sergent, 1992). Yet the evidence from investigations of prosopagnosia continues to point toward the possibility of face-specific deficits in some, very rare cases. Our chosen reading for Chapter 4 (McNeil & Warrington, 1993) provides a particularly compelling example in which the deficit affected mainly *human* faces; when McNeil and Warrington's (1993) prosopagnosic patient took up farming, he was able to learn to recognise his sheep, and correctly identified several of them from photographs of their faces! A similar report has been made with another case, RM (Sergent & Signoret, 1992b). When asked to recognise famous faces, RM could only identify Mikhail Gorbachev (from his birthmark) out of 300 faces shown. However, RM was very interested in cars, and was still able to give the manufacturer's name, model, and approximate year of manufacture to 172/210 pictures of cars. In this task, RM outperformed six normal controls, whose best score was 128/210.

Although they are exceptionally rare, such cases imply that the possibility of face-specific deficits must be taken seriously. We therefore need to ask why this can happen. The most common type of explanation emphasises some aspect of the *visual* demands of face recognition; faces form a category with a particularly large number of very similar exemplars (Gross, 1992), they place special demands on whole-based encoding mechanisms (Farah, 1991), and so on. However, although it has seldom been suggested, we think it equally plausible that it will prove to be the *semantic* properties of faces that are the principal cause. In other words, it is the need to access rapidly previously stored knowledge of familiar individuals that may dictate the creation of a domain-specific recognition mechanism.

The force of this argument can be seen by considering neuropsychological cases that involve loss of memory for people. Ellis, Young, and Critchley (1989) worked with KS, who suffered severe loss of memory for people following a history of epilepsy and a right anterior temporal lobectomy. This was quite different from a prosopagnosia, because people were poorly recognised from their faces or from their names, suggesting a more central loss of information. Yet KS was highly intelligent and certainly not amnesic (her

Memory Quotient of 122 was in line with her IQ of 119). She also showed no generalised semantic memory deficit; for example, being able to classify correctly a penguin as a bird even though she could not remember that Tchaikovsky was a composer. However, although her problem was strikingly circumscribed, it was not entirely restricted to people; KS was also poor at recognising famous animals, famous buildings, and familiar product names.

A similar problem has been documented as part of a progressive impairment associated with right temporal lobe atrophy for case VH (Evans, Heggs, Antoun, & Hodges, 1995). VH initially presented symptoms of prosopagnosia, being unable to recognise faces of many people whose names she recognised with ease, but on follow-up 9 months later she was found to be impaired at recognising both faces and names, even though she remained highly intelligent (IQ 117 on initial presentation, 119 at follow-up) and did not show any pronounced deterioration of other cognitive skills.

For a member of a social species, inability to remember things about other people can have a devastating impact. Our observations of KS (Ellis et al., 1989) revealed her to be severely handicapped in everyday life. Conversations had to be kept to straightforward concrete matters, as any reference to other people or the things they had done could rapidly lead to incomprehension. KS seldom initiated conversations herself, because without being able to remember much about the person she was talking to, she could think of little to say. She worked in a library, but had to be taken off the front desk and given clerical duties when she was found to be unable to answer inquiries because she no longer recognised the names of famous authors.

An important feature of face-processing impairments is that they can also be specific to certain aspects of face perception, and further strong evidence has been found of dissociable impairments affecting the determination of identity and expression from the face (Young, Newcombe, de Haan, Small, & Hay, 1993). At present, though, much more is known about impaired recognition of identity (and especially prosopagnosia) than is known about impaired recognition of expression. A recent striking finding concerning facial expressions of emotion suggests that there may be some emotion-specific deficits; recognition of facial expressions of fear was found to be differentially severely affected by bilateral damage to the amygdala (Adolphs, Tranel, Damasio, & Damasio, 1994, 1995). This implies that the functional component labelled "expression analysis" in Fig. 4.1 (p. 88) needs to be carefully investigated to see whether it may fractionate along fault lines corresponding to certain basic emotions.

Chapter 4 proposes a rough division of prosopagnosias into those reflecting defective perception of the face and those based on impaired memory of previously stored appearances of familiar people. This distinction is challenged by a certain type of connectionist model, which uses the same processing units to represent both perception and memory (Farah, 1994). However, clinical reports continue to demonstrate a degree of independence between perceptual and mnestic prosopagnosias, suggesting that this particular connectionist interpretation is incorrect (De Renzi, Faglioni, Grossi, & Nichelli, 1991). One way to tease apart these accounts is through investigating face imagery. If perceptual and memory representations involve a common representational system, as in Farah's (1994) connectionist model, prosopagnosia will always involve impaired face imagery (i.e. inability to describe the appearances of familiar people from memory). In contrast, the proposal of separate perceptual and memory representations (as in Fig 4.1, p. 88, which separates structural encoding from face recognition units) leads to the prediction that prosopagnosias due primarily to impaired perception (i.e. problems in structural encoding) may be associated with relatively preserved face imagery, whereas memory-based prosopagnosias (involving problems at the face recognition unit level) will involve loss of face imagery. This latter prediction has been supported by detailed case studies (Young, Humphreys, Riddoch, Hellawell, & de Haan, 1994).

Although the type of connectionist account favoured by Farah (1994) therefore runs into problems accounting for the evidence, other connectionist approaches look promising. Burton and his colleagues have managed to implement certain key features of the architecture shown in Fig. 4.1 into a connectionist computer simulation (Burton, 1994; Burton & Bruce, 1993; Burton, Bruce, & Johnston, 1990). It turns out that when it is damaged in a certain way, this computer model can simulate many of the properties of covert recognition in prosopagnosia described in Chapter 4 (Burton, Young, Bruce, Johnston, & Ellis, 1991). This advance has opened up the possibility that understanding covert recognition may be a more tractable problem than it first appeared, although it does not solve some of the more difficult conceptual and philosophical issues associated with awareness of recognition.

REFERENCES

Adolphs, R., Tranel, D., Damasio, H., & Damasio, A. (1994). Impaired recognition of emotion in facial expressions following bilateral damage to the human amygdala. *Nature, 372,* 669–672.

Adolphs, R., Tranel, D., Damasio, H., & Damasio, A.R. (1995). Fear and the human amygdala. *Journal of Neuroscience, 15,* 5879–5891.

Burton, A.M. (1994). Learning new faces in an interactive activation and competition model. *Visual Cognition, 1,* 313–348.

Burton, A.M. & Bruce, V. (1993). Naming faces and naming names: exploring an interactive activation model of person recognition. *Memory, 1,* 457–480.

Burton, A.M., Bruce, V., & Johnston, R.A. (1990). Understanding face recognition with an interactive activation model. *British Journal of Psychology, 81,* 361–380.

Burton, A.M., Young, A.W., Bruce, V., Johnston, R., & Ellis, A.W. (1991). Understanding covert recognition. *Cognition, 39,* 129–166.

De Renzi, E., Faglioni, P., Grossi, D., & Nichelli, P. (1991) Apperceptive and associative forms of prosopagnosia. *Cortex, 27,* 213–221.

Ellis, A.W., Young, A.W., & Critchley, E.M.R. (1989). Loss of memory for people following temporal lobe damage. *Brain, 112*, 1469–1483.

Evans, J.J., Heggs, A.J., Antoun, N., & Hodges, J.R. (1995). Progressive prosopagnosia associated with selective right temporal lobe atrophy: a new syndrome? *Brain, 118*, 1–13.

Farah, M.J. (1991). Patterns of co-occurrence among the associative agnosias: implications for visual object representation. *Cognitive Neuropsychology, 8*, 1–19.

Farah, M.J. (1994). Neuropsychological inference with an interactive brain: a critique of the "locality" assumption. *Behavioral and Brain Sciences, 17*, 43–104.

Gross, C.G. (1992). Representation of visual stimuli in inferior temporal cortex. *Philosophical Transactions of the Royal Society London, B335*, 3–10.

Gross, C.G., & Sergent, J. (1992). Face recognition. *Current Opinion in Neurobiology, 2*, 156–61.

McNeil, J.E. & Warrington, E.K. (1993). Prosopagnosia: a face-specific disorder. *Quarterly Journal of Experimental Psychology, 46A*, 1–10.

Sergent, J. & Signoret, J.-L. (1992a). Functional and anatomical decomposition of face processing: evidence from prosopagnosia and PET study of normal subjects. *Philosophical Transactions of the Royal Society London, B335*, 55–62.

Sergent, J. & Signoret, J.-L. (1992b). Varieties of functional deficits in prosopagnosia. *Cerebral Cortex, 2*, 375–388.

Young, A.W., Humphreys, G.W., Riddoch, M.J., Hellawell, D.J., & de Haan, E.H.F. (1994). Recognition impairments and face imagery. *Neuropsychologia, 32*, 693–702.

Young, A.W., Newcombe, F., de Haan, E.H.F., Small, M., & Hay, D.C. (1993). Face perception after brain injury: selective impairments affecting identity and expression. *Brain, 116*, 941–959.

Prosopagnosia: A Face-specific Disorder

Jane E. McNeil and Elizabeth K. Warrington

National Hospital, London, U.K.

A follow-up study of a patient, WJ, with a very severe prosopagnosia is reported. After a stroke he became a farmer and acquired a flock of sheep. He learnt to recognize and name many of his sheep, and his performance on tests of recognition memory and paired-associate learning for sheep was significantly better than on comparable tests using human face stimuli. It is concluded that in some instances prosopagnosia can be a face-specific disorder.

Experimental studies of face perception have shown a double dissociation between the ability to perceive unknown faces and the ability to recognize familiar faces (Tranel, Damasio, & Damasio, 1988; Warrington & James, 1967). However, one of the continuing controversies is whether or not prosopagnosia, the inability to recognize familiar faces, is specific to faces. Bodamer (1947) first described the syndrome as a specific disorder of the face recognition system, but more recent authors have suggested that the deficit may also apply to other within-category discriminations. Damasio, Damasio, and Van Hoesen (1982) suggested that prosopagnosia was not specific to human faces, but would be found for all "visually ambiguous stimuli whose recognition depends on contextual memory evocation" (p. 331).

Recent studies have suggested that prosopagnosia itself may not be a unitary disorder. De Renzi (1986; De Renzi, Faglioni, Grossi, & Nichelli, 1991) has proposed two distinct types of prosopagnosia. The first he terms "perceptual" or "apperceptive prosopagnosia" and the second "mnestic" or "associative prosopagnosia". He also proposes that it is among patients with the associative form that a face-specific disorder is most likely to be observed. Indeed Case 4 from his 1986 paper appeared to be a case of the

We are grateful to Ms Anne-Marie Regan for supplying us with photographs of Irish sheep. Thanks are also due to Dr Gordon Plant for providing us facilities to carry out this investigation.

associative form of prosopagnosia, a deficit that was selective for faces. He was unable to recognize close friends or relatives but could identify his own belongings from others of the same category, sort foreign from Italian coins, and pick out particular breeds of cats from photographs. However, it could be argued that that these types of tasks are easier than distinguishing between two faces.

In our alternative classification (McNeil & Warrington, 1991) we have treated apperceptive difficulties as an associated deficit and would wish instead to emphasize the presence or absence of covert recognition. So, rather than distinguishing between apperceptive and associative forms, we suggested that the two forms could be seen as being due to either a disconnection of the face recognition units or damage to the units themselves. However, this issue of face specificity still exists.

Davidoff (1986) has argued that visual stimuli need to be equated for familiarity and difficulty of discrimination before a selective deficit for faces can be inferred. At the very least, within-category discriminations for other visually difficult categories should be tested.

There are a few papers in the literature that have attempted to test prosopagnosic patients' abilities to make other within-category discriminations by using animals that were previously familiar to them. Bornstein (1963) reported the case of a bird watcher who could no longer identify birds, and Bornstein, Sroka, and Munitz (1969) describe a prosopagnosic farmer who was no longer able to recognize his own cows. Bruyer et al. (1983) provide a clinical description of a farmer (Mr W) who could not recognize faces but who could identify his own cows and dogs. A further case by Assal, Favre, and Anderes (1984) showed the converse pattern. They describe a farmer, MX, who was initially impaired at recognizing human faces and his livestock (cows). However, when he was retested after 6 months, he had recovered the ability to recognize faces but still unable to recognize his cows.

These studies provide some evidence that prosopagnosic patients can be unimpaired on other visually similar and confusable stimuli and there-ιore do appear to have a face-specific disorder. The aim of the present study is to describe our further observations of a very severe case of prosopagnosia, who had a stable and longstanding impairment for recognizing very familiar people but who nevertheless learnt to identify a flock of sheep.

CASE REPORT

WJ was a 51-year-old right-handed professional man with a history of at least 3 vascular episodes. On examination he was found to have a profound prosopagnosia, normal visual acuity, and a dense right homonymous hemianopia with a relative scotoma in the upper left quadrants. A CT scan showed low-density lesions in the left occipital lobe and left frontal and temporal lobes. There was also low attenuation in the right occipital lobe.

Neuropsychological Investigation

WJ showed a significant impairment on the Peformance scale of the WAIS but was unimpaired on the Verbal Scale (PIQ = 116, VIQ = 143). He had a selective visual memory impairment, scoring at a chance level on the visual version of the Recognition Memory test but in the average range on the verbal version (Warrington, 1984). He had excellent naming skills, and he achieved a high score (24/30) on a proper names test (McKenna & Warrington, 1980). He performed normally on tests of shape detection and shape discrimination. He was impaired on some perceptual tests including unusual views and object silhouettes. However, his most marked impairments were on tasks that required the perception and recognition of faces. He was able to identify only 2 out of 12 very well-known faces, and it seemed that even for the faces that he correctly identified he was performing the task through the use of deductive strategies rather than by actually recognizing them. He was also unable to judge the age, sex, or facial expression of faces and was impaired on tests of face matching, including the Benton and Van Allen (1968) test (WJ's score = 36/54, which is in the moderately impaired range). (For further details, see McNeil and Warrington, 1991, Case 1.)

EXPERIMENTAL INVESTIGATION

1. Famous Face Familiarity

Our aim in this experiment was to confirm WJ's poor face recognition abilities and to replicate our original observations of covert recognition of faces. This test consisted of 30 arrays of three faces: one famous face and two unfamiliar distractors, which were similar in appearance (see Figure 1 for an example of the stimuli used). The famous faces were all contem-

TABLE 1
Scores on Famous Face Familiarity Tests

	Date Tested	
	10 June 1991	31 Oct. 1991
Face only	10/30	13/30
Face and name	20/30	25/30

FIG. 1.   An example of face familiarity stimuli.

porary personalities (this is an updated version of the original test material used by Warrington & McCarthy, 1988). The patient was merely required to pick out the famous face from the two unfamiliar distractor stimuli. WJ was administered this test on two occasions (6 months apart). His results were close to chance on both occasions (see Table 1).

The same test stimuli were re-presented together with the name of the famous face. So, rather than being asked, "which is the famous face?" he was asked, "which is Michael Aspel?" The number correct on each occasion was significantly greater than when he was merely pointing to the famous face: sign tests, $n = 16$, $x = 4$ and $n = 18$, $x = 3$, 1-tailed $p < 0.05$. WJ maintained that he was guessing on this task, even though his performance dramatically improved.

These findings provide a very robust replication of our original observations and suggest that WJ has covert face recognition abilities.

2.   Sheep Identification

Our earlier study did not address the issue of face specificity. We reported that WJ was able to name 9/10 famous buildings, 7/7 breeds of dog, 7/7 makes of car, and 14/15 flowers. But although these tasks test within-category discrimination, they do not test identification of unique individual exemplars within a category, as is the case for faces. The following experiments will attempt to test this by looking at WJ's abilities to recognize sheep.

WJ had recently (2 years previously) acquired a flock of 36 sheep, which he kindly photographed for the purposes of these experiments. Each of the 36 sheep had a number (ranging from 1 to 59) which was written on a tag in its ear, so that they could be individually identified. A sub-set of 16 sheep photographs was re-photographed so that only the face of each sheep, without a tag, was visible. WJ's first task was to tell us the number label of each of the sheep. He was able to identify, by number, 8/16 sheep; however, this is probably an underestimate of his actual knowledge of his sheep, as in several instances he would say things like, "I know that sheep very well, she's the one that had three lambs last year, but I can't remember her number". Obviously all answers like this had to be scored as incorrect as there was no way to check his answers. Nevertheless, WJ still shows a striking ability to recognize his sheep.

3. Recognition Memory for Sheep

To eliminate the need for WJ to recall the number labels of the sheep, a Yes/No recognition test was devised: 8 of the photographs of sheep faces were presented singly at a 3-sec presentation rate (see Figure 2). An orienting task was used, in which WJ had to say whether he thought the sheep was pleasant/not pleasant. Recognition memory was then tested by presenting the 8 stimuli and 8 distractors in a random order. WJ was required to say whether or not each item had been in the stimulus list.

Two subjects, in the same age range, who had also recently retired (4 years) and acquired a flock of sheep, were tested as controls; 5 age- and profession-matched controls were also tested.

FIG. 2.   Examples of "known" sheep.

TABLE 2
Recognition Memory for Faces of Sheep and People

| | | Mean Percentage Correct (Range) | |
| | | Controls | |
	WJ	Profession Matched	Sheep Experienced
Familiar sheep	87	66 (44–81)	59 (44–75)
Unfamiliar sheep	81	69 (56–81)	63 (44–81)
Faces	50	89 (75–100)	100

Two further versions of this recognition memory test were devised. The first used a different breed of sheep that were unknown to WJ and the second photographs of unknown human faces (with the hair masked). In each test there were again 8 stimuli and 8 distractors, and in each a pleasant/ not pleasant orienting test was used. Both recognition memory tests were administered to WJ and the control subjects using the same Yes/No recognition procedure. The percentage correct for each test for WJ and the mean percentage correct (and range) for the control subjects are shown in Table 2.

The pattern of test scores for WJ is the opposite to that obtained by the control subjects. The profession-matched controls were significantly better at the unfamiliar face version than the unfamiliar sheep version: Wilcoxon test, $N = 5$, $T = 0$, $p < 0.05$. The two subjects with experience with sheep performed within the range of the profession-matched control group. However, WJ obtained significantly higher scores on both the familiar and unfamiliar sheep versions of this test than on the face version: $\chi^2 = 7.27$ and 9.6, respectively, $p < 0.05$. It is worth noting that the control subjects' performance was very similar on the tests using WJ's sheep and those using the sheep unfamiliar to WJ; it therefore seems reasonable to assume that WJ's sheep are not particularly easy to recognize.

4. Paired Associate Learning for Sheep and Faces

This test was a modification of a paired-associate learning task originally used by De Haan, Young, and Newcombe (1987) to demonstrate covert knowledge of faces. It consisted of 6 photographs of unknown sheep faces, which were paired with 6 plausible sheep "names" (e.g. "Frisky"). Figure 3 shows an example of the sheep stimuli used. The 6 photographs were presented one at a time, and WJ was told the name that was to be associated with each face. He was then tested on his ability to recall the name for each sheep face photograph. The faces were presented in a

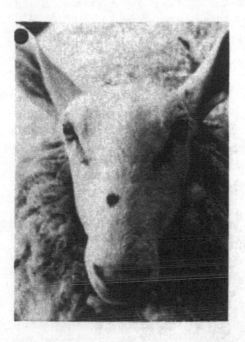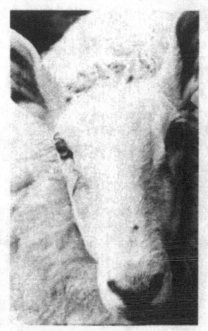

FIG. 3. Examples of "unknown" sheep.

different random order on each trial, and incorrect answers and no responses were corrected immediately by giving the correct answer. A second version of this task was devised using human faces, which were paired with similar descriptor names matched for frequency (e.g. "Friendly"). Five learning trials were given on each version of the test. The number of names correctly recalled across all the trials by WJ and the control subjects is given in Table 3.

TABLE 3
Paired Associate Learning for Sheep and People

	Mean Percentage Correct		
		Controls	
	WJ	Profession Matched	Sheep Experienced
Faces	23	71	78
Sheep	57	41	55

The control subjects were significantly better at paired-associate learning of names for human faces than for sheep faces: Wilcoxon test, $N = 5$, $T = 0$, $p < 0.05$. An identical pattern was observed in the two subjects with experience of sheep. However, WJ did not show this normal human face advantage. His pattern of performance was the converse of that obtained by the control subjects, so that he was significantly better at learning sheep faces: $\chi^2 = 5.625$, $p < 0.05$.

This pattern of results is the same as that obtained on the recognition memory tests and indicates that WJ is unimpaired on tests involving sheep but performs poorly on learning and memory tasks involving human faces.

DISCUSSION

It has been shown that WJ continues to exhibit a profound prosopagnosia. In contrast, however, he has a remarkable ability to recognize another group of visually and easily confusable stimuli, the faces of sheep. He was able to identify his own sheep and claimed to recognize them more easily than faces. But, perhaps more surprisingly, he was also able to perform recognition memory tasks using photographs of sheep that were unfamiliar. It seems difficult to explain these results in terms of difficulty of discrimination, as the profession-matched controls found the sheep stimuli incredibly difficult to recognize (subjects complained that they "all looked the same"). It also cannot be explained in terms of familiarity with sheep, as the sheep-experienced controls were only marginally better. Unlike the other previously reported cases, WJ had no experience of sheep before he developed his prosopagnosia. His current abilities to recognize sheep must have been learnt since his stroke, added to which it would seem implausible that he was now more familiar with sheep than with faces. It therefore seems as if WJ does in fact exhibit a face-specific recognition problem whilst remaining able to recognize other visually difficult and confusable stimuli.

According to De Renzi's classification, WJ should be termed a perceptual or apperceptive prosopagnosic (as he is severely impaired on tests of face perception) and should therefore be less likely to show a face-specific impairment. However, WJ does appear to have a face-specific deficit, as he can perform recognition memory tasks involving visually difficult stimuli other than faces. It seems implausible that his perceptual difficulties are only relevant for the recognition of faces, as the sheep stimuli used were just as perceptually demanding as faces. This seems further reason to suppose that his perceptual difficulties are insufficient to explain his prosopagnosia and should be seen as an associated deficit.

How WJ has learnt to recognize sheep is a matter for debate. It is possible that he has developed a sheep "prototype", which enables the effective encoding of sheep facial features. What is quite surprising, however, is the extent to which his abilities appear to generalize to other visually dissimilar breeds of sheep. Perhaps the more remarkable finding is that WJ has been totally unable to overcome his prosopagnosia. He has been seen in the department regularly over the past three years, and he is no better at recognizing faces now than when first seen in 1988. He seems unable to utilize the sorts of strategies he has learnt to use for sheep. This would suggest that his damaged face recognition system is actually still operating to such an extent that it prevents him from developing new strategies for use with faces. Previously we interpreted his performance on tests of face familiarity and famous face/name matching with reference to the Bruce and Young (1986) model of face perception and suggested that for WJ the problem lay at the output from the face recognition units to the person identity nodes and could be considered a disconnection. The units themselves are undamaged but are disconnected from the person identity nodes. It is possible that the existence of intact but disconnected face recognition units prevents the development of alternative methods of perceptual encoding.

Our patient provides further evidence that prosopagnosia can occur as a face-specific deficit. Other visually complex and difficult-to-discriminate stimuli were processed normally, indicating that prosopagnosia cannot be seen as a more general impairment for within-category discriminations. For some cases, at least, prosopagnosia appears to be a face-specific impairment.

REFERENCES

Assal, G., Favre, C., & Anderes, J.P. (1984). Non-reconnaissance d'animaux familiers chez un paysan: Zooagnosie ou prosopagnosie pour les animaux. *Revue Neurologique, 140*, 580–584.

Benton, A.L., & Van Allen, M.W. (1968). Impairment in facial recognition in patients with cerebral disease. *Cortex, 4*, 344–358.

Bodamer, J. (1947). Die Prosop-Agnosie. *Archiv für Psychiatrie und Nervenkrankheiten, 179*, 6–53.

Bornstein, B. (1963). Prosopagnosia. In L. Halpern (Ed.), *Problems of dynamic neurology*. Jerusalem: Hadassah Medical School.

Bornstein, B., Sroka, M., & Munitz, H. (1969). Prosopagnosia with animal face agnosia. *Cortex, 5*, 164–169.

Bruce, V., & Young, A.W. (1986). Understanding face recognition. *British Journal of Psychology, 77*, 305–327.

Bruyer, R., Laterre, C., Seron, X., Feyereisen, P., Strypstein, E., Pierrard, E., & Rectem, D. (1983). A case of prosopagnosia with some preserved covert remembrance of familiar faces. *Brain and Cognition, 2*, 257–284.

Damasio, A.R., Damasio, H., & Van Hoesen, G.W. (1982). Prosopagnosia: Anatomic basis and behavioral mechanisms. *Neurology, 32*, 321–341.

Davidoff, J.B. (1986). The specificity of face perception: Evidence from psychological investigations. In Bruyer, R. (Ed.), *The neuropsychology of face perception and facial expression*. Hillsdale, NJ: Lawrence Erlbaum Associates, Inc.

De Haan, E.H.F., Young, A.W., & Newcombe, F. (1987). Face recognition without awareness. *Cognitive Neuropsychology, 4*, 385–415.

De Renzi, E. (1986). Current issues in prosopagnosia. In H.D. Ellis, M.A. Jeeves, F. Newcombe, & A.W. Young (Eds.), *Aspects of face processing* (pp. 243–252). Dordrecht: Martinus Nijhoff.

De Renzi, E., Faglioni, P., Grossi, D., & Nichelli, P. (1991). Apperceptive and associative forms of prosopagnosia. *Cortex, 27*, 213–221.

McKenna, P., & Warrington, E.K. (1980). Testing for nominal dysphasia. *Journal of Neurology, Neurosurgery and Psychiatry, 43*, 781–788.

McNeil, J.E., & Warrington, E.K. (1991). Prosopagnosia: A reclassification. *Quarterly Journal of Experimental Psychology, 43A*, 267–287.

Tranel, D., Damasio, A.R., & Damasio, H. (1988). Intact recognition of facial expression, gender and age in patients with impaired recognition of face identity. *Neurology, 38*, 690–696.

Warrington, E.K. (1984). *Recognition memory test*. Windsor, Berks: NFER-Nelson Publishing Co. Ltd.

Warrington, E.K., & James, M. (1967). An experimental investigation of facial recognition in patients with unilateral cerebral lesions. *Cortex, 3*, 317–326.

Warrington, E.K., & McCarthy, R.A. (1988). The fractionation of retrograde amnesia. *Brain and Cognition, 7*, 184–200.

Revised manuscript received 25 May 1992

Chapter 5   Producing Spoken Words

Hanley, J.R. (1995). Are names difficult to recall because they are unique? A case study of a patient with anomia. *Quarterly Journal of Experimental Psychology*, *48A*, 487–506.

Chapter 5 is concerned with the production of individual spoken words. In the clinic that process tends to be investigated using the 'confrontation naming task' in which patients are asked to name pictures of familiar objects. Standardised tests such as the Graded Naming Test (McKenna & Warrington, 1983) will indicate whether or not a naming problem is present, but such tests may not, on their own, indicate how and where the problem is arising.

One possible cause of a naming deficit is an agnosic difficulty in recognising objects; this can be investigated using the techniques described in Chapter 2. In Chapter 5, we distinguished two further levels of naming breakdown. One is a conceptual semantic disorder that affects the patient's understanding of what objects are. Such a disorder will affect both the comprehension and the production of words, and will tend to lead to semantic errors in both input and output. Patient JCU of Howard and Orchard-Lisle (1984) was used to illustrate this type of disorder in Chapter 5 (see pp. 118–119 and 123–124). Other aphasic patients have since been described who make semantic errors in both comprehension and production (e.g. patient KE of Hillis, Rapp, Romani, & Caramazza, 1990), and central semantic deficits have been identified in patients with degenerative dementing conditions (Patterson & Hodges, 1994).

The second level of naming breakdown identified in Chapter 5 concerns the mapping from semantic representations to the object's name. We illustrated this with case EST (Kay & Ellis, 1987). However, a major theoretical development since 1988 concerns the way that we think about the processes involved in getting from a conceptual understanding of an object to its spoken name. In Chapter 5 we treated this as a one-stage process, but current accounts of word retrieval suggest that we should be identifying at least two stages. A characteristic of these models is that they seek, quite properly, to situate word retrieval more firmly in the context of sentence production (e.g. Butterworth, 1989; Levelt, 1989).

Suppose you are trying to name a picture of a settee. Your conceptual knowledge of settees tells you that they are padded seats capable of holding more than one person. But you might also refer to the same object as a "sofa" or a "couch". The first step in *lexicalisation* (i.e. word retrieval) is, therefore, to decide between these alternatives and to activate a representation that modern theories call a *lemma*. This is a word-specific representation, so there are separate lemmas for the words settee, sofa, and couch. Each lemma contains syntactic and semantic information about such things as a word's grammatical class (settee is a noun, not a verb or an adjective) and whether it is singular or plural. In the majority of the world's languages, the lemma for settee would also indicate that word's gender (e.g. whether it is masculine or feminine; English is unusual in not employing gender).

The lemma level is intimately involved with the process of sentence construction—deciding what the structure of the sentence is to be, and where the different elements will go. At the lemma level you do not, however, know the actual sound-form of the target word. Spoken word-forms are called *lexemes*, so the next step in successful word retrieval occurs when the word's lemma succeeds in activating the correct lexeme (the lexeme level corresponds roughly to the speech output lexicon of Chapter 5). Badecker, Miozzo, and Zanuttini (1995) described an Italian-speaking aphasic who was unable to name many objects, but could reliably say whether their names were masculine or feminine. This, they argue, is precisely the pattern one would expect in a patient who could still access lemmas but could no longer retrieve the spoken word-forms held at the lexeme level. A patient like EST (Kay & Ellis, 1987; see pp. 119–123) who could often get part of the way towards accessing spoken word-forms (e.g. knowing the number of syllables in a word and its initial sound) might be interpreted as being able to access lemmas but having problems at the lexeme level.

Hanley (1995) considers the applicability of the lemma/lexeme distinction to understanding his anomic patient NP in the paper's General Discussion. The main thrust of Hanley's (1995) paper is, however, directed at a different issue. We all experience difficulties from time to time in remembering names, and the names of people seem to be particularly problematic. Everyone has tried to negotiate a conversation with someone without revealing the fact that they cannot recall the person's name. You can typically remember what the person does, and where you know him or her from, while the name remains tantalisingly elusive.

Why should people's names cause such difficulties? People's names differ from the names of other objects in a number of respects. If we are talking about the names of politicians, film stars, and other celebrities whose faces are typically used to assess the naming of people, then we probably use their names less often than the names of familiar objects (i.e. they are of lower frequency). Celebrity names are often learnt later in life than object names, and Hirsh and Ellis (1994) have suggested that aphasic word-finding difficulties may reflect age of acquisition, with greater problems for late-acquired words than for words learned early in life. In this respect, peoples' names are especially interesting, because we carry on learning new names throughout our lives, as we encounter new people. After childhood, changes in other forms of vocabulary are often relatively slight.

Another feature of names is their arbitrariness. To know that someone is called Henry Smith tells you little about the person, other than this person is probably male. This high degree of arbitrariness may be important in understanding why selective deficits of proper name retrieval are sometimes found after brain injury (Semenza, 1995; Semenza & Zettin, 1989).

The possibility considered by Hanley (1995) is, however, that raised by Burton and Bruce (1992) who developed a simple account of name retrieval problems from their connectionist computer model of person recognition (Burton, Bruce, & Johnston, 1990). Burton and Bruce (1992) suggested that people's names are hard to recall because they are unique to each person, and therefore highly distinctive. When shown a picture of a celebrity, NP was often able to state the person's occupation but seldom the name; for example, knowing that George Bush was a former American President without being able to name him. But the occupation "President" is one shared by several familiar people, whereas there is only one famous person called George Bush. Thus, "George Bush" is more distinctive than "President", and it may be its lack of integration with other semantic information that makes the name harder to retrieve. Hanley (1995) sought to evaluate this account by assessing NP's ability to access and name other unique attributes of famous people, such as the identity of their spouses. His findings show clearly that at least some person-specific facts can be recalled, even when the name is unobtainable. Harris and Kay (1995) conducted a very similar study, arriving at broadly equivalent conclusions.

We have chosen the Hanley (1995) paper for two reasons. The first is that it uses patient data to test theories of normal cognitive functioning, something dear to the heart of cognitive neuropsychologists. The second is that it forms a link to Chapter 4, which is about face processing. Chapter 4 discusses how we recognise familiar faces and access stored knowledge about the people concerned; Hanley's (1995) paper starts at that point and asks how we then assign names to those people. Like all disciplines, cognitive neuropsychology tends to fragment naturally; people working on face processing disorders may claim ignorance of language processing disorders, and vice versa. Yet simple questions such as why is it that we find faces so hard to name, or why is it that a patient can tell you the occupations of celebrities but not their names, highlight the fact that although minds may be modular, disciplines cannot afford to be.

REFERENCES

Badecker, W. Miozzo, M., & Zanuttini, R. (1995). The two-stage model of lexical retrieval: evidence from a case of anomia with selective preservation of grammatical gender. *Cognition, 57*, 193–216.

Burton, A.M. & Bruce, B. (1992). I recognise your face but I can't remember your name: a simple explanation? *British Journal of Psychology, 83*, 45–60.

Burton, A.M., Bruce, V. & Johnston, R.A. (1990). Understanding face recognition with an interactive activation model. *British Journal of Psychology, 81*, 361–380.

Butterworth, B. (1989). Lexical access in speech production. In W. Marslen-Wilson (Ed.), *Lexical representation and process*. London: MIT Press.

Harris, D.M. & Kay, J. (1995). I recognise your face but I can't remember your name: is it because names are unique? *British Journal of Psychology, 86,* 345–358.

Hillis, A.E., Rapp, B.C., Romani, C., & Caramazza, A. (1990). Selective impairment of semantics in lexical processing. *Cognitive Neuropsychology, 7,* 191–243.

Hirsh, K.W. & Ellis, A.W. (1994). Age of acquisition and aphasia: a case study. *Cognitive Neuropsychology, 11,* 435–458.

Howard, D. & Orchard-Lisle, V.M. (1984). On the origin of semantic errors in naming: evidence from the case of a global aphasic. *Cognitive Neuropsychology, 1,* 163–190.

Kay, J. & Ellis, A.W. (1987). A cognitive neuropsychological case study of anomia. *Brain, 110,* 613–629.

Levelt, W.J.M. (1989). *Speaking: from intention to articulation.* Cambridge, Mass.: MIT Press.

McKenna, P. & Warrington, E.K. (1983). *Graded naming test.* Windsor, UK: NFER-Nelson.

Patterson, K.E. & Hodges, J.R. (1994). Disorders of semantic memory. In A. Baddeley, B. Wilson & F. Watts (Eds), *Handbook of memory disorders.* Hove, UK: Lawrence Erlbaum Associates Ltd.

Semenza, C. (1995). How names are special: neuropsychological evidence for dissociable impairment and sparing of proper name knowledge in production. In R. Campbell & M.A. Conway (Eds), *Broken memories. Case studies in memory impairment* (pp. 366–378). Oxford: Blackwell.

Semenza, C. & Zettin, M. (1989). Evidence from aphasia for the role of proper names as pure referring expressions. *Nature, 342,* 678–679.

Are Names Difficult to Recall
because They Are Unique?
A Case Study of a Patient with Anomia

J. Richard Hanley

Department of Psychology, University of Liverpool, Liverpool, UK

According to Burton and Bruce (1992), names are more difficult to recall than biographical information about people, such as their occupation, because names are unique or highly distinctive. It follows from this that anomic patients who have great difficulty in recalling names should also find it difficult to recall other information that is unique to a particular individual. This paper attempts to evaluate this claim by examining the case of NP, a patient who has severe anomic word-finding difficulties following the rupture and repair of a posterior cerebral artery aneurysm. NP's ability to recall biographical information about people that she cannot name was investigated in a series of experiments. These revealed that she can answer specific questions about the occupations and appearance of well-known people and can recall distinctive meaningful information about them such as the identity of their spouse, even though she is unable to recall their name. It is argued that these results support the view that names are represented in a store separate from that for semantic information about people that we know. The findings are therefore consistent with the sequential stage model of face identification put forward by Bruce and Young (1986) and are explained in terms of the theory of speech production put forward by Levelt (1989).

Anomia is a problem with the retrieval of words during speech production and writing. Although word-finding problems are very common in patients with acquired language disorders, anomia can occur in the absence of the general language impairments that are found in global aphasia. Speech in anomic patients can therefore be grammatical and fluent, even though the word-finding problem means that it is sometimes empty of content (see Ellis & Young, 1988, for further discussion).

In some cases of anomia, patients can readily recognize and repeat words that they are unable to retrieve, and they seem to have a good grasp of the meaning of these words. For instance, when patient EST (Flude, Ellis & Kay, 1989; Kay, 1992; Kay & Ellis, 1987) was

---

I would like to thank Wendy Best, Mike Burton, Mark Craigie, David Howard, and Andy Young for their extremely helpful comments on an earlier version of this manuscript. I would also like to thank Andy Young and Edward De Haan for lending me the materials that were used in Experiment 1, and Sarah Irving for enabling me to make contact with the patient described in this paper.

shown a set of pictures of objects that he had been unable to name, he was able to point to the appropriate picture when the name was spoken to him. Naming performance was also improved by the auditory presentation of the first phoneme of the target word. Sometimes, when EST was unable to recall a word, he would produce a phonological error. For example, he once referred to a *strawberry* as a *sumberry*. According to Kay and Ellis (1987), EST's impairment comes about because the connections between a word's representation in the semantic system and its phonological specification in the speech output lexicon have become weakened. In addition, the phonological errors that EST makes suggest damage to some of the representations within the speech output lexicon itself (Kay, 1992).

The literature on anomia has great relevance for current theories of face processing. For example, a lot of interest has recently been generated by the finding that the naming impairment observed in certain anomic patients can be very selective indeed. Although EST, like many anomic patients, has a word-finding problem that affects all types of stimuli, two cases who appear to have a problem that is confined to the retrieval of *proper* names have been reported (Semenza & Zettin, 1988, 1989). These patients have no general difficulty in retrieving words during speech production but can recall the names of hardly any people or places. Furthermore, McKenna and Warrington (1980), Lucchelli and De Renzi (1992), and Carney and Temple (1993) have all described cases whose problems appear only to affect the retrieval of names of *people*. There are also reports of patients whose ability to produce proper names is relatively well preserved despite a severe problem in retrieving all other word forms (Cipolotti, McNeil, & Warrington, 1993; Semenza & Sgaramella, 1993).

It is clearly important that future theories of face processing should be able to explain the basis of these dissociations. The focus of the present paper, however, is on the implications that studies of anomia have for the theories of name retrieval put forward by Bruce and Young (1986) and Burton and Bruce (1992). According to Bruce and Young's sequential stage model, names of familiar people are stored at a different level in the person recognition system from biographical information that is known about these people, such as their occupation or where they are typically encountered. Biographical information about a familiar person is directly accessible from their person identity node in semantic memory, whereas their name is stored in a separate output lexicon. The model is sequential in that Bruce and Young argue that recall of a name from a face occurs subsequent to, and is contingent upon, recall of biographical information about the person from their person identity node. In other words, it is not possible to retrieve a person's name from the output lexicon in response to seeing their face unless one can also retrieve semantic information about them from their person identity node.

Studies that provide support for the sequential stage model can be divided into two basic categories. First, there are studies that demonstrate that a person's name is more difficult to retrieve from memory than other types of biographical information. For example, reaction-time studies have shown that it takes significantly longer to recall a person's name in response to seeing their face than it does to recall their occupation or whether they are dead or alive (Johnston & Bruce, 1991; Young, Ellis, & Flude, 1988). Names have also been found to be more difficult to learn than occupations, even when the same words are used in both tasks, such as *Mr. Baker* versus *a baker* (Cohen, 1990; McWeeny, Young, Hay, & Ellis, 1987).

The second type of study suggests that retrieval of a person's name may be *contingent upon* recalling biographical information about people. Studies of this kind have revealed that a familiar face is never named unless a subject is also able to recall some piece of biographical information about them, such as their occupation (Hanley & Cowell, 1988; Hay, Young, & Ellis, 1991; Young, Hay, & Ellis, 1985). Craigie and Hanley (1993) have shown that the converse is also true; retrieval of facial information about a familiar person in response to seeing their name appears to be contingent upon the recall of their occupation. Finally, investigations of the effects of recall cues have shown that it is when a cue acts at the point in the Bruce and Young model at which a subject's retrieval attempt has faltered that it will be most likely to help the subject recall a previously inaccessible name (Brennen, Baguley, Bright, & Bruce, 1990; Hanley & Cowell, 1988).

Studies of anomia support the sequential stage model because they reveal that anomic patients can accurately discriminate familiar from unfamiliar faces and can frequently recall biographical information about people, even though they cannot retrieve their names. For example, patient EST (Flude et al., 1989) was able to provide the occupation associated with 30 out of 40 famous faces (controls recalled a mean of 32) but was able to recall the name of only 3 of them (controls recalled a mean of 25). If names are stored alongside occupations, then one might have expected that such a patient should be able to recall names if they can recall occupations. Furthermore, there has never been a convincing published report of a patient who could recall names of faces without also recalling the appropriate occupations; it appears to be the case that whenever a patient has difficulty in retrieving biographical information about people, then that person will also have a problem in recalling their names (de Haan, Young, & Newcombe, 1991; Ellis, Young, & Critchley, 1989; Hanley, Young, & Pearson, 1989).

Despite this, the sequential stage model has not gone unchallenged. Burton and Bruce (1992) have recently claimed that it is not necessary to postulate that names are stored in a separate location from other types of biographical information about people. The problems that are encountered in recalling names, they argued, arise because names tend to be unique to an individual, whereas biographical information is more likely to be shared by a number of different people. Burton and Bruce used the Interactive Activation and Competition model (IAC) put forward by Burton, Bruce, & Johnston (1990) to demonstrate precisely how the uniqueness of an item might hinder its retrieval from memory.

According to the IAC model, each fact that we know about a person is stored as a node in a semantic information pool. Each node is linked via excitatory bi-directional connections to the person identity node of every person to whom that fact applies. A shared piece of semantic information will thus start to activate a large number of person identity nodes as its own activation level begins to rise. Activation will then start to feed back from the person identity nodes to the piece of semantic information itself. The greater the number of person identity nodes thus activated, the more rapid will be the activation of the piece of semantic information in question. The ease with which a piece of information about a person will reach threshold in the semantic information pool is therefore dependent upon the number of other people possessing that attribute who are represented in the system.

In a computer simulation exercise using the IAC model, Burton and Bruce (1992) were able to show that unique facts about people were more difficult for the model to retrieve than information that is common to more than one person. As names tend to be unique or highly distinctive relative to most other facts we know about people, this provides a possible explanation of why it is more dificult to recall a person's name than their occupation. Consequently, Burton and Bruce argued that it is unnecessary to postulate a sequential stage model and claimed that both names and occupations are represented as semantic information units in the *same* memory store.

Such an account leads to a novel interpretation of the problems that anomics suffer when attempting to recall the names of familiar people. According to Burton et al. (1990), the functional deficit in anomia comes about because the person identity node is unable to provide the semantic information units with their normal level of activation. The activation level may be enough to allow general information about people to be recalled, such as their occupation, but the level of activation is not strong enough to allow highly distinctive information about them to be accessed. Because the link between a person identity node and a name is generally unique, it follows that anomics will be unable to recall people's names.

According to Burton and Bruce, therefore, the problems that a patient such as EST encounters in naming faces arise because names are highly distinctive. It follows from this that anomics should have a difficulty in recalling not just names, but any piece of highly distinctive information that is associated with a person. This account can, of course, explain why EST is able to recall occupations but not names (Flude et al., 1989). Unlike a name, occupations such as *politician* or *film-star* tend to be shared by a large number of celebrities that we know.

Nevertheless, the claim that patients such as EST are suffering from a semantic level impairment runs counter to the views expressed by both Kay and Ellis (1987) and Flude et al. (1989). Furthermore, some of the anecdotal evidence that is contained in published reports of anomic patients does not appear to rest easily alongside Burton and Bruce's (1992) claim that anomic patients cannot recall unique information about people they are unable to name. For example, Semenza and Zettin (1988) report that the anomic (Italian) patient PC was able to respond "Prime minister, he is the first socialist holding this position in our country" when shown a photograph of Bettino Craxi, but could not recall his name.

No published study has specifically reported whether or not anomic patients can *consistently* recall biographical information of this quality about people that they cannot name, however. The purpose of the present investigation, therefore, was to examine whether the biographical information that an anomic patient can typically retrieve about a person is as detailed and distinctive as the information that is available to control subjects. It was anticipated that this would provide critical evidence as to whether or not Burton and Bruce's (1992) account does genuinely constitute a viable alternative to the theory of name retrieval put forward by Bruce and Young (1986).

CASE REPORT PATIENT NP

Clinical Details. NP is a 47-year-old woman who lives in the North-West of England and was employed as a secretary at the time of her illness. In early 1993 she was admitted to hospital after acute onset of headache, followed by a grand mal seizure. A CT scan showed a substantial posteriorly placed left temporal intracerebral clot. An angiogram showed this to be due to an aneurysm at the origin of the left posterior communicating artery. The aneurysm was clipped via left craniotomy without interference of the clot. The operation was successful, and she made a good clinical recovery. There was no evidence of hemianopia or of hemiparesis. She was discharged from hospital approximately three weeks after her operation.

Psychological Testing.   The tests reported in this paper commenced approximately a month after her discharge in April 1993 and continued over a 12-month period. Her score of 33 on the Standard Progressive Matrices (Raven, 1958) was in the middle of the normal range and suggested that her general intellectual functioning is unimpaired. Since her illness, however, NP has complained of two major cognitive impairments: a problem with reading and a difficulty in remembering common and proper names. Detailed investigation revealed slow but accurate word recognition—she read 30/50 words correctly from Nelson's (1982) National Adult Reading Test (consistent with an estimated WAIS-R IQ of 106)—and preserved spelling. In the early stages of her recovery, NP would often say the letter names aloud as she read a word. Her reading speed improved significantly between April and September 1993, but she continued to take a long time to read words aloud, and reading latency increased as a function of the number of letters in a word. This indicates that NP can be classified as a letter-by-letter reader (cf. Patterson & Kay, 1982).

NP's ability to name objects was extremely poor. On the Boston Naming test (Kaplan, Goodglass, & Weintraub, 1983), she was able to name only 18 of the pictures when tested in April 1993. The mean score for normal controls is 54.4/60 ($SD = 3.47$). She did not benefit at all from semantic cues, but her performance rose to 46 when she was presented with phonemic cues. When re-tested five months later, her score was 29, and she was able to name all but two of the items in response to a phonemic cue. Performance had therefore improved, but it was still severely impaired. She had a score of 0/30 on the Graded Naming Test (McKenna & Warrington, 1983) when tested in April 1993. She was, however, able to give an accurate description of the function of most of the objects, suggesting that her problem was anomic rather than visual. After 5 months, her score had improved to 5/30 on this test. Her score remained at 5/30 when this test was re-administered in March 1994, after a further 6 months had elapsed. On no occasion did she make any phonological errors.

In order to investigate further the nature of her naming impairment, NP was administered a picture-naming test (no. 54) from the PALPA battery (Kay, Lesser, & Coltheart, 1992). In this test, the subject must name 60 pictures taken from the set devised by Snodgrass and Vanderwart (1980): 20 pictures are of high frequency (e.g. *window, train*) and have a mean frequency value of 176.5 (range = 76–591) according to the norms of Kucera and Francis (1967); 20 are of medium frequency (e.g. *shirt, bird*), having a mean frequency value of 32.5 (range = 18–65); 20 are of lower frequency, but are still relatively common words (e.g. *clown, frog*), having a mean frequency value of 5.7 (range = 1–15). The high-, medium-, and lower-frequency sets are matched for number of letters and name agreement. NP's picture-naming ability showed a highly significant effect of frequency ($p < 0.001$): she named 20/20 high-frequency items, 18/20 medium-frequency items, and only 10/20 lower-frequency items. As in the case of EST (Kay & Ellis, 1987), therefore, NP's ability to retrieve a word appears to be closely related to its frequency in the language. Only twice did NP produce what might be considered a semantic error, responding "sweeping brush" to a picture of a *broom*, and "screw" to a picture of a *nut*. On the remaining trials, when she was unable to provide the name, she gave a correct description of the item (e.g. "they are in hot places like Egypt, they carry you on their back" in response to a picture of a *camel*).

Face Processing.   In order to establish that NP, like EST (Flude et al., 1989), had no difficulty in forming structural descriptions of faces (Bruce & Young, 1986), she was given Benton, Hamsher, Varney, and Spreen's (1983) test of unfamiliar face matching. Her score of 44 was within the normal range. She also scored 48/48 on a forced-choice test of expression recognition, and 48/48 on a forced-choice lip-reading test created by Brenda Flude and Andrew Young. These tests had previously been used by Dewick, Hanley, Davies, Playfer, and Turnbull (1991) and were similar in form to those used by Parry, Young, Saul, and Moss (1991). Performance was also good on Warrington's (1984) Recognition Memory test for faces, in which a subject is shown 50 unfamiliar faces, which they are then asked to recognize on a forced-choice recognition test. NP scored 46/50, which is similar to a mean score of 43.33 (SD = 3.63) achieved by Warrington's normal controls.

Naming Famous Faces.   A series of tests was undertaken to examine whether NP was as poor at naming the faces of celebrities as at recalling the names of objects. First of all, she was given the set of 52 famous faces used by Hanley, Pearson and Young (1990). She found 50/52 of the famous faces to be familiar and made only one false alarm on the 26 unfamiliar faces. Table 1 shows that her ability to recall the occupations of the famous faces was slightly higher than that of the controls for people who had become famous

TABLE 1
NP's Ability to Recall Occupations and Names of
Famous Faces

	Recall of Occupations		Recall of Names	
Pre 1980				
NP	24		0	
Controls (*SD*)	21.2	(2.9)	18.2	(4.0)
Post 1985				
NP	20		0	
Controls (*SD*)	18.2	(1.9)	13.7	(3.4)

Note: Occupations and names of the 52 Famous Faces used by Hanley et al. (1990), 26 of which were famous before 1980 and 26 of which have become famous since 1985. Controls are 10 subjects matched to NP in sex and age.

before 1980 and for people who had become famous after 1985. She was unable to name any of the faces, however.

Despite her problems with name recall, NP was able to recall the appropriate occupation at a level slightly above that of the controls when shown the names of the same people during a subsequent testing session. For the pre-1980 names she was correct on 26/26, and for the post-1985 names she was correct on 20/26. Ten matched controls scored 25.0 ($SD = 1.6$) for the pre-1980 names, and 15.3 ($SD = 4.7$) on the post-1985 names.

NP's ability to identify the Lancaster/Radcliffe famous faces line-up that was used by Flude et al. (1989) with patient EST is shown in Table 2. Once again, her ability to recall occupations was good, both for very famous people and those slightly less famous, and her ability to recall these people's names was severely impaired: she was able to recall the names of only two (Margaret Thatcher and Marilyn Monroe). Her overall performance on this test was very similar to that of EST, who recalled 30/40 occupations and 3/40 names. In the course of administering this test, NP's ability to recognize the names that she could not recall was also investigated. At the end of each trial she was shown a card on which were written four names, one of which was the correct name, and three of which were the names of people of similar age and occupation. NP was able to indicate correctly the name that went with the face on 36/40 trials.

The final faces line-up was a set of 48 currently famous faces created by Brenda Flude and Andrew Young. This involved an initial forced-choice decision between a famous and a matched non-famous face. NP made the correct decision on 47/48 trials. Eight female control subjects matched for age and occupation with NP were correct on 45.88 familiarity decisions ($SD = 3.00$). NP was then able to recall the occupation of 46 of the familiar faces and the name of 6 of them. Controls recalled the occupation of 45.50 of the familiar faces ($SD = 4.07$) and the names of 38.25 ($SD = 6.56$). When this test was repeated a year later, in March 1994, NP's performance was virtually unchanged. She made 48/48 correct familiarity judgements and was able to recall the occupation for 48/48 of the faces, but she was able to name only 6 of them.

TABLE 2
NP's Ability to Recall Occupations and Names of
Famous Faces

	Recall of Occupations		Recall of Names	
High Familiarity:				
NP	17		2	
Controls (*SD*)	18.9	(1.2)	16.3	(2.8)
Low Familiarity:				
NP	15		0	
Controls (*SD*)	13.1	(4.5)	9.4	(4.4)

Note: Occupation and names of the 40 Famous Faces used by Flude et al. (1989), 20 of which were of high familiarity, and 20 of which were of slightly lower familiarity. Control data are taken from Flude et al.

With this set of faces, the effects of cues on NP's naming ability were also investigated. Whenever NP failed to recall the name of a face within a 1-min period but had success-fully recalled the occupation, she was given either an additional minute to recall the name, or else a card containing the initials of the person. For the face of George Bush, for instance, she was given G—— B—. Such cues are particularly useful for name recall when normal subjects are in a tip-of-the-tongue state (Brennen et al., 1990; Hanley & Cowell, 1988). NP recalled 0/20 names when given an additional minute, but she recalled the name on 10/20 trials in which she was given the initials. NP was clearly able to benefit from these orthographic cues in the recall of proper names, therefore, just as she was able to benefit from phonological cues when attempting to recall object names on the Boston naming test.

On virtually every occasion that NP failed to name a face, she responded simply that she did not know the answer. She never produced a neologistic response of the kind occasionally made by EST (Flude et al., 1989), that was phonologically related to the name that she was attempting to recall. She made hardly any semantic errors (e.g. recalling the name of someone of a similar occupation). The only exceptions were that she named a photo of Princess Anne as "Princess Margaret" and a photo of Prince Charles as "Prince Phillip". Occasionally she would say an incorrect first name aloud but would dismiss it as incorrect within a few seconds. To a photo of David Dimbleby, for example, she responded "Ian? Robert? No." Nevertheless, this was a relatively rare occurrence; on the Lancaster/Radcliffe famous-faces line-up, for instance, it happened on only four occasions. It was equally unusual for her to have available any partial phonological information about the name when she was unable to recall it; on the Lancaster/Radcliffe line-up, the only examples of this were that she said Winston Churchill had "a long name that starts with C", and Henry Cooper's name "started with an O". She also said that she thought John McEnroe had an "Irish name".

NP and the same eight control subjects were also given a series of verbal fluency tests to discover whether NP's problem in recalling names would be observed only when she has to name a specific face. She was given a minute to generate boys' names, a minute to generate girls' names, and a minute to generate as many names of famous people as she could. She was also given a standard FAS verbal fluency test in which she was asked to recall as many words starting with F, with A, and with S as she could recall in a minute. Performance was within the normal range on the FAS test: NP generated 37 words, and controls generated 43.29 (SD = 8.48, range = 32–58). This was particularly interesting given that the mean score by these controls on the Graded Naming Test was 20.43 (SD = 2.94, range = 17–25), compared to NP's score of zero. However, NP was able to generate the names of only 10 boys, 12 girls, and zero celebrities; controls generated the names of 20.86 boys (SD = 2.19, range = 18–24), 23.57 girls (SD = 3.21, range = 20–29), and 11 celebrities (SD = 4.40, range = 4–15).

In many respects, NP's pattern of performance on face-processing tasks is similar to that of EST. Neither of them has any problem on tests of structural processing such as unfamiliar face matching. In addition, both NP and EST are able to recognize the names of people and match them to faces, even though they cannot recall them. The only differences are that NP benefits from cues, whereas Flude et al. (1989) report that phonemic cues did not help EST to name people and that NP, unlike EST, virtually never recalled partial phonological information about a name that she could not recall. Like EST, NP has similar problems in recalling the names of pictures of objects as she has in recalling the names of people. However, NP's speech appears to be more fluent than that of EST; her performance on the FAS test of verbal fluency was within the normal range, and her conversation does not appear to be as slow or faltering as that of EST (see Flude et al., 1989, p. 67).

Like EST, NP is clearly able to distinguish familiar from unfamiliar faces and can recall the occupation of familiar faces just as accurately as controls. She is also good at recognizing names. In the terms of Bruce and Young (1986), she can be seen as having no problems in forming and accessing structural codes of faces, in activating face recognition units and name recognition units for familiar people, nor in retrieving biographical information about people from their person identity nodes. Her problem lies in accessing the output lexicon in which these names are stored. This difficulty in recalling names occurs both while naming famous faces and on a fluency task.

The tests described so far, however, are unable to distinguish such an account from the one put forward by Burton and Bruce (1992) in which names are stored alongside other pieces of information that we know about people. Burton and Bruce argue that the role of the person identity nodes is to make units available within the semantic information pool. NP's problems could, therefore, be seen to be a consequence of an inability on the part of her person identity nodes to activate fully semantic information units about people. This would make it impossible for her to retrieve highly distinctive information about them such as their name. A series of experiments, therefore, investigated whether or not NP's difficulties in naming people occurred in the context of a general inability to recall unique information about people.

EXPERIMENT 1

In the first experiment, the issue was whether NP's performance would start to deteriorate as the information that she was asked to retrieve about people became more specific. She was therefore given a series of forced-choice tests in which she was asked to decide which of two faces was famous, which of two famous celebrities was associated with a general occupation (e.g. politician, sportsperson), and which of two famous faces was associated with a more specific occupation (e.g. Labour politician, tennis player). If NP's performance is worse than that of the control subjects on the more specific questions, then this would provide strong support for Burton and Bruce's (1992) model.

Method

This experiment contained 160 trials. On each of them, the subject was shown photographs of two faces simultaneously and was asked to point to one of the pair. There were four different conditions.

On 40 of the trials, one face was that of a famous person and one was that of an unfamiliar person of similar age and physical appearance. Subjects were asked to indicate which face was famous.

On 40 of the trials, subjects were shown two famous faces, together with a general occupation (sportsperson, politician, TV personality, actor). For example, the face of politician John F. Kennedy and footballer Emlyn Hughes appeared together on one trial, along with the general occupation "politician". Subjects were asked to indicate which of the two faces was associated with the occupation. All the faces on these trials were the same as those on which the subjects made the familiarity decisions.

On 40 of the trials, subjects were shown two famous faces, together with a specific occupation (e.g. Labour politician, US President, comedian, Western actor, tennis player, sports commentator). The faces of the same famous people were again used, but they were arranged into different pairs such that the non-target face was always a member of the same general occupation as the target face. For example, the face of John F. Kennedy and former prime minister Harold Macmillan appeared together on one trial, along with the specific occupation "US President". Subjects were asked to indicate which of the two faces was associated with the specific occupation.

On 40 of the trials, subjects were shown two famous faces, together with a first name (e.g. David, Norman, Robin). The faces of the same famous people were again used. The non-target item was always someone with a different name, but from the same precise occupation as the target face. For example, the faces of John Kennedy and Ronald Reagan appeared together on one trial, along with the name "John". Subjects were asked to indicate which of the two faces was associated with that name.

Results and Discussion

NP's performance on this task can be seen in Table 3, together with that of nine female control subjects matched with her for age and occupation. It is clear that her scores are equivalent to those of the control subjects, and there is no evidence that her performance declines as the questions become more specific.

In order to investigate whether NP's score of 37/40 when presented with first names came about because the first name had enabled her to retrieve the full name, she was re-presented with the stimuli at the end of the experiment and was asked to attempt to recall the full name of the person whose first name was visible. She was successful on 17/40 trials, indicating that the first name had indeed acted as a successful retrieval cue on some of the trials. On the remaining trials, she claimed to have been guessing, even though her performance was clearly above chance. Sometimes, when normal subjects are in a tip-of-the-tongue state, they are able to retrieve partial information about the word that they are unable to recall (see Brown, 1991). It is therefore possible that NP was able to achieve such a high score by retrieving partial information about the name of one of the faces and matching it with the first name that she had been shown. NP explicitly denied that this was the case, however. Furthermore, as was pointed out earlier, NP is very rarely able to offer such partial information when she is unable to recall a name. Alternative explanations of how she was able to perform so well in response to first names are discussed later.

TABLE 3
NP's Performance on Forced Choice Tests

	Familiarity	General Occupation	Precise Occupation	First Name
NP	38	40	39	37
Controls (SD)	38.3 (2.5)	39.2 (1.1)	39.1 (1.4)	38.6 (2.0)

Note: Forced choice tests measure the ability to access general and more specific information about faces of famous people (max score = 40).

Although NP's ability to recall specific information about people means that the experiment did not provide strong support for Burton and Bruce (1992), neither does it provide strong evidence against their theory. A specific occupation is not as distinctive a piece of information about a person as their name. In Burton and Bruce's terms, it is possible that the person identity node is providing enough activation for a specific occupation—but not a name—to be recalled. Although her good performance in the first-name condition does suggest that she *can* access distinctive information about people she cannot name, it is not obvious how Bruce and Young's (1986) model could explain her performance here either.

EXPERIMENT 2

The purpose of Experiment 2 was to establish whether NP knows exactly who a person is when she cannot name them, or whether she only has a general notion as to who they are. NP's ability to access visual information about people whose names she cannot retrieve was therefore investigated. NP was presented with a set of biographies and was asked to recall each person's name and a distinctive piece of information about their face.

Method

NP was shown a set of 64 cards, each of which contained biographical information about a different famous person. An example was "French actor whose recent films include *Green Card* and *1492: Conquest of Paradise*" (Gerard Depardieu). The materials were the same as those used by Craigie and Hanley (1993, Experiment 2). The 64 famous people selected all possessed one, and only one, of four facial features: 16 of them had a balding head, 16 had a beard, 16 wore glasses, and 16 had long hair. In addition, 16 of the 64 famous people had surnames that start with the letters A–F, 16 had surnames that start with the letters G–L, 16 had surnames that start with the letters M–R, and 16 had surnames that start with the letters S–Z.

When NP was presented with a biography, she was asked to indicate which of the four name categories and which of the four facial categories applied to the person. As in Craigie and Hanley (1993), the instructions were designed to discourage guessing. NP was therefore told not to respond unless she was reasonably confident of getting the answer correct.

Results and Discussion

NP made 22/64 correct decisions regarding the facial features and 2/64 correct decisions regarding the name of the celebrities. The 20 normal subjects used by Craigie and Hanley (1993) made 24.8 correct decisions about facial features ($SD = 7.2$) and 21.9 correct name decisions ($SD = 8.3$). Although these control subjects were not specifically matched to NP, it appears reasonable to conclude from these results that NP's ability to recall visual information about people from semantic information is preserved, even though her ability to recall their name is as severely impaired as it is when she is shown a face.

In order to recall, say, that a particular person wears glasses, it would appear necessary either to generate a mental image of that person's face or to access a structural description of that person's face, which may perhaps be the face recognition unit activated in a top-down manner (Craigie & Hanley, 1993; Valentine, Bredart, Lawson, & Ward, 1991).

Either way, NP's ability to do this task suggests that she can retrieve very specific information about a person she cannot name. In Bruce and Young's (1986) terms, it suggests that NP's person identity nodes can activate visual information about familiar people even though they cannot activate the appropriate lexical codes.

EXPERIMENT 3

In Experiment 3, the quality of the descriptions that NP is able to provide when she sees a face was investigated. If NP is unable to retrieve distinctive information about a person that she cannot name, then it should prove very difficult for a normal subject to identify the person in question from examining NP's description of them.

Method

The faces of 18 people whom NP had never been able to name on any of the previous occasions that she had seen them were selected. These were again shown to NP, who was asked to recall as much detail about them as she could, including their name if possible. In fact, she recalled none of the names. The same faces were also presented to eight female control subjects matched to NP in age and occupation. The controls were also told that it was important that they provide as much biographical detail as they could about each celebrity in addition to recalling their name.

The quality of the descriptions that NP produced was then compared with that of the best control subject who successfully recalled the name of 17 out of the 18 faces. For example, the biographical detail provided by the normal subject for Kenny Dalglish was:

> One of the best managers that Liverpool football team ever had. I was once on a plane going to Spain with him and his wife and children. He resigned and then took on another appointment. I forget which team he's managing right now.

The description provided by NP was:

> I think he used to run Liverpool football club. He's retired now and runs another football club. He did very well when he was the manager. He's from Scotland. He's very shy, he doesn't interview very well.

Each description made by NP and the control subject was transcribed and written on a separate index card. These cards were then shown to a further 10 control subjects, who were asked to provide the name of the celebrity. Of the famous people, 9 were randomly allocated to Set A and 9 to Set B. Each of the 10 control subjects received 9 of the descriptions provided by NP and 9 of the descriptions provided by the normal subject. Five of the controls received NP's descriptions of the Set A celebrities and the normal subject's descriptions of the Set B celebrities. The remaining 5 controls received NP's descriptions of the Set B celebrities and the normal subject's descriptions of the Set A celebrities.

Results and Discussion

The 10 control subjects were able to recall 6.3/9 names on average in response to NP's descriptions, and 6.2/9 names on average in response to the descriptions made by the normal subject. The descriptions provided by NP proved therefore equally likely to elicit recall of the name of the face as did the descriptions generated by the normal control subject. If subjects are consistently able to work out the face that NP is looking at from her descriptions, then it seems to follow that NP can access information that uniquely identifies that person. Such a finding would appear to be more compatible with the views of Bruce and Young (1986) than those of Burton and Bruce (1992).

EXPERIMENT 4

In Experiment 4, NP was presented with the faces of people who are highly distinctive. These people were selected on the basis that they were famous for two reasons. For instance, the singer Bob Geldof is famous not just because he is a pop singer, but also because of the work that he did to try and help starving people in Africa. If NP is unable to access very distinctive information about people, then it might be expected that she would be able to recall one but not both pieces of information about these celebrities. She might, for instance, recall that John F. Kennedy was an American President, but not that he was assassinated.

Method

NP was presented with the faces of 20 highly distinctive celebrities, none of whom she was able to name. These included Seb Coe (athletics champion and Conservative MP), and Glenda Jackson (film actress and Labour MP). The same faces were shown to 7 female control subjects matched with NP for age and occupation. All subjects were asked to provide as much detail as they could about all of the faces.

Results and Discussion

NP was able to retrieve both pieces of biographical detail about 16/20 of the faces, one piece of information about three of the faces, and no information about one of the faces. The control subjects were able to recall full biographical information about 14.3/20 of the celebrities (SD = 2.6). NP's ability to describe people who are highly distinctive is, therefore, at least as good as that of control subjects.

EXPERIMENT 5

Experiment 5 tested NP's ability to recall one highly distinctive piece of information about a person. One unique fact about most people is the identity of their husband or wife, and NP was therefore asked to indicate the identity of famous people's spouses. This is not a task that it is possible to perform successfully simply by recalling many facts about the person that are not in themselves unique. If Burton and Bruce (1992) are correct to argue that an anomic patient cannot recall unique information about people that they cannot name, then it follows that NP should be significantly impaired at recalling the spouses of famous people.

Method

NP was shown a photograph of the faces of 22 well-known people, all of whom have or used to have a famous spouse. NP was asked to recall the name of the person in the photograph and to recall the identity of their spouse. If NP could not recall the name of the spouse, then she was asked to identify them by providing biographical details about them. Examples of the faces used (with spouses in brackets) are John McEnroe (Tatum O'Neill), Rula Lenska (Dennis Waterman), Pamela Stephenson (Billy Connolly), Raisa Gorbachev (Mikhail Gorbachev). The procedure was repeated with 10 control subjects matched to NP in age and occupation.

Results and Discussion

NP successfully named 5/22 of the celebrities from their photographs. The mean number named by the control subjects was 17.1 ($SD = 2.28$). NP was able to identify correctly the spouses of 17/22 of the faces. The mean number identified by the control subjects was 16.7 ($SD = 2.27$). NP identified all of the spouses by providing details of their occupation rather than their name, whereas the control subjects were on average able to provide the name for 91% of the spouses that they could identify from occupation. The quality of the biographical information that NP was able to provide about the spouses was just as high as it had been in the previous experiments. For example, in response to a photo of Bob Geldof, she responded that his spouse (Paula Yates) was "little and slim with dyed blonde hair. She does interviews on television on pop music".

Despite being severely impaired at recalling the names of the faces, therefore, NP performed well at recalling their spouses. Of course, NP could not recall the names of the spouses any more than she could recall the names of the people in the photographs themselves. The key point, though, is that NP recalled enough biographical information about the spouse to demonstrate that she knew who they were. This means that NP is clearly able to retrieve a unique piece of information about a person, even though she is poor at recalling their name.

EXPERIMENT 6

There are a small number of other facts about people, in addition to their name and the identity of their spouse, that are highly distinctive or unique to them. One of these is a person's telephone number. It is interesting to note that Lucchelli and De Renzi's (1992) anomic patient was unable to recall the telephone numbers of his acquaintances despite claiming to know many numbers before his illness. One important difference between these two types of information is that whereas the identity of a spouse is highly meaningful, a telephone number is arbitrary and relatively meaningless, as is the case with a person's name (Cohen, 1990; Semenza & Zettin, 1989). It was therefore by no means clear that NP would be as successful at recalling a person's telephone number as she was at recalling the identity of a person's spouse.

Method and Results

When NP was questioned about her knowledge of telephone numbers, she replied that she was poor at remembering phone numbers. The only number that she was able to recall was her own home telephone number. She was unable to recall her husband's work number despite using it several times every week. She claimed that she had never been particularly good at remembering phone numbers at any time in her life, but was now much worse than she had been before her illness, when she knew at least 10 numbers of other people.

NP's performance was compared with that of 5 control sujects of similar age and sex to NP who also worked as secretaries. They were asked to recall the phone numbers of as many friends (including their own) or organizations as possible. One of them recalled 8 separate numbers, one recalled 9 numbers, two recalled 11 numbers, and one recalled 20 numbers. When checked, 90% of the numbers recalled turned out to be correct.

Discussion

The level of performance achieved by the control subjects suggests that NP is impaired at recalling telephone numbers. Her ability to recall a person's telephone number does not, therefore, appear to be as well preserved as her ability to recall the identity of a person's spouse. Although it appears that NP can recall unique *meaningful* facts about people, it does not seem to be the case that she can recall unique *meaningless* facts about people. The possible significance of this distinction is discussed at the end of the paper.

EXPERIMENT 7

The previous experiments have demonstrated that NP's ability to recall meaningful biographical information about familiar people such as their occupation is extremely well preserved relative to her ability to recall their names. It is important to bear in mind, however, that phonological representations of names of occupations, just like phonological representations of names of people, are stored in the speech output lexicon rather than in the semantic system. How is it that NP can access the speech output lexicon to retrieve the former but not the latter? One possibility is that the recall of names of occupations is an area of preserved ability amongst NP's word-finding difficulties. More probably, NP's ability to recall names of occupations relative to names of people is related to their frequency of usage, as it was demonstrated in an earlier experiment that her ability to recall the name of a picture is strongly influenced by word frequency. In the final experiment, therefore, NP's ability to recall the names of occupations was investigated.

Method

A total of 30 short definitions of occupations was read to NP, and she was asked to supply the name of each occupation. Some examples of the definitions used were "A tutor of the highest rank in a university", and "A person trained to care for the sick or disabled" for the occupations *professor* and *nurse*, respectively. Although she was allowed as much time and as many attempts as she wanted, NP was told that in order to be credited with having recalled an occupation correctly, she had to provide the exact name that the experimenter had in mind. In other words, in response to the definition for *sailor* ("one who serves in the navy or works on a ship"), a response such as 'seaman" would be counted as incorrect. The procedure was repeated with seven subjects matched to NP in age, sex, and occupation.

Results and Discussion

NP successfully produced the name of 18/30 of the occupations. The mean number recalled by the control subjects was 26.9/30 (SD = 2.2). When the mean score that the controls achieved on each of the 30 occupation names was correlated with whether or not NP recalled it, the result was highly significant (r = 0.54, p < 0.01). It is therefore clear that NP is severely impaired on this task, and that her performance appears to be closely related to item difficulty.

There is thus no evidence that NP's ability to recall the names of occupations is any better preserved than her ability to recall the names of people. It seems that her ability to retrieve phonological forms from the speech output lexicon, whether they be names of pictures, names of people, or names of occupations, is strongly related to frequency of usage and/or item difficulty. It appears to be the case, therefore, that a vocabulary restricted to a set of relatively high-frequency words is sufficient to enable NP to produce excellent detailed biographical information about familiar people, even though it is not sufficient to enable her to recall the names of most of the people that she knows.

GENERAL DISCUSSION

In this study, we have described the case of an anomic patient with a severe difficulty in recalling the names of familiar people. Despite this, it has been demonstrated that she knows both the general and the more specific occupation of these people, that she can recall both pieces of information about people who are famous for more than one reason, and that she knows the identity of the spouses of famous people that she sees in photographs. She can also recall a specific fact about a person's facial appearance when she is presented with biographical detail about that person, even though she cannot name them. In addition, when her descriptions of famous people are presented to normal control subjects, they can readily name the celebrity in question.

None of the tests given to NP, therefore, has revealed any evidence of a semantic deficit in her knowledge of familiar people. As far as one can tell, her ability to recall meaningful information about people is entirely preserved, even when this information is unique or highly distinctive. This would appear to be inconsistent with Burton and Bruce's (1992) claim that anomic patients find it difficult to recall people's names because names are highly distinctive. NP can recall other unique information about people, but she cannot recall their names.

The case of NP, therefore, seems at odds with Burton and Bruce's suggestion that names might be represented in the same memory store as the other information that we know about people. If names were stored alongside other facts, then why does NP find it so difficult to recall names? It is also important to bear in mind, however, that NP's inability to recall proper names occurs in the context of a general anomia. That is, she is also impaired at recalling common names of objects and at recalling the names of occupations. It seems likely that a major factor that determines whether she is able to recall a particular word form is its frequency of usage. Might it therefore be possible to argue that the model put forward by Burton and Bruce (1992) could be retained, but with frequency of usage rather than uniqueness being the critical factor that determines how easily a particular item can be retrieved from within the semantic pool?

The main problem with such an approach is that it confuses the retrieval of word forms with the retrieval of semantic information. A word form is associated with one specific linguistic term. A conceptual representation within the semantic system, in contrast, is likely to play a role in determining the meaning of a variety of different linguistic terms. For instance, "movie-star" and "film-star" are distinct linguistic terms, but both are presumably linked to a virtually identical set of conceptual nodes within the semantic system. It is thus the *concept* of being a film-star or a tennis player that is part of the semantic system rather than any specific word forms (cf. Fodor, 1976). The phonological or orthographic form(s) in which that concept can be expressed linguistically will be stored in a separate output lexicon. In this sense, much of the information that we use to categorize and distinguish the people that we know is conceptual rather than linguistic. It is therefore likely to be stored at a different level in the system from a person's name, which is nothing more than a set of phonemes and/or letters.

Recent models of speech production such as those put forward by Butterworth (1989) and Levelt (1989) also draw a distinction between a non-linguistic semantic system and the representation of specific word forms (see also Burke, Mackay, Worthley, & Wade, 1991). Butterworth (1989) and Levelt (1989) postulate the existence of a semantic lexicon that provides the interface between the language system and our conceptual knowledge of the world. Each entry—to which Levelt refers as a "lemma"—in the semantic lexicon is connected to a particular set of nodes in the non-linguistic semantic system. A lemma becomes selected when it receives sufficient activation from the appropriate nodes in the non-linguistic semantic system. Once the lemma has been activated, it then becomes possible to access the word's phonological representation, to which Levelt refers as a "lexeme".

Perhaps the best way of conceptualizing the role of a lemma for a proper name is to think of it as an address to the phonological specification of a name. There is therefore no need to store the phonological form of, for instance, *John* separately for all of our acquaintances who are called "John". Every person that we know will have their own address, which, if the system is working properly, will provide access to the phonological representation of the name(s) associated with that person in an output lexicon. The address will itself become active when sufficient semantic information about the person is accessed within the non-linguistic conceptual system.

In the terms of this model, it would appear that NP has a normally functioning semantic system, which enables her to retrieve unique semantic information about people such as the identity of their spouse. Such an account is not inconsistent with NP's inability to recall telephone numbers. Telephone numbers, like names, are meaningless symbols, and so they are also likely to be stored outside the semantic system (cf. Cohen, 1990). The fact that telephone numbers are probably of at least equally low familiarity relative to names may well be the reason why NP, like other anomic patients, has such severe problems in recalling them. It seems probable that the recall of a telephone number will also involve the retrieval of a lexical address that will provide access to the phonological representations of the numbers themselves in an output lexicon.

NP's problems would seem to occur because either the lemmas (addresses) or the phonological lexemes for words of relatively low frequency cannot be activated, thus preventing her from recalling proper names, telephone numbers, and a large number of ordinary words. There is, however, one reason why it appears slightly more likely that in NP's case the impairment occurs *after* the appropriate lemma in the semantic lexicon has been activated, but before the lexeme has been retrieved. This was the finding in Experiment 1 that she was able to indicate successfully which of two faces was associated with a particular first name, even when she was unable to recall the full name of the person in question. It would seem possible that the lemma could be the source of this match—that is, the appropriate lemma may provide enough activation of the first-name lexeme for it to be distinguished from the incorrect lemma, even when there is insufficient activation of the lexeme for the name to be fully retrieved.

The idea that an impairment between the lemma and the lexeme is the source of the word-finding difficulties experienced by anomic patients such as NP enables one to distinguish her problems from cases of anomia that appear to be more semantically based. Anomics such as the patient who made semantic errors in naming, as described by Howard and Orchard-Lisle (1984), can therefore be seen as suffering from an impairment at the level of the lemma or semantic lexicon itself. This would disrupt the patient's ability to distinguish words of similar meaning without necessarily impairing their general conceptual knowledge of the world.

In NP's case, there is no evidence for any additional damage to the phonological representations themselves, as she does not make phonological errors in naming people. This is not the case with EST (cf. Kay, 1992) and may be the reason why, unlike EST, NP's ability to recall names is improved by the presentation of a cue that is phonologically or orthographically related to the target item.

In conclusion, then, the difficulties that NP experiences in attempting to retrieve the names of familiar people are difficult to explain in terms of Burton and Bruce's (1992) model, as she is often able to recall unique semantic information about people whom she cannot name. The results that have been obtained with NP are consistent with the sequential stage model of name retrieval put forward by Bruce and Young (1986) and with the idea that semantic information about a person (in the form of conceptual knowledge) is stored at a different level in the person recognition system from their name. Bruce and Young's model, however, offers no account of exactly how the phonological form of a name might be retrieved once semantic information about the person has been accessed. Consistent with the views of Bredart and Valentine (1992), the results of the present study suggest that the most profitable approach is to integrate Bruce and Young's sequential stage model of face identification with theories of speech production of the kind put forward by Butterworth (1989) and Levelt (1989).

REFERENCES

Benton, A.L., Hamsher, K., Varney, N.R., & Spreen, O. (1983) *Facial recognition*. New York: Oxford University Press.

Bredart, S., & Valentine, T. (1992). From Monroe to Moreau. An analysis of face naming errors. *Cognition, 45*, 187–223.

Brennen, T., Baguley, T., Bright, J., & Bruce, V. (1990). Resolving semantically induced tip-of-the-tongue states for proper nouns. *Memory and Cognition, 18*, 339–347.

Brown, A.S. (1991). A review of the tip-of-the-tongue experience. *Psychological Bulletin, 109*, 204–223.

Bruce, V., & Young, A.W. (1986) Understanding face recognition. *British Journal of Psychology, 77*, 305–327.

Burke, D.M., Mackay, D.G., Worthley, J.S., & Wade, E. (1991) On the tip-of-the-tongue: What causes word finding failures in young and old adults. *Journal of Memory and Language, 30*, 542–579.

Burton, A.M., & Bruce, V. (1992). I recognize your face but I can't remember your name: A simple explanation? *British Journal of Psychology, 83*, 45–60.

Burton, A.M., Bruce, V., & Johnston, R.A. (1990). Understanding face recognition with an interactive activation model. *British Journal of Psychology, 81*, 361–380.

Butterworth, B. (1989). Lexical access in speech production. In W. Marslen-Wilson (Ed.), *Lexical representation and process*. Cambridge, MA: MIT Press.

Carney, R., & Temple, C.M. (1993). Prosopanomia? A possible category-specific anomia for faces. *Cognitive Neuropsychology, 10*, 185–195.

Cipolotti, C. McNeil, J.E., & Warrington, E.K. (1993). Spared written naming of proper nouns: A case report. *Memory, 1*, 289–311.

Cohen, G. (1990). Why is it difficult to put names to faces. *British Journal of Psychology, 81*, 287–297.

Craigie, M., & Hanley, J.R. (1993). Access to visual information about a face is contingent on access to identity specific semantic information. *Memory, 1*, 367–391.

de Haan, E.H.F., Young, A.W., & Newcombe, F. (1991). A dissociation between the sense of familiarity and access to semantic information concerning familiar people. *European Journal of Cognitive Psychology, 3*, 51–67.

Dewick, H.C., Hanley, J.R., Davies, A.D.M., Playfer, J., & Turnbull, C. (1991). Perception and memory for faces in Parkinson's disease. *Neuropsychologia, 29*, 785–802.

Ellis, A.W., & Young, A.W. (1988). *Human cognitive neuropsychology*. Hove: Lawrence Erlbaum Associates Ltd.

Ellis, A.W., Young, A.W., & Critchley, E.M.R. (1989). Loss of memory for people following temporal lobe damage. *Brain, 112*, 1469–1483.

Flude, B.M., Ellis, A.W., & Kay, J. (1989). Face processing and name retrieval in an anomic aphasic: names are stored separately from semantic information about familiar people. *Brain & Cognition, 11*, 60–72.

Fodor, J.A. (1976). *The language of thought*. Brighton: Harvester.

Hanley, J.R., & Cowell, E.S. (1988). The effects of different types of retrieval cues on the recall of names of famous faces. *Memory and Cognition, 16*, 545–555.

Hanley, J.R., Pearson, N., & Young, A.W. (1990). Impaired memory for new visual forms. *Brain, 113*, 1131–1148.

Hanley, J.R., Young, A.W., & Pearson, N. (1989). Defective recognition of familiar people. *Cognitive Neuropsychology, 6*, 179–210.

Hay, D.C., Young, A.W., & Ellis, A.W. (1991). Routes through the face recognition system. *Quarterly Journal of Experimental Psychology, 43A*, 761–791.

Howard, D., & Orchard-Lisle, V. (1984). On the origin of semantic errors in naming: Evidence from the case of a global aphasic. *Cognitive Neuropsychology, 1*, 163–211.

Johnston, R.A. & Bruce, V. (1991). Lost properties? Retrieval differences between name codes and semantic codes for familiar people. *Psychological Research, 52*, 62–67.

Kaplan, E., Goodglass, H., & Weintraub, S. (1983). *The Boston naming test*. Philadelphia, PA: Lea & Febiger.

Kay, J. (1992). The write stuff. In R. Campbell (Ed.), *Mental lives*. Oxford: Blackwell.

Kay, J., & Ellis, A.W. (1987). A cognitive neuropsychological case study of anomia: Implications for psychological models of word retrieval. *Brain, 110*, 613–629.

Kay, J., Lesser, R., & Coltheart, M. (1992). *Psycholinguistic assessment of language processing in aphasia*. Hove: Lawrence Erlbaum Associates Ltd.

Kucera, H., & Francis, W.N. (1967). *Computational analysis of present day American-English*. Providence, RI: Brown University Press.

Levelt, W.J.M. (1989). Speaking: From intention to articulation. Cambridge, MA: MIT Press.

Lucchelli, F., & De Renzi, E. (1992). Proper name anomia. *Cortex, 28*, 221–230.

McKenna, P., & Warrington, E.K. (1980). Testing for nominal dysphasia. *Journal of Neurology, Neurosurgery & Psychiatry, 43*, 781–788.

McKenna, P., & Warrington, E.K. (1983). *The graded naming test.* Windsor: NFER Publishing Company.

McWeeney, K.H., Young, A.W., Hay, D.C., & Ellis, A.W. (1987). Putting names to faces. *British Journal of Psychology, 78*, 143–151.

Nelson, H. (1982). *The new adult reading test.* Windsor: NFER Publishing Company.

Parry, F.M., Young, A.W., Saul, J.S., & Moss, A. (1991). Dissociable face processing impairments after brain injury. *Journal of Clinical and Experimental Neuropsychology, 13*, 545–558.

Patterson, K., & Kay, J. (1982). Letter-by-letter reading: Psychological descriptions of a neurological description. *Quarterly Journal of Experimental Psychology, 34A*, 411–441.

Raven, J.C. (1958). *Raven's standard progressive matrices.* London: H.K. Lewis.

Semenza, C., & Sgaramella, T.M. (1993). Production of proper names: A clinical case study of the effects of phonemic cueing. *Memory, 1*, 265–280.

Semenza, C. & Zettin, M. (1988). Generating proper names: A case of selective inability. *Cognitive Neuropsychology, 5*, 711–721.

Semenza, C., & Zettin, M. (1989). Evidence from aphasia for the role of proper names as pure referring expressions. *Nature, 342*, 678–679.

Snodgrass, J.G., & Vanderwart, M. (1980). A standardized set of 260 pictures: Norms for name agreement, image agreement, familiarity, and visual complexity. *Journal of Experimental Psychology: Human Learning and Memory, 6*, 174–215.

Valentine, T., Bredart, S., Lawson, R., & Ward, G. (1991). What's in a name? Access to information from people's names. *European Journal of Cognitive Psychology, 3*, 147–176.

Warrington, E.K. (1984). *Recognition memory test.* Windsor: NFER-Nelson.

Young, A.W., Ellis, A.W. & Flude, B.M. (1988). Accessing stored information about familiar people. *Psychological Research, 50*, 111–115.

Young, A.W., Hay, D.C., & Ellis, A.W. (1985). The faces that launched a thousand slips: Everyday difficulties and errors in recognizing people. *British Journal of Psychology, 76*, 495–523.

Revised manuscript received 23 June 1994

Chapter 6 Recognising and Understanding Spoken Words

Franklin, S., Howard, D., & Patterson, K. (1994). Abstract word meaning deafness. *Cognitive Neuropsychology, 11*, 1–34.

Chapter 6 is concerned with the processes that make possible the comprehension and repetition of heard words, and with the disorders that can occur when those processes are damaged. The theoretical model represented in Fig. 6.1 (p. 145) implies that the route from sound to meaning involves at least three stages. First, the auditory analysis system identifies the different speech sounds present in the sound wave. The results of that process of analysis are communicated to the second stage, the auditory input lexicon. It contains representations of all the words known to the listener in spoken form. If a sound sequence identified by the auditory analysis system matches a stored representation in the auditory input lexicon, then the heard word carries with it a feeling of familiarity—no more at this stage. If the word is to be *understood*, then it must activate its meaning (semantic representation) in the third stage, the semantic system. That system is also involved in comprehending written words and objects, so has multiple inputs.

If this sequence of processes, or anything like it, underlies normal auditory comprehension, then we should be able to see a range of qualitatively different patterns of auditory comprehension disorder associated with malfunction at each of the different stages. "Pure word deafness" is the term used in Chapter 6 to describe patients whose deficit appears to lie within the auditory analysis system and who therefore have difficulty identifying the sounds of speech. The condition is also sometimes known as "word-sound deafness". The model predicts that a second type of disorder should exist that is caused by damage to the auditory input lexicon. Such patients should hear speech clearly, but should be unable to recognise words, and hence be unable to distinguish spoken words from nonwords. No patients of this type had been reported when Chapter 6 was written, although putative cases have since been described by Howard and Franklin (1988; patient MK) and Franklin (1989; patient AH).

Damage to the semantic system itself should affect the comprehension of spoken words, written words and objects equally and in the same way. Such across-the-board semantic losses, as might be seen in forms of dementia (Patterson & Hodges, 1994), were beyond the scope of Chapter 6. This list does not, however, exhaust the set of auditory comprehension disorders. The reason it does not is because brain damage can affect not only components like the auditory input lexicon and the semantic system, but also the transmission of information (or activation) between such components. That is what is assumed to have happened in the case of patients suffering from "word-meaning deafness".

Imagine that the auditory analysis system and auditory input lexicon are still functioning satisfactorily, but that activating a word in the auditory input lexicon no longer guarantees that the corresponding meaning will be activated in the semantic system because the links between the auditory input lexicon and the semantic system are damaged. Perception of speech sounds should be preserved, as should the ability to make auditory lexical decisions, because the auditory analysis system and auditory input lexicon are still functioning. Comprehension of heard words would be compromised, although comprehension of written words would be intact. The patient should also be able to repeat heard words and nonwords using the pathways between input and output that by-pass the semantic system (see Fig. 6.1, p. 145).

In Chapter 6 we were only able to illustrate this pattern by reference to a very old report by Bramwell (1897), plus a relatively brief description by Kohn and Friedman (1986). The publication by Franklin, Howard, and Patterson (1994) of case DRB provides us with a much fuller account, and a better basis on which to evaluate the claim that word-meaning deafness constitutes a distinct form of auditory comprehension disorder. As Franklin et al. (1994) acknowledge, DRB falls some way short of the ideal just outlined of a "pure" case of word-meaning deafness. For example, he has naming problems in production, and his repetition is impaired.

Although this complicates the picture, it also makes DRB more representative of real-life aphasics, who typically have multiple speech and language problems. It also makes it more of a challenge for the cognitive neuropsychologist to dissect the auditory comprehension disorder out from the patient's other impairments.

Franklin et al.'s (1994) analysis of DRB is extremely thorough, and a follow-up investigation of his word-finding problems (which also turn out to be more severe for abstract than concrete words) is reported in Franklin, Howard, and Patterson (1995). Franklin et al. (1994) take pains to contrast a diagnosis of word-meaning deafness from alternative possible explanations, such as that DRB's pattern of deficits arises from a combination of a mild problem in speech perception allied to a mild deficit within the semantic system. In seeking to probe the status of DRB's semantic system, the authors also carry out experiments looking at his reaction times in various tasks. Such experiments are very seldom done. Cognitive neuropsychologists usually base their inferences solely on a patient's *accuracy* on various tasks. One might, however, query the wisdom of relying entirely on this. If, for example, a patient performs a task without error, but takes three times as long as control subjects, would we be justified in saying that the patient is unimpaired?

Auditory comprehension deficits remain relatively underinvestigated, but Franklin et al.'s (1994) study provides, in our view, a model of how such investigations should be conducted.

REFERENCES

Bramwell, B. (1897). Illustrative cases of aphasia. *Lancet, 1*, 1256–1259. Reprinted in 1984 as: A case of word meaning deafness. *Cognitive Neuropsychology, 1*, 249–258.

Franklin, S. (1989). Dissociations in auditory word comprehension: evidence from nine fluent aphasics. *Aphasiology, 3*, 189–207.

Franklin, S.E., Howard, D., & Patterson, K. (1995). Abstract word anomia. *Cognitive Neuropsychology, 12*, 549–566.

Howard, D. & Franklin, S. (1988). *Missing the meaning? A cognitive neuropsychological study of processing of words by an aphasic patient.* Boston, Mass.: MIT Press.

Kohn, S. & Friedman, R. (1986). Word-meaning deafness: a phonological-semantic dissociation. *Cognitive Neuropsychology, 3*, 291–308.

Patterson, K.E. & Hodges, J.R. (1994). Disorders of semantic memory. In A. Baddeley, B. Wilson & F. Watts (Eds), *Handbook of memory disorders*. Hove, UK: Lawrence Erlbaum Associates Ltd.

Abstract Word Meaning Deafness

Sue Franklin

University of York, York, UK

David Howard

Birkbeck College, London, UK

Karalyn Patterson

MRC Applied Psychology Unit, Cambridge, UK

We report the case of a patient, DRB, who shows impaired auditory comprehension of abstract but not concrete words, in the context of preserved
comprehension of all types of written words. Good performance on auditory
lexical decision for abstract words indicates that DRB is able to access these
lexical entries. This pattern may be termed "abstract word meaning deafness."

Repetition is also more impaired for abstract words than concrete words.
DRB is unable to repeat nonwords or write them to dictation. He makes
semantic errors in real word repetition, which is compatible with the view
that his repetition is semantically mediated. Exactly the same pattern of
semantic errors and a particular difficulty with abstract words is found in
tasks where DRB is required to write to dictation. DRB's auditory comprehension and repetition impairments are not affected by word frequency.
Performance on specific words is inconsistent, and is improved following a
written cue.

INTRODUCTION

Auditory Comprehension Impairments

Cases of "word deafness," a comprehension deficit specific to the auditory
modality, have been reported in the literature for over a hundred years.
In 1886, Ziehl distinguished two types: word sound deafness ("Wortlaut-

---

We are grateful to Andrew Ellis and the anonymous reviewers for useful suggestions for revisions.
The staff at the City University Dysphasic Group referred DRB to us and kindly allowed us to test him
there. We are profoundly grateful to DRB himself for tolerating such extensive testing: We have been
rewarded by his interest in our work and his great sense of humour. This research was supported by the
Medical Research Council.

taubheit") and word meaning deafness ("Wortsinntaubheit"). Word sound deafness was an inability to process speech sounds (in the absence of deafness), and was necessarily associated with disorders in repetition and writing to dictation. Word meaning deafness was an inability to derive the meaning of the word and was distinguished from word sound deafness by the patient's ability to repeat and write to dictation, indicating that he was able to process speech sounds adequately. In this classical definition, the deficit was seen primarily as one of the *auditory* modality (hence the term "deafness"). Whether this should be accompanied by an equivalent deficit for written comprehension depended on whether written comprehension was conceptualised as depending on auditory comprehension.

Word meaning deafness has been reported much less frequently than word sound deafness; a notable exception is the recently republished case history by Bramwell (1897, reprinted with an introduction by Ellis, 1984). The data presented by Bramwell are anecdotal (he only gave one actual example of a comprehension failure, when the patient was unable to understand "Do you like to come to Edinburgh" until she had written it down). There is no evidence of a single word comprehension impairment (when asked to point to named objects the patient made no mistakes), but the patient's ability to repeat and write a sentence that she was apparently unable to comprehend does suggest a form of word meaning deafness.

More detailed descriptions exist of cases of "transcortical sensory aphasia," analogous to word meaning deafness in that it is an impairment of auditory comprehension with spared repetition, but unlike the "pure form" in that the patient has other aphasic symptoms, such as anomia. However, this definition of transcortical sensory aphasia does not rule out the possibility that the patient has a general semantic problem (i.e. one that affects comprehension of both written and spoken language), so unless other modalities are shown to be spared, this cannot be considered to be a specific "deafness" for word meanings. Indeed, in the most detailed description of a patient with transcortical sensory aphasia, Berndt, Basili, and Caramazza (1987) demonstrated that, although their patient had impaired auditory comprehension and intact repetition, he also had impaired written comprehension and naming. They did, however, establish that RR's difficulty in understanding spoken words was a post-lexical impairment by showing that he performed well in auditory lexical decision tests. Likewise the two patients of Buckingham and Kertesz (1974) are described as having a "rather severe anomia," and since performance in written comprehension was not tested, this pattern of performance would be consistent with a general semantic problem.

Heilman, Rothi, McFarling, and Rottmann (1981) described a patient with poor auditory comprehension and spared repetition. On the limited testing carried out, he achieved higher scores in naming than in auditory comprehension (which they argue indicates an impairment specific to the auditory modality); nonetheless he was impaired in both naming and written comprehension. Unlike Berndt et al. they do not rule out this patient having a pre-lexical auditory impairment.

Although word meaning deafness and transcortical sensory aphasia are recognised "syndromes" in the aphasia literature, no good description of a patient exists that demonstrates an impairment of access to meaning for understanding spoken words in the absence of a deficit in the comprehension of written words. The "syndromes" of pure word deafness and transcortical sensory aphasia are defined in terms of co-occurring deficits. In this paper we want to adopt a rather different approach in trying to understand how the performance of our patient may be understood in terms of information processing models of lexical organisation.

Forms of "Word Deafness" and Lexical Organisation

The information processing model of lexical organisation in Fig. 1 is taken from Patterson and Shewell (1987), and is a development of Morton's (1980) revision of the logogen model. In this model, the auditory comprehension of words requires (1) auditory analysis of the incoming acoustic signals, resulting in (2) access to the correct word form in an auditory input lexicon, which representation gives (3) access to a representation of the words' meanings in the cognitive system. The processes involved in the comprehension of written words are separate from those involved in spoken word comprehension up until the level of the modality-independent cognitive system.

Impairments to each of the stages involved in spoken word comprehension should result in different patterns of impairment. A deficit in auditory analysis should result in the classical pattern of "pure word sound deafness." Kohn and Friedman (1986) differentiate two patterns of impairment to auditory comprehension in patients in whom speech sound perception is apparently normal. Their notion of "post-access" word deafness seems to correspond most closely to the notion of classical word meaning deafness; that is an inability to understand in the absence of a difficulty in word sound perception. They describe a patient, HN, who, when he is unable to understand spoken words, is still able to write them correctly. Kohn and Friedman point out that this can occur with words such as "thigh" that are irregular in terms of their sound-to-spelling correspondences. They argue that the correct spelling of the word could only be achieved if the appropriate entry had been accessed in the auditory input lexicon; the patient's difficulty must therefore occur after lexical access and before access to meaning. The data on which this claim is based are, unfortunately,

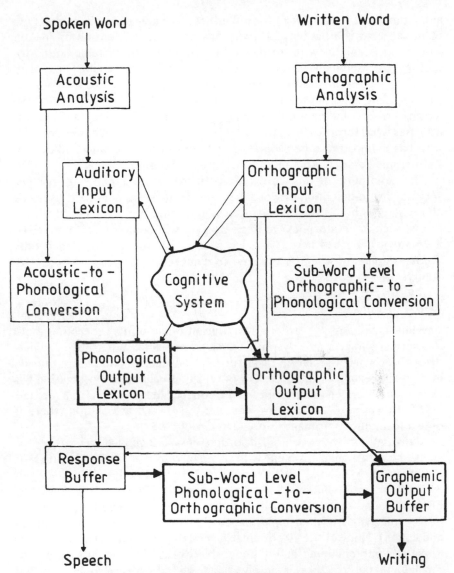

FIG. 1   A model of lexical processing (Patterson & Shewell, 1987).

rather scanty; Kohn and Friedman cite only eight words where HN is
unable to understand a spoken word, and their diagnosis of a post-lexical
deficit rests on his successful writing to dictation of three words whose
spellings were not predictable from their phonological form ("knee" and
"thigh," which are both irregular in their spelling, and "hair," which has
an ambiguous spelling). Kohn and Friedman (1986) distinguish this pattern
of impairment from "pre-access word deafness" (also described by Howard

and Franklin, 1988 as "word form deafness"). Their example of this type of impairment is a patient, LL, who has poor comprehension of spoken words but is able to write to dictation words with predictable sound-to-spelling correspondences. As the patient tends to mis-spell words with exceptional correspondences, they suggest that he is unable to use a lexical routine. This is not an entirely convincing argument, however, since the writing errors could be a reflection of other deficits. Franklin (1989) characterises word form deafness more simply in the description of patient AH, who has unimpaired repetition (even of nonwords), but who makes substantial numbers of errors in auditory lexical decision.

The description of this third type of word deafness makes possible a very narrow re-definition of word meaning deafness, as a modality-specific deficit, but with no impairment in tasks requiring the accessing of lexical forms, such as auditory lexical decision. We will demonstrate that DRB, the patient described here, has such a deficit. However, the deficit only becomes apparent when he is asked to comprehend words of low imageability.

Word Imageability[1]

The imageability of a word has a significant effect on its processing, both for normal subjects and dysphasic/dyslexic subjects. When given lexical decision or word association tasks, normal subjects respond more quickly to high-imageability words (De Groot, 1989). A significant interaction has been found between imageability and frequency in lexical decision (James, 1975). However, in an overtly semantic task, word association, there is only a main effect of imageability (De Groot, 1989).

Many patients with acquired disorders of language have been reported as having a particular problem with abstract words in reading (Coltheart, Patterson, & Marshall, 1980), repetition (Howard & Franklin, 1988) or comprehension (Franklin, 1989). In a series of 20 fluent aphasic patients, Franklin found that 13 were significantly worse at comprehending words of low imageability (than high-imageability words matched in frequency and length). None of the 20 patients showed the opposite pattern, of being worse at comprehending highly imageable words. This might lead one to conclude that abstractness is simply an index of difficulty, a conclusion that receives some intuitive support (consider, for example, trying to explain the meaning of "process" rather than "eagle!"). However, patients have been reported who appear to be more impaired at comprehending concrete than abstract words (Warrington, 1975; 1981).

---

[1]Most of the tests used here contrast performance with high- and low-imageability words. Imageability and concreteness correlate very highly: we have therefore used both "high-imageability" and "concrete," and "low-imageability" and "abstract" interchangeably. We have no data that allow us to determine whether the relevant variable is truly imageability or concreteness.

Access and Storage Impairments

We will argue in this paper that DRB has an impairment of semantic access for abstract words from auditory input. This claim is based on two arguments: first we will try to establish that pre-semantic levels in auditory word recognition are unimpaired; secondly, we will argue that semantic access from written input is normal both for concrete and abstract words. Our claim that this is an impairment of access to central semantic representations, which are involved in the comprehension of both spoken and written words, thus depends on excluding other levels of impairment.

There is a second way in which attempts have been made to distinguish between disorders of access to semantics and degradation of semantic representations. This is in terms of the characteristics of the word comprehension impairment. A set of empirical criteria were developed by Shallice and Warrington, which, it is claimed, can distinguish between access and storage impairments (Shallice, 1987; 1988; Warrington & Shallice, 1979). Disorders that result from impaired stored semantic representations are said to show the following features:

1. Performance is consistently poor for specific items on repeated presentation.
2. Semantic representations of low-frequency words are more impaired than those of high-frequency words.
3. Performance cannot be improved by priming or changes in rate of presentation.
4. Access to superordinate semantic information can be preserved when subordinate or attribute information cannot be retrieved.

Semantic access impairments, in contrast, show the following features:

1. Performance is inconsistent item-by-item across different presentations of the same items.
2. Performance is unaffected by word frequency.
3. Semantic access can be improved by priming, or by changes in rate of presentation.
4. Attribute information should be no more impaired than superordinate information where the superordinate information can be accessed.

These proposals for empirical distinctions between access and storage deficits have been quite widely criticised (e.g. Howard, Note 4; Riddoch, Humphreys, Coltheart, & Funnell, 1988; Rapp & Caramazza, 1992). The criticisms take broadly three lines.

First, these distinctions only apply to a particular set of models of access to semantics. Shallice and Warrington initially described these impairments in terms of a model where aspects of meaning are accessed by progress down a semantic tree. This is initially accessed at a superordinate level, and as the process of access proceeds down a tree, increasingly specific components of meaning become available. Storage impairments consist of pruning of trees corresponding to low-frequency words, such that the lower branches (corresponding to subordinate and attribute information) are no longer present. Access impairments, on the other hand, correspond to a reduced probability of being able to proceed further down the tree, which may result in blocked access at any node in the tree. Although the predictions on the characteristics of access and storage follow reasonably simply from application of a model of this kind, it has been pointed out that other proposals concerning the organisation of semantic knowledge can make very different predictions. As Rapp and Caramazza (1992) demonstrate, under certain circumstances, both item consistency and a frequency effect may follow from an impairment of access to intact stored representations.

The second principal line of criticism has been empirical; to what extent do the patients with putative impairments of access and storage show all the set of criterial features? As Rapp and Caramazza show, there are a number of patients who show some of the features set out earlier but not others; the interpretation of such patterns of performance is not clear cut. Furthermore, as Howard (Note 4) and Coltheart and Funnell (1987) show, application of the criterion of consistency is not straightforward. This is for two reasons; first, significant consistency may arise not from any item-specific effects but simply due to a pronounced effect of some variable (such as frequency or concreteness) on performance. Second, even where there is complete item consistency, actual measured performance can appear to be very inconsistent in tasks with substantial chance probabilities of success.

The third criticism is more general. Rapp and Caramazza (1992) argue that there is no point in making any pre-theoretical distinction between access and storage deficits; claims about the underlying level of breakdown can only be made in relation to a theory of the process of semantic access.

We do not propose to deal in detail with these matters in this paper. Having established, by exclusion, that DRB has an impairment in semantic access, we will then evaluate whether his pattern of performance is consistent with Shallice's criteria. Thus we will investigate whether he shows item-by-item consistency; whether performance is affected by word frequency; whether auditory semantic access can be improved by a visually presented prime; and whether he has partial semantic information available when complete semantics are unavailable.

Before this we will demonstrate that DRB provides a clear example of a patient with word meaning deafness, defined as an impairment of word comprehension, specific to the auditory modality. He is especially impaired at comprehending words of low imageability. DRB is not a *pure* case of word meaning deafness; he is also impaired in tasks of repetition and writing to dictation. However, we will argue that this is a consequence of a severe impairment in the ability to repeat or write heard sounds by a direct mapping of input phonology to output phonology/orthography.

CASE HISTORY

DRB has a history of hypertension and diabetes, and had a coronary thrombosis in 1969. In 1985, when he was 54, he had a left CVA (he is right-handed), of which the only presenting symptom was dysphasia (although he has subsequently been shown to have a mild weakness of the right arm). A subsequent CT-scan showed evidence of a left middle cerebral infarct. His hearing, which was tested using pure tone audiometry, is normal.

For three years after his stroke DRB received speech therapy three times per week, and he now attends a maintenance group. Because of the CVA he gave up his work, which had been organising a motorcycle dispatch service for a travel agency, as well as his hobby of semi-professional photography. Although unable to work because of his language disability, he still drives, has become skilled at marquetry, and has no episodic memory or intellectual impairments.

All the testing reported here was carried out between 1987 and 1989, when DRB was between 2 and 4 years post-onset. DRB has impaired auditory comprehension, but his comprehension for single written words appears intact (although he is mildly "surface" dyslexic in *oral* reading). His speech is fluent and syntactically well formed (see Appendix 1), although with some function word errors and with pausing, characteristic of an anomic deficit. His anomia is not particularly evident in picture naming tests, where he performs just outside the normal range. However, word fluency tests suggest that he finds it difficult to find words in more abstract categories (e.g. he was able to produce six words to do with religion; a matched normal control produced double this number). His repetition is impaired, even at a single word level, and is more impaired when he is unable to lip read.

Results of Formal Testing

Raven's Standard Progressive Matrices (Raven, Court, & Raven, 1977). DRB scored on the 75th percentile (48/60) for age-matched norms, indicating good performance on this nonverbal task.

British Picture Vocabulary Scale—Spoken Presentation (Dunn, 1965). Although this test gives no norms for DRB's age group, he scored on the 80th percentile (113/150) for the eldest group tested (16–18 year olds).

Test for Reception of Grammar—Spoken Presentation (Bishop, 1982).
A score of 50/80 on this test (9 blocks passed, age equivalent 5 years)
indicated a severe impairment in sentence comprehension. Some of the
errors may have been due to an inability to comprehend function words
(which of course tend to be highly abstract).

TESTS OF COMPREHENSION

Since DRB's main problem appeared to be an impairment of auditory
word comprehension, testing was initially focussed on this area. We gave
him two types of comprehension test, the first looking at his ability to
understand pictures and picturable words. The second type of test compared the comprehension of high- and low-imageability (or concrete and
abstract) words. In order to establish whether the impairment was modality
specific, the latter tests were given in both a spoken and a written form.
DRB was asked to turn away from the experimenter when tests were
presented auditorily, to ensure he was not able to lip read. A summary of
the results of all the auditory comprehension tests can be seen in Table 1.

Comprehension Tests Using Picturable Items

The Pyramids and Palm Trees Test (Howard & Patterson, 1992)

This test was given in two versions; the first was a picture version, where
DRB had to judge which of two response pictures was most closely related
in meaning to a target picture. The two response pictures are themselves
closely related (e.g. for the target WEB the choice is between pictures of
a SPIDER and a BEE). Howard and Orchard-Lisle (1984) argue that good
performance on this test requires the ability to make fine semantic distinctions. The other version given to DRB also required a choice between the
two response pictures, but on this occasion each target item was a spoken
word. There are 52 items in this test, and Howard and Patterson found
that the normal range of performance is 0–3 errors. DRB made 2 errors
with picture targets, and 4 errors with spoken word targets, suggesting that
for some picturable items at least he is able to access fine semantic information from the spoken word. His performance may, however, have been
enhanced by the pictorial information priming the heard words.

PALPA Word-to-picture Matching Test (Kay, Lesser, & Coltheart, 1992)

This test requires the patient to match a heard word to a corresponding
picture. As well as the correct picture (e.g. AXE), there are four distractor
items: a close semantic distractor (e.g. HAMMER), a more remote
semantic distractor (e.g. SCISSORS), a visual distractor (e.g. FLAG), and

TABLE 1
Tests of Spoken and Written Comprehension

Test	Spoken Stimuli		Written Stimuli	
1. Pyramids & Palm Trees	0.92		—	
2. PALPA word-to-picture matching test (n = 40)	0.98		1.00	
	Hi Im	Lo Im	Hi Im	Lo Im
3. Synonym judgments (n = 38)	0.95	0.61	1.00	0.95
4. Concrete/abstract picture-word matching (n = 30)	0.97	0.47	1.00	0.83
5. Word "associations" (n = 40)	0.93	0.43	1.00	0.90

an item semantically related to the visual distractor (e.g. KITE). Thus, in order to do this test successfully, the patient has to access a reasonably precise meaning of the word he hears. As with the previous test, DRB was able to select the correct pictures in response to a heard word; he scored 39/40 correct (error = "underpants" → vest).

Comprehension Tests Contrasting Words of Low and High Imageability

Although it was clear that DRB was having considerable difficulty comprehending what people said to him, the word-to-picture matching tests described earlier, which are typical of the tests generally used to assess comprehension, had failed to uncover any significant deficit. Knowing that word imageability can be an important factor in patients with acquired disorders of reading, we gave him a number of tests that required comprehension of words low in imageability (= abstract words). As mentioned earlier, all these tests were given (on separate occasions) in an identical form in both the written and the spoken modalities.

Synonym Judgments Test (Coltheart, Note 1)

This test requires the subject to judge whether two words have similar meanings (e.g. marriage/wedding, throng/crowd). The dissimilar pairs are produced by random reallocation of the same items; these pairs are thus not semantically related. The test comprises 76 pairs, half of which are words with high-imageability ratings (e.g. crop/battle) and half with low-imageability ratings (e.g. truth/reality). The high- and low-imageability sets are matched for word frequency. Control subjects made between 0 and 3 errors on the 76 items (Anne Edmundson, personal communication).

DRB performed normally on the written version of this test (High 38/38, Low 36/38), but was significantly worse on the spoken version (High 36/38, Low 23/38, McNemar Test, $z = 3.87$, $P < 0.001$). Even for the high-imageability words he performed (just) outside the normal range, perhaps supporting the notion that his good performance in the word/picture tests reflects the use of picture semantics to prime auditory input. However, what is most striking about his performance on this test is his extremely low score on the low-imageability spoken words (low is significantly worse than high: Fisher Exact Test, $z = 2.63$, $P < 0.01$), where chance performance would be 50%. Since imageability is presumably a function of meaning, the difference in performance between the spoken and written modalities is intriguing. It suggests that DRB has a *modality-specific* deficit for low-imageability words.

Concrete and Abstract Word-to-picture Matching Test (Shallice & McGill, unpublished)

This test requires the patient to select the picture corresponding to the stimulus word from a choice of four pictures. The abstract word items are conceptually more difficult in that, whereas the concrete words correspond directly to the picture (e.g. wigwam → picture of a wigwam, propeller → picture of a propeller), for the abstract words it is necessary to make inferences to select the correct picture (e.g. skill → someone playing a musical instrument, democracy → a group of people all with their hands raised). It is not therefore surprising that, although DRB made no errors on the concrete items (with written presentation), he scored only 0.83 on the written abstract items. Although this constitutes a significant difference between written abstract and concrete items (Fisher Exact, $z = 1.85$, $P < 0.05$), it is well within normal performance on this test, since Warrington (1981) reported that the *mean* normal performance for abstract items was 0.86.

In the spoken word condition, he scored 97% on the concrete word items and was significantly worse (47%) with the abstract words (Fisher Exact, $z = 3.85$, $P < 0.01$). Since he was able to select the correct picture for most of the items with written presentation, poor performance with abstract items cannot be wholly attributable to a difficulty in interpreting the pictures. These results are further support for DRB having a modality-specific abstract word impairment.

Word "Associations"

In the final test of this series, DRB either heard or saw a word and was then asked to produce a single word "association" indicating that he knew some aspect of the meaning of the word. The list used was Howard and

Franklin's (1987) 80-item imageability × frequency list. The imageability ratings are taken from norms in the MRC Psycholinguistic Database (Coltheart, Note 2), in which the words were rated on a 7-point scale, where 1 is the least and 7 the most imageable. Forty of the words in the list were highly imageable (range: 5.72–6.37), the other 40 were low in imageability (range: 3.15–3.97). Half of each imageability set were low-frequency words (5–19 words per million), the other half were high-frequency words (100–199 words per million). Word frequency counts were taken from Kuçera and Francis (1967). Whether the responses were acceptable "associations" was decided by an independent judge who was not told either the purpose of the experiment or the modality of the stimulus presentation.

Examples of "associations" judged correct are:

Written Presentation	*Spoken Presentation*
RADIO → "wireless"	"radio" → "TV"
CLAY → "plasticine"	"clay" → "wax"
CULT → "Marx"	"cult" → "ghost"
DEBUT → "the first"	"theory" → "idea"

The results (Table 1) indicate that, despite being mildly anomic, DRB was able to produce an appropriate associate to most of these words when they were in written form. When he heard the words, however, he was significantly worse at producing "associations" to words of low imageability (Fisher Exact Test, $z = 4.61$, $P < 0.01$). The majority of incorrect responses were no responses.

In summary, DRB's single word comprehension is characterised by a striking interaction between modality of presentation and word imageability, with a significant impairment only for spoken abstract words. Since imageability is necessarily a *lexical* property, the discrepancy cannot be explained entirely by any peripheral impairment, such as a difficulty in word sound perception. There are, however, still two possible accounts of the deficits underlying DRB's pattern of performance. One is that he has a true abstract word *meaning* deafness; that is, although word forms (for spoken abstract words) and meaning representations (for abstract words) are both intact, he cannot access the latter from the former. The other possibility is that he has a mild central semantic deficit, which is too mild to produce errors in written word tasks, but which becomes evident in auditory comprehension because of an additional, more peripheral, auditory deficit. Since, as will be demonstrated in a later section, DRB does have severely impaired word repetition, this latter account must be given serious consideration. The next section therefore addresses the issue of whether DRB has an impairment of processing input phonology.

TESTS OF AUDITORY INPUT

According to the information processing model in Fig. 1, in order to understand a word it is necessary to access the corresponding word-form in the auditory input lexicon, as well as carrying out pre-lexical auditory processing. This is supported by neuropsychological evidence showing that patients, although able to carry out pre-lexical analysis (as demonstrated, for example, by adequate discrimination of minimal pairs), may have a problem specifically at the level of word form access (Howard & Franklin, 1988; Franklin 1989). Therefore, in order to rule out the possibility of a phonological input deficit, it is necessary to assess DRB's performance on tests requiring both processing of specific speech sounds (i.e. minimal pair discrimination) and access to word forms in the auditory modality (i.e. lexical decision tests). The results of both the minimal pair tests and the auditory lexical decision tests are summarised in Table 2. DRB was prevented from lip reading during the administration of all these tests.

Minimal Pair Tests

DRB was given two phoneme discrimination tests, where he had to decide whether the two members of each pair of spoken strings were identical or different. The different pairs differed only on one phoneme. The first test (Franklin, 1989) used CV syllables. On half the dissimilar items the phoneme contrast differed by 1 distinctive feature; on the other

TABLE 2
Tests of Auditory Input

Phoneme Discrimination	(n)	Correct		
CV syllables	(40)	0.95		
CVC nonwords	(36)	0.89		

	Correct		Errors	
Lexical Decision	[Visual]	Auditory	Real Word	Nonword
Easy lexical decision (n = 50)	[0.98]	0.98	0	1
320-item test	[0.98]	0.96	5"	8
Syllable length (n = 180)				
1-syllable		0.98	0	1
2-syllables		0.93	3	1
3-syllables		0.93	2	2

"Three high-imageability words, two low-imageability words missed.

half it differed by 3 distinctive features. DRB made 2 errors on this 40-item test. The PALPA test (Kay et al., 1992) used 36 CVC nonword pairs, with the contrast occurring initially or finally. DRB made 3 false positive errors with initial contrasts and 1 false positive error with final contrasts (feature contrasts in incorrect pairs were 2 manner, 1 place, and 1 voice). Although not perfect, DRB achieved around 90% correct overall in these tests, indicating that he has no severe impairment of auditory analysis.

Auditory Lexical Decision Tests

Two tests of auditory lexical decision were initially given to DRB. The first is Coltheart's (Note 1) "Easy lexical decision test," the second is a test derived from a set of 160 words varying in imageability and frequency, with the nonwords made by changing a single letter/phoneme in the real words. For the auditory version of the tests, DRB was asked to give a yes/no response; he was asked to tick the real words in the written versions. There was no time constraint, but DRB responded without hesitation on all items. As can be seen in Table 2, DRB shows no impairment in lexical decision for either written or spoken words. Finally we devised a lexical decision test using words and nonwords of 1, 2, and 3 syllables and again he achieved 95% accuracy. When asked to make a lexical decision in response to an abstract word, DRB commonly responds, "Yes it's a word, but I don't *hear* it."

Tests of "Phonological Confusability"

Word-to-picture Matching with Phonologically Related Foils

DRB's good performance on lexical decision tests suggests that he is not impaired at the level of the auditory input lexicon. However, lexical decision is hardly a measure of "normal" language processing, and it could be argued that DRB has developed a particular strategy to deal with such a peculiar task. If DRB has any impairment of phonological or lexical access in auditory comprehension he should have difficulty with tests where there are phonologically related foils. A test from the PALPA Battery (Kay et al., 1992), where the patient hears a word and has to point to the corresponding picture, was therefore administered. There are two picture distractors representing phonologically related words (e.g. "fan" with pictures of fan, van, man). DRB was able to point to 36/40 of the pictures correctly, which, although below the mean score of the normal control subjects, is within the range of normal (control mean 39, sd 1.70; Kay et al., 1992). As with the minimal pair tests, DRB's performance is not perfect, but neither is it seriously impaired.

Picture Decision Test

The Picture Decision Test (Howard & Franklin, 1988) was devised to test more searchingly the patient's ability to access the correct lexical form. The items from the 100 Picture Naming Test were used, excluding 3 items that had no phonological real-word neighbours (thermometer, mermaid, and stethoscope). The patient saw a picture, heard a word, and had to say whether the word was a correct name for the picture. There were four conditions (e.g. picture of an iron):

appropriate → "iron"
semantically related word → "press"
phonologically related real word → "lion"
phonologically related nonword → /baiən/

Each of the 97 items was tested in each condition. The results (Table 3) show that DRB very rarely rejected the appropriate name for a picture (miss errors) but accepted a substantial number of semantically related inappropriate names. The small number of errors in the real and nonword phonologically related conditions is inconsistent with a deficit of phonological or lexical access.

Word Associations Using Words of Differing Lengths

If DRB's impairment is at a post-lexical level, we would predict that his ability to define words would be independent of stimulus length. We asked him to give word associations to 180 words that were either 1, 2, or 3 syllables in length, half of which were high-imageability words and half low-imageability words. Although, as would be expected, there was a dramatic effect of imageability on association accuracy, it can be seen in Table 4 that there was no effect of syllable length. (It is of interest to note that when asked to give word associations, he never provides an association appropriate to a word that is phonologically related to the stimulus.)

TABLE 3
Picture Decision Test

Correct (n = 388)	361
Errors	
Misses	4
Semantic errors	15
Phonological real-word errors	4
Phonological nonword errors	4

TABLE 4
"Associations" to Imageability × Length List

No. of Syllables	High Imageability	Low Imageability
1 syllable	0.87	0.17
2 syllables	0.93	0.23
3 syllables	0.90	0.20

n = 30 in each cell.

All the tests in this section indicate that DRB shows none of the characteristics of a patient who has difficulty accessing lexical forms: He performs normally in auditory lexical decision, he does not make "phonological" errors in word comprehension, and his understanding of words is unaffected by their length. His difficulty in understanding spoken words, particularly when they are abstract, must therefore lie in the access to semantic representations from an auditory input lexicon.

REPETITION AND WRITING TO DICTATION

In the preceding section we argued that DRB's auditory comprehension impairment represents a deficit in the process of access to lexical/semantic representations rather than a deficit at a phonological/lexical level. Can this account be sustained in the light of his impaired performance in repetition and writing to dictation? The model in Fig. 1 offers three routines for word repetition, (1) via sub-lexical auditory-to-phonological conversion, (2) via the direct link from the auditory input lexicon to the phonological output lexicon, and (3) via access to meaning representations in the cognitive system. We will argue that DRB is only able to repeat words via their semantics, and that both the sub-lexical and direct lexical routes must be unavailable. This entails that DRB's word repetition should be affected by the same variables that affect word comprehension; that is, he should be poor at repeating low-imageability words, but repetition should be unaffected by other factors such as word length and word frequency. In the model shown in Fig. 1, there are no direct lexical or sub-lexical routes from auditory input to written output (see Patterson & Shewell, 1987, for a justification of this architecture of the model). All the routes for writing spoken words to dictation that do not involve semantic mediation involve output phonological representations as an intermediate stage. If, as we have suggested, he has neither the routine for sub-lexical auditory-to-phonological conversion, nor the direct route from the auditory input lexicon to the phonological output lexicon available for word repetition, this model predicts that writing to dictation should only be possible via semantic mediation. Thus, writing to dictation should resemble word repetition in being affected by the variables that determine his success in word comprehension.

DRB's deficits in repetition and writing to dictation will be explored by looking first at his ability to repeat and write nonwords, then at the characteristics of his word repetition and writing. As for all previously described tests involving auditory presentation, DRB was prevented from lip reading.

Repetition and Writing to Dictation of Nonwords

DRB was given the same list of nonwords, on different occasions, for repetition, for oral reading, and for writing to dictation. There were 20 pronounceable phoneme strings of between 3 and 5 phonemes. Table 5 shows DRB's performance on this test, as well as the types of error he produces. Although unable to repeat or write a single nonword, he was able to read aloud 17/20 correctly. His poor performance when these strings were presented auditorily for repetition or writing cannot be explained wholly by an output deficit as he can produce nonwords in reading; neither can the deficit be at the level of pre-lexical input, since he is able to perform well with minimal pairs and lexical decision. We conclude that he must have a deficit in the processes of sub-word level auditory to phonological conversion. The fact that some of the responses bear no clear relation to the target, coupled with the fact that he was unable to reproduce even one heard nonword correctly, indicates the severity of this impairment.

Repetition and Writing to Dictation of Words

If DRB is unable to use the sublexical repetition routine, then his repetition and writing to dictation will reflect the use of either the semantic routine and/or the direct lexical routines. If the direct lexical routines are available, then real-word repetition should be unimpaired. Alternatively, if DRB can only repeat via semantics, his repetition will be sensitive to the same property as his comprehension, that is, word imageability. If his repetition

TABLE 5
Repetition, Writing to Dictation, and Reading Nonwords

Stimulus	Repetition	Dictation	Reading
Correct	0/20	0/20	17/20
Errors			
No response	4	3	0
Real word	14	17	1
Phonologically related nonword	0	0	2
Neologism	2	0	0

is impaired, and is worse for abstract words, it will show that he is unable to access output lexical forms directly from the input lexicon. It would not be possible to conclude from this whether such access exists in normal language processing, or whether it is an additional impairment for DRB. Since it is hypothesised that other routines for writing to dictation are dependent on prior lexical/phonological access, DRB will also be forced to write heard words via semantics. His writing to dictation should therefore be sensitive to imageability.

Imageability × Frequency List (Howard & Franklin, 1987)

DRB was asked to repeat the 80-item imageability × frequency list used earlier to produce word associations. The results are shown in Table 6. It can be seen that, in addition to a general impairment in word repetition (due in part to his anomic problems?), he is significantly worse at repeating low-imageability than high-imageability words (Fisher Exact Test, $z = 2.35$, $P < 0.01$). There is no significant effect of word frequency. His responses for all the items in this test can be seen in Appendix 2. The majority of the 47 errors were failures to respond (= 33). The remaining errors were unrelated real words (3), semantic errors (8, including 2 that

TABLE 6
Word Repetition and Writing to Dictation

Word Repetition	High Imageability		Low Imageability	
	Hi Freq.	Lo Freq.	Hi Freq.	Lo Freq.
Imageability × Frequency				
Howard Test (n = 80)	0.80	0.70	0.15	0.10
PALPA Test 1 (n = 80)	0.85	0.70	0.05	0.10
PALPA Test 2	0.95	0.85	0.20	0.15
Imageability				
200 Item Test 1	0.92		0.47	
200 Item Test 2	0.94		0.52	
Imageability × Syllable length (n = 180)				
1 syllable	0.63		0.00	
2 syllables	0.67		0.03	
3 syllables	0.67		0.00	

Writing to Dictation	High Imageability	Low Imageability
Imageability × Syllable length (n = 180)		
1 syllable	0.77	0.23
2 syllables	0.37	0.13
3 syllables	0.40	0.10

are also phonologically similar), morphological errors (2 plurals) and phonological errors (2). This error pattern is reflected in all the other tests given for repetition: To the majority of items, DRB produces either the correct word or nothing. Clear phonological errors are rare. The overall pattern of responses, a particular difficulty with abstract words and some semantic errors, indicates that DRB is repeating via the semantic routine.

To confirm these findings, we gave DRB another 2 lists for repetition; the first was the 80-item imageability × frequency list taken from the PALPA battery (Kay et al., 1992), and the other was a list of 100 high-imageability words and 100 low-imageability words, matched for length and frequency (Howard & Franklin, 1988). The results of these tests, each administered twice, can also be seen in Table 6. There is exactly the same pattern of results in each test; on each administration, DRB was significantly worse at repeating the low-imageability words.

Syllable Length List

When describing DRB's ability to access lexical forms, we demonstrated that his comprehension was unaffected by word length. If DRB is repeating via the semantic route, the same should hold for repetition. It is important to demonstrate this since, in the auditory comprehension tasks, a length effect might be masked by an ability to use only partial information. In a repetition test, however, the precise word has to be produced, and there is no additional contextual information.

The list used to investigate the effect of length on DRB's repetition was the 180-word imageability × syllable length list that had been used earlier for the word "associations" task. The results can be seen in Table 6. DRB showed no significant difference between syllable lengths, although, as would be expected, there was a clear effect of imageability (high-imageability words, 0.66 correct; low-imageability words, 0.01 correct).

In summary, DRB's word repetition shows no effect of word length or frequency, but a dramatic impact of word imageability. This pattern, coupled with the occurrence of semantic errors in repetition, demonstrates that he repeats via the semantic route, and it is further evidence for a deficit at a lexical/semantic level rather than a phonological/lexical level. The absolute proportion of errors across the three different tests, shown in Table 6, varies considerably. However, performance across different administrations of the same test remains fairly constant.

Writing to Dictation: Syllable Length List

We predicted earlier that DRB should be impaired in tasks requiring him to write to dictation, and that as in repetition, performance should be affected by imageability. As he makes semantic errors in repetition, he should also make semantic errors in writing to dictation. To test these predictions, we asked him to write the words in the syllable length list described earlier. (This was several months after we had used the test for repetition.) The results are shown in Table 6. As predicted, there was a significant effect of imageability on performance (high-imageability words, 0.54 correct, low-imageability words, 0.16 correct: Fisher Exact Test, $z = 4.81$, $P < 0.001$). In contrast to the repetition results, there was also a significant effect of syllable length (1-syllable, 0.50 correct; 2-syllable, 0.25 correct; 3-syllable, 0.25 correct: Jonckheere Trend Test, $z = 2.80$, $P < 0.005$). DRB's poorer performance with longer words appeared to be explicable in terms of an additional spelling impairment. As with repetition, many of DRB's errors were either no responses or semantic errors (e.g. "hurricane" $\rightarrow$ WIND). However, he also made a large number of spelling errors on the longer words (e.g. "scissors" $\rightarrow$ SISSORS; "carnation" $\rightarrow$ CARNASATION), along with semantic-then-spelling errors (e.g. "lobster" $\rightarrow$ CRAMB; "bracelet" $\rightarrow$ PREASANT).

DRB writes heard words, as well as repeating them, via meaning. This is demonstrated by the fact that he produces errors in both tasks which are semantically related to the target. The large effect of word imageability on DRB's performance in auditory comprehension is also found in both writing and repetition.

CHARACTERISTICS OF DRB'S COMPREHENSION

Having established the locus of deficit in DRB's comprehension as mapping from lexical forms to meaning, we conducted further tests of his auditory comprehension and repetition to establish the characteristics of his access impairment.

The Effect of Word Frequency

Although we have already demonstrated that there are no main effects of word frequency, nor an interaction between frequency and imageability, in DRB's repetition, null results are always difficult to interpret; here we report some more searching attempts to find word frequency effects.

Frequency and Imageability in Spoken Word Association and Repetition

We used a list of 180 words, half of which were of high imageability and half of low imageability, in three word frequency bands (frequency values from Kuçera & Francis, 1967): low-frequency (0–5 occurrences per million), mid-frequency (6–15), and high-frequency (16–150). DRB was asked to repeat the 180 items on one occasion and to provide an association to each word on a different occasion, in both cases without seeing the experimenter's lips as the items were spoken. As expected, substantial effects of word imageability were observed in both tasks (*association*: high-imageability = 91%; low-imageability = 11%, chi-squared [1] = 115.26, $P < 0.0001$; *repetition*: high-imageability = 78%, low-imageability = 12%, chi-squared [1] = 78.14, $P < 0.0001$). Our central question is about the effects of word frequency; these are illustrated in Fig. 2. There was no significant effect of frequency in either association (chi-squared [2] = 0.31), or repetition (chi-squared [2] = 3.72, $P > 0.10$). There was also no significant interaction between frequency and imageability in either word association or repetition.

Frequency × Levels of Imageability

For a more stringent test of the effects of frequency in repetition, we used a list of 160 items from more widely separated frequency ranges; half were high-frequency words (98–150 per million) and half low-frequency words (10–20). There were 20 high-frequency items and 20 low-frequency items in each of 4 imageability ranges; sets were matched for length, across imageability bands they were matched for word frequency, and between frequency ranges they were matched for word imageability.

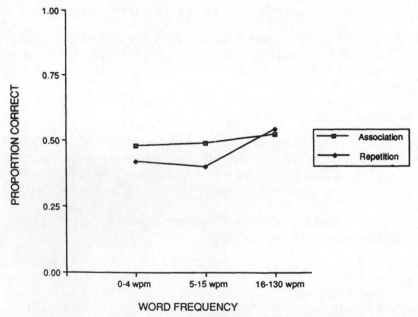

FIG. 2   The effect of frequency on repeating and defining heard words.

The results of DRB's repetition of these items without lip reading, shown in Fig. 3, reveal the usual substantial effect of word imageability (chi squared [3] = 50.21, $P < 0.0001$), but no significant effect of word frequency (chi squared [1] = 0.94) and no interaction between imageability and frequency (chi squared [3] = 3.69, ns). There appears to be no critical level of imageability that predicts DRB's performance, rather there is a gradual decline in performance as word imageability decreases.

Item Consistency

We have argued that DRB's comprehension deficit is one of access, and that he has reasonably intact semantic representations. Shallice (1987) predicts that patients with access deficits will perform inconsistently on individual items. Does DRB consistently fail to comprehend particular items?

In neuropsychology, consistency has often been assessed by comparing performance on one set of items tested in two different sessions, computing a chi squared test for independence between the two sessions, and then calculating from this the contingency coefficient C. Although some researchers have taken significant values of chi squared as showing that there is item-by-item consistency (e.g. Silveri & Gainotti, 1988), this is not a valid conclusion.

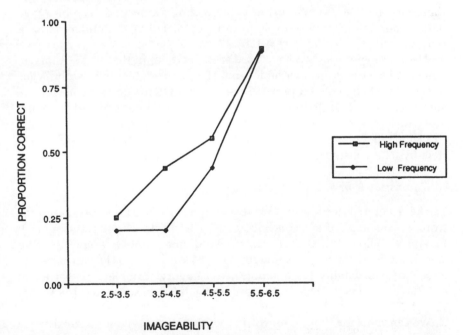

FIG. 3   The effect of imageability and frequency on word repetition.

The calculation of chi squared is against the null hypothesis that the probability of being correct is equal for all items. Where performance is significantly affected by any other variable—for instance, with DRB, word imageability, or for Silveri and Gainotti's (1988) patient, semantic category —we know a priori that the null hypothesis is false. In such cases, consistency in performance can only be assessed where either (1) the set of items used to test for consistency do not vary on any of the variables that affect the patient's performance, or (2) the effects of any confounding variables are partialled out.

Consistency in Word Repetition

In a separate session more than a month later, DRB repeated the set of 160 items drawn from 4 imageability ranges for a second time. Overall 72% of items repeated correctly on the first occasion were repeated correctly on the second occasion, whereas only 28% of those incorrect in the first test were correct on the second. A contingency coefficient based on these figures alone gives chi squared (1) = 27.89, $C = 0.385$, $P < 0.001$.

This result is, however, meaningless given that repetition accuracy is a function of word imageability. If we assume, as a more plausible null hypothesis, that the probability of a correct response is equal for each item *within each of the four imageability bands*, then we would expect 65% of the items correct on the first test to be correct on the second and 33% of those incorrect on the first test to be correct on the second. The observed data do not differ significantly from those predicted by *this* null hypothesis (chi squared [1] = 2.52, $C = 0.124$).

The null hypothesis we have used here is crude, in that it takes imageability to be a categorical variable. In fact, of course, the items within each imageability band cover a range of values, and DRB's performance, as we suggested earlier, probably varies continuously with word imageability. Nevertheless, taking the effects of word imageability into account, even in this simple manner, is sufficient to demonstrate the absence of significant item-by-item consistency in DRB's repetition performance.

Consistency in Word Association

The list of 180 items used to assess frequency effects was presented for word associations on a second occasion. The results are straightforward: Failure to allow for the effects of word imageability would indicate significant consistency (chi squared [1] = 74.75, $C = 0.541$); but once the effects of imageability (as a simple two-category variable) are partialled out, the consistency effect disappears completely (chi squared [1] = 0.983, $C = 0.074$).

We can conclude that, as in word repetition, there is no item consistency in DRB's ability to provide adequate word associations.

Priming Effects

Given that DRB's deficit is one of semantic access and that performance is not consistent on specific items, does his comprehension improve with additional information from another modality? Shallice (1987) suggests that one of the criteria for an access deficit is that performance will improve with priming.

Synonym Priming

Given the items from Coltheart's (Note 1) "synonym judgments" task, DRB was asked to repeat one item from each pair in the presence of the second item in written form. This word would either be a synonym or an unrelated word. All the items were presented twice; half occurred first with a written synonym cue, and half with an unrelated cue. If semantic information from the written item can improve semantic access for the spoken word, DRB should be better at word repetition in the synonym condition. The results (Table 7) show a significant advantage for repetition in the presence of a written synonym cue (McNemar's Test, $P < 0.01$). Two more tests were designed to investigate whether he had access to any semantic information about the spoken word, even when he did not attempt to repeat it.

Binary Judgements Test

In the "binary judgements test," DRB was asked to repeat a series of words; on each occasion where he was unable to attempt a response, he was given two written words from which to select the one related in meaning to the word he had heard. The list of 200 high- vs. low-image-ability words was used for this test; meaning-related words were generated for all items, and each was paired with an unrelated word (generated by randomly re-assigning the appropriate items). Since the majority of DRB's errors in repetition and comprehension are failures to respond, nothing can be inferred about whether any activation of the semantic system has taken place. However, *partial* information accessed in the semantic system,

TABLE 7

Word Repetition in the Presence of a Written Synonym Cue
and an Unrelated Written Cue (n = 19 in Each Cell)

	Synonym Cue	Unrelated Cue
High imageability	0.84	0.68
Low imageability	0.37	0.05
Total	0.61	0.37

though an insufficient basis from which to produce any output, could be sufficient for making the binary judgement. If DRB's performance in the binary judgements test is significantly above chance, it will suggest that partial access has occurred.

DRB was surprisingly good at the binary judgements task; for the 136 words that he was unable to repeat, he was able to select 131 synonyms correctly. It should be stressed that the word he had failed to repeat was not re-presented, so that in this task he was given the auditory stimulus *before* the written ones.

Synonym Judgements Test

DRB was given the Coltheart synonym judgements test once again, but this time with one spoken word and one written word for each pair. Table 8 indicates that, despite essentially chance-level performance on spoken pairs of low-imageability words, changing just one word of each pair from spoken to written form makes all the difference. This again suggests the availability of some information for the heard word even when, given an abstract word, DRB often insists that he has not heard it.

IS WRITTEN COMPREHENSION NORMAL?

In an earlier section we demonstrated that DRB had no apparent impairment in written comprehension: In terms of response accuracy, he was at ceiling in various tests. Although this allows us to conclude that he is significantly better at comprehending written words than spoken ones, it is a more difficult matter to assert that his written comprehension is actually *unimpaired*. Since all of these tests are very easy for normal subjects, it is possible that the tests are insufficiently sensitive to reveal that DRB is actually performing less well than control subjects. To enable a more sensitive comparison of DRB's written-word comprehension with normal subjects, we administered a test that included close semantic distractors, where normal subjects do not necessarily perform at ceiling, and two further tests where response *latencies* could be measured.

TABLE 8
Synonym Judgments: Spoken/Written vs.
Single Modality Versions

	High Imageability	*Low Imageability*
Spoken	0.95	0.61
Written	1.00	0.95
Spoken/written	1.00	0.95

Kay's Semantic Association Test (Unpublished)

DRB was given a target word (spoken or written) and had to select the word closest in meaning from a choice of four written response words. The four alternatives include: a word closely related in meaning (= the correct response); a word more distantly related in meaning, and two unrelated words. Thus this test requires more specific information than the synonym judgements task, where only random foils are given. On the other hand, since the response words are always written, irrespective of the modality of presentation of the target word, DRB should find this task easier than one where all items are given in the auditory modality. Half the items in this test are highly imageable words; the other half comprise words with low imageability ratings.

When DRB was given the target words in written form, he made only one error on each of the high- and low-imageability sets, which compares extremely favourably with the norms collected by Kay (personal communication). With spoken targets his performance was significantly worse with the low- than the high-imageability items (14/15 vs. 7/15: Fisher Exact Test, $z = 2.35$, $P < 0.01$). This again supports the view that his written word comprehension is unimpaired but that he is poor at comprehending spoken words of low imageability.

Associative Priming in Visual Lexical Decision

We used the materials and methods of Lupker's (1984) experiment 6, where printed words and nonwords are preceded by real-word primes presented for 550msec immediately before the target items. The subject makes no response to the prime, but has to make a word/nonword decision to the second item, which remains in view until a response is made. There were 60 prime words; each occurred once (in each of 3 sessions) paired with a semantically associated real word, an unrelated real word, or a nonword. No primes or targets were repeated within sessions, and different orders of conditions across sessions were equally frequently across the items. The results from DRB and from the young student subjects of Lupker (1984) are shown in Table 9. DRB performed lexical decision with an error rate comparable to the young controls, and had latencies somewhat above their mean, as is typical for older subjects (see, e.g., Cerella, 1985). Critically, though, DRB showed a significant difference of 58msecs between related and unrelated pairs (related $t[46] = 2.57$, $P < 0.01$), which is comparable in magnitude to the priming effect found with the controls (47msecs). This shows that rapid semantic access from a written prime influences DRB's processing of a subsequent word to a normal extent.

TABLE 9
Associative Priming, DRB and Student Controls (n = 60 in Each Cell)

	Error Rates		Latencies (msecs)	
	DRB	Controls	DRB	Controls
Related pairs				
COW MILK	3.3%	1.2%	691	538
Unrelated pairs				
STEEL MILK	1.7%	3.7%	749	585
Nonwords				
COW MULK	3.3%	7.4%	913	674

Synonym Judgements Test: Response Latencies

Two new synonym judgements tests were administered (Turner, un-published), using exactly the same procedure as for the Coltheart (Note 1) set. One test comprised (different) high- and low-imageability words, whereas the other comprised high- and low-frequency words. As with the Coltheart test, the non-synonymous items were constructed by randomising the pairs used for the synonyms. This test was given to DRB and 12 normal subjects (students and academic staff) and their response latencies were measured. There was no difference between his performance and that of the controls in terms of accuracy (see Table 10). In Fig. 4, for each subject, the size of (a) the imageability effect and (b) the frequency effect is plotted against the mean response times for the "Yes" trials. Despite the fact that the controls are considerably younger than DRB (age range 16–24), his performance is within the normal range. (His performance on these tests in an auditory, untimed condition can be seen in Table 10.) Although one can never state categorically that DRB would perform normally on every conceivable test of written word comprehension, it does appear that he

TABLE 10
Turner Synonym Judgements Tests: Errors (n = 40 in Each Cell)

	DRB		Controls	
	[Untimed Auditory]	Written	Range	Mean
High Imageability	[8]	1	0–3	1.6
Low Imageability	[16]	0	0–5	2.8
High Frequency	[5]	1	0–7	2.7
Low Frequency	[10]	1	0–5	1.5

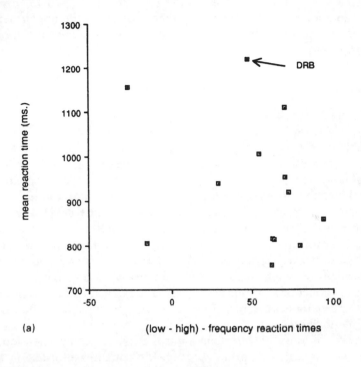

(a)   (low - high) - frequency reaction times

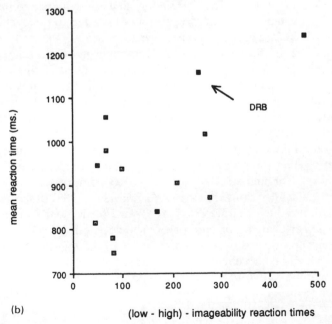

(b)   (low - high) - imageability reaction times

FIG. 4   Synonym judgements tests: DRB and controls.

shows a strong, *classical* dissociation (see Shallice, 1988 for discussion) between auditory and written comprehension, with the impairment being one of accessing semantic representations corresponding to auditorily presented words.

DISCUSSION

DRB has an impairment in understanding spoken words, and the more abstract a word is, the less likely he is to comprehend it. There are two possible explanations for such an impairment. The first is that an impairment of processing phonological input is interacting with a mild central semantic deficit for abstract words. The absence of a corresponding peripheral deficit for orthographic input would account for his success in comprehending written abstract words. There are two lines of evidence in support of this explanation. The first is that DRB has impaired repetition of both words and nonwords, suggesting that he must have some impairment of sublexical (phonological) processing. Secondly, he has both an impairment of input (auditory comprehension) and of output (anomic in speech production). A mild central semantic deficit could account for both input and output problems. However it is equally plausible that DRB has multiple deficits.

The more compelling explanation is that DRB's comprehension impairment reflects a deficit in the accessing of semantic information from an auditory input lexicon. There are many lines of evidence to make this the preferred explanation. Extensive testing has failed to uncover any impairment in DRB's comprehension of written words; this is true for word/picture matching tests, synonym judgements, and definitions in the form of word associations. He performs within the normal range even in Kay's Semantic Association Test, where normal subjects are not necessarily at ceiling and where very fine semantic judgements on abstract words are required. It is even possible to argue that he comprehends written words, not just as accurately, but also as rapidly as control subjects. DRB's comprehension impairment appears to be specific to the auditory modality.

Equally there is no evidence for an impairment of lexical access. This was initially argued on the basis of DRB's impressive ability to make correct lexical decisions. Howard and Franklin (1988) described a patient, MK, whom they characterised as "word-form deaf" on the basis of impaired performance on auditory lexical decision. They demonstrated the further consequences of such a deficit: (1) phonologically related errors in repetition and comprehension, (2) a deficit in repeating or comprehending short words relative to longer words, and (3) difficulty in word comprehension with phonologically related foils. DRB shows none of these features of a lexical access deficit and is at or close to ceiling on all tests of auditory lexical decision, irrespective of the length, imageability, or frequency of the words used. Although his repetition is impaired, the pattern of the repetition impairment is entirely consistent with a semantic access deficit combined with the sublexical routine being unavailable.

The most surprising characteristic of DRB's word meaning deafness is the very strong effect of word imageability in all tests of auditory word comprehension and repetition. This is the only factor which significantly predicts success in comprehension; performance is unaffected by word frequency and phoneme length. When asked to repeat words with decreasing levels of imageability, DRB shows a gradient of difficulty rather than a specific level of imageability below which errors occur. Although he is quite consistent, across occasions, in the words correctly comprehended, it can be shown that this is purely due to a variation in the probability of a correct response as a function of the imageability of the words.

What is happening when DRB fails to comprehend a word? The majority of his responses are "don't know's;" indeed, he often reports that he cannot hear the word. It is, however, unlikely that his comprehension is "all or nothing," given that he sometimes makes semantic errors in comprehension and repetition. Moreover, his auditory comprehension and repetition are improved by priming, and, as shown in the binary judgements test, he is able to recover some aspects of the meaning of a spoken word to match with a related word presented *after the heard word*.

Since imageability is a function of meaning, one might have predicted that significant effects of imageability would always reflect a *central* semantic deficit. What does this very large effect of imageability associated with an access deficit suggest about the nature of that deficit? There are at least two possible characterisations.

The first is that the deficit represents an undifferentiated impairment of access, something like a reduction in activation or additional noise. The imageability effect is merely a reflection of the normal working of the semantic system; abstract words are the items that tend not to be activated when the system is below par. The slower processing times for abstract words, shown by normal subjects in tests of lexical decision and comprehension, provide support for this notion. Furthermore, for the vast majority of patients with a differential impairment in the understanding of abstract and concrete words, it is abstract words that are disadvantaged. A clear prediction results from this: All patients with a modality-specific access deficit will be worse at comprehending abstract than concrete words.

To our knowledge, there is no description of a patient with a modality-specific impairment for concrete words. Although Warrington (1981) described her patient CAV as a "concrete word *dyslexic*," she also demonstrated that CAV had impaired auditory comprehension of concrete words; his impairment was therefore not modality specific.

The second characterisation of DRB's deficit would be that some aspect of the access process itself is disrupted. If access to representations of meaning somehow differs for words with and without concrete referents, then a modality-specific access deficit could favour either class of words; indeed there might be deficits specific to even more constrained categories. Although no such modality-specific comprehension deficits have been described, there are cases of category-specific deficits in naming only, without any apparent central semantic impairment (Semenza & Zettin, 1988). This suggests that mapping between meaning and word-forms can be impaired in quite specific ways.

To what extent does DRB's word comprehension show the characteristics which Shallice (1987; 1988) suggests are characteristic of access impairments? In general there is a good fit. DRB shows no item-specific consistency in either word definition or word repetition, once the effects of word imageability have been partialled out. His performance is unaffected by word frequency. Word repetition, which, we have argued, depends on semantic access, is improved by a visually presented synonym prime; and DRB is able to gain partial access to semantic information (in the binary judgements task) for words he cannot repeat.

Since we have *independent* grounds for our claim that DRB's difficulty is one of semantic access, rather than impaired representation, this outcome could be taken as support for Shallice's claim that these characteristics can be found in patients with access impairments. But no stronger conclusions follow. In particular, we would not like to argue that all access impairments will necessarily show these characteristics, nor that impairments of semantic representation could not, under some circumstances, show a subset of these features (for further discussion see Franklin, Note 3; Howard, Note 4).

DRB, we would claim, is the clearest example in the literature of word meaning deafness: That is, a comprehension deficit restricted to the auditory modality. The sensitivity of this impairment to word abstractness is intriguing, and it remains to be seen whether other patients with modality-specific comprehension deficits will show the same pattern.

Manuscript received 8 November 1990
Revised manuscript received 6 October 1992

REFERENCES

Bishop, D.V.M. (1982). *Test for reception of grammar*. Abingdon: Thomas Leach Ltd.
Berndt, R.S., Basili, A., & Caramazza, A. (1987). Dissociation of functions in a case of transcortical sensory aphasia. *Cognitive Neuropsychology*, *4*, 79–107.
Bramwell, B. (1897). Illustrative cases of aphasia. *Lancet*, *1*, 1256–1259. Reprinted in 1984 as: A case of word meaning deafness. *Cognitive Neuropsychology*, *1*, 249–258.

Buckingham, H.W., & Kertesz, A. (1974). A linguistic analysis of fluent aphasia. *Brain and Language*, *1*, 43–62.

Cerella, J. (1985). Information processing rates in the elderly. *Psychological Bulletin*, *98*, 67–83.

Coltheart, M., & Funnell, E. (1987). Reading and writing: One lexicon or two? In A. Allport, D. MacKay, W. Prinz, & E. Scheerer (Eds.), *Language perception and production: Relationships between listening, speaking, reading and writing*. London: Academic Press.

Coltheart, M., Patterson, K.E., & Marshall, J.C. (Eds.) (1980). *Deep dyslexia*. London: Routledge & Kegan Paul.

De Groot, A.M.B. (1989). Representational aspects of word imageability and word frequency as assessed through word association. *Journal of Experimental Psychology: Learning, Memory, and Cognition*, *15*, 824–845.

Dunn, A. (1965). *The Peabody Picture Vocabulary Test*. Minneapolis: American Guidance Service.

Franklin, S. (1989). Dissociations in auditory word comprehension: Evidence from nine "fluent" asphasic patients. *Aphasiology*, *3*, 189–207.

Hart, J., Berndt, R.S., & Caramazza, A. (1985). Category-specific naming deficit following cerebral infarction. *Nature*, *316*, 439–430.

Heilman, K.M., Rothi, L., McFarling, D., & Rottmann, A.L. (1981). Transcortical sensory aphasia with relatively spared spontaneous speech and naming. *Archives of Neurology*, *38*, 236–239.

Howard, D., & Franklin, S. (1987). Three ways for understanding written words, and their use in two contrasting cases of surface dyslexia. In A. Allport, D. MacKay, W. Prinz, & E. Scheerer (Eds.), *Language perception and production: Relationships between listening, speaking, reading and writing*. London: Academic Press.

Howard, D., & Franklin, S. (1988). *Missing the meaning?* Cambridge, Mass.: MIT Press.

Howard, D., & Orchard-Lisle, V.M. (1984). On the origin of semantic errors in naming: Evidence from the case of a global dysphasic. *Cognitive Neuropsychology*, *1*, 163–190.

Howard, D., & Patterson, K.E. (1992). *The Pyramids and Palm Trees Test; A test of semantic access from words and pictures*. Bury St Edmunds: Thames Valley Test Company.

James, C.T. (1975). The role of semantic information in lexical decisions. *Journal of Experimental Psychology: Human Perception and Performance*, *104*, 130–136.

Kay, J., Lesser, R., & Coltheart, M. (1992). *Psycholinguistic Assessments of Language Processing in Aphasia (PALPA)*. London: Lawrence Erlbaum Associates Ltd.

Kohn, S., & Friedman, R. (1986). Word-meaning deafness: A phonological-semantic dissociation. *Cognitive Neuropsychology*, *3*, 291–308.

Kuçera, H., & Francis, W.N. (1967). *Computational analysis of present-day American English*. Providence: Brown University Press.

Lupker, S.J. (1984). Semantic priming without association: A second look. *Journal of Verbal Learning and Verbal Behaviour*, *23*, 709–733.

Morton, J. (1980). The logogen model and orthographic structure. In U. Frith (Ed.), *Cognitive processes in spelling*. London: Academic Press.

Patterson, K.E., & Shewell, C. (1987). Speak and spell: Dissociations and word-class effects. In M. Coltheart, R. Job, & G. Sartori (Eds.), *The cognitive neuropsychology of language*. Hillsdale, NJ: Lawrence Erlbaum Associates Inc.

Rapp, B., & Caramazza, A. (1992). *On the distinction between deficits of access and deficits of storage: A question of theory*. Report 91-5 of the Cognitive Neuropsychological Laboratory: Johns Hopkins University.

Raven, J.C., Court, J.H., & Raven, J. (1977). *Standard progressive matrices*. London: H.K. Lewis.

Riddoch, M.J., Humphreys, G.W., Coltheart, M., & Funnell, E. (1988). Semantic system or systems? Neuropsychological evidence re-examined. *Cognitive Neuropsychology, 5,* 3–25.

Semenza, C., & Zettin, M. (1988). Generating proper names: A case of selective inability. *Cognitive Neuropsychology, 5,* 711–721.

Shallice, T. (1987). Impairments in semantic processing: Multiple dissociations. In M. Coltheart, R. Job, & G. Sartori (Eds.), *The cognitive neuropsychology of language.* London: Lawrence Erlbaum Associates Ltd.

Shallice, T. (1988). *From neuropsychology to mental structure.* Cambridge: Cambridge University Press.

Silveri, M.C., & Gainotti, G. (1988). Interaction between vision and language in a category-specific semantic impairment. *Cognitive Neuropsychology, 5,* 677–709.

Warrington, E.K. (1975). The selective impairment of semantic memory. *Quarterly Journal of Experimental Psychology, 27,* 635–657.

Warrington, E.K. (1981). Concrete word dyslexia. *British Journal of Psychology, 72,* 175–196.

Warrington, E.K., & Shallice, T. (1979). Semantic access dyslexia. *Brain, 102,* 43–63.

REFERENCE NOTES

1. Coltheart, M. (1980). *Analysing acquired disorders of reading.* Unpublished manuscript. Birkbeck College: London.
2. Coltheart, M. (1981). *MRC psycholinguistic database user manual: Version 1.* Unpublished manuscript. (Available from the author on request.)
3. Franklin, S. (1989). *Understanding and repeating words: Evidence from aphasia.* Unpublished PhD thesis: City University, London.
4. Howard, D. (1985). *The semantic organisation of the lexicon: Evidence from aphasia.* Unpublished PhD thesis: University of London.

APPENDIX 1

DRB's Spoken Description of the Story of Cinderella

This is a story about /silli/, /sində/, Oh my God, Cinderella. And they had four sisters. Three of them were ugly sisters. And Cinders has very beautiful. But she was done lots of work. The Cinders had to do all the housework and cooking. But the /ʌglə/, ugly sisters, didn't do anything. Then they had to go to a ball. And they had beautiful clothing for the /ʌglə/ sisters. But Cinders couldn't go because he had no clothes. In the evening the /ʌŋ/, /eŋ/, ugly sisters went to the ball. And Cinders was sitting by the fire. And then a beautiful fairy arrived and said "why don't you go to the ball?" And so he said "I've got no clothes." So she said "I will give you some." So they got a big wands and they've got a beautiful gown with a little (tari:ə/ and beautiful glass slippers. Then had a big /pʌntʃən/, /pʌmpʃən/, one of them things. And the wand arrived and then the coach arrived. Then had the wand four mouse. And /wɒnd/ it, /weind/ it, oh my God. And made into four horses. She said "You can go to the ball, but you must go home at twelve o'clock."

APPENDIX 2

Repetition of Imageability × Frequency List

Low imageability high frequency

4   answer → *correct*
7   type → DK
13 fear → /f/ – "no"
15 theory → "fairy"
20 modern → DK
27 idea → DK
30 late → "liver"
38 simple → DK
39 easy → "answer"
40 reach → DK
42 unit → DK
50 chance → DK
51 issue → DK
56 deal → DK
57 rest → *correct*
63 moral → DK
66 fine → DK
70 care → DK
74 piece → *correct*
77 trade → "business"

Low imageability low frequency

2   plead → DK
8   cult → "colt"
9   relax → DK
11 pardon → /pasən/
16 meek → DK
21 pity → DK
22 frieze → DK
29 span → "saw"
33 sullen → "silent, no"
34 custom → DK
44 saint → DK
45 debt → DK
49 idiom → DK
53 dumb → *correct*
55 heir → DK
61 ardent → DK
64 lend → DK
71 debut → DK
72 keen → *correct*
78 wary → DK

High imageability high frequency

1   river → "water"
3   radio → *correct*
10 window → *correct*
12 army → *correct*
14 heart → *correct*
23 plant → "plants"
24 summer → "today, no"
26 fire → *correct*
28 clay → DK
32 dark → *correct*
43 square → DK
47 ball → *correct*
48 road → *correct*
52 book → *correct*
58 doctor → *correct*
69 wall → *correct*
75 blood → *correct*
76 market → *correct*
79 hair → *correct*
80 pool → *correct*

High imageability low frequency

5   pole → *correct*
6   mouse → *correct*
17 rabbit → *correct*
18 nail → "nails"
19 pill → *correct*
25 hawk → *correct*
31 lawn → *correct*
35 kiss → *correct*
36 apple → *correct*
37 cigar → *correct*
41 whip → DK
46 infant → DK
54 cake → *correct*
59 arrow → DK
60 hammer → *correct*
62 elbow → DK
65 swim → *correct*
67 collar → DK
68 dusk → *correct*
73 bubble → "like a balloon"

Chapter 7 Spelling and Writing

Behrmann, M. & Bub, D. (1992). Surface dyslexia and dysgraphia: dual routes, single lexicon. *Cognitive Neuropsychology, 9,* 209–251.

We noted in Chapter 7 that, compared with the vast amount of research into reading and its disorders, spelling and writing have been little studied. Broadly speaking, that remains the case, although Brown and Ellis (1994) have charted an encouraging gradual improvement in the proportion of articles published on spelling as compared to reading.

The model of spelling and writing proposed in Chapter 7 remains in use, although as has happened in the field of reading research, some theorists have questioned the strict separation of lexical and nonlexical routes or procedures. In Fig. 7.1 (p. 175) the spellings of familiar words are retrieved as whole strings from the graphemic output lexicon in response to inputs from the semantic system and the speech output lexicon. In contrast, the spellings of unfamiliar words or invented nonwords are assembled using a knowledge of the sound-to-spelling correspondences of English. It may be that these two aspects of spelling are not so separate and that, for example, writers use analogies with the spellings of familiar words when attempting to assemble a plausible spelling for a similar-sounding nonword (Barry & Seymour, 1988). Alternatively, we might think of mappings between phonology (spoken word-forms) and orthography (written word-forms) as operating at every level from whole words, through syllables, down to single sounds and letters. This is the approach that is often preferred by connectionist modellers of both reading and spelling (Brown & Loosemore, 1994; Olson & Caramazza, 1994).

The paper selected to accompany Chapter 7 addresses a related, but different issue, namely the extent to which reading and spelling are mediated by distinct or shared processes. In the composite model of reading and spelling presented in Fig. 8.3 (p. 222), the processes responsible for reading and spelling are presented as being largely distinct, with separate lexicons for reading (the visual input lexicon) and spelling (the graphemic output lexicon), and separate sublexical processes for grapheme–phoneme (reading) and phoneme–grapheme (spelling) conversion. We acknowledge, however, on pp. 233–236 the fact that some theorists believe that there is more sharing of processes between reading and spelling. For example, Allport and Funnell (1981) argued that a single orthographic lexicon might be responsible for both visual word recognition in reading and the retrieval of spellings in writing.

When orthographic lexicons are damaged, patients are unable to recognise or retrieve written word-forms on a whole-word basis. They must resort instead to assembling pronunciations or spellings using letter–sound correspondences. These should still give the correct results for the reading and/

or spelling of regular words, but irregular words are likely to be misread (*trough* → "truff") or misspelled ("castle" → CASSELL). Such "regularisation" errors are characteristic of *surface dyslexia* and *surface dysgraphia*, respectively. Now, if the visual input lexicon and the graphemic output lexicon are two distinct things, then it should be possible to find patients who have damage to one but not the other. That is, it should be possible to find patients who have surface dyslexia but not surface dysgraphia, or surface dysgraphia but not surface dyslexia. As Behrmann and Bub (1992) point out, such patients have proved elusive; to date, surface dyslexia and surface dysgraphia have gone hand in hand. Behrmann and Bub (1992) present a detailed report of one such patient, MP, whose surface dyslexia was the subject of an earlier report by Bub, Cancelliere, and Kertesz (1985) (see Chapter 8, pp. 207–208).

One possible explanation of the association between surface dyslexia and surface dysgraphia—the one preferred by Behrmann and Bub (1992)—is that there is only one orthographic lexicon, damage to which creates problems with whole-word recognition in reading and whole-word retrieval in spelling. If this is the case, then it follows that the particular words that create problems in reading should be the same words that create problems in spelling, and part of Behrmann and Bub's (1992) paper is devoted to trying to discover if that is true. An alternative interpretation that readers may wish to consider is that reading and spelling irregular words require some contribution from semantic representations (see Patterson & Hodges, 1992; 1994), and that the reason surface dyslexia and surface dysgraphia cooccur is that patients with those disorders tend also to have semantic impairments.

One component of the writing process that *has* received considerable theoretical attention in recent years is what we refer to in Chapter 7 as the *grapheme level*. That is the stage at which letter strings are represented in abstract form, and which serves as input to processes responsible for handwriting, typing, spelling aloud, etc. Spellings retrieved from the graphemic output lexicon are held there, as are spellings assembled by phoneme–grapheme conversion. Hence, damage to the grapheme level should result in a patient making similar errors in spelling words and nonwords, and the same sorts of errors should be manifested in handwriting, typing and spelling aloud. The first reports of such a patient by Miceli, Silveri, and Caramazza (1985; 1987—see Chapter 7, pp. 181–182) have been followed by a spate of further descriptions combined with detailed theorising about just what representations at the grapheme level might look like (see Kay & Hanley, 1994; Shallice, Glasspool, & Houghton, 1995).

Finally, Hillis and Caramazza (1989; Caramazza & Hillis, 1991) reported a patient who made errors at the ends of words and nonwords in both writing and spelling aloud. This implies a problem at the grapheme level.

Interestingly, the same patient also made errors at the ends of words and nonwords in *reading*. On the strength of this association, Hillis and Caramazza speculated that the same graphemic representations may be involved in both reading and spelling/writing. If so, this would be another example of processes shared between input and output.

REFERENCES

Allport, D.A. & Funnell, E. (1981). Components of the mental lexicon. *Philosophical Transactions of the Royal Society of London, B295*, 397–410.

Barry, C. & Seymour, P.H.K. (1988). Lexical priming and sound-to-spelling consistency effects in nonword spelling. *Quarterly Journal of Experimental Psychology, 40A*, 5–40.

Brown, G.D.A. & Ellis, N.C. (1994). Issues in spelling research: an overview. In G.D.A. Brown & N.C. Ellis (Eds), *Handbook of spelling: Theory, process and intervention*. Chichester: Wiley.

Brown, G.D.A. & Loosemore, R.P.W. (1994). Computational approaches to normal and impaired reading and spelling. In G.D.A. Brown & N.C. Ellis (Eds), *Handbook of spelling: Theory, process and intervention*. Chichester: Wiley.

Bub, D., Cancelliere, A., & Kertesz, A. (1985). Whole-word and analytical translation of spelling to sound in a nonsemantic reader. In K. Patterson, J.C. Marshall, & M. Coltheart (Eds.), *Surface dyslexia*. London: Lawrence Erlbaum Associates Ltd.

Caramazza, A. & Hillis, A.E. (1991). Levels of representation, co-ordinate frames, and unilateral neglect. *Cognitive Neuropsychology, 7*, 391–445.

Hillis, A.E. & Caramazza, A. (1989). The graphemic buffer and attentional mechanisms. *Brain and Language, 36*, 208–235.

Kay, J. & Hanley, R. (1994). Peripheral disorders of spelling: the role of the graphemic buffer. In G.D.A. Brown & N.C. Ellis (Eds), *Handbook of spelling: Theory, process and intervention*. Chichester: Wiley.

Miceli, G., Silveri, C., & Caramazza, A. (1987). The role of the phoneme-to-grapheme conversion system and of the graphemic output buffer in writing: Evidence from an Italian case of pure dysgraphia. In M. Coltheart, G. Sartori, & R. Job (Eds), *The cognitive neuropsychology of language*. London: Lawrence Erlbaum Associates Ltd.

Olson, A. & Caramazza, A. (1994). Representation and connectionist models: The NETspell experience. In G.D.A. Brown & N.C. Ellis (Eds), *Handbook of spelling: Theory, process and intervention*. Chichester: Wiley.

Patterson, K. & Hodges, J.R. (1992). Deterioration of word meaning: Implications for reading. *Neuropsychologia, 30*, 1025–1040.

Patterson, K. & Hodges, J.R. (1994). Disorders of semantic memory. In A. Baddeley, B. Wilson, & F. Watts (Eds), *Handbook of memory disorders*. Hove, UK: Lawrence Erlbaum Associates Ltd.

Shallice, T., Glasspool, D.W., & Houghton, G. (1995). Can neuropsychological evidence inform connectionist modelling? An analysis of spelling. *Language and Cognitive Processes, 10*, 195–225.

Surface Dyslexia and Dysgraphia: Dual Routes, Single Lexicon

M. Behrmann
Rotman Research Institute of Baycrest Centre, Ontario and University of Toronto, Canada

D. Bub
Montreal Neurological Institute and Centre Hospitalier Cote-de-Neiges, Montreal, Canada

The dual route interpretation of surface dyslexia as a deficit in word-specific activation has been challenged recently by computational models that incorporate a unitary print-to-sound mechanism. The most current of these makes no allowance for word-specific nodes, but obtains the pronunciation of regular and exception words by weighted connections between graphemic and phonemic units. Damaging the model in a variety of ways produces a pattern that appears consistent with the performance of many surface dyslexic patients. Exception words are mispronounced more often than regular words, though accuracy deteriorates on both categories. In addition, frequency has no clear-cut effect on the probability of reading an exception word correctly. We describe the existence of a variant of the syndrome that is not fully captured by the above simulations. MP, a surface dyslexic, demonstrates a dissociation between lexical and nonlexical pronunciation of written words. We also show that performance on irregular words varies as a function of their frequency. We provide evidence that the locus of the subject's deficit arises at the level of the representations in a single orthographic lexicon that subserves both reading and writing.

This work was supported by an Ontario Ministry of Health Personnel Development Award to the first author and grants from the Medical Research Council, Fonds de la Recherche en Sante du Quebec to the second author.

The authors thank Elizabeth Hampson for her contribution in the early stages of the research project, Derek Besner for assistance in the N-count analysis, Gloria Waters for her advice on what constitutes regularity, and Sandra Black for her interest and valuable input. We also thank Max Coltheart, Sue Franklin, David Howard and Karalyn Patterson for their constructive suggestions. The authors also thank Marian Villa for providing access to the patient and, most of all, we thank MP for her contribution.

INTRODUCTION

Acquired reading disorders in previously literate adults are now frequently analysed to test hypotheses concerning the functional architecture of the normal system. One form of acquired dyslexia that has continued to be the focus of considerable interest is surface dyslexia, taken by many as support for a dual process account of the mechanism by which printed words are converted to sound. The dual process model of reading distinguishes between the activation of units corresponding to whole-words, which map onto phonology via semantics, and an alternative, nonlexical procedure, which uses smaller orthographic segments to assemble pronunciation.

The performance of patients with surface dyslexia is interpreted within the dual route framework as the outcome of damage to the whole-word component; the patients read pronounceable nonsense words quite accurately (though the level of proficiency varies from case to case), implying adequate translation of nonlexical spelling patterns into sound. Words that obey regular principles of translation between orthography and phonology (for example, MINT) also yield accurate performance (though again, not all patients are capable of error-free responding) because their pronunciation can be obtained via the same procedure that permits reading of nonsense words. Many errors are observed, however, when the patient is asked to read words with irregular spelling-sound correspondences (for example, PINT)—these items necessarily require the word-specific procedure for correct translation but impairment to this component renders them inaccessible or lost. The patient is thus forced to read by applying the nonlexical procedure to words that violate the regular correspondences between spelling and sound, and the resulting incorrect output is either directly based on the pronunciation given by the nonlexical orthographic segments or on a more complex procedure that retrieves a word in the phonological lexicon, approximating the output of the nonlexical routine (see Patterson & Coltheart, 1987, for further discussion of these options). In addition to regularity, reading performance may be affected in some cases by word frequency; pronunciation accuracy for exception words diminishes as word frequency decreases, whereas accuracy scores remain consistently high for regular words (Bub, Cancelliere, & Kertesz, 1985).

The foregoing interpretation of surface dyslexia has not gained universal acceptance, however. One problem is that many of the patients first documented were found to make errors when reading regular words (and nonsense words) as well as exception words, so that the predicted dissociation between the two reading procedures was not completely obtained. The argument in terms of the model is that the difficulty with regular correspondences must reflect an additional—though moderate—impairment to the nonlexical route, but the failure to observe a surface dyslexic who retains a normal command of the regularities between spelling and sound has prompted questions about the ultimate validity of the dual route framework. More recently, a few cases have been described who do show excellent ability to read orthographically regular words coupled with severely impaired reading of exception words (Shallice, Warrington, & McCarthy, 1983). This discrepancy between patients has led to a classification of the syndrome into Type I and Type II variants (Shallice & McCarthy, 1985). Type I cases demonstrate highly accurate naming of regular words and pronounceable nonsense words at normal response latencies. Errors occur in reading exception words, the vast majority of responses being the more frequent pronunciation (regularisation) of the spelling pattern. Type II patients are poorer at reading exception words than regular words, although performance on regular words (and nonsense words) is also impaired. Response latencies are abnormally slow, and the patient may produce a series of approximations when attempting to read a word.

The existence of variable forms of surface dyslexia complicates the interpretation of the phenomenon. We should note that the extra assumption required by the dual process model to account for Type II patients— i.e. that damage must have occurred to both the nonlexical routine and the whole-word mechanism—has been made entirely by default. The inference would be valid if the model is correct, but proof of the claim requires additional evidence that the pattern of performance in one variant of surface dyslexia is the outcome of two separate functional deficits.

A further challenge to the conventional account of surface dyslexia (and to the dual route interpretation as a whole) has come from attempts to simulate the disorder by damaging a working computational architecture of word recognition and pronunciation. Seidenberg and McClelland (1989) have devised a model incorporating a unitary (rather than dual route) print-to-sound mechanism that learns to activate the phonology of both regular and exception words and is subsequently able to activate the phonology of nonsense words. This network consists of three layers of simple processing units: orthographic, phonological, and an intermediate layer of hidden units. There is complete connectivity between layers but units within a single layer are not connected. A pattern of activation distributed across the phonological units represents the network's response and the accuracy of the network's output is then assessed (see Seidenberg & McClelland, 1989, and Patterson, 1990, for details). This single route model is able to simulate a wide range of experimental results in normal readers, including the frequency-by-regularity interactions reported by Seidenberg and his colleagues (Seidenberg, Waters, Barnes, & Tanenhaus, 1984; Seidenberg, 1985).

The model has recently been extended to account for qualitative and quantitative aspects of acquired dyslexia. Patterson, Seidenberg, and

McClelland (1989) have "damaged" the model by zeroing a proportion of the connections or units at specific "lesion" sites. The results may be summarised as follows: The location of the damage had minimal effect on performance. After sufficiently extensive damage, however, exception words were pronounced as the regular correspondence in approximately 50% of the trials whereas "other" errors, bearing orthographic and/or phonological resemblance to the target, made up the remaining 50%. Thus, although the model is able to produce the regularisation errors observed in surface dyslexia, the error distribution differs from that produced by the patients in whom regularised pronunciations occur on about 85% of the trials and "other" errors occur on the remaining 15% of the trials. In the model, error scores for regularly spelled words also rose as a function of damage. This profile and a number of related effects mimic the pattern associated with the Type II variant of surface dyslexia.

One surprising outcome from the simulations that should be emphasised was the notable absence of any frequency effects on the accuracy of irregular word reading. The authors (Patterson et al., 1989, p.45) comment: "it is clear that being very common does not protect the word from reversing[1] when it is damaged." Interestingly, in a recent paper (Patterson, 1990) reporting an update of the simulation work, in which an alternative method of assessing the network's performance is utilised, a trend toward the frequency-by-regularity interaction is reported. When 20% of the hidden units are "lesioned," the network names high-frequency regular and exception words equally well (93% and 86% respectively). Performance on low-frequency regular words also remains high (93%), but accuracy on low-frequency exception words is decreased (78%).

These computational simulations offer a promising approach to capturing a number of basic aspects of the reading impairments in surface dyslexia. The absence of significant frequency effects together with the ability to depict only one variant of the syndrome (i.e. Type II), however, leaves their account incomplete. The authors offer a number of possible reasons for the incompatibility of the model with the full range of existing behavioural data. They also leave open the possibility that further adjustment of the current model might yield frequency effects under appropriate conditions. For example, they suggest that the complete dissociation between regular and exception words, characteristic of Type I surface dyslexia, might be obtained by leaving the representations intact and by imposing a ceiling on the activations feeding the unit. Finally, they consider whether, in fact, Type I patients may be reading via a procedure that has little to do with the normal mechanism. As the authors put it (Patterson et al., 1989, pp.63–64), these patients: "may utilise other types

---

[1]Reversing refers to the assignment of the regular pronunciation to the spelling pattern.

of knowledge relevant to pronunciation. It is possible that readers may have formed explicit generalisations about the correlations between spelling-sound correspondences . . . which merely come into play when the normal system is nonfunctional." The achievement of frequency effects and/or a clean dissociation between regular and irregular words without radical alteration of the existing parallel distributed processing model may or may not be feasible. Since it is often very difficult to predict the behaviour of computational models without actually running them, such claims must remain indeterminate.

In view of the questions relating to the different profiles of surface dyslexia, and the potential importance of the frequency effects documented in some cases, the present article is concerned with a detailed analysis of the performance of a patient who exemplifies the characteristics of Type I surface dyslexia. We initially replicate the pronounced frequency effects on naming of irregular words, and extremely high accuracy for orthographically regular words. We then demonstrate that a similar effect holds for writing to dictation. Further, we provide evidence from which we infer that the locus of the deficit arises at the level of orthographic representations rather than at some other point that could also affect the whole-word reading procedure.

Having documented the importance of frequency as a constraint on the patient's ability to recover the orthographic description of a word, we then go on to evaluate whether the same items are affected in reading and writing. The rationale for this enterprise derives from the controversy surrounding the number of orthographic lexicons available for single word processing. Several authors have proposed that reading and writing (together with oral spelling) are mediated by separate components holding orthographic knowledge. Some of this work is based on experimental work done with normal subjects whereas other evidence is obtained from dissociations observed in subjects with impaired reading and writing.

Results of experiments with normal subjects on tasks of reading and writing have not yielded a clear answer to the question of number of lexicons. Monsell and Banich (in Monsell, 1987) have shown that writing a word with no visual feedback (i.e. blind) failed to prime later lexical decision, suggesting that the representations subserving input and output must be independent. In a second experiment, however, subjects were required to write a spoken word, then match it to a visually presented definition, and then finally perform a lexical decision task on the same target. Under these conditions (orthographic output → visual input), facilitation was observed. This latter finding is consistent with the notion that a single item is represented by the same underlying code irrespective of input or output modality. These conflicting outcomes preclude a strong interpretation of the data based on the claim that the two tasks share a lexicon. At most, they are consistent with the notion that separate but linked orthographic lexicons may exist.

Data from patients with reading and/or writing deficits also remains ambiguous on the issue of single or dual lexicons. Campbell (1987) described two young adults who consistently failed to detect the errors in their habitually misspelled words but were able to identify the correct form as well as control subjects. Campbell favoured the interpretation that, for these impaired subjects, a description of the item is available in the reading lexicon but that the description is not adequately specified in a separate writing lexicon. Beauvois and Derouesné (1981) have reached a similar conclusion with respect to a patient who showed a discrepancy in reading and writing performance. Since the patient could read irregular words correctly but could not spell them, they argued that separate processes mediate reading and writing (see also Behrmann, 1987). These dissociations, however, are subject to an alternative interpretation; Allport and Funnell (1981) have argued that they are equally compatible with an access view as with a view of separable representational systems. On this account, all representations exist within a single intact central lexicon but errors in reading or writing arise from selective damage to functionally distinct input or output procedures (see Caramazza & Hillis, 1991, for illustrative case studies).

The evidence from neuropsychology based on dissociations has not added clarity to the rather confusing picture obtained from normal subjects, as we have seen. However, a potentially more revealing method might consist of examining the item-by-item association between reading and writing in selected patients (Caramazza & McCloskey, 1991). Coltheart and Funnell (1987), for example, have described HG, a surface dyslexic and dysgraphic patient, who showed similar performance in reading and spelling. The authors obtained a set of homophone words (Set A) yielding consistent accuracy on a test of lexical reading, and a further set (Set B) that produced errors on at least one out of two occasions. HG's spelling of Set A was found to be much better than that of Set B even when frequency effects were partialled out. The authors conclude (Coltheart & Funnell, 1987, p.337) that the symmetrical disturbance in reading and writing observed for Set B words indicates: "that there is a single orthographic lexicon, used both for reading and spelling, and the entry for each of these words in this lexicon has been impaired."

We will apply a similar logic to MP's performance. We claim that her surface dyslexia, demonstrating much more severe impairment for low-frequency exception words, is the outcome of damage to their orthographic descriptions. We then examine her ability to spell these same words to dictation and compare her performance across the two modalities. Given appropriate methodological precautions (Coltheart & Funnell, 1987), which are discussed at a later point, it is possible to draw inferences about the modular organisation of orthographic representations. A high degree of item consistency for reading and spelling exception words would support the claim of a unitary lexical component underlying performance.

In summary, we will examine whether the dissociation between lexical and nonlexical procedures obtains for MP and whether these procedures are differentially affected by word frequency. We will then go on to determine whether writing performance parallels that of reading and will provide evidence that the deficit arises in a locus shared by reading and writing, thus giving rise to symmetrical performance in input and output.

CASE HISTORY

MP, a 67-year-old right-handed female, was struck by a motor vehicle on April 11, 1979. The accident resulted in extensive herniation of the left temporal lobe and has produced severe and lasting impairment to MP's comprehension of both spoken and written language. At the time of the present testing, MP was co-operative and alert and was able to follow instructions and comprehend the task. Her speech was fluent but anomic and consisted of a mixture of semantic jargon, neologisms, and literal paraphasias. Results from the previous study (Bub et al., 1985), primarily concerned with MP's oral reading, revealed the following:

1. On a visually presented version of the Peabody Picture Vocabulary Test, MP's raw score was 31, yielding an age-equivalent of 2.8 years. The results on an auditorily presented version were similar (raw score 21, age equivalent 2.0 years).

2. MP performed poorly on a word-word and picture-word matching task when semantic relatedness formed the basis of the match.

3. MP did not show semantic priming effects in an oral reading task using written words as stimuli although she named high-frequency words more rapidly than low-frequency words.

4. MP's oral reading was good relative to her limited comprehension— she read a large variety of words accurately and rapidly provided that they had regular spelling-to-sound correspondences. Reading accuracy for irregular words fell systematically as word frequency diminished (80% correct with high-frequency words, 62% for mid-frequency words, and 40% for low-frequency words). The predominant error pattern was one of regularisation; for example, BEAR is read as /biːr/ to conform to words like "hear" and "gear."

In sum, MP shows surface dyslexia together with a severe semantic deficit manifested in her auditory and written language comprehension. The following section contains a detailed examination of MP's reading and writing.

READING AND WRITING OF NONWORDS

Prior to documenting the dissociation in MP's performance on regular and irregular words, we describe the results of tasks designed to evaluate the integrity of the nonlexical route.

Nonword Reading

A list of nonwords was presented to MP one at a time on a Macintosh computer using Psychlab experimental software (Bub & Gum, 1988) for oral reading. Following a central fixation point, a single target item appeared in the centre of the screen in upper-case 24-point Geneva bold font for an unlimited duration until MP named the item into a microphone. Voice latency was recorded and a 2sec inter-trial interval ensued. The items were a subset of Glushko's (1979) list in which the monosyllabic nonwords are generated by changing the first letter of either a regular (n = 22) or an irregular word (n = 22) (see Appendix 1 for stimuli and MP's responses). A response was considered correct if it was pronounced in a manner analogous to a real word containing the same orthographic pattern. MP named 42 items correctly. The errors were visual confusions (NUST → "must" and SUFF → "duff"). Interestingly, MP pronounced both SHEAD and WEAD to rhyme with HEAD rather than with BEAD. Although her responses do not contain the most frequent pronunciation, these items were still counted as correct by the definition given (also see Masterson, 1985, for discussion on normal subjects' possible pronunciations). MP's reaction time was 817.6msecs, with a mean of 801.7msecs and 831.1msecs for regular and irregular items respectively.

Nonword Writing

A list of 62 monosyllabic nonwords was given to MP for writing to dictation (see Appendix 2 for stimuli and responses). A single item was presented auditorily and then MP was required to repeat it before writing it. Four items were excluded from the analysis as MP could not repeat them correctly. MP wrote 55/58 items correctly. The errors consisted of vowel confusions such as /plak/ → "pluck," /cadʒ/ → "cuje" and /lɔt/ → "lot."

Her high degree of accuracy in both reading and writing nonwords and her speed of response in reading confirms the integrity of the nonlexical route in which constituent spelling or sound elements can be assembled according to standard grapheme-phoneme (or phoneme-grapheme) correspondences. Having established that this nonlexical route is well preserved, we then go on to examine MP's lexical processing ability.

READING AND WRITING OF IRREGULAR WORDS

To document the dissociation between lexical and nonlexical processes and to determine the effects of frequency and regularity, a list of regular and irregular words was presented to MP, first for reading aloud and then for writing to dictation. Given her previous performance on a similar test (Bub et al., 1985), we predicted that MP would pronounce words with near perfect accuracy if they conformed to principles of regular spelling-sound correspondences, but that exception words would yield many regularisation errors, which would become more prevalent as word frequency diminished. We predicted the same deterioration in writing performance on exception words and a similar, though possibly less marked, decrease in accuracy for regular words. The reason for the hypothesised effect of word frequency in writing regular words lies in the asymmetry between the constraints on the pronunciation of an orthographic segment, and the weaker constraints on the orthographic values of most phonemes in English (for example, BAIT, BATE, and BAYT are all sensible written renditions of the word /beɪt/ although there are no alternative reading pronunciations for each of them). Since regularity was defined with respect to the translation of spelling to sound, i.e. for reading, many words would be unpredictable when the mapping is reversed and translation from sound to spelling is required.

Reading Regular and Irregular Words

Procedure

A set of 392 words was compiled, half of which were defined as regular and the other half irregular according to Venezky's (1970) criteria, which divide spelling-to-sound correspondences on the basis of the regularities at the level of the individual grapheme as follows:

1. words which have an invariant assignment of phonemes regardless of their position or the orthographic context;
2. words whose letters necessitate consideration of the surrounding orthographic context (for example, "c" before a, o, u is pronounced /k/ otherwise /s/); and
3. words whose letter-sound correspondences are not predictable by 1 or 2 above.

Half the items were drawn from groups 1 and 2 (regular words, n = 196), whereas the second half (irregular or exception words, n = 196) came from group 3 (see Appendix 3 for stimuli). The words exemplified a variety of orthographic patterns including variations of vowel and consonant patterns. Both regular and irregular words consisted of mono- and polysyllabic words. Furthermore, the list included items drawn from a wide range of frequency values ranging from high-frequency items (more than 200 per million, Kuçera & Francis, 1967), to low-frequency items (less than 10 per million). The words were presented to MP on white cards in black upper-case letters for an unlimited time for reading aloud. Responses were tape-recorded and phonetically transcribed. On a second occasion, these same words were presented in randomised order for writing to dictation. Each word was dictated and repeated if necessary and MP was allowed to take as much time as necessary to produce a response.

Results

Almost all reading and writing errors were phonologically plausible albeit incorrect renditions of the target words (see Appendix 3 for error corpus). In addition to the regularisation errors, MP made occasional stress errors, particularly on polysyllabic words (see also case CD, Coltheart et al., 1983). The percentage of regular and irregular words correctly read by MP as a function of frequency is shown in Fig. 1.

Performance on regular words was significantly better than on irregular words (collapsed across frequency, $\chi^2(1) = 88.8$, $P < 0.001$), confirming

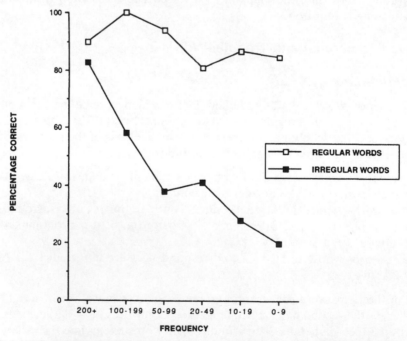

FIG. 1   Accuracy of pronunciation of regular and irregular words (defined according to Venezky) as a function of frequency.

the dissociation between reading of lexical and nonlexical items. Regression curves, plotted with accuracy against frequency, revealed a significant linear trend for irregular words ($r = 0.98$, $P < 0.001$) but not for regular words ($r = 0.72$, $P < 0.10$), reflecting the frequency by regularity interaction previously observed by Bub et al. (1985). The effect of frequency across the six frequency bandwidths was statistically significant ($\chi^2[5] = 30.4$, $P < 0.001$), confirming the effect of frequency on irregular word reading.

Because the definition of what constitutes regularity is problematic and multiple definitions exist, we re-analysed this data using an alternative scheme to that proposed by Venezky. According to this scheme, which takes into account varying levels of regularity (Shallice et al., 1983), very irregular words contain multiple irregularities or exceptional correspondences, mildly irregular words contain a single grapheme-phoneme correspondence that is not the most common correspondence, and regular words contain the major or most frequent grapheme-phoneme correspondence. The words were also divided according to frequency: high (50–200+), mid (10–50), and low frequency (<9) according to Kuçera and Francis (1967). Accuracy of reading performance (expressed as percentage correct) as a function of frequency is shown in Fig. 2.

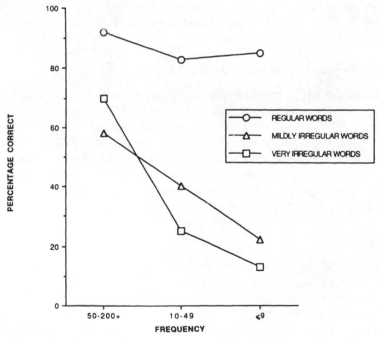

FIG. 2   Accuracy of pronunciation of words defined by varying levels of regularity (according to Shallice et al., 1983) as a function of frequency.

The pattern of findings confirms the frequency × regularity interaction noted earlier with performance on regular words remaining high across all levels of regularity. An analysis of the difference between mildly and very irregular words, done as the analysis of the difference of confidence intervals at $P < 0.05$ at each level, shows a significant difference between the proportion of correct words (mildly and very irregular) at each frequency. The direction of the difference changes across frequency since, on mid- and low-frequency items, mildly irregular words are named significantly better than very irregular words, whereas the converse is true for the highly frequent words. This latter effect is probably attributable to the fact that many of the highly frequent, very irregular words are commonly used everyday words such as ARE, COME, VERY, and GIVE, whereas the mildly irregular, high-frequency words are less commonly used. In general, in contrast to the regular words, performance on both mildly and very irregular words remains good only for high-frequency words but not for mid- or low-frequency words. The frequency by regularity interaction shown here provides further support for the pattern observed earlier using the Venezky definition of regularity.

The findings from both these analyses demonstrate a systematic breakdown in performance on irregular words as frequency declines whereas accuracy for regular words remains consistently high. These results replicate the findings of Bub et al. (1985), which show the frequency by regularity interaction.

Writing Regular and Irregular Words

The analysis of MP's writing to dictation also showed a significant difference between regular and irregular words (see Fig. 3) (collapsed across frequency, $\chi^2[1] = 83.1$, $P < 0.001$). As in reading, accuracy for irregular words deteriorates, as seen in the significant linear trend of accuracy against frequency ($r = 0.93$, $P < 0.01$), whereas no linear frequency effect is observed with regular words ($r = 0.59$, $P < 0.10$). The effect of frequency on accuracy in irregular word writing was confirmed statistically (Pearson $\chi^2[5] = 18.5$, $P < 0.001$).

Discussion

MP's writing of regular words was not as well preserved as her reading of regular words (compare Figs. 1 and 3), as we had predicted. This can be explained by the fact that regularity was defined with respect to print-sound correspondences rather than with respect to sound-print mappings, as would be the case for writing. Overall, the reading and writing data demonstrate a striking symmetry between the two modalities, with scores showing a significant discrepancy between performance on regular and

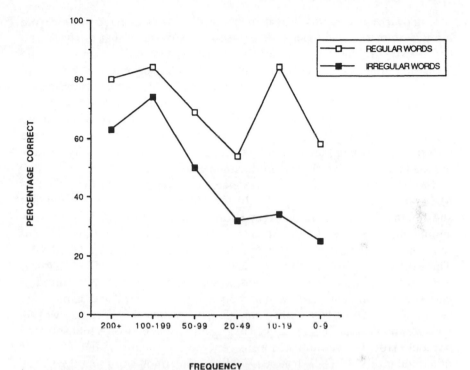

FIG. 3.   Accuracy of writing regular and irregular words as a function of frequency.

irregular words. In addition, scores on regular words remain consistently high across the spectrum of frequencies, especially in reading, whereas scores for irregular words fall off as frequency declines. It is interesting to note that, even at very low frequencies, MP has retained the ability to pronounce and write some items correctly. In the next section we look for evidence that allows us to specify more precisely the locus of the deficit underlying these results.

LOCUS OF THE DEFICIT IN WORD-FORM ACTIVATION

Until now, we have assumed that MP's surface dyslexia and dysgraphia are due to an impairment in the ability to activate the orthographic descriptions of whole-words. However, at this point we have no direct basis for this claim, given that the properties of surface dyslexia taken to define the syndrome may reflect impairment to one of several functional loci. In fact, Coltheart and Funnell (1987) point out that the dual-process model of reading aloud predicts seven types of damage that would force dependence on sub-lexical processes, and thus cause regularisation errors in the transcoding of irregular words. Impairments as diverse as damage to the visual input system (which impedes the pathway between visual analysis and lexical orthographic codes) or destruction or inaccessibility to entries in the lexical phonological codes could yield the regularisation errors produced by MP. A common assumption is that surface dyslexia usually reflects a partial loss of the whole-word orthographic component and, although this has been the standpoint in the present case report, there is as yet no independent proof of this claim. This, together with the considerable differences between patients, only adds further to the uncertainty regarding the functional disturbance producing a given instance of the syndrome.

In this section, we look for evidence that would specify the origin of MP's reading disorder more precisely. One of us has previously argued that she retains the orthographic description of many words, and that a substantial number of regularisation errors occur because the pronunciation of the word unit cannot be retrieved in the output lexicon (Bub et al., 1985). The evidence in favour of this conclusion is derived from MP's performance on a word-nonword discrimination task, in which she was required to choose the real item from a pair consisting of a word and a matched pseudoword. Trials were made up of orthographically irregular words, consistently misread by MP, as well as regularly spelled words that she read without error. Nonsense words were generated by changing the first letter of a regular (e.g. PLOCK from BLOCK) or exception word (e.g. MACHT from YACHT) to preserve overall spelling pattern, and were paired with words so that all combinations of regular and irregular words were equally represented (word regular, nonword irregular; word irregular, nonword regular, etc.).

MP did rather well on this task, even when both items of the pair contained irregular spelling patterns (82% correct). By contrast, she did very poorly, scoring below chance (41% correct), on trials consisting of irregular words matched against a regular nonword. Bub and colleagues reasoned that MP tended to base her decisions on orthographic familiarity (as opposed to lexical status) under most circumstances—therefore opting for a more common nonword spelling pattern rather than a legitimate word having a less frequent orthography—but that she retained enough whole-word information to respond correctly once orthographic familiarity no longer differed between words and nonwords. They concluded from the evidence (Bub et al., 1985, p.29) that "at least some of MP's regularisations involve defective retrieval of phonology, while the ability to recognise the target lexically remains intact."

For a variety of reasons, we now have some doubts about the validity of the claim that MP's difficulty in reading exception words is the outcome of a disturbance in the mapping of whole words onto their phonological description rather than a failure to activate their orthographic representation. First, forced-choice lexical discrimination is not an on-line measure and partial activation of an item may be enough to yield a response. Thus, a damaged orthographic representation might be sufficient to yield accurate judgements on such a forced-choice task. In addition, we should note that MP's performance on word-nonword discrimination, though certainly above chance, was far from perfect, leading the authors to concede (op. cit., p.30) that any regularisation errors "might well reflect global impairment to whole-word orthographic addresses." A second problem is that the discrimination task failed to sample a wide range of frequencies, so that we do not know whether accuracy deteriorates as words become less familiar. Finally, the effect of prior exposure to many of the words, repeatedly presented to MP on other test occasions, must be considered as a possible confound, spuriously guiding some of her responses. Bub et al. have argued that MP's rejection of many irregular words in favour of regular (and completely novel) nonsense words stands against the view that her decisions are only based on the familiarity of items encountered during previous testing. But the lack of adequate controls for word repetition effects does not allow us to determine whether this factor plays a significant role on other trials. We may claim that the choice of orthographically common nonword patterns over irregular words as the alternative indicates that decisions are not always determined by episodic familiarity effects. There is no reason to assume, however, that this factor is not the basis for MP's ability to discriminate words from nonwords when orthographic familiarity has been equated between choices.

Can we obtain further evidence on the nature of the disturbance preventing MP from deriving the word-specific pronunciation of many lexical items? Is the deficit orthographic in origin, or does it occur subsequent to the activation of visual word forms, where phonology is addressed from print? Our attempt to clarify the issue relies on the fact that under limited viewing conditions, perceptual recovery of letters in words is enhanced relative to their perception in less familiar contexts. The word superiority effect was initially thought to have little bearing on direct perception; many authors considered it to be a relatively trivial consequence of guesswork or "filling in" of unidentified letters matching a highly predictable sequence. Later work by Reicher (1969) and Wheeler (1970), however, has demonstrated convincingly that the advantage for words must be perceptual in origin.

The technique devised, which eliminates the possible contribution of guessing, typically requires the brief presentation of a four-letter word or random string followed by a pattern mask. The subject is then given two choices for recognition of a letter in a particular position. In the case of words as targets, both response alternatives would furnish plausible completions of the array on the basis of the remaining three letters. For example, if the target is WORD, the alternatives might be ——K or ——D. With this testing procedure, many researchers have documented substantially better performance for words than unstructured sequences even for individual letters. The implication of this is that familiarity must affect the actual formation of a visual representation before the reader produces an overt response (McClelland & Johnston, 1977). The stored knowledge responsible for the word superiority effect appears to include both larger and smaller orthographic units. Normally, words are perceived slightly better than pseudowords with comparable spelling patterns (e.g. FORK versus LORK), indicating an advantage for whole-word units. Pseudowords, in turn, yield better recognition than random letters, providing support for the contribution of more general knowledge dealing with orthographic structure. We have previously adopted the forced-choice procedure of Wheeler (1970) and Reicher (1969) to evaluate a theoretical claim with respect to a case of letter-by-letter reading; namely that this particular syndrome is the outcome of such extensive damage to stored knowledge of orthography that no higher-level influence of context would be observed on the patient's (JV) ability to recognise a briefly presented string of letters (Bub, Black, & Howell, 1989). Here, we are interested in a more specific question, concerning the range of orthographic descriptions available to a patient with surface dyslexia. Clearly, MP does have access to some word units, given that her reading of exception words is good for high-frequency items and only deteriorates as word frequency declines. She also must be capable of readily activating subword units, as she reads pronounceable nonwords accurately and with normal speed. Thus, we learn little by merely demonstrating that MP yields the pattern typically found in research on the word superiority effect, i.e. a small advantage (usually around ten percent) for words relative to pseudowords and a much bigger advantage for pseudowords relative to random letter sequences. We need, if possible, a version of the paradigm that would produce a strong advantage for words over pseudowords, permitting a clear inference about the status of word units separate from more general effects of their orthographic familiarity. In addition, we must examine the word-specific advantage across a range of different frequencies, because any pathological constraints on word-level activation are more likely to emerge for less familiar targets.

The task appropriate to these requirements entails verbal report of all the letters that can be identified in briefly displayed words and matched pseudowords. Researchers have tended to avoid the use of free report in evaluating the word superiority effect, because of the criticism that results may be contaminated by postperceptual guessing. Evidence has accumulated, however, that this factor plays a negligible role if certain precautions are taken. McClelland and Johnston (1977) have argued that subjects can be prevented from using contextual information to guess unperceived letters by deployment of a post-display mask that may limit the time available to formulate a reasonable guess on the basis of fragmentary visual cues. Instructions to report the target letter-by-letter, and to avoid filling in the unseen portion, can further reduce the contribution of educated guessing (also see Estes, 1975; Johnston, 1978, for further evidence on the role of guessing in the free report paradigm).

A number of studies have demonstrated substantial advantages for words relative to orthographically regular nonwords using verbal report of the constituent letters as the dependent measure. The difference can range from 20% (McClelland & Johnston, 1977) to as much as 50% or greater (Adams, 1979), depending on the details of the stimulus presentation. The discrepancy between verbal report and forced-choice results, which, as we have mentioned, yields a much weaker superiority (in some cases non-existent) for words over pseudowords, can be attributed to the reduced sensitivity of the forced-choice procedure, where 50% accuracy corresponds to chance performance. McClelland and Johnston (1977, p.258) also point out that word familiarity may affect perception of the entire string without enhancing the recovery of a fragment once perception of the whole fails. Thus: ". . . any measure of perceptual encoding of a single letter should reflect influences on encoding the string as a whole much more weakly than a measure of the probability of encoding all the letters. A correct forced-choice response can potentially be based on encoding of only the critical letter, and some correct forced choices undoubtedly result from pure guesses when no information about the critical letter is extracted from the stimulus at all."

The foregoing comments provide the necessary background and rationale for the next experiment, which investigates MP's ability to report constituent letters in four-letter words and pseudowords under limited viewing conditions. Targets were pattern masked and MP was instructed to respond letter-by-letter to minimise the influence of guessing on performance. These restrictions, and the fact that she has a very severe semantic and naming disorder, with numerous neologisms occurring in spontaneous speech, make it quite unlikely that her identification of briefly presented targets will be determined by guessing the word on the basis of partial information. Note that we return to this point when discussing the results of the task.

The logic of the experiment is as follows: If MP can activate a whole-word orthographic unit, free report of all the constituent letters should be reliably better than report of a pseudoword matched for structural familiarity. If her decreased performance on irregular words is a result of an impairment in word-specific orthographic units, or loss of access to visual word forms, then we might expect to see less of a word superiority effect as item frequency decreases. The prediction we derive, then, is that MP will show a perceptual advantage for high-frequency words compared to pseudowords but that accuracy should drop sharply with decreasing word frequency, greatly reducing and finally eliminating the differences between words and pseudowords. Evidence from normal readers suggests that they should not be so heavily influenced by the effects of word frequency. Johnston (1978) examined the relative accuracy of free reports for letters in words chosen from the highest and lowest frequency quartiles of a sample, and found only an 8% difference between them. We should note that many of the words in their low-frequency group were so unfamiliar as to be hardly distinguishable from nonwords, for example, FIFE, BOLL, LAVE, and TING. Similar modest effects of word frequency were observed by McClelland and Johnston (1977), with low-frequency values again selected from the lowest possible frequency values. In view of these results, our working assumption is that, when frequency values are sampled across a broad range and still permit unambiguous differentiation of less familiar words from nonsense words, normal elderly subjects will either show a greatly reduced effect of word frequency or potentially no effect whatsoever.

Procedure

A set of 96 4-letter words was compiled so that an equal number had frequency values of more than 100 per million, 50–75, 25–49, and 10–25 per million (Francis & Kuçera, 1982). Each word had at least one other possible completion when a single letter was changed, for example, the alternatives for BANK were BAND, BANG, BANS, etc. and for CARE were CARP, CART, and CARD. A further 96 pseudowords were generated by changing the first or last letter in each word (e.g. PANK for BANK), matched as closely as possible to the original for single-letter position frequency and for bigram frequency (Mayzner & Tresselt, 1965) (see Appendix 4 for stimuli as well as frequency, bigram, and N counts).

Word or pseudoword targets were presented by means of Psychlab software on a Macintosh Plus computer in upper-case letters, black 24-point Geneva font on a white background. MP sat at a distance of 40cm from the screen. Each trial consisted of the following sequence. The word "ready" appeared on the screen until a keypress, and was immediately replaced by a central fixation point for 1sec. A 500msec delay was then introduced prior to the appearance of the target word or pseudoword. Exposure duration was adjusted on practice trials to yield an accuracy of 70% complete report correct (on all 4 letters) for MP and for each normal subject on words taken from the highest frequency range. The exposure selected for MP was 83msecs whereas for the normal subjects it ranged between 33 and 83msecs. Words selected for practice trials were not the same as those used in the experimental set. Targets were immediately followed by a random pattern mask displayed for 50msec. Words and pseudowords were presented according to a blocked design (48 items per block) and word frequency was randomised within blocks (cf. McClelland & Johnston, 1977). Blocked presentation of materials was selected since the word advantage over pseudowords is generally rather small if the subject knows that the stimuli include pseudowords. For this reason, trials are usually blocked so subjects can adopt the optimum strategy for each type of material (see McClelland & Rumelhart, 1981, pp. 395–396). This was considered to be particularly important for MP, to encourage her to treat the word targets as specific orthographic units. MP was instructed to report verbally all the letters she could discern in the target without attempting to guess at letters that were not identified. The same instructions were given to a group of 10 normal age-matched controls (mean 59.3 years) with a mean educational level of 14.2 years and no history of neurological illness.

Results

The performance of MP and the age-matched controls is shown in Fig. 4, which contains the accuracy of reporting all four letters correctly for words and pseudowords as a function of frequency. We should re-emphasise the fact that accuracy for all subjects has been titrated on high-frequency words, so that any difference between MP and normal readers cannot be attributed to a difference in absolute levels. As it turns out, there is some variability in performance between subjects, resulting in a slightly higher baseline than the titration threshold. The second point to note is the complete absence of a word frequency effect in the control group, despite a clear separation of the curves for words and pseudowords with closely matched orthographic structure. Normal readers, at least under the conditions of the present experiment, benefit substantially from the whole-word status of a spelling pattern, and show no restriction of access to word units as they become less familiar.

The total absence of any contribution of word frequency may appear rather surprising in view of the major importance of this variable in tasks like lexical decision and naming. It should be mentioned, however, that even our least familiar words (e.g. DEER, MINT, and HOOP) were considerably more frequent than the lowest frequency item typically used in research on masked perception of visual words. We suggest that the modest effects of frequency observed by some investigators are either the outcome of a greater contrast between items (i.e. the effect may not appear until a particular cutoff point is reached along the frequency dimension) or is merely an artifact due to a blurring of the distinction between very low-frequency words and pseudowords (see Paap, Newsome, McDonald,

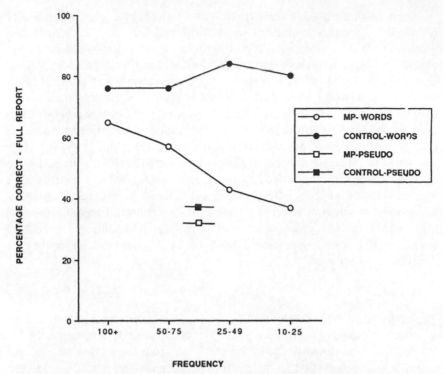

FIG. 4. Percentage of whole-word correct report as a function of frequency for MP and matched controls. (Note: Performance in pseudowords is represented as a single point even though the items were derived from the words across all frequency bands.)

& Schvaneveldt, 1982, for persuasive arguments in favour of this latter explanation). Although it is possible that other, more difficult testing conditions may induce a frequency effect in the normal subjects, 80% overall performance on our task is below ceiling and should have uncovered a frequency effect if one were present.

Given that normal readers show no effect of frequency on word perception under these masked conditions, MP's performance appears strikingly discrepant. Accuracy deteriorates systematically with decreasing word frequency, so that words in the lowest frequency group approach the baseline level obtained for completely unfamiliar words. The same general pattern of findings is observed when counting the number of letters (rather than full words) reported by MP. She reports 285/384 (74%) of letters in nonwords and 326/384 (82.9%) of letters in words, reflecting a word superiority effect. The effect of frequency on number of letters reported is still present, though somewhat less marked than when whole-words are counted, with 93%, 88%, 76%, and 71% for targets in the 100–150, 50, 25, and 10 per million frequency bands respectively.

Further analysis of the results indicates that the word superiority effect and its dramatic reduction across frequency bands are not due to possible differences in orthographic structure between words and pseudowords (nor between words from different frequency groups). There was no significant difference between the mean single letter frequency for words (mean frequency 331.57) and pseudowords (mean frequency 335.05) ($t[95] = 0.09$, $P < 0.10$), so this could not account for the difference in accuracy on these items. Although we matched words and pseudowords as closely as possible on bigram frequency, because target selection was subject to other constraints (four letters only, contains alternative completions, etc.), there was still a small but significant difference in summed bigram frequency across the two lists (mean summed bigram for words 61.08 and for pseudowords 56.53, $t[95] = 2.65$, $P < 0.05$). However, it is unlikely that MP was influenced by summed bigram since there were no major differences in her accuracy of reporting words across the four summed bigram quartiles. She correctly reported 10/24 from the top quartile range (mean summed bigram 114.9), 10/24 correctly from the next highest range (mean 64.5), 12/24 from the second lowest range (mean 44.2), and 9/24 from the lowest quartile (mean 15.9).

Finally, in order to determine the extent of orthographic overlap between words and pseudowords, we calculated the N count (i.e. the total number of English words that can be formed from each word by substituting one letter at a time in each serial position, cf. Coltheart, Davelaar, Jonasson, & Besner, 1977). The mean value of N for the words (6.4) was slightly, though significantly, higher than the N count for pseudowords (4.2) ($t[190] = 4.98$, $P < 0.01$). Inspection of the data, however, reveals no direct relation between N and accuracy of report. In fact, performance on words falling in the lowest quartile in the N count range (mean 2.3) was significantly higher than performance in the words falling in the top quartile (mean 11) ($\chi^2[1] = 3.9$, $P < 0.05$).

Having ruled out orthographic structure as the explanation for MP's pattern, we need to consider whether guessing is responsible for these findings. If guessing had occurred, one might have expected that MP would produce more word than nonword errors and that the error responses were likely to be higher in frequency than the target. This was not the case—of the 57 errors in reporting words, 29 were nonwords and, of the word responses, 12 were higher in frequency than the target whereas 16 were lower in frequency. These results argue against a strategy in which a high-frequency target word is guessed and provided as the response to the briefly exposed target.

Our conclusion, therefore, is that word-specific activation of orthographic codes (rather than orthographic structure) must be responsible for the advantage displayed by MP for high-frequency words over pseudowords and by normal subjects across a wide range of frequencies. The letters comprising a word are reported better than the letters in a pseudoword because they are mapped onto a permanent description of the word as a perceptual unit, whereas no such representation exists for a comparable pseudoword. Apparently, under pattern masking, frequency plays no role in visual word identification, a finding which has previously been reported by Paap et al. (1982) using a forced-choice paradigm, and which we have now replicated with the more sensitive free-report procedure. Paap et al. (1982) have argued that word frequency does not influence the activation of word units, but that the variable exerts its influence on subsequent stages required to verify the output of perceptual analysis.

Although the exact location affected by frequency remains controversial, MP clearly demonstrates a fundamental disturbance in visual encoding of word units when normal readers have full access to a much wider range of items. We note that MP's results on whole report of visually masked four-letter words closely resemble the accuracy profile derived from her pronunciation of printed exception words. The evidence points to a partial loss of whole-word orthographic activation as the basis for impairment on both tasks. Better perception of masked words than pseudowords requires activation of lexical units, each corresponding to a particular sequence of letters. Attenuation of the word-specific advantage implies that the normal range of visual word units is not available to MP, with lower-frequency items being reduced to the perceptual status of orthographically legal but unfamiliar spelling patterns. Failure to contact a word unit would also limit MP's ability to read exception words; a naming response must be assembled from subword units incorporating the more general correspondence between a letter sequence and its pronunciation, leading to a regularisation error. It is reasonable to assume, therefore, that the inability to use lexical representation to recover constituent letters from briefly displayed strings underlies MP's surface dyslexia and that the frequency effect is a direct consequence of the inaccessibility or deletion of the lower-frequency words within the lexicon itself. The most convincing demonstration of this argument would be to show that a word superiority effect exists for those items she can read correctly but not for those items that she cannot read. This result has no yet been demonstrated.

ONE ORTHOGRAPHIC LEXICON OR TWO?

We have established that MP has a deficit affecting the activation of whole-word orthographic units. One possible outcome of such a deficit is that, if the same set of lexical codes subserve both reading and writing, then we should expect to see errors on identical items in both modalities. There are, however, major methodological problems to be dealt with in using item-to-item correspondence as evidence for a single shared lexicon for reading and writing (Coltheart & Funnell, 1987). Since MP's performance is frequency-sensitive, any item consistency effect may be merely artifactual (the result of differing probabilities of accuracy in modalities). Thus, item-to-item correspondence may be driven purely by frequency. The same holds true for other potentially significant variables such as word length and word imageability, which have been shown to affect performance in other surface dyslexic patients. If MP's performance in both modalities can be accounted for by a variable such as frequency, any conclusions regarding the orthographic lexicon must be treated with caution. Before reaching conclusions about orthographic representations, then, the role of any contributing variable must be assessed and partialled out. Only then can item-by-item consistency be assessed.

A second consideration, which must be kept in mind before making claims about a single orthographic store, is that only certain stimuli can shed light on this issue. Only those items that necessarily require lexical processing (and cannot be produced correctly without it) can be included in the analysis to test the single lexicon hypothesis. If some irregular items can be produced nonlexically, "chance level" (probability of correct response without lexical processing) would not be zero and statistical interpretation of the data becomes impossible (Coltheart & Funnell, 1987).

Using only the irregular items, we first considered the contribution of frequency, which we know to affect MP's performance. Thereafter, we also investigated the effect of the other potentially relevant variables (word length and imageability) on item-to-item consistency.

The Contribution of Frequency

Procedure and Results

The 92 irregular words that had been given to MP for reading and writing and that fell into the mid-frequency range (between 10 and 99 per million) were included in this analysis. The mid-range items only were used to circumvent the potential floor and ceiling effects produced by frequency. These items were subjected to a Kappa agreement analysis in order to determine, after correcting for chance, the extent of item consistency (i.e. whether correct reading of an item co-occurs with the correct writing of that same item). A sample Kappa of 0.62 ($P < 0.001$; 99% confidence limits $0.40 <$ sample Kappa < 0.84) was obtained, reflecting a moderate to good association between items across modalities.[2] NcNemar's test of symmetry confirms these findings, showing no significant difference in

---

[2]According to Fleiss (1981), 0.4 to 0.6 sample Kappa values suggest a moderate to good association, whereas values above 0.75 reflect very good item-to-item association.

MP's performance across modalities in the mid-frequency range ($\chi^2[1] = 0.35$, $P > 0.05$). The data were further broken down into smaller bandwidths to ascertain whether this moderate-to-good association held throughout the mid-frequency range or perhaps was simply the result of the higher-frequency items in the group. Data for the items in the three bandwidths (10–19 per million [n = 32 pairs], 20–49 [n = 44 pairs], and 50–99 [n = 16 pairs]), were subjected to individual tests of symmetry. Table 1 reflects the number of words read correctly that were not spelled correctly and vice versa as a function of frequency.

There was no significant difference in performance on reading and writing in any of these three groups (McNemar's test $\chi^2[1] = 2.0$, $P > 0.05$, $\chi^2[1] = 1.0$, $P > 0.05$, and $\chi^2[1] = 1.0$, $P > 0.05$ for three bands respectively). The sample Kappa values for the three ranges were 0.86, 0.51, and 0.50 (all $P < 0.001$) respectively, indicating a moderate-to-good association between all items in the mid-frequency range including those in the lowest mid-frequency range. These results suggest that, even when frequency effects are controlled, there is good item-to-item consistency (and no significant asymmetry) across modalities. This finding is consistent with the hypothesis of a single lexicon, which, when damaged, gives rise to consistent performance across modalities.

The Contribution of Other Potentially Relevant Variables

In order to assess the contribution of frequency relative to other variables on MP's performance, a step-wise logistic regression analysis was carried out on the full list of irregular words (n = 392, 196 reading and 196 writing). The binary dependent measure was accuracy (1 = correct;

TABLE 1
Irregular Words Read Correctly/Incorrectly Crossed
with Words Spelled Correctly/Incorrectly as a
Function of Mid-frequency Bandwidth (per Million)

		Reading					
		10–19 (n = 32)		20–49 (n = 44)		50–99 (n = 16)	
		+	−	+	−	+	−
Writing	+	9	2	11	3	5	3
	−	0	21	7	23	1	7

0 = incorrect). Three variables were entered into the regression equation as possible predictors (three-variable analysis): modality (reading, writing), frequency, and word length. Because we wanted to include imageability as a variable but only had imageability scores for a small subset of items, we conducted a separate analysis (four-variable analysis) with modality, frequency, word length, and imageability (n = 54; norms taken from Paivio, Yuille, & Madigan, 1968) as factors. We predicted that frequency in combination with some other variables might account for the majority of the variance in MP's data but that modality would not be a significant predictor of performance. In other words, when the effect of the significant variables is removed, a clearer pattern of symmetry between the modalities might be observed, yielding a more accurate test of the single lexicon hypothesis.

Because the distribution of frequency counts of the items was skewed, a log transformation was performed, yielding a more normal distribution of the frequency scores. On the three-variable analysis, log frequency was entered initially as the most significant variable ($\chi^2[1] = 55.9$, $P < 0.001$), supporting the previous analysis that frequency is a major determinant of response outcome. A small improvement in prediction was noted when word length entered the regression equation with the incremental change still being significant at the $P < 0.05$ level ($\chi^2[1] = 6.9$, $P < 0.009$). Modality was not a significant determinant of performance. At the termination of the regression, the overall goodness of fit of this model was still significant ($\chi^2 = 405.6$, $P < 0.001$), suggesting that there may be an additional variable, not currently included in the model, that may improve the overall fit and account for the remaining variance. On the four-variable analysis, a similar pattern was noted with frequency (log) accounting for most of the variance at the outset ($\chi^2[1] = 14.2$, $P < 0.001$). Not word length, modality, nor imageability added any more predictive power over and above the contribution of frequency. This model was seen as more stable than on the three-variable analysis, with the goodness of fit at termination being nonsignificant ($\chi^2 = 599$, $P = 0.2$) and thus showing that the existing model adequately captures all the variance.

These findings suggest that, even when the contribution of potentially relevant variables is removed, there still remains a high association across reading and writing. Once the effect of frequency is partialled out (and also the smaller contribution of word length), performance across the two modalities is indistinguishable. The outcome of these analyses strongly supports the notion that reading and writing share the same orthographic lexicon and that deficits in the lexical representations give rise to a symmetrical impairment in reading and writing.

GENERAL DISCUSSION

A variety of functional deficits can give rise to the regularisation errors that are the hallmark of surface dyslexia. Although the heterogeneity of cases reported in the literature is doubtless a reflection of these multiple possible causes, patients have generally not been described in sufficient detail to produce a comprehensive taxonomic breakdown of the syndrome. The distinction has been made between one variant of surface dyslexia—characterised by the misreading of exception words, laborious deciphering of print, and incomplete command of the regularities between spelling and sound—and another subtype displaying rapid and accurate reading of words with regular spelling-sound correspondences. The underlying pathologies responsible for these variants remain at issue, though it has generally been assumed by dual routine theorists that the disturbance in at least one form of surface dyslexia occurs at the level of the stored orthographic word units, with relative sparing of smaller units below the whole word.

A recent computational model of phonological reading (Seidenberg & McClelland, 1989), incorporating one routine and thus departing from previous dual routine accounts, has also been applied to surface dyslexia in an attempt to clarify further the nature of the disorder (Patterson, 1990; Patterson et al., 1989). The model, capable of simulating a variety of normal effects in the translation of spelling to sound, has no localist lexical representations for the orthography or pronunciation of words, nor any distinct procedures for reading words and nonsense words. Instead, orthographic and phonological codes are represented as patterns of activation distributed over a set of more primitive units. Damage to various locations in the model produced essentially the same pattern of results: Error scores increased for both regular and exception words, although exception words were more vulnerable to damage. In addition, frequency had minimal or no effect on impaired performance; reading of both very familiar and less familiar words was found to be equally compromised.

The profile of surface dyslexia captured by this analysis clearly does not resemble the profile observed in MP. We have documented reliable effects of frequency on MP's reading and writing of exception words, along with the apparently normal speed and ability to convert regular spelling patterns to sound. Conceivably, as argued by Patterson et al. (1989), this rather extreme outcome—involving a dissociation between reading of regular and exception words—may be less crucial to our understanding of surface dyslexia than the more conventional variant, especially in view of the discrepant performance of the recent computational model. These authors raise the possibility that some cases, MP among them, may not be reading via knowledge representations that form part of the normal mechanism. Instead, explicit generalisations regarding the correspondences between spelling and sound, formed during the learning process, are used to pronounce common spelling patterns. The authors note, however (p.64), that such rule-based translation is "of limited applicability" and cannot be understood to "reflect the actual underlying computational mechanism."

We have devised a method of testing the extent to which MP can map letter identities onto whole-word knowledge, using a modified version of the procedure originally developed by Reicher (1969) and Wheeler (1970). Free report of letters in words presented briefly and followed by a pattern mask was compared to free report of letters in orthographically matched pseudowords under equivalent conditions of exposure. We assume that the task, which simply requires the subject to report the letters identified in a four-item display, provides a relatively direct measure of word activation, placing very little burden on memory or decision-making. Any differences favouring words over matched pseudowords can be attributed to the benefit derived from word-specific information that enhances the recover-ability of letter identities compared to orthographically legal but unfamiliar spelling patterns.

Results indicate that normal readers show a robust word superiority effect without any changes in report accuracy as a function of frequency. The complete absence of a frequency effect is noteworthy given the large contribution of this variable observed in other tasks (e.g. speeded naming and lexical decision). However, previous studies examining the influence of frequency on the perception of visually masked words have found similar weak (McClelland & Johnston, 1978) or absent effects (Paap et al., 1982). Interestingly, word frequency may also be seen to play a negligible role in the auditory modality, under circumstances when clear differences are observed between legitimate words and pseudowords. Samuel (1981) has reported that phoneme restoration—the illusory perception of a deleted segment as remaining present in the target utterance—is not reliably dependent on the frequency of a word but is strongly determined by lexical status (i.e. phoneme restoration is much less marked in nonsense words than in words).

The automatic restoration of phonemes in auditory words and the comparable enhanced recovery of letters forming visual words are both due to the contextual influences of whole-word units in the processing of lower-level codes. A spoken or written stimulus makes contact with the stored lexical representation in memory, and the resultant activation is sufficiently strong to overwrite the deletion of a missing acoustic segment or to prevent the loss of letter identities by visual masking. Apparently, these contextual effects are less crucially determined by the frequency of a word than by its existence as a unit in a person's vocabulary; if the letter (or phonemic) sequence corresponds to a legitimate word, perception can be shown to differ relative to structurally comparable nonsense items.

The foregoing comments will serve to highlight the dramatic change in

MP's full report of masked 4-letter words as their frequency diminishes from 150 per million to 10 per million, her performance ultimately converging with the baseline accuracy obtained for orthographically legal pseudowords. We have demonstrated that the advantage for words over pseudowords—occurring at higher frequencies—is in no way due to a discrepancy in single or in bigram frequency, nor to a potentially larger orthographic neighbourhood (measured by number of lexical items sharing 3 letters with the target) shared by words and pseudowords. We therefore conclude that any difference in the familiarity of orthographic structure would not account for the substantially better perception of letters in high-frequency words; instead, the advantage must reflect the activation of word-specific perceptual units from print. The evidence reveals that access to whole-word representation for MP is abnormally dependent on frequency—common words, like SHOP and WIND, are reported more accurately than the corresponding nonwords (SHOM, LIND), but the advantage for words rapidly diminishes as they become less familiar. We note that the effect of frequency of MP's free report of visually masked four-letter words is strikingly comparable to the effect on her ability to read orthographic exception words like PINT displayed for an unlimited exposure duration. Although it has been shown that patients may show widely differing patterns of performance on reading words aloud compared to their ability to report letter-by-letter from an array (Howard, 1991), we think that MP's performance on these two tasks is comparable because of the overall qualititative similarity in performance. Quantitative similarity cannot be evaluated since the letter report task, but not the word reading task, was subject to titration. Our claim, then, is that the same functional deficit accounts for her performance in both situations; whole-word knowledge becomes increasingly unavailable for lower-frequency items, leading to regularisation errors when exception words are displayed in free vision, and a major attenuation of the advantage for words over matched pseudowords under conditions of limited viewing. The most convincing test that would link these two tasks would be the free-report task using irregular words that can be read and spelled as well as those that cannot. If loss of access to whole-word representations mediates performance, then we should expect to see a word superiority effect only for the former but not for the latter items.

We should re-emphasise that perceptual identification of letters in words obscured by a pattern mask is a most direct test of the higher-level codes available to a reader, one that can reasonably be considered to reflect the operation of the underlying computational mechanism in real time. The fact that MP demonstrates an overall advantage for words compared to pseudowords, and that the word superiority effect appears to be unrelated to structural factors like single-letter, bigram, or N counts, makes it hard to assume that her reading is mediated entirely by a secondary procedure that has little to do with normal reading. We infer that MP's surface dyslexia is due to a partial loss of word-level descriptions contacted from letter identities, but that her reading knowledge, in other respects, is based on the same knowledge available to fluent readers of English.

MP's loss of certain word descriptions is also observed on a writing task in which items are dictated for spelling. Are the representations mediating her reading the same as those used for spelling or are they functionally separate? Friedman and Hadley (1992), in accounting for the association of letter-by-letter reading with surface dyslexia and dysgraphia in patient BL, have argued that a single orthographic lexicon subserves both reading and writing. Since BL demonstrated spelling difficulty pre-morbidly, the authors suggest that his orthographic lexicon was already mildly degraded. Access to this lexicon was then compromised by his stroke, resulting in letter-by-letter reading. Thus, the degradation of the single lexicon in association with the access difficulty gives rise to surface dyslexia, surface dysgraphia, and letter-by-letter reading. Like Friedman and Hadley (1992), we have concluded that a single lexicon is responsible for both reading and writing. In the first instance, MP's curves for reading and writing, plotted as a function of frequency, have exactly the same form, indicating a similar pattern of deficit across input and output. This equivalence could arise simply because a comparable degree of impairment in input and output could produce quantitatively similar findings. This, however, is insufficient to demonstrate that the behaviours arise from a single underlying mechanism. Analysis of the item-to-item correspondence reveals substantial consistency across individual items in the two modalities. Even when the contribution of frequency and other pertinent variables is subtracted out, a high degree of association for individual items is observed. Items that are impaired in one modality are likely to be impaired in the second modality as well. This evidence, based on associations of function, is consistent with a single orthographic lexicon rather than with a model of functionally independent input and output lexical codes.

Manuscript received 8 March 1990
Revised manuscript received 13 August 1991

REFERENCES

Adams, M.J. (1979). Models of word recognition. *Cognitive Psychology, 11*, 133–176.
Allport, A. & Funnell, E. (1981). Components of the mental lexicon. *Philosophical Transactions of the Royal Society of London, B295*, 397–410.

Beauvois, M.F. & Derouesné, J. (1981). Lexical or orthographic agraphia. *Brain, 104*, 21–49.

Behrmann, M. (1987). The rites of righting writing: Homophone remediation in acquired dysgraphia. *Cognitive Neuropsychology*, 4(3), 365–384.

Bub, D., Black, S.E., & Howell, J. (1989). Word recognition and orthographic context effects in a letter-by-letter reader. *Brain and Language, 36*, 357–376.

Bub, D., Cancelliere, A., & Kertesz, A. (1985). Whole-word and analytic translation of spelling to sound in a nonsemantic reader. In K. Patterson, J.C. Marshall, & M. Coltheart (Eds.), *Surface dyslexia*. London: Lawrence Erlbaum Associates.

Bub, D. & Gum, T. (1988). *Psychlab software*. Montreal: McGill University.

Campbell, R. (1987). One or two lexicons for reading and writing words: Can misspellings shed any light? *Cognitive Neuropsychology*, 4(4), 487–499.

Caramazza, A. & Hillis, A.E. (1991). Lexical organisation of nouns and verbs in the brain. *Nature, 349*, 788–790.

Caramazza, A. & McCloskey, M. (1991). The poverty of methodology. *Behavioural and Brain Sciences, 14*(3), 444–445.

Coltheart, M. & Funnell, E. (1987). Reading writing: One lexicon or two? In D.A. Allport, D.G. MacKay, W. Prinz, & E. Scheerer (Eds.), *Language perception and production: Shared mechanisms in listening, speaking, reading, and writing*. London: Academic Press.

Coltheart, M., Davelaar, E., Jonasson, J.T., & Besner, D. (1977). Access to the internal lexicon. In S. Dornic (Ed.), *Attention and performance VI*. Hillsdale, N.J.: Lawrence Erlbaum Associates Inc., 535–555.

Coltheart, M., Masterson, J., Byng, S., Prior, M., & Riddoch, J. (1983). Surface dyslexia. *Quarterly Journal of Experimental Psychology, 35A*, 469–495.

Estes, T. (1975). The locus of inferential and perceptual processes in letter identification. *Journal of Experimental Psychology: General, 104*, 122–145.

Fleiss, J.L. (1981). *Statistical methods for rates and proportions*. Second Edition. London: Wiley Interscience.

Francis, W.N. & Kuçera, H. (1982). *Frequency analysis of English usage*. Boston: Houghton Mifflin Company.

Friedman, R.B. & Hadley, J.A. (1992). Letter-by-letter surface alexia. *Cognitive Neuropsychology*, 9(3), 185–208.

Glushko, R.J. (1979). The organisation and activation of orthographic knowledge in reading aloud. *Journal of Experimental Psychology: Human Perception and Performance, 5*, 674–691.

Howard, D. (1991). Letter-by-letter readers: Evidence for parallel processing. In G.W. Humphreys & D. Besner (Eds.), *Basic processes in reading: Visual word recognition*. London: Lawrence Erlbaum Associates Ltd.

Johnston, J.C. (1978). A test of the sophisticated guessing theory of word perception. *Cognitive Psychology, 10*, 123–153.

Kuçera, H. & Francis, W.N. (1967). *Computational analysis of present-day American English*. Providence, R.I.: Brown University Press.

Masterson, J. (1985). Nonword reading in different populations. In K. Patterson, J.C. Marshall, & M. Coltheart (Eds.), *Surface dyslexia*. London: Lawrence Erlbaum Associates Ltd.

Mayzner, M.S. & Tresselt, M.E. (1965). Tables of single-letter and digram frequency counts for various word-lengths and letter-position combinations. *Psychonomic Monograph Supplement, 1*, 13.

McClelland, J.L. & Johnston, J.C. (1977). Preliminary letter identification in the perception of words and nonwords. *Journal of Experimental Psychology: Human Perception and Performance, 2*, 80–91.

McClelland, J.L. & Rumelhart, D. (1981). An interactive activation model of context effects in letter perception: Part 1. An account of basic findings. *Psychological Review*, 88(5), 375–407.

Monsell, S. (1987). Nonvisual orthographic processing and the orthographic input lexicon. In M. Coltheart (Ed.), *Attention and performance XII: The psychology of reading*. London: Lawrence Erlbaum Associates Ltd.

Paap, K.R., Newsome, S.K., McDonald, J.E., & Schvaneveldt, R.W. (1982). An activation-verification model for letter and word recognition: The word superiority effect. *Psychological Review*, 89, 573–594.

Paivio, A., Yuille, J.C., & Madigan, S. (1968). Concreteness, imagery, and meaningfulness values for 925 nouns. *Journal of Experimental Psychology Monograph Supplement*, 76(1), Part 2, 1–25.

Patterson, K.E. (1990). Alexia and neural nets. *Japanese Journal of Neuropsychology*, 6, 90–99.

Patterson, K.E. & Coltheart, V. (1987). Phonological processes in reading: A tutorial review. In M. Coltheart (Ed.), *Attention and performance XII: The psychology of reading*. London: Lawrence Erlbaum Associates Ltd.

Patterson, K.E., Seidenberg, M.S., & McClelland, J.L. (1989). Connections and disconnections: Acquired dyslexia in a computational model of reading processes. In R.G.M. Morris (Ed.), *Parallel distributed processing: Implications for psychology and neurobiology*. Oxford: Oxford University Press.

Reicher, G.M. (1969). Perceptual recognition as a function of meaningfulness of stimulus material. *Journal of Experimental Psychology*, 81, 274–280.

Samuel, G. (1981). The role of bottom-up confirmation in the phoneme restoration illusion. *Journal of Experimental Psychology: Human Perception and Performance*, 7, 1124–1131.

Seidenberg, M.S. (1985). The time-course of phonological code activation in two writing systems. *Cognition*, 19, 1–30.

Seidenberg, M.S. & McClelland, J.L. (1989). A distributed, developmental model of visual word recognition and naming. *Psychological Review*, 96, 523–568.

Seidenberg, M.S., Waters, G.S., Barnes, M.A., & Tanenhaus, M.K. (1984). When does irregular spelling or pronunciation influence word recognition? *Journal of Verbal Learning and Verbal Behaviour*, 23, 383–404.

Shallice, T. & McCarthy, R. (1985). Phonological reading: From patterns of impairment to possible procedure. In K. Patterson, J.C. Marshall, & M. Coltheart (Eds.), *Surface dyslexia*. London: Lawrence Erlbaum Associates Ltd.

Shallice, T., Warrington, E.K., & McCarthy, R. (1983). Reading without semantics. *Quarterly Journal of Experimental Psychology*, 35A, 111–138.

Venezky, R.L. (1970). *The structure of English orthography*. The Hague: Mouton.

Wheeler, D.D. (1970). Processes in word recognition. *Cognitive Psychology*, 1, 59–85.

APPENDIX 1

Nonword Stimuli and MP's Responses for Reading Aloud (taken from Glussko, 1979)

Regular		*Irregular*	
Stimulus	*MP's Response*	*Stimulus*	*MP's Response*
hoil	/hɔɪl/	mear	/miːr/
grool	/gruːl/	shead	/ʃɛd/
cath	/hæθ/	wull	/wʌl/
nust	/mʌst/	brove	/broɒv/
wote	/woɒt/	wead	/wɛd/
heef	/hiːf/	pove	/poɒv/
weat	/wiːt/	moof	/muːf/
prain	/preɪn/	sost	/sɑst/
sheed	/ʃiːd/	heen	/hiːn/
bink	/bɪnk/	coth	/kɑθ/
moop	/muːp/	steat	/stiːt/
speet	/spiːt/	gome	/goɒm/
sweal	/swiːl/	domb	/dɑmb/
feal	/fiːl/	bood	/buːd/
lole	/loɒl/	pomb	/pɑmb/
bort	/bɔrt/	bint	/bɪnt/
dold	/dɑld/	drood	/druːd/
suff	/dʌf/	haid	/heɪd/
pode	/poɒd/	lome	/loɒm/
dore	/dɔːr/	pild	/pɪld/
pilt	/pɪlt/	wush	/wʌʃ/
beed	/biːd/	sweak	/swiːk/

APPENDIX 2

Nonword Stimuli and MP's Responses for Writing to Dictation

Stimulus	*MP's Response*	*Stimulus*	*MP's Response*
/biːl/	beel	/dreɪt/	drate
/bloɒm/	blome	/nɛld/	neld
/sɛk/	sek	/dɑld/	dold
/kɔːm/	caum	/koɒb/	cobe
/mɛl/	mell	/flæm/	flam
/tʃæm/	cham	/bɔːs/	bauce
/spæl/	spal	/læts/	lats
/hiːn/	heen	/dɪmp/	dimp
/kɛd/	ked	/sʌf/	suff
/diːtʃ/	deetch	/woɒl/	wole
/fleɪt/	flate	/wʌʃ/	wush

Stimulus	MP's Response	Stimulus	MP's Response
/liːm/	leem	/rɪlt/	rilt
/driːs/	dreece	/pliːk/	pleak
/seɪt/	sate	/riːs/	reese
/skərl/	skirl	/hɔɪs/	hois
/kadʒ/	cudge	/maɪs/	mise
/niːtʃ/	neech	/keɪl/	kail
/frɪm/	frim	/fɛnt/	fent
/swiːm/	sweam	/dɛgs/	degs
/nɪlt/	nilt	/rɛl/	rell
/muːp/	moop	/stald/	stold
/trɪst/	trist	/plak/	pluck
/teɪz/	taze	/skɪm/	skim
/fliːp/	fleep	/rag/	rog
/hɔɪl/	hoil	/pɛtʃ/	petch
/bliːm/	bleam	/blɪk/	blick
/briːs/	brease	/lat/	lot
/gɛd/	ged	/friːtʃ/	freech
/wiːtʃ/	weech	/nuːd/	nood

APPENDIX 3

Corpus of Reading and Writing Responses for MP for Regular and Irregular Words (Divided by Frequency Bands)

There are a total of 392 words (196 irregular and 196 matched regular words). The reading errors are phonetically transcribed using the phonetic alphabet in Patterson, K.E., Marshall, J.C., & Coltheart, M. (1985). *Surface dyslexia*. London: Lawrence Erlbaum Associates Ltd.

Sound-spelling correspondences are considered irregular if they are not predictable from the single grapheme-to-phoneme match or from the surrounding context. An irregular word may appear twice if it is being tested for two different irregular components, for example, "massage" is tested for the irregular /g/ correspondence as well as the irregular /a-e/ correspondence.

The frequency bands are determined by the irregular words. The regular words are matched as closely as possible for the sound-spelling correspondence and then for the frequency.

The * indicates which of the irregular words were classified as very irregular on the Shallice, Warrington, and McCarthy (1983) scheme.

	Writing	Reading
A. Below 9 per million		
(a) Irregular		
womb	woom	/wamb/
*choir	quire	/tʃɔɪr/
chrome	crome	/tʃroom/
anarchy	enarkey	/ænartʃi/
mustache	mustash	/muːstæʃ/

	Writing	Reading
parachute	+	/pærətʃuːt/
chef	shef	/tʃɛf/
*sew	so	/soʊ/
chivalry	shivare	/tʃɪvælri/
*yacht	yaut	/jætʃət/
massage	mesage	/mæseɪdʒ/
camouflage	camaflash	+
*debris	debree	/dɛbrɪs/
*debut	dabue	/dɪbʌt/
corsage	corsosh	/kɔrseɪdʒ/
massage	mesage	/mæseɪdʒ/
sabotage	sebatosh	/sæbʊteɪdʒ/
barrage	berosh	/bɛreɪdʒ/
*awe	aw	/oʊ/
*facade	fesad	/fækeɪd/
*clientele	clientale	+
ravine	+	/rəvaɪn/
*malice	malus	/mælaɪs/
dove	+	+
*shone	shaun	/ʃoʊn/
*safari	sufire	/səfeɪri/
siren	syren	/sɪrən/
*urine	yuren	/juraɪn/
*mural	+	/mjuræl/
spiral	spirow	/spiræl/
hind	hinde	/hɪnd/
*draught	draft	/drɔt/
endeavour	endeaver	+
dread	+	+
pheasant	fesent	/fiːzænt/
sweat	swet	/swiːt/
yearn	yurn	/jiːrn/
*sieve	sive	/saɪv/
*lingerie	lanjerine	/lingəriə/
*coyote	ciotee	/kɔɪaɪoʊt/
*leopard	lepard	/liːoʊpɒrd/
soot	+	+
crook	+	/kruːk/
hook	+	/huːk/
brook	+	+
vow	+	+
*sponge	spunj	+
*coupon	cupon	/kjupɒn/
*bouquet	bucay	/boʊkwɛt/
*suave	swav	+
*cough	+	/kɒʊf/
biscuit	+	/bɪskjuət/
trough	+	/trʌf/

	Writing	*Reading*
*cough	+	/kaɔf/
shove	shuv	/ʃoɔv/
(b) Regular Words		
ebb	eb	/ebəbə/
thimble	+	/θɪmbʌl/
crumble	+	/krʌmpəl/
orchard	orched	+
chore	+	+
preach	+	+
chess	ches	+
cherry	chary	+
chive	+	+
chant	+	+
punch	+	+
garlic	garlek	+
fragrant	fegrent	/fragrænt/
crusade	+	+
pity	+	+
ornate	ornature	+
sage	+	I
sedate	+	+
shave	+	+
skate	+	+
bake	+	+
revere	ravere	+
serene	sereen	+
hive	+	+
recite	resight	+
dole	+	+
mole	mol	+
beware	+	+
arid	ared	+
horrid	hored	+
tariff	tereph	+
borrow	borow	+
mint	+	+
wilt	+	+
auction	+	+
spear	speer	+
breach	+	+
peach	+	+
defeat	defeet	+
siege	+	/si:ʒ/
niece	neese	/nis/
voice	+	+
noise	+	+
tycoon	ticoon	+
broom	+	+

	Writing	*Reading*
spoon	spoone	+
coil	+	+
rouse	roose	+
bounty	+	/boɑnti/
sour	+	+
abound	+	/abʌnd/
bounce	+	+
slaughter	slauter	+
neighbour	naber	+
gaze	+	+

B. *Between 10–19*
(a) Irregular Words

	Writing	*Reading*
tomb	tume	/toɑmb/
ache	ake	/eɪtʃ/
chemistry	cemestry	/tʃɛmistri/
echo	eco	/ɛtʃoɑ/
chaos	kaos	/tʃeɪəz/
anchor	ancor	/æntʃɔr/
*champagne	shampane	/tʃæmpeɪn/
*receipt	reseete	/risipt/
*morale	morel	/mɔreɪl/
*allege	alege	/əlidʒ/
*elite	alete	/əlaɪt/
*pint	pinte	/pɪnt/
shove	+	+
glove	+	+
irony	+	+
virus	vires	/virʌs/
*concerto	consherto	/kɑnkertoɑ/
mild	+	/mild/
*gauge	gaje	/gaɑdʒ/
sweater	+	+
deaf	def	/di:f/
feather	+	+
*tortoise	tortis	/tɔrtɔɪz/
wool	+	+
brow	+	+
plow	+	+
soup	+	+
boulevard	bulavard	/boɑləvɑrd/
*sword	sord	/swɔrd/
dough	doe	/dʌf/
ton	tun	/tɑn/
shoe	+	/ʃoɑ/

	Writing	Reading
(b) Regular Words		
grumble	+	+
curb	+	+
hub	+	+
pinch	+	/pinətʃ/
chimney	chemanee	+
arch	+	+
couch	+	+
crusade	+	+
champion	+	+
apricot	+	+
behave	+	+
adhere	+	+
slice	+	+
hint	+	+
grove	+	+
dose	+	+
orange	+	+
ranch	+	+
alarm	+	+
fist	+	+
limb	+	/lɪmb/
launch	+	+
heap	+	+
teach	+	+
oyster	oister	+
boot	+	+
pillow	pelow	+
glow	+	+
mouse	+	/maɒz/
boundary	boundarene	+
switch	swich	/swɪtʃt/
ditch	+	+
C. Between 20–49		
(a) Irregular Words		
*debt	det	/dɛbt/
subtle	suttle	/sʌbtəl/
stomach	stomak	+
architect	arketict	/artʃɪtɛkt/
prestige	presteesh	/prɛstaiʒ/
regime	reshime	/rɛgaɪm/
scheme	skeem	/stʃɪːm/
garage	garash	/gæreidʒ/
mortgage	morgij	/mɔrtgeɪdʒ/
*honour	+	/hɑnaɒr/
tour	+	+
*honest	+	+
sugar	+	+

	Writing	Reading
garage	garash	/gæreɪdʒ/
motive	+	/moʊtaɪv/
regime	reshime	/rɛgaɪm/
grow	gro	/groʊ/
routine	rutine	/ru:taɪn/
prestige	presteesh	/prestaɪʒ/
*bury	burry	/bjuri/
*thorough	thorow	/thoʊrʌf/
*scarce	scarse	+
breath	breth	/bri:θ/
sergeant	sargine	+
grind	grinde	/grɪnd/
blind	blinde	/blɪnd/
*aunt	+	/aɒnt/
breast	brest	/bri:st/
thread	+	+
meadow	medow	+
wealth	+	+
realm	relm	/ri:lm/
leather	+	+
pleasant	+	+
ceiling (homo)	sealing	+
routine	rutine	/rutaɪn/
tough	+	+
rough	+	+
*circuit	sirket	/sɔrkjuət/
*exaggerate	ecajerate	+
*colonel	curnel	/kɑlanɛl/
touch	tuch	+
bread	+	+
roll	+	+
(b) Regular Words		
button	butten	+
globe	+	+
debate	+	+
branch	+	+
preach	+	+
magnificent	magnifent	/mægnɪfɪʃent/
merchant	merchent	/merchænt/
cigarette	cigaret	+
humour	humer	+
hill	heal	+
sudden	suden	+
shame	+	+
slice	+	+
compromise	compremise	/kɑmpramɪs/
define	+	+
enterprise	+	+

	Writing	*Reading*
cure	+	+
borrow	borow	+
carve	carf	+
storm	+	+
milk	+	+
fond	+	+
lost	+	+
treat	+	+
freight	frate	/fraɪt/
authorise	autherise	+
breach	+	+
creature	creacher	/kriːeɪtʃər/
dean	deen	+
lean	leene	+
repeat	repeet	+
teach	+	+
veil	vail	+
mountain	+	/maʊnteɪn/
mount	+	+
bound	+	+
colony	caluernee	+
trap	+	+
reveal	+	/rɛviːl/
strip	+	+
yard	yarde	+
song	song	+
sweet	sweat	+
clean	+	+

D. *Between 50–99*
(a) Irregular Words

orchestra	orcestra	/ɔːrtʃɛstrə/
village	+	+
engine	enjin	/ɛndʒaɪn/
wild	wyld	/wɪld/
*laugh	+	+
pleasure	+	/pliʒuːr/
spread	+	+
*height	hitc	+
*broad	braud	/brɔʊd/
foot	fut	/fuːt/
*key	+	/keɪ/
cook	+	/kuːk/
shook	shuk	/ʃuːk/
*lose	+	+
bought	+	+
learn	lurn	/liːrn/

	Writing	Reading
(b) Regular Words		
chest	+	+
frame	+	+
advice	edvice	+
bond	+	+
list	+	+
pitch	pich	/pɪtʃt/
gaudy	gody	/gaʊdi/
repeat	repeet	+
goal	+	+
obey	obay	+
proof	+	+
boot	+	+
round	+	+
air	+	+
wage	+	+
nine	+	+

E. Between 100–199

(a) Irregular Words

	Writing	Reading
*doubt	dout	+
character	carecter	/tʃæræktər/
machine	+	/mæʃain/
police	+	+
above	+	+
heavy	+	+
healthy	+	+
ready	+	+
*blood	blud	/blu:d/
stood	+	/stu:d/
couple	+	+
trouble	+	+
shoulder	sholder	+
enough	+	+
*answer	+	/ænswər/
gone	gon	/goʊn/
heart	+	+
month	+	/mɑnθ/
meant	+	/mi:nt/

(b) Regular Words

	Writing	Reading
husband	+	+
charge	+	+
leave	+	+
spoke	+	+
lost	+	+
wish	+	+
easy	+	+
fear	feer	+

	Writing	*Reading*
peace	+	+
pool	+	+
soon	soone	+
south	+	+
ground	+	+
sound	+	+
west	+	+
brown	+	+
shot	+	+
hear	heer	+
green	+	+

F. *200+*
(a) Irregular Words

	Writing	Reading
*island	iland	/izlænd/
*sure	+	+
often	offen	+
*give	+	+
*move	moove	/moɒv/
*come	+	+
*very	+	+
*are	ar	+
child	+	/tʃɪld/
kind	kind	/kɪnd/
behind	behinde	+
*said	sead	+
again	+	/əgeɪn/
death	+	+
head	+	+
*friend	+	+
book	+	+
good	+	+
allow	alow	+
how	+	+
now	+	+
could	coud	/ku:ld/
country	+	/kaɒntri/
should	shood	+
group	croop	+
young	+	+
*build	+	+
*two	+	+
both	+	+
*front	+	+

(b) Regular Word

	Writing	Reading
basic	basik	/bæsik/
summer	+	+
point	+	+

	Writing	*Reading*
five	+	+
those	+	+
close	+	+
more	+	+
save	+	+
think	+	+
beyond	+	+
firm	ferm	+
grove	+	+
wait	wate	+
reach	+	+
each	+	+
calorie	calaree	/kæloriə/
food	+	+
tool	+	+
low	+	+
below	+	+
show	+	+
about	+	+
mouth	+	+
house	+	+
found	+	+
ground	+	+
suit	sute	/su:ət/
sound	+	+
twenty	+	+
black	blak	+

APPENDIX 4

Stimuli used in Word Superiority Effect Experiment (Frequency Calculated per Million, Francis & Kuçera, 1982)

	Frequency		
>100	*50*	*25*	*10*
BORN	FOLK	SANG	FLOP
LOAN	COPY	MARS	GUSH
PAIN	LEAP	TILE	FUSE
SALE	ROOF	VEIL	LIMB
SING	TALL	LAMP	GOAT
RISE	PALE	PORT	MENU
SELL	BEND	BARE	TOME
BANK	CARD	BEEF	MINT
BOND	FLEE	BELL	HAZE
DARK	RUSH	BULK	OATH
CARE	MOOD	COIN	FORT
EASY	GRIN	SPIN	FLAP
WIND	MEAL	SOAP	DEER
ARMS	COAT	SLUG	LURE
POEM	FIST	RAIL	BEAD
COOL	CORE	CHIN	HULK
FILM	MOOD	SLAM	BEEP
ROLL	DISK	CURB	HOOP
DENY	MILK	CAFE	CLOT
POOR	GRAB	LOOP	CLAP
SHOP	COLD	LEND	HULL
MAIN	LUCK	POLE	CORD
FAIL	CAST	SCAR	DART
TEAM	PACK	BOLD	CLOG

Mean bigram frequency (summed across all bigrams):

66.1	65.2	50.5	62.5

Mean single letter frequency (summed across all letters):

317	341	299	368

Mean N count:

6.4	6.8	6.8	5.9

Chapter 8   Reading

Patterson, K. (1990). Alexia and neural nets. *Japanese Journal of Neuropsychology, 6,* 90–99.
Patterson, K. (1994). Reading, writing and rehabilitation: a reckoning. In M.J. Riddoch & G.W.
Humphreys (Eds), *Cognitive neuropsychology and cognitive rehabilitation.* Hove, UK: Lawrence
Erlbaum Associates Ltd.

The two papers chosen to accompany Chapter 8 are both by Karalyn Patterson, one of the leading researchers in the field of visual word recognition and acquired dyslexia. The first introduces an area of real advance since 1988— that is, the application of computer-based connectionist (or "neural net") models. These models consist of large numbers of simple processing elements (units) that are connected one to another but are typically grouped together into "pools". Each pool handles different types of representations. Thus, a model of reading might have a pool of orthographic units that represent the letter structure of words, a pool of semantic units that represent word meanings, and a pool of orthographic units that represent spoken word-forms. The model is trained to associate different letter combinations (written words) with particular meanings and pronunciations. Training involves cycling many times through a set of items, gradually modifying the strengths of the connections between units within and between pools until a given input (here a letter string) reliably produces the required output (in this case, a meaning and a pronunciation).

As Patterson (1990) observes, such models are an advance over their "box-and-arrow" predecessors because they embody a set of theoretical assumptions about what goes on at each processing stage. They have been enormously influential within cognitive psychology and cognitive neuropsychology (Quinlan, 1991; Plaut & Shallice, 1994). There is a great deal one can do with a working, implemented computer model. Once trained, its behaviour can be compared with that of humans performing the same task. For example, does the model have difficulty with the same sorts of items that cause humans problems? Does it make the same sorts of errors? If it is presented with novel items that were not part of its training, does it respond in the same way that humans do? Patterson considers the issues of item difficulty and error types by comparing the effects of word frequency and regularity on the accuracy and the errors of human readers and a connectionist model (that of Seidenberg & McClelland, 1989). The question of generalisation to novel items can be addressed by presenting the model with nonwords it has not seen before and comparing the accuracy with which it assigns pronunciations to them with the accuracy of skilled adult readers given the same nonwords to read aloud.

Another possibility with a trained connectionist model is to "lesion" it.

There are a variety of ways of doing this, including switching off a proportion of the units, adding "noise" to the system, or weakening connection strengths. All of these have been employed at one time or another in attempts to simulate a range of neuropsychological disorders from prosopagnosia (Burton, Young, Bruce, Johnston, & Ellis, 1991) to deep dyslexia (Plaut & Shallice, 1994). The particular disorder chosen for simulation by Patterson, Seidenberg, and McClelland (1989) was surface dyslexia. The attempt was made using a model that, crudely speaking, converts letter strings to speech via pools of orthographic and phonological units. There are no semantic units in this particular model.

Despite our general enthusiasm, connectionism has not proved an entirely unmixed blessing for cognitive neuropsychology. One of its dangers is of being caught up by overenthusiasm for what can sometimes be relatively superficial analogies between the performance of a damaged computer model and the impairments suffered by someone with a brain injury. One of the best tests of a computer model lies in its ability to simulate a range of phenomena, and to simulate fine-grained performance. We are therefore especially impressed by the way Patterson (1990) always grounds her points securely in data, showing the rich interplay between simulation and careful documentation of cognitive deficits. Although Karalyn Patterson would doubtless no longer agree with everything she wrote in the Patterson (1990) reading, it stands as a model of clear and concise exposition of the basic aims and rich promise of the enterprise.

Some recent and very interesting work describes attempts to retrain damaged neural networks, drawing explicit analogies between that and the efforts of the damaged brain to re-acquire lost skills (Plaut, 1996). This represents just one aspect of a growing interest among cognitive neuro-psychologists in recovery and rehabilitation. As Patterson (1994) notes in the second of our two selected papers, when cognitive neuropsychologists have reflected on the possible contribution of their subject to therapy, their assessments have ranged widely; from pessimistic to optimistic (e.g. Caramazza, 1989; Ellis, Franklin, & Crerar, 1994; Hillis, 1993; Wilson & Patterson, 1990).

Patterson (1994) discusses some of the issues involved in applying cognitive neuropsychology to treatment and summarises the findings of a number of attempts to remediate the reading disorders of patients with pure alexia (letter-by-letter reading), surface dyslexia, and deep dyslexia. The outcomes are, inevitably, mixed. But after decades in which countless patients have given generously of their time to help the cognitive neuropsychologist to understand disorders of mental functioning, such attempts by cognitive neuropsychologists to give something back in return can only be applauded.

REFERENCES

Burton, A.M., Young, A.W., Bruce, V., Johnston, R., & Ellis, A.W. (1991). Understanding covert recognition. *Cognition, 39*, 129–166.

Caramazza, A. (1989). Cognitive neuropsychology and rehabilitation: an unfulfilled promise? In X. Seron & G. Deloche (Eds), *Cognitive approaches in neuropsychological rehabilitation.* Hillsdale, N.J.: Lawrence Erlbaum Associates Ltd.

Ellis, A.W., Franklin, S., & Crerar, M.A. (1994). Cognitive neuropsychology and the remediation of disorders of spoken language. In M.J. Riddoch & G.W. Humphreys (Eds), *Cognitive neuropsychology and cognitive rehabilitation.* Hove, UK: Lawrence Erlbaum Associates Ltd.

Hillis, A.E. (1993). The role of models of language processing in rehabilitation of language impairments. *Aphasiology, 7*, 5–26.

Patterson, K.E., Seidenberg, M.S., & McClelland, J.L. (1989). Connections and disconnections: acquired dyslexia in a computational model of reading processes. In R.G. Morris (Ed.), *Parallel distributed processing: implications for psychology and neurobiology.* Oxford: Oxford University Press.

Plaut, D.C. (1996). Relearning after damage in connectionist networks. *Brain and Language, 52*, 25–82.

Plaut, D.C. & Shallice, T. (1994). *Connectionist modelling in cognitive neuropsychology: A case study.* Hove, UK: Lawrence Erlbaum Associates Ltd.

Quinlan, P.T. (1991). *Connectionism and psychology: a psychological perspective on new connectionist research.* Hemel Hempstead, UK: Harvester-Wheatsheaf.

Seidenberg, M.S. & McClelland, J.L. (1989). A distributed, developmental model of word recognition and naming. *Psychological Review, 96*, 523–568.

Wilson, B. & Patterson, K.E. (1990). Rehabilitation for cognitive impairment: does cognitive psychology apply? *Applied Cognitive Psychology, 4*, 247–260.

Alexia and Neural Nets

K. E. Patterson
MRC Applied Psychology Unit, Cambridge, UK

A neural net model (developed by Seidenberg & McClelland, 1989) computes phonological representations for alphabetic letter strings. Learning, over a series of training experiences with English words, corresponds to changes in weights on connections between units at different layers in the model. After training, the performance of the model simulates many features of the word-naming performance of adult English readers. "Lesioning" the trained model also yields at least some features of one prominent form of acquired alexia. The distributed representations used by this and other neural net models have important implications for modelling cognitive impairments that result from brain lesions.

Traditional theorizing in the field of cognitive psychology and neuro-psychology relies on descriptive process models consisting of boxes and arrows. The diagram in Figure 1, for example, postulates that a written word (in the English alphabetic writing system) can be pronounced by using one of three different routines. One routine proceeds via orthographic word recognition and semantics, a second via orthographic recognition followed by word level transcoding from orthography to phonology, and a third via sub-word level transcoding. Such a model is utilized in neuropsychology by inferring, on the basis of a patient's performance, that the neural substrate corresponding to one or more boxes and/or arrows has been damaged, making a particular routine unavailable and therefore forcing the patient to rely on an alternative routine to perform a cognitive task. In the domain of acquired disorders of reading, deep dyslexia (Coltheart, Patterson & Marshall, 1980) and surface dyslexia (Patterson, Marshall & Coltheart, 1985) might be described in the framework of Figure 1 as follows: for a deep dyslexic patient, pronunciation of written words can only be accomplished by the routine involving ortho-graphic recognition and semantics; for a surface dyslexic patient, this same task is largely restricted to the routine involving sub-word level transcoding from orthography to phonology.

This kind of descriptive model has served a useful function in helping researchers to think clearly about the component processes required for complex skills like reading and writing. Such models have been particularly valued in neuropsychology because they represent hypotheses about which processes are truly separable, in the sense that a brain lesion can damage one process but leave another intact (Shallice, 1988).

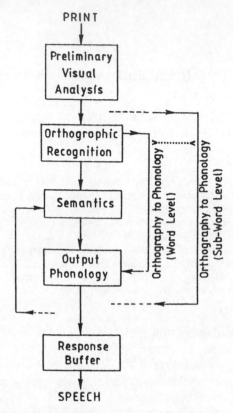

FIG. 1. A descriptive model of hypothesized processes for pronouncing a written word (from Patterson, Marshall & Coltheart, 1985, General Introduction, p. XXI).

Despite the recent popularity of this approach, many researchers now consider that it is limited, primarily because such a model merely states that a particular function is handled by some box or arrow, without specifying precisely how the necessary computation occurs. Neural net models are, in part, a response to this limitation. They represent one way of specifying the operation of boxes and arrows because they are working computational simulations. A neural net model does not just describe a cognitive process like the transcoding of a written word to a phonological representation: the model performs the process.

A neural net model of pronouncing written words in English has been developed by Seidenberg & McClelland (1989), and some initial explorations of this model with regard to acquired disorders of reading have been performed by Patterson, Seidenberg & McClelland (1989). The general framework of the model is shown in Figure 2, where it can be seen that, unlike Figure 1 with its three routines for written word naming, this model postulates

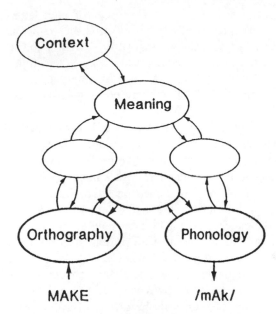

FIG. 2. A general framework for orthographic, phonological and semantic processing of words: the part of the framework in bold outline has been implemented as a neural net model by Seidenberg & McClelland (1989).

only two: one direct computation from orthography to phonology, and one indirect computation to phonology via meaning or semantics. Furthermore, although the theory acknowledges the necessity for both of these routines, the initial implementation of the model includes only the processes in bold outline—that is, only the direct computation of phonology from orthography.

Like most neural net or connectionist models, this one consists of simple processing elements (units) with connections between them. As Figure 2 indicates, this network has three levels or layers of units: in the simulations to be described here, 400 units code the orthographic information in a word presented to the model, 460 units code the phonology of the pronunciation computed by the network; and 200 units intervene at a "hidden" layer. These are called hidden units because they do not directly reflect any features of the real world (such as orthography or phonology) but are completely internal to the functioning of the model. In this neural net, units within a single layer are unconnected and therefore do not influence one another's operation, but there is complete connectivity between layers: every unit at the orthographic input level is connected to every hidden unit, and every hidden unit is connected to every unit at the phonological output level.

Details about the orthographic and phonological representations can be found in Seidenberg & McClelland (1989). For present purposes, it is sufficient to note just a few facts. The order of both letters and phonemes is represented not in terms of explicit position, but rather in terms of relative, position: the letter K in the written word MAKE is coded not as the letter K in position 3 but as the letter K preceded by A and followed by E; likewise /k/ in the spoken word "make" is coded as the phoneme /k/ preceded by the sound of a long /A/ and followed by nothing (a word boundary). The other thing to be noted here is that phonological units in the model do not actually correspond to triplets of phonemes, but rather to triplets of phonetic features of phonemes such as place of articulation, voicing, etc. This phonological coding scheme was borrowed from the past-tense verb learning connectionist model developed by Rumelhart & McClelland (1986).

The current network was trained on a vocabulary of almost 3000 words, which is not all but most of the monosyllabic and monomorphemic words in the English language. Training was carried out in a series of "epochs"; during each epoch, around 500 words were presented to the net for processing. The items were selected from the vocabulary at random but modulated as a function of word frequency, with the function closely related to the log of word frequency as tabulated by Kucera & Francis (1967).

Connections between units in the different layers carry weights which are given random values at the beginning of training. Over the series of training trials, the weights on these connections are gradually altered, using the back-propagation learning algorithm (Rumelhart, Hinton & Williams, 1986), to reduce the discrepancy between the model's computed pronunciation for a letter string and the correct pronunciation.

In fact, this simulation model of written word pronunciation does not pronounce words: it has not been implemented with a voice. The model simply computes a pattern of activation across the 460 phonological units, where each unit is either "off" or is activated to some degree approaching maximum. The performance of the model can be evaluated in one of two ways. The qualitative measure attempts to determine whether the pattern of activation across the phonological units computed by the model is closer to the correct pattern for the presented word than to the pattern for any other word or string. This measure is similar to assessing a human subject's accuracy (per cent correct) in naming printed words. It would be cumbersome to compare the model's output to a very large number of alternative patterns; the current version of the simulation (see Seidenberg & McClelland, 1989 for details) compares the model's output to the correct pronunciation and to any pronunciation deviating from the correct one by a single phoneme, and reports the best fit. The second performance measure is quantitative: for each phonological unit, the dis-crepancy in activation level between expected (what the model would compute if it were performing perfectly) and observed (what the model has actually computed) is squared and the squared difference values from all phonological units are then combined to give an "error" score. The advantage of this quantitative performance measure is that two words which are both correct (in the qualitative sense noted above) can still yield different error scores. A low error score can be thought of as the model's equivalent of quick, efficient, noise-free processing. Error scores are intended to provide a simulation of real subjects' reaction times in naming written words.

Figure 3 shows the performance of the model over 250 training epochs on a set of words from an experiment by Taraban & McClelland (1987). The stimulus list contained 96 words, 24 in each of four classes: high frequency regular words (like the word MUST) are English words that occur very commonly and also have a regular spelling-to-sound relationship; high frequency exception words (e.g. HAVE) are also common individual items but do not exemplify the common pronunciation of their spelling patterns (SAVE, GAVE and WAVE are regular examples contrasting with HAVE); low frequency regular words (like BANG) are less commonly encountered items with regular spelling-to-sound correspondences; and low frequency exception words (LOSE) have both lower familiarity as whole items and also embody an atypical correspondence (regular examples of this spelling pattern are POSE and HOSE).

Figure 3 reveals that performance as measured by the quantitative error score improves over the training period for all four word classes. How do the independent variables of word frequency and spelling-to-sound regularity influence the model's performance at various stages of training? Early in training (for example, at epoch 20), there are major effects of both frequency and regularity: the low frequency words, represented by squares, have larger error scores than the high frequency words, represented by triangles; and the exception words, represented by open symbols, have larger error scores than the regular words, represented by filled symbols. This pattern is of interest because it corresponds to the characteristics of word naming performance by children who are learning to read in English: as demonstrated by Backman, Bruck, Hebert & Seidenberg (1984), children's success in reading aloud is facilitated by both familiarity and regularity. Late in training (epoch 200, for example), there are no longer two independent effects but rather an interaction: for low frequency words (the squares), regularity still influences the model's performance; but for words on which the model has had many training experiences (high frequency words, the triangles), there is no longer a significant advantage for items with regular correspondences. This interaction is of interest because it is characteristic of word naming performance by adult skilled readers of English (Seidenberg, Waters, Barnes & Tanenhaus, 1984; Taraban & McClelland, 1987). The model shows a close, quantitative simulation of the effects of these two stimulus variables on word naming by both novice and experienced readers of English. Simulations of other effects can be found in Seidenberg & McClelland (1989).

As indicated earlier in the paper, the broader theory of which the implemen-

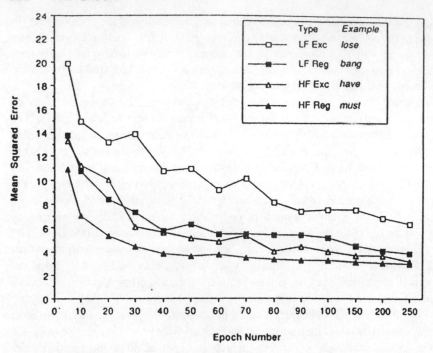

FIG. 3. Performance of the neural net model on four types of words over a series of training epochs (from Seidenberg & McClelland, 1989, p. 535).

ted model is a part postulates two routines by which a reader can compute the pronunciation of a written word. In attempting to capture a whole range of human performance characteristics with the implementation of just one of these routines, the model represents a bold hypothesis that the majority of word naming is handled by this single procedure. Although more traditional information processing models like the one displayed in Figure 1 have been somewhat agnostic about the role of the semantic routine in normal word naming, the proposers of such models have thought it necessary to postulate two other, more-or-less independent, procedures: one involving "addressed" (word level) and another involving "assembled" (sub-word level) phonology (see Coltheart, 1980, 1987 for reviews of the evidence underlying this distinction). One of the major sources of this evidence has been studies of neurological patients with acquired disorders of reading.

Of particular relevance to the present neural net model is the form of acquired dyslexia known as "surface" dyslexia (Marshall & Newcombe, 1973). In its purest form (see Bub, Cancelliere & Kertesz, 1985; McCarthy & Warrington, 1986; Shallice, Warrington & McCarthy, 1983), this reading disorder is characterised by (a) relatively fluent and correct naming of words with a regular spelling-to-sound correspondence (e.g. MUST and BANG from the list in Figure 3); (b) a significantly higher error rate on words with an exceptional spelling-to-sound correspondence (e.g. HAVE and LOSE) ; and (c) a predominance of one specific error type on exception words: the patient's response represents a "regularized" or typical pronunciation of the spelling pattern (e.g. LOSE pronounced to rhyme with "pose" or "hose").

The general question to be addressed now is whether the model, so successful in accounting for word naming by normal readers, can also advance our understanding of the breakdown of this skill as a consequence of neurological damage. The specific question is whether some form of "lesion" or damage to the trained network can simulate the characteristics of surface dyslexia mentioned above. There are two major reasons for selecting the "pure" form of surface dyslexia as a test of the model's ability to capture impaired as well as intact word naming performance. First of all, such patients have severely impaired word comprehension, suggesting that their word naming performance is largely uninfluenced by the routine, available to normal readers, in which the computation of phonology from orthography is mediated by word meaning. Since the neural net also knows nothing of word meanings, its parallel to surface dyslexia has at least face validity.

The second point concerns the striking claim of this neural net model that a single procedure for the direct computation of phonology from orthography can handle all types of words and letter strings in English. As already noted, traditional information processing models have not managed without two different procedures to explain a number of features of both normal and impaired performance, and surface dyslexia has been one of the sources of evidence claimed to support this multiple-routine view. It is simple enough to "explain" the pattern of reading performance in surface dyslexia in terms of a model like Figure 1: an English reader forced (by damage to alternative procedures) to rely primarily on an intact sub-word level routine should name regular words correctly but give regularized pronunciations to exception words. A challenge for a single-process account like the neural net model is whether some form of disruption to the single computational process can also produce the surface dyslexic pattern of reading.

The trained network can be disrupted in various ways: processing structures can be eliminated or noise can be added to the processing procedures. It can also be damaged in various locations: in the present model, for example, either hidden units or connections from hidden units to phonological output units could be disrupted. Finally, the net can be lesioned to varying degrees: different proportions of units or connections can be affected. Some of the features associated with these options for damaging the network have been explored in Patterson, Seidenberg & McClelland (1989). Here, just one lesion experiment will be reported, in which 20% of hidden units were damaged: that is, after training to 250 epochs, the activation values of 40 hidden units (selected at random from the 200 units at the hidden layer) were fixed at zero so that they could not contribute to the model's computations. The model was tested on the Taraban & McClelland (1987) high and low frequency regular and exception words 10 times, each time with a new random 20% of the hidden units zeroed. The model's damaged performance, averaged over the 10 tests, was then compared to the performance of two surface dyslexic patients asked to name comparable words. The two patients selected from the literature were KT, a patient with a diagnosis of pre-senile dementia (McCarthy & Warrington, 1986) and MP, a patient with severe left-temporal damage following a road traffic accident (Bub, Cancelliere & Kertesz, 1985).

It is important to note that, since (a) the patients were studied prior to the development of the model, and (b) the precise word-sets used with patients are not always reported in detail, it was not possible to compare network and patients on identical lists. One of the impressive features of Seidenberg & McClelland's evaluation of their computational model with respect to normal readers is the use of identical stimulus materials. Assessment of future surface dyslexic patients will permit tighter control in this regard; for the moment, it is merely possible to assess performance on similar classes of words. Data for MP were taken from Bub et al (1985, Table 1. 2, p. 21); performance for KT (R. McCarthy, personal communication) includes virtually all of the Taraban & McClelland exception words on which the model was tested, but somewhat different (though comparable) lists of regular words.

Table 1 shows the performance of the patients. As always in neuro-psychology, there is considerable variation amongst patients with the same general symptom complex: KT was dramatically poorer at naming exception than regular words, even for high frequency words. For MP, the regularity effect was restricted to lower frequency words. In fact, MP basically shows in accuracy of word naming what normal adult readers show in speed of word naming: an interaction between regularity and frequency effects.

The performance of the model with 20% of hidden units lesioned is also shown in Table 1. The model shows a small effect of regularity for high frequency words and a somewhat larger effect for low frequency words: essentially, a rather good match to MP's performance. The lesioned model represents a less satisfactory simulation of KT's very substantial regularity effects. It might seem an obvious step (towards a closer simulation of KT) to inflict a greater degree of damage on the net, but the model's performance on regular words begins to decline when larger proportions of hidden units are eliminated. Thus far, our lesioning explorations have not reproduced the dramatic pattern of performance shown by KT.

What about the other major feature of surface dyslexic performance noted above, the predominant type of error on exception words? Since the simulation compares the model's computed pattern of activation over the phonological

TABLE 1.
Word naming performance (per cent correct) on high and low
frequency regular and exception words by two surface dyslexic
patients (KT: McCarthy & Warrington, 1986; MP: Bub,
Cancelliere & Kertesz, 1985) and by the neural net model with
20% of its hidden units "lesioned".

	High Frequency		Low Frequency	
	Regular	Exception	Regular	Exception
KT	100	47	89	26
MP	95	93	98	73
Model	93	86	93	78

output units to each pattern differing from the correct one by a single phoneme and reports the best fit, one can assess whether the model's "pronunciation" errors are a good match for the patients' errors. Across a large number of exception words, both MP and KT produced the regularized pronunciation (e.g. PINT named as if it rhymed with "hint" and "mint") on about 85% of error responses. The other 15% of their erroneous responses were pronunciations with some orthographic/phonological resemblance to the target word (e.g. PINT named as "paint"). The lesioned model's errors on the Taraban & McClelland exception words were split almost exactly 50/50 between exact regularizations and these other kinds of pronunciation errors. Thus the network successfully simulates the occurrence of the right kinds of errors in surface dyslexia, though not necessarily the precise proportions of these error types that are observed in specific patients.

These preliminary results suggest a promising start in considering alexia within the neural net approach. There is much work to be done, both to improve the simulation of surface dyslexia and to attempt the simulation of other reading disorders such as deep and phonological dyslexia. Detailed modelling of these other varieties of alexia will require the implementation of other parts of the theory (shown in Figure 2 but not in bold outline): the transcoding procedure from orthography to meaning (see Hinton & Shallice, 1989, for a neural net model of this computation) and thence from meaning to phonology.

Since this paper originally formed part of a symposium on various approaches to the study of alexia, it seems appropriate to conclude with a comment on an aspect of the neural net approach which has implications for our general understanding of cognitive disorders and their rehabilitation. Like many neural net models, this one embodies the principle of distributed representations. As contrasted with local representations, where one meaningful entity (for example, the phonological form of a particular word) is represented by one element or location in the model, here a word is represented by many different units, and many different connections are involved in its processing. Likewise, no given unit or connection in the model can be considered to belong to a particular word: rather that element or connection participates in the representation of and processing of many different words.

The consequences of distributed representations for lesioned performance seem to fit the behaviour of real patients in several important ways. One of these is so-called "graceful degradation" with damage: as the model is incrementally damaged, its performance degrades gradually rather than in an all-or-none fashion. Most neuropsychologists would concur with Allport's (1985) observation that the performance of brain-lesioned patients on cognitive tasks is also not all-or-none: the most typical feature of performance by an aphasic or alexic patient trying to compute the pronunciation of a word is that performance is less efficient and less reliable than normal. The patient is likely to be slow, and may achieve only a partially correct representation, or may indeed fail altogether; but on another occasion, the patient may succeed on that same word. As Allport (1985) emphasises this pattern fits neatly with the idea of distributed representations: since no one element or connection is essential to success on a particular item, partial damage to the network should result in precisely this observed variability.

The second point involves generalization of learning, whether this is initial learning or re-learning in treatment for cognitive impairment. In the neural net, all learning corresponds to changes in the weights on connections. Since any given connection is involved in processing many different words, it is a prediction of this kind of model that there should always be some degree of generalization of learning or re-learning (Hinton, McClelland & Rumelhart, 1986). Training on one particular group of items (say, set A) should have maximum implications for the processing of items in group A, because it is the connections specifically relevant to A items which are being exercised and altered; but since those same connections are also used to some extent by other, similar items (in set B), the effects of training on A items should generalise to some degree to untreated B items. Coltheart & Byng (1989) have shown precisely this pattern of generalization effects in their treatment of a surface dyslexic patient (see also Wilson & Patterson, 1990, for further discussion).

Generalization of treatment effects indicates the relevance of neural net models to rehabilitation only at a very general level. One can, however, hope for a future stage offering more detailed interaction between theory and therapy. As neural net models grow in scope and detail, neuropsychologists may be able to use these models as a source of hypotheses as to which items and which types of training might provide maximum generalization and benefit.

REFERENCES

1. Allport, D.A. Distributed memory, modular subsytems and dysphasia. In *Current Perspectives in Dysphasia* (ed. by Newman, S.K. & Epstein, R.), Churchill Livingstone, Edinburgh, 1985.
2. Backman, J., Bruck, M., Hebert, M. & Seidenberg, M.S. Acquisition and use of spelling-sound information in reading. *Journal of Experimental Child Psychology, 38*, 114–133, 1984.
3. Bub, D., Cancelliere, A., & Kertesz, A. Whole-word and analytic translation of spelling to sound in a non-semantic reader. In *Surface Dyslexia* (ed. by Patterson, K., Marshall, J.C. & Coltheart, M.), Erlbaum, London, 1985.
4. Coltheart, M. Reading, phonological recoding, and deep dyslexia. In *Deep Dyslexia* (ed. by Coltheart, M., Patterson, K. & Marshall, J.C.), Routledge & Kegan Paul, London, 1980.
5. Coltheart, M. Cognitive neuropsychology and the study of reading. In *Attention and Performance XI* (ed. by Posner, M.I. & Marin, O.S.M.), Erlbaum, Hillsdale NJ, 1985.
6. Coltheart, M. & Byng, S. A treatment for surface dyslexia. In *Cognitive Approaches in Neuropsychological Rehabilitation* (ed. by Seron, X. & Deloche, G.), Erlbaum, Hillsdale NJ, 1989.
7. Coltheart, M., Patterson, K. & Marshall, J.C. *Deep Dyslexia*. Routledge & Kegan Paul, London, 1980.
8. Hinton, G.E., McClelland, J.L. & Rumelhart, D.E. Distributed representations. In *Parallel Distributed Processing*. Volume 1 (ed. by Rumelhart, D.E. & McClelland, J.L.), MIT Press, Cambridge Mass, 1986.
9. Hinton, G.E. & Shallice, T. Lesioning a connectionist network: investigations of acquired dyslexia. University of Toronto (Department of Computer Science), technical report CRG-TR-893.
10. Kucera, H. & Francis, W. N. *Computational Analysis of Present-Day American English*. Brown University Press, Providence RI, 1967.
11. McCarthy, R. & Warrington, E.K. Phonological reading: phenomena and paradoxes. *Cortex, 22*, 359–380, 1986.
12. Marshall, J.C. & Newcombe, F. Patterns of paralexia: a psycholinguistic approach. *Journal of Psycholinguistic Research, 2*, 175–199, 1973.
13. Patterson, K., Marshall, J. C. & Coltheart, M. *Surface Dyslexia*. Erlbaum, London, 1985.
14. Patterson, K., Seidenberg, M.S. & McClelland, J.L. Connections and disconnections: acquired dyslexia in a computational model of reading processes. In *Parallel Distributed Processing: Implications for Psychology and Neurobiology* (ed. by Morris, R.G.M.), Oxford University Press, Oxford, 1989.
15. Rumelhart, D.E., Hinton, G.E. & Williams R.J. Learning internal representations by error propagation. In *Parallel Distributed Processing*. Volume 1 (ed. by Rumelhart, D.E. & McClelland, J.L.), MIT Press, Cambridge Mass, 1986.
16. Rumelhart, D.E. & McClelland, J.L. On learning the past tenses of English verbs. In *Parallel Distributed Processing*. Volume 1 (ed. by McLelland, J.L. & Rumelhart, D.E.), MIT Press, Cambridge Mass, 1986.
17. Seidenberg, M.S. & McClelland, J.L. A distributed, developmental model of word recognition and naming. *Psychological Review, 96*, 523–568, 1989.
18. Seidenberg, M.S. Waters, G.S., Barnes, M.A. & Tanenhaus, M.K. When does irregular spelling or pronunciation influence word recognition? *Journal of Verbal Learning and Verbal Behavior, 23*, 383–404, 1984.
19. Shallice, T. *From Neuropsychology to Mental Structure*. Cambridge University Press, Cambridge, 1988.
20. Shallice, T., Warrington, E.K. & McCarthy, R. Reading without semantics. *Quarterly Journal of Experimental Psychology, 35A*, 111–138, 1983.

21. Taraban, R. & McClelland, J.L. Conspiracy effects in word recognition. *Journal of Memory and Language, 26,* 608–631, 1987.
22. Wilson, B. & Patterson, K. Rehabilitation for cognitive impairment: does cognitive psychology apply? *Applied Cognitive Psychology, 4,* 247–260, 1990.

Reading, Writing, and Rehabilitation: A Reckoning

Karalyn Patterson
MRC Applied Psychology Unit, Cambridge, UK

INTRODUCTION

In the late 1980s and early 1990s, a number of books and even a new journal have appeared documenting research in neuropsychological rehabilitation. One possible reaction to this is to revise the gloomy assessment made by Beauvois and Derouesne (1982, p.167): "Rapports entre recherche et reeducation—ce qui n'existe pas". On the other hand, unbridled optimism may be premature. The arrival of *Neuropsychological Rehabilitation* and the recent books does not necessarily reflect significant integration between theory and therapy. An equally plausible hypothesis is that the current major increase in rehabilitation research is occurring in parallel with, but for the most part independently of, cognitive neuropsychology. In other words, even if theoretical and applied cognitive neuropsychology are both thriving, they may as yet be failing fully to communicate. It is worth briefly considering why this might be.

If applied neuropsychologists (i.e. people whose primary concern is the rehabilitation of cognitive deficits) are unenthusiastic about theoretical neuropsychology, this is probably because they do not perceive it as offering any genuine applicability. In a recent debate as to whether cognitive theory is pertinent to treatment, it was suggested on the negative side by Wilson and Patterson (1990, p.248) that "... theories about the nature of the deficit do not relate to questions that have to be asked in treatment or rehabilitation". Cognitive neuropsychology is *about* the nature of various deficits and what they imply for our understanding of cognitive mechanisms. If this is of no use in rehabilitation, then perhaps the field of rehabilitation research *ought* to proceed more or less independently of theoretical neuropsychology. There is, however, an opposing point of view (expressed hesitantly by Howard & Patterson, 1989; rather more forcefully by Mitchum & Berndt, 1990; and on the positive side of their debate by Wilson & Patterson, 1990) suggesting that treatment could in principle be guided by cognitive theory, even if this rarely occurs in practice.

On the other side of the non-communicating artery, why might theoretical neuropsychologists be failing to engage in or attend to rehabilitation research? One reason may be simply the daunting prospect of properly designed and executed cognitive rehabilitation research. The rare examples of this (e.g. Byng, 1988; De Partz, 1986) demonstrate that the enterprise requires everything in a good cognitive neuropsychology study (the background assessments, the deficit analysis, etc.) plus all the added work and complications of the treatment programme itself, the necessarily longitudinal nature of the research, the need to rule out explanations other than the treatment for any obtained effects, etc. It is hard work. A second possible reason is that the potential to learn something of real theoretical significance from the outcome of treatment may not be apparent (or convincing) to many neuropsychologists. Howard and Patterson (1989) argued that treatment studies may offer insights into cognitive architecture that are not (or at least not so easily) obtained from more standard experimental neuropsychology; but this view may not be widely shared.

As the issue of what theory and therapy have to offer one another is clearly a matter of both opinion and degree, it is time to turn to something more concrete and less speculative: a review of some current rehabilitation research. The studies included here were selected by the intersection of three defining features: (1) they involved treatment for acquired disorders of written language processing, either reading or writing; (2) whether or not the choice of treatment technique was genuinely guided by cognitive theory, most of these studies were conducted in a framework and spirit of cognitive neuropsychology; (3) they worked—i.e. the patient's performance improved as a result of the treatment.

ACQUIRED DISORDERS OF READING

Figure 19.1 shows a very simplified (and despite its simplicity, speculative and probably controversial) sketch of the processes involved in recognising, pronouncing and comprehending written words. The implication of such a scheme is firstly that all and only these components

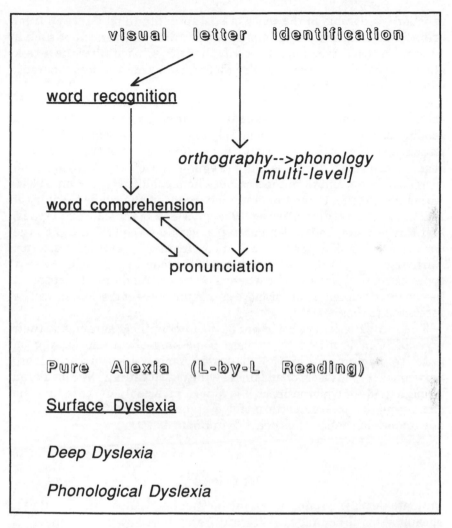

FIG. 19.1. A simplified descriptive scheme for the processes involved in recognising, comprehending and pronouncing a written word, with an indication of the disorders of reading likely to arise from selective impairments to these processes.

(and pathways of communication between them) are necessary to account for the performance of normal adult readers (of English) when they succeed in pronouncing or comprehending a written word, and secondly that each process and/or pathway is—though not independent of the other parts of the system in its normal activity and function—separable in the sense of susceptibility to malfunction from brain injury. These are the implications of a strong version of such a "theory"; a weaker version claims only that this scheme allows us to talk about and compare various reading disorders in a more or less coherent, even if under-specified, fashion.

When cognitive neuropsychological studies of reading began to get established, it appeared that there were four major patterns of acquired reading disorder, differentiable mainly on the basis of sensitivity of the patient's reading performance to various dimensions of the word to be read, such as word length, regularity of spelling-to-sound correspondence, and word concreteness/imageability (Patterson, 1981). Although these four "syndromes" do not map out the whole territory of reading disorders (Ellis & Young, 1988, give labels to at least eight types, and furthermore distinguish sub-types within some of the eight), the earlier four remain perhaps the most frequently studied patterns. Furthermore, as they (or at least three of the four) appear to be the only types of reading impairment where systematic reading rehabilitation has been attempted in one or more cases, the current discussion will be restricted to these patterns.

The four varieties are listed in Fig. 19.1 under the diagram, and their style of print is meant to indicate something about the location of putative impairment in the diagram. Again, this correspondence between observed disorder and underlying deficit can only be considered a rough guide or hypothesis, as it is almost invariably the case that the same symptom or even pattern of symptoms can arise from more than one underlying deficit (Coltheart & Funnell, 1987).

Pure Alexia

Patients displaying pure alexia (also commonly called "alexia without agraphia" in the neurological literature and "letter-by-letter reading" in the neuropsychological literature) are poor at identifying written words, where poor always means slow—with word-naming speed a monotonic function of word length, hence the sobriquet letter-by-letter reading—and often inaccurate as well. By contrast, these patients typically show excellent performance at recognising words spelled aloud to them. This combination of features is compatible with the suggestion by various authors (e.g. Farah & Wallace, 1991; Howard, 1991; Price, 1990) and in Fig. 19.1 (indicated by shadowed print) that pure alexia may be attributable to a deficit in visual letter identification (or perhaps the transmission of information from letter identification to word recognition).

Surface Dyslexia

Three prominent features of reading performance in patients displaying surface dyslexia are:

1. A major advantage in word naming (and sometimes in other tasks, such as lexical decision, as well) for words with a regular or typical spelling-sound correspondence (e.g. MINT) as compared to 'exception' words (like PINT).
2. A high probability that the patient's errors in naming exception words will be to regularise them, that is to assign the more typical phonological correspondences.
3. Many surface dyslexic patients have severe comprehension deficits for both written and spoken words (e.g. Bub, Cancelliere, & Kertesz, 1985). For those who do not, reading comprehension is often determined by phonological rather than orthographic characteristics of the word. This feature has several symptomatic consequences, including frequent errors in comprehending both exception words (BEAR might be defined as an alcoholic drink) and homophones (VAIN might be defined as something like an artery).

These three features suggest, as indicated by underlining in Fig. 19.1, that surface dyslexia usually arises from a deficit somewhere in the set of processes from letters to pronunciation via word recognition and comprehension. Written words must therefore be processed by direct computation of phonology from orthography, a procedure that is sensitive to the spelling-sound regularities of English.

Deep and Phonological Dyslexia

Patients with these two patterns of reading disorder show severe or even total impairments in the ability to assign pronunciation to unfamiliar letter strings (e.g. nonwords such as RINT), and their accuracy in real word naming is unaffected by spelling-sound characteristics of the word. As suggested by use of italic print in Fig. 19.1, the procedure that translates directly from orthography to phonology is disrupted in both phonological and deep dyslexia, and the patients can only deal with letter strings that have meaning.

The differentiation between these two patterns of reading impairment, at least in the scheme of Fig. 19.1, comes from the status of the word recognition/comprehension routine. This appears to be relatively intact in phonological dyslexic patients, hence they can correctly name most real words (although many patients classified as phonological dyslexics do in fact make some errors in word naming, most notably when given function words and/or morphologically complex words). Deep dyslexic patients, on the other hand, typically make many errors in naming real words (including semantic errors such as GUILTY → "judge"), and are especially disadvantaged with abstract words. Some researchers have therefore concluded that, in addition to complete malfunction of the direct computation of phonology from orthography, the computation of meaning from orthography and/or pronunciation from meaning is also partially disrupted in deep dyslexia (see Coltheart, Patterson, & Marshall, 1987, for discussion).

ACQUIRED DISORDERS OF WRITING

Although the skills involved in written language as a receptive task (reading) and as a productive task (writing) differ in undoubted and important ways, they also of course have significant similarities. In particular, it seems probable that the competent writer develops several different procedures or routines for computing an orthographic representation for a spoken word, parallel to those illustrated in Fig. 19.1 for computing a pronunciation for a written word. This view is supported by patterns of break-down observed in writing or spelling tasks, following brain injury in a previously literate adult. As with reading, the most basic distinction in disorders of writing is whether the patient is either forced to rely too heavily, or unable to rely sufficiently, on general knowledge governing the translation between phonology and orthography, independently of specific word recognition and comprehension. The former pattern, borrowing its designation from the domain of reading, is often referred to as surface dysgraphia, or sometimes lexical dysgraphia (Beauvois & Derouesne, 1981) or phonological writing (Hatfield & Patterson, 1983). Loss of the ability to write phonologically is (again, as with reading) typically subdivided into phonological dysgraphia (Shallice, 1981) and deep dysgraphia (Bub & Kertesz, 1982), depending on the degree of intactness of real-word writing and its sensitivity to variables such as word concreteness.

As in most aspects of research on reading and writing, studies of rehabilitation for impairments of writing are less common than those of reading; only three could be found in the literature that fitted the general approach of this review chapter.

STUDIES OF TREATMENT FOR ACQUIRED
DISORDERS OF READING AND WRITING

Pure Alexia

Gonzalez-Rothi and Moss (1989) devised a treatment technique for a pure alexic patient on the basis of three theoretical assumptions or principles. Firstly, these authors hypothesised that, at least for some patients with this reading disorder, the deficit is not one of visual letter identification *per se*, but rather of the ability to match perceived letters to stored word knowledge. Secondly, given demonstrations for several pure alexic patients of above-chance performance on word comprehension tasks with stimulus presentation too brief to allow explicit word identification (e.g. Coslett & Saffran, 1989; Shallice & Saffran, 1986), Gonzalez-Rothi and Moss assumed that some word comprehension can be achieved without the word recognition stage of Fig. 19.1, that is, direct from an incompletely specified letter array to meaning. Finally, they suggested (along with Landis, Regard, & Serrat, 1980) that the explicit letter-by-letter (L-by-L) strategy of such patients may in fact inhibit word comprehension activated directly from the letter-array stage. The treatment devised by Gonzalez-Rothi and Moss was designed to disengage the patient's L-by-L strategy and to encourage his direct (even if partial) word comprehension.

The technique involved brief tachistoscopic presentation of letter strings, followed by one of three types of yes-no judgements. In the first task, the presented item was always a homophonic word (e.g. REIGN); the patient was subsequently given a spoken sentence (e.g. "It will rain today"), and asked to judge whether the written and spoken homophones were the same or different. In task 2, the patient was asked to judge whether a printed word (e.g. HORSE) was an instance of a subsequently named category ("Is it an animal?"). In task 3, the letter string was either a word or a nonword (e.g. BLIKE), and the patient was asked to make a lexical decision.

The exposure duration for each task was initially set to yield a maximum of 75% accuracy. The goal of the therapy was both to improve accuracy and to reduce exposure duration. The initially selected duration for each task was reduced during treatment in 50ms steps if the patient's accuracy improved to 90% on three consecutive sessions. Treatment consisted of 20 sessions (2/day, 10/week for 2 weeks).

Table 19.1 shows the patient's accuracy and exposure duration for the three tasks at session 1 and session 20. Accuracy increased in all three tasks, though only in task 2 was the improvement large and stable enough to permit a reduction of exposure duration.

TABLE 19.1
Results of Treatment by Gonzalez-Rothi and Moss (1989)
for a Pure Alexic Disorder

	Task		
	1	2	3
Accuracy			
Pre-treatment	72%	71%	57%
Session 20	100	90	90
Exposure Duration			
Pre-treatment	450ms	500ms	500ms
Session 20	450	400	500

Examples from the three yes/no judgement tasks:
TASK 1:   Visually presented REIGN: Same word as in spoken sentence
                "It will rain today"?
TASK 2:   Visually presented HORSE: Is it an animal?
TASK 3:   Visually presented BLIKE: Is it a word?

How did Gonzalez-Rothi and Moss evaluate the more general effects of their treatment on the patient's reading ability? Pre-treatment, his word naming had been accurate but very slow; for example, he required two minutes to name a list of 10 words. Post-treatment, they were able to show that his word-naming speed had improved by an average of 21%. This sounds like a significant gain, and is certainly a major step in the right direction. It is however difficult to evaluate therapeutic effectiveness in clinical terms (usefulness to the patient). Moody (1988) makes this point in assessing the improvement of reading speed (measured in syllables/second in oral reading of text) in a pure alexic patient whom she treated with a technique developed by Moyer (1979). At the beginning of treatment, the patient was given a novel text (passage 1) for timed oral reading. He then practised reading this same text aloud at home for 20 minutes each day. At the end of a week, the patient was timed in reading both passage 1 (practised) and passage 2 (novel); this procedure carried on for 15 weeks, with one old and one new text being assessed each week. Although the patient's speed on both measures improved from the beginning to the end of treatment (see Table 19.2), Moody concluded that this improvement was more

TABLE 19.2
Results of Treatment by Moody (1988) for a Pure Alexic Disorder,
using the Moyer Technique of Practised Text Reading

	Speed in syllables/second	
	Novel	Practised
Text 1	0.18	0.25
Text 15	0.52	0.74

statistically than clinically significant (my own very informal measurements suggest that a normal reader manages about 5 syllables/sec on novel text, a far cry from the patient's speed even on practised text).

To the extent that one can generalise from two cases of treatment, it appears that pure alexic patients who are slow (though not particularly inaccurate) in recognising letters and words can, via two quite different forms of treatment, achieve a measurable improvement in speed. It is unclear whether, when Gonzalez-Rothi and Moss (1989) and Moody (1988) stopped treating their patients, the improvements obtained amounted to the improvements obtainable, or whether further treatment might eventually have achieved reading speeds approaching normal.

One final set of observations about more severely alexic patients suggests that the 'trajectory' of improvement following treatment is not always what one might expect. Wilson (1987) treated two alexic patients who were certainly not typical L-by-L readers because their letter recognition skills were too poor to support L-by-L reading. These patients were trained on letter recognition, in one case by re-teaching the sounds of letters (this patient is also discussed in Wilson & Patterson, 1990), in the other case by a combination of visual discrimination and letter sounding. As these two patients improved enough to begin to read some words, both turned out to be (or turned into) surface dyslexic readers. This point will be mentioned again in the discussion.

Surface Dyslexia and Dysgraphia

The treatment of a surface dyslexic patient by Coltheart and Byng (1989) probably represents the most thorough, and also the most explicitly cognitive, rehabilitation study in the area of written language skills. This is because, before deciding on a treatment technique, the authors took several other steps. First, they identified three different stages in a cognitive model at which abnormality of function might give rise to a surface dyslexic pattern of reading. In the terms of Fig. 19.1, these stages are word recognition, word comprehension, and the retrieval of phonological word forms (pronunciation). Coltheart and Byng then carried out tests specifically designed to determine which of these alternative deficits was responsible for this particular patient's surface dyslexia.

A phonological form deficit? No. Although the patient (E.E.) did have problems with retrieving spoken word forms in tasks other than oral reading (e.g. object naming), the authors argued that this could not be the main source of his surface dyslexia, for the following reason: it was rarely the case that E.E. understood a written word but failed to name it correctly; if he misnamed a written word, usually he also misunderstood it.

A comprehension deficit? No. E.E. had adequate comprehension of spoken words, and on the (rather standard) assumption that spoken and written words are merely two different forms of input to a common semantic system, this would seem to rule out a comprehension deficit as the primary source of E.E.'s surface dyslexia.

A written word recognition deficit? Yes. Coltheart and Byng drew this conclusion not just because it was the sole remaining alternative, but also due to E.E.'s frequent errors in comprehension of a particular kind of written word, namely homophones. Suppose that a patient defines the written word TAIL as a story and/or the written word TALE as the thing at the back of an animal (as E.E. was prone to do). Then, according to Coltheart and Byng, it is clear that the patient is comprehending those words by the following stages in Fig. 19.1: letter identification, translation of orthography to phonology, pronunciation, word comprehension. The source of impairment, then, must be in written word recognition (or perhaps access from it to word comprehension).

Coltheart and Byng thus concluded that any attempt to improve E.E.'s reading should be specifically targeted at the stage of visual word recognition, and their chosen technique paired written words with pictures and various other mnemonics that would enable E.E. to associate a particular orthographic form with the correct meaning. Table 19.3 shows the results of two (of several) studies based on this procedure. The first study focused on words such as BOUGH, ROUGH, COUGH, THROUGH, etc; the spelling pattern -OUGH is one of the most inconsistent in the English orthography, and surface dyslexic patients are predictably stumped by it. Twenty four words containing this spelling pattern were selected and, following a test to assess E.E.'s pre-treatment naming of these words, were divided into two sets. In the first treatment phase, E.E. was trained on group-1 words only; Table 19.3 demonstrates that two weeks of this therapy resulted in perfect performance on the treated words and also noticeable improvement on the untreated -OUGH words. In the second phase, group-2 words were treated and, by the end of that phase, E.E. named all 24 -OUGH words correctly. Furthermore, when re-assessed a year later, this perfect performance had been maintained.

The other treatment study summarised in Table 19.3 was not restricted to a particular spelling pattern causing difficulty for E.E. but simply included all of the items that he had previously misnamed from a list of words with frequencies of occurrence between 100 and 200 per

TABLE 19.3
Results of Treatment by Coltheart and Byng (1989)
for a Surface Dyslexic Disorder

Study 1	(24 -OUGH words): Number correct				
	Pre-test	Group 1 words treated		Group 2 words treated	
	Week 1	Week 2	Week 3	Week 4	Week 5
Group 1 words	4/11	7/11	12/12	11/12	12/12
Group 2 words	1/12	3/12	7/12	9/12	12/12

Study 3	(101 mis-named words in frequency range 100-200/million): Proportion correct			
	Pre-treatment		Post-treatment	
	Test 1	Test 2	Test 1	Test 2
Treated words	0.45	0.63	1.00	0.96
Untreated words	0.48	0.52	0.78	0.70

million. The outcome was identical to study 1 in two respects: (a) performance on treated words became virtually error-free; (b) the benefits of treatment generalised to untreated words: performance on these, although not as good as on the treated words, was significantly altered as a result of therapy. The issue of generalisation will be taken up further in the discussion.

The strategy of identifying a patient's specific underlying impairment in the context of a cognitive model and then attempting to direct treatment at that specific processing function is, of course, the hallmark of the cognitive neuropsychological approach to rehabilitation. This approach is often advocated (e.g. Howard & Patterson, 1989; Mitchum & Berndt, 1990), but there are as yet few actual examples of it in the literature. Thus Coltheart and Byng's (1989) study is cognitive neuropsychological rehabilitation at its (existing) best. Even better (though, at least to my knowledge, not presently existing) would be the following strategy: having hypothesised that surface dyslexia can arise from deficits at each of three 'locations', Coltheart and Byng might have specified what treatment technique would be most appropriate to each of the three alternatives. Then, despite their conclusion that E.E.'s deficit was at the level of word recognition, they might have treated him (with three different sets of materials) using each of these techniques. If the one putatively directed at the stage of word recognition produced the most benefit, we would have some convincing support for the author's analysis either of E.E.'s deficit or of the link between it and the treatment (or both). When it is such hard work to evaluate the effects of even one technique, we should scarcely be surprised not to see such treatment-comparison studies. However, the link between deficit and treatment is often rather loose, and almost always intuitive; for example, in what sense can Coltheart and Byng's technique of indicating meaning for written words be said to affect word recognition as opposed to word comprehension? Eventually, therefore, treatment comparisons will be needed to achieve progress beyond the intuitive stage.

Another study of treatment for surface dyslexia, by Scott and Byng (1989), tackled the patient's problem with comprehension of homophones. Like E.E. (Coltheart & Byng), J.B. (Scott & Byng) frequently misunderstood a homophonic word as its mate; for example, she defined the written word VAIN as "veins and arteries", LYNX as "in your clothes ... jewellery as well", and FINED as "we went all over to find her". The treatment devised by Scott and Byng required J.B. to select the correct (homophonic) orthographic form, from one of six alternatives, to complete 136 sentences. For the sentence THE LADIES SERVED CREAM— , the six randomly ordered alternatives consisted of the correct word (TEAS), its homophonic word mate (TEASE), a homophonic nonword (TEEZE) and three orthographically similar word foils (TENS, TEAM, TENSE). Treatment took place over 29 sessions, during which J.B. was given feedback about the correctness of each of her choices. During treatment, J.B.'s accuracy in the completion task climbed steadily from about 70% correct choices to nearly perfect; furthermore, the time required for her to perform the task dropped steadily from a very slow speed of about 20 seconds/sentence at the beginning of therapy to around 3 seconds at the end.

J.B.'s overall performance, before and after the therapy programme, was assessed by a sentence sorting task: each of 270 homophonic words (135 pairs, half assigned to the treated set and half assigned to the control set) was embedded in both an appropriate sentence and an inappropriate sentence (e.g. *The angry child bawled at the top of her voice; The man with no hair is bawled*), and J.B. was requested to sort these 540 sentences into correct and incorrect sets. From pre- to post-therapy, there was a highly significant improvement in her performance on the sentences containing treated words, and also a significant (though numerically smaller) improvement on the untreated items. Although significant generalisation occurred across items, Scott and Byng did not find generalisation from the reading domain to the spelling domain. As a surface dysgraphic as well as a surface dyslexic, J.B. made many errors in writing homophonic words to dictation (of course these were disambiguated for her by a sentence context); following therapy, her error rate on the homophonic writing assessment had not changed significantly, even on those words that had been amongst the set treated for reading comprehension.

Behrmann (1987), in a study paralleling the treatments just described for surface dyslexia, trained a surface dysgraphic patient C.C.M. on the written production of homophonic words like RIGHT - WRITE - RITE. Being surface dysgraphic, C.C.M. had no problem in producing a plausible spelling for the phonological form /rait/ but rather in achieving the particular spelling appropriate to a given lexical/semantic context. Therefore Behrmann used various techniques, including picture matching and sentence completion, to help C.C.M. to link specific homophonic words to their meanings. Behrmann selected 25 pairs of homophones (e.g. BREAK/BRAKE, BY/BUY, etc.) from a set of 69 pairs on which C.C.M. was originally tested; in the pre-treatment testing, C.C.M. had incorrectly spelled either both or at least one of the members of each of these 25 pairs. Training was administered on the homophones as pairs, to focus C.C.M.'s attention on the difference between the precise spelling patterns of BREAK and BRAKE, FOR and FOUR, and so on.

This procedure produced a significant improvement in C.C.M.'s writing of homophonic words, from 49% of the whole set of 138 words (69 pairs) pretreatment to 67% post-therapy. Two other features of the effects of C.C.M.'s therapy warrant comment. Firstly, as well as an improvement in accuracy, Behrmann found a change in the pattern of C.C.M.'s errors after the treatment programme: whereas pre-treatment the patient had produced many phonologically plausible nonword spellings as well as (the largest error category) productions of the opposite member of the homophone pair, post-treatment C.C.M.'s errors were almost exclusively homophonic words rather than nonwords. Secondly, unlike the results discussed above from the treatments for surface dyslexia by Coltheart and Byng (1989) and Scott and Byng (1989), Behrmann did not find significant item generalisation: C.C.M.'s writing performance on the untreated homophones did not improve from pre- to post-therapy. Somewhat puzzlingly however, the patient's writing of 75 words with an irregular correspondence between phonology and orthography (e.g. COMB, DOUBT, etc) was significantly better after than before the homophone therapy. This study therefore yields a mixed picture regarding the issue of generalisation across items, though Behrmann emphasises that homophones appear to require word-specific remediation.

Deep Dyslexia and Dysgraphia

As indicated earlier in the brief summary on various patterns of acquired reading disorder, deep dyslexic patients appear to have lost the ability to translate directly from orthography to phonology. In her treatment programme, De Partz (1986) set out to re-teach this knowledge, in the form of associations between graphemes and phonemes, to the deep dyslexic patient S.P. It would come as no surprise to many researchers concerned with reading acquisition (e.g. Morais,

Cary, Alegria, & Bertelson, 1979) that, in order to accomplish manipulations involving individual phonemes, S.P. had to re-learn certain basic skills often summarised under the term "phonological awareness". Thus, after establishing a standard link word for each written letter of the alphabet (e.g. A → "Allo", B → "Bebe", C → "Carole", etc.), De Partz taught S.P. to segment the initial phoneme from each spoken link word. The sequence from the letter A to the spoken word "Allo" and thence to the single phoneme /a/ should (and did, in S.P.'s case) eventually enable the direct association A → /a/. After S.P. had mastered grapheme-phoneme correspondences for individual letters, De Partz trained him to blend individual phonemes into simple words and nonwords. Finally she tackled the problem that single phonemes sometimes correspond to letter sequences rather than single letters, by use of various mnemonics: for example, S.P. was taught to associate the letter sequence AU with the meaningful word "eau". At the end of these four stages of treatment, requiring nine months of intensive work, S.P.'s word naming had improved significantly on all word classes (see Table 19.4).

It is interesting to note the almost perfect parallel between the rehabilitation devised by De Partz for deep dyslexia in an alphabetic writing system and a rehabilitation programme devised by Monoi and Sasanuma (see Sasanuma, 1980) for acquired disorders in reading the Japanese syllabic/phonetic script, kana. It seems likely that this programme should be even more efficacious for Japanese kana than for the French or English alphabet, because individual characters of written kana correspond to morae of spoken Japanese (roughly speaking, morae are syllables, almost all CV or plain V). Therefore the crucial stage of the therapy programme where the patient must re-learn to segment words into component sounds only requires segmentation at the level of the syllable; and syllables form an easier unit for segmentation than

TABLE 19.4
Results of Treatment by De Partz (1986) for a Deep Dyslexic Disorder

	% correct	
	Pre	Post
Part of Speech (N = 10 each)		
Nouns	50	90
Adjectives	20	80
Verbs (infinitive)	10	100
Verbs (conjugated)	0	40
Adverbs	10	70
Prepositions	0	100
Pronouns	0	80
Nonwords (N = 20)	0	90

phonemes (e.g. Mann, 1986). Furthermore kana, with its highly predictable print-sound relationships, does not suffer from the complications of the French and English writing system, namely the frequent irregularities and context sensitivities of print-sound correspondences.

The force of these complexities can be seen in the fact that, as a result of the treatment described above, S.P. became a surface dyslexic reader; in any writing system with one-to-many mappings between letters and sounds, a *successful* training programme based on one-to-one mappings is virtually guaranteed to produce this outcome. In French (as in English), C is pronounced /k/ if it is followed by the vowel A or O but /s/ if the succeeding vowel is E; thus the function word CELLE has the pronunciation /sel/. Before his treatment, the deep dyslexic patient S.P. was unable to produce any oral reading response to the word CELLE; after therapy in which he learned the sequence C → "Carole" → /k/, the surface dyslexic patient S.P. named the word CELLE as /kel/. Thus De Partz had to extend S.P.'s basic four stages of treatment with instruction about the context-sensitive pronunciations of certain letters, a technique appropriate for surface dyslexia.

In a research field as young as cognitive rehabilitation, attempts at replication are rare; but they are of course important, mainly for the standard scientific goal of establishing a body of reliable phenomena, but also for another reason. As emphasised repeatedly in recent literature on cognitive neuropsychology, the relationship of deficits to symptoms in patients (like that of graphemes to phonemes in English) is not a one-to-one mapping. The ways in which reading can be symptomatically impaired are rather limited (at least when considered in some summarised, coherent form rather than a complete listing of each patient's responses); but the possible underlying impairments giving rise to these symptoms are more numerous and graded. For example, patients A and B may be described as deep dyslexics because both fail in nonword naming and make semantic errors in real-word naming; but their anatomical and functional lesions may well be different. Thus it is by no means guaranteed that the same rehabilitation techniques will be effective for both (Wilson, 1987). If the technique shown to help patient A is applied to patient B, successful replication increases one's confidence in the usefulness of the treatment; but a failure to replicate may also be theoretically informative in highlighting differences in impairment between the superficially similar cases.

This point is well illustrated in an application of the De Partz (1986) rehabilitation programme to a study of a deep dyslexic patient by Nickels (1992). Before treatment, T.C. was unable to name any novel words (nonwords) and, despite showing the imageability effect in word reading characteristic of all deep dyslexic patients, was actually rather more impaired at naming high imageability words than S.P. (see Table 19.5). In therapy, he mastered the first two stages of De Partz's programme successfully; then, despite all efforts on the therapist's part, T.C. failed totally at stage 3, phoneme blending. If a patient can produce the individual phonemes for a simple nonword but cannot blend them into a single spoken syllable, then his nonword naming score will remain zero (as shown post-therapy for T.C. in Table 19.5).

Why then did the treatment lead to a marked increase in T.C.'s naming of high imageability words? The answer is that initial-phoneme cuing helped T.C.'s word naming, and as a result of stages 1 and 2 of his rehabilitation programme, he was able to produce his *own* initial phoneme cues in reading. The same cuing phenomenon (combined with the fact that T.C. was significantly better at producing written than spoken names for objects or pictures) accounts for the beneficial effect of the therapy on his spoken picture naming: given a picture to name aloud, he could often (internally) produce its written name, then use the technique learned in therapy to provide himself with the initial phoneme that could serve as a phonemic cue to oral naming.

In summary, when the therapy technique that had worked well with S.P. (De Partz, 1986) was administered to T.C. (Nickels, 1992), in one sense it failed completely (no improvement in T.C.'s ability to name novel words) due to a difference between the two patients in basic impairments. In another sense, the treatment worked well for T.C. (a significant improvement in word naming); but even the benefit experienced by the two patients requires different accounts. Further discussion of the efficacy of this rehabilitation programme can be found in the chapter by Mitchum and Berndt in this volume.

TABLE 19.5
Results of Treatment by Nickels (1992) for a Deep Dyslexic Disorder

	Proportion Correct		
	Pre [12/88]	Post 1 [4/89]	Post 2 [9/89]
Word Reading			
Hi Imag	0.28	0.70	0.55
Lo Imag	0.00	0.05	0.13
Nonword Reading	0.00	0.00	0.00
Picture Naming			
Spoken	0.12	0.62	0.58
Written	0.65	0.78	0.78

Hatfield (1982; 1983) utilised a rather different approach to ameliorating some of the deficits in three patients with deep dyslexia/dysgraphia. Her technique, which she applied particularly in the writing domain, bears more resemblance to stage 4 of De Partz' programme than to stages 1-3: that is, Hatfield tried to exploit some of the patients' retained knowledge rather than re-teaching impaired procedures. As is typical in deep dyslexia/dysgraphia, Hatfield's patients had a particularly severe deficit in producing function words like prepositions and auxiliary verbs. Recall that in stage 4, De Partz used S.P.'s knowledge of the word EAU as a link to the pronunciation of the letter combination AU. Similarly, Hatfield used her deep dysgraphic patients' retained knowledge of the spelling of certain content words (e.g. INN and BEAN) as a strategy to help them produce the orthographically similar function words IN and BEEN. Function words were selected for treatment on the basis of one or both of two criteria: (1) words that seemed particularly useful to the patients (locative prepositions such as IN and ON, pronouns such as HIM, etc.), and (2) function words such as BEEN with an obvious content-word mate (BEAN) to serve as the link word. Link words were chosen individually for, and in consultation with, each patient.

Following establishment of the link words, therapy sessions consisted of the patients first writing the content link word, and then attempting to produce the corresponding function word (from dictation of a sentence containing the function word). In the third "direct" stage, the patients were not required (though they were always encouraged, if it helped) to engage in explicit use of the link words on the way to writing the target function words. These therapeutic procedures yielded somewhat variable results across the three deep dysgraphic patients; best results, for patient B.B., showed an improvement from 34% to 64% correct for a set of 18 function words. For patients with severe and multi-modality agrammatism, as Hatfield comments (1983, p.166), "Improvement, rather than mastery, would be a more realistic aim". Although this rehabilitation study is perhaps not the most rigorous in terms of some of the features that later research has incorporated (e.g. comparing treated vs. untreated items and/or tasks), it deserves mention here because Hatfield was one of the pioneers of this approach to treatment; a number of subsequent rehabilitation studies acknowledge her influence (e.g. De Partz, 1986). A sophisticated use of the link-word (or "lexical relay") technique can be found in the treatment of an Italian patient with a severe dysgraphia (Carlomagno & Parlato, 1989).

CONCLUDING REMARKS

Given the infancy of cognitive neuropsychological rehabilitation, this review could not hope to be more than an interim reckoning: we will need many more individual studies, followed by attempts to find key recurring features across the individual studies, before we can begin to reckon up the practical benefits of this sort of rehabilitation and the theoretical benefits of this sort of rehabilitation research. Even at this early stage, however, it could be argued that a few general points are emerging from the specific findings. With regard to practical benefits, one can at least point to a number of significant (and in some cases, long-lasting) changes for the better in the treated patients' performance. A number of the effective treatment methods mentioned in this review took place many years after the patient's brain insult, years during which the patient had often received considerable amounts of therapy of one sort or another. Although rigorous comparisons of different therapy techniques are virtually non-existent, the success of treatment inspired by cognitive analysis in the absence of significant change consequent upon other techniques at least suggests that cognitive neuropsychological rehabilitation may be on to something.

With regard to theoretical implications, I would like to conclude with three points of a somewhat more speculative nature.

1. Table 19.6 lists instances, from the studies reviewed above, of both positive and negative answers to two questions about generalisation of treatment effects: Namely, is there generalisation across items (from treated to untreated words) and is there generalisation across tasks (from reading to writing or vice versa)? Whether one observes these two types of generalisation is of some consequence. This is of course true in a practical sense, because the therapist always hopes that the benefit of treatment will extend beyond the necessarily limited set of items practised in therapy (although, as was pointed out in discussion at the meeting of the book, such generalised benefit is not a pre-requisite for considering the treatment a success: if the therapist selects to-be-treated items that are of particular utility to the patient, improved performance restricted to those items may be well worth achieving). It is also true in a theoretical sense. Very different predictions about generalisation across words are made by theories that assume that individual words have discrete, local representations in the brain and by theories which contrastingly assume that words are represented by interconnected micro-features shared by many different words (for further discussion of this point, see Coltheart & Byng, 1989; Hinton, McClelland & Rumelhart, 1986; Patterson, 1990; Wilson & Patterson,

TABLE 19.6
Generalisation of Treatment Effects

---

1. *From treated to untreated items (words): relevant to issue of localist vs.*
   distributed representations
   YES   Coltheart & Byng, 1989
            Scott & Byng, 1989
   NO   Behrmann, 1987

2. *From treated to untreated task (reading to writing or vice versa): relevant to*
   issue of shared vs. separate procedures for reading/writing
   YES   Carlomagno & Parlato (1989)
   NO   Scott & Byng (1989)

1990). Likewise, predictions about generalisation between reading and writing will depend on whether one's theory assumes, for example, that the orthographic representations underlying word recognition in reading and word production in writing are different or the same. Table 19.6 is not meant to offer a conclusion about either of these generalisation issues; indeed it could not do, given the small number of studies, not to mention differences amongst them in both procedure and outcome. Table 19.6 is included merely to highlight one way in which rehabilitation studies can make a unique contribution to theoretical issues.

2. Table 19.7 lists my summary of various issues or controversies that have recently characterised research on reading, both normal and impaired. There has been no attempt to make this list exhaustive, nor do I claim that it presents a clear or balanced view of this research field. The aim of Table 19.7 is merely to convey some of the detailed complexities exercising the minds of reading researchers. Compare this with Table 19.8, which lists my summary of the main types of treatment that have been applied to disorders of reading. There is, of course, an element of comparing chalk and cheese here; but I suggest that some of the lack of integration between theory and therapy (to which I drew attention in the introduction of this chapter) may derive from the startling difference in the questions addressed by typical theoretical and therapeutic research. If a theorist is doing experiments to inquire about inter-letter redundancies and a therapist is doing experiments where patients practise judging that a horse is an animal, perhaps it is not surprising if the common ground between them tends to appear meagre (Wilson & Patterson, 1990).

By the way, this contrast is not necessarily meant to favour the theoreticians. The treatment techniques in Table 19.8 may tend to look rather simplistic; but it is quite possible that Table 19.7 with all its complexity represents theorists' brains reflecting on reading processes

TABLE 19.7

A Sample of Theoretical Controversies Regarding the Nature of Processes and Representations Underlying Reading Skills

---

Early Processing in Reading
How are letters recognised?
Does word recognition require (complete) letter identification?
Does word recognition use word shape?
Does word recognition use inter-letter redundancies?

Lexical Access
Is lexical access:
  active/passive?
  serial/parallel?
Is there a discrete stage best characterised as lexical access?
Do representations correspond to words or morphemes?
Are representations localised or distributed?

Orthography → Phonology
Is there a separate non-lexical routine?
  If so, what size (or sizes) of unit does it operate on?
Is there a separate lexical non-semantic routine?

Orthography → Semantics
Is word comprehension ever/always mediated by phonology?
Are there separate semantic systems for:
  objects vs. words?
  concrete vs. abstract words?
  perceptual vs. conceptual information?

TABLE 19.8

Types of Treatment Utilised in Studies Reviewed in this Chapter

---

Letter → Sound
Wilson (1987)
De Partz (1986)
Nickels (1992)

Word → Meaning
Gonzalez-Rothi & Moss (1989)
Coltheart & Byng (1989)
Scott & Byng (1989)
Behrmann (1987)

Word via Other Word
Hatfield (1982; 1983)
Carlomagno & Parlato (1989)

General Practice
Wilson (1987)
Moody (1988)

---

rather better than it represents readers' brains computing these processes. One of the most important potentials of computational models that learn to perform their computations is that they may reveal complex patterns of performance emerging from simple learning algorithms.

3. Finally, ending on a lighter note, it sometimes seems as if all paths lead to surface dyslexia and dysgraphia. For example, (1) as I commented earlier, patients treated for various other forms of acquired reading disorder sometimes evolve into surface dyslexics (e.g. De Partz, 1986; Wilson, 1987). (2) Patients with severe comprehension disorders typically become surface dyslexic and dysgraphic (e.g. Bub, Cancelliere, & Kertesz, 1985; McCarthy & Warrington, 1986). (3) Perfectly normal children learning to read and write make errors typical of surface dyslexia and dysgraphia. A 6-year-old child of my acquaintance has already learned a lot about writing but displays imperfect grasp of the context sensitivities of English (e.g. the fact that the sound /k/ must be represented by the letter K rather than the letter C in certain contexts); thus, in a letter where he wanted to express affection for someone, he wrote I LICE YOU. This spelling error is perhaps just a more amusing reminder than the other observations mentioned above that, even in a "quasi-regular" (Seidenberg & McClelland, 1989) alphabetic system like English, statistical regularities are powerful and always lurking in the background.

REFERENCES

Beauvois, M. F., & Derouesne, J. (1981). Lexical or orthographic agraphia. *Brain, 104,* 21-49.

Beauvois, M. F., & Derouesne, J. (1982). Recherche en neuropsychologie et reeducation: Quels rapports? In X. Seron & C. Laterre (Eds.), *Reeduquer le Cerveau.* Brussels: Mardaga.

Behrmann, M. (1987). The rites of righting writing: homophone remediation in acquired dysgraphia. *Cognitive Neuropsychology, 4,* 365-384.

Bub, D, Cancelliere, A., & Kertesz, A. (1985). Whole-word and analytic translation of spelling to sound in a non-semantic reader. In K. E. Patterson, J. C. Marshall & M. Coltheart (Eds.), *Surface dyslexia.* London: Lawrence Erlbaum Associates Ltd.

Bub, D., & Kertesz, A. (1982). Deep agraphia. *Brain and Language, 17,* 146-165.

Byng, S. (1988). Sentence processing deficits in aphasia: theory and therapy. *Cognitive Neuropsychology, 5,* 629-676.

Carlomagno, S., & Parlato, V. (1989). Writing rehabilitation in brain-damaged adult patients: a cognitive approach. In X. Seron, & S. Deloche (Eds.), *Cognitive approaches in neuropsychological rehabilitation.* Hillsdale, N.J.: Lawrence Erlbaum Associates Inc.

Coltheart, M., & Byng, S. (1989). A treatment for surface dyslexia. In X. Seron & G. Deloche (Eds.), *Cognitive approaches in neuropsychological rehabilitation*. Hillsdale, N.J.: Lawrence Erlbaum Associates Inc.

Coltheart, M., & Funnell, E. (1987). Reading and writing: One lexicon or two? In D. A. Allport, D. G. MacKay, W. Prinz, & E. Scheerer (Eds.), *Language Perception and Production: Shared Mechanisms in listening, reading and writing*. London: Academic Press.

Coltheart, M., Patterson, K., & Marshall, J. C. (1987). Deep dyslexia since 1980. In M. Coltheart, K. Patterson & J. C. Marshall (Eds.). *Deep dyslexia*, (2nd edition). London: Routledge and Kegan Paul.

Coslett, H. B., & Saffran, E. M. (1989). Evidence for preserved reading in 'pure alexia'. *Brain, 112*, 327-359.

De Partz, M. (1986). Reeducation of a deep dyslexic patient: Rationale of the method and results. *Cognitive Neuropsychology, 3*, 149-177.

Ellis, A. W., & Young, A. W. (1988). *Human cognitive neuropsychology*. London: Lawrence Erlbaum Associates Ltd.

Farah, M. J., & Wallace, M. A. (1991). Pure alexia as a visual impairment: A reconsideration. *Cognitive Neuropsychology, 8*, 313-334.

Gonzalez-Rothi, L. J., & Moss, S. (1989). *Alexia without agraphia: A model driven therapy*. Paper presented at the Academy of Aphasia. Santa Fe, New Mexico, October 1989.

Hatfield, F. M., (1982). Diverses forms de desintegration du langage écrit et implications pour la reeducation. In X. Seron & C. Laterre (Eds.), *Reeduquer le Cerveau*. Brussels: Mardaga.

Hatfield, F. M. (1983). Aspects of acquired dysgraphia and implications for reeducation. In C. Code & D. J. Müller (Eds.), *Aphasia therapy*. London: Edward Arnold.

Hatfield, F. M., & Patterson, K. (1983). Phonological spelling. *Quarterly Journal of Experimental Psychology, 35A*, 451-468.

Hinton, G. E., McClelland, J. L., & Rumelhart, D. E. (1986). Distributed representations. In D. E. Rumelhart & J. L. McClelland (Eds.), *Parallel distributed processing*, Vol 1. Cambridge, Mass: MIT Press.

Howard, D. (1991). Letter-by-letter reading: evidence for parallel processing. In D. Besner & G. W. Humphreys (Eds.), *Basic processes in reading: Visual word recognition*. Hillsdale, N.J.: Lawrence Erlbaum Associates Inc.

Howard, D., & Patterson, K. (1989). Models for therapy. In X. Seron & G. Deloche (Eds.), *Cognitive approaches in neuropsychological rehabilitation*. Hillsdale, N.J.: Lawrence Erlbaum Associates Inc.

Landis, T., Regard, M., & Serrat, A. (1980). Iconic reading in a case of alexia without agraphia caused by a brain tumor: A tachistoscopic study. *Brain & Language, 11*, 45-53.

McCarthy, R., & Warrington, E. K. (1986). Phonological reading: phenomena and paradoxes. *Cortex, 22*, 359-380.

Mann, V. A. (1986). Phonological awareness: The role of reading experience. *Cognition, 24*, 65-92.

Mitchum, C. C., & Berndt, R. S. (1988). Aphasia rehabilitation: an approach to diagnosis and treatment of disorders of language production. In M. G. Eisenberg (Ed.), *Advances in clinical rehabilitation*. New York: Springer.

Moody, S. (1988). The Moyer reading technique re-evaluated. *Cortex, 24*, 473-476.

Morais, J., Cary, L., Alegria, J., & Bertelson, P. (1979). Does awareness of speech as a sequence of phones arise spontaneously? *Cognition, 7,* 323-331.

Moyer, S. B. (1979). Rehabilitation of alexia: A case study. *Cortex, 15,* 139-144.

Nickels, L. (1992). The autocue? Self-generated phonemic cues in the treatment of a disorder of reading and naming. *Cognitive Neuropsychology, 9,* 155-182.

Patterson, K. (1981). Neuropsychological approaches to the study of reading. *British Journal of Psychology, 72,* 151-174.

Patterson, K. (1990). Alexia and neural nets. *Japanese Journal of Neuropsychology, 6,* 90-99.

Price, C. J. (1990). *Simultanagnosia, letter-by-letter reading and attentional deficits in reading.* Unpublished PhD thesis, University of London.

Sasanuma, S. (1980). A therapy program for impairment of the use of the kana-syllabary of Japanese aphasic patients. In M. Taylor Sarno & O. Hook (Eds.), *Aphasia: Assessment and treatment.* Stockholm: Almqvist & Wiksell.

Scott, C., & Byng, S. (1989). Computer assisted remediation of a homophone comprehension disorder in surface dyslexia. *Aphasiology, 3,* 301-320.

Seidenberg, M. S., & McClelland, J. L. (1989). A distributed, developmental model of word recognition and naming. *Psychological Review, 96,* 523-568.

Shallice, T. (1981). Phonological agraphia and the lexical route in writing. *Brain, 104,* 413-429.

Shallice, T., & Saffran, E. (1986). Lexical processing in the absence of explicit word identification: Evidence from a letter-by-letter reader. *Cognitive Neuropsychology, 3,* 429-458.

Wilson, B. A. (1987). *Rehabilitation of memory.* New York: Guilford.

Wilson, B. A., & Patterson, K. (1990). Rehabilitation for cognitive impairment: Does cognitive psychology apply? *Applied Cognitive Psychology, 4,* 247-260.

Chapter 9   Further Language and Communication Processes

Mitchum, C.C., Haendiges, A.N., & Berndt, R.S. (1995). Treatment of thematic mapping in sentence comprehension: implications for normal processing. *Cognitive Neuropsychology, 12*, 503–547.

Chapter 9 covers a very wide range of topics, from syntactic disorders through "nonpropositional speech' to prosody and gesture. It is impossible to find one or two papers that would update our coverage of all of these issues. We have chosen a paper that is concerned with disorders of sentence comprehension and production (cf. Chapter 9, pp. 241–251), and that continues the theme of the application of cognitive neuropsychology to therapy that was introduced by Patterson (1994) in the second companion paper to Chapter 8.

We noted in Chapter 9 the existence of patients whose comprehension of individual words is reasonably good but whose understanding of sentences is flawed. If patients of this sort hear a sentence like "The cat is chasing the dog", they often interpret it correctly because they can understand the individual words and they employ a strategy that treats the first noun phrase (the cat) as the person or thing doing the action and the second noun phrase (the dog) as the person or thing that is on the receiving end of the action. This will produce a correct interpretation of "The cat is chasing the dog", but will lead to an incorrect interpretation of "The dog is being chased by the cat", where the dog will be assumed to be doing the chasing rather than being chased.

Sentences like "The dog is being chased by the cat" are termed "semantically reversible" because the two noun phrases (*the cat* and *the dog*) can be swapped over to produce another plausible sentence. This is unlike, say, "The milk is being drunk by the cat", where the reversed form ("The cat is being drunk by the milk") could only make sense in a carefully constructed story setting. Semantically reversible sentences are widely used in testing for grammatical deficits in sentence comprehension. A patient will typically hear (or read) a reversible sentence and have to point to the picture that depicts the sentence. The correct picture will be accompanied by one that shows the reversed interpretation plus others in which, for example, the same participants are engaged in a different activity (a dog is sleeping next to a cat) or different participants are involved in the same activity (a cat is chasing a mouse). A grammatical deficit is diagnosed when a patient has a tendency to select the reverse role distractor picture while successfully avoiding the others.

Mitchum et al. (1995) note that several suggestions have been made concerning the precise nature of the grammatical disorder in patients with grammatical deficits. Their preferred view (at least for the patient considered in the paper) is that the problem is caused by a "mapping deficit". The basic idea of a mapping deficit is not too difficult to grasp. Sentence–picture matching requires you to look at a set of pictures and determine what is going on in each one. When you look at the picture of a cat chasing a dog, your perceptual and cognitive processes must create a representation of what is happening in that particular picture. This representation will include the fact that there is an action (chasing), that the creature engaged in the action (the "agent") is a cat, and that the creature being chased (the "patient") is a dog. This, note, is a conceptual not a linguistic representation; it is similar to the representation that we would expect an intelligent but nonverbal animal like a chimpanzee to create on viewing the same scene (perhaps in the flesh rather than in a picture). Comparable representations of the goings-on in the other pictures will also be created. You then hear the sentence "The dog is being chased by the cat". Linguistic processes go to work on the sentence and determine that it is a "passive" sentence (the "active" version being "The cat is chasing the dog") in that "dog" is the grammatical subject and "cat" the grammatical object. (Just because you may not be able to articulate these processes does not mean that they are not happening.)

Finally, you must decide which picture depicts the sentence you have just heard and decoded. That is, you must decide which of the four conceptual representations you have derived from the pictures *maps onto* the linguistic representation derived from the sentence. It is this mapping process that Mitchum et al. (1995) believe to be impaired in many patients with grammatical comprehension deficits, including the patient who formed the subject of their investigation. They admit, though, that damage to other linguistic processes such as sentence parsing (dividing a sentence into its grammatical constituents) and assigning grammatical roles like subject and object to elements of the sentence could result in similar problems. If these processes are part of what the brain does when it understands sentences, then there should exist patients in whom those processes are damaged. One challenge for the future is to tease apart the different possible causes of grammatical difficulty and devise suitable tests for distinguishing between them.

Mitchum et al.'s (1995) assessment of their patient, ML, was extremely thorough. It was also accompanied by an attempt at treatment that is a good example of how to determine for an individual case whether or not a therapy is effective. The accumulation of such reports is establishing beyond doubt that therapy can have some efficacy, even for patients with long-standing impairments (Berndt & Mitchum, 1995; Code & Müller, 1995; Riddoch & Humphreys, 1994).

Mitchum et al. (1995) also examined the extent to which their treatment *generalised* to other items and other situations. Therapists obviously like the benefits of their treatments to generalise. Hence Mitchum et al. looked to see whether a treatment of auditory sentence comprehension carried out using one set of sentences generalised to the auditory comprehension of other sentences, to written sentence comprehension, and to sentence production. The results were mixed but informative, serving to demonstrate that the results of therapy studies, as well as being of practical importance, can also be theoretically significant.

References

Berndt, R.S. & Mitchum, C.C. (Eds) (1995). *Cognitive neuropsychological approaches to the treatment of language disorders*. Hove, UK: Lawrence Erlbaum Associates Ltd.

Code, C. & Müller, D. (1995). *The treatment of aphasia: from theory to practice*. London: Whurr.

Riddoch, M.J. & Humphreys, G.W. (Eds.) (1994). *Cognitive neuropsychology and cognitive rehabilitation*. Hove, UK: Lawrence Erlbaum Associates Ltd.

Patterson, K. (1994). Reading, writing and rehabilitation: A reckoning. In M.J. Riddoch & G.W. Humphreys (Eds.), *Cognitive neuropsychology and cognitive rehabilitation*. Hove, UK: Lawrence Erlbaum Associates Ltd.

Treatment of Thematic Mapping in Sentence Comprehension: Implications for Normal Processing

Charlotte C. Mitchum, Anne N. Haendiges, and Rita Sloan Berndt

University of Maryland School of Medicine, Baltimore, USA

The inability of some aphasic patients to interpret semantically reversible sentences has been hypothesised to arise from failure to link the grammatical roles of nouns (e.g. subject, object) to their corresponding thematic roles (e.g. agent, patient). Several previous attempts to improve patients' thematic mapping abilities have demonstrated a range of treatment effects of considerable relevance to the development of cognitive models of sentence processing. This study reports a new treatment approach to thematic mapping impairment; it succeeded in improving auditory sentence comprehension in a chronic aphasic patient with a long-standing comprehension deficit. Generalisation of improvement to auditory comprehension of sentences with untreated verbs, to comprehension of written sentences, and to tests using pictorial and videotaped materials not used in treatment, place constraints on the range of possible interpretations of the functional locus of treatment effects. Two areas that did not show significant improvement following treatment included auditory comprehension of sentences lengthened with modifiers, and spoken production of active and passive sentences that express correct thematic roles. These null effects are also interpreted as providing information relevant to models of sentence processing, including the role of working memory in sentence comprehension and the nature of thematic mapping procedures in comprehension and production.

INTRODUCTION

A large share of recent research on aphasic sentence comprehension has focused on a pattern of impairment in which patients demonstrate good comprehension of single-word meanings, and of sentences that can be

This project was supported by grant number R01-DC00262-10 from the National Institutes of Health. A preliminary version of this paper was presented at the Academy of Aphasia, Toronto, in October, 1992. The authors are grateful to Anastasia Raymer and Michael Weinrich for helpful comments and to Maryne C. Glowacki for assistance in preparation of the manuscript.

understood on the basis of single-word meanings, but fail to demonstrate consistently correct comprehension of sentences that require interpretation of syntactic (morphological and/or configurational) cues (see Berndt, 1991, for a review). Although several recent reports have investigated comprehension of a wide range of sentences, including those with subordinate clauses and various types of complements (e.g. Caplan & Hildebrandt, 1988; Friederici & Frazier, 1992), most attention has been directed at syntactically simple, semantically reversible, declarative sentences that use transitive verbs to encode actions (e.g. Jones, 1984; Schwartz, Saffran, & Marin, 1980).

The study of patients' comprehension of semantically reversible sentences frequently includes testing of active and passive voice counterparts of the same basic sentence (but see Gallaher & Canter, 1982; Jones, 1984). Most often, sentence interpretation is assessed in a task of sentence-to-picture matching in which the patient must select between the correct picture and a distractor picture that shows a reversal of the thematic roles of the sentence nouns. For example, the sentence "the boy is kissing the girl" would be presented with the target depiction and a distractor picture showing a girl kissing a boy. Other probes detect lexical interpretation errors by including a distractor that is incongruent with the sentence's lexical content (e.g., the sentence "the boy is kissing the girl" shown with the target depiction and a distractor showing a boy hugging a girl). A long-standing and consistent finding reveals that aphasic performance is frequently poor for reversible distractor conditions, in contrast to normal or near normal performance with lexical distractors (see Berndt, Mitchum, & Haendiges, in press, for a summary of such data from recent studies).

Early interpretations of patients' impaired understanding of semantically reversible sentences described the failure as an impairment in the operations required to extract syntactic constituents (subject, object) from auditory input (i.e. as an inability to parse the sentence into a hierarchically interpretable structure) (e.g. Berndt & Caramazza, 1980). More recently, the idea that aphasic comprehension impairment can be explained by failure early in the time course of processing events—that is, to parsing operations—has generally given way (but see Zurif & Swinney, 1994) to an account in which patients' impairments are located later in the process, at a point at which sentence constituents are linked to possible thematic roles. Based on a series of experiments, Saffran and Schwartz (1988) have argued that the pattern of "asyntactic" comprehension stems neither from a general failure to recover the grammatical constituents of sentences (see Linebarger, Schwartz, & Saffran, 1983), nor from a specific impairment in carrying out the parsing operations required for sentence analysis (see Schwartz, Linebarger, Saffran, & Pate, 1987). Instead, these authors argue that the failure of patients to interpret sentence meaning arises from an inability to assign the appropriate thematic role(s) of nouns (e.g. agent, patient) to their grammatical roles (e.g. subject, object). The view that asyntactic sentence comprehension arises from difficulty in linking grammatical and thematic roles is widely known as the "mapping deficit hypothesis" (see Saffran & Schwartz, 1988, for a summary).

Attempts to locate patients' deficits more precisely within the processes involved in "mapping" between grammatical and thematic roles have been undermined by the lack of any widely accepted model describing what the assignment of thematic roles entails. Within theoretical linguistics, there is little consensus regarding the proper formal characterisation of thematic roles and how they are represented (see, for example, selections in Wilkins, 1988). Added to a vague notion of formal representation is an extreme paucity of information (e.g. from psycholinguistics) about the processing requirements that serve to transcode syntactic constituents into interpretable semantic functions (see, for example, papers in Carlson & Tanenhaus, 1989). Nevertheless, there seems to be some consensus that the semantic representation of the verb contains specific information (an argument structure, a subcategorisation frame, and/or a "thematic grid") that constrains the selection of mapping relations that can obtain for a particular predicate and its noun arguments (although a detailed description of verbs along these lines has yet to be developed). In addition to some type of critical information encoded in the verb, researchers interested in processing (rather than in formal representation) have postulated a set of procedures by which verb information is used in the assignment of thematic roles to nouns (see Saffran & Schwartz, 1988).

Despite the lack of a coherent theory of how sentence surface structures are mapped to thematic roles, apparent failure of mapping between constituent and thematic roles has been the target of numerous treatment studies. Moreover, findings from treatment studies have expanded the database upon which a theoretical model of thematic mapping can be built. In one of the earliest studies, Jones (1986) carried out a series of intervention tasks with a non-fluent patient (BB) who showed very circumscribed problems in sentence processing. BB demonstrated clear appreciation of how sentences should be parsed into phrasal constituents (NP, VP), and he seemed to have retained considerable knowledge of the meaning of nouns and verbs. However, in tasks requiring sentence production and comprehension, BB consistently failed to demonstrate an appreciation of how surface phrase order related to underlying sentence meaning. In most production tasks, there was a notable absence of lexical main verbs. Stages of an intervention programme designed to improve BB's sentence processing focused on the identification of sentence constituent phrases, with the verb phrase taking on a role of primary importance. Following identification of the verb, words filling the roles of agent, theme, and location were identified using instructive queries ("who," "what," and "where" questioning). Initial stages of treatment used exclusively written materials and were focused on enhancing comprehension. When improvement was noted in verb retrieval and sentence *production* as a result of the early stage of comprehension treatment, additional treatment was carried out that practised spoken sentence production. Indications of generalisation to production from the initial comprehension treatment suggested that the mapping mechanism might serve both production and comprehension. Although Jones further noted generalisation of treatment effects to interpretation and use of prepositional phrases, the use of locative phrases in some stages of treatment make this finding difficult to interpret.

Whereas Jones' finding of comprehension-to-production generalisation was not anticipated, Byng (1988) set out to measure the effects on spoken production of treatment that was directed at written sentence comprehension. One subject of Byng's study, BRB, was a chronic, non-fluent aphasic patient with poor interpretation of semantically reversible sentences. The intervention was designed primarily to measure generalisation from treatment focused exclusively on mapping NPs around a *prepositional phrase* in reversible locative sentences to mapping NPs around a *lexical verb phrase*. Post treatment analyses of BRB's sentence processing revealed improvement of spoken sentence production, which was not treated, and significantly better auditory comprehension of sentences with verbs (although only written locative sentences were used in treatment).

The results of the two treatment studies reported by Jones (1986) and Byng (1988) have been interpreted as indicating that the functional mechanism that supports thematic mapping is (1) central to production and comprehension of sentences and (2) relevant for at least two types of predicates: lexical verbs and prepositions. However, other studies of patients' responses to treatment designed to improve thematic mapping provide results that suggest a somewhat more complicated picture. A second patient (JG) reported by Byng (1988) did not improve following the treatment designed for BRB. A new series of treatment tasks developed for JG improved his comprehension and production of reversible sentences, but had no effect on his comprehension of sentences constructed with locative prepositions. Several subsequent attempts to replicate JG's sentence comprehension therapy program with other patients have resulted in a variety of outcomes. Such inconsistent response to the same treatment among patients with apparently similar impairments at the start of treatment has been interpreted as an indication that the impairments were, in fact, fundamentally different. However, it was not until the completion of intervention that critical discrepancies in performance were revealed (see Byng, Nickels, & Black, 1994; Nickels, Byng, & Black, 1991).

A number of patients with poor comprehension of reversible sentences have undergone treatment, designed by Schwartz et al. (1994), which is modelled closely after the Jones study (described earlier). These authors also reported substantial variability in the outcome of the intervention, with the consistent finding that patients with poor appreciation of the meaning of the WH terms that are used as the basis of the treatment queries failed to make significant gains in the treatment. Saffran and co-workers further reported that, among the patients who demonstrated improved sentence comprehension following treatment, there was most often discernible improvement in sentence production.

From the review presented here, it would seem that the findings from continued attempts to treat a specific impairment of sentence processing have served mainly to underscore the complexity of the problem. Each patient who has undergone a controlled intervention directed at sentence comprehension has responded in a unique manner. These variations in treatment effects indicate that "thematic mapping" should not be viewed as a unitary entity that either is, or is not, affected in an individual patient. Rather, thematic mapping seems to involve a number of poorly understood operations and representations that are needed for the linking of surface structures to meaning. Variations in response to intervention may be due to important differences among patients in the functional impairment that underlies the comprehension deficit.

Despite the lack of a coherent set of results among intervention studies, however, the finding of improvement in sentence *production* following treatment directed at *comprehension* suggests that the functional mechanism that improves from such treatment may involve very general principles that can be used both in understanding and producing sentences. The potential theoretical importance of this finding to the development of models of sentence processing motivates further scrutiny of previous studies and continued exploration. It is not clear, for example, that previous studies have prevented practice of spoken production along with the comprehension training, since treatment exercises seemed to have included some verbal practice (e.g. oral reading of written sentences). It is also not clear precisely how patients' spoken sentences improved following treatment, especially in terms of their ability to express thematic roles in various surface structures.

The study reported here describes an attempt to improve the comprehension of reversible sentences by a patient (ML) for whom this task had been a chronic problem. Attempts were made to control aspects of intervention in such a manner that generalisation of the treatment effects to untreated functions could be measured. Since particular emphasis was placed on the assessment of generalisation from comprehension to production, the treatment was strictly limited to auditory comprehension. Further controls included an assessment of generalisation from a set of treated to untreated stimuli in an effort to address issues regarding the influence of specific verbs. Manipulations of the stimuli and variation in elicitation procedures were integrated into the overall design to provide a means of assessing whether or not results were dependent on factors specific to the treatment materials and procedures. Finally, comprehension of written sentences was evaluated before and after treatment to probe the possibility that modality-independent mechanisms could respond to treatment of thematic mapping.

The treatment designed for ML (described in detail later) was somewhat different from the treatments described earlier, as his comprehension of the WH-words used in previous mapping treatments was poor. Instead, the approach used positive and negative feedback to help ML develop a basis for interpreting semantically reversible active and passive sentences. This approach to intervention was based upon a general theoretical view that successful learning requires the establishment and maintenance of a correct hypothesis about sentence meaning, along with rejection of incorrect hypotheses. The technique essentially involved providing the patient with a spoken sentence (with the availability of unlimited repetitions), along with one or two candidate interpretations of that sentence. No explicit information was given about which elements of the spoken sentences provided the necessary cues for interpretation, and no written words were used in training. One question of interest was whether ML could, over time, learn which surface structure cues were relevant, and in what ways they were relevant. The design of the study also allowed assessment of whether the information acquired in this way was specific to the training task and the modality of input.

CASE HISTORY AND PRELIMINARY INVESTIGATIONS

ML is a right-handed male who suffered a massive left fronto-parietal CVA in 1983 at the age of 47. In addition to chronic aphasia, ML continues to demonstrate (very) mild dysarthria and residual right hemiparesis, more pronounced in the upper than in the lower extremity. Based on his premorbid education and work history (as an attorney), it is assumed that ML's language skills were well within normal limits prior to the onset of aphasia.

ML's initial speech/language treatments focused on impairment of both spoken and written language production and comprehension. According to progress reports, functional performance at the single-word level was emphasised, and steady progress was obtained in basic reading and writing, as well as in single-word production and comprehension. At about 4½ years post onset, ML's language functions reportedly stabilised, and he was discharged from treatment. Upon discharge, the characteristics of his aphasia were consistent with a clinical classification of Wernicke's aphasia—speech was fluent, paragrammatic and relatively "empty"; auditory comprehension was impaired.

Since an initial research evaluation in 1987, ML has been the subject of several cognitive neuropsychological investigations. An extensive evaluation of ML's ability to read aloud revealed a pattern of performance on the continuum of deep/phonological alexia: imageable words were read significantly better than non-imageable words; nouns were read better than verbs, which were read better than function words. Nouns and verbs were read with greater accuracy when presented in the uninflected (root) form than when presented with a suffix or derivational ending. Reading aloud of nonsense words was virtually impossible, and no advantage was observed in reading of pseudohomophones versus control nonword strings. Most errors of oral word reading were semantically or visually related to the target.

Several additional research investigations have been directed at ML's sentence production (Mitchum, 1992; Mitchum & Berndt, 1988, 1994). The results of extensive diagnostic testing indicated a relatively circumscribed impairment of language production. Despite fluent, well-articulated speech, ML was unable to construct a meaningful sentence. Systematic evaluation revealed that his impaired production was the functional consequence of at least three distinct, but possibly related impairments: (1) poor verb retrieval in production of both single words and sentences; (2) limited and often incorrect use of verb-related grammatical morphemes (auxiliary verbs and inflections); and (3) incorrect realisation of the logical relations between the verb and the nouns in a sentence.

ML's difficulty producing a spoken, well-formed, and meaningful sentence was addressed in treatments carried out prior to the initiation of the study described here. The first two of the three functional impairments were targeted separately for intervention (Mitchum & Berndt, 1988). Based on the hypothesis that poor main verb retrieval contributed to his difficulty in producing sentences, an initial treatment attempted to improve retrieval of main verbs. Despite successful facilitation of ML's ability to produce a set of trained main verbs in a single-word action naming paradigm, there was no effect on ML's ability to produce the same verbs embedded successfully in an S + V + O sentence. This result was interpreted as an indication that a disturbance other than impaired main verb retrieval posed a fundamental deficit within the sentence construction process.

A second intervention targeted ML's use of verb-related grammatical morphemes. Instruction in the use of the auxiliary verbs and inflections that signal tense was carried out using sequential action pictures. Increased production of trained grammatical elements was observed in a variety of sentence production tasks, including *un*trained S + V + O sentence structures (Mitchum & Berndt, 1994). In addition, it was observed that the therapeutically facilitated use of the grammatical elements around the main verb enhanced the retrieval of a wide range of unpractised main verbs. However, despite clear generalisation to untrained active sentences, there was no effect of treatment observed in sentence structures that were not trained. Most notably, no change was observed in *production* of passive sentences that used the same surface auxiliaries and inflections (albeit for a different purpose) that ML embedded successfully in past tense active sentences. Thus, effects of the treatment that targeted production of verb-relevant grammatical elements were observed, but only under relatively circumscribed sets of elicitation conditions, and only in the trained sentence structure.

Production of Passive Voice Verb Morphology

One of the goals of targeting ML's sentence comprehension disorder was to investigate some of the issues (raised earlier) regarding the relationship between thematic mapping procedures in comprehension and production. Consequently, it was important to demonstrate that ML could consistently produce the morphological elements needed to express a passive voice sentence. Even though ML frequently produced all of the morphological elements of passive voice when speaking spontaneously, our goal of ultimately exploring his ability to express thematic roles in production required a clear demonstration of meaningful control over these morphological elements.

Production of passive structure was gradually shaped by repetition and modelling of a passive sentence that described a picture. Following six sessions of "practice," ML's ability to produce a passive sentence structure (using the passivisation ". . . is being [verb]ed by . . .") was significantly improved from baseline performance (production of 16 passive sentence structures increased from 0.13 to 0.81 correct; $P = 0.001$, McNemar test)[1]. ML's ability to realise phonetically and to sequence the grammatical morphemes that distinguish active from passive voice suggests that a late-

---

[1]Four nonparametric statistical tests were used in this investigation. For evaluation of differences in the number correct when test items could not be matched pairwise (i.e. when comparison is for different tests, or different items within a test), the Fisher's Exact Test (FI) was used for small samples ($N \leqslant 20$) and the Chi-square Test (χ^2) for larger samples. The McNemar Change Test was used to test for significance of the change in the number of correct responses to pairwise matched items "before" and "after" intervention (Siegel & Castellan, 1988). Since cell sizes were small, exact probabilities were computed directly from the permutation statistic for the McNemar Test using Statxact (Mehta & Patel, 1991). For one-sample cases, the Binomial Test was used to determine if the observed proportion correct was significantly different from chance.

stage impairment of automatic sound-sequencing procedures or phonetic encoding did not contribute to his failure to realise thematic roles in production. Such late-stage impairment has been invoked as one possible account of at least some types of "agrammatic" omissions (Schwartz, 1987), and can preclude any meaningful test of patients' ability to express thematic roles in active and passive sentences (for discussion, see Caramazza & Berndt, 1985).

Comprehension of Locative Sentences

As documented later, ML's comprehension of reversible sentences remained poor following the series of interventions directed at sentence production, described earlier. Comprehension was particularly poor for sentences that required interpretation of surface structure cues to meaning, including noun order and verb morphology. To assess his ability to use the cue of noun order around a predicate in assigning meaning, we administered a short version of a locative sentence–picture matching task originally described by Schwartz et al. (1980) and modified for treatment by Byng (1988). The task includes one picture set with spatial distractors probing understanding of preposition *meaning*, and a separate set with reversal distractors probing appreciation of *noun order*. ML performed poorly in both conditions (0.57 correct for each distractor type, $N = 14$).

Since improvement in use of *order* cues can only come about if the meaning of the predicate is clear, it was necessary to teach ML the meanings of the prepositions. A series of exercises targeting 10 prepositions used real objects and pictures with abstract geometric shapes. ML repeatedly named the target preposition, and arranged the objects to represent the target spatial relation in five one-hour sessions. Practice in the production of sentences containing the prepositions was encouraged. Following these procedures, administration of an expanded version of the baseline comprehension task revealed significantly improved interpretation in the spatial distractor condition (from 0.57 of 14 items to 0.88 of 40 items, $FI = 5.40$, $P = 0.02$), but performance in the condition with reversal distractors remained at chance (0.38 correct in 40 trials, $P = 0.15$).

Once interpretation of preposition meaning was established, ML's pattern of performance was similar to that demonstrated by Byng's patient BRB prior to treatment. Accordingly, ML was treated using the protocol described for BRB, which includes practice in both the comprehension and production of reversible locative constructions (Byng, 1988, pp. 644–646; see also Byng, unpublished, for details). Remarkably, after only 3 sessions ML's ability to use noun order to understand reversible locative sentences improved from 0.38 to 0.95 correct in 80 trials. Notwithstanding some insignificant fluctuation, this performance level has been maintained over subsequent maintenance probes. Further, his ability to produce reversible sentences using prepositions improved (from a baseline of 0.43 correct to 0.98 correct in the 80 depictions used in treatment).

Like Byng's patient BRB, ML responded favourably to treatment that used prepositions to demonstrate information about noun order in sentences. Unlike BRB, ML's improved appreciation of noun order in locative sentences had no impact on his comprehension of sentences with lexical verbs. Performance on a set of 24 reversible active and passive voice sentences (described more fully later) remained at chance following improved comprehension of locative sentences. The different outcomes for the two patients presumably reflect differences in the nature of their comprehension impairment. If failure to appreciate the importance of noun *order* in interpreting reversible sentences were the patient's sole problem (as may have been the case with BRB), sentences with verbs as predicates would be expected to improve as a result of treatment with locative sentences. If additional problems involving interpretation of grammatical morphemes were also present (as may have been the case for ML), generalisation to sentences with verbs from locative treatment would not be expected.

At the initiation of the treatment reported here, the status of ML's sentence processing could be described as follows: Despite significant improvement in sentence production, particularly in the realisation of verb phrase morphology and lexical main verbs, and despite a new ability to understand semantically reversible locative sentences, ML continued to have difficulty interpreting declarative sentences with transitive verbs when two nouns were available that could reasonably fill the role of agent of the action. The study described next was undertaken to address this remaining impairment, and to evaluate the impact of any improvements that could be produced on other aspects of sentence processing.

BASELINE ASSESSMENT

Sentence Comprehension

Materials and Methods

Three sentence comprehension tasks were constructed to assess ML's ability to interpret sentences describing simple action scenes in a variety of different conditions. Two of the sentence comprehension tests were administered first in an auditory presentation and later (in another session) with written presentation. All verbs used in sentence tasks were transitive action verbs that could be depicted clearly.

Sentence–picture Matching: Short and Long Sentences. Twelve semantically reversible (e.g. "the boy is kissing the girl") and 12 non-reversible (e.g. "the boy is kicking the ball") sentences were constructed using a variety of transitive action verbs ($N = 19$, mean cumulative frequency $= 141$; SD $= 127$). Professional-quality black-and-white line drawings were constructed to represent each sentence. Pictures were arranged vertically in pairs such that each target stimulus was paired with a reversed-role distractor for reversible sentences (e.g. a boy kissing a girl vs. a girl kissing a boy), or a lexical distractor for non-reversible sentences (a boy kicking a ball vs. a boy hitting a ball). Each picture pair appeared four times in the test, serving once each as either the target or the distractor, for an active or a passive sentence structure. The sentences were arranged into four blocks so that the target/distractor pairs did not appear more than once in a block. Sentences contrasting active and passive structures, as well as those contrasting semantic reversibility, were interspersed randomly within each block. In auditory trials the sentence was spoken aloud only once as ML viewed the response choices; he then selected one of the two pictures. In written presentation, the printed sentence was shown to ML as he viewed the response choices before selecting one picture. No time limit was imposed in either condition.

Two versions of this task were administered using the same pictures, but with either a short or long variation of a target sentence. The short version of sentences included an unelaborated NVN structure (e.g. "The man is pushing the woman"). A second version of the task retained the same basic sentence content, but elaborated the targets by preceding each major lexical item with a modifier (e.g. "The *friendly* man is *gently* pushing the *stubborn* woman"). The modifying terms were not probed by the picture stimuli and thus served primarily to lengthen the stimulus. The task was given in its entirety using all standard length (unelaborated) targets and later (in subsequent sessions) using the padded (elaborated) targets. Auditory presentation preceded written presentation of the same stimuli by several sessions.

Sentence–video Scene Matching. Thirty-four[2] semantically reversible sentences were constructed using 17 transitive action verbs (mean cumulative verb frequency $= 49.5$; SD $= 84$). Each scene was played out in a 10sec videotaped scenario. Distractor scenes were also created in which the same action was carried out by the same actors, but the role of the actors was reversed. Thirty-four targets (each sentence presented once as an active and once as a passive structure) were presented for forced choice against reversed-role distractors in the following manner. One scene was presented on the right half of a television monitor followed by a 2sec grey blank. A second scene was presented on the left half of the monitor and

---

[2]Three verbs included in our video–sentence matching test (where $N = 20$) were inadvertently included as treatment verbs. These verbs were excluded from results of pre/post assessment of sentence comprehension reported in this study (where $N = 17$).

followed by a 2sec grey blank. The scenes were then presented simultaneously on their respective sides of the screen. A sentence that matched only one of the scenes was spoken aloud by the examiner prior to viewing of the individual scenes, and was repeated during the simultaneous presentation of scenes. The patient was instructed to point (during the simultaneous presentation) to the side of the screen that best depicted the spoken sentence. Auditory presentation was carried out several weeks prior to written presentation.

The scenes were edited for random presentation and integrated into a larger set of stimuli that probed other distractor conditions. Although a total of 84 sentences were included in the task, only the 34 trials in which role reversibility was contrasted are discussed in the present study.

Agent Identification. The reversible sentences from the sentence-picture matching task were used in conjunction with drawings of the sentence nouns, depicted individually. For example, based on the stimulus sentence "the boy is kissing the girl," a picture of a boy was presented along with a separate picture of a girl. The nouns were depicted unengaged in any obvious action (e.g. the boy and girl would be shown standing with their hands at their sides), and there were no extraneous objects in the picture. The same picture pair was used for both the active and passive sentences (12 each). Active and passive sentences were randomised with the constraint that sentences requiring the same stimulus picture were not assessed in the same session. This task was administered only in the auditory modality.

As the sentences were spoken aloud, the pair of noun pictures were shown. Instructions were to point to "the one that is doing the action." Additional instruction was given by example using eight practice trials (semantically reversible and non-reversible noun pairs), in which performance feedback was used to demonstrate the task requirements. Feedback during the practice trials was limited to pointing out errors and repeating the spoken sentence.

Results

ML's performance on the sentence comprehension tests is shown in Table 1. Results for *auditory* sentence–picture matching are consistent with periodic testings obtained for the same type of task over several years (see Mitchum, 1992; Mitchum & Berndt, 1988), i.e. non-reversible sentences were comprehended well, with poor performance on reversible sentences. Active reversible sentences were at or near ceiling, with chance or below-chance performance with passives. This pattern of results was repeated across all variants of the task. The apparent superiority of active voice comprehension may not indicate genuine understanding of this structure,

TABLE 1
Proportion Correct Responses in Pre-intervention Assessment in
Sentence Comprehension

	Auditory	Written
Sentence-picture Matching		
Short (standard)		
Reversible		
Total (24)	0.67	0.50
Active (12)	1.00	0.92
Passive (12)	0.33	0.08
Non-reversible		
Total (24)	1.00	0.96
Active (12)	1.00	0.92
Passive (12)	1.00	1.00
Long (padded)		
Reversible		
Total (24)	0.71	0.54
Active (12)	1.00	0.75
Passive (12)	0.42	0.33
Non-reversible		
Total (24)	1.00	1.00
Active (12)	1.00	1.00
Passive (12)	1.00	1.00
Sentence-video Matching		
Reversible		
Total (34)	0.53	0.82
Active (17)	0.82	1.00
Passive (17)	0.24	0.65
Agent Noun Identification		
Reversible		
Total (24)	0.54	
Active (12)	1.00	DNT
Passive (12)	0.08	

but could signal a strategy of assigning the thematic role of agent to the
first noun in the sentence (see Caplan & Futter, 1986). The task in which
ML was required to identify the agent noun unengaged in specific action
most clearly revealed a pattern of error consistent with this interpretation:
All active sentence agents appeared to be correctly identified whereas
passive sentences were (almost) always misinterpreted. This pattern
suggests a complete inability to discriminate between the two structures
when a full depiction of the action was not available. Consequently, we
interpret ML's performance across all tasks as reflecting potential problems
in understanding both active and passive sentences.

ML's comprehension of *written* sentences was similar to the basic "asyntactic" pattern of sentence comprehension found for the auditory picture-matching tasks. Non-reversible sentences (regardless of length) were comprehended well; reversible sentences were at chance, with active better than passive. However, matching of written reversible sentences to videotaped scenes (0.82) was significantly more accurate than ML's auditory matching of the same sentences and scenes (0.53; FI = 8.32, $P = 0.007$). There is no obvious explanation for ML's good performance in the written video–sentence matching task, which also differed significantly from his performance matching written sentences to pictures (0.50; FI = 10.04, $P = 0.001$). These differences primarily reflect improved performance with passives in written video to a level that is still not significantly different from chance (0.65 in 34 trials; $P = 0.12$). This outcome is most conservatively attributed to chance variation on multiple versions of similar materials.

Sentence Production

Materials and Methods

Two sentence production tasks were designed to assess ML's ability to construct verbally a syntactically well-formed and meaningful sentence. Active and passive voice sentences were included in each task. Seventeen of the transitive action verbs selected for use in the production tasks were also used in the sentence comprehension tasks described earlier.

Picture Description. Sixteen professional-quality line drawings were constructed to depict scenes that could be described using simple noun + verb + noun sentences. Each sentence showed an animate agent clearly engaged in an action scene that could be described with a transitive action verb (mean cumulative verb frequency = 98; SD = 75). Half the target sentences were semantically reversible, and half were non-reversible. Two sentences were elicited from each picture in two blocked conditions: one in which the response was constrained to begin with the agent noun (e.g. *the boy* is kissing the girl), and one constrained to begin with the non-agent noun (e.g. *the girl* is kissed by the boy). The systematic use of constraints, and blocked elictation format for active vs. passive sentences, permitted an assessment of ML's ability to produce these structures under the optimal condition in which the same morphological elements could be used in successive trials.

The sentence production task was administered in separate sessions: once to obtain active and later to obtain passive spoken responses. No cues, other than giving the initial constraining noun phrase, were provided. Each administration was initiated with four practice trials that served to orient the patient to the task. During the practice trials, modelling of sentence targets was provided if necessary, and production of a single sentence response was encouraged.

Video Scene Description.   A subset of items from the sentence–video scene matching task (described earlier) was selected for use in a sentence production paradigm. Fourteen different videotaped action scenes were used to elicit semantically reversible active and passive sentences. All scenes could be described accurately with an NVN sentence using a transitive action verb (mean cumulative verb frequency = 67, SD = 84). Each scene appeared on the full screen of the television monitor for 10sec, at which time it was replaced by a blackened screen that was maintained throughout the production of the response.

The constraint to produce either an active or passive sentence description was again induced by providing ML with the first noun in the sentence prior to the start of the video scene. Thus, presentation of active targets was immediately preceded by instruction to start with the agent noun phrase, whereas passive targets were preceded by instruction to start with the non-agent noun phrase. Unlike picture description, production of active and passive targets was randomly intermixed within a block, with each structure elicited in half of the trials. Active and passive sentences describing the same videotaped scene were not elicited in the same session.

Results

There was no ambiguity in determining the "scorable" response since ML produced a single, fluently articulated response to each stimulus. All responses were evaluated for three aspects of spoken sentence production (overall correctness; production of the target lexical verb; and correct use of the targeted morphological structure of the sentence). Each response was also judged for correct expression of the depicted noun thematic roles. Interjudge agreement (between two of the authors) was calculated for 52 responses at 100%, 96%, and 100% respectively, for each aspect of structure and content described earlier. Agreement regarding the accuracy of thematic role expression was obtained in 100% of 60 responses. As shown in Fig. 1, only about half of the sentences produced by ML were entirely correct—that is, no lexical, morphological, or thematic role errors were detected.

More correct responses were elicited from pictures than from video enactments (FI = 6.33; $P = 0.01$). Production of target lexical verbs was relatively good and comparable in the two elicitation conditions (FI = 2.34, $P = 0.07$). However, production of the target morphosyntactic structure was significantly more accurate in response to pictured (vs. video) stimuli

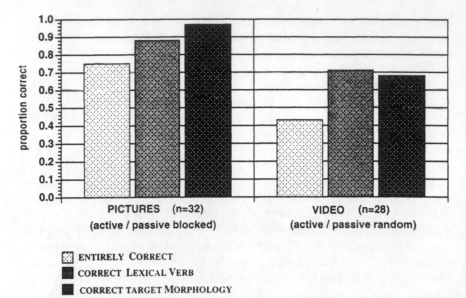

FIG. 1. Results of three analyses of sentence production responses elicited from pictures ($N = 32$) and video scenes ($N = 28$) prior to intervention (active and passive targets combined).

($FI = 9.09$; $P = 0.02$). Differences in performance for the picture and video description tasks (in overall correctness and morphosyntactic accuracy) are attributed to the method of presentation: Active and passive structures were elicited in random order in the video task, and were blocked in the picture task. The repeated (blocked) elicitation of a particular structure type appeared to enhance ML's ability to produce the targeted morphology and, consequently, to produce a correct sentence response.

Quantification of accuracy in thematic role expression in the sentence elicitation tasks was carried out by considering *jointly* ML's active and passive responses to each verb.[3] ML correctly expressed the target thematic roles in both the active and passive condition in only 21% (+3/14 pairs) of video targets, but was significantly more accurate when describing the picture targets (+10/16 pairs; $FI = 4.98$, $P = 0.03$). Among those responses counted as incorrect, six responses were purely errors of

[3]The rationale for the requirement of correct production of *both* active and passive descriptions of each scenario was based on a desire to reduce the probability that sentences would be correct by chance. Since ML was able to produce both sentence structures with relative ease, the probability of correct thematic role expression by chance approached 0.5. Requiring that both active and passive structures convey the appropriate roles for each picture or video enactment reduced this probability to 0.25 and seemed to be a reasonable criterion for an attribution of "correct" thematic role expression.

thematic role expression in well-formed sentences (e.g. "The girl is kicking the boy" → "The girl is kicked by the boy"). Of these, five were incorrect production of passive morphology for active targets; one was production of active morphology for a passive target. Five responses were not interpretable due to ambiguity of the morphological structure (e.g. "The man is stabbing the woman" → "The man is knife the girl"). The remaining responses contained ambiguous or incorrect lexical content (e.g. "The girl is hitting the boy" → "The girl is being shin the girl").

SUMMARY OF BASELINE RESULTS

ML's ability to understand semantically reversible sentences was characterised by difficulty in correctly assigning the thematic role of agent to nouns in the sentence. Difficulty along these lines was noted in all tests of auditory sentence comprehension. Written sentence comprehension was similarly impaired. Use of video scenes for sentence matching resulted in somewhat improved written sentence comprehension, although interpretation of passive sentence structures remained at "chance" level.

Sentence production elicited from ML was fluent and well-articulated, thus providing an unusual opportunity to assess production of the morphosyntactic elements required to construct active and passive voice sentences. Although production of some correctly realised sentence structures was observed, responses included errors such as incorrect main verb selection, morphological aberrations, and incorrect expression of noun thematic roles. Even when elicitation of active and passive voice structures was blocked—thus providing the greatest likelihood of success—ML demonstrated considerable difficulty expressing thematic roles correctly.

Evidence of poor thematic role expression was obtained in both production and comprehension of reversible sentences. Since we had established that ML could produce passive sentence morphology (see Case History), it was apparent that he lacked appreciation of the link between sentence surface structure cues (verb morphology, noun order) and sentence meaning. Based on this interpretation of the production impairment, it seemed reasonable that ML's failure to comprehend sentence meaning might similarly arise from an inability to interpret structural cues to sentence meaning. A treatment was designed with the goal of establishing appreciation of the complex relationship between syntactic, lexical semantic, and thematic aspects of semantically reversible sentences. Treatment was aimed directly toward improvement of reversible sentence comprehension without any practice of sentence production. In fact, practice in production was explicitly avoided in an effort to provide an opportunity to measure unpracticed generalisation from "treated" sentence comprehension to "untreated" sentence production.

INTERVENTION

Materials

Ten transitive verbs that were not used in the baseline assessment (mean cumulative frequency = 250; SD = 322) were used in the treatment materials. Half the verbs were expressed with regular and half with irregular past tense. Line drawings were constructed to depict two actors engaged in the target action. Position of the agent noun in the picture was equated across all conditions in an attempt to obviate the use of positional strategies (Deloche & Seron, 1981). All pictures were easily described by a semantically reversible sentence.

Procedures

Treatment was carried out in two separate (but related) stages, always in the auditory modality. The same pictures were used in each stage. In the first stage, only one picture was shown to ML as a sentence was spoken aloud. ML was instructed to say "yes" if the sentence described the picture and "no" if it did not. Each of the 10 verbs was targeted in 16 different presentations that completely crossed sentence voice, "yes/no" response, identity of the agent (e.g. man/woman), and position of the agent (left/right) in the picture. The resulting 160 trials were arranged in a predetermined, pseudo-random order that avoided presentation of a target verb within four items of any previous presentation of that target. Active and passive sentences were staggered so that no more than five consecutive sentences used the same syntactic structure. All "no" trials were semantic reversals of the target. In stage II, two pictures were shown as the target sentence was spoken aloud: The target picture was shown along with its reversal. ML was instructed to point to the picture that best matched the spoken sentence. Stage II included a total of 80 trials (8 presentations of the 10 verbs).

The same basic therapeutic regimen was used in both stages I and II of the treatment. Thematic role information was conveyed implicitly through feedback intended to highlight the relationship between noun phrase order and verb morphology. Cues and examiner reactions were predetermined (as much as possible) to ensure consistency of feedback within each treatment session. Correct and incorrect responses were met with positive and negative feedback, respectively. As illustrated in Fig. 2, positive feedback was provided by telling ML that his response was correct. The sentence was then repeated by the examiner. To highlight the relationship between sentence surface structure and sentence morphology, the content words depicted in the target were pointed out as the sentence was slowly spoken aloud (e.g. "The boy," point to the boy; "is touching," move from the

Scenario: WOMAN SPLASHING MAN

FEEDBACK TO CORRECT RESPONSES

(Stimulus)	(Target)	(Response)	(Feedback)
(Active Sentences)			
"The woman is splashing the man."	Yes	"Yes"	"That's right... The woman is splashing the man."
"The man is splashing the woman."	No	"No"	"Right, it's the other way... The woman is splashing the man."
(Passive Sentences)			
"The man is splashed by the woman."	Yes	"Yes"	"That's right... The man is splashed by the woman."
"The woman is splashed by the man."	No	"No"	"Right, it's the other way... The man is splashed by the woman."

FEEDBACK TO INCORRECT RESPONSES

(Stimulus)	(Target)	(Response)	(Feedback)
(Active Sentences)			
"The woman is splashing the man."	Yes	"No"	"It's yes.. The woman is splashing the man."
"The man is splashing the woman."	No	"Yes"	"No, it was wrong... The woman is splashing the man."
(Passive Sentences)			
"The man is splashed by the woman."	Yes	"No"	"It's yes... The man is splashed by the woman."
"The woman is splashed by the man."	No	"Yes"	"No, it was wrong... The man is splashed by the woman."

FIG. 2.   Example of treatment materials and feedback procedures used with ML in stage I of intervention to improve sentence comprehension.

boy to the girl at the point where they touch: "the girl"; point to the girl). In negative feedback, ML was told immediately that his response was incorrect and, as the correct sentence was slowly spoken, the depiction was linked to a correct spoken sentence. In cases requiring feedback with a sentence that differed from the original stimulus (e.g. false acceptance in stage I), the verb morphology (i.e. sentence voice) was maintained, and the noun order was changed (see Fig. 2). Feedback in the forced-choice condition (stage II) reinforced a correct response or negated an incorrect response by pointing out the depicted content words in the correct picture as the original target sentence was repeated. Spoken practice of the sentence by ML was inhibited at all times.

Results

Each treatment session consisted of as many of the items as ML could tolerate in one sitting. In the earliest sessions, only a portion of the items could be presented. In subsequent sessions, when ML became more proficient, it was possible to complete the entire "round" of stimuli (and more) within one sitting. As shown in Fig. 3, two full rounds given without feedback (i.e. "treatment baseline") revealed gross misinterpretation of the reversible sentences constructed for treatment, with a pattern suggesting use of a "first noun is agent" strategy. Once treatment was initiated (i.e. once feedback was begun), ML showed immediate improvement in his response choices. Analysis of this rapid improvement indicated that the change in performance within the initial round was attributable to a significant increase in correct rejection of target "no" responses between the early (1–80) vs. later (81–160) trials of Round 1 (proportion of correct responses to target "no" = 0.65 in trials 1–80 vs. 0.86 in trials 81–160; FI = 4.59, P = 0.037). Thus, this initial change in performance is largely the result of a general improvement in correct rejection of a sentence/picture mismatch.

Another factor in ML's immediate response to the initiation of feedback might involve the response strategy that we have hypothesised is responsible for the apparent advantage of active vs. passive sentence interpretation. The feedback could have given ML a clear indication that his tendency to assign agency to the first sentence noun was incorrect, and he was able to substitute a more appropriate interpretation with relative ease. In any event, although he showed occasional signs of reverting to the pre-treatment pattern of active sentences interpreted more accurately than passives (see sessions marked by asterisks on Fig. 3), he never returned to the strikingly disparate performance levels shown at baseline. The fact that both active and passive performance remained consistently above chance, but never sustained ceiling levels, suggests that the feedback procedures induced ML to respond with some care to *both* sentence types.

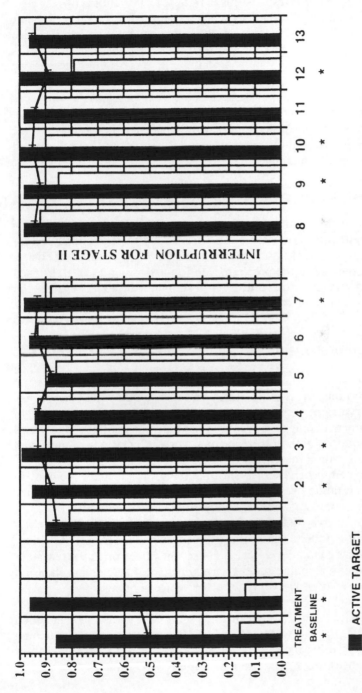

FIG. 3. Proportion correct responses in active and passive targets presented over 13 administrations of the full set of 160 treatment items ($N = 80$ per bar).

ACTIVE TARGET

PASSIVE TARGET

— MEAN OF ACTIVE/PASSIVE

* (difference in active vs. passive correct: * p<.04; chi 2)

After seven full rounds of stage I (yes/no) treatment, the second stage (requiring a forced-choice response) was initiated. The choice of response between two competing alternatives has been argued to be more difficult for some patients than is verifying a single sentence/picture match (Cupples & Inglis, 1993); thus, it was of interest to determine whether ML's improved performance could be maintained in this training condition. Seven rounds of stage II training yielded performance levels that were comparable to those obtained in stage I: Sub-ceiling performance that was consistently better than chance for both active and passive targets. A return to training using the stage I procedures showed maintenance of this pattern, along with qualitative improvement in response time that had continued throughout the treatment rounds.

POST-INTERVENTION ASSESSMENT

Generalisation of the treatment effect was assessed in a variety of conditions. In an attempt to identify the nature of any therapeutically established changes, specific aspects of the stimulus and/or conditions of elicitation were manipulated in the post-intervention assessment. All tasks used to assess performance before and after treatment employed exactly the same materials and procedures described in the pre-intervention assessment.

Sentence Comprehension

Auditory Sentence–picture Matching

Re-administration of the baseline sentence–picture matching task (unelaborated version) permitted assessment of ML's performance in sentence–picture matching of reversible sentences essentially like those used in treatment but with untreated main verbs. Performance improved significantly following intervention ($P = 0.02$, McNemar Test on pre- vs. post-treatment items correct). As shown in Fig. 4, the improvement in sentence interpretation was accompanied by a change in performance pattern: Active sentences were no longer interpreted without error, but performance on active and passive targets were now *both* significantly above chance ($P = 0.04$). Again, this pattern shift (though not at ceiling) suggests that ML's ceiling-level performance on actives prior to treatment was a reflection of a response strategy, rather than of true comprehension of the thematic relations conveyed in active voice sentences.

To explore ML's sensitivity to specific surface structure cues for comprehension, his ability to interpret truncated sentences (a task not included in baseline testing) was assessed. The 24-item sentence–picture matching test was repeated, using the same picture stimuli, to test interpretation of truncated sentences (e.g. "The man is pushed"; "The man is pushing").

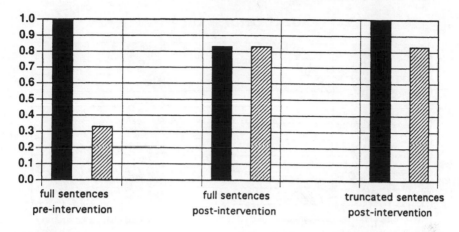

FIG. 4.   Proportion correct responses to active and passive targets in an auditory sentence-picture matching task before and after intervention and in the same task with truncated sentences after intervention ($N = 12$ per bar).

As shown in Fig. 4, ML's post-treatment performance in sentence–picture matching was as good with truncated as with the fully expressed version of reversible sentences. This finding indicates that ML was sensitive to the variation in verb form, rather than simply to the presence or absence of the "by" phrase, to interpret auditory sentences following intervention.

Generalisation of reversible sentence comprehension to depictions *unlike* those used in training was assessed in two conditions. As shown in Fig. 5, re-administration of the agent identification task used in the baseline assessment revealed significant post-treatment improvement over baseline (from 0.54 to 1.00 correct active and passive combined; $P = 0.0005$, McNemar Test), thus providing evidence that what ML learned to use in comprehending reversible sentences did not require explicit depiction of both actors and the action in the picture. Further evidence that ML's improved sentence comprehension was not dependent on specific types of action depictions was indicated by a significant improvement in the post-intervention interpretation of reversible sentences enacted in video scenes (mean proportion correct of combined active and passive increased from 0.53 to 0.94, $N = 34$; $P = 0.0003$, McNemar Test).

Using the same picture-matching stimuli described in the baseline assessment, the longer ("padded") versions of the reversible sentences were tested for auditory interpretation. In striking contrast to good post-treatment performance with the unelaborated, but otherwise identical sentences (shown in Figs. 4 and 5), ML's auditory interpretation of "padded" sentences did not change in response to the treatment (see Fig. 6).

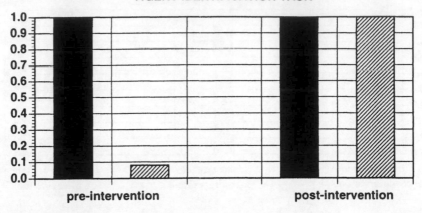

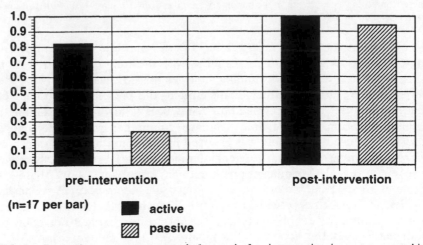

FIG. 5.   Proportion correct responses before and after intervention in sentence matching under two conditions: agent identification (using pictures with unengaged actors) and sentence comprehension (using videotaped enactments).

Written Sentence–picture Matching

Three of the reversible sentence comprehension tasks described earlier were administered as part of the post-treatment assessment measures using written stimuli. Written sentence-to-picture matching of reversible sentences (see Fig. 7) improved from 0.50 correct to 0.96 correct following intervention ($P = 0.001$, McNemar Test). Interpretation of written sentences padded with adjectives and adverbs also improved (from 0.54 to

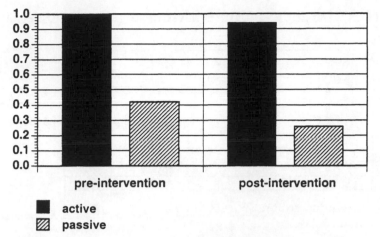

FIG. 6. Proportion correct responses before and after intervention in auditory sentence picture matching with lengthy (padded) sentences ($N = 12$ per bar).

0.92, $P = 0.01$, McNemar Test). Performance for written sentence-to-video scene matching changed from 0.82 correct to 0.91 correct ($N = 34$), but this effect was not significant because of the relatively high level of performance even at baseline ($P = 0.50$, McNemar Test).

As with auditory sentence comprehension, it was possible to assess ML's appreciation of elements of verb morphology in the sentence–picture matching task by modifying the sentences to a truncated form. Again, the truncated version of the task followed the same procedures and used the same materials as the full-sentence version. ML's interpretation of written truncated sentences was quite poor. Although his performance with active sentences was errorless, he correctly matched only one written passive truncated sentence to its correct depiction ($N = 12$ trials). This result suggests that full active and passive written sentences were interpreted on the basis of the "by" phrase.[4] When that cue was not available, as in truncated sentences, comprehension based on the written verb morphology alone was poor.

---

[4] During the post-treatment assessment, ML was asked to read aloud the sentence stimuli used in the standard sentence–picture matching task. Slightly more than half of the sentences were read aloud without error (0.61 correct in 48 trials), with no difference in response to reversible and non-reversible targets. Active and passive targets elicited about the same proportion of correct responses. Errors ($N = 19$) were equally distributed across two types: about half (0.53) of all errors were incorrect reading of the main verb inflection, and more than one-third of responses (0.37) involved a lexical substitution. Inflection errors did not tend to substitute one suffix for all responses (e.g. ML did not always read the inflection as "ing"); rather, ML tended to produce either "ing" or "ed" without particular regard to the target. In contrast to this relatively poor reading of verb inflections, ML's oral reading of the preposition "by" in passive structures was excellent. The term "by" was read correctly in all (24) presentations of passive targets. Although ML falsely included "by" in the reading of three active targets, he expressed awareness of this error at least once.

WRITTEN SENTENCE - PICTURE MATCHING (STANDARD LENGTH)

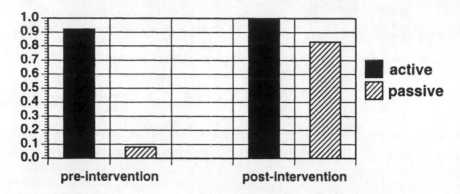

WRITTEN SENTENCE -PICTURE MATCHING (PADDED)

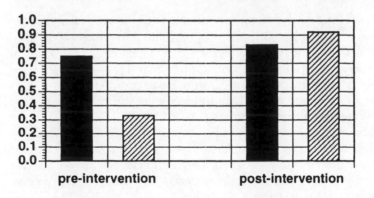

WRITTEN SENTENCE - VIDEO MATCHING

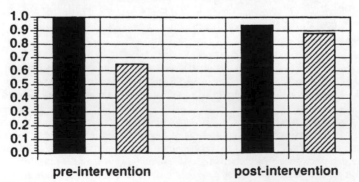

FIG. 7.   Proportion correct responses before and after treatment in three written sentence comprehension tasks: sentence-picture matching using standard and lengthy (padded) sentences ($N = 12$ per bar), and sentence-video scene matching ($N = 17$ per bar).

Sentence Production

The same procedures described for analysis of baseline sentence production performance were used to assess post-treatment performance obtained under two elicitation conditions: picture description and video scene description.[5] As shown in Fig. 8, there was no significant change in the adequacy of ML's responses in either the picture description or the video scene description tasks obtained before and after intervention. The lack of change in sentence production cannot be attributed to a ceiling effect, since there was clearly an adequate margin available to demonstrate improvement. The discrepancy between sentences elicited from pictures and those elicited from video scenes was maintained following intervention. In order to verify that poorer performance in the video condition was a function of the random elicitation of active and passive targets, the picture description task was re-administered with random elicitation of active and passive sentences. As shown in Fig. 9, the pattern of responses obtained in the video and random picture description tasks was quite similar; the picture condition with blocked active/passive elicitation was

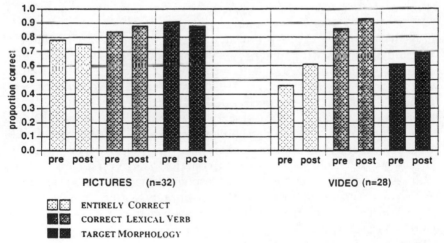

FIG. 8.   Results of three analyses of production responses elicited from pictures ($N = 32$) and video scenes ($N = 28$) before (pre-) and after (post-) intervention.

---

[5]Five verbs used in baseline sentence comprehension tasks were used as treatment stimuli (three in the video condition and two in the picture condition). These items were excluded from baseline/post-test comparisons of comprehension, where we needed to assess generalisation to untrained verbs. The goal in assessment of generalisation to production is somewhat different. In order to provide the strongest challenge to the null hypothesis (that sentence production remained unchanged), pre/post comparisons were based on the full set of elicitations, including responses elicited for a few "treated" verbs.

622 MITCHUM, HAENDIGES, BERNDT

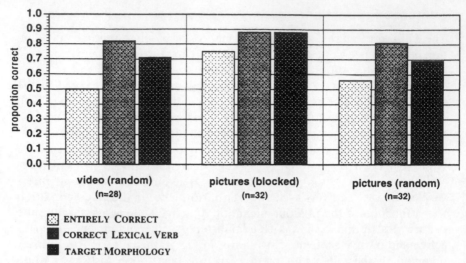

FIG. 9. Comparison of post-intervention sentence production responses elicited from (1) video scenes with randomly ordered active and passive targets; (2) pictures under blocked active vs. passive target conditions; and (3) pictures with randomly ordered active and passive targets.

markedly superior. Clearly, repeated elicitation of a specific surface structure enhanced ML's ability to produce an adequate sentence.

Further analysis of ML's sentence production was required to determine whether or not the comprehension treatment affected his ability to convey thematic roles. Only the sentences obtained under random elicitation conditions were evaluated, since these responses most accurately reflected ML's command of sentence morphology and lexical order. Many of the sizeable proportion of sentences that were not judged to be "entirely correct" in the earlier analysis might contain frank reversal of thematic roles, as was observed at baseline. In response to video scenes, the active and passive version of each target was entirely correct in five paired responses. This result represented no significant change from thematic role expression at baseline ($P = 0.62$, McNemar Test). Following treatment, ML continued to produce a pattern of responses quite similar to those obtained before treatment. When describing videotaped scenes, he produced four well-formed sentences that clearly reversed thematic roles (e.g. "The girl is kicked by the boy" to describe a scene of a girl kicking a boy). These types of errors were observed in response to both active and passive targets. The remaining errors involved incorrect verbs (kick/hit), or production of "mixed" verb morphology ("the girl is kissing by the boy").

ML's performance in the picture description task with random elicitation of active and passive targets was also quite poor (0.75 active; 0.38 passive, entirely correct). Only 4/16 pairs were correct in both the active and passive condition. Errors of mixed morphology ($N = 8$) and/or verb substitutions ($N = 6$) that precluded clear expression of thematic roles accounted for a large portion (86%) of the 14 incorrect responses. Two errors were well-formed reversals of thematic roles, including the response "the bike is riding the girl" elicited for a passive target. Taken together, the results of sentences produced under video and picture elicitation conditions suggest that ML's much improved *comprehension* of thematic roles in active and passive reversible sentences had very little effect on his ability to *produce* thematic roles in the same types of sentences.

Summary of Results

The primary goal of treatment, i.e. to improve auditory comprehension of semantically reversible sentences, was clearly achieved. More importantly, however, the results of post-treatment assessment revealed a clear pattern of generalisation of treatment effects in a variety of tasks that were not practised in treatment. Systematic manipulation of the stimuli and elicitation procedures provided a means of assuring that improved performance did not result from ML's adoption of a response strategy that was effective only for interpreting treatment materials. Since the treatment repeatedly linked the lexical/semantic interpretation of the stimulus to its full and static depiction, it was quite plausible that ML's sentence comprehension ability was dependent upon the presence of a detailed depiction of events. However, post-treatment improvement in a task that depicted only the agent or patient of the sentence, unengaged in any action, indicated that ML was not relying on explicit depiction of the action/actor link to support sentence comprehension. Furthermore, if ML were dependent upon picture interpretation, he should have performed poorly in matching sentences to videotaped scenes; rather, his post-treatment sentence/video matching was excellent.

In addition to these results, which seem to rule out a variety of possible performance artifacts, other generalisation results have more theoretical importance. First, consistent with other studies of treatment of thematic role assignment, ML easily generalised his new skills to sentences using verbs that had not been trained. This result, as discussed later, essentially rules out an interpretation of the results requiring a verb-by-verb acquisition of mapping rules in this case (but see Berndt et al., in press). Second, post-treatment generalisation to interpretation of written reversible sentences is of particular significance, since no written materials were used in treatment. This "spontaneous" cross-modal improvement, in a patient with impaired ability to read inflections and function words, suggests that the locus of improvement might have involved abstract representations or procedures that are not tightly bound to the nature of the input. The question of how ML made the connection between the *spoken* surface structure cues he learned to interpret in treatment, and their *written* correlates, is considered in the General Discussion.

In contrast to these consistent findings of generalisation of treatment results to a variety of new situations *within* the function of comprehension, our results did not show evidence of significant generalisation to sentence production. Using a more rigorous definition of the effect that improved thematic mapping would be expected to have on production than has previously been employed, we found only small changes in ML's ability to express thematic roles in surface structures. In fact, the continued production of frank role reversals and persistence of sentences with mixed morphology was rather striking in the light of nearly perfect performance in various tasks testing sentence comprehension.

There was a marked contrast between ML's ability to comprehend unelaborated auditory sentences and his inability to interpret the same sentences lengthened with three modifier terms. This difference in performance suggests that the longer sentences may have exceeded ML's limited memory capacity. An additional three tasks were administered in an attempt to assess this possibility and to address the source of this auditory/written discrepancy in sentence comprehension.

PROBING THE INTERACTION OF MEMORY AND LENGTH

Recent investigations by Saffran and Martin (1990; see also Martin & Saffran, 1990) indicate that analysis of the repetition performance of patients with impaired short-term memory can reveal how the language capacities that support short-term retention may be compromised selectively. In an attempt to uncover possible interactions between language processing and short-term verbal memory in ML, several manipulations of the sentence comprehension stimuli were constructed. The following tasks were aimed at assessing how ML's auditory comprehension of sentences was at risk of loss from memory as sentence length was extended, and what influence might be exerted from limited phonological retention of sentence information.

Word List Repetition

Repetition of word lists with increasing numbers of concrete, high-requency words (mean frequency = 96.1, Francis & Kuçera, 1982) revealed a pattern of performance that is consistent with that obtained from patients characterised as demonstrating phonologically based STM deficits (cf. Vallar & Shallice, 1990). As shown in Fig. 10, ML's auditory repetition span was less than four words, with poor recall of the terminal

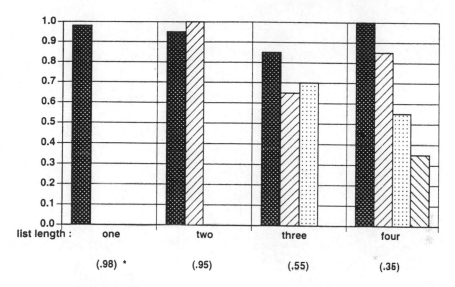

list length :   one   two   three   four

   (.98) *   (.95)   (.55)   (.36)

  * proportion full sets correct (n=10)

FIG. 10.   Proportion correct, immediate serial recall of high-frequency, concrete words presented in one-, two-, three-, and four-word lists.

items in supra-span conditions. This finding indicates an impairment of phonologically based short-term storage, with relatively better reliance on lexical or semantic support (from early list positions) (see Saffran, 1990, for a comprehensive review of the interpretation of word list repetition performance).

Sentence Repetition (Short and Long Sentences)

If phonological retention of auditory information is limited for ML, then it is of interest to determine the extent to which lexical information can support retention of meaningful sentences. In an attempt to reveal the influence of sentence length and grammatical class on ML's performance, we asked him to repeat verbatim the sentence stimuli that were used in the sentence/picture matching assessment tasks. This provided an index of retention of both short and long (padded) NVN active and passive sentences. As shown in Fig. 11, ML was able to repeat the shorter (unelaborated) sentences nearly perfectly, but he had considerable difficulty repeating the lengthier (padded) stimuli.

Examination of repetition performance in the long sentence condition demonstrated that ML's retention of the sentence was not simply abolished for items at the terminal position (as in list repetition), but rather was influenced by the nature of the word to be repeated, as well as by its position in the sentence. The adjective in the *first* noun phrase was accur-

626

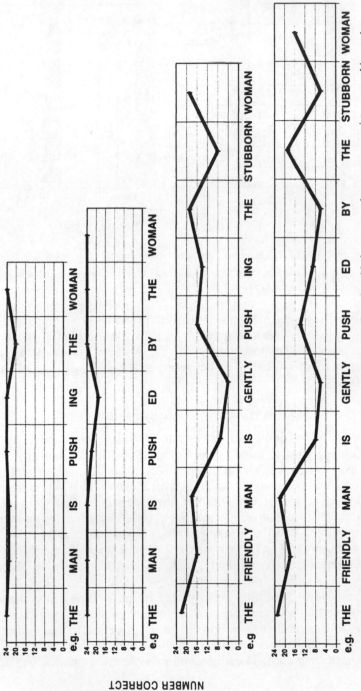

FIG. 11. Number of words repeated at each word position in standard length and padded sentences from sentence-picture matching tasks (*N* = 24/sentence type).

ately reproduced in 0.85 of the total trials (active and passive combined). In contrast, the adjective contained in the *second* noun phrase was correctly reproduced significantly less often (0.35 of 48 trials; FI $= 25.9, P < 0.001$). Errors of commission (semantic substitutions) characterised the majority of incorrect adjective responses (0.92 and 0.87 of errors to the early and late adjectives, respectively). Substitutions were primarily repeated (but not "perseverative") use of a few adjectives ("little," "young," and "new") produced with no apparent relationship to the target adjectives. Noun errors in sentence repetition were primarily semantic substitutions (0.69; e.g. "girl" for "woman"), and some omissions (0.31). By far the most poorly reproduced elements from the longer sentences involved items in the verb phrase (VP): adverb, auxiliary verb, inflections, and (in passives) the preposition "by." Even the main verb was repeated relatively poorly, and significantly less often than sentence nouns (FI $= 4.23, P < 0.05$). Most (0.74) of the adverb errors were omissions, indicating that ML was either unaware of the presence of the adverb or was unable to produce a suitable (e.g. within-class) substitution, having failed to retain the target. Errors on inflections and "by" were also primarily omissions. Only one sentence repeated by ML reversed the order of sentence nouns, indicating that retention of lexical term *order* was not especially vulnerable and there-fore could not account for failed interpretation of the sentences under sentence–picture matching conditions. Rather, to the extent that poor comprehension of these longer sentences can be argued to reflect memory limitations that also undermine repetition, it appears that the particular vulnerability of VP elements, especially of "by" in passive sentences, is responsible for ML's poor comprehension of padded sentences.

Sentence Repetition with Constituent Segmentation

The sentence repetition results suggest that ML can reproduce the sentence quite successfully if it is not beyond his immediate auditory span, but under conditions of supra-span recall he selectively loses from memory the struc-tural cues that distinguish active from passive. An alternative interpretation of the detrimental effect of the padding manipulation is that the addition of modifiers interfered with ML's ability to parse the sentences into con-stituents. A direct test of this possibility was carried out. Measures of verbal and written sentence parsing were obtained using the standard and padded sentence stimuli described in the sentence–picture matching task. Follow-ing presentation of several practice trials, ML was easily induced to carry out verbal segmentation by repeating the sentence (spoken to him with natural, uninterrupted inter-word intervals), to indicate the way that he would "parse" (or segment) the sentence constituents into logical "parts." All standard sentences were given first, followed immediately by the padded sentences. Written sentence parsing was similarly preceded by several practice trials. To obviate the use of visual–spatial cues, which may have been available from the written sentence, the padded and standard sentences were alternated for the visual presentation condition.

The results of verbal and written parsing were exactly comparable to the results obtained in post-treatment assessment of comprehension of the same sentences. Verbal responses to standard sentences were perfectly parsed, without hesitation, into constituents. In contrast, the fully padded spoken sentences caused ML some difficulty, and forced him to request a large number of stimulus repetitions. However, much of the problem demonstrated with the padded sentence condition was related more to ML's poor verbatim repetition (e.g. six adverbs were omitted, eight adjectives were substituted with another adjective) than to his inability to "parse" the sentence using phrasal boundaries. Scoring of the parsing of padded sentences *without* regard to accuracy of the repetition, but *with* respect to the logical division of the repeated segments, revealed correct parsing in 8/10 responses. These findings indicate that ML was able to parse the parts of the sentence that he was able to retain for reproduction; the omission of information he could not retain did not undermine his appreciation of the basic sentence structure. Written parsing was easily and accurately executed without error.

GENERAL DISCUSSION

If the only goal of this study were to demonstrate an effective result of intervention, then clearly the treatment was successful. ML's post-treatment performance suggested that he had indeed learned how to relate the order in which nouns occur around particular verb forms to an interpretation of sentence meaning. As noted earlier, controls built into the treatment, as well as patterns of generalisation of testing formats not used in treatment, suggest that what was learned was abstract enough for ML to apply it to a wide range of sentence comprehension situations. This result is another indication that processing changes can be induced in chronic aphasic patients even many years following onset; as yet no "upper limit" on the time available for such changes has been established (see, for example, Byng, 1988; Jones, 1986; Schwartz et al., 1994).

Does this mean that ML's comprehension of sentences of this type has returned to normal? It is not possible to say that the processes ML employs to perform these tests following intervention are the same as the processes used by normal listeners. Although his response times during treatment and in the post-tests have declined, ML's approach to the performance of these tasks remains considerably slower and more analytic than would be expected of a normal subject. The question of whether he assigns thematic roles to nouns "on-line," with the possibility of easy, "low-cost" role re-assignment (as argued by Carlson & Tanenhaus, 1989), can be addressed only with tasks designed to describe the time course of sentence processing. From the perspective of off-line comprehension, however, ML seems to have regained information about how surface structures should be related to thematic roles.

Although it is useful to consider the functional significance of our results to the patient's language comprehension, the primary questions of interest in evaluating the effect of treatment in studies modelled on cognitive neuro-psychological investigation are not so much concerned with how well the patient did in the treatment as with how the treatment influenced aspects of processing that were not directly practised. Assessment of the extent to which generalisation of treatment effects can be detected in untrained materials, new elicitation conditions, and across input and output modal-ities provides a unique methodology for characterisation of the functional relationship among various processing components (see Mitchum, 1992). That is, improved performance with untreated stimuli, or in untrained modalities, may be indicative of a functional relationship between the treated and untreated processing components. Similarly, the lack of gener-alised effect might indicate a lack of, or weak, functional relationship between components. Thus, in addition to identifying the use of superficial strategies and/or specific limitations in post-treatment processing, it is also possible to use the assessment procedures to address questions of theor-etical interest. In this view, the question of most relevance is how well we can characterise the processing changes that resulted from treatment.

Auditory Comprehension

The treatment involved the repeated association of spoken sentences with pictured interpretations of those sentences. Feedback maintained sentence voice and, if necessary, changed noun order to demonstrate how the target sentence described the picture. From these exercises, it appears that ML successfully extracted the combinations of surface elements that provide structural cues to meaning, and could apply them to verbs that were not trained.

Generalisation to comprehension of sentences containing untrained main verbs has been interpreted as indicating that the source of a patient's mapping deficit prior to treatment was not an impairment of information within the verb representation, but to a set of mapping "procedures" that relate surface structures to thematic roles (Saffran & Schwartz, 1988; Schwartz et al., 1994). That is, if the mapping deficit were caused by an impairment of information that is represented uniquely for each verb, then treatment would need to be carried out with each verb to effect improve-ment. Another possibility can be raised, however. Although treatment verbs were not intended to encode specific semantic properties or argument structures, the requirement of picturability resulted in the inclusion of agentive, action verbs that systematically map the d(eep)-structure subject of the verb onto the thematic role of Agent, (i.e. verbs such as "receive," that map d-structure subject onto the thematic role of "Goal," for example, were not included in this study). ML may have learned a single mapping rule that, although not verb-specific, happened to work for all of the items included here (and in fact would work quite well for many transitive verbs).

It should be noted that this type of account is at variance with most discussions of this issue, in which detailed verb-specific mapping information is viewed as part of a unique lexical representation for verbs. Further, although all of the verbs used in this study could enter into two-argument constructions with direct objects, some verbs (e.g. "pay") allowed other configurations as well. Nonetheless, if it is the case that ML learned a general mapping rule in treatment, it may not be necessary to postulate a separate set of mapping procedures to account for the results. Thus, unlike Schwartz et al. (1994), we do not believe that generalisation of treatment effects to untrained verbs necessarily favours a "procedural" interpretation of the mapping deficit; a general mapping rule might suffice to improve verb-based mapping for many verbs, including those tested in this study.

Schwartz and co-workers (1994) have, in fact, demonstrated some (non-significant) generalised improvement from treatment with agentive verbs to verbs that map subject to the thematic role of Experiencer ("hear," "see," etc.), but even this result can be incorporated into an account that favours improvement based on a general mapping rule. For example, Schlesinger (1992) has argued that nouns that fill the thematic role of Experiencer are assimilated into the category of Agent. Consequently, Experiencers are judged to have more control of the situation and more intention than other candidate nouns in constructions with Experiencer verbs. An even more radical proposal along the same lines has been offered by Dowty (1991), who favours broad prototype categories for only two thematic roles—Proto-Agent and Proto-Patient—that subsume other traditional thematic role categories such as Experiencer, Instrument, Theme, and Goal. Verbs are classified as typically assigning their logical subject to Proto-Agent by examining a cluster of semantic entailments (Dowty, 1991, p. 572) including "volitional involvement in the event or state; sentience (and/or perception); causing an event or change of state . . . ; movement relative to the position of another participant," etc. Under this analysis, Experience is a Proto-Agent (sentience without volition or causation), as is Instrument (causation and movement without volition or sentience). Similarly, a set of entailments can be defined for Proto-Patient that results in the classification of traditional roles such as Theme and (usually) Goal as Proto-Patients. This type of "fuzzy" classification of thematic roles allows a motivated basis for findings of cross-verb treatment generalisation to a wide range of verb types. If patients retain or relearn something about the semantic entailments of Proto-Agents, and how those characteristics are linked to meaning via sentence surface structures, then such knowledge should serve for a very wide range of different types of verbs. This type of analysis may explain the common finding of treatment generalisation across verbs, while at the same time predicting a failure of generalisation to other predicates such as locative prepositions.

The failure of treatment generalisation from mapping around reversible locative prepositions to mapping around verbs, found in this study as well as by others (e.g. patient JG reported by Byng, 1988; Nickels et al., 1991), also provides information about the nature of the information patients learn to use in accomplishing thematic mapping. ML required explicit treatment of preposition meaning, and a separate programme focused on interpretation of order. Although these interventions resulted in consistently correct interpretation of reversible locatives, comprehension of reversible sentences with verbs remained poor, with much better performance on active than passive voice (baseline data for this study). We interpret these results as suggesting that the preposition treatment cued ML to attend to noun order, which was sufficient for sentences with prepositions (assuming intact lexical meaning), but was not sufficient in active and passive voice sentences with verbs (which also requires attention to verb morphology). In fact, the preposition treatment may have inappropriately reinforced reliance on noun order cues, leading to the adoption of a strategy of assigning agent status to the first noun in both active and passive sentences.

The mapping treatment that is the primary focus of this report appears to have succeeded in adding to ML's repertoire of useful structural cues those elements that distinguish active from passive voice—verb inflections and (possibly) the occurrence of a noun phrase vs. a prepositional phrase (with "by") in the verb phrase. Successful integration of the verb inflection with noun order was indicated by ML's good performance with truncated sentences presented aurally, and rules out strategic reliance on the presence or absence of "by" that we have found for another patient (EA) who has completed the mapping treatment (Haendiges, Berndt, & Mitchum, submitted). The important point about ML's use of these cues is that the details of precisely *how* they combine to constrain sentence interpretation were never explicitly pointed out to him; rather, he extracted these details from repeated association of structure and meaning.

Written Sentence Comprehension

ML's demonstration of much-improved comprehension of written sentences following treatment in the auditory modality was not anticipated, since it was not clear how he would make the connection between these surface structure cues in the auditory and visual modalities. As noted in the Case Report, ML's reading of grammatical morphemes was generally poor, with many in-class substitutions; there was also very little evidence that he had retained any information about letter/sound correspondences. Post-testing suggests that verb inflections are particularly poorly realised in his oral reading of sentences, but that the preposition "by" could be read aloud consistently following treatment of auditory comprehension. Although comparable data are not available on oral *sentence* reading prior to treatment, it is possible that his ability to read "by" was a result of repeated exposure to passive sentence structures in treatment. Following treatment, ML frequently produced in-class errors when reading the function words in the sentences that had been used in training, but he did not substitute other prepositions for "by" when reading aloud. It is reasonable to assume that (auditory) comprehension treatment reduced the range of reading options to one possibility for "by" in these sentences, since ML had heard no other prepositions in treatment. In contrast, the treatment materials repeatedly exposed him to two *different* verb inflections and appears to have done little to constrain his choice of inflection when reading aloud. Whatever the source of his ability to read "by" following treatment for auditory comprehension, it appears from his poor performance on *written* truncated sentences that he relied on the presence or absence of that word, in conjunction with noun order, to interpret written sentences. These two cues were apparently sufficient for ML to carry out the assignment of thematic roles in written sentences, even those lengthened with modifiers.

Auditory Comprehension and Memory

ML's improved comprehension of *spoken* sentences was not apparently based only on the presence or absence of the "by" phrase that he used to interpret written sentences. Performance with spoken truncated sentences at a level comparable to full sentences following treatment indicates that auditory comprehension was not based solely on the nature of the post-verbal phrase. Rather, ML apparently succeeded in integrating information about the order of sentence nouns with the morphological form of the verb in his comprehension of spoken standard and truncated sentences. This success was remarkably limited, however, and did not extend to longer sentences of the same type. There are two potential explanations for ML's failure to understand these longer sentences following treatment. The addition of modifiers to the sentences might have interfered with ML's ability to extract the necessary surface structure cues from the sentence input, i.e. to parse the sentence into syntactic constituents. An alternative explanation is that ML's ability to retain information obtained through the auditory modality is reduced, as it is for many aphasic patients (Vallar,

Corno, & Basso, 1992), and that this memory impairment undermines comprehension when some critical length is exceeded.

There is little evidence that the sentence modifiers interfered with ML's ability to parse the input sentences. His repetition of the padded sentence generally retained the NVN structure of the targets, suggesting successful recovery of those constituents. Moreover, when asked explicitly to segment (verbally) the longer sentences into coherent parts, ML largely succeeded in reproducing sentence constituents despite poor retention of the "padding" words (i.e. adjectives and adverbs).

The suggestion that reduced memory capacity contributed to ML's failure to extend his new abilities to longer sentences, though perhaps more compelling, is based on a controversial assertion that short-term memory and auditory comprehension are functionally related. Early enthusiasm for the idea of a necessary compromise of comprehension in patients with short-term memory impairment (e.g. Caramazza, Basili, Koller, & Berndt, 1981; Saffran & Marin, 1975) has given way to widespread appreciation of the complexity of any relationship that might obtain (Caplan & Waters, 1990; Martin, 1990; Saffran, 1990). There is currently considerable consensus among researchers, focused primarily on memory limitations, that traditional repetition span tasks provide a poor indication of the various ways that memory for auditory information can be impaired (see Saffran, 1990, for review). The emphasis from this perspective is on the design of tasks that fractionate the working memory system into different components, only some of which may relate to impaired sentence comprehension (see Martin, 1993, for an example). A very different perspective comes from other researchers, whose concept of the memory requirements of comprehension tasks is more global: A unitary pool of limited processing resources is tapped during sentence processing as an increasing function of sentence complexity (Just & Carpenter, 1992). This "capacity limitation" view of comprehension has recently been applied to explain data from aphasic patients, and is argued to predict a hierarchy of structural difficulty reported in several group studies (Friederici & Frazier, 1992; Miyake, Carpenter, & Just, 1994).

In our view, the hypothesis that specific patterns of sentence comprehension impairment (e.g. failure *only* on complex sentences) result from a general limitation of resources or memory capacity can be supported only if the patient can be shown to be capable of performing the processing required by the task under some conditions (i.e. with maximum resources available). There are many reasons why aphasic patients might succeed with short, simple sentences, and fail with longer, more complex constructions; indeed, most accounts of aphasic sentence comprehension would predict this general pattern. For these reasons, we believe that our finding, that ML failed to comprehend aurally presented lengthy sentences of the same structural type that he could comprehend in a shorter version, is important evidence that memory limitations may interact systematically with sentence comprehension (see also Berndt, Mitchum, & Price, 1991, for a similar argument).

Rather than postulating a very general resource limitation, however, we think it may be possible to specify more directly the type of information that a patient finds most difficult to maintain during sentence comprehension. The tasks added to our post-treatment assessment helped to characterise the nature of ML's difficulty in comprehending lengthy sentences. His sentence repetition, although not definitive as an isolated measure, lends converging evidence that when capacity was exceeded (in padded sentences), he preferentially lost information about the representation of the verb—both the identity of the lexical verb and, more strikingly, information about its morphological structure. Retention of the preposition "by" in passive structures was particularly vulnerable.

It is not clear *why* these elements were especially at risk. Selective loss from memory may represent underlying difficulty in the lexical representation of these elements (verbs and their related grammatical morphemes), necessitating reliance on the phonological memory that the repetition span task indicates was impaired for ML. Alternatively, it may simply reflect the particular vulnerability of elements that happen to fall in middle serial positions in sentences. Regardless of the source of the impairment, it is clear that it emerged only in the longer sentences, and thus appears to reflect some effect of exceeding the patient's limited span of retention. The consequence of this impairment is hypothesised to be a loss from memory of some of the surface structure cues ML had learned to use in mapping from sentence constituents to thematic roles.

Thematic Mapping in Sentence Production

One finding of particular theoretical interest from this study was a relative lack of improvement in ML's ability to express thematic roles in active and passive sentences, despite his improved ability to understand the same kinds of sentences. Several treatment studies have demonstrated improvement of sentence production following treatment that succeeded in establishing changes in sentence comprehension. In the study reported here, there was little indication that ML was able to apply what he had learned about thematic mapping for sentence comprehension to the correct expression of noun thematic roles in sentence production. There are several potential explanations for our failure to find generalisation to production.

Some of these are primarily methodological. For example, in some treatment studies that report improved sentence production from training of sentence comprehension, patients may not have been entirely prevented from practising production. Many of the procedures that have been used to re-train thematic mapping, in fact, require the patient to read active and passive sentences before analysing the relationship between the nouns and verb. Sometimes these sentences are read aloud, either as part of the training protocol, or by choice of the patient (e.g. Jones, 1986; Schwartz et al., 1994). Under these conditions, it is possible that the effects of having practised sentence production (despite the lack of direct focus) may have contributed in some way to improved post-treatment sentence production.

Another factor to be considered is the manner in which changes to sentence production are assessed and described. One way of reporting changes in sentence production following thematic mapping treatment has been to count the number of verb arguments produced in narrative speech before and after intervention. In several cases, the number of verb arguments increased significantly, even though the production of multi-argument sentences was not the aim of treatment (see Byng, 1988; Nickels et al., 1991). However, the extent to which increased production of verb arguments reflects enhanced thematic mapping of sentence nouns can be questioned. First, treatment protocols have necessarily focused on sentences with two noun arguments; not surprisingly, much of the reported post-treatment increase in the number of arguments results in a change from one- to two-argument structures. Although repeated exposure to sentences with two noun arguments might well underlie such improvements, it is difficult to claim that improved *thematic role mapping* is a critical element in such improvement. For example, a change in production might arise from a new awareness of verb transitivity, but such an awareness does not necessarily indicate clear appreciation of the link between structure and thematic roles.

A related point is that correct mapping is more a question of the placement, rather than the *number*, of arguments. Clearly, a patient could produce a sentence that contained numerous noun phrases to fill argument slots, but if nouns are misordered around the verb and sentence meaning is incorrectly expressed, then it is difficult to claim that improved thematic mapping is responsible for improved production. The cases reported to date have not constrained sentence production in ways that allow for examination of whether or not the noun order correctly expresses thematic roles.[6] In this study, we found clear evidence of noun order reversals in post-treatment tasks of constrained spoken picture description.

In addition to these methodological and analytic considerations, there are other potential differences between this study and previous work. Most obvious is the possibility that ML's impairments prior to treatment differed qualitatively from those of other patients. Many sources of evidence

---

[6]Other studies have examined changes in narrative production following treatment of sentence comprehension. Since narrative production tasks place little (or no) constraint on choice of lexical content and sentence structure, it is difficult to analyse reliably the accuracy of thematic role expression in narrative context.

support the idea that comprehension of reversible sentences can break down for a number of quite different reasons (see Berndt et al., in press, for review). Our results with ML do not preclude the possibility that a patient could be found whose comprehension impairment, though superficially similar to ML's, arises from an impairment to some processing component that is shared in comprehension and production. Successful treatment of such a deficit would presumably result in improvement in both functions.

The hypothesis that some abstract thematic mapping mechanism exists that could support both comprehension and production has not been offered only within the context of intervention studies. Caramazza and Miceli (1991) reported a detailed study of a patient with an apparent thematic mapping impairment (difficulty with reversible sentences) and intact morphological processing in both comprehension and production. Although they assume a common mechanism, these authors point out a variety of ways in which mapping for comprehension differs from mapping for production, especially regarding the utility of heuristics to aid performance. A similar set of arguments can be offered to account for ML's persistent problems with sentence production, but these arguments appear to weaken considerably the notion of common mapping procedures.

Our analysis of the source of ML's improved comprehension has stressed his extraction and interpretation of several surface structure cues that distinuish active from passive voice sentences. The mapping "procedures" used for comprehension must take these cues as input, in combination with lexical/semantic information in the predicate, and yield an output that is largely conceptual in nature (i.e. sentence "meaning"). Comparable "procedures" for production, though they would involve the same lexical meanings, surface structure cues, and concepts, shift the burden of serialisation onto the speaker. That is, the starting point is the concept, and the speaker is responsible for placing the nouns and surface elements into the correct linear string. Although ML clearly had the articulatory control and phonetic distinctions needed to produce all of these elements, there is little indication in his production that he could consistently *begin with* the functional relationships he wanted to express and carry out the "procedures" required to produce and sequence these morphological elements correctly. We undertook no explicit steps to point out to ML the relationship between the cues he could use in comprehension, and their utility in sentence production, and it is possible that what he learned in comprehension could be exploited in an explicit treatment designed to improve *expression* of thematic roles. The important point is that knowing how to accomplish structure-to-meaning mapping in comprehension, though it may be necessary, is not sufficient to support meaning-to-structure mapping in production, even when the patient does not suffer from additional impairments to late-stage production components. This finding leads us to the conclusion that, although comprehension and production may share representational information such as verb argument structure, conceptual/ thematic information, and so forth, the actual "procedures" required to put that information to use in the service of comprehension and production are quite different.

In this study, we demonstrated two related, but independent points regarding current notions of aphasia treatment. First, this report provides another contribution toward the growing compilation of studies (only some of which are cited here) demonstrating that intervention with chronic aphasic patients is not only feasible and effective, but may product long-lasting effects on processing that can be built upon over time. This report of intervention with ML is one in a series of studies linking the outcome of one intervention to the motivating rationale of a subsequent study. The second major issue here regards the contribution of intervention studies toward the goal of understanding the functional relationships among processing mechanisms engaged in various cognitive operations. In this report, we attempt to characterise the generalisation of effects in order to address questions about sentence processing that are of topical theoretical importance. It is our hope that the findings reported here will help to elucidate issues surrounding thematic role assignment in sentence processing. As a larger goal, we anticipate that future studies of the effects of controlled intervention will similarly contribute to the therapeutic resolution of cognitive dysfunction, while developing new methodological approaches to the study of normal cognition.

Manuscript received 26 May 1993
Revised manuscript received September 1994
Revised manuscript accepted October 1994

REFERENCES

Berndt, R.S. (1991). Sentence processing in aphasia. In M.T. Sarno (Ed.), *Aquired aphasia* (2nd Edn.) (pp. 223–270). San Diego, CA: Academic Press.

Berndt, R.S., & Caramazza, A. (1980). A redefinition of the syndrome of Broca's aphasia: Implications for a neuropsychological model of language. *Applied Psycholinguistics, 1*, 225–278.

Berndt, R.S., Mitchum, C.C., & Haendiges, A.N. (in press). Comprehension of reversible sentences in "agrammatism." *Cognition*.

Berndt, R.S., Mitchum, C.C., & Price, T.R. (1991). Short-term memory and sentence comprehension: An investigation of a patient with crossed aphasia. *Brain, 114*, 263–280.

Byng, S. (1988). Sentence processing deficits: Theory and therapy. *Cognitive Neuropsychology, 5*(6), 629–676.

Byng, S. (unpublished). *Sentence processing deficits in aphasia: Investigations and remediation*. Unpublished doctoral dissertation, University of London, 1986.

Byng, S., Nickels, L., & Black, M. (1994). Replicating therapy for mapping deficits in agrammatism: Remapping the deficit? *Aphasiology*, *8*(4), 315–342.

Caplan, D., & Futter, C. (1986). Assignment of thematic roles by an agrammatic aphasic patient. *Brain and Language*, *27*, 117–134.

Caplan, D., & Hildebrandt, H. (1988). *Disorders of syntactic comprehension*. Cambridge, MA: MIT Press.

Caplan, D., & Waters, G.S. (1990). Short-term memory and language comprehension: A critical review of the neuropsychological literature. In G. Vallar & T. Shallice (Eds.), *Neuropsychological impairments of short-term memory* (pp. 337–389). Cambridge: Cambridge University Press.

Caramazza, A., & Berndt, R.S. (1985). A multicomponent view of agrammatic Broca's aphasia. In M.L. Kean (Ed.), *Agrammatism* (pp. 27–64). New York: Academic Press.

Caramazza, A., & Miceli. G. (1991). Selective impairment of thematic role assignment in sentence processing. *Brain and Language*, *41*, 402–436.

Caramazza, A., Basili, A.G., Koller, J.J., & Berndt, R.S. (1981). An investigation of repetition and language processing in a case of conduction aphasia. *Brain and Language*, *14*, 235–271.

Carlson, G.N., & Tanenhaus, M.K. (1989). Thematic roles and language comprehension. In W. Wilkins (Ed.), *Syntax and semantics: Thematic relations* (pp. 263–300). San Diego, CA: Academic Press.

Cupples, L., & Inglis. A.L. (1993). When task demands induce "asyntactic" comprehension: A study of sentence interpretation in aphasia. *Cognitive Neuropsychology*, *10*, 201–234.

Deloche, G., & Seron, X. (1981). Sentence understanding and knowledge of the world: Evidences from a sentence–picture matching task performed by aphasic patients. *Brain and Language*, *14*, 57–69.

Dowty, D. (1991). Thematic proto-roles and argument selection. *Language*, *67*(3), 547–619.

Francis, W.N., & Kuçera, H. (1982). *Frequency analysis of English usage: Lexicon and grammar*. Boston, MA: Houghton-Mifflin.

Friederici, A.D., & Frazier, L. (1992). Thematic analysis in agrammatic comprehension: Syntactic structures and task demands. *Brain and Language*, *42*, 1–29.

Gallaher, A.J., & Canter, G.J. (1982). Reading and listening comprehension in Broca's aphasia: Lexical versus syntactical errors. *Brain and Language*, *17*, 183–192.

Haendiges, A.N., Berndt, R.S., & Mitchum, C.C. (1992). *Phonological contributions to non-lexical reading impairments*. Paper presented at the annual meeting of the Academy of Aphasia, Toronto, Canada.

Haendiges, A.N., Berndt, R.S., & Mitchum, C.C. (in press). Assessing the elements contributing to a "mapping" deficit: A targeted treatment study. *Brain and Language*.

Jones, E.V. (1984). Word order processing in aphasia: Effects of verb semantics. In F.C. Rose (Ed.), *Advances in neurology: Progress in aphasiology*. New York: Raven Press.

Jones, E.V. (1986). Building the foundations for sentence production in a non-fluent aphasic. *British Journal of Disorders of Communications*, *21*, 63–82.

Just, M.A., & Carpenter, P. (1992). A capacity theory of comprehension: Individual differences in working memory. *Psychological Review*, *99*, 122–149.

Linebarger, M.C., Schwartz, M.F., & Saffran, E.M. (1983). Sensitivity to grammatical structure in so-called agrammatic aphasics. *Cognition*, *13*, 361–392.

Martin, R.C. (1990). Neuropsychological evidence on the role of short-term memory in sentence processing. In G. Vallar & T. Shallice (Eds.), *Neuropsychological impairments of short-term memory* (pp. 390–427). Cambridge: Cambridge University Press.

Martin, R.C. (1993). Short-term memory and sentence processing: Evidence from neuropsychology. *Memory and Cognition*, *21*, 176–183.

Martin, N., & Saffran, E.M. (1990). Repetition and verbal STM in transcortical sensory aphasia: A case study. *Brain and Language, 39*, 254–288.

Mehta, C., & Patel, N. (1991). *Statxact*. Cambridge, MA: Cytel Software Corporation.

Mitchum, C.C. (1992). Treatment generalization and the application of cognitive neuro-psychological models in aphasia therapy. In J. Cooper (Ed.), *Aphasia treatment: Current approaches and research opportunities* (pp. 99–116). Bethesda, MD: NIDCD Monograph.

Mitchum, C.C., & Berndt, R.S. (1988). Aphasia rehabilitation: An approach to diagnosis and treatment of disorders of language production. In M.G. Eisenberg (Ed.), *Advances in clinical rehabilitation*, II (pp. 160–185). New York: Springer.

Mitchum, C.C., & Berndt, R.S. (1994). Verb retrieval and sentence construction: Effects of targeted intervention. In G.W. Humphreys & M.J. Riddoch (Eds.), *Cognitive neurology and cognitive rehabilitation* (pp. 317–348). Hove: Lawrence Erlbaum Associates Ltd.

Miyake, A., Carpenter, P.A., & Just, M.A. (1994). A capacity approach to syntactic comprehension disorders: Making normal adults perform like aphasic patients. *Cognitive Neuropsychology, 2*(6), 671–717.

Nickels, L., Byng, S., & Black, M. (1991). Sentence processing deficits: A replication of therapy. *British Journal of Disorders of Communication, 26*(2), 175–201.

Saffran, E.M. (1990). Short-term memory impairment and language processing. In A. Caramazza (Ed.), *Advances in cognitive neuropsychology and neurolinguistics* (pp. 137–168). Hillsdale, NJ: Lawrence Erlbaum Associates Inc.

Saffran, E.M., & Marin, O.S.M. (1975). Immediate memory for word list and sentences in a patient with deficient auditory short-term memory. *Brain and Language, 2*, 420–433.

Saffran, E.M., & Martin, N. (1990). Short-term memory impairment and sentence processing: A case study. In G. Vallar & T. Shallice (Eds.), *Neuropsychological impairments of short-term memory* (pp. 428–447). Cambridge: Cambridge University Press.

Saffran, E.M., & Schwartz, M.F. (1988). "Agrammatic" comprehension it's not: Alternatives and implications. *Aphasiology, 2*(3/4), 389–394.

Schlesinger, I.M. (1992). The experiencer as an agent. *Journal of Memory and Language, 31*, 315–332.

Schwartz, M.F. (1987). Patterns of speech production deficit within and across aphasia syndromes: Application of a psycholinguistic model. In M. Coltheart, G. Sartori, & R. Job (Eds.), *The cognitive neuropsychology of language* (pp. 163–199). Hillsdale, NJ: Lawrence Erlbaum Associates Inc.

Schwartz, M.F., Saffran, E.M., & Marin, O.S.M. (1980). The word order problem in agrammatism: Comprehension. *Brain and Language, 10*, 249–262.

Schwartz, M.F., Linebarger, M.C., Saffran, E.M., & Pate, D.S. (1987). Syntactic transparency and sentence interpretation in aphasia. *Language and Cognitive Processes, 2*, 85–113.

Schwartz, M.F., Saffran, E.M., Fink, R., Myers, J., & Martin, N. (1994). Mapping therapy: A treatment programme for agrammatism. *Aphasiology, 8*(1), 19–54.

Siegel, S., & Castellan, N.J. (1988). *Nonparametric statistics for the behavioural sciences*. (Second Edn.). New York: McGraw-Hill Book Company.

Vallar, G., & Shallice, T. (Eds.) (1990). *Neuropsychological impairments of short-term memory*. Cambridge: Cambridge University Press.

Vallar, G., Corno, M., & Basso, A. (1992). Auditory and visual verbal short-term memory in aphasia. *Cortex, 28*(3), 383–389.

Wilkins, W. (Ed.) (1988). *Syntax and semantics: Thematic relations*. San Diego, CA: Academic Press.

Zurif, E., & Swinney, D. (1994). The neuropsychology of language. In M. Gernsbacher (Ed.), *Handbook of psycholinguistics*. San Diego, CA: Academic Press.

Chapter 10   Memory

Hodges, J.R. & McCarthy, R.A. (1995). Loss of remote memory: a cognitive neuropsychological perspective. *Current Opinion in Neurobiology, 5*, 178–183.
Wilson, B.A., Baddeley, A., Evans, J., & Shiel, A. (1994). Errorless learning in the rehabilitation of memory impaired people. *Neuropsychological Rehabilitation, 4*, 307–326.

Nearly everything we do involves some form of memory. To come home from work in a car you need to remember where you left it, how to get in it, how to start the engine, what the controls do, the conventions obeyed by other road users, and so on. To talk to a friend on the telephone you must remember what the number is and how to dial it, which piece of the handset you speak into, what the words you are using mean, and you need to bring to mind specific facts you may need such as what your friend has been doing recently, what you want to say, etc.

Memories thus have a pervasive influence on almost all the topics we have discussed in this book; something of the range of memory impairments can be seen in the collection edited by Campbell and Conway (1995). Even so, the study of memory *per se* still retains some separation from the rest of cognitive neuropsychology. Chapter 10 shows that, historically, this has in part derived from its emphasis on the classical amnesic syndrome, as shown by a person like HM, or in Korsakoff's amnesia. Amnesic patients often cannot remember what they were doing a few hours or even minutes ago. Their inability to do this has profound consequences for their lives.

Consider the importance of memories to maintaining a sense of self and orientation in the world. This can be seen very clearly through case CW, who suffered herpes simplex encephalitis in 1985 (Wilson & Wearing, 1995). Before his illness, CW had been an exceptionally talented musician with a most promising career. He was a specialist in early music, and an authority on the 16th-century composer Lassus. He was chorus master with the London Sinfonietta, and had joined the staff of the BBC in 1983.

Since 1985, CW has been able to remember little about his adult life other than his wife and his being a musician who had worked for the BBC. When asked to give as many names as possible of famous musicians, he could think of only four in one minute: Mozart, Beethoven, Bach, and Haydn. He remembered no famous painters or artists, and only one writer (Dickens). On the Rivermead Behavioural Memory Test (Wilson, Cockburn, & Baddeley, 1985) CW's screening score was 0/12, and he was also very poor on other tests of remembering visual or verbal material. Wilson, an exceptionally experienced clinical neuropsychologist, considered him the most densely amnesic patient she had ever seen (Wilson & Wearing, 1995).

A most striking feature of CW's case was that the world seemed to him to be in a state of flux. He made comments like "You weren't wearing blue just now. No, no, it was yellow or pink but it certainly wasn't blue". When playing patience with a pack of cards, he kept thinking that the cards were changing whenever he looked away from them, so he devised a system for writing down their positions, to try to work out what was going on. He also began to keep a diary of what was happening to him, carefully recording the time, the date, and the observation that he was now fully conscious, as if he had just woken up after his long illness. Diary entries to this effect were made hundreds of times across more than 9 years, and the same feelings were evident in CW's everyday life. In the words of his wife, CW's world

> now consists of a *moment* with no past to anchor it and no future to look ahead to. It is a blinkered moment. He sees what is right in front of him but as soon as that information hits the brain it fades. Nothing registers. Everything goes in perfectly well ... he perceives his world as you or I do, but as soon as he's perceived it and looked away it's gone for him. So it's a moment to moment consciousness as it were ... a time vacuum (Wilson & Wearing, 1995, p. 15).

CW's case shows dramatically how important our memories are to orientation in time and place. Although fully conscious, CW often has no adequate idea of who he is, where he is, or why he is there. Without memory, he is in a state graphically described by Wilson and Wearing (1995) as a "prisoner of consciousness".

In Chapter 10, though, we argue that concentrating too much on the classical amnesic syndrome may limit our insight into the true range of memory disorders, and that exploring the full range of disorders will be crucial to the development of a better articulated theory (Hanley & Young, 1994). One of the main problems that arises in this context is to define different potential forms of memory. Theorists often draw a distinction between our memory for specific episodes that have happened to us (e.g. remembering your holiday last year) and semantic memories, where the item is known from so many sources that it is no longer linked to any specific episode (e.g. remembering that Paris is the capital of France; you know this is correct, but not where or how you first learnt it). Clearly, CW's episodic memory was grossly impaired. However, people with amnesias often show relative sparing of semantic memory, but this was not found for CW, whose semantic memory was also markedly abnormal; for example, when asked to define "eyelid" he said "I don't know that word, it must be used by a great specialist". When this semantic memory loss was investigated in detail, CW was found to show especially poor knowledge of semantic information for living things. As we saw in Chapter 2, this differentially severe deficit for living things has been noted in other studies of post-encephalitic patients.

Despite his severe memory loss, CW remained able to sight-read music, transpose keys and extemporise, and he could still conduct his choir. None the less, his wife felt that his musical skills had deteriorated, but the changes would not be evident to nonmusicians (Wilson & Wearing, 1995). In these examples, though, whatever deficits CW showed in relation to his likely premorbid level of functioning were relatively limited in comparison to his devastating amnesia.

The importance of such findings is that all of these abilities depend on past learning; any problems remembering how to do them can therefore be considered a form of retrograde amnesia. A key area of investigation has thus become the fractionation of retrograde memory impairments into different types. This is explored in the first of our supplementary readings, in which Hodges and McCarthy (1995) show how detailed analysis of retrograde amnesias has begun to reveal dissociations between semantic memory, autobiographical memory, and memory for people. This work forges strong links between studies of memory disorders and the topics considered elsewhere in this book, especially those discussed in Chapter 2 (Object recognition), Chapter 4 (Face processing), and Chapter 5 (Producing spoken words); and much the same points are now being widely discussed in the research literature (De Renzi, Liotti, & Nichelli, 1987; Greene and Hodges, 1996a, b; Hodges, Patterson, Oxbury, & Funnell, 1992; Hodges, Patterson, & Tyler, 1994). We consider this a very positive development, both showing that the cognitive neuropsychological approach is as valuable in understanding memory impairments as for any of the other types of disorder we have discussed, and helping to bridge what are actually somewhat arbitrary boundaries we create between abilities we find it convenient to describe as "perception", "recognition", "memory", or even "understanding".

Some of the things CW could still do, like sight-reading or transposing music, seem like skills that would be so ingrained in a professional musician with his experience as to be almost habitual. In Chapter 10, we note several other examples of preserved skills and even skill-learning in cases of amnesia. One way to think about these is that perceptuo-motor learning may be a special case, distinct from other types of memory. This may be so, but there is also a great deal of current interest in the nature of the tasks used to reveal preserved or impaired memory. In cases such as CW, performance can be at chance in direct tests of memory. Direct tests would include recalling the items from a list learnt earlier, picking them out from a list of previously learnt items and new distractors, and so on. However, the performance of amnesics is often less severely impaired if memory is tested indirectly, using tasks that do not require one to know that something has been remembered.

The path breaking studies were carried out by Warrington and Weiskrantz (1968, 1970), who asked amnesic patients to identify fragmented pictures or words, and showed that subsequent identification of the same stimuli was facilitated. For amnesics, just as much as for normal people, it becomes easier to recognise a fragmented picture of an object if you have already had to recognise the same object before. This type of finding can be obtained even when the amnesic patients fail to remember having taken part in any previous testing sessions! Hence amnesics show a form of nonconscious memory, in which their performance can be affected by previous experiences they may completely fail to remember overtly. The phenomenon is often called "implicit memory". Examining the reasons why this might happen has become central to much current research on memory impairment (Mayes, 1992; Schacter, 1992).

One of the reasons for the great upsurge of interest in implicit memory is that, if we could understand how it comes about that amnesics can do so well in this type of test, we might have a better idea of how to rehabilitate or mitigate some of the consequences of the memory problems. As yet, though, there are only scant indications that this can be done successfully, and a number of problems have been noted by Baddeley (1992). One of the most intriguing of these comes from thinking about what explicit memory might be for. A plausible speculation is that explicit memory is one of the things that helps us to correct errors we made in the past, whereas implicit memory by its nature tends to lead to one's previous errors being repeated. If this is the case, then amnesics will be actually be disadvantaged by their relatively preserved implicit memory abilities if they are free to make errors during learning; without explicit memory, their erroneous responses can become more likely to be repeated (i.e. more "memorable" than the correct ones. This observation has led to a very promising method described in our final reading, based on errorless learning (Wilson, Baddeley, Evans, & Shiel, 1994). The principle used in errorless learning derives from a long tradition in behavioural psychology; in essence, one structures the conditions under which learning takes place in order to minimise or prevent the possibility of mistakes. Wilson et al. (1994) showed that amnesics do indeed learn better if they are prevented from making mistakes, and gave examples of the application of this finding to some of the real-life problems of memory-impaired people.

REFERENCES

Baddeley, A.D. (1992). Implicit memory and errorless learning: a link between cognitive theory and neuropsychological rehabilitation? In L.R. Squire & N. Butters (Eds), *Neuropsychology of memory* (pp. 309–314). New York: Guilford Press.

Campbell, R. & Conway, M.A. (Eds). (1995). *Broken memories. Case studies in memory impairment*. Oxford: Blackwell.

De Renzi, E., Liotti, M., & Nichelli, P. (1987). Semantic amnesia with preservation of autobiographic memory. A case report. *Cortex, 23,* 575–597.

Greene, J.D.W. & Hodges, J.R. (1996a). Identification of famous faces and famous names in early Alzheimer's disease. Relationship to anterograde episodic and general semantic memory. *Brain, 119,* 111–128.

Greene, J.D.W. & Hodges, J.R. (1996b). The fractionation of remote memory. Evidence from a longitudinal study of dementia of Alzheimer type. *Brain, 119,* 129–142.

Hanley, J.R. & Young, A.W. (1994). The cognitive neuropsychology of memory. In P.E. Morris

& M.M. Gruneberg (Eds), *Theoretical aspects of memory* (pp. 238–272). London: Routledge.

Hodges, J.R. & McCarthy, R.A. (1995). Loss of remote memory: a cognitive neuropsychological perspective. *Current Opinion in Neurobiology, 5,* 178–183.

Hodges, J.R., Patterson, K., Oxbury, S., & Funnell, E. (1992). Semantic dementia: progressive fluent aphasia with temporal lobe atrophy. *Brain, 115,* 1783–1806.

Hodges, J.R., Patterson, K., & Tyler, L.K. (1994). Loss of semantic memory: implications for the modularity of mind. *Cognitive Neuropsychology, 11,* 505–542.

Mayes, A.R. (1992). Automatic memory processes in amnesia: how are they mediated? In A.D. Milner & M.D. Rugg (Eds), *The neuropsychology of consciousness* (pp. 235–261). London: Academic Press.

Schacter, D.L. (1992). Implicit knowledge: new perspectives on unconscious processes. *Proceedings of the National Academy of Science, USA, 89,* 11113–11117.

Warrington, E.K. & Weiskrantz, L. (1968). New method of testing long-term retention with special reference to amnesic patients. *Nature, 217,* 972–974.

Warrington, E.K. & Weiskrantz, L. (1970). Amnesia: consolidation or retrieval? *Nature, 228,* 628–630.

Wilson, B., Cockburn, J., & Baddeley, A.D. (1985). *The Rivermead Behavioural Memory Test.* Bury St Edmunds, UK: Thames Valley Test Company.

Wilson, B.A., Baddeley, A., Evans, J., & Shiel, A. (1994). Errorless learning in the rehabilitation of memory impaired people. *Neuropsychological Rehabilitation, 4,* 307–326.

Wilson, B.A. & Wearing, D. (1995). Prisoner of consciousness: a state of just awakening following herpes simplex encephalitis. In R. Campbell & M.A. Conway (Eds.), *Broken memories. Case studies in memory impairment* (pp. 14–30). Oxford: Blackwell.

Loss of Remote Memory: A Cognitive Neuropsychological Perspective

John R. Hodges and Rosaleen A. McCarthy
Addenbrooke's Hospital and University of Cambridge, Cambridge, UK

Recent, cognitively based neuropsychological studies have established that retrograde amnesia is not a single entity. Profound loss of autobiographical memory, with relative sparing of knowledge of word meaning, facts about other people and personal semantic information, may arise from either disruption of thematic retrieval frameworks or a loss of individual memory traces. The opposite pattern of profound loss of general semantic information with preservation of autobiographical memory also occurs. Finer-grained loss of semantic information, involving famous persons or other categories have also been described, providing important clues regarding the representation and organization of such knowledge.

INTRODUCTION

In this review, we propose a cognitive neuropsychological account of the various patterns of retrograde amnesia—the phenomenon of loss of memory for material acquired prior to the onset of pathology. Until very recently, investigators have tended to regard retrograde memory as a single entity concentrating on the presence or absence of retrograde amnesia and whether patients with retrograde amnesia show a temporally graded pattern (that is, relative sparing of more distant memories).[1-10]

In the past decade, cognitive neuropsychology has begun to make substantial contributions towards the study of remote memory loss, leading to some new questions and changes of emphasis in research: first, in the application of single-case methodology, and second by the use of cognitive models to account for specific deficits in remote memory. This shift in focus has allowed a more detailed, theoretically motivated exploration of the quantitative and qualitative attributes of patients' retrograde knowledge and has led to a greater emphasis on dissociations and double dissociations of function within the retrograde domain.

FRACTIONATING RETROGRADE AMNESIA: EPISODIC VERSUS SEMANTIC MEMORY

The various aspects of retrograde memory can be fractionated in different ways; one of the major dissociations distinguishes between memory for premorbid events or episodes (episodic memory) and knowledge of facts (semantic memory).[11] Conventionally, the label episodic memory is used to denote the long-term storage of information that is coded both with respect to its temporal and contextual content. Tasks dependent on episodic memory include story recall and word list learning. By contrast, semantic memory applies to that component of long-term memory that represents knowledge of objects, facts and concepts, as well as words and their meaning. Tasks dependent on semantic memory include object naming, generation of definitions for spoken words, word–picture and picture–picture matching, the generation of exemplars on category fluency tests (e.g. animals, vegetables, etc.) and the identification of famous faces or buildings.

More recently, there has been a further refinement of the 'episodic/semantic' dichotomy. The concept of autobiographical memory has been introduced to refer to personally relevant memories, which may be further subdivided into personal episodes and personal semantics. For example, remembering the details of last year's holiday constitutes an episodic autobiographical memory, whereas recalling your marital status, occupation and educational background would be an example of autobiographical (personal) semantics.[12, 13] However, the fundamental question of whether these distinctions relate to true dichotomies (whether at the level of neural processing or in cognitive science), or rather are points on a continuum remains a controversial issue.

Knowledge of word meaning, facts about other people and personal semantic information may be relatively spared in the presence of profound amnesia for events or episodes.[14-16, 17*, 18**] For example, McCarthy and Warrington[16] described a patient who could retrieve semantic information about famous people and personal acquaintances, but who was unable to access information about events involving the same individuals. By contrast, patients with impaired semantic knowledge who fail to recognize common objects and words but with preserved memory for episodes have been reported by several investigators.[19-21, 22**] Although the evidence for this dissociation is compelling, recently it has become clear that a full theoretical understanding will have to incorporate some explicit consideration of the interaction between episodic and semantic representations. Snowden et al.[23**] have stressed the functional and practical utility of ongoing personal experience in the maintenance and support of semantic knowledge. They described patients with a grave semantic memory disorder whose knowledge of people, places and objects was strongly tied to current personal experience: "what appeared most readily available from a name was information about specific events, and it was this information that invested the name with significance".[23]** They argued that their findings indicated a strong and dynamic interaction between semantic and episodic memory.

AUTOBIOGRAPHICAL MEMORY

Neuropsychological studies of autobiographical memory began only 10 years ago with the advent of more standardized assessment techniques.[12, 13] In parallel with the growing literature on the effects of brain pathology, experimental psychologists have also shown a considerable interest in the organization and structure of memories with autobiographical content as compared with memories for public events and episodes.[24] Of interest here has been the issue of whether memories for personally experienced events differ from public events in terms of their representation and/or organization.[25] The narrative structure of one's own life is continuously recreated, edited, reinterpreted and updated. By contrast, memory of public events is often imposed and encoded in a relatively 'fixed' format by the media.

Contemporary cognitive theories of autobiographical memory emphasize the view of memory as a complex, distributed system. The overall processes of retrieval and remembering are viewed as a dynamic cognitive operation involving the integration of problem solving, cross checking, verification and inference.[24, 25] For example, if you are asked to recall last year's holiday, the relevant information needs to be differentiated from other holidays or journeys; you also need to select the portion that is relevant and appropriate to introduce into a specific conversation; you also need to verify that you are recalling true memories rather than wishful thinking; and you have to impose a structure on your recall so that a continuous and overlapping series of occurrences is retrieved as coherent discourse. As the previous example makes clear, autobiographical information is not simply read out from a store, but is reconstructed in accordance with social conditions, task demands, and with reference to records of various sorts.

One way of conceptualizing this operation, which we have applied[18]**, is in terms of thematic retrieval frameworks, see Fig. 1. According to this model, the higher-level retrieval frameworks are organized thematically, in terms of major life-events or lifetime periods. At the lowest level are the elements of autobiographical records that may be relatively fragmentary and cognitively unstructured. The major role of the retrieval frameworks is in providing pointers, and an organizational structure, for guiding retrieval and integration of the lower level records.

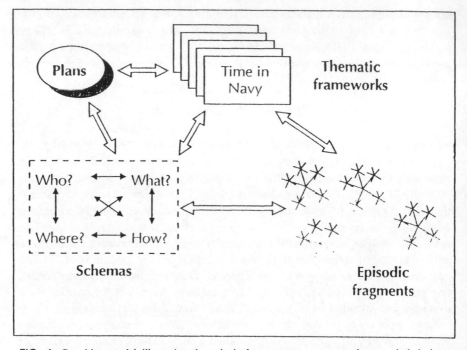

FIG. 1. Cognitive model illustrating the principal memory access procedures and their inter-relationship as discussed in the text. Memory is thought to have a basic hierarchical structure with 'thematic frameworks' providing pointers or indices to lower level records. These lower level records include 'schemas' composed of inter-linked databases of factual semantic knowledge (e.g. concerning people, things, places, etc.) and less structured, event-specific, 'episodic fragments'. In the case of 'autobiographical memory', thematic frameworks may be organized in terms of important (personally salient) life-time epochs such as 'Time at University', 'Time in Navy', 'Businessman', etc. Neuropsychological evidence suggests that the integration of thematic frameworks and schemas is mediated via thalamo-frontal links under the modulatory control of the attentional and planning systems of the frontal lobes. Factual semantic information is critically dependent on locally specialized temporal cortical subsystems. Event-specific episodic fragments may be retrievable or reconstructed from those same temporal, parietal and occipital processors that are implicated in the initial processing of input.

In terms of neurological substrates, it has been suggested that the dynamic control of memory search relies on procedures supported by the frontal lobes. Semantic information is probably represented in temporal (and possibly inferior parietal) cortical areas and under the appropriate circumstances such semantic records may be accessed directly, without recourse to the frontally supported retrieval procedures. The individual elements of autobiographical information are probably stored according to sensory and motor properties; as such they are likely to involve multiple and distributed regions of association cortex.

A disorder at the thematic retrieval framework level can explain the pattern of memory impairment seen in patient P.S. who suffered from profound autobiographical amnesia following bilateral thalamic infarction, and yet, who retained remarkable knowledge of famous people[18**]. P.S.'s performance on tasks relating to autobiographical recall was gravely impaired, confusing events such as his own marriage and that of his children, and failing to retrieve or recognize information about the births of his children. Despite this grave deficit of personal knowledge, P.S. was found to be surprisingly accurate when asked to identify famous faces, to provide information about the events that had made people famous, or to place people in an appropriate temporal order. Because of the close anatomical and functional inter-relationship between the thalamus and prefrontal cortex, P.S.'s lesions were critically sited to disrupt the operation of thematic retrieval frameworks, which we postulate depend on the interaction of frontal and posterior association cortices.

A similar type of cognitive explanation has been advanced by other researchers to explain the autobiographical amnesia and confabulation found in a subgroup of patients with frontal damage and in patients with Korsakoff's syndrome.[17*, 26**]

Loss of autobiographical memory could also arise from destruction of individual traces rather than organizing thematic frameworks. This may explain the pattern reported in patients with disproportionate retrograde amnesia, most of whom have sustained damage to the polar regions of the temporal lobes, particularly on the right.[27,28,29*] Pursuing the importance of specific classes of memory trace, O'Connor et al.[30] and Ogden[31*] suggested that their patients' pronounced visual agnosic and visuospatial deficits might have compromised their ability to generate and manipulate visual images, resulting in a disproportionate loss of autobiographical memories. However, data from group studies of patients with right or left temporal lobectomy suggest a more complex interaction between test materials and memory impairments.[32]

PEOPLE AND THEIR NAMES

Assessing knowledge and retrieval of proper names has become a central area of cognitive research. Most models have emphasized a distinction between semantic and lexical levels of processing: a 'lexicon' is one's store of known names, whereas the term 'semantics' refers to the specific, and often unique, information about a person that is normally accessed when viewing their face, hearing or seeing their name or hearing their voice, etc.[33*,34] Disproportionate impairments in semantic knowledge associated with particular people has been described.[35,36,37*,38**] For instance, patient V.H.[38**] presented with difficulty recognizing previously familiar and famous people, which was initially modality-specific, but progressed so that she was unable to recognize people from their face or to provide appropriate information when presented with their name. This pattern indicates a loss of semantic information about people, which, in this case, occurred in the absence of a more general semantic memory disorder. By contrast, patients with selective lexical impairments in retrieving the names of people have also been documented.[39,40,41]* As difficulty in retrieving people's names is, in fact, a common manifestation of ageing, it is important to note that some anomic patients may demonstrate a selective preservation of this category.[42] Disorders of knowledge about other people do not necessarily affect an individual's ability to access previous autobiographical or public events: in at least some cases, autobiographical memory appears to be normal unless specific people are critical to the particular event or episode.[35]

Thus, there is emerging evidence that both knowledge about, and the specific names of, people are represented independently of other forms of knowledge. The neural basis of person-specific semantic knowledge is not well understood, but it is intriguing to note that the three most clearly documented cases with specific deficits in this domain all had right temporal lobe pathology.[35,36,38]**

OTHER SEMANTIC CATEGORIES

Neuropsychological disorders of semantic knowledge are sometimes selective to particular categories of information. Even when the possible roles of confounding variables, such as stimulus familiarity, frequency or visual complexity are taken into account, substantial category-specific effects may remain. The most widely documented category-specific profile involves a disproportionate impairment of stimuli drawn from biological categories (e.g. animals, plants, foods) with sparing of knowledge of man-made objects (e.g. furniture, tools).[43-45] The converse pattern has also been documented.[44-46] This double dissociation rules out the possibility that such effects are merely a product of task difficulty. It has been suggested that things that are primarily distinguished in terms of their sensory properties, such as animals, foods, etc. might be encoded and stored differently from things known in terms of their functional attributes—such as man-made objects.[43,44,47] A semantic knowledge base that was locally organized to exploit information from different sensory or motor sources might manifest a category-specific pattern of breakdown if injury were appropriately located. Farah and McClelland[48] have shown how a simple scheme of this type can be instantiated in a computational model.

RELEVANCE TO NEUROLOGICAL DISORDERS

Severe retrograde amnesia also has been shown in a variety of chronic conditions including Huntington's disease,[8] Parkinson's disease[9] and frontal lobe dementia (Pick's disease).[49] In each of these diseases, an impairment in the retrieval of old memories secondary to disruption of fronto-striatal circuits has been postulated. Marked retrograde deficits are also typical following temporal cortical lesions resulting from herpes simplex encephalitis[50-52] and radiation necrosis.[53*] These deficits can be thought of in terms of destruction of cortical memory stores.

A major recent development has been the delineation of the syndrome of 'semantic dementia', which has the following characteristics: selective impairment of semantic memory causing severe anomia, impaired single-word comprehension (both spoken and written), reduced generation of exemplars on category fluency tests and an impoverished fund of general knowledge; relative sparing of other components of language output, notably syntax and phonology; normal perceptual skills and non-verbal problem solving abilities; and relatively preserved autobiographical and day-to-day (episodic) memory.[21,22**,23**] Neuroradiological studies of patients with semantic dementia have shown selective atrophy of the left temporal neocortex involving the pole, inferior and middle gyri but with sparing of the hippocampal formation. Such patients are impaired on traditional tests of remote public knowledge but may have sparing of autobiographical memory.[21,23**]

A pervasive disorder of semantic memory is also a fairly universal feature of Alzheimer's disease.[54,55,56*,57] Patients with Alzheimer's disease are impaired on tests of remote public information, based on both famous faces[8,58*] and famous events.[9,10] The current evidence points to a loss of stored semantic knowledge about the person or event represented, rather than a failure of access.[58*] Autobiographical memory is also impaired from early in the course of the disease[9,10,12] with deficits in both personal semantic and episodic knowledge. It remains to be clarified whether the autobiographical impairment in Alzheimer's disease represents breakdown at the thematic frameworks level or is entirely attributable to a loss of stored knowledge, but recent work suggests that both factors may play a role.[59]

CONCLUSIONS

Over the past few years the detailed analysis of patients with retrograde amnesia has started to reveal theoretically important dissociations. Based on these findings, we propose a tentative model that stresses both the processes involved in the retrieval and verification of old memories and the type of information stored: thematic retrieval frameworks appear critical for the retrieval of autobiographical memories and are mediated by frontal lobe systems; loss of autobiographical memory may also arise from destruction of the individual traces in higher-order cortical association areas; within the domain of semantic memory there is evidence for the separation of person-based from general semantic memory, as well as for other consistent dissociations within the semantic system, most notably between biological and man-made categories. There remain many unanswered questions that will, we hope, be resolved as further methods of assessment evolve and are applied to patients with disorders of remote memory.

REFERENCES AND RECOMMENDED READING

Papers of particular interest, published within the annual period of review, have been highlighted as:
* of special interest
** of outstanding interest

1. Sanders H.I., Warrington E.K. Memory for remote events in amnesic patients. *Brain* 1971, *94*, 661–668.

2. Seltzer B., Benson D.F. The temporal gradient of retrograde amnesia in Korsakoff's disease. *Neurology* 1974, *24*, 527–530.

3. Marslen-Wilson W.D., Teuber H.L. Memory for remote events in anterograde amnesia. Recognition of public figures from news photographs. *Neuropsychologia* 1975, *13*, 353–364.

4. Albert M.S., Butters N., Levin J. Temporal gradients in the retrograde amnesia of patients with alcoholic Korsakoff's disease. *Arch Neurol* 1979, *36*, 211-216.

5. Meudell P.R., Northern B., Snowden J.S, Neary D. Long-term memory for famous voices in amnesic and normal subjects. *Neuropsychologia* 1980, *18*, 133–139.

6. Cohen N.J., Squire L.R. Retrograde amnesia and remote memory impairment. *Neuropsychologia* 1981, *19*, 337-356.

7. Zola-Morgan S., Cohen N.J., Squire L.R. Recall of remote episodic memory in amnesia. *Neuropsychologia* 1983, *21*, 487–500.

8. Beatty W.W., Salmon D.P., Butters N., Heindel W.C., Granholm E. Retrograde amnesia in patients with Alzheimer's and Huntington's disease. *Neurobiol Aging* 1988, *9*, 181–186.

9. Sagar H.J., Cohen N.J., Sullivan E.V., Corkin S., Crowden J.H. Remote memory function in Alzheimer's disease and Parkinson's disease. *Brain* 1988, *111*, 185–206.

10. Kopelman M.D. Remote and autobiographical memory, temporal context memory and frontal atrophy in Korsakoff and Alzheimer patients. *Neuropsychologia* 1989, *27*, 437–460.

11. Tulving E. *Elements of Episodic Memory.* New York, Oxford University Press; 1983.

12. Dall'Ora P., Della Sala S., Spinnler H. Autobiographical memory. Its impairment in amnesic syndromes. *Cortex* 1989, *25*, 197-217.

13. Kopelman M.D., Wilson B., Baddeley A. The autobiographical interview – a new assessment of autobiographical and personal semantic memory in amnesic patients. *J Clin Exp Neuropsychol* 1989, *11*, 724–744.

14. Warrington E.K., McCarthy R.A. The fractionation of retrograde amnesia. *Brain Cogn* 1988, *7*, 184–200.

15. Dalla Barba G., Cipolotti L., Denes G. Autobiographical memory loss and confabulation in Korsakoff's syndrome: a case report. *Cortex* 1990, *26*, 525–534.

16. McCarthy R.A., Warrington E.K. Actors but not scripts: the dissociation of people and events in retrograde amnesia. *Neuropsychologia* 1992, *30*, 633–644.

17. Dalla Barba G. Confabulation: knowledge and recollective experience. *Cogn Neuropsychol*
* 1993, *10*, 1–20.
The performance of an amnesic patient with confabulations restricted to episodic memory was assessed using a comprehensive battery of neuropsychological tasks.

18. Hodges J.R., McCarthy R.A. Autobiographical amnesia resulting from bilateral paramedian
** thalamic infarction: a case study in cognitive neurobiology. *Brain* 1993, *116* 921–940.
A detailed case study of a patient who sustained bilateral paramedian thalamic infarction resulting in profound autobiographical amnesia with relative sparing of knowledge about famous events, and particularly of famous faces. These findings were interpreted as reflecting a disorder at the 'thematic frameworks' level of memory organization.

19. Warrington E.K. The selective impairment of semantic memory. *Q J Exp Psychol* 1975, *27*, 187–199.

20. DeRenzi E., Liotti M., Nichelli P. Semantic amnesia with preservation of autobiographical

memory: a case report. *Cortex* 1987, *23*, 575–597.
21. Hodges J.R., Patterson K., Oxbury S., Funnell E. Semantic dementia: progressive fluent aphasia with temporal lobe atrophy. *Brain* 1992, *115*, 1783–1806.
22. Hodges J.R., Patterson K., Tyler L.K. Loss of semantic memory: implications for the
** modularity of mind. *Cogn Neuropsychol* 1994, *11*, 505–542.
A longitudinal follow-up study of a patient with semantic dementia with a profound and global loss of knowledge, including memory of famous people, but relative preservation of episodic memory and other non-semantically mediated abilities.
23. Snowden J., Griffiths H., Neary D. Semantic dementia: autobiographical contribution to
** preservation of meaning. *Cogn Neuropsychol* 1994, *11*, 265–289.
This important study of five patients with semantic dementia proposes a role for autobiographical experience in the maintenance of meaning of words and objects.
24. Conway M.A. Verifying autobiographical facts. *Cognition* 1987, *26*, 39–58.
25. Baddeley A.D. What is autobiographical memory? In *Theoretical Perspectives on Auto-biographical Memory*. Edited by Conway M.A., Rubin D., Wagenaar W., Spinnler H. Amsterdam: Kluver Academic Publishers; *1992*, 13–29.
26. Della Sala S., Laiacona M., Spinnler H., Trivelli C. Autobiographical recollection and frontal
** damage. *Neuropsychologia* 1993, *31*, 823–839.
Anterograde and autobiographical memory, as well as executive function, were investigated in 16 patients with computer tomography-verified frontal lobe lesions. Of the 16, six were impaired on autobiographical retrieval and eight on supra-span verbal learning. Autobiographical memory correlated poorly with anterograde learning, but very significantly with executive abilities. The authors propose that the attentional systems involved in the retrieval of remote memory and in learning new information are qualitatively distinct.
27. Kapur N., Ellison D., Smith M.P., McLellen D.L., Burrows E.H. Focal retrograde amnesia following bilateral temporal lobe pathology. *Brain* 1992, *115*, 73–85.
28. Markowitsch H.J., Calabrese P., Liess J., Haupt M., Durwen H.F., Gehlen W. Retrograde amnesia after traumatic injury of the fronto-temporal cortex. *J Neurol Neurosurg Psychiatry* 1993, *6*, 988–992.
29. Kapur N. Focal retrograde amnesia in neurological disease: a critical review. *Cortex* 1993,
* *29*, 217–234.
A comprehensive review of the neuropsychological and anatomical data on isolated retrograde amnesia.
30. O'Connor M., Butters N., Miliotis P., Eslinger P., Cermak L.S. The dissociation of anterograde and retrograde amnesia in a patient with herpes encephalitis. *J Clin Exp Neuropsychol* 1992, *14*, 159–178.
31. Ogden J.A. Visual object agnosia, prosopagnosia, achromatopsia, loss of visual imagery and
* autobiographical amnesia following recovery from cortial blindness: case M.H.. *Neuropsychologia* 1993, *31*, 571–589.
The young RTA victim reported in this single-case study was shown to have a dense autobiographical amnesia which the author argues is related to deficits in visual long-term memory and visual imagery.
32. Barr W.B., Goldberg E., Wasserstien J., Novelly R.A. Retrograde amnesia following unilateral temporal lobectomy. *Neuropsychologia* 1990, *28*, 243–255.
33. Cohen G., Burke D.M. Memory for proper names: a review. *Memory* 1993, *1*, 249–265.
*A very useful review of the literature on memory for proper names with special reference to normal ageing.
34. Burton A.M., Bruce V. Naming faces and naming names: exploring an interactive model of person recognition. *Memory* 1993, *1*, 457–481.
35. Ellis A.W., Young A.W., Critchley E.M.R. Loss of memory for people following temporal lobe damage. *Brain* 1989, *112*, 1469–1483.

36. Hanley J.R., Young A.W., Pearson N.A. Defective recognition of familiar people. *Cogn Neuropsychol* 1989, *6*, 179–210.

37. De Renzi E., Lucchelli F. Dense retrograde amnesia, intact learning capacity and abnormal
* forgetting rate: a consolidation deficit. *Cortex* 1993, *29*, 449–466.
Following anoxic brain damage, a 24 year old presented with a dense retrograde amnesia for events, persons and events that spanned his whole life. Anterograde memory was marked by very efficient learning capacity with almost perfect retention of information after 4 hours and pathologically rapid forgetting at longer delays indicative of defective consolidation.

38. Evans J.J., Heggs A.J., Antoun N., Hodges J.R. Progressive prosopagnosia associated with
** selective right temporal lobe atrophy: a new syndrome? *Brain* 1995, *118*, 1–15.
The first reported case with a disorder of face recognition progressing to loss of person-specific semantic knowledge in the absence of a more general semantic disorder. Selective right temporal lobe atrophy was shown on magnetic resonance imaging.

39. Lucchelli F., De Renzi E. Proper name anomia. *Cortex* 1992, *28*, 221–230.

40. Shallice T., Kartsounis L.K. Selective impairment of retrieving people's names: a category specific disorder? *Cortex* 1993, *29*, 281–291.

41. Hittmair-Delazer M., Denes G., Semenza C., Mantova M.C. Anomia for people's names.
* *Neuropsychologia* 1994, *32*, 465–476.
A case study of a patient with a deficit in retrieving the phonological form of people's names with intact semantic memory.

42. Semenza C., Sgaramella T.M. Production of proper names: a clinical case study of the effects of phonological cueing. *Memory* 1993, *1*, 265–281.

43. Warrington E.K., Shallice T. Category specific semantic impairments. *Brain* 1984, *107*, 829–854.

44. Warrington E.K., McCarthy R.A. Categories of knowledge: further fractionations. *Brain* 1987, *110*, 1273–1296.

45. Hillis A.E., Caramazza A. Category specific naming and comprehension impairment—a double dissociation. *Brain* 1991, *114*, 2081–2094.

46. Sacchett C., Humphreys G.W. Calling a squirrel a squirrel but a canoe a wigwam: a category specific deficit for artefactual objects and body parts. *Cogn Neuropsychol* 1992, *9*, 73–86.

47. Warrington E.K., McCarthy R.A. Multiple meaning systems in the brain: a case for visual semantics. *Neuropsychologia* 1994, *32*, 1465-1473.

48. Farah M.J., McClelland J.L. A computational model of semantic memory impairment: modality specificity and emergent category specificity. *J Exp Psychol [Gen]* 1991 *120*, 339–357.

49. Hodges R., Gurd J. Remote memory and lexical retrieval in a case of frontal Pick's disease. *Arch Neurol* 1994, *51*, 821–827.

50. Cermak L.S., O'Connor M. The anterograde and retrograde retrieval ability of a patient with amnesia due to encephalitis. *Neuropsychologia* 1983, *21*, 213-233.

51. Damasio A.R., Eslinger P.G., Damasio H., Van Hoesen G.W., Cornell S. Multimodal amnesic syndrome following bilateral temporal and basal forebrain damage. *Arch Neurol* 1985, *42*, 252–259.

52. Squire L.R., Zola-Morgan S., Cave C.B., Haist F., Musen G., Suzuki W.A. Memory: organisation of brain systems and cognition. *Cold Spring Harb Symp Quant Biol* 1990, *55*, 1007–1023.

53. Kapur N., Ellison D., Parkin A., Hunkin N.M., Burrows E., Sampson S.A., Morrison E.A.
* Bilateral temporal lobe pathology with sparing of medial temporal structures: lesion profile and pattern of memory disorder. *Neuropsychologia* 1994 *32*, 23–35.
A detailed study of a patient with radiation-induced bilateral necrosis of the temporal neocortex.

54. Chertkow H., Bub D., Caplan D. Constraining theories of semantic memory processing: evidence from dementia. *Cogn Neuropsychol* 1992, *9*, 327–365.

55. Hodges J.R., Salmon D.P., Butters N. Semantic memory impairment in Alzheimer's disease:

failure of access or degraded knowledge? *Neuropsychologia* 1992, *30,* 301–314.

56. Chan A.S., Butters N., Paulson J.S., Salmon D.P., Swenson M., Maloney L. An assessment of
*   the semantic network in patients with Alzheimer's disease. *Cogn Neurosci* 1993, *5,* 254–261.
The application of multidimensional scaling to the category fluency deficit in Alzheimer's patients.

57. Hodges J.R., Patterson K. Is semantic memory consistently impaired early in the course of
     Alzheimer's disease: diagnostic and neuroanatomical implications. *Neuropsychologia* 1995, *33,*
     441–459.

58. Hodges J.R., Salmon D.P., Butters N. Recognition and naming of famous faces in Alzheimer's
*   disease: a cognitive analysis. *Neuropsychologia* 1993, *31,* 775–788.
The first detailed analysis of the cognitive deficits underlying Alzheimer's disease patients' inability
to identify and name famous faces. This study established that the primary deficit is not one of name
retrieval but an actual loss of stored information of the person represented.

59. Greene J, Hodges J.R., Baddeley A.D. Autobiographical memory and executive frontal
     function in early dementia of Alzheimer's type. *Neuropsychologia* 1995, in press.

Errorless Learning in the Rehabilitation
of Memory Impaired People

Barbara A. Wilson, Alan Baddeley, Jonathan Evans

MRC Applied Psychology Unit, Cambridge, U.K.

Agnes Shiel

Rehabilitation Research Unit, University of Southampton, U.K.

We report six experiments comparing errorful and errorless learning in the teaching of new information to neurologically impaired adults with severe memory problems. The first experiment is a group study in which amnesic subjects, young controls, and older controls were required to learn two lists of words under two conditions. One of these required subjects to generate guesses that produced incorrect responses, and the other prevented guessing—permitting only correct responses. Conditions and lists were counterbalanced across subjects. People with amnesia scored significantly higher under the errorless condition. We further explored the principle of errorless learning in five single case studies in which severely memory impaired people were required to learn information analogous to that needed in everyday life. Tasks included learning names of objects and people, learning how to programme an electronic aid, remembering orientation items, and learning new items of general knowledge. In each case, errorless learning was superior to errorful learning.

INTRODUCTION

Memory problems are common after brain injury (Brooks, 1984; Schacter & Crovitz, 1977) and prevent many people from returning to work or independent living. It seems unlikely that neuropsychologists, therapists, or others can restore memory functioning in brain-injured people (Wilson, 1992a) although some 30% of this population show a noticeable improvement on tests of memory following treatment (Wilson, 1991a).

Attempts to help memory-impaired people have concentrated on teaching the use of compensatory aids (Sohlberg & Mateer, 1989) or on using mnemonics to enhance learning (Wilson, 1987a). Theoretical influences on treatment have for the most part been limited to areas of cognitive neuropsychology or behavioural psychology. As an example of the former, Wilson (1992a), provides some general guidelines for helping memory-impaired people to encode, store, and retrieve information more effectively. An alternative view is that these methods help anyone—including people with amnesia—make the most of their memory.

Glisky and Schacter (1987, 1989) developed a teaching technique also based on cognitive neuropsychological theory when they employed the "method of vanishing cues" to teach compensatory skills to amnesic people. The authors wanted to use the intact implicit learning skills typically shown by amnesic subjects. Implicit learning is that which occurs without awareness, and can be seen in a variety of tasks including the learning of certain motor skills, recognising degraded pictures, and word-stem completion tasks (see Squire, 1987 and Tulving & Schacter, 1990 for a more detailed discussion).

Glisky and Schacter (1987, 1989) based their "method of vanishing cues" on the word-stem completion procedure, in which subjects are first given a list of words and then tested by being presented with the first three letters of each of those words, and are asked to supply the first word that comes to mind. In these circumstances amnesic patients are likely to provide the correct words, even though they do not remember having seen or heard the originals a short time previously.

Glisky and Schacter used a computer screen to teach the meaning of words commonly associated with computing, so that, in the first stage for example, a subject might be presented with "A repeated segment is called a LOOP". In the second stage, the last letter of LOOP would be omitted, then the last two and so on until there were no letters of the word LOOP on the screen. Amnesic subjects were successful in learning the computer terminology and other computer-related tasks using this procedure over a lengthy period of time and after considerable effort.

Although the procedure adopted by Glisky and Schacter was derived from theoretical studies of implicit learning, the actual learning resulting from the "method of vanishing cues" was slower and more effortful than that taking place in the more typical implicit learning studies, where it occurs without apparent effort or realisation on the part of the subject. It could also be argued that the "method of vanishing cues" is, in essence, no different from behavioural chaining, used for many years in teaching people with severe learning difficulties (Yule & Carr, 1987). In behavioural chaining a task is broken down into its component parts (or links in the chain) and the steps are taught one at a time. Both forward chaining—in which the first step is taught first—and backward chaining—beginning with the last step and working backwards—are used, although the latter is probably employed more frequently. There is no doubt that Glisky and Schacter achieved a notable success in teaching computing skills to severely memory impaired individuals, but so far there has been little extension from this work to either theoretical neuropsychology or rehabilitation.

The second major theoretical influence on remediation of memory deficits has come from behavioural psychology. Wilson (1987a, 1991b, 1992a) discusses how behavioural assessment and treatment techniques, emanating from learning theory, can be modified and adapted to plan memory therapy programmes. Single-case experimental designs, originating in behavioural psychology, have also begun to play a part in evaluating the effectiveness of neuropsychological rehabilitation (Gianutsos & Gianutsos, 1987; Wilson, 1987b).

Another potentially useful application from behavioural psychology is the errorless learning technique first described by Terrace (1963, 1966). Terrace taught pigeons to discriminate a red from a green key with very few or no errors; for pigeons this is a difficult discrimination to make. Terrace achieved success by teaching a pecking response to the red key first. When this response was well established the red key was darkened and exposed very briefly while the pigeon was not in a good position to peck, thus preventing the bird from making an incorrect response. The darkened key was shown for increasing lengths of time as well as gradually changing from red to green. The result was that the pigeon only pecked the red key. This fading procedure was also used to teach an even more complex discrimination between horizontal and vertical lines. Terrace reported that the pigeons showed less emotionality when the errorless learning procedure was employed than they did under trial and error learning.

In 1967 Sidman and Stoddard taught mentally handicapped children to discriminate between circles and ellipses using an errorless learning procedure similar to Terrace's.

Errorless learning has not, as far as we know, been used in memory rehabilitation prior to the studies we report here. Nor has implicit learning had the impact on rehabilitation expected a decade or so ago. However, as Baddeley (1992) suggests, the reason why it is so difficult to apply implicit learning to rehabilitation may lie in the fact that implicit learning is poorly equipped to deal with errors. He presents three pieces of evidence in favour of this idea. First, amnesic patients may not necessarily show normal performance on implicit learning tasks. Wilson, Baddeley, and Cockburn (1989) attempted to teach 100 brain-injured patients and 50 controls to enter the date and time into an electronic memory aid. The operation involved six stages and all controls mastered it within three trials. In contrast, 41% of the brain-injured subjects failed to learn the task within three trials. Two subjects with a pure amnesic syndrome failed to learn it after 25 trials. The task itself is one where implicit learning would be expected, given that explicit recollection of the learning experience is not required for performance. Despite this, subjects with poor episodic memory found the task very difficult or impossible to learn. Baddeley (1992) suggests that the amnesic subjects failed because they were unable to remember and eliminate their errors.

The second piece of evidence comes from a much earlier study (Brooks & Baddeley, 1976), where tasks showing preserved learning in amnesic subjects were those where errors were few and where performance was typically measured in faster performance or more time on target. The third piece of evidence comes from Green (1993), who used the stem completion technique with amnesic subjects. In one condition she presented each word fragment (the stem) and asked subjects to guess the word *before* presenting the complete word.

The amnesic subjects showed very poor learning in contrast to the standard procedure whereby the whole word is presented first and the stem later. Again, it would appear that, once errors are produced or elicited, amnesic subjects have great difficulty eliminating them.

Evidence from these studies encouraged us to ask two questions. First, "Do amnesic subjects learn better if prevented from making mistakes during learning?" and, second, "If so, can we apply this finding to the practical, everyday life problems faced by memory-impaired people?" Experiment 1 answers the first of these questions; it is described briefly here; a more detailed account and analysis is given in Baddeley and Wilson (in press).

EXPERIMENT 1: DO AMNESIC SUBJECTS LEARN BETTER IF PREVENTED FROM MAKING MISTAKES, AND IS ERRORLESS LEARNING MORE BENEFICIAL TO THEM THAN TO CONTROLS?

Method

Subjects.   Three groups were included:

1. Sixteen subjects with severe memory impairment, i.e. a delayed prose recall score of 0 on the Wechsler Memory Scale-Revised (Wechsler, 1987), and a screening score of 3 or less (maximum equals 12) on the Rivermead Behavioural Memory Test (Wilson, Cockburn, & Baddeley, 1985). This group comprised 11 men and five women, ages ranged from 20 to 69 years (mean = 44; SD = 17). Diagnoses were encephalitis ($n = 6$), traumatic brain injury ($n = 4$), anterior communicating artery aneurysm (ACoA) rupture ($n = 2$), posterior cerebral anterior aneurysm (PCoA) rupture ($n = 1$), thalamic stroke ($n = 1$), Korsakoff's syndrome ($n = 1$) and carbon monoxide (CO) poisoning ($n = 1$).

2. Sixteen younger control subjects (ten men and six women) aged between 20 and 58 years (mean = 35; SD = 12), selected to represent a broadly equivalent range of intellectual abilities to those of the amnesic subjects.

3. An older control group of 16 subjects (eight men and eight women) aged between 61 and 79 years (mean = 67 years; SD = 4). Again, these were selected to represent a broadly equivalent range of intellectual abilities.

Procedure

Each subject attempted to learn two lists of five-letter words using a stem completion procedure. In order to avoid floor and ceiling effects, the lists contained five words for the amnesic subjects and ten words for the controls. One list was presented in such a way as to ensure errors were made during the initial learning trials. The other list was presented in such a way as to prevent errors during the same period. Lists and order of presentation were counterbalanced so that half the subjects received one list in the errorless condition and the other in the errorful, with the lists switched for the remaining subjects. In addition, the errorful condition was presented first and second on an equal number of occasions.

In the errorful condition subjects were told, "I am thinking of a five-letter word beginning with TH" (or whatever the initial letters were). "Can you guess what the word might be?" If the correct response had not occurred within 25 seconds, or if the subject made four incorrect responses (whichever came first) the subject was told the correct word (e.g. THUMB) and asked to write it down. If the subject's first response happened to be the correct one a substitute word was used to ensure that at least one error had been made for each word.

Lists were presented three times in succession so that each correct word was written down three times. Guesses were not written down by the subject. These first three trials were called "the learning trials". Following these, subjects were tested by the researcher saying, "One of the words you wrote down just now began with TH. Can you remember what the word was?" Feedback was provided on whether or not the word was correct, and the correct word supplied if necessary. If there was no response subjects were asked, "Can you think of any word beginning with TH?" Again feedback was provided.

In all there were nine test trials (in three blocks) spread over a 20–25-minute period. The first three test trials were presented immediately after the learning trials. A break of 5 to 7 minutes was given before the second set of test trials, then another break before the final set.

Subjects were not asked to guess in the errorless condition. They were told, "I am thinking of a five-letter word beginning with ST and the word is STORY. Please write that down". Once again there were three learning trials. These were followed by nine test trials that were identical in both errorful and errorless condition. None of the target words generated began with the same initial letters.

Results

Every one of the 16 amnesic subjects made more correct responses under the errorless than the errorful condition. Of the elderly control subjects, ten of the 16 did better with the errorless procedure, and so did 11 of the younger subjects, although these were close to ceiling on both occasions.

Figure 1 shows the performance of all three groups under both conditions. Scores are plotted in terms of percentage correct in order to allow a direct comparison between the amnesic subjects who were learning five word lists and the controls who were learning ten.

An analysis of variance (ANOVA) indicates that there was a group effect (df = 2,45; $F = 55.36$; $P < 0.0001$), a condition effect (df = 1,45; $F = 55.32$; $P < 0.0001$) and an interaction effect (df = 2,45; $F = 21.87$; $P < 0.0001$), with the amnesic patients being significantly more affected by learning method than either the elderly or the young controls.

Discussion

There is no doubt that our amnesic subjects found the errorless learning far more beneficial than the errorful, both in terms of enhanced learning and reduced forgetting. In a comparison paper (Baddeley & Wilson, in press) we argue that this is because implicit learning is poorly equipped to deal with errors. Young control subjects, with presumably good episodic memory, use both episodic and implicit memory skills to show ceiling effects on the word list learning. The older controls also use both episodic and implicit memory skills but, for some of these at least, episodic memory presumably shows an age-related decline, leading to poorer performance than is found in the younger subjects.

The amnesic subjects, however, have very poor episodic memory, and so rely almost exclusively on their implicit memory, which is assumed to be particularly sensitive to interference. For a further discussion of this topic and of the elimination of errors, see Baddeley and Wilson (in press).

The implication of these findings for rehabilitation would appear to be that rehabilitationists should, as far as possible, prevent mistakes occurring when trying to teach new information to people with amnesia.

Following this experimental study we wanted to know whether the errorless learning would succeed when applied to the everyday problems experienced by people with severe memory impairment. In an attempt to answer this question, and to discover ways of applying errorless learning in practical situations, five single case studies were conducted.

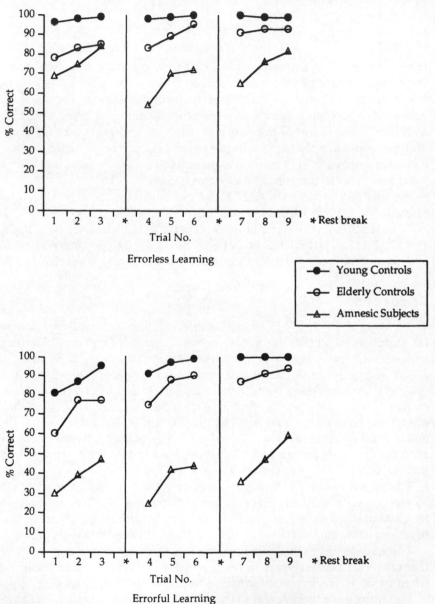

FIG. 1.   Performance of subjects on learning words in Experiment 1.

EXPERIMENT 2: ERRORLESS VERSUS ERRORFUL LEARNING IN TEACHING OBJECT NAMES TO A MAN WITH VISUAL OBJECT AGNOSIA

Method

Subject JBR was a 34-year-old man who became amnesic, agnosic, and dyslexic following herpes encephalitis at the age of 23 years. A description of his agnosia can be found in Warrington and Shallice (1984). He remains severely amnesic with a screening score of 0/12 on the Rivermead Behavioural Memory Test (Wilson et al., 1985), and a delayed index score of below 50 on the Wechsler Memory Scale-Revised (Wechsler, 1987).

Procedure

The Renfrew Pictures (Renfrew, 1975) were presented to JBR and he was asked to name them. He named 17/50 correctly; gave incorrect responses to 20 of them (e.g. "teapot" for WATERING CAN); correctly described eight others without supplying the names (e.g. "thing to help you park a ship" for ANCHOR); mispronounced one ("caddle" for SADDLE); and replied "Don't know" to the remaining four.

Six of the pictures that JBR described without naming and two of the "don't knows" were selected for treatment, as being pictures on which JBR had failed, but not made overt errors. Four items were randomly allocated to each of the two conditions of errorful and errorless learning.

The procedure was similar to that described above, in that three learning trials were followed by nine test trials in three blocks of three. For the errorless condition JBR was shown the pictures one at a time and told, "This is an ANCHOR, HINGE, etc. Please write that down." For the errorful condition JBR was first asked to guess what the picture might represent or free-associate, or say anything it made him think of. One picture, for example, was of a flame. JBR said, "It could be a leaf or a tree or a plant". After 25 seconds he was given the correct answer and asked to write it down. Once again, only the correct answers were written down and each was written three times.

Results

The mean number of correct responses during the nine test trials (maximum equals 36) were 33 for errorless and 19 for errorful. Eight of the nine trials resulted in superior performance of errorless over errorful. A sign test (Siegel, 1956) showed these results to be significantly different ($P < 0.005$).

EXPERIMENT 3: ERRORFUL VERSUS ERRORLESS LEARNING IN PROGRAMMING AN ELECTRONIC MEMORY AID

Method

Subject RM was a 35-year-old man who was diagnosed as having Korsakoff's syndrome several months prior to a referral for memory therapy. On neuropsychological assessments he was estimated to be: (1) functioning in the low average range of ability overall; (2) with an intact immediate memory; (3) showing severe impairment on tests of delayed memory and new learning; (4) showing a temporal gradient on tests of remote memory; (5) exhibiting normal procedural memory; (6) experiencing difficulty on a test of executive functioning; and (7) showing a tendency to confabulate.

Procedure

Two tasks were selected, both of which involved programming an electronic memory aid. Both involved six steps (entering a telephone number and writing a memo). The steps were as follows:

Entering a Telephone Number.
1. Switch ON button
2. Press TEL
3. Write in "BARBARA"
4. Press ENTER
5. Write in 355294
6. Press ENTER

Write a Memo.
1. Switch ON button
2. Press MEMO
3. Write in "SEE ALAN"
4. Press ENTER
5. Press CALENDAR
6. Switch OFF

The two tasks were randomly allocated to an errorful (write a memo) or errorless (enter telephone number) learning condition. In the errorful condition the six steps were demonstrated to RM who was then asked to enter the telephone number himself. He was given feedback after each of the six steps and corrected when necessary. (This procedure is almost identical to that reported by Wilson et al., 1989.) Thirteen trials were given in total; the first nine trials were given in succession, followed by a 5-minute break before going on to the final four trials.

In the errorless condition RM was asked to remember the first step for only two trials, then to remember steps one and two for a further trial. The plan was to use a forward chaining procedure in an attempt to reduce errors. RM, however, became bored with this so the procedure was modified. In trials four to nine inclusive RM was required to follow written instructions in order to prevent errors. A 5-minute break was given before the final four trials were adminsitered. No written instructions were provided for these trials, although RM was watched carefully to pre-empt any errors.

Results

RM failed to learn the task under the errorful condition. In the errorless condition, following the written instructions, he was able to complete trials 10–13 with 100% success without prompting. These results can be seen in Figure 2.

EXPERIMENT 4: USING ERRORLESS LEARNING TO TEACH NAMES

Subject

PS sustained a thalamic stroke at the age of 68 years. As a consequence he became densely amnesic with a retrograde amnesia of approximately 45 years. His IQ was in the average range and he was severely impaired on tests of episodic memory.

Procedure

We attempted to teach PS names of fictitious people using a similar paradigm to that used in Experiments 1 and 2. Ten common first names and ten surnames were selected. Half were randomly allocated to an errorful procedure and half to an errorless. In the errorful condition PS was told, "This man's name begins with M or D (or whatever). Can you guess what his name might be?" After three guesses PS was told the correct name and asked to write it down. There were three learning trials in succession followed by nine test trials in blocks of three spread over a 30-minute period. In the errorless condition PS was told, "This man's name begins with H or W (or whatever) and his name is HARRY. Please write that down." Again, there were three learning trials followed by nine test trials. First names were subjected to the errorful and errorless condition first followed by surnames.

Results

First Names.   The total numbers correct under both errorful and errorless conditions was 32/45, thus no differences occurred.

Trials	Steps					
	1	2	3	4	5	6
1	✓	✗	✗	✓	✓	✗
2	✓	✗	✗	✗	✓	✗
3	✓	✗	✗	✓	✓	✗
4	✓	✗	✗	✓	✓	✗
5	✓	✓	✗	✗	✓	✗
6	✓	✗	✗	✓	✓	✗
7	✓	✗	✓	✗	✓	✗
8	✓	✗	✗	✓	✓	✗
9	✓	✗	✓	✓	✓	✗
5 minute break						
10	✓	✗	✗	✓	✓	✗
11	✓	✗	✓	✓	✓	✗
12	✓	✗	✓	✓	✓	✗
13	✓	✗	✗	✓	✓	✗

	Trials	Steps					
		1	2	3	4	5	6
	1	✓					
	2	✓					
	3	✓	✓				
written instructions provided	4	✓	✓	✓	✓	✓	✓
	5	✓	✓	✓	✓	✓	✓
	6	✓	✓	✓	✓	✓	✓
	7	✓	✓	✓	✓	✓	✓
	8	✓	✓	✓	✓	✓	✓
	9	✓	✓	✓	✓	✓	✓
		5 minute break					
no help provided	10	✓	✓	✓	✓	prevented from making error	✓
	11	✓	✓	✓	✓	✓	✓
	12	✓	✓	✓	✓	✓	✓
	13	✓	✓	✓	✓	✓	✓

FIG. 2. (Top) RM: programming an electronic aid (trial and error method). Steps performed correctly (√) and incorrectly (×). (Bottom) RM: programming an electronic aid (errorless learning). Steps performed correctly (√) and incorrectly (×).

Surnames.   The total number correct under the errorful condition was 20 and under errorless it was 36. Of the nine test trials eight resulted in superior performance after errorless learning (significant difference on sign test $P < 0.005$).

EXPERIMENT 5: LEARNING NAMES OF STAFF AND ITEMS OF ORIENTATION DURING POST-TRAUMATIC AMNESIA

Subject

ED sustained a very severe head injury at the age of 25 years. He was in coma for 86 days. His screening score on the Rivermead Behavioural Memory Test (RBMT) was 3 (severely impaired range). In addition he had a spastic quadriplegia and severe dysarthria. He communicated principally by means of an alphabet board whereby he pointed to individual letters to spell out words. This was supplemented by occasionally spelling out words orally. ED had no receptive language problems. He was believed to be in post-traumatic amnesia (PTA) as assessed by the Modified Westmead PTA Test (Horn et al., 1991) when seen for this study. The length of PTA was estimated to be 319 days in total. At the time of inclusion in the study ED was on the 251st day of PTA.

Procedure

Names of Staff.   ED was a patient on the rehabilitation ward, and names of staff working on this ward were selected and placed in three groups. The groups were matched (as far as possible) for frequency so that people working closely with ED, or less closely, were equally represented in all three groups. Photographs of the staff involved were obtained and allocated appropriately to one of the three groups. One of the groups was randomly allocated to an errorful condition, one to an errorless, and one to a no treatment condition. In the errorful condition ED was shown a photograph and was asked, "Who is this?" He was encouraged to guess if he did not know. Following three guesses, ED was told the correct answer.

In the errorless procedure ED was first shown the photograph with the name written underneath. A vanishing cues procedure was then adopted whereby ED was provided with the name minus one letter and asked to complete the full name. He then completed the name with the last two letters missing and so forth. When there were only one or two letters he was asked *not* to guess if he was not sure. Approximately the same amount of time was spent in each condition.

Five learning trials were given in each condition, followed by 30 test trials in blocks of three given over 4 days. After 30 test sessions two further names were added in each condition.

At the end of the second week when ED was at ceiling identifying the photographs in both of the treatment conditions, he was asked to identify the members of staff who came into the testing room one by one. He made only one mistake—one of the staff members had changed both her hair length and the colour of her hair since her photograph was taken.

The five names allocated to a "no treatment" condition were tested three times during the trial. ED failed to learn any of these names and was at floor throughout. When the trial was completed these names were taught to ED using the errorless learning procedure. Again he learned rapidly and retained the information. The errorless procedure has been used successfully to teach ED other facts, e.g. details of the several cars he had owned and renovated in the two years prior to his injury. At present ED frequently refuses to guess when asked questions. For example, when he is asked to name pictures during speech therapy he usually asks to be told the correct answer.

Results. As can be seen in Figure 3, ED learned in both conditions but took far longer to learn the names in the errorful condition.

Orientation. A similar procedure was used to teach ED six items of orientation. Age, month, and home address were randomly allocated to

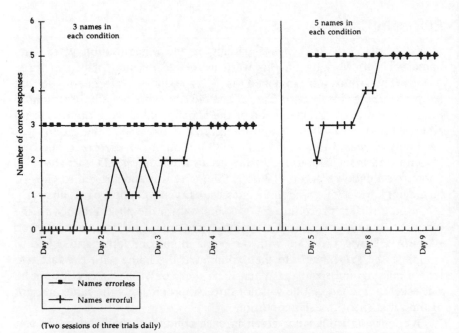

(Two sessions of three trials daily)

FIG. 3.   ED: number of correct responses in learning names using errorful and errorless procedures.

the errorless procedure and year, time of day (i.e. am or pm; sessions were always held in the morning), and current place (i.e. name of the ward and hospital) were allocated to the errorful procedure.

Results.   Once again, ED learned under both conditions but learning took place far more rapidly under the errorful condition, as can be seen in Figure 4.

EXPERIMENT 6: LEARNING NAMES (FROM PHOTOGRAPHS) AND ITEMS OF GENERAL KNOWLEDGE

Subject

LR, aged 31, had a right anterior communicating artery rupture, which was clipped. Assessment 2 months post-surgery showed a severe memory deficit (RBMT Screening Score = 2). Reassessment 1 year post-insult showed that the memory deficit persisted (RBMT = 3). Other cognitive functions were unimpaired.

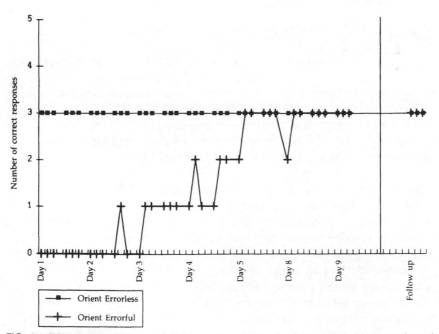

FIG. 4.   ED: number of correct responses in learning items of orientation using errorful and errorless procedures.

Procedure

Two tasks were used in the experiment—learning names and learning general knowledge facts. Five names or facts were randomly allocated to an errorful condition and five to an errorless condition. Five learning trials were administered in each condition. In the errorful condition, LR was shown a photograph (or asked a general knowledge question). After three incorrect guesses the correct answer was given and LR wrote it down. In the subsequent trials feedback was given, i.e. LR was told the correct answer, if he guessed wrongly, and he wrote it down each time. In the errorless condition the correct answer was given in the first administration and was written down. In subsequent learning trials a series of prompts was given where the written answer with a missing letter was given. On each subsequent trial further letters were removed until no prompts were required. The correct answer was also written down each time. LR was also instructed *not* to guess during these learning trials.

Following the learning trials there was a 10-minute break. This was followed by four blocks of five test trials with a 10-minute gap between trials. Feedback was given during the test trials but the correct answer was not written down. Recall was also tested in two blocks of five test trials one week later.

Results

Names. The results are displayed in Figure 5. In the errorless condition LR was almost at ceiling throughout. In the errorful condition recall on the first trial was very poor, but he continued to learn and reached ceiling. The trials 1 week later showed that LR reached ceiling on those names learned in the errorless condition more quickly than on those names learned in the errorful condition. Wilcoxon signed rank tests showed that the difference was significant ($Z = 2.83$, $P < 0.01$).

Facts. The results of these trials are displayed in Figure 6. In the errorful condition, LR remembered none of the facts on the first trial but reached ceiling on the fourth test trial. In the errorless condition he was at ceiling throughout. Recall 1 week later demonstrated that he had retained the facts learned in the errorless condition almost at ceiling (4/5 correct on the first trial and all correct thereafter) whereas he failed to reach ceiling on the facts learned in the errorful condition. When asked, LR had no recollection of learning the facts 1 week earlier and stated that these were facts of general knowledge, which he had always known. The differences in recall between these two conditions was significant in this case ($Z = -3.41$, $P < 0.001$).

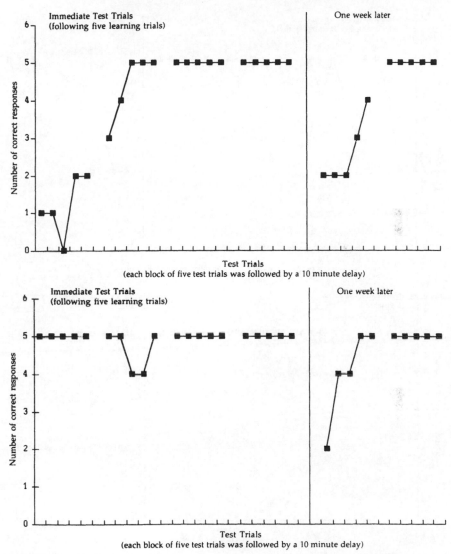

FIG. 5 (Top) LR: number of correct responses learning facts using errorful procedure. (Bottom) LR: Number of correct responses learning facts using errorless procedures.

GENERAL DISCUSSION

Errorless learning appears to be superior to trial-and-error learning for people with severe memory impairments. In each of our experiments, covering a wide range of neurologically impaired people, learning was superior when errors were avoided (or greatly reduced) during the learning

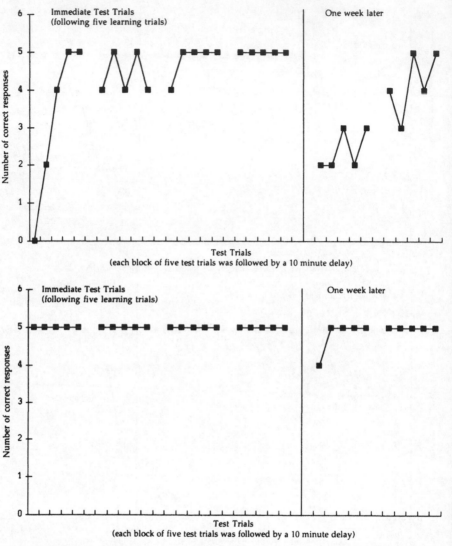

FIG. 6   (Top) LR: number of correct responses learning names using errorful procedure. (Bottom) LR: Number of correct responses learning names using errorless procedures.

process. Furthermore, this was true in a variety of tasks including learning lists of words, object names, names of people, orientation items, general knowledge, and learning to programme an electronic aid. In some ways this finding is counterintuitive, or at least contrary, to rehabilitation practice. Most of us in rehabilitation will say to a patient something along the lines of, "Can you remember my name? No? Well guess—you might be right." This could be an appropriate strategy for those without significant memory impairment but, as we point out in the discussion following Experiment 1, if these subjects are relying almost exclusively on implicit memory, it will encourage errors, which they will then find difficult to eliminate. Explicit memory is required if we want to benefit from past mistakes. Consequently, we should try to avoid errors in order to prevent those same errors from being reinforced through repetition.

Errorless learning is not perfect. Our results, for example, cannot be compared to those of Terrace (1963, 1966) working with pigeons. Errors creep in during the test phases, possibly because we have used within-subject design, with the result that interference occurs between the errorful and errorless conditions, which typically take place within an hour or two of each other. It seems likely that such interference would be reduced by not carrying out errorless and errorful conditions too close together in time. In studies aiming to compare the effectiveness of each approach it might be better to allow a week's separation of the two conditions.

Nevertheless, the principle appears to be effective for most of the people with severe memory impairments we have tested so far. We are not, of course, suggesting that errorless learning is in itself sufficient. It is clearly desirable that it should be combined with other principles from learning theory. For example, one should probably teach one thing at a time to people with any kind of learning disability, and in particular in the case of those with cognitive impairments arising from neurological insults. Thus, instead of teaching five words or five names, we should teach one before introducing a second. Errorless learning can also be combined with expanding rehearsal (as described by Landauer & Bjork, 1978) whereby the information to be learned is presented, tested immediately, then tested after a brief delay, next after a very slightly longer delay and so on. In other words, the test interval is gradually expanded. This method is likely to increase the robustness and durability of learning. We are currently engaged in studies to determine whether or not this is true. We are also trying to shed further light on the question of when to stop the errorless learning procedure and to risk allowing the subject to proceed alone. In clinical practice we often "feel" that the person has learned the step well enough to proceed without help. Furthermore, we are alert and prepared to step in if the subject appears to be about to make a mistake (see Figure 2B for example). Eventually, however, we need to be able to set clear guidelines for others.

We also believe it is important to ensure the active participation of the subjects. Simply listening to correct answers, or even writing them down, may not be sufficient to ensure adequate learning. One way to increase active participation might be to use anagrams or closure tasks (e.g. completing J–A–NA for JOANNA in name learning) as we did with LR in Experiment 6.

A further question of interest is whether the errorless learning principle is better than trial-and-error learning with other groups, such as elderly people, children with dyslexia, or patients with language disorders. It would appear from our results in Experiment 1 that our older subjects showed a tendency to do better with errorless learning but, because of ceiling effects with some of our sample, we cannot be certain of this. We would need to design a harder task. We would hope that other researchers would investigate the possibilities of errorless learning with language impaired adults, children with dyslexia and other patients with cognitive impairments.

REFERENCES

Baddeley, A.D. (1992). Implicit memory and errorless learning: A link between cognitive theory and neuropsychological rehabilitation? In L.R. Squire & N. Butters (Eds.), *Neuropsychology of memory* (2nd ed.) (pp. 309–314). New York: The Guilford Press.

Baddeley, A.D., & Wilson, B.A. (in press). When implicit learning fails: Amnesia and the problem of error elimination. *Neuropsychologia*.

Brooks, D.N. (1984). *Closed head injury*. Oxford: Oxford University Press.

Brooks, D.N., & Baddeley, A.D. (1976). What can amnesic patients learn? *Neuropsychologia, 14*, 111–122.

Gianutsos, R., & Gianutsos, J. (1987). Single case experimental approaches to the assessment of interventions in rehabilitation psychology. In B. Caplan (Ed.), *Rehabilitation psychology* (pp. 453–470). Rockville, MD: Aspen Corporation.

Glisky, E.L., & Schacter, D.L. (1987). Acquisition of domain specific knowledge in organic amnesia: Training for computer related work. *Neuropsychologia, 25*, 893–906.

Glisky, E.L., & Schacter, D.L. (1989). Extending the limits of complex learning in organic amnesia: Computer training in vocational domain. *Neuropsychologia, 27*, 107–120.

Green, R.E.A. (1993). *Investigations of intentional and automatic processing in amnesic, healthy elderly, and healthy young subjects*. Unpublished PhD Thesis, University of Cambridge.

Horn, S., Watson, M., Campbell, M., McLellan, D.L., & Wilson, B.A. (1991). Assessing post traumatic amnesia (abstract). *Journal of Clinical and Experimental Neuropsychology, 13*, 19.

Landauer, T.K., & Bjork, R.A. (1978). Optimum rehearsal patterns and name learning. In M.M. Gruneberg, P.E. Morris, & R.N. Sykes (Eds.), *Practical aspects of memory* (pp. 625–632). London: Academic Press.

Renfrew, E. (1975). *Word finding* (3rd ed.). Oxford: Renfrew Language Test Publishers.

Schacter, D.L., & Crovitz, H.F. (1977). Memory function after closed head injury: A review of the quantitative research. *Cortex, 13*, 159–176.

Sidman, M., & Stoddard, L.T. (1967). The effectiveness of fading in programming simultaneous form discrimination for retarded children. *Journal of Experimental Analysis of Behavior, 10*, 3–15.

Siegel, S. (1956). *Nonparametric statistics for the behavioral sciences*. New York: McGraw-Hill.

Sohlberg, M.M., & Mateer, C.A. (1989). Training use of compensatory memory books: A three stage behavioral approach. *Journal of Clinical and Experimental Neuropsychology, 11*, 871–891.

Squire, L.R. (1987). *Memory and the brain*. New York: Oxford University Press.

Terrace, H.S. (1963). Discrimination learning with and without "errors". *Journal of Experimental Analysis of Behavior*, 6, 1–27.

Terrace, H.S. (1966). Stimulus control. In W.K. Honig (Ed.), *Operant behavior: Areas of research and application* (pp. 271–344). New York: Appleton Century Crofts.

Tulving, E., & Schacter, D.L. (1990). Priming and human memory systems. *Science*, 247, 301–306.

Warrington, E.K., & Shallice, T. (1984). Category specific semantic impairments. *Brain*, 107, 829–854.

Wechsler, D. (1987). *The Wechsler Memory Scale-Revised*. San Antonio: The Psychological Corporation.

Wilson, B.A. (1987a). *Rehabilitation of memory*. New York: Guilford Press.

Wilson, B.A. (1987b). Single case experimental designs in neuropsychological rehabilitation. *Journal of Clinical and Experimental Neuropsychology*, 9, 527–544.

Wilson, B.A. (1991a). Long term prognosis of patients with severe memory disorders. *Neuropsychological Rehabilitation*, 1, 117–134.

Wilson, B.A. (1991b). Behaviour therapy in the treatment of neurologically impaired adults. In P.R. Martin (Ed.), *Handbook of behavior therapy and psychological science: An integrative approach* (pp. 227–252). New York: Pergamon Press.

Wilson, B.A. (1992a). Memory therapy in practice. In B.A. Wilson & N. Moffat (Eds.), *Clinical management of memory problems* (2nd ed.) (pp. 120–153). London: Chapman & Hall.

Wilson, B.A. (1992b). Rehabilitation and memory disorders. In L.R. Squire & N. Butters (Eds.), *Neuropsychology of memory* (2nd ed.) (pp. 315–321). New York: The Guilford Press.

Wilson, B.A., Baddeley, A.D., & Cockburn, J.M. (1989). How do old dogs learn new tricks: Teaching a technological skill to brain injured people. *Cortex*, 25, 115–119.

Wilson, B., Cockburn, J., & Baddeley, A.D. (1985). *The Rivermead Behavioural Memory Test*. Bury St Edmunds, Suffolk: Thames Valley Test Company.

Yule, W., & Carr, J. (Eds.) (1987) (1987). *Behaviour modification for people with mental handicaps*. London: Croom Helm.

Author index

Subject index